An Introducti
Quantitative Re
Methods for Marketing

This introductory text covers the foundational concepts and statistical applications of quantitative research techniques using SPSS and R.

Using step-by-step examples throughout, the book is broken down into six core sections: Part I covers an introduction to quantitative research methods and how to get started with SPSS and R; Part II covers basic concepts in measurement, data descriptions, and distributions; Part III discusses hypothesis testing and basic statistical tests; Part IV covers regression analysis; Part V discusses advanced topics in regression analysis and analysis of variance; and finally Part VI covers advanced statistical methods. Each chapter contains learning objectives and summaries to structure learning, while breakout boxes provide tips and draw students' attention to dos and don'ts in statistical research. SPSS and R Action Boxes present step-by-step instructions on how to perform statistical tests and procedures with SPSS and R. Review questions prompt self-reflection on concepts taught in each chapter and are complemented by exercises that allow students to put their learning into practice.

A very applied text designed to make this complex subject accessible to students with no background in quantitative methods, this book is valuable recommended and core reading for advanced undergraduate and postgraduate students studying business and marketing research methods, business analytics, marketing analytics, statistical skills, and quantitative methods.

Online supplementary resources include datasets and programming files.

Ahmad Daryanto is Professor of Marketing at Lancaster University Management School in the United Kingdom.

An Introduction to Quantitative Research Methods for Marketing

Tools and Techniques Using SPSS and R

Ahmad Daryanto

Routledge
Taylor & Francis Group
LONDON AND NEW YORK

Designed cover image: paulau83/Getty Images

First published 2025
by Routledge
4 Park Square, Milton Park, Abingdon, Oxon OX14 4RN

and by Routledge
605 Third Avenue, New York, NY 10158

Routledge is an imprint of the Taylor & Francis Group, an informa business

British Library Cataloguing-in-Publication Data
A catalogue record for this book is available from the British Library

ISBN: 978-1-032-52566-2 (hbk)
ISBN: 978-1-032-52564-8 (pbk)
ISBN: 978-1-003-40722-5 (ebk)

DOI: 10.4324/9781003407225

Typeset in Palatino
by Apex CoVantage, LLC

Access the Support Material: www.routledge.com/9781032525648

Contents

Part V Advanced Topics in Regression and ANOVA

Part VI Advanced Statistical Methods

Figures

Tables

Preface

This book provides a concise introduction to quantitative research methods without complicated mathematical details. Most of the contents of this book grew out of the teaching materials and tools that I used in my module taught at Lancaster University. My students came from various undergraduate backgrounds with little exposure to statistics or, otherwise, have forgotten much what they had learned in their undergraduate statistics classes. This book is intended, in particular, for such audience, including upper undergraduate and postgraduate students in business and management, in general. The book focuses on various statistical techniques at a basic, intermediate, and advanced levels, with much emphasis is placed on analysing self-reported data collected via a questionnaire, although the techniques can also be applied to direct measures, such as metrics data (e.g., unit sales). The book is written with emphasis on providing the conceptual understanding of the methods followed by practical approaches with SPSS and R.

Each chapter discusses different statistical techniques and takes the readers through a step-by-step approach working with an example using those software programs. Attempts to replicate SPSS results are demonstrated in the R section.

Features

Every chapter contains several pedagogical features.

- **'Abstract'**, placed at the very beginning of each chapter, provides an overview of the chapter.
- **'SPSS Action'** presents step-by-step instructions on how to perform a statistical test with SPSS.
- **'R Action'** shows how to perform a statistical procedure or task using R in a step-by-step fashion.
- **'R Code'** is a block of R code to draw certain graphs or perform certain task. When I read a book and find a beautiful graphs, I was always amazed and curious how the graphs were produced. This part should fulfil the curiosity of the readers.

  However, unlike the R action, there is no detailed explanation about the logic of the code as this is not a R programming book. Nonetheless, with basic knowledge in R and what the code does, readers can modify the code to suits their need (e.g. changing line colour). I hope that the availability of the code encourages readers to enhance their programming skills in R.
- **'Summary'** summarizes key learning points discussed in the chapter.

- **'Review Questions'** are self-assessment questions for students to check their understanding on the concepts being discussed in the chapter.
- **'Exercises'** require students to perform mathematical operations and/or conduct statistical procedures using SPSS or R.

Organization of the Book

The book consists of 23 chapters organized into six parts, described briefly as follows:

Part I covers the introduction to quantitative research methods, how they differ with qualitative research methods, the important of data and model in research, and introduces statistical software covered in the book, namely, SPSS and R, and basic functions for data processing and manipulation.

Part II explains the notion of constructs, their operationalizations, and how to describe quantitative data. It also covers statistical distribution, which includes normal and standard normal distribution, sampling distribution, and distributions derived from the normal distribution.

Part III covers the concept of hypothesis testing and basic statistical tests in the frequentist approach. This includes proportion test and correlational analysis.

Part IV discusses regression analysis which includes a simple linear regression, a multiple regression, and diagnostic tests to check the assumptions of the linear regression model.

Part V discusses fundamental essential topics in regression and analysis of variance (ANOVA). This includes testing mediation, moderation, ANOVA, and experimentation.

Finally, **Part VI** discusses advanced techniques in quantitative research methods, which include cluster analysis, principal component analysis (PCA), exploratory factor analysis (EFA), and logistic regression.

Online Support

The book has supplementary materials hosted at www.routledge.com/9781032525648 and https://github.com/ahdar1/iqrm, which include the following:

- **Slide presentations for each chapter**
- **SPSS datasets** and **ahdar** R data package, which contains datasets discussed in R action sections of the book

Acknowledgement

Alam takambang jadi guru. (The unfolding nature is our greatest teacher.)

– *Minangkabau proverb*

This book is dedicated to my late father, Mirwan Apen, and my late mother, Jusmihanum, who were always my constant motivation. I take this opportunity also to thank my wife, Rilda Oelangan Taneko, and my son, Ilham Idraki Ahmad, for their constant support and understanding.

I wish to thank anonymous reviewers for their invaluable feedback. I would like to thank several colleagues on their insightful comments and feedback: Didier Soopramanien, Jingxi Huang, Zening Song, Ralf van der Lans, and Raja Patricia Sharah. I would also like to take this opportunity to thank the statisticians, researchers, and R scientists who created the freely available R packages I used in this book, which have helped me expand my statistical knowledge and skills.

Lastly, I wish to express my thanks to Sophia Levine and Nicole Doyle at the Routledge Publisher for their support during the writing of this book, especially for keeping me on schedule. Lastly, any remaining errors, if any, or oversights are entirely my own.

About the Author

Ahmad Daryanto (Anto) is a Professor of Marketing at Lancaster University Management School in the United Kingdom. He received his BSc degree in environmental engineering from Bandung Institute of Technology in Indonesia, a MSc degree in engineering mathematics from Twente University in the Netherlands, and a PhD degree in marketing from Maastricht University in the Netherlands. He has published in top international journals such as the *Journal of Consumer Psychology, Journal of the Academy of Marketing Science, Journal of Service Research, Industrial Marketing Management, Personality and Individual Differences, Cities,* Handbook of Partial Least Squares, and *Journal of Business Research,* among others. Anto currently acts as an associate editor of an Elsevier journal, Sustainable Futures, and acted as a co-chair session on marketing analytics and big data at the prestigious AMA winter conference. Anto held a visiting scholar position at Beijing Foreign Studies University under the scheme of the High-End Foreign Expert Program of the Government of China, and has acted as an external grant reviewer for UK Research Innovation (UKRI) future leadership and a lead reviewer for the British Academy small research grants. He is currently an external examiner at International Business School of Xi'an-Jiaotong Liverpool University for its Marketing degree programs, and Regents' University of London for its new MSc program in Data Science and Business. He was an external examiner at Imperial College Business School, London, for its MSc in Strategic Marketing program. Anto is a keen chess player and runs a chess club at the Lancaster public library in the UK.

Part I

Getting Started

1

An Introduction

This chapter explains what constitute quantitative research methods and how they differ with qualitative research methods. The important of data and model as the approximation of how things work in a real-life are emphasized. An example of a simple model is presented with the aim of illustrating how a model can never be able to perfectly explain the reality but it can be more useful than other potential models. The concept of model parsimony – a model with few variables but can explain data well – is also discussed.

Learning Objectives:

- Know what constitutes quantitative research methods.
- Explain the difference between quantitative and qualitative research methods.
- Be aware of the importance of data and model in quantitative research methods.

1.1 Why Quantitative Research?

The objective of this book is to introduce you to various quantitative research methods, not qualitative research methods. The main feature of quantitative research methods lies on their emphasis on the use of statistics (e.g. regression analysis, factor analysis) as tools to analyse data that are expressed as numbers (i.e. numerical data) typically gathered from experiments and/or surveys with closed-ended questions. Qualitative research methods, on the other hand, focuses on non-statistical approaches (e.g. text analysis, content analysis, thematic analysis, discourse analysis) in analysing data that are not in numerical forms (e.g. text, audio, video) typically gathered from focus groups, interviews, peer observations, survey with open-ended questions, and social media. While qualitative research focuses on extracting meanings from data that can be very subjective (e.g. different researchers can interpret the same text differently), quantitative research focuses on objectivity as it relies on standard procedure to collect and analyse data. For example, different researchers can use the same scale to measure consumer attitude toward a brand, and the results can be interpreted in the same way. Nowadays, the objectivity in quantitative research methods is enhanced by the increasing demands for researchers to report their detailed descriptions of how they collect and analyse their data. Three important elements of quantitative research methods are hypothesis, data, and model. The former is treated in Chapter 9. Data and model are described in the following subsections.

DOI: 10.4324/9781003407225-2

1.2 Data

Quantitative research methods, in general, require quantitative data. What is quantitative data? it simply refers to data that communicate numbers. The numbers can be produced from the process of counting and measurement. For example, the number of products being sold is a quantitative data. The number is produced from a counting the number of products that are sold to customers. Measurement, which is the topic discussed in Chapter 4, produces a number that is a result of something being measured or being assigned. For example, you take a test that measures how you know a subject, which produces a number (e.g. test score) that indicates your level of knowledge about the subject. Another example is a customer who chooses number 7 ('very satisfied') in a survey.

Nowadays, many data come as unstructured (e.g. text, image, video, and voice; see Balducci & Marinova (2018) on the discussion about the use of unstructured data in marketing). These data do not communicate a number. Text is a form of data, but text per se does not constitute a quantitative data. However, certain aspects of it can be turned into one. For instance, from a text or a narrative paragraph, we can calculate the frequency of occurrence of a certain word. The process of counting the occurrence of words that exist in a paragraph results in a number, which communicates quantity. The majority of data discussed in this book are regarded as those collected from surveys using closed-ended questions. For the sake of learning, the book also uses fake data that I generated to mimic the survey data.

1.3 Model

When I was a postgraduate student, I always thought that quantitative research methods were all about statistics with its statistical jargon and terminologies – you will learn some in this book. Another aspect that I was not fully aware back then was that quantitative research methods is also about building a model, which depicts how we think the variables of our interests relate to each other in reality. To quote Lazer (1962): 'A model is simply the perception or diagramming of a complex or a system. In marketing, it involves translating perceived marketing relationships into constructs, symbols, and perhaps mathematical terms.' Thus, model is our tool to approximate a real-world phenomenon – it is not an exact representation of the reality. As an approximation, it would contain errors or noises. For example, we can hypothesize that advertising exposure will have a positive influence on brand purchase (i.e. the more consumers are exposed to an advert, the higher their intention to purchase the brand being advertised). We could illustrate this hypothesized relationship using a diagram representing a model, in this case, which is quite simple: advertising exposure → purchase intention. This diagram is actually a visual representation of a mathematical or statistical relationship between the two variables – it is a simple linear model that we will learn in Section 12. The model glues our hypothesis. We never know whether this model is `correct`. What we can do is we can collect data and investigate whether data will support our hypothesized research model. We can improve the quality of the approximation – hence reducing the noises, by including other factors that might also affect purchase intention. Perhaps, we can include perceived brand price as this variable can have a stronger influence on purchase intention. Now, we have two variables affecting purchase intention. Perhaps, we are not yet satisfied with the expanded research model that only include only two variables explaining purchase intention. Perhaps, word-of-mouth should also be included – recommendations from our friends are usually influential. Now, we have three variables affecting purchase intention. The list of the variables can be very long when we are tempted to include all factors that might influence purchase intention. We might come up with 10–15 variables. Having many variables, however, should be avoided as adding more variables means adding more uncertainty with regard to how we are going to estimate the fit of the model to the data. Having many variables also in conflict with the principle of *model parsimony (Occam's razor)* – choose a simple model over the complex one if both equally explain the data well. In other words, the simplest explanation is the better. Therefore, models with few variables are parsimonious, whilst those with ten variables are not despite both are supported by data.

Nevertheless, despite the long list of variables, we would never be able to exactly explain purchase intention. The model with the long list of variables is still an approximation. All these models are wrong in the sense that they can not perfectly explain reality, but the model with only two variables may be more useful that the model with only one variable or fifteen variables. To quote the famous saying of the British statistician, George Box: 'All models are wrong but some are useful.' A research model is like a map. A map cannot exactly describe how a region looks like, but it is useful. In this book, I hope, you will learn how to build a model that is useful to address your research enquiries.

1.4 Further Reading

Jaccard, J. & Jacoby, J. (2019), *Theory construction and model-building skills: A practical guide for social scientists*. Guilford Publications.

Lazer, W. (1962), 'The role of models in marketing', *Journal of Marketing* **26**(2), 9–14.

1.5 Review Questions

1. Explain the difference between quantitative vs. qualitative research.
2. What is the role of a research model in quantitative research methods?

2

Getting Started with SPSS

This chapter provides a brief introduction to SPSS, which is a statistical package used in this book along with R. SPSS stands for Statistical Package for Social Science, founded in 1975 and currently owned by IBM since 2009. SPSS is one of the most widely used statistical software in academics and industry. SPSS comes with various *standard* statistical procedures that can be assessed from its menu.[1] Nevertheless, SPSS has a flexibility to allow users to install an add-on statistical procedure that is not available in its menu. This add-on procedure is called an SPSS macro. This book relies on several macros with majority of them developed by the author. The end of the chapter explains how to install an SPSS macro.

Learning Objectives:

- Know how to enter data into SPSS manually.
- Know to open an existing SPSS data.
- Know how to assess statistical procedures in SPSS menu.
- Understand basic operations in SPSS.
- Know what an SPSS syntax is and how to run it.
- Know what an SPSS macro is and how to install it.

2.1 SPSS Versions

In nearly every chapter of this book, it contains an 'SPSS Action' section, which demonstrates a step-by-step procedure in performing a statistical task or procedure in SPSS. To make use of the 'SPSS Action' section, you must ensure that you have SPSS installed on your computer. SPSS comes with many versions, the latest of which is version 30; however, this book uses version 28, however, in some parts, I show how to perform some tasks using version 29. There are no significant differences between these two versions with regard to the statistical procedures discussed in the book. In fact, older versions, such as versions 26 and 27, can also be used to follow the SPSS instructions as there is little variation in the outputs produced by the newer versions and the older versions.

[1] The latest version is 30. Majority of the chapters use version 28, unless stated otherwise.

DOI: 10.4324/9781003407225-3

2.2 Let's Get Started

I assume that you have managed to install SPSS on your machine. The first thing you should be able to do is knowing how to enter raw data into an SPSS data file.

We consider the following data and will enter it manually into an SPSS data file.

Data in Table 2.1 shows a record of number of telephone calls made by five salespersons during a given week. Data is displayed in a rectangular format where each row in the first column of the table provides the names of the salespersons, and data in the second column provides the number of calls made by the salespersons. Let us open a new data file on SPSS by clicking: File→New→Data (see Figure 2.1)

TABLE 2.1

Salesperson and Number of Calls Made to Customers in a Week

Name	Number of calls
Alex	12
Donna	13
Lou	14
Dylan	12
Millam	11

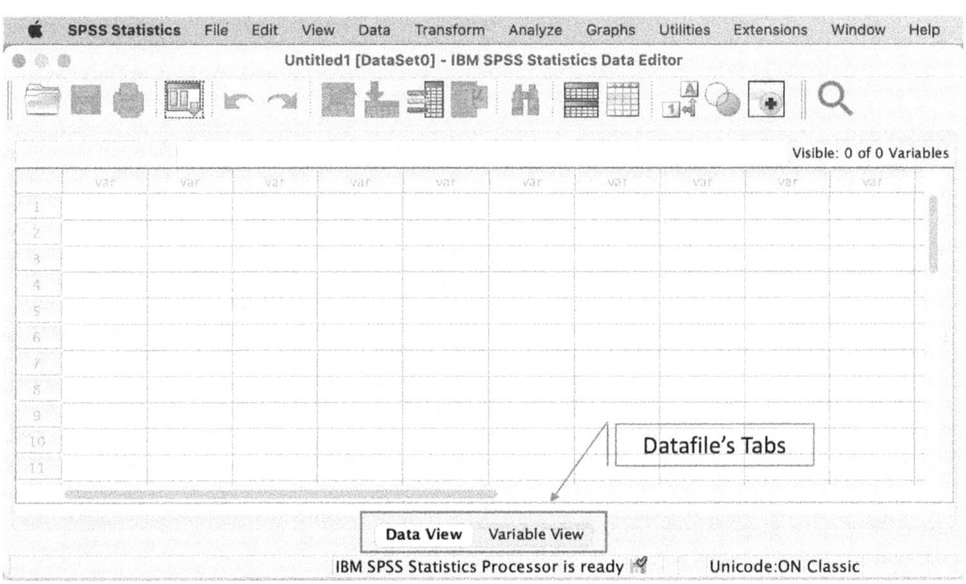

FIGURE 2.1
An empty SPSS data file.

As you can see from Figure 2.1, SPSS shows two types of View – `Data View` and `Variable View` – which you can switch from one to another by clicking the data file tabs named at the bottom. `Data View` shows the actual data where each row represents a case or observation or respondent and each column corresponds to a variable. `Variable View` shows the detail about your variables.

Now, click `Variable View` tab, and write down the name of the variable (salesperson, ncalls). On the column *Type*, choose *string* for salesperson, and choose *Numeric* for ncalls. *string* data can hold multiple characters and cannot be used for a mathematical operation like taking summation. It is usually used to record a text variable, such as names of salespersons. Unlike *string* data, *numeric* data type is used to store values or numbers that can be used for a mathematical operation and/or statistical analysis. Next, write down the description of salesperson and ncalls under the *label* column (e.g. name of salesperson, number of calls made in a week). For the time being, you can ignore column next to *Label* (e.g. *Values, Measures*), which allow you to specify the variables further. We will revisit these features again in the future. Your `Variable View` should look like the image in Figure 2.2.

Next, click `Data View` to enter the data. You have to type in salespersons' names in the first column and the number of calls in the second column. Your `Data View` should look like the image displayed in Figure 2.3. Save the data to *salesrecord.sav* by clicking File→Save.

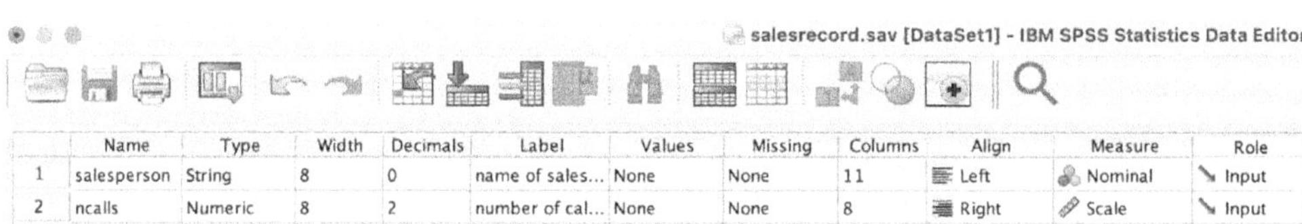

FIGURE 2.2
`Variable View` of sales record data.

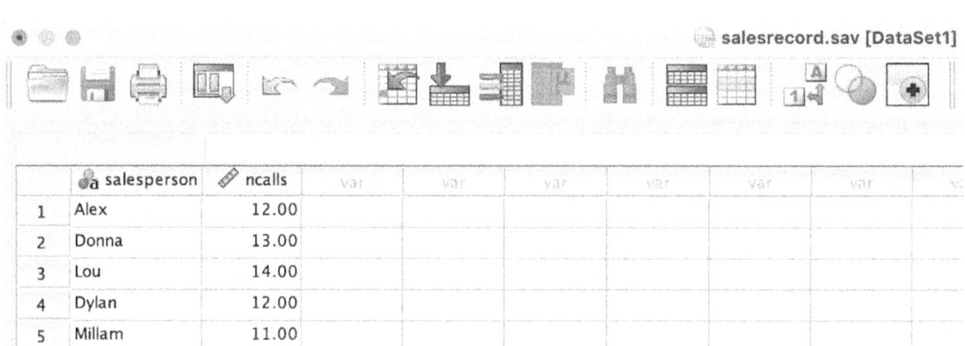

FIGURE 2.3
`Data View` of sales record data.

2.3 Opening a Data File

Data file in SPSS has an extension `.sav`. This section requires you to download SPSS data *empathyinit.sav* from the book website. This data was gathered via a survey with a questionnaire. Launch SPSS and open the data by clicking: File → Open → Data. When the data is opened on SPSS, you should see Data View displayed in Figure 2.4 and `Variable View` in Figure 2.5. On the `Variable View`, on the second row, you can see variable `MI1`. On the `Label` column, you can see the full details of what has been measured: 'It would make me feel good to be a person who has these characteristics', and the `Values`

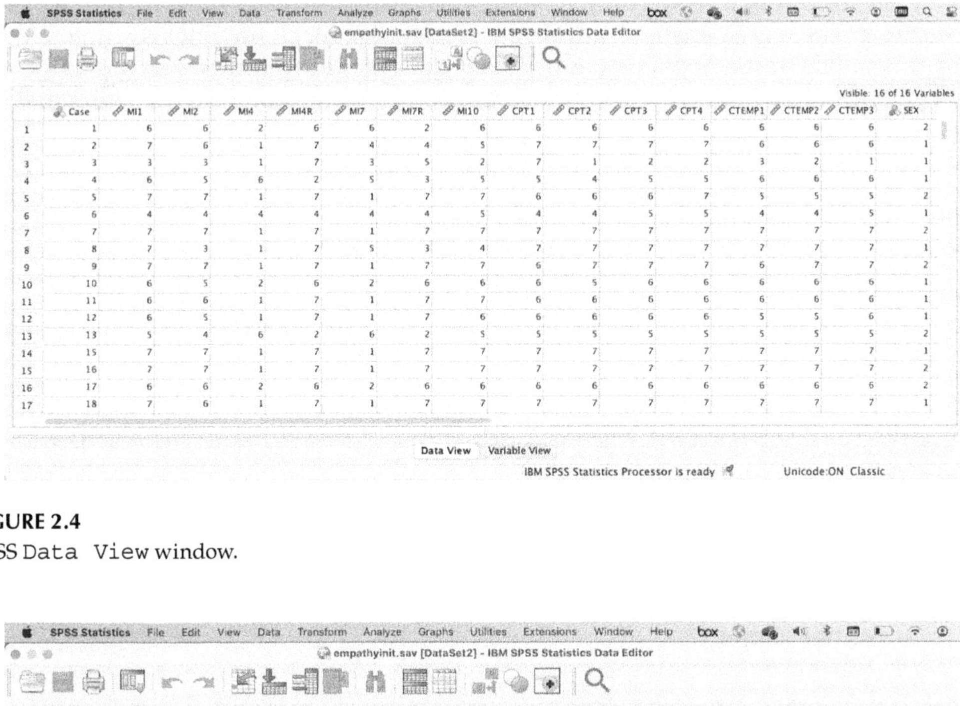

	Case	MI1	MI2	MI4	MI4R	MI7	MI7R	MI10	CPT1	CPT2	CPT3	CPT4	CTEMP1	CTEMP2	CTEMP3	SEX
1	1	6	6	2	6	6	2	6	6	6	6	6	6	6	6	2
2	2	7	6	1	7	4	4	5	7	7	7	7	6	6	6	1
3	3	3	3	1	7	3	5	2	7	1	2	2	3	2	1	1
4	4	6	5	6	2	5	3	5	5	4	5	5	6	6	6	1
5	5	7	7	1	7	1	7	7	6	6	6	7	5	5	5	2
6	6	4	4	4	4	4	4	5	4	4	5	5	4	4	5	1
7	7	7	7	1	7	1	7	7	7	7	7	7	7	7	7	2
8	8	7	3	1	7	5	3	4	7	7	7	7	7	7	7	1
9	9	7	7	1	7	1	7	7	6	7	7	7	6	7	7	2
10	10	6	5	2	6	2	6	6	6	5	6	6	6	6	6	1
11	11	6	6	1	7	1	7	7	6	6	6	6	6	6	6	1
12	12	6	5	1	7	1	7	6	6	6	6	6	5	5	6	1
13	13	5	4	6	2	6	2	5	5	5	5	5	5	5	5	2
14	15	7	7	1	7	1	7	7	7	7	7	7	7	7	7	1
15	16	7	7	1	7	1	7	7	7	7	7	7	7	7	7	2
16	17	6	6	2	6	2	6	6	6	6	6	6	6	6	6	2
17	18	7	6	1	7	1	7	7	7	7	7	7	7	7	7	1

FIGURE 2.4
SPSS `Data View` window.

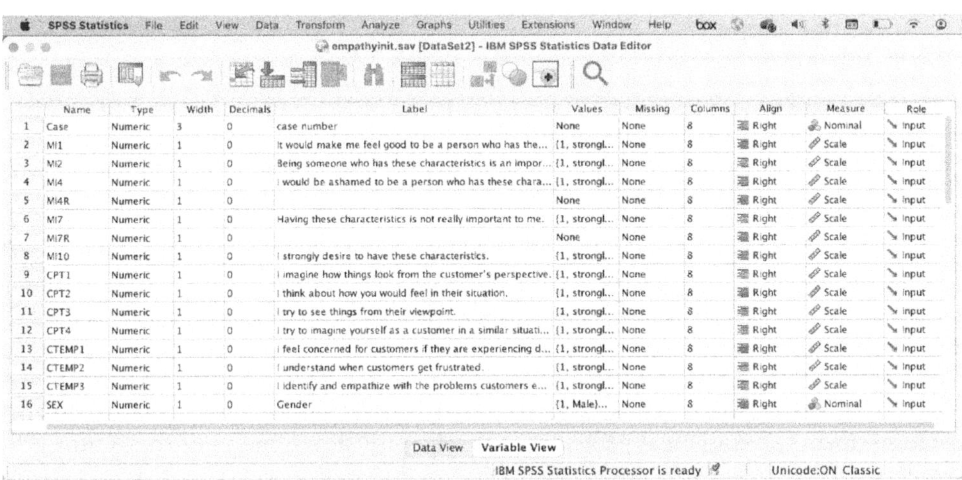

	Name	Type	Width	Decimals	Label	Values	Missing	Columns	Align	Measure	Role
1	Case	Numeric	3	0	case number	None	None	8	Right	Nominal	Input
2	MI1	Numeric	1	0	It would make me feel good to be a person who has the...	{1, strongl...	None	8	Right	Scale	Input
3	MI2	Numeric	1	0	Being someone who has these characteristics is an impor...	{1, strongl...	None	8	Right	Scale	Input
4	MI4	Numeric	1	0	I would be ashamed to be a person who has these chara...	{1, strongl...	None	8	Right	Scale	Input
5	MI4R	Numeric	1	0		None	None	8	Right	Scale	Input
6	MI7	Numeric	1	0	Having these characteristics is not really important to me.	{1, strongl...	None	8	Right	Scale	Input
7	MI7R	Numeric	1	0		None	None	8	Right	Scale	Input
8	MI10	Numeric	1	0	I strongly desire to have these characteristics.	{1, strongl...	None	8	Right	Scale	Input
9	CPT1	Numeric	1	0	I imagine how things look from the customer's perspective.	{1, strongl...	None	8	Right	Scale	Input
10	CPT2	Numeric	1	0	I think about how you would feel in their situation.	{1, strongl...	None	8	Right	Scale	Input
11	CPT3	Numeric	1	0	I try to see things from their viewpoint.	{1, strongl...	None	8	Right	Scale	Input
12	CPT4	Numeric	1	0	I try to imagine yourself as a customer in a similar situati...	{1, strongl...	None	8	Right	Scale	Input
13	CTEMP1	Numeric	1	0	I feel concerned for customers if they are experiencing d...	{1, strongl...	None	8	Right	Scale	Input
14	CTEMP2	Numeric	1	0	I understand when customers get frustrated.	{1, strongl...	None	8	Right	Scale	Input
15	CTEMP3	Numeric	1	0	I identify and empathize with the problems customers e...	{1, strongl...	None	8	Right	Scale	Input
16	SEX	Numeric	1	0	Gender	{1, Male}...	None	8	Right	Nominal	Input

FIGURE 2.5
SPSS `Variable View` window.

represent what the imputed numbers represented in the questionnaire, e.g. 1 = strongly disagree and 7 = strongly agree.

2.4 SPSS Syntax

To allow SPSS to execute a procedure given in the pull-down menu, SPSS provides two options: clicking `OK` or `Paste`. If you click `OK`, SPSS executes the procedure and produce outputs in an output window. If you click `Paste`, SPSS open a syntax editor, which contains scripts or commands to run the SPSS procedure. The script must be Run for SPSS to execute it. There is a benefit of working with a syntax file. It provides documentation, saves time, and can be applied to a different data file. Furthermore, if you work in a team, you can share this script to other team members, which allow them to understand what you had done.

```
get file '/Users/ahmaddaryanto/OneDrive -
Lancaster University/dataspss/salesrecord.sav'
```

For a demonstration, let us run a frequency analysis for ncalls variable. From the SPSS pull down menu, click:

- Analyze → Descriptive Statistics → Frequencies.
- Insert `ncalls` to `Variable(s)` box.
- Click `Paste`.

SPSS will open a syntax editor. If you save this file, it will have an extension `.sps`. I provided the syntax file of this code in *my_first_syntax.sps*, which you can download from the book's online support.

```
DATASET ACTIVATE DataSet1.
FREQUENCIES VARIABLES=ncalls
        /ORDER=ANALYSIS.
```

The first command tells you the data file that is active: `DataSet1`. SPSS assigns a different name for a dataset. You can see a dataset name inside a bracket term next to filename (see Figure 2.6). The same data file can be assigned a different dataset name depending on the order the data is opened.

In the syntax command, dataset name can be removed as long as the command is applied to data file that is active. The command in the syntax file needs to be run in order to perform the statistical procedure. On the pull-down menu of the syntax editor:

- Click `Run`
- Choose `All`
- Inspect the output window

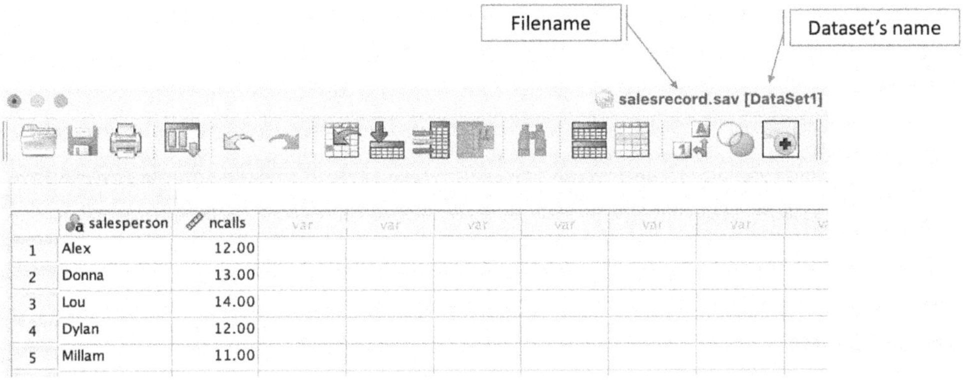

FIGURE 2.6
Data filename and dataset name.

If you open syntax file that I provided *my_first_syntax.sps*. The first line begins with an asterisk *. Any line beginning with * is not going to be processed by SPSS – it is good for annotation. The second line contains `get file [filename]` command. This command opens an SPSS file if you run it. With this command, you do not have to open the SPSS data file when you begin your SPSS session.

2.5 SPSS Macros

SPSS macro is a special SPSS scripts that contains commands to perform a specific statistical procedure that can be installed on SPSS; therefore, it is not necessarily available under the SPSS menu when you install SPSS for the first time. An SPSS macro can be developed by end users. I have written several macros, which you will learn in certain chapters. There are also macros developed by other researchers discussed in this book. To use these SPSS macros, they need to be installed on SPSS. Table 2.2 shows list macros used in the book and the chapter they are discussed.

TABLE 2.2
List of SPSS Macro Used in This Book

Macro	Chapter
NORMDIST and QNORMDIST	6
CHIDIST and QCHIDIST	7
TDIST and QTDIST	7
FDIST and QFDIST	7
D2prop	10
CENTERING	11
HeteroskedasticityV3	14
Process	15 and 16
EndoS	17
Corrmat	22

2.5.1 Installing an SPSS Macro

SPSS macro has an extension *spd* or *spe*. Macros used in this book has an *spd* extension. To install the SPD file onto SPSS, you can double-click the SPD file provided that you have an admin right on your machine. If do not have an admin right, you will be prompted by an error message – that's how you find out that you do not have an admin right. Alternatively, you can install the macro by clicking: Extensions → Utilities → Install Custom Dialog.

2.6 Summary

This chapter provides a brief introduction to SPSS, which is a statistical package used in this book, along with R, SPSS syntax, and SPSS macros.

2.7 Review Questions

1. Explain the difference between a data filename and dataset name.
2. What is an SPSS syntax? Explain the advantages of working with an SPSS syntax.
3. What is an SPSS macro? Explain the advantages of working with an SPSS macro.

3

Getting Started with R

This book covers how to perform calculations, statistical tests, produce graphs not only with SPSS but also with a free open-source software R. R is supported by groups of volunteers from the Comprehensive R Archive Network (CRAN) team (https://cran.r-project.org) and hosted at various mirror servers around the world. R can be downloaded from this website – https://cloud.r-project.org – which will automatically pick the mirror server closer to users. In this chapter, steps to working with R and R code editor, RStudio (now called Posit), are demonstrated, covering several key functions for importing, exporting, viewing, and modifying data. The final section introduces ggplot and ggpubr packages for data visualization.

Learning Objectives:

At the end of this chapter you will know

- how to install RStudio (Posit), R, and R packages,
- the notion of R objects,
- several basic functions in R,
- how to read and export an SPSS data to R,
- how to use R pipe operators,
- how to install and call tidyverse packages,
- how ggplot package works, and
- how to create graphs with ggplot and ggpubr.

3.1 RStudio (Posit)

RStudio is an IDE, which stands for `integrated development environment`. It is essentially a software application that can be used to write and execute R programming code. RStudio is now called Posit, but I will refer to RStudio as this name is a generic name used in the R community.

We can install RStudio by visiting the website https://posit.co/downloads/. During the process of installation, we will be prompted to install R software in our computer. If R is already installed on our machine, we can skip this step. Figure 3.1 shows a screenshot of RStudio in my computer.

DOI: 10.4324/9781003407225-4

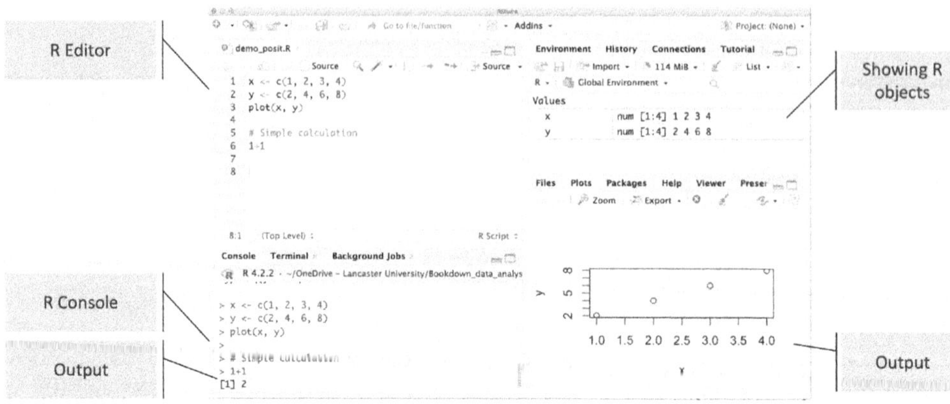

FIGURE 3.1
RStudio (Posit) screenshot.

Let me explain the key elements displayed in the figure:

- `R editor` pane allows us to write R code, also called R script, if it is saved as a file. R script will have an extension `file.r`. We can create an R script using RStudio by clicking: *File* → New File → R script.
- `R console` pane can also be used to write our code. On the console, to run the code, we have to press enter. The output is also printed on the pane, e.g. the result of running `1+1` is printed as `[1] 2`. Any code that we write in the `R editor` will be printed on the console along with the outputs.

  ```
  1+1
  ```

  ```
  [1] 2
  ```

  `[1]` refers to a row number, and the number 2 next to the row number is the answer to `1+1`, which is quite obvious.

IMPORTANT

Hereafter, outputs of code in this book, will be shown after `## sign`. I set it up this way for ease of reading. The R outputs in your `R console` will not have the same format as mine.

```
1+1
```

```
## [1] 2
```

- In the `Output` on the right of the image, you see a graph displayed as a result of running `plot(x,y)`.
- In the `Global Environment` pane, RStudio list `R objects` that are active in our `R` session. R is an object-oriented programming language, which means that everything we created with R code come as an object. As we can see on the pane, there

are two R objects: `x` and `y`. These two R objects were created as a result of running `x <- c(1, 2, 3, 4)` and `y <- c(2, 4, 6, 8)`. These two R objects are 'alive' in our computer or our R workspace during an R session. As they are alive, they consume energy taken from our computer RAM (random access memory). If we close an R session, the objects are removed from workspace.

```
x <- c(1, 2, 3, 4)
y <- c(2, 4, 6, 8)
```

Run the following command to show R objects that are active in your R session:

```
ls() # see the results in your R console or global environment pane
```

```
## [1] "has_annotations" "x"      "y"
```

All R objects that you create can be removed from your R session by running the following command.

```
rm(list=ls())
# inspect the Global Environment' pane, the objects are disappeared
```

Let us check whether the two R objects x and y were indeed already deleted.

```
ls()
```

```
## character(0)
# x and y were gone.
```

IMPORTANT

Executing Code in R editor

- To run a particular line, select the line with your cursor and click the `Run` toolbar button.
- To run multiple lines, select the entire lines, and click the `Run` toolbar button.
- To run the entire code in your script, click the `Source` toolbar button.

In the next section, I provide a brief introduction to R. There are many useful functions out there, more than we can cover in this book, as there are thousands of R packages that exist. In the next section, I cover several useful R packages and functions that can get you going with R. In my research work, I use SPSS data mostly for data cleaning (which can also be done in R) then import the data to R to perform statistical calculations. Nevertheless, in other occasion, I do everything in R. Indeed, you could do many things R if you like writing code.

3.1.1 R Package

An R package is a collection of functions. A function is programming code that acts as a tool to make things work. For example, `ggplot2` is an R package that contains various functions to create graphs. When we install R, it comes with several standard packages referred to, hereafter, as R base (the name is a bit of misnomer, because 'base' is one of the packages among other packages supplied by R Core Team). These packages enable R to be used as a scientific programming language. For example, one of the packages included in the R base is `stats` package, which contains functions to run a wide variety of statistical procedures, some of which are covered in this book (e.g. `lm()` function for conducting regression analysis – see Chapters 12 and 13). You can run the following command in your R console to see the complete lists of function in this package.

```
library(help = "stats")
```

As a result of running this code, a new window will pop up in your RStudio: `Documentation for package 'stats'`. Click it and see the list of function that belongs to the `stats package`.

NOTE

How many R packages are there? The answer is thousands! The list can be viewed at https://cran.r-project.org. On the left pane of the site, under `Software`, click `Packages`. At the end of December 2022, the website listed 18,960 packages. As I am typing this line on 8 December 2023, the number of packages has risen to 20,162. Thus, just within a year, there is an increase of 1202 packages!

In dealing with an R package, there are two functions that we will frequently use to access functions contained the package. The first function is:

```
install.packages("package1")
```

The `install.packages()` function will install a package called `package1`. Just for your info, there is no package called 'package1', so do not try to install it. If you want to install a particular package, replace 'package1' with the name of the package.

We can install multiple packages at once by running:

```
install.packages("package1", "package2", "package3")
```

The second function is:

```
library(package1)
```

The `library()` will load `package1`. To **load** a package means making it available in a workspace during an R session. When a package is available in a workspace, it can be searched by R. R is automatically loaded with standard R packages or R base when we start an R session. This means, we can use any functions from the R standard packages straightaway.

> **NOTE**
>
> As you advance in R, you may become interested in creating your own package. The following book is one of the best resources in learning on how to develop your own R package: https://r-pkgs.org. One of the authors of the book is the inventor of the famous tidyverse package, which will discuss very soon:

Now, run the following code, which will display all packages that are active in your R session:

```
search()
```

```
## [1] ".GlobalEnv"        "package:stats"  "package:graphics"
## [4] "package:grDevices" "package:utils"  "package:datasets"
## [7] "package:methods"   "Autoloads"      "package:base"
```

This output shows the list of packages that are currently active in my current R session. Of course, your outputs will be different than mine.

3.1.2 Help File

Suppose that you just download a package and are not sure what it does and what function it contains. For this, you can read the documentation of the package by running `?package`. Similarly, for a function, you can run `?function`. For an illustration, run the following commands in your R console: `?base and ?sum`.

3.1.3 Data Package

An R package typically contain datasets. However, many R packages are created to store only data without including functions for performing mathematical or statistical procedures. This package is called a data package. As explained in the preface, many chapters of this book contain R sections. The R sections show you how to perform a statistical procedure using R in a step-by-step fashion. Data used in the R section are available in a data package called `ahdar`. Ahdar package is available to download from the book's online support mentioned in the preface. The name of the file is ahdar_0.1.0.tar.gz. If you manage to download the data package, we can install the package from R studio via the following steps.

- Click Tools → Install Packages.
- Under `Install from`, select Package Archive File (.zip, .tar.gz)
- Find `ahdar _ 0.1.0.tar.gz` on the download folder of your compute unless you have moved it to a different folder.
- Click `Open`.
- Click `Install`.

Alternatively, the package can be installed directly using `install.packages()` function by specifying the local path where the package is located. The format of the code is:

```
install.packages("path/ahdar_0.1.0.tar.gz")
```

Replace the path in the code with the corresponding path. If the package is located in the download folder of my mac, the path is `/Users/ahmaddaryanto/Downloads`.

Continue reading this page, which will allow you to make use of data in the ahdar package.

3.2 Creating Data

When you have a really small data, which is good to learn R, you can type this data directly on the R editor in RStudio. Let us record the following data that we used earlier in SPSS:

```
# Record names of salespersons

salesperson <- c("Alex", "Lou","Donna", "Dylan", "Millam")

# number of calls made in a week
ncalls <- c(12,13,14,12,11)

# number of positive responses from clients
npos <- c(4,6,4,6,5)
```

I have recorded three information: the number of salespersons (stored in `salesperson`), the number of calls each salesperson made to clients in a week (stored in `ncalls`), and the number of positive responses that each salesperson receives from making that class (stored in `npos`). The three `objects` (`salesperson, ncalls, npos`) that I used to record the information are `variables`. The symbol <- is an assignment operator, which is equivalent to the = sign. The symbol c stands for **combine**. The " " sign are used to store strings. The symbol # is used to insert comment, which is good for documenting your code especially if you have long code – # is not processed by R.

Now, let us apply the `mean` function from R base to calculate averages.

```
# average number of calls made
avg _ ncalls <- mean(ncalls)
# average number of positive responses received
avg _ npos <- mean(npos)
```

Show the results:

```
avg_ncalls
```

```
## [1] 12.4
```

```
avg_npos
```

```
## [1] 5
```

NOTE

To output the results, you can also `print()` command:
`print(avg _ npos)` `## [1] 5`

You can combine the three variables into one data frame using either `cbind()` or `data.frame()`. These two functions come from R base. As the package is pre-loaded, you can use the functions straight away.

```
dat_sales <- cbind(salesperson, ncalls)
dat_sales <- data.frame(salesperson, ncalls, npos)
```

These two new datasets created do not contain the same data. In the first code, two variables are assigned to `dat _ sales` whereas in the second code, three variables get assigned. R stores only the recent object because if the objects have the same name, the previous object was overwritten. As can be seen in the `Global Environment` pane, there exists only one `dat _ sales` containing three variables.

Let us view the newly created data by running `head(data)` – this function belongs to `utils` package, which is one of the R standard packages. `head()` returns the first five rows of a specified data, which means showing the entire contents of `dat _ sales`.

```
head(dat_sales)
```

```
##    salesperson ncalls  npos
## 1 Alex             12     4
## 2 Lou              13     6
## 3 Donna            14     4
## 4 Dylan            12     6
## 5 Millam           11     5
```

The output shows our data in an R standard data frame format.

Now, load the `tibble` package. We are going to use it to convert our data from the traditional R data frame format into a `tibble` format, which works better with the `tidyverse`, which is a modern package for working with data.

```
library(tibble)
dat_sales <- as_tibble(dat_sales)
```

Let us view it again:

```
head(dat_sales)
```

```
## # A tibble:   5 x 3
##   salesperson  ncalls  npos
##   <chr>         <dbl> <dbl>
## 1 Alex             12     4
## 2 Lou              13     6
## 3 Donna            14     4
## 4 Dylan            12     6
## 5 Millam           11     5
```

Regardless of their formats (i.e. data.frame or tibble), you can access an individual column by placing the dollar sign $ in front of the data name. For example, you can calculate the average of `ncalls` and npos:

```
mean(dat_sales$ncalls)
```

```
## [1] 12.4
```

```
mean(dat_sales$ncalls)
```

```
## [1] 12.4
```

3.2.1 Loading Data

3.2.1.1 From an R Package

Run the following to see list of data in your R.

```
data()
```

If you have successfully installed `ahdar` package, type the following command to see the list of data within the package:

```
library(ahdar)
data(package="ahdar")
```

One of the datasets within the package is `youtube`. Let us load this data:

```
data(youtube)
```

`youtube dataset` is now available in your R workspace as an R object and listed in the

`Global Environment pane.`

```
# view the first few rows of youtube dataset
head(youtube)
```

```
## # A tibble:  6 x 3
##    Group  Likes Subscribers
##    <dbl> <dbl>        <dbl>
## 1      1      1           3
## 2      1      2           2
## 3      1      1           3

## 4      2     12           4
## 5      2     11           5
## 6      2     12           4
```

If you do not want to work directly with `youtube` dataset but instead want to work on it as a different object, you can load it by assigning a different name.

```
dat <- youtube
```

Now, look at the `Global Environment` pane, you should see `dat` listed under `Data`.

3.2.2 From Your Computer

For this section, we use haven package and `read _ sav("file.sav")` function to read data from SPSS.

```
library(haven) # load the package
# reading an SPSS data from my Mac

dat _ empathy <-
read _ sav("/Users/ahmaddaryanto/Documents/Data1/empathy2.sav")

# check Global Environment pane
# dat _ empathy should appear there.
```

If you have data in formats used by software such as STATA or SAS, visit this page https://haven.tidyverse.org. For Excel, you can refer to this page https://readxl.tidyverse.org

3.3 Exporting Data to SPSS Format

To export data into an SPSS format, we can use `write _ sav` function written in the format: `write _ sav(data, "file.sav")`. See the following code:

```
library(haven)
write_sav(dat_sales,
"/Users/ahmaddaryanto/Documents/Data1/dat_sales_temp.sav")
```

3.4 Viewing Data

You can view the contents of the data using `view()`function that belongs to tibble package. You can load it by typing `library(tibble)`.

```
library(tibble) # to use view(dat)

view(dat_sales)
# a new window is created in RStudio.
# showing the contents of the data.
```

You can check the structure of our data with `glimpse()` function from the `dplyr` package.

```
library(dplyr)

glimpse(dat_sales)
```

```
Rows: 5
Columns: 3
$ salesperson <chr> "Alex", "Lou", "Donna", "Dylan", "Millam"
$ ncalls              <dbl>  12, 13, 14, 12, 11
$ npos         <dbl>  4, 6, 4, 6, 5
```

If you want to see only the list of variables:

```
names(dat_sales) # names() is from R base.
```

```
## [1] "salesperson" "ncalls"     "npos"
```

You can read the first n rows of a data

```
head(dat_sales, 3) # view the first 3 row
```

```
#  A tibble:  3 x 3
  salesperson ncalls   npos
  <chr>          <dbl>  <dbl>
1 Alex              12      4
2 Lou               13      6
3 Donna             14      4
```

and the last n rows.

```
tail(dat_sales, 3) # view the last 3 row
```

```
## # A tibble: 3 x 3
##   salesperson ncalls npos
##   <chr>          <dbl> <dbl>
## 1 Donna             14     4
## 2 Dylan             12     6
## 3 Millam            11     5
```

3.5 Pipe Operator

The %>% and >| symbols are called pipe operators, which belongs to the `magrittr` package and loaded automatically if you used the `dplyr` package. Both operators do similar tasks, and for the tasks you are doing in this book, you can use either one of them. The operator %>% is the predecessor of the >| operator. %>% comes from the magrittr package (Bache et al. 2022). If we use the tidyverse package (see Section 3.7), we can use the %>% operator without loading the magrittr package. In this book, I used the two operators interchangeably.

Run `version` or `R.version` in your console to find out the R version you are using.

```
version
```

You can use %>% or >| operator in your code to pass the result of one command to another command in a sequence. This operator is very handy to use if you have a long sequence of code or procedure applied to the same data.

To demonstrate the benefit of using the pipe operator, continue reading to the next section where I discuss some useful functions that can be used to work with data.

3.6 Some Useful Functions

3.6.1 mutate()

You can use `mutate()` function to add new variables to your existing data. This function belongs to the `dplyr` package.

Suppose that I receive a new information about the actual number of orders received by salespersons, which can be stored in a variable called `norders`. I will add this new variable to our previous data `dat_sales` and save the newly augmented data into a new R object called `expanded_dat_sales`. However, I forgot to add a variable to indicate the sex of salespersons and I want to add this information. The following code shows how I add `norders` and `sex` to the existing data using `data.frame` and pipe operator. Instead of having `sex` as a column in my data, I choose `gender` showing you that you do not have to retain the same name. Note that using pipe |>, the code is easy to read and appears to be logically sound.

```
library(magrittr)
library(dplyr)

# create another data
norders <- c(3,5,5,4,3)
sex <- c(1,0,0,1,1) # 0 = female, 1 = male

# set sex as a factor
sex <- as_factor(sex)

# add norders and sex, save to dat_sales1
dat_sales1 <- data.frame(dat_sales,norders, sex)

# using >| operator, save to dat_sales2

dat_sales2 <- dat_sales |>
   mutate(norders = norders) |>
   mutate(gender = sex)
```

Let us view dat_sales

```
dat_sales2
```

```
# A tibble: 5 x 5
  salesperson ncalls  npos  norders  gender
  <chr>        <dbl> <dbl>    <dbl>   <fct>
1  Alex           12     4        3       1
2  Lou            13     6        5       0
3  Donna          14     4        5       0
4  Dylan          12     6        4       1
5  Millam         11     5        3       1
```

You may notice in the output that under variable names within < > sign, each variable is assigned to a specific type: *chr, dbl,* and *fctr. chr* stands for character. `salesperson` is assigned to *chr* because its value is a text or usually called in R as a string type. *dbl* stands for double. `ncalls` is a *dbl* type because it contains numerical values. Although `ncalls` always a solid number, *dbl* accommodates real number, which can take a decimal value. A solid number in R is called an *int* type that stands for integer. *fctr* stands for factor to represent variable in a category (e.g. 0 = female, 1 = male). Sex is assigned to a factor type as a result of running: `sex <- as _ factor(sex)`. Without `as _ factor()` `function, '0,1'` value in `sex` will be declared as *dbl.*

3.6.2 relocate()

Now, we have column `gender` that appears in the last column of the dataset. Ideally, I should have placed it next to `salesperson` as I can see the names of each person along with their respective genders. You can do this by running `relocate(variable,. after = variable)`.

Run the following code:

```
library(magrittr)
library(dplyr)
dat_sales2 <- dat_sales2 |>
relocate(gender,.after = salesperson)

 dat_sales2
```

```
## # A tibble:    5 x 5
##    salesperson    gender ncalls   npos norders
##    <chr>           <fct>  <dbl>  <dbl>   <dbl>
## 1 Alex                 1     12      4       3
## 2 Lou                  0     13      6       5
## 3 Donna                0     14      4       5
## 4 Dylan                1     12      6       4
## 5 Millam               1     11      5       3
```

If you missed `dat _ sales2` <- in the code and run `dat _ sales2`, the result is unchanged because the new operation was not saved to the data.

3.6.3 select()

You can use `select()` function that belongs to `dplyr` package to select columns.

```
library(magrittr)
library(dplyr)
# select CPT_avg and store into a new variable dat_success

dat_success <- dat_sales2 %>%
  select(salesperson, norders)

head(dat_success)
```

```
## # A tibble: 5 x 2
##   salesperson norders
##   <chr>         <dbl>
## 1 Alex              3
## 2 Lou               5
## 3 Donna             5
## 4 Dylan             4
## 5 Millam            3
```

Check RStudio's `Global Environment` pane and locate the new R objects.

3.6.3.1 filter()

Sometimes we have to work on a subset of our data (e.g. male only). We can use `filter()` function that belongs to `dplyr` package to select a subset of our data.

```
library(magrittr)
library(dplyr)

# select male only data
# in our data, male is coded as '1'.

dat_male <- dat_sales2 %>%
  filter(gender == 1)

head(dat_male)
```

```
## # A tibble:   3  x 5
##   salesperson      gender ncalls  npos  norders
##   <chr>             <fct>  <dbl> <dbl>    <dbl>
## 1 Alex                  1     12     4        3
## 2 Dylan                 1     12     6        4
## 3 Millam                1     11     5        3
```

3.6.4 add_row()

Imagine that you just realized that you missed out one salesperson's record whose name is Amy. You can add new information about Amy to the `dat _ sales2` data by using `add _ row()` function and save the result again to `dat _ sales2`. The function `add _ row()` belongs to the tibble package.

```
library(tibble)

dat_sales2 <- dat_sales2 %>%
  add_row(salesperson = "Amy",
          gender = "0", ncalls = 10,
          npos = 6, norders = 4)

dat_success
```

```
## # A tibble: 5 x 2
##   salesperson norders
##   <chr>         <dbl>
## 1 Alex              3
## 2 Lou               5
## 3 Donna             5
## 4 Dylan             4
## 5 Millam            3
```

WARNING

When adding new data for Amy using the `add _ row()` function, I put the " " sign in `gender = "0"`. The " " sign is required because gender is a *fctr* (read: factor) type. Try to remove the " " sign, and inspect your Console.

3.6.5 rowMeans()

Imagine that you want to compute the average score of three variables, which are measures of response of several individuals. For instance, you have three variables – *SAT1, SAT2, SAT3* – and you want to calculate the average score of the three variables for every individual in your dataset. The `rowMeans` is handy for this purpose. In the following code, we have a record of four individuals on three variables. A new variable *SAT_avg* is created to store the average score of the three variables. Then, the new object is combined with the original data frame.

```
SAT1 = c(1,5,6,7)
SAT2 = c(2,3,4,6)
SAT3 = c(3, 5, 6, 5)
dat <- data.frame(SAT1, SAT2, SAT3)
```

```
SAT_avg <- dat %>%
  select(SAT1, SAT2, SAT3) %>%
  rowMeans()

dat <- cbind(dat, SAT_avg)
dat
```

```
##   SAT1 SAT2 SAT3  SAT_avg
## 1    1    2    3 2.000000
## 2    5    3    5 4.333333
## 3    6    4    6 5.333333
## 4    7    6    5 6.000000
```

3.7 All-in-One Package: Tidyverse

At this point, you have used the following packages: `dplyr` and `tibble`. The two packages belong to `tidyverse` https://www.tidyverse.org package, which is a collection of packages useful for data science. Nowadays, `tidyverse` is regarded as the language of modern data science in R. Currently, there are eight packages in tidyverse, each with its own website.

```
install.packages("tidyverse")
```

and load it:

```
library(tidyverse)
```

IMPORTANT

`tidyverse` works with **tidy** data. Data is called **tidy** if its rows and columns refer to observations (or cases) and variables, respectively. For example, `dat _ sales is tidy data.`

3.8 Creating Graphs

R base provides functions to create plots. For example, the `plot()` function can be used to plot data points in x-y coordinate – called a scatter plot.

```
p <- plot(dat_sales2$ncalls, dat_sales2$norders)
p
```

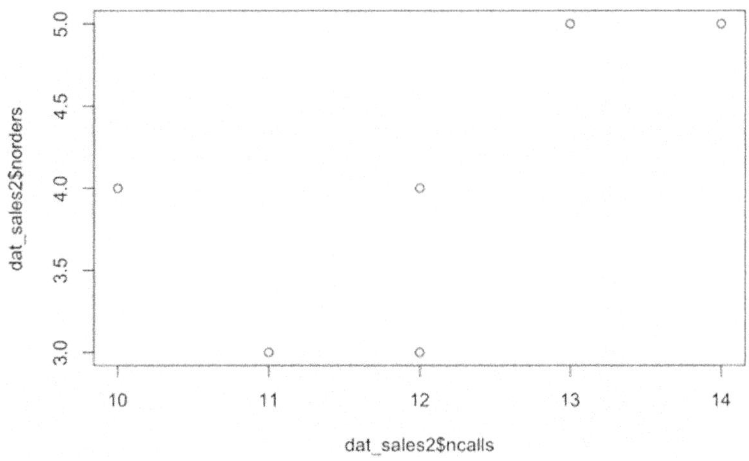

FIGURE 3.2
A scatter plot produced by plot() function.

As you can see from the image, the scatter plot looks basic. Now let us try to `ggplot2`:

```
library(ggplot2)

p <- ggplot(data = dat_sales2,
     mapping = aes(x = ncalls, y = norders)) +
geom_point() +
labs(x = "Number of Calls",
     y = "Number of Orders",
     title = "My first plot using ggplot")
```

You have just created a new R object p. You should see p listed in the `Global Environment` pane – it is placed under `Data`.

NOTE

You do not have to store your graph as an R object. Without storing into an R object, the graph will be produced to output once the line is executed. However, I prefer to store it as an R object because in doing so, I can place the object at any place inside my code.

Now, run the following:

```
p
```

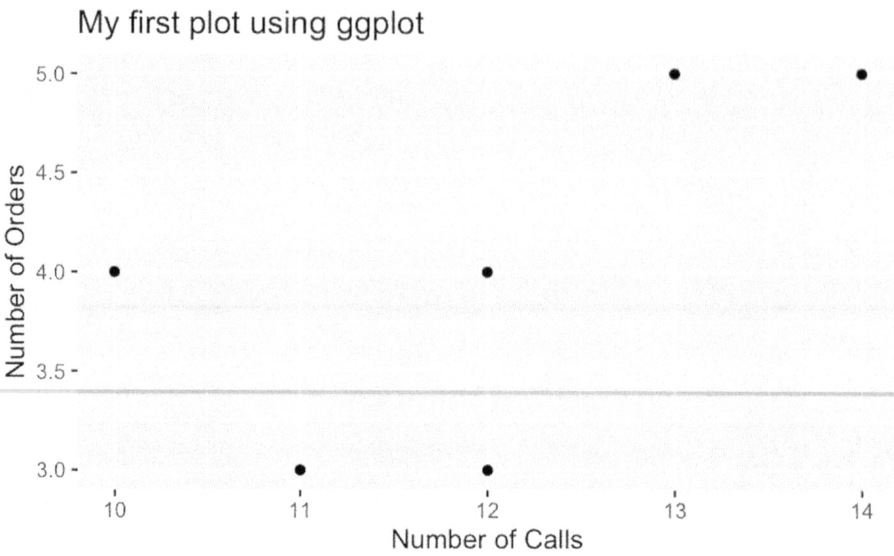

FIGURE 3.3
A ggplot image.

As you can see from the new image, the graph looks more advanced than the basic graph produced by the `plot()` function.

3.8.1 How ggplot2 works

ggplot2 is a system of creating graphs that allow users to develop graphs by adding layers in successive orders (Wickham 2016). ggplot2 implemented the philosophy of building graphs called grammar of graphics introduced by (Wilkinson 2012).

Let us break down the code that we just used to see what is happening line by line.

1. Type in the following:

```
library(ggplot2)

p <- ggplot()
p
# Just a blank grey canvas.
```

FIGURE 3.4
Just a blank grey canvas.

2. How about this code? We declare that we are going to use our data dat_success.

```
p <- ggplot(data = dat_sales2)
p
# will be just a blank grey canvas.
```

3. How about this one? We tell ggplot2 to map our variables `ncalls` and `norders` to x-axis and y-axis in the graph, respectively. In the ggplot terminology, we are mapping our variables into **aesthetic** (aes). **Aesthetic** is the visual property of object in the plot such as its size, shape, and colour.

```
p <- ggplot(data = dat_sales2,
            mapping = aes(x = ncalls, y = norders))
p
```

4. Finally, run this code in which we add `geom_point`. `geom` stands for geometry and point is a type of geometry we want to see on the graph.

   There are a variety of `geom`, some of which will be covered in subsequent chapters.

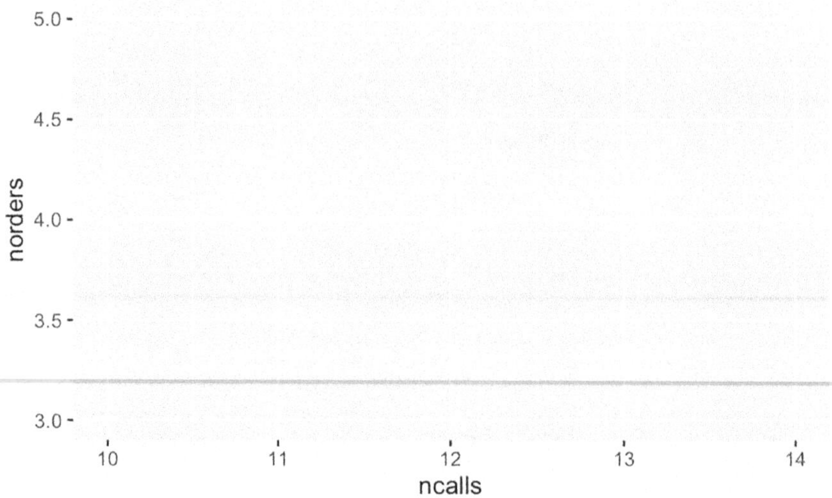

FIGURE 3.5
Grey canvas showing a coordinate system.

```
p <- ggplot(data = dat_sales2, mapping = aes(x = ncalls, y =
norders)) +
        geom_point()
p
```

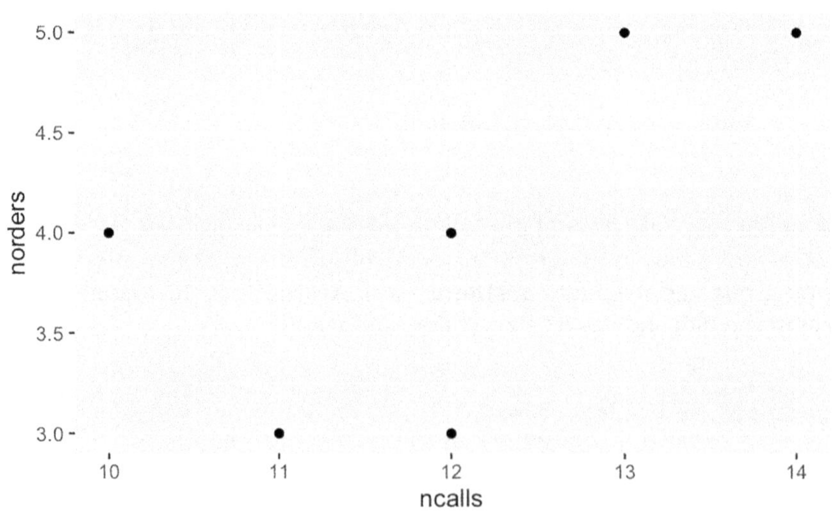

FIGURE 3.6
An image produced by geom_point().

As you might notice, the + sign must be placed at the end of a line if a new task or element is to be added on the graph. The + sign behaves like a pipe operator that we discussed previously. At the time ggplot2 was invented, the pipe operator does not yet exist.

Now, let us put labels and title on the graph.

```
p <- ggplot(data = dat_sales2,
            mapping = aes(x = ncalls,
                          y = norders)) +
      geom_point() +
      labs(x = "Number of Calls",
           y = "Number of Orders",
           title = "My first plot using ggplot")
p
```

What I have presented to you is that breaking down the code line by line even to its most basic from (step 1) and see what it returns. In my opinion, this is the best way to understand what a code does.

The code can be simplified by removing `data` and `mapping` from the first line as ggplot2 will pick up the order of the information supplied on the code.

```
p <- ggplot(dat_sales2, aes(x = ncalls, y = norders)) +
      geom_point() +
      labs(x = "Number of Calls",
          y = "Number of Orders",
          title = "My first Plot")
p
```

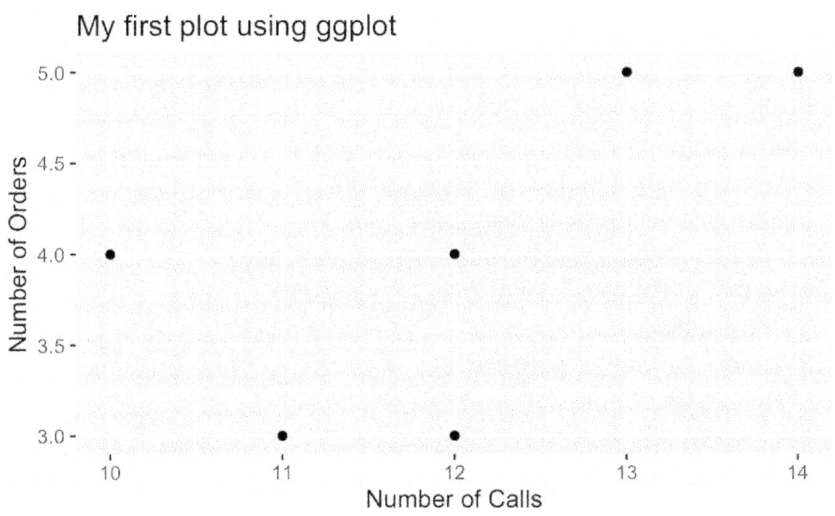

FIGURE 3.7
x-y labels and title were added to the plot.

We can differentiate the shape of the points for different category of gender by adding `shape = gender`, and increase the size of the point by adding `size = 2`.

```
p <- ggplot(dat_sales2,
       aes(x = ncalls, y = norders,
           shape = gender, size = 2)) +
  geom_point() +
  labs(x = "Number of Calls",
       y = "Number of Orders",
       title = "My first Plot") +
  guides(size = "none") +
  scale_shape_discrete(name="Gender",
                       labels=c("Female", "Male"))
```

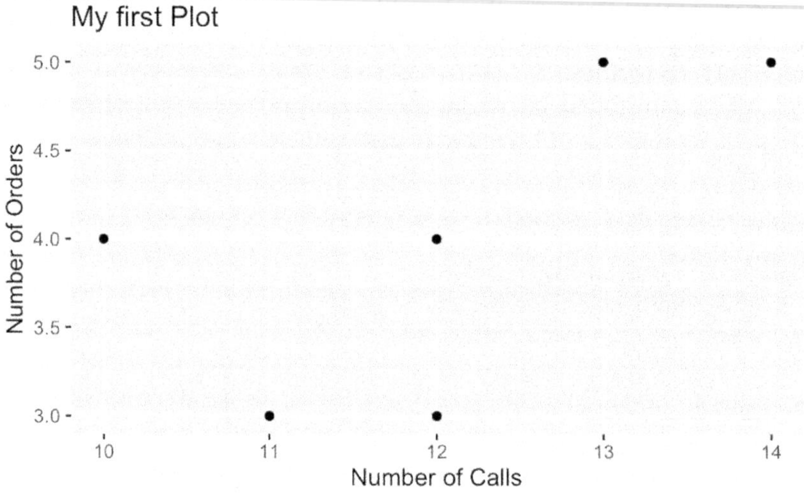

FIGURE 3.8
Another plot.

```
# Note:
# guides(size = "none") removes legend for size
# scale_shape_discrete() changes the legend"
p
```

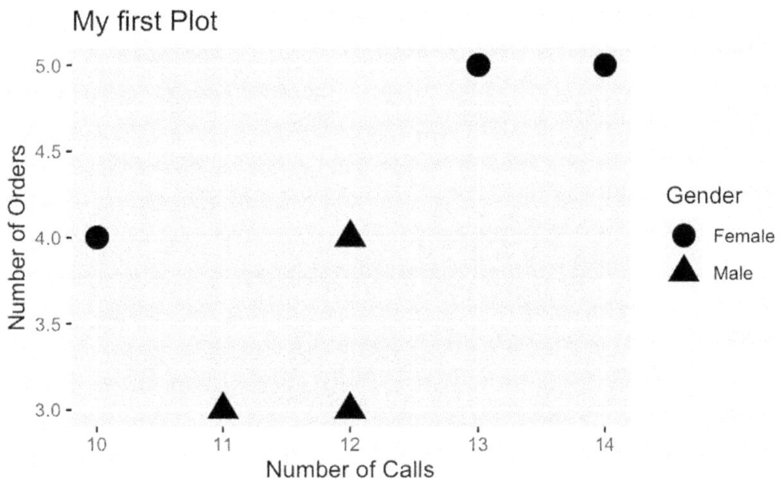

FIGURE 3.9
Adding shape=gender and increasing size of the points.

There is more than one way to produce a plot. Instead of setting **aes()** in the ggplot, you can set **aes()** in the `geom()` layer. The following code will return the same plot.

```
p <- ggplot(dat_sales2) +
  geom_point(aes(x=ncalls,y=norders,shape=gender,size= 2))+
  labs(x="Number of Calls",
       y="Number of Orders",
       title="My first Plot")+
       guides(size="none") +
       scale_shape_discrete(name="Gender",
       labels=c("Female","Male"))
p
```

Putting it all together

The following is my final code. I use data.frame() function to save my data into an R object. I also use set as.factor(), which is a function from R base, to declare gender as a categorical variable:

```
library(tidyverse)
 dat_sales2 <- data.frame(
salesperson = c("Alex", "Lou","Donna", "Dylan", "Millam", "Amy"),
gender = as.factor(c(1,0,0,1,1,0)),
ncalls = c(12,13,14,12,11,10),
 npos = c(4,6,4,6,5,6),
 norders =    c(3,5,5,4,3,4)
 )
```

```
dat_sales2 <- as_tibble(dat_sales2)

p <- ggplot(dat_sales2,
        aes(x = ncalls, y = norders,
            shape = gender, size = 2)) +
    geom_point() +
    labs(x = "Number of Calls",
        y = "Number of Orders",
        title = "Sales Record This Month") +
      guides(size = "none") +
      scale_shape_discrete(name="Gender",
                           labels=c("Female", "Male")) +
  # showing salespersons' names on the plot
  geom_label(aes(label = salesperson),
      nudge_x = 0.25, nudge_y = 0.25)
p
```

3.8.2 Alternative with ggpubr()

Creating a graph with ggplot2 involves adding layers in a successive order. For those who are not familiar with coding, may find this endeavour cumbersome. For this, you can use `ggpubr` package, which is a wrapper for ggplot2. Using this package makes the task of plotting a graph quite straightforward as you do not have to type in "+" sign at the end of a line to add a new layer.

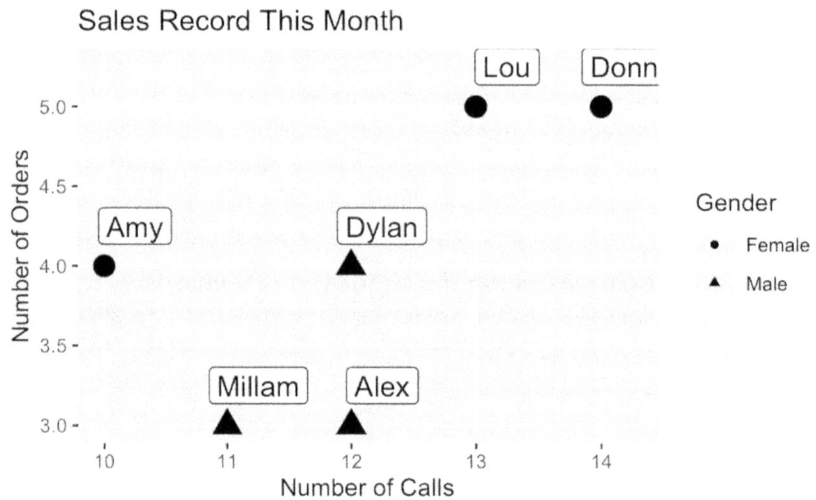

FIGURE 3.10
A nice looking image.

`Install ggpubr package:`

```
install.packages("ggpubr")
```

Use `ggscatter()` function from ggpubr to create a scatter plot:

```
library(ggpubr)

# first part
p2 <- ggscatter(data = dat_sales2,
          x = "ncalls", y = "norders",
          shape = "gender",
          size = 5,
          xlab = "Number of Calls",
          ylab = "Number of Orders",
          title = "My first Plot",
          ggtheme = theme_gray())

# second part: modifying legend

p2 <- p2 +
   scale_shape_discrete(name="Gender", labels=c("Female", "Male"))
 p2
```

The first part of the code is just one long syntax where adding layers were handled internally inside ggpubr:

```
p2 + ggscatter(data,x,y,shape,size,xlab,ylab,title,ggtheme)
```

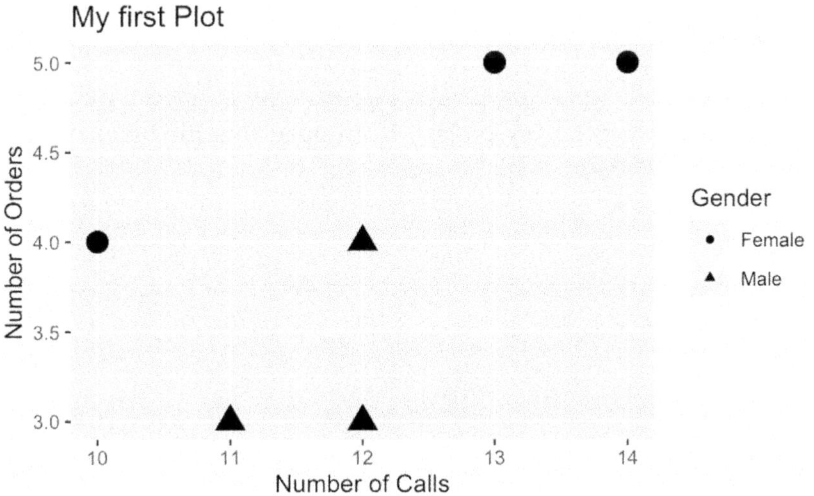

FIGURE 3.11
A scatter plot using ggscatter() from ggpubr() package.

3.9 Working on a Project

If you are working on a specific project that requires writing several R scripts, you can create an R project from RStudio by clicking: *File* → New Project.

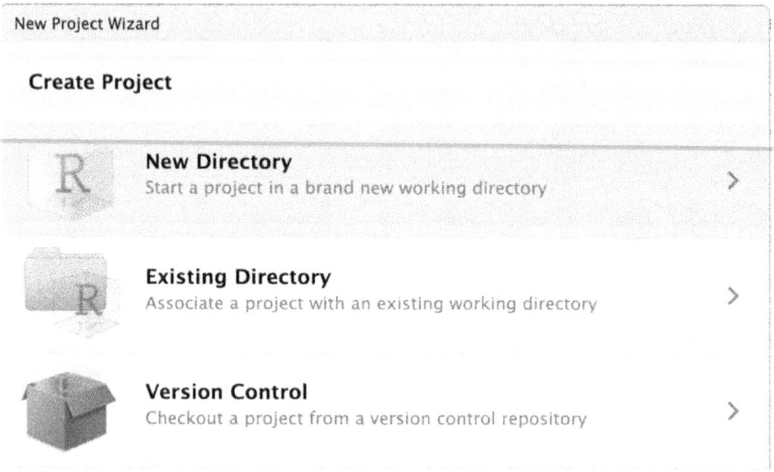

FIGURE 3.12
Next, click New Directory.

- Choose `New Directory`.
- Click `New Project` (untick `Create Git Repository`) and type in your project name, e.g. MyProject.

I have just created a new folder in my directory. It contains a file with extension.*Rproj*. Every time I want to work on my project, I can open this file by clicking File Reject Project$, then select *MyProject*.

FIGURE 3.13
Next, click `New Project`.

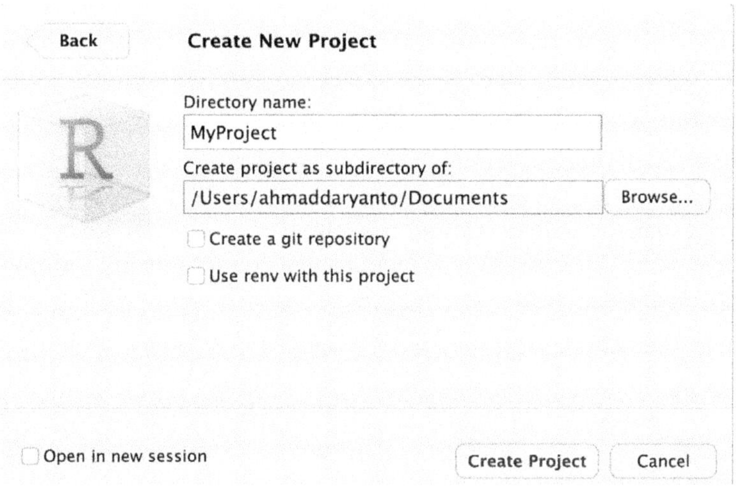

FIGURE 3.14
Type in a directory name and untick `Create a git repository`.

FIGURE 3.15
A folder contains.Rproj.

Any R scripts that I created will be saved to *MyProject* folder. For example, I have created one R script *first_script.R* saved into the folder.

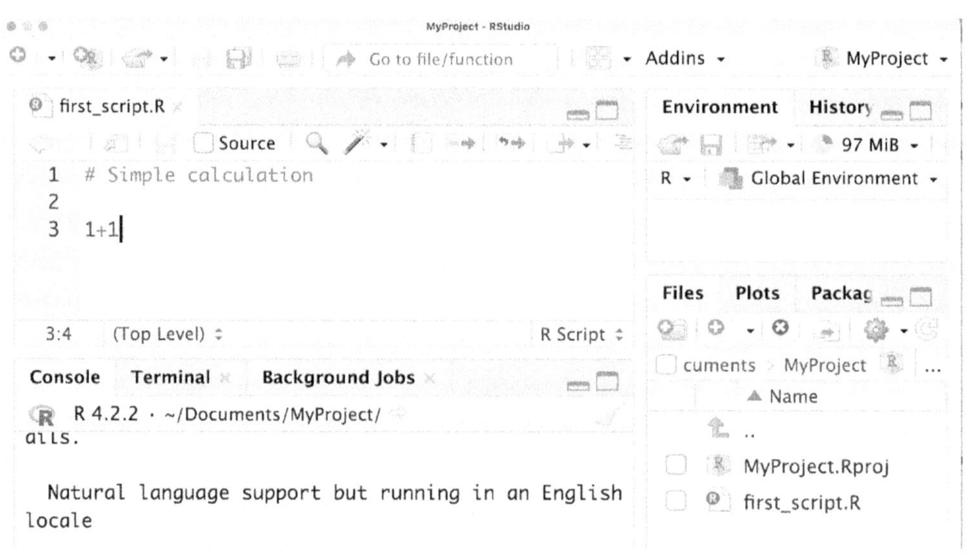

FIGURE 3.16
The folder contains one R script.

I can check which my directory I am working in by typing – it should return

```
getwd()
```

```
# [1] "/Users/ahmaddaryanto/Documents/MyProject"
```

3.10 What Else Can You Do with R?

If you are comfortable using R and RStudio, it opens up an enormous opportunity that you can do with R. R and RStudio are not only great tools for data and statistical analysis, but they can also be used to produce reports, presentation slides, books, and even animations. For example, some parts of this book were initially written using the `quarto()` package, which I compiled to LaTeX documents (you can learn more about LaTeX by visiting this website, https://www.latex-project.org).

3.11 Summary

This section produces a brief introduction to R and RStudio. It shows how to work with R packages and R functions to import, export, view, and modify data. This section also introduces `ggplot2` and `ggpubr` packages for creating beautiful graphs using R.

3.12 Review Questions

1. What is an R object?
2. What is the different between R functions and R packages?
3. Explain how ggplot2 works.
4. What are the advantages of working with the tidyverse package?

3.13 Exercises

1. Install `ISRL` package in your Posit or RStudio. This package contains datasets used in the book *An Introduction to Statistical Learning with Applications in R*, by James, Witten, Hastie, and Tibshirani. How many datasets are in this package?
2. Load dataset `Carseats` from the ISLR package. How many variables are in this data?

3.14 Further Reading

I recommend the following R books if you want to delve deeper into R. These books are great learning resources on R and available online. These books are actively maintained by their authors.

Wickham, H. (2016), *Package 'ggplot2': Elegant graphics for data analysis*, Springer-Verlag, New York. https://doi.org/10.1007/978-3-319-24277-4_9, https://ggplot2-book.org

Wickham, H., Çetinkaya-Rundel, M. & Grolemund, G. (2023), *R for data science*, O'Reilly Media, Inc. https://r4ds.hadley.nz

Part II

Basic Concepts in Measurement, Data Descriptions, and Distributions

4

Construct and Measurement

Constructs are at the heart of research in social sciences. They are employed to comprehend our social environments, such as family, schools, consumers, etc. Many of these constructs are latent, meaning that they are not directly observable, even though they are commonly used in everyday conversations and hold a central position in our attention. For example, everyone seems to possess a preconceived idea about consumer satisfaction, although it cannot be directly observed. Furthermore, satisfaction may hold different meanings for different people. Therefore, a clear definition of what constitutes a construct that everyone is agreed upon is needed. Without this, multiple interpretations can arise merely because individuals discuss the same thing but may actually mean different things. This chapter delves into what constitutes a latent construct, its operational definition, and how it can be transformed into a variable during data analysis. Following the discussion of a construct, the concept of a measurement scale is covered, followed by an exploration of how to assess its reliability and validity. The assessment of reliability using tools, such as SPSS and R, is also demonstrated.

Learning Objectives:

- Understand what constitute a (latent) construct and its operationalization.
- Understand the use of a scale to measure a construct.
- Understand the difference between a reflective and a formative latent construct.
- Understand the four levels of measurement scale.
- Understand the notion of reliability and validity.
- Be able to conduct reliability analysis using SPSS and R.

4.1 Marketing Construct

Let us look at the following phrases that can be used to state research objectives. Similar statements like these can be found in the front page of an introduction section of a research report or research article.

- To determine the effect of *perceive ease of use* on *customer intention to revisit a website*
- To determine the effect of *compulsive buying* on *satisfaction toward a product*
- To determine the effect of *gender* on the *attitude toward a print ad*

DOI: 10.4324/9781003407225-6

Some words in those sentences are *underlined*. They are called constructs or to be more precise, latent psychological constructs or latent constructs, for short. A latent construct is not easily observable without involving some kinds of measurement or overt observations – that way, it is *latent*. For instance, we will not know whether a consumer will buy a product by just observing the way she walked around in a shop unless we wait until she makes a purchase. Alternatively, we can approach her and ask whether she intend to buy something in the shop. Here, the latent construct we are uncovering is her purchase intention. I include gender in this example. Gender can also be considered as a latent construct unless we know for certain the gender of an individual. As in an anonymous survey, the gender of the respondents is unknown by researchers; hence, it is latent. The key research challenge is that how we are going to measure these latent constructs and ensure we are really measuring them.

4.1.1 Definition

You must have heard the term 'concept', which refers to a general idea about something (e.g. a cat, a table). A latent construct is just the abstract version of the concept, which can stem from individual trait, attitude, motivation, perception, and preferences. For example, extrovert is a construct, which as personality trait. Attitude toward a brand is an attitudinal construct that is used to represent consumer's evaluation of a brand. A brand preference is a construct that describes the extent to which a consumer prefers a certain brand over another brand. These constructs can be measured by presenting individuals with a single or a set of statements or questions. We discuss ways of measuring constructs in the following section.

4.1.2 Construct Operationalization

One construct can be measured in different ways. For example, to measure consumer loyalty toward a store, we can present consumers with set of statements and ask them to indicate their opinion about the statements (e.g. 1 = strongly disagree, 7 = strongly agree). One such statement is 'I will continue buying from this store'. Alternatively, we can ask them to indicate their willingness to recommend a store to their friends by responding to this question: 'I will recommend this store to my friends'. Another option is by asking them to indicate how often they visit the store in a week. These different ways of measuring a construct are called **construct operationalization** or **operational definition** of a construct.

4.1.3 Variable

A variable can be treated as a synonym for a construct, but it is mostly used when working with data. A variable contains values that vary from one observation (e.g. person's height) to another observation. If a construct is measured with multiple questions or multiple items, each item belonging to the construct is a variable. When working with data, researchers commonly refer to a variable instead of a construct and the variable's name is not necessarily the same as a construct it represents. For instance, gender is a construct. Any names can be assigned to represent gender in a data file. We can use 'GEND' as a variable in our data file to record gender. Take satisfaction as another example. If satisfaction is measured with three items, we can use variables 'SAT1' 'SAT2', and 'SAT3' to represent each of the three items in our data file.

4.2 Scale

A scale is the set of statements or questions to measure constructs. For instance, consumer impulsiveness scale is the scale to measure consumers' tendency to buy things impulsively. This scale is developed by Rook & Fisher (1995), which consists of 9 items. Two sample items of the impulsiveness scale are (1) 'I often buy things spontaneously' and (2) 'I often buy things without thinking'. These statements require respondents to indicate their agreement of disagreement using a 7-point Likert scale ranging from 1 = strongly disagree to 7 = strongly agree.

The relationship between a latent construct and their measurement items can be visually described by a diagram. Figure 4.1 shows the relationship between satisfaction and its three measurement items. As we can see from the figure, satisfaction is a latent construct. As a convention, a latent construct in a diagram is usually represented by an oval. Each of the three items measuring satisfaction is represented by a rectangle that is typically used to represent observable items. In the diagram, satisfaction and its measurement items is connected by an arrow. As we can see in the figure, the direction of the arrow is from satisfaction to the measurement items. This arrow direction infers that satisfaction exerts an influence on the items. That is, the existence of satisfaction influences how consumers provide responses to the three measurement items. Consequently, any changes in the three measurement items should occur due to changes in satisfaction. In other words, the three measurement items are the manifestation of satisfaction. A latent construct that determines the values of the measurement items, is known in literature as a **reflective construct**.

Some constructs are composed of multiple items, each of which can itself be considered as a construct. In this case, the direction of influence is from the items to the construct. That is, the directions of the arrows in a diagram are from items to constructs implying that that a latent construct exists because it is formed by the items. In other words, it is the items that give rise to the construct.

Such a latent construct is called a **formative construct**. For example, **SES** (socio-economic status) is a good example of a formative construct that is formed all together by education, income, and status (see Figure 4.2). In-depth discussion on the distinction between reflective and formative constructs in marketing can be read in Jarvis et al. (2003).

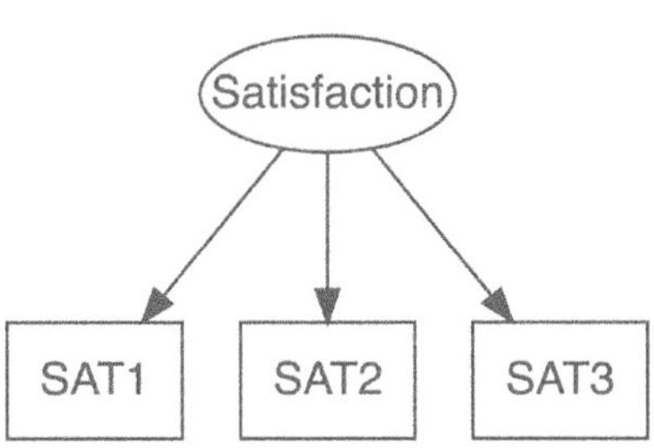

FIGURE 4.1
Satisfaction measured with three reflective items.

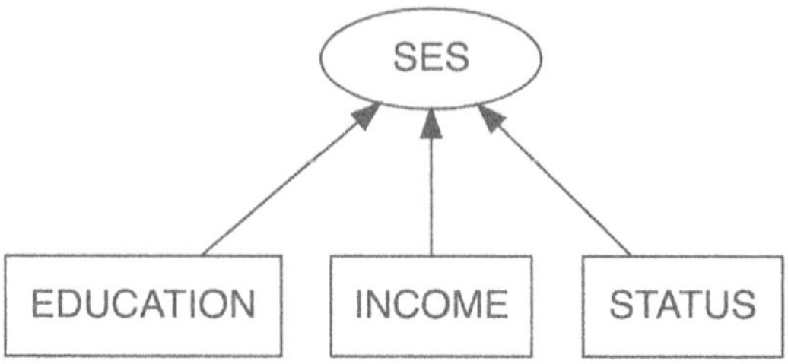

FIGURE 4.2
SES is a formative construct.

NOTE

It is worth noting that, in empirical research, reflective constructs are predominantly used than formative constructs. For example, in a tourism research, for measuring destination image, 88% of articles treated it as a reflective rather than a formative construct (Mikulić & Ryan 2018).

Developing a scale involves a lengthy and complex scientific procedure, which is beyond the scope of this book. Nevertheless, nearly every day a new scale is developed. It is highly likely that the scale we need for our research already exists, so we do not need to invent a new scale. This Wikibooks textbook contains documentations of scales used in management research: https://en.wikibooks.org/wiki/Handbook_of_Management_Scales. Other resources worth looking are the handbook of scales written by Bearden & Netemeyer (1999), Bruner et al. (2005), and Zarantonello & Pauwels-Delassus (2015). Articles in academic journals are also excellent resources for scales especially newly invented scales. The whole statements in the scale are usually placed in an appendix or a method section of the article.

TIP

Scale development process is a serious scientific endeavour. Therefore, many researchers relied on scales developed by other researchers who had developed their scale through a rigour scale development process. Borrowing a scale from others, more often, requires changing elements of the scale to fit into your research context (e.g. translating the scale from English to other language). Scale adaption requires a justification of why the scale needs to be adapted (see (Heggestad et al. 2019) who provides an excellent discussion on this topic).

4.3 Using a Scale

Imagine that we have collected data on consumer satisfaction. Our consumer satisfaction scale consists of three items, each measured with a 7-point semantic scale with 1= very dissatisfied and 7 = very satisfied. Let us assign SAT1, SAT2, and SAT3 as variables representing these items. So how would we determine the level of consumer satisfaction, suppose a particular consumer provides SAT1 = 4, SAT2 = 5, and SAT = 6?

4.3.1 Summated Score

One alternative we can use to represent satisfaction is by creating a composite score by summing or adding together the response to each item making up the summated scale, i.e. SAT1 + SAT2 + SAT 3 = 4 + 5 + 6 = 15. The drawback of this option is that it is not directly obvious to us how to translate score of 15 into something that is easy to communicate and meaningful: what does '15' mean?

4.3.2 Mean Score

Another option is to calculate the average score of the items or mean score. The advantage of a mean score is that it has a meaning when translated back to options in the response answers. For example, the mean score of the three satisfaction items is equal to $\frac{4+5+6}{3} = 5$. Translating back to the 5-point satisfaction scale, score '5' means 'satisfied'. A mean score of satisfaction is more meaningful than the summated score of satisfaction, and as easy as the summated score to calculate. For these reasons, a mean score is a favourite metric to use to represent a construct.

4.3.3 Problem with Mean Score

Nevertheless, taking a mean score to represent a construct is not without a problem. By taking a mean score, we implicitly assume that respondents react to the three satisfaction items in the same way. In calculating the mean score of satisfaction, we implicitly assume that each measurement item contributes equally to the formation of mean score of satisfaction (see Figure 4.3). This means, that in the calculation, each item has an equal weight: $\frac{1\times 4+1\times 5+1\times 6}{3} = 5$.

A mean score is a special case of a weighted mean (W) given by the following formula:

$$W = \frac{\sum_{i=1}^{N} w_i v_i}{\sum_{i=1}^{N} w_i}$$

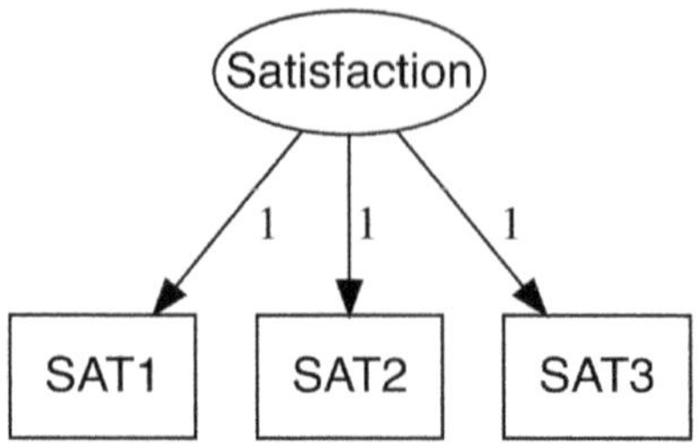

FIGURE 4.3
The three items contribute equally to satisfaction.

where w_i is the weight applied to the v_i values. For example, if the weight applied to SAT1 is 60%, and those applied to SAT2 and SAT3 are only 30%, then the weighted mean of satisfaction is equal to:

$$W_{SAT} = \frac{0.6 \times SAT1 + 0.3 \times SAT2 + 0.3 \times SAT3}{0.6 + 0.3 + 0.3}$$
$$= \frac{0.6 \times 4 + 0.3 \times 5 + 0.3 \times 6}{0.6 + 0.3 + 0.3} = 4.75$$

The weighted mean score is 4.75, which is lower than the ordinary mean score with equal weights. However, if the items have similar weight regardless the size of the weights, the consistent weights will produce a weighted average that is also equal to an ordinary mean score. For example, for weight = 30%:

$$W_{SAT} = \frac{0.3 \times SAT1 + 0.3 \times SAT2 + 0.3 \times SAT3}{0.3 + 0.3 + 0.3}$$

Generally, if the weights of all items are equal ($w_i = w$), with a simple algebra, it can be shown that:

$$\begin{aligned} W &= \frac{\sum_{i=1}^{N} w_i v_i}{\sum_{i=1}^{N} w_i} \\ &= \frac{\sum_{i=1}^{N} w v_i}{\sum_{i=1}^{N} w_i} \\ &= \frac{w \sum_{i=1}^{N} v_i}{Nw} \\ &= \frac{\sum_{i=1}^{N} v_i}{N} \\ &= \bar{W} \end{aligned} \tag{4.1}$$

where $\bar{W}$ is an ordinary mean.

Nevertheless, assigning equal weights to measurement items sounds quite unrealistic as, in this case, we expect respondents to react to measurement items in the same way.

This assumption might not be achieved in a real-life research setting. Now, let us assign a different weight to each of the three items: *SAT* 1 = 50%, *SAT* 2 = 50%, and *SAT* = 40%:

$$
\begin{aligned}
W_{SAT} &= \frac{0.5\times 4+0.5\times 5+0.4\times 6}{0.5+0.5+0.4} \\
&= 4.92
\end{aligned}
$$

The result is quite close to the ordinary mean. These simple exercises show us that taking into account the individual contribution of measurement items to the calculation of mean score might best represent the construct than just using the ordinary mean score. However, taking mean score for our three satisfaction items is not a bad idea provided that the weights are not small (e.g. greater than 0.5).

Finding the weights of items of a known construct is a serious research endeavour. Furthermore, calculating scores that best represent a construct is far from simple than our exercise shows. In real life, errors can be induced when respondents react to measurement items, which introduce measurement errors. For example, the mood that the respondents have when filling in a survey can produce answers that might not truly reflect the true opinions. One statistical technique that can be used to deal with measurement errors is **factor analysis (FA)**, which is discussed in Chapter 22.

4.4 Combining Two Scales

We can combine two scales to make up a new scale. I have devised two instruments to measure my students' attitude toward quantitative and qualitative research. You can see the response of one of my students who participated in my survey in Figure 4.4. As you can see in the figure, five items are used to measure attitude toward quantitative research and five items to measure attitude toward qualitative research. In each of the

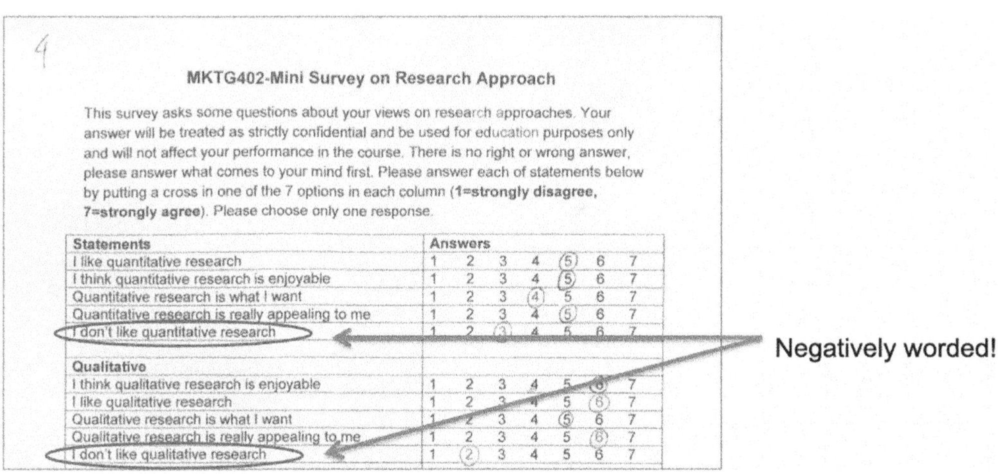

4

MKTG402-Mini Survey on Research Approach

This survey asks some questions about your views on research approaches. Your answer will be treated as strictly confidential and be used for education purposes only and will not affect your performance in the course. There is no right or wrong answer, please answer what comes to your mind first. Please answer each of statements below by putting a cross in one of the 7 options in each column (**1=strongly disagree, 7=strongly agree**). Please choose only one response.

Statements	Answers						
I like quantitative research	1	2	3	4	(5)	6	7
I think quantitative research is enjoyable	1	2	3	4	(5)	6	7
Quantitative research is what I want	1	2	3	(4)	5	6	7
Quantitative research is really appealing to me	1	2	3	4	(5)	6	7
I don't like quantitative research	1	2	(3)	4	5	6	7
Qualitative							
I think qualitative research is enjoyable	1	2	3	4	5	(6)	7
I like qualitative research	1	2	3	4	5	(6)	7
Qualitative research is what I want	1	2	3	4	(5)	6	7
Qualitative research is really appealing to me	1	2	3	4	5	(6)	7
I don't like qualitative research	1	(2)	3	4	5	6	7

FIGURE 4.4
Two scales administered to measure attitude toward quantitative/qualitative research.

subscale, there is one item that is worded negatively: 'I don't like quantitative research' and 'I don't like qualitative research'. Including negatively worded items are a nice tactic to check whether respondents are paying enough attention to our questionnaire. If all items are worded in the same directions (e.g. all positively worded), there is a possibility that respondents will just tick the same position in a survey or apply a slight variation (e.g. zigzag ticking). These kinds of response style might introduce a bias in research findings known as a common method variance (Podsakoff et al. 2012).

In my survey, the response answers are given in a 7-point Likert scale format ranging from 1 = strongly disagree to 7 = strongly agree. Before proceeding to analysis, the two negative items in the survey need to be reverse-coded. A simple rule to reverse code an item is by summing the maximum and minimum point, then subtracting the original value:

TIP

reverse code = (maximum point + minimum point) – original value

In Figure 4.4, the response answer of the negative item 'I don't like quantitative research' being reverse coded is $(7+1)-3=8-3=5$. The original score of 3 (somewhat disagree), after being reverse coded to 5, corresponds to somewhat agree. If we do not reverse code the original score and straightly take the average of all items to represent the score of the scale, the result would be misleading.

For the response answer in Figure 4.4, respondent's score for attitude toward quantitative research (AQ) is computed as here.

$$AQ=\frac{5+5+4+5+(\mathbf{8}-\mathbf{3})}{5}=4.8 \tag{4.2}$$

$$AL=\frac{6+6+5+6+(\mathbf{8}-\mathbf{2})}{5}=5.8 \tag{4.3}$$

Having the scores for *AQ* and *AL*, we can invent an index, say, and index of **method orientation**, which reflects the extent to which one is predominantly oriented toward quantitative or qualitative research. **Method orientation** can be operationalized as the difference between *AQ* and *AL* score: *AQ* – *AL*. That is, if $AQ > 0$, then a respondent is predominantly oriented toward quantitative research, and if $AQ < 0$, the respondents is predominantly oriented toward qualitative research.

4.5 Scale Evaluation

How to evaluate whether a scale used to measure a construct is good? Here, good means the scale should be both reliable and valid. Scale evaluation requires a **reliability** and **validity** analysis.

4.5.1 Reliability

Reliability is an indicator of a scale consistency, which measures the extent to which a scale is free from a random error. Reliability also means consistency or stability. If a scale is administered to the same respondents at two separate points in time and if the results of both measurements are the same, provided the condition between the first and second measurement are the same, then the consistency is achieved showing the scale is reliable. For a scale that has multiple items, it would be reliable if responses on those items are relatively consistent. To check for item consistency, we can calculate a **Cronbach's alpha** or **coefficient alpha** invented by Cronbach (1951). This is an indicator or reliability that is widely used and reported by researchers.

WARNING

Cronbach's alpha is denoted by α. Significant level, which we are going to learn in subsequent chapters, is also denoted by level α. Do not get confused between the two.

Cronbach's alpha is a measure of consistency among items calculated by using data provided by respondents. It assesses the extent to which items in a scale get together in measuring a construct. Its value is ranging from 0 to 1. It is equal to 0 if the scale is totally unreliable, which means no consistency among the items. It is equal to 1 is the scale is perfectly reliable – perfect reliability is impossible to achieve in reality.

IMPORTANT

Cronbach's alpha of 0.7 is generally considered satisfactory and acceptable in research.

4.5.2 Validity

Validity is a measure the extent to which the items of a scale really measure the intended construct. There are three types of validity:

- Face validity refers to whether scale items appear to reflect the construct it is supposed to measure – do the items read as representing the intended construct? A simple way to inspect whether a scale achieves face validity is simply by reading out loud each item in the scale. Imagine, the variable LOY1 reads as 'I like the brand', while LOY2 and LOY3 read as 'I would recommend this brand to my family and friends' and 'I buy this brand whenever I can', respectively. If we use these three items to measure brand loyalty, the scale would not achieve face validity because LOY1 does not seem to measure brand loyalty but brand liking. Brand liking and brand loyalty are two distinct constructs; therefore, we cannot use LOY1 as an item to measure brand loyalty (see Table 4.1).

TABLE 4.1

Loyalty Items (One Is Not)

Item	Wording	Construct
LOY1	I like the brand	Brand liking
LOY2	I would recommend this brand to my family and friend	Brand loyalty
LOY3	I buy this brand whenever I can	Brand loyalty

- Convergent validity refers to the extent to which a scale is positively correlated with other scale that measures a positively-related construct. For example, scale items measuring brand liking should be positively correlated with those measuring loyalty – if you like a brand, you are highly likely to say positive things about the brand to your friends.
- Discriminant validity refers to the extent to which a scale is negatively correlated or uncorrelated to other scales from which it is supposed to differ. For example, scale items measuring brand liking should be negatively correlated with those measuring brand hate – responses to brand hate and brand like should be in an opposite direction unless you can love and hate a brand at the same time!

4.5.3 Reliability vs. Validity

It is important to note that a reliable scale is not necessarily valid. If you step on a scale to measure your weight and if it repeatedly shows 80 kg, you would ignore the scale when your weight is just 65 kg. However, the scale is reliable because it shows a consistent number every time you step on it. However, despite being stable, the scale is not valid because it is not showing your true weight. For a scale to be valid, it should also be reliable.

IMPORTANT

A good scale is one that is both **reliable** and **valid.**

4.6 Response Formats

Majority of research in social science used a scaled-response formats. The formats utilized a continuum (e.g. 5- or 7-point scale) chosen by the researcher to measure respondent's attitudes, feelings, judgements, and perceptions. These response options permit the measurement of the intensity of a respondent's answers. The Likert scale is a widely favoured set of response options employed by researchers. It typically includes a 5-point scale, where responses range from 1 for 'disagree' to 5 for 'agree'. Alternatively, it might utilize a 7-point scale, with options labelled from 1 for 'strongly disagree' to 7 for 'strongly agree'. The scale was invented by an American social scientist, Rensis Likert, in 1932 (Likert 1932). There is an interesting article about the history of the Likert scale by Edmondson (2005) – please read it.

Another popular format is the semantic differential scale. The scale was developed by a psychologist Charles E. Osgood (Osgood 1964). The characteristics of the semantic differential scale is that the end-points have bipolar labels (e.g. bad – good; negative – positive; powerless – powerful).

4.7 Level of Measurement

A variable can have one of the four levels of measurement: nominal, ordinal, interval, and ratio. These levels of measurement refer to the mathematical nature of the numbers assigned to the variable. Knowing these four levels of measurement is very important because it dictates the choice of statistical tests that we can use.

- **Nominal.** Keyword: **labelling.** Nominal assigns a label to an object or observation for identification purposes. For example, a consumer' ID number on a water bill is nominal data. One's student ID is just a number to differentiate the student with others.
- **Ordinal.** Keywords: **labelling + ordering.** Ordinal data preserves the property of the nominal data (i.e. labelling) but also gives information about the order, ranking or the position of the observations in a response answer. For example, a response answer to this question: How often do you click our YouTube channel in a day? (1 = always, 5 = never) is ordinal data. Viewers who tick '1' are obviously more loyal than those who tick '5'.
- **Interval.** Keywords: **labelling + ordering + distance.** Interval scale retains the property of the nominal and ordinal data but also gives information about the distance between the points in a scale. For example, satisfaction rating measured with 7-point scale with 1 = very unsatisfied and 7 = very satisfied is an interval scale. Age measured in years is also an interval scale. The distance, which is the difference between two points is meaningful in an interval scale. If one aged 30 and another person aged 20. The difference between the age, which is 10 years, is meaningful.
- **Ratio.** Keywords: **labelling + ordering + distance + zero.** The ratio scale is seemingly similar to the interval scale. The only addition to the definition of the ratio scale is that the origin of the scale or the zero point on the scale is clearly defined or meaningful. For example, income in pounds is a ratio scale where zero income means a person receives no income or possibly unemployed.

Interval and ratio variables are quantitative in nature because we can apply a mathematical formulation to manipulate the scores of the variables. For example, we can compute an average score of an interval or ratio variable. However, we cannot calculate the average score of a nominal or ordinal variable. For this reason, nominal and ordinal variables are both classified as qualitative variables. Nominal, ordinal, and interval

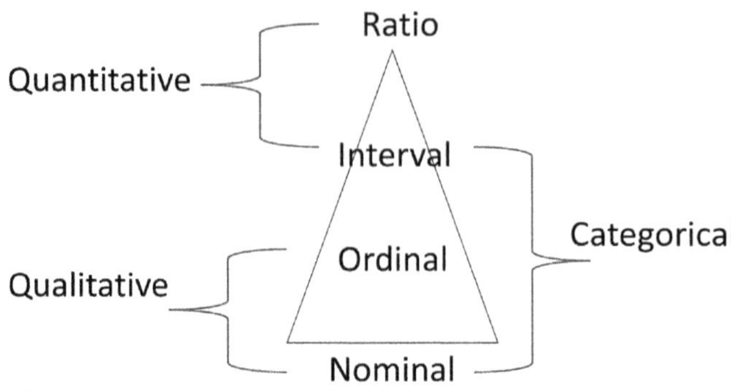

FIGURE 4.5
Level of measurement.

variables are in a discrete form because the scores of these variables are whole numbers. A discrete variable can be obtained from a counting process (e.g. counting the number of brands in the market). A ratio variable can be discrete or continuous. A continuous variable has a value in any place on a ruler and can contain decimal places (e.g. 42.195 km). Any variable in the upper level can be transformed to other type below the hierarchy. For example, a customer satisfaction scores is a ratio variable and can be transformed to an ordinal variable to classify customers into two categories: satisfied and unsatisfied customers. However, having known a customer to be a satisfied customer is uninformative about the person's actual satisfaction score unless the score is revealed to us. In other words, a variable in a lower category cannot be transformed into that of the upper category. These explanations can be summarized in Figure 4.5.

4.8 Different Ways of Measuring the Same Construct

A construct can be measured in multiple ways using different types of level of measurements. For example, satisfaction can be measured using either a nominal, interval, or ratio scale. This is illustrated by the following example.

- Nominal

  Are you satisfied with our mobile app?

  ______Yes ______No
- Ordinal

  Compared to other mobile app you have used, how is your satisfaction with our mobile app?

  ______Lower______About the same______Higher
- Interval

  Please indicate your level of satisfaction with our mobile app

  ______Very unsatisfied______Unsatisfied______Satisfied______Very satisfied

TIP

Which level of measurement should we use? In some situations, we may not have a choice about which level of measurement to be used. For example, gender will always be a nominal scale. When we do have a choice, it is advisable to use a higher-order level of measurement because the choice of the statistical analysis that can be implemented is wider compared to a lower-order level.

4.9 Reliability Analysis

If a scale intended to measure a construct consists of multiple items, we can conduct a reliability analysis to check the consistency of the items, that is, whether the multiple items belong together in measuring the construct. For this purpose, we can calculate a Cronbach's alpha and inspect whether it is greater than the recommended value of 0.7.

Suppose that brand trust is measured with four items and response answers of 500 customers were gathered. The brand trust's items are presented thus:

- I trust this brand (BT1)
- I rely on this brand (BT2)
- This is an honest brand (BT3)
- This brand is safe (BT4)

4.9.1 SPSS Action and Interpretation

Data: retailerbrand.sav

Follow the following step to get Cronbach's alpha. Steps:

- Analyze → Scale → Reliability Analysis.
- Insert BT1, BT2, BT3, and BT4 into the `Items box`.
- Click `Statistics`.
- Tick Descriptives for `Items`, `Scale`, and `Scale if items deleted`.
- Click `OK` or `Paste` if you want to work with an SPSS syntax, and inspect the output window.

Clicking `Paste` produces the following syntax:

```
RELIABILITY
   /VARIABLES=BT1 BT2 BT3 BT4
   /SCALE('ALL VARIABLES') ALL
   /MODEL=ALPHA
   /SUMMARY=TOTAL.
```

Reliability Statistics

Cronbach's Alpha	N of Items
.793	4

Item-Total Statistics

	Scale Mean if Item Deleted	Scale Variance if Item Deleted	Corrected Item-Total Correlation	Cronbach's Alpha if Item Deleted
BT1	14.49	8.270	.694	.695
BT2	15.49	7.882	.535	.795
BT3	14.27	8.994	.647	.723
BT4	14.13	9.603	.583	.754

FIGURE 4.6
SPSS outputs of the reliability analysis.

From the outputs shown in the last figure, you only look at two key information:

- Cronbach's alpha, which is greater than 0.7 indicating a good reliability coefficient. Some researchers accept a cut-off value of 0.6.
- Item-Total Statistics table shows reliability coefficient if an item is dropped from the analysis. The table provides a list of alpha if one item is not selected. For example, if we omit BT1, the Cronbach's alpha of the remaining items is 0.895. However, as the Cronbach's alpha for the four items is already good and retaining more items is better than a fewer one – omitting an item means losing an information – therefore, BT1 is kept as a part of measurement items. We can conclude that we have a good indication that BT1, BT2, BT3, and BT4 are reliable items for measuring brand trust.

4.9.2 R Action

To calculate the reliability coefficient in R, you can use the `alpha()` function that belongs to the `psych package`.

```
install.package("pysch")
```

In the following code, I use the same data to calculate the reliability coefficient.

```
library(tidyverse)
library(haven)
library(psych)
library(ahdar)
```

```
dat2 <- retailerbrand %>%
      select(BT1, BT2, BT3, BT4)

res <- alpha(dat2)
res
```

```
Reliability analysis
Call: alpha(x = dat2)

  raw_alpha std.alpha G6(smc) average_r S/N ase   mean sd median_r
       0.79       0.8    0.77      0.51 4.1 0.015  4.9 0.95     0.55

    95% confidence boundaries
         lower alpha upper
Feldt     0.76  0.79  0.82
Duhachek  0.76  0.79  0.82

Reliability if an item is dropped:
   raw_alpha std.alpha G6(smc) average_r S/N alpha se   var.r med.r
BT1     0.69      0.72    0.64      0.46 2.5    0.024 1.3e-02  0.45
BT2     0.80      0.80    0.72      0.57 3.9    0.016 3.5e-05  0.57
BT3     0.72      0.74    0.67      0.48 2.8    0.021 1.4e-02  0.54
BT4     0.75      0.76    0.69      0.52 3.3    0.019 3.4e-03  0.54

Item  statistics
      n raw.r std.r r.cor r.drop mean sd
BT1 500  0.84  0.84  0.77   0.69  5.0 1.2
BT2 500  0.78  0.74  0.60   0.53  4.0 1.5
BT3 500  0.80  0.82  0.73   0.65  5.2 1.1
BT4 500  0.75  0.78  0.68   0.58  5.3 1.0

Non missing response frequency for each item
       1    2    3    4    5    6    7 miss
BT1 0.01 0.03 0.05 0.22 0.34 0.29 0.07    0
BT2 0.06 0.11 0.18 0.30 0.18 0.13 0.04    0
BT3 0.00 0.01 0.04 0.22 0.32 0.30 0.11    0
BT4 0.00 0.00 0.03 0.19 0.29 0.37 0.11    0
```

`alpha()` function produces lots of outputs of which you need only two key information:

- raw_alpha = 0.79. If you want to get the reliability coefficient and omit the rest of the outputs, you can type in your RStudio console:

```
res$total
```

- Reliability if item is dropped. This provides a list of alpha if one item is not selected. As our alpha is good, you do not need to drop an item.

4.10 Summary

This chapter discusses the notion of (latent) constructs, their measurements, and the assessments of their reliability and validity. Few key points worth mentioning when conducting research. First, measuring a construct with multiple items are always preferable to using a single item. Second, developing a scale involves a rigorous scientific procedure; therefore, it is recommended to look for existing scales rather than thinking of inventing a new scale. An existing scale can be adapted to our research context providing that scale adaption is justified. Third, mean scores can be used to represent a construct provided that its measurements items are valid and reliable.

4.11 Further Reading

DeVellis, R. F. & Thorpe, C. T. (2021), *Scale development: Theory and applications.* Sage publications.

Heggestad, E. D., Scheaf, D. J., Banks, G. C., Monroe Hausfeld, M., Tonidandel, S. & Williams, E. B. (2019), 'Scale adaptation in organizational science research: A review and best-practice recommendations', *Journal of Management* **45**(6), 2596–2627.

Jarvis, C. B., MacKenzie, S. B. & Podsakoff, P. M. (2003), 'A critical review of construct indicators and measurement model misspecification in marketing and consumer research', *Journal of Consumer Research* **30**(2), 199–218.

Peter, J. P. (1981), 'Construct validity: A review of basic issues and marketing practices', *Journal of Marketing Research* **18**(2), 133–145.

Podsakoff, P. M., MacKenzie, S. B. & Podsakoff, N. P. (2016), 'Recommendations for creating better concept definitions in the organizational, behavioral, and social sciences', *Organizational Research Methods* **19**(2), 159–203.

4.12 Review Questions

1. What is the level of measurement of the following questionnaire item in the following figure?

```
Please indicate your age:

1. Under 15 years
2. 16-20 years
3. 21-25 years
4. 26-30 years
5. 31-35 years
6. 36 and above
```

2. Explain the difference between discriminant and convergent validity.
3. Explain why using your self-developed scales is not a good idea?

4.13 Exercises

Use retailerbrand.sav. BV1, BV2, and BV3 are items meant to measure perceived brand value. Can they be used to measure brand value? Conduct a reliability analysis with SPSS and R.

5

Describing Quantitative Data

This chapter discusses how to describe quantitative data and visualize the data with graphs. Quantitative data can be described with measures of central tendency, such as mean, and measures of central dispersion, such as standard deviation. The chapter also explains the concept of percentiles or quartiles to describe positions of data values. The chapter also covers the five summary measures, which include the minimum, first quartile, third quartile, and maximum. These five numbers summarize quantitative data in a concise manner and can be visually presented by a box plot. The use of a box plot in detecting potential outliers are also discussed.

Learning Objectives:

- Understand measures of central tendency: mean, mode, median.
- Understand measures of central dispersion: variance, standard deviation, range, interquartile range (IQR).
- Know how to construct a histogram and a boxplot using SPSS and R.
- Know how to construct a boxplot and use it for detecting potential outliers.

5.1 Summary Measures

5.1.1 Mean

Mean is as a measure of central tendency (also referred to as central location) that tells us the centre of a set of values. Mean is what we call as 'average' value in our daily conversations. The mean of a set of values is the sum of the values divided by total number of values.

$$\overline{X} = \frac{\sum_{i=1}^{N} x_i}{N} \tag{5.1}$$

where $\overline{X}$ (read: *X* bar) denotes mean. x_i refers to a specific value, N is the total number of values, and the symbol $\sum$ (read: `sigma`) describes the summation of values.

In the following table, we have a record of the number of books purchased by 5 customers selected randomly from all customers who visited a store in a particular week.

DOI: 10.4324/9781003407225-7

Name	Count
Alex	2
Elizabeth	3
Donna	4
Dylan	2
Millam	1

Any number in the table is an x. If x_i is the number of books purchased by customer i, then i is an index from 1 to 5. The total number of books bought by the customers is given by:

$$\sum_{i=1}^{5} x_i = x_1 + x_2 + x_3 + x_4 + x_5$$

$$= 2 + 3 + 4 + 2 + 1 \quad (5.2)$$

The mean of the number of books purchased by the 5 customers is $\frac{12}{5} = 2.4$.

Two symbols associated with mean:

- μ denotes a population mean.
- $\overline{X}$ denotes a sample mean.

A population mean μ is a numerical characteristic of a population regarded as a parameter of the population whose value is mostly unknown in most research situations. A sample mean $\overline{X}$ is a numerical characteristic of a sample whose values are varied from sample to sample, thus called as a statistic.

Properties of Mean

Every interval or ratio variable has a mean. The sum of the deviations of each value from the mean is zero. For an illustration, consider this set of values: 1, 3, 8. The mean value is 4.

$$\sum_{x=1}^{3} \left(x_i - \overline{X}\right) = (1-4) + (3-4) + (8-4) = -3 - 1 + 4 = 0 \quad (5.3)$$

The mean can be considered as the balance point of a set of data (see Figure 5.1). If you put cylinders of equal weight on a ruler at numbers 1, 3, and 8, the balance point is 4. If you subtract the mean score from each value, the result gives a distance of the point to the mean where the sum of all the distances (distance to the left of zero is considered to be negative) to the mean is equal zero.

The presence of extremely high values in data can distort the mean. Imagine that if a young billionaire had a lunch at your university canteen. At the same time, a marketing researcher distributed a questionnaire in the canteen to study students' weekly spending. The billionaire could inadvertently participate in the survey making the average students' weekly spending to be higher than that was expected.

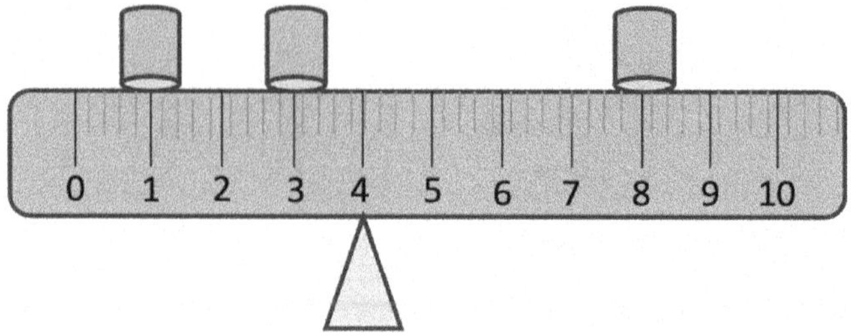

FIGURE 5.1
Mean as a balance point. The sum of the distances of each point to the mean is 0.

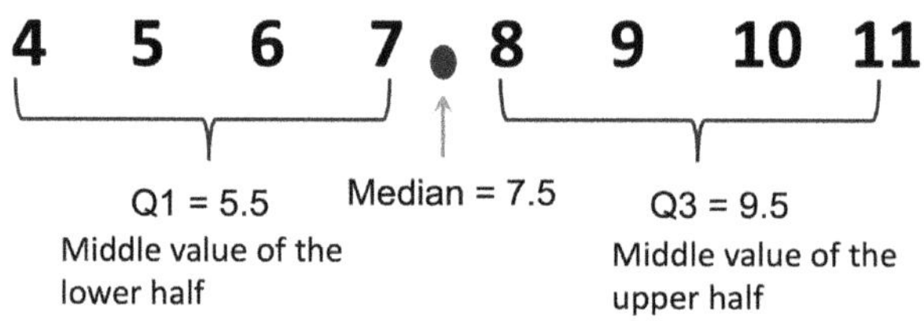

FIGURE 5.2
Median of odd number of cases.

5.1.2 Quartiles

Median is the middle value of data also refer to as the second quartile (Q2). Quartiles are special cases of quantiles that divide set of values into four quarters where data is arranged in an increasing order. The lower quartile (Q1), or first quartile, is the value under which 25% of data points are found. The upper quartile (Q3), or the third quartile, is the value under which 75% of data points are found.

To find the median, if the number of values is odd, median is the value in the middle of the values that are in an ascending order. If the number of values is even, median is found by calculating the average of the two numbers that lie in the middle. In the same way, Q1 is found by taking the middle value of the half part to the left of the median, and Q3 is found by taking the middle value of the half part to the right of the median (e.g. see Figure 5.2).

IMPORTANT: PERCENTILES

Percentiles are terms to locate the position of data values. An *X*-th percentile is a value below which an *X* percentage of cases fall. For example, if your exam score is in the 90th percentile, this means that you are better than 90% of students in your cohort (10% of them scored higher than yours). The 25th percentile is called the lower quartile (Q1), the 75th percentile is called the upper quartile (Q3), and the 50th percentile is called the median.

While percentile is defined in terms of a percentage, quantile is defined in terms of a decimal. For example, the 25th percentile (or 25%) is the same as 0.25 quantile. Quartile is a special case of quantile (lower quartile, middle quartile, and upper quartile).

Data 1	4	5	6	7	8	9	10
Data 2	4	5	6	7	8	9	100

FIGURE 5.3
Median is unaffected by an unusual value.

Properties of Median

Every quantitative data has a median. Median is preferable if data contains unusual values (e.g. extremely high values) or if the distribution of data is skewed because median is not affected by the presence of these unusual values (see Figure 5.3). The median value of the two datasets in Figure 5.3 are the same despite data 2 contains an extremely high value.

5.1.2.1 SPSS Action

Data: quantile.sav

Here, I am going to show you how to calculate the 25th (Q1), 50th (Q2), and 75th (Q3) percentile using SPSS.

Steps:

- Analyze → Descriptive Statistics → Frequency.
- Insert a variable into `Variable(s) box`.
- Click `Statistics`.
- Tick `Percentiles`.
- Insert `25` into the empty box next to the percentile requesting SPSS to produce the 25th percentile. Click `Add`. Repeat this for the `50th` and `75th` percentiles.
- Click `Continue`.
- Click `OK` or `Paste` if you want to work with an SPSS syntax, and inspect the output window.

Clicking `Paste` produces the following syntax:

```
FREQUENCIES VARIABLES=value
  /PERCENTILES=25.0 50.0 75.0
  /ORDER=ANALYSIS.
```

As you can see from Figure 5.4, Q1 = 5.25, Q2 = 7.5, and Q3 = 9.75. To your surprise, these results are not the same as those we manually calculate previously. The explanation is that our data is considered as a sample by SPSS. The method implemented by the `Frequencies` procedure ensures that it is the unbiased estimate of the population percentile.[1]

[1] https://www.ibm.com/support/pages/how-does-spss-statistics-calculate-percentiles-frequencies-or-ctables

Statistics

value

N	Valid	8
	Missing	0
Percentiles	25	5.2500
	50	7.5000
	75	9.7500

FIGURE 5.4
Percentiles from SPSS.

NOTE

Perhaps to your surprise, there is more than one method to calculate the percentiles. Hyndman & Fan (1996) discussed nine methods applied by various statistical software, including S-plus, which is a predecessor of R.

5.1.2.2 R Action

```
library(ahdar)

dat <- quantile

out <- quantile(dat$value)
out
```

```
  0%   25%   50%    75%  100%
4.00  5.75  7.50  9.25 11.00
```

There is no gold standard for calculating percentiles, as different statistical software programs use different methods, which may produce different results. The good news is that results reported by SPSS and R are identical.

5.1.3 Variance and Standard Deviation

The standard deviation is typically reported in tandem with the mean. While mean describes the central position of the data, standard deviation tells us about how data points are spread out. Technically speaking, standard deviation measures the average distance of data to its mean. That is, how the data on average deviates from the mean, hence the name 'deviation'.

Consider again this set of values: 1,3, 8. You learned from Section 5.1.1 that the sum of the distance to its mean is zero, so the average distance is also zero. However, there is a trick to avoid zero in the summation in order to say something about the spread of these three values to their mean. You can calculate the squared distance of each point to the mean, then calculate the sum of the squared distance, which is equal to 26 (see

Equation 5.4). Next, you divide the sum by the number of data points to represent the average squared distance, which is 26 / 3 = 8.67. Because the number is nonzero, you can take the square root of the sum, to represent the average distance of points to their mean, which is equal to 2.94. This number is called as the **standard deviation** of the set of values 1, 3, and 8.

$$\sum_{x=1}^{3}(x_i - \bar{X})^2 = (1-4)^2 + (3-4)^2 + (8-4)^2 = (-3)^2 + (-1)^2 + 4^2 = 26 \quad (5.4)$$

Formally, to calculate standard deviation, first, you need to calculate the variance of set of values. Taking the square root of variance gives standard deviation. Actually, variance, rather than standard deviation, is frequently used to refer to variation in data. The mathematical forms of variance denoted by $Var(X)$ and standard deviation are given by Equation 5.5.

$$Var(X) = \frac{\sum_{i=1}^{N}(x_i - \bar{X})^2}{n} \quad (5.5)$$

$$SD(X) = \sqrt{Var(X)} \quad (5.6)$$

5.1.3.1 Sample Variance

If you want to calculate the variance of a sample, the numerator that you should use is $N - 1$, not N (see Equation 5.7), otherwise you will underestimate the population variance. This is because the sample variance is used to infer the population variance.

$$Var(X) = \frac{\sum_{i=1}^{N}(x_i - \bar{X})^2}{N-1} \quad (5.7)$$

. . .

. . .

Table 5.2 presents a step-by-step calculation of sample variance and sample standard deviation.

TABLE 5.2

Step-by-Step Calculation of Sample Variance and Sample Standard Deviation

i	x	$\bar{X}$	$x - \bar{X}$	$(x - \bar{X})^2$
1	2	2.4	−0.4	0.16
2	3	2.4	0.6	0.36
3	4	2.4	1.6	2.56
4	2	2.4	−0.4	0.16
5	1	2.4	−1.4	1.96
Sum				3.2

The variance is the sum of values in the far-right column (= 3√ 2) divided by 5 – 1, which is 3.2 / 4 = 0.8. Therefore, the standard deviation equals 0.8 = 0.89.

5.2 Visualizing Data

5.2.1 Histogram

Histogram gives an idea how a variable is distributed. It arises from grouped frequency data. Figure 5.5 shows a histogram of weekend spending of 100 students with the height of each bar showing the number of students that fall in the associated interval. You noticed that in a histogram, there are no gaps between bars or intervals.

The histogram in Figure 5.5 is actually created using Excel as a proxy for manual drawing. It is constructed from grouped frequency data presented in Table 5.3. The numbers shown in the x-axis of the histogram in Figure 5.5 are the interval midpoints – see the third column of Table 5.3.

The SPSS version of the histogram in Figure 5.5 is presented in Figure 5.6. This histogram is created using raw data (actual values) as SPSS is not capable of creating a histogram from grouped frequency data.

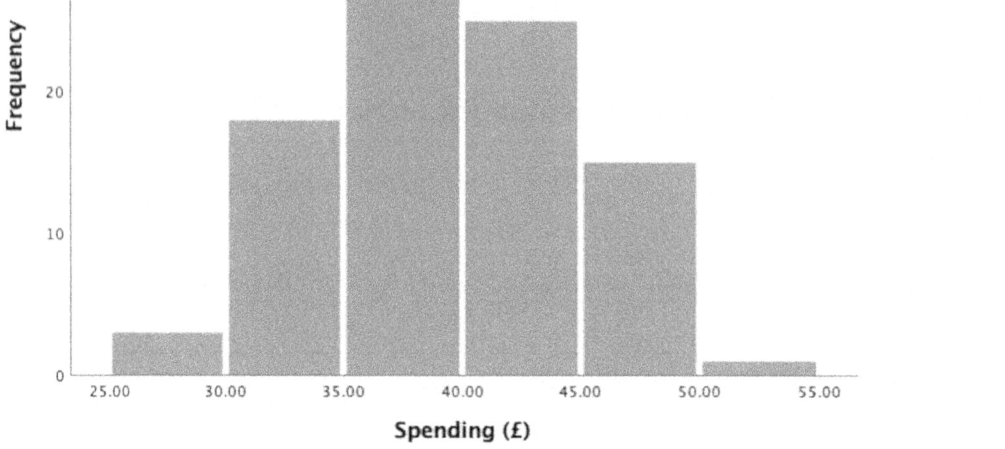

FIGURE 5.5
A histogram of weekend spending created in Excel.

TABLE 5.3
Grouped Frequency Table

Lower Limit	Upper Limit	Midpoint	Frequency
25	30	27.5	3
30	35	32.5	18
35	40	37.5	38
40	45	42.5	25
45	50	47.5	15
50	55	52.5	1

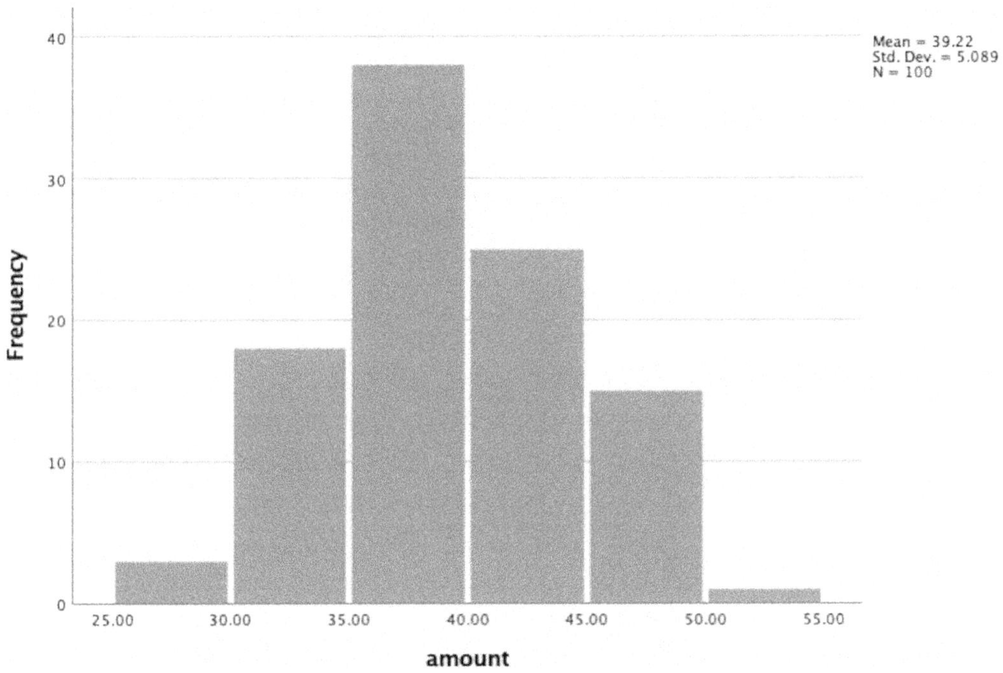

FIGURE 5.6
A histogram of weekend spending created with SPSS.

5.2.1.1 SPSS Action

Data: spending.sav
Steps:

- Graphs → Legacy Dialogs → Histogram. (In SPSS version 29: Graphs→ Histogram.)
- Insert a variable into `Variable` box.
- Click `OK` or `Paste` if you want to run the syntax, and inspect the output window. The SPSS syntax:

```
GRAPH
  /HISTOGRAM=amount.
```

The histogram produced by SPSS, by default, was printed in a blue colour, and as displayed, its shape was not quite the same with that of the one we have seen earlier in Figure 5.6. In the current histogram, it has many bins whilst in the previous histogram, it contains only 6 bins. This is because I have modified the current histogram and make it into 6 bins. The step I had taken to create the histogram with 6 bins is as follows:

- Move your cursor to the image in the SPSS output window, double-click the image. The chart editor must pop-up on your screen.
  - Double-click bars in the image. You will see the windows shown in Figure 5.7.
- Choose 'Binning'.
- Under 'x-axis', tick 'Custom', and insert 6 – you are requesting SPSS to modify the histogram to reduce the number of bars into 6.

You will get the histogram as seen in Figure 5.6. You can modify the appearance of the histogram, for instance, by clicking 'Fill & Border' to change the colour of the bars. You can also hide the major grid lines (on the chart window, right-click on the lines and choose `Hide Grid Lines` or click **Options** → Hide Grid Lines), and add title to the graph by clicking **Options** → Title.

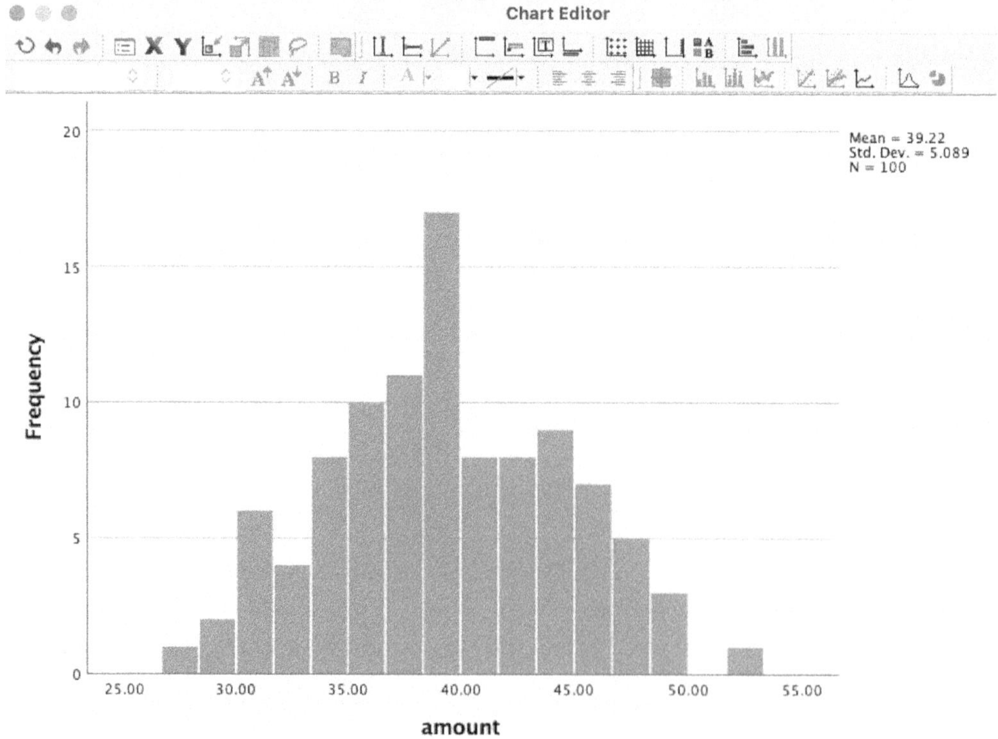

FIGURE 5.7
An SPSS chart editor.

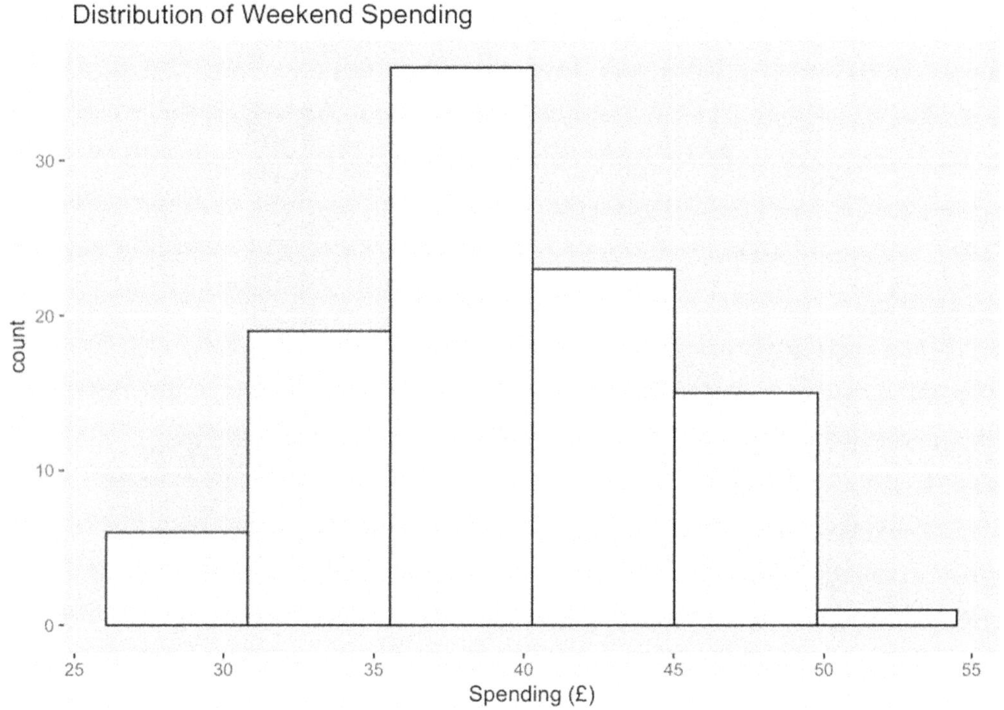

FIGURE 5.8
A histogram of weekend spending.

5.2.1.2 R Action

To create a histogram using R, you can use hist() function from R base, and the `geom_histogram()` function from the ggplot2() package. To use `hist()` is straightforward. If *X* is a variable of your interest and you want to plot a histogram of X, you can type in `hist(X)`. Why not try it yourself?

In the code, bin = 6 sets the number of bins to 6. You can set it to a different number and see how it affects the shape of the histogram.

```
rm(list = ls(all=TRUE)) # make a fresh start
library(ggplot2)
library(ahdar)

dat <- spending.sav

p <- ggplot(dat, aes(amount)) +
       geom_histogram(bins = 6,
              color="black",
              fill="white") + labs(x="Spending (£)"
              ,title =" Distribution of Weekend Spending ")

p
```

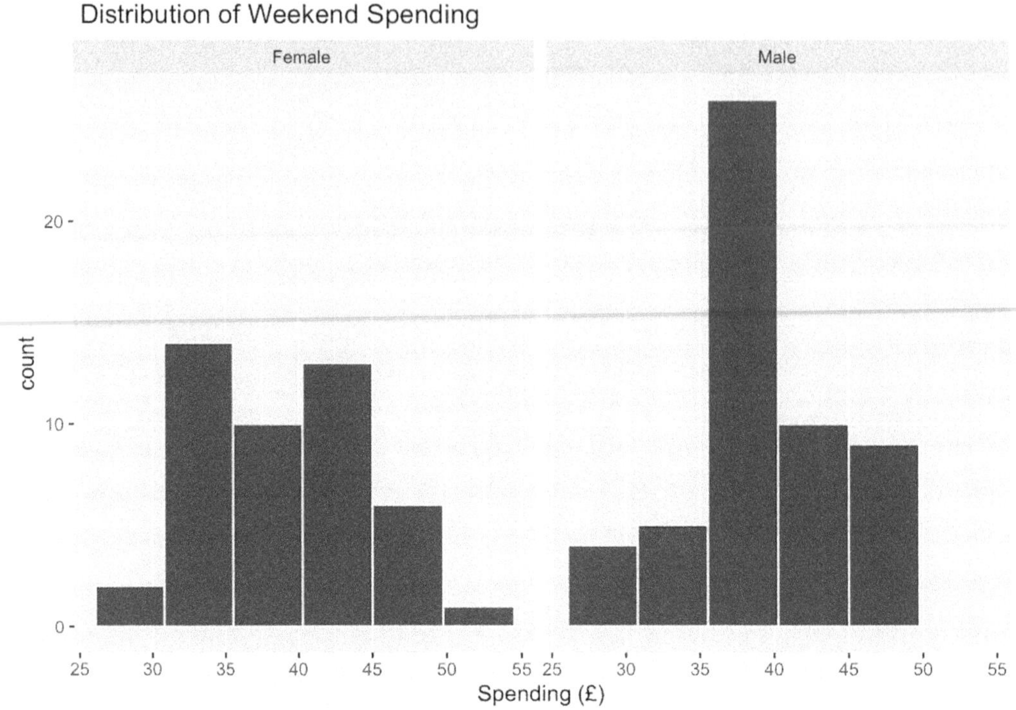

FIGURE 5.9
Histograms of weekend spending for female and male samples.

As you have a categorical variable `gender in dat _ spending` (1 = male, 0 = female), you can produce a histogram for each category to compare the distribution of spending for male vs. female. The following code produced two histograms for male and female as a result of setting `facet _ wrap(~ gender, ncol = 2)`. If you delete this expression, only one graph is returned.

```
library(ggplot2)
library(ahdar)
dat_spending <- spending.sav

p <- ggplot(dat_spending, aes(amount)) +
        geom_histogram(bins = 6,
               color="white",
               fill="gray28") +
               facet_wrap(~ gender, ncol = 2) +
               labs(x="Spending (£)"
               , title = " Distribution of Weekend Spending ")

p
```

Alternatively, you can use `gghistogram()` function from the ggpubr package. `face.by()` is the wrapper function for the `face _ wrap()` of the `geom _ histogram`.

The following code is presented (see Figure 5.10):

```
library(ggpubr)
library(ahdar)

dat_spending <- spending

p <- gghistogram(dat_spending,
            x="amount",
            bins=6,
            color="black",
            fill="white",
            facet.by = "gender",
            xlab="Spending (£)",
            title = " Distribution of Weekend Spending ") +
            theme_grey()
p
```

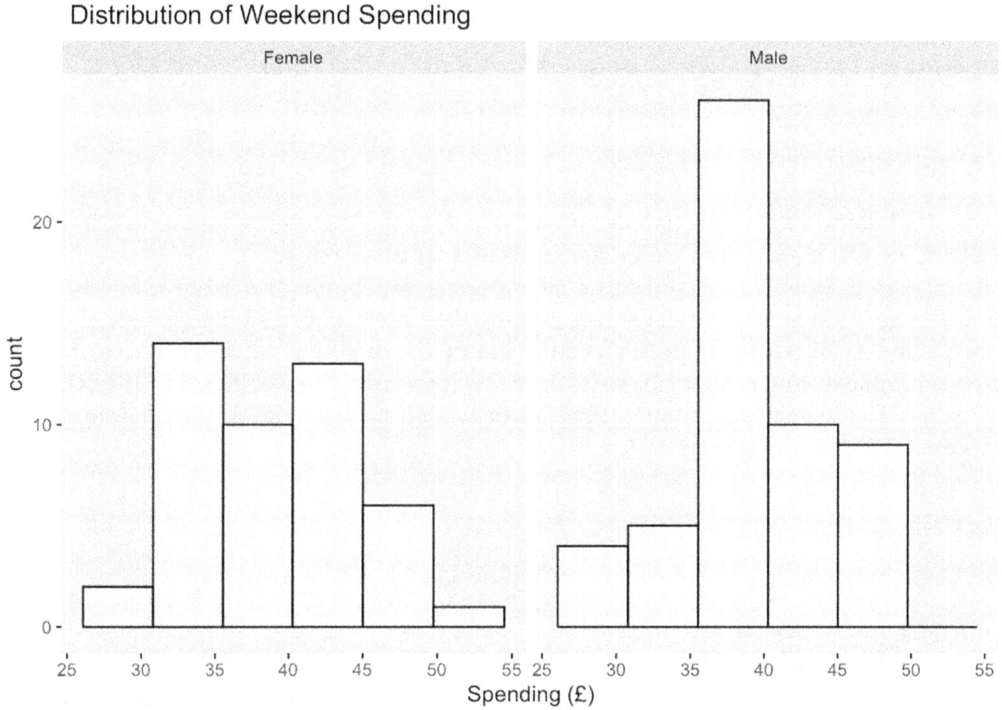

FIGURE 5.10
Histograms of weekend spending for female and male samples produced by gghistogram().

5.2.2 Boxplot

The five number summary (minimum, Q1, Q2, Q3, maximum) can be visualized by displaying a **boxplot**. A boxplot also shows any values that are suspected to be unusual (outliers). To understand how a boxplot displays outliers, you need to know other features of a boxplot called fences:

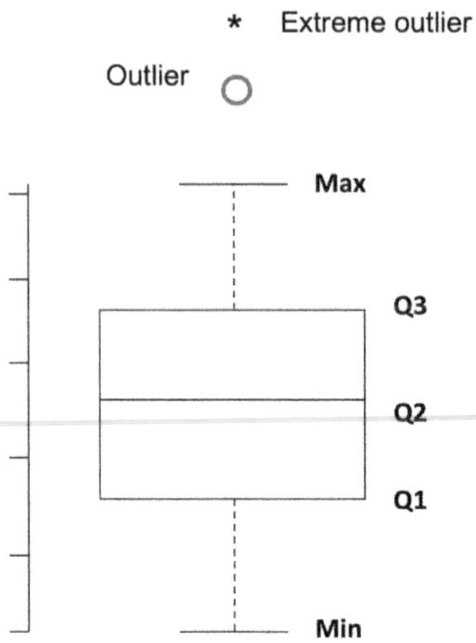

FIGURE 5.11
A boxplot.

- lower inner fence: Q1 – 1.5*IQR
- upper inner fence: Q3 + 1.5*IQR
- lower outer fence: Q1 – 3*IQR
- upper outer fence: Q3 + 3*IQR

where IQR stands for interquartile range, which is the difference between Q3 and Q1 (IQR = Q3 – Q1). IQR is considered as a **measure of dispersion.**

An observation is considered to be an outlier if it is below inner fence or above out inner fences. That is, any observations outside this interval: Q1 – 1.5*IQR, Q3 + 1.5*IQR, is suspected as an outlier. If an observation lies below or above the outer fences, it is considered as an extreme outlier (those beyond the interval: Q1 – 3*IQR, Q3 + 3*IQR).

Figure 5.11 illustrates a boxplot. SPSS indicates an outlier with a white circle, and an extreme outlier with an asterisk *.

5.2.3 Illustration

You have this data: 8, 9, 6, 7, 5, 4, 1, 2, 16, 3. Find Q1, Q2, Q3. Is 16 an outlier?

Solutions:

Reordering: 1, 2, 3, 4, 5, 6, 7, 8, 9, 16

Q1 = 3, Q2 = 5.5, Q3 = 8 IQR = Q3 – Q1 = 5

Outer fence:

Upper fence: Q3 + 1.5*IQR = 8 + 1.5*5 = 15.5
Lower fence: Q1 – 1.5*IQR = 3 – 1.5*5 = – 4.5

Therefore, 16 is an outlier because 16 is above the upper fence.

Min = 1, max = 9. Min and max are the lowest and highest value that are not an outlier.

5.2.4 SPSS Action

Data: order.sav

Let us create a boxplot of data used in the previous section: 8, 9, 6, 7, 5, 4, 1, 2, 16, 3. Steps:

- Open order.sav
- On the SPSS menu, click Graphs → Legacy Dialogs → Boxplot. For SPSS version 29, click Graphs → Boxplot.
- Click `Simple` and `Summaries of separate variables.`
- Insert a variable into `Box Represent.`
- Click `OK` or `Paste` if you want to work with syntax, and inspect the output window. The SPSS syntax:

```
EXAMINE VARIABLES=order
    /COMPARE VARIABLE
    /PLOT=BOXPLOT
    /STATISTICS=NONE
    /NOTOTAL
    /MISSING=LISTWISE.
```

5.2.5 R Action

Here, we use the `boxplot.stats()` and `boxplot()` functions from R base. The first function is useful to locate outliers, and the second function can be used to create a boxplot.

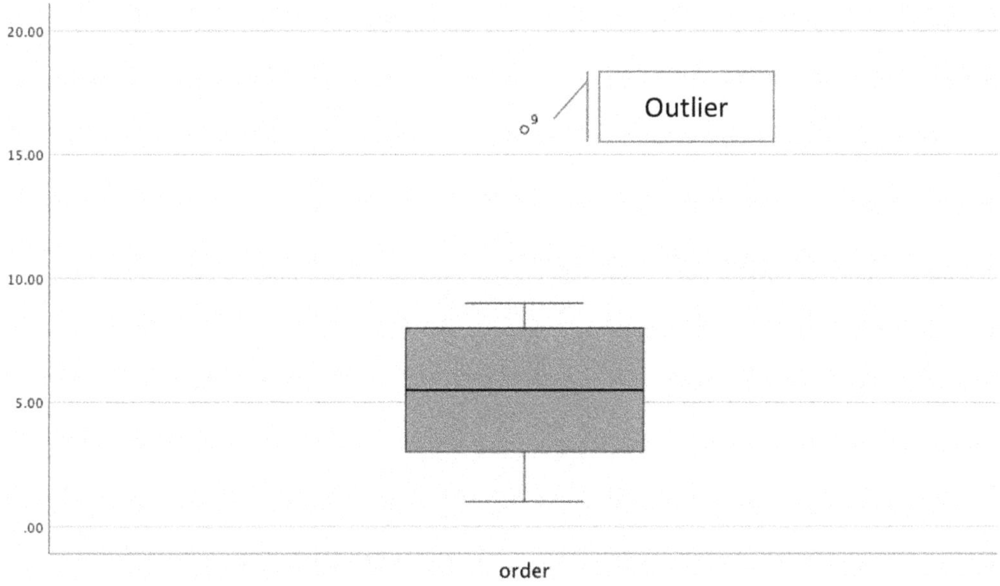

FIGURE 5.12
A boxplot produced by SPSS.

```
library(tidyverse)

 # record our data
 dat <- c(8, 9, 6, 7, 5, 4, 1, 2, 16, 3)

 detected_outlier <- boxplot.stats(dat)$out

# view
 head(dat)

# show outlier
detected_outlier

# use which() to locate row that corresponds with the outlier

# locate the row
which_case <- which(dat %in% c(detected_outlier))

# show the row
which_case

# create boxplot
boxplot(dat,
  ylab = "Value",
  main = "Boxplot"
)
mtext(paste("Outlier: ", paste(detected_outlier,
collapse = ", ")))
```

Using geom_boxplot()

You can also use geom _ boxplot() function from the ggplot2() package. dat has to be converted to tibble with as _ tibble(). By default, the name of the variable in the dat as a tibble is 'value'. To set aes in the ggplot, only one value needs to be supplied, either

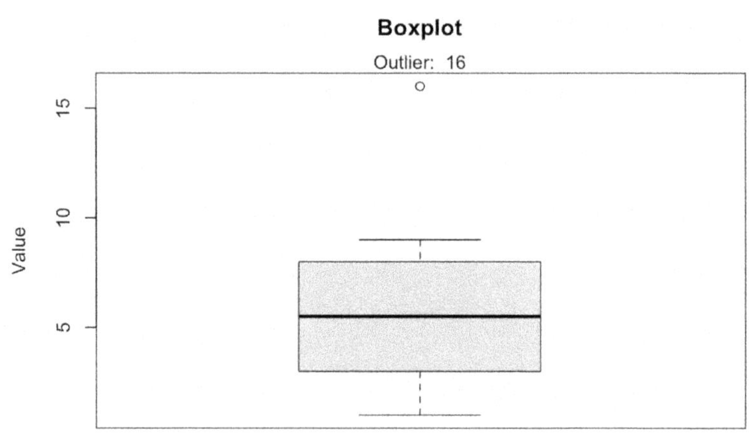

FIGURE 5.13
A boxplot produced by boxplot() and a potential outlier.

FIGURE 5.14
A boxplot produced by geom_boxplot().

Note:

- Setting aes(x = `value`) will return a horizontal boxplot.
- The expression `outlier.shape` = '1' marked an outlier with a blank-circle shaped.

aes(x = value) or aes(y=value). The former produces a horizontal boxplot, whereas the latter produces a vertical boxplot. The following code uses a vertical boxplot.

```
library(tidyverse)
library(haven)

 dat <- as_tibble(c(8, 9, 6, 7, 5, 4, 1, 2, 16, 3))

p <- ggplot(dat, aes(y=value)) +
      geom_boxplot(outlier.shape = 1)+
      labs(y=" Value")
p
```

Using ggboxplot()

```
library(ggpubr)
ggboxplot(dat, y="value", orientation = "vertical",
outlier.shape = 1)+
   theme_grey()
```

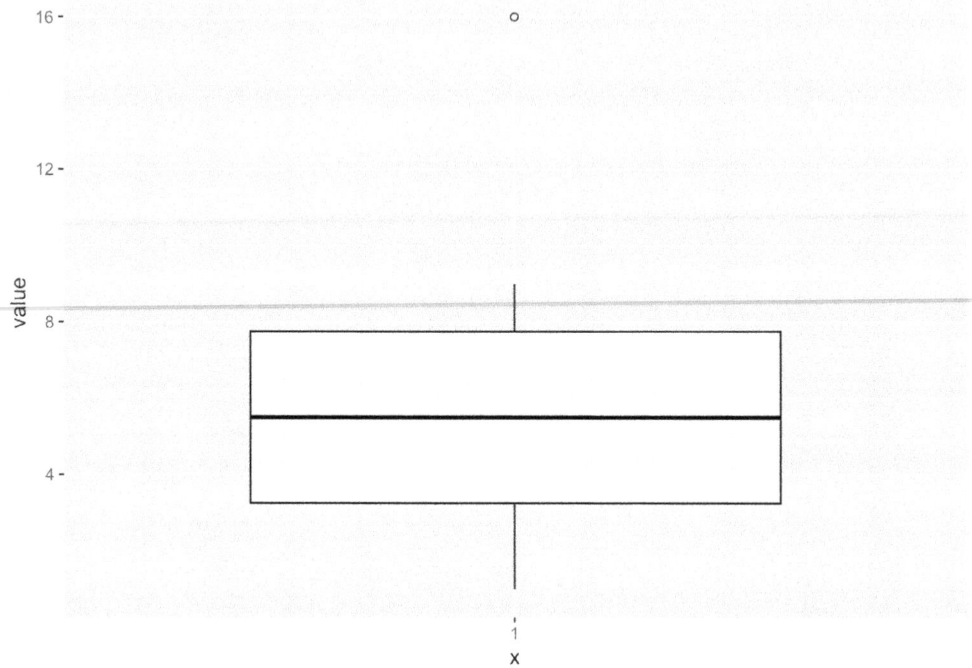

FIGURE 5.15
A boxplot produced by ggboxplot().

5.3 Further Reading

On percentiles:

Hyndman, R. J. & Fan, Y. (1996), 'Sample quantiles in statistical packages', *The American Statistician* **50**(4), 361–365. Note: This is a mathematical text that is quite challenging to read for non-mathematical-oriented readers. I included here as a reference only.

On data storytelling and visualization:

Chang, W. (2018), *R graphics cookbook: Practical recipes for visualizing data*, O'Reilly Media. This book, which is also freely available at https://r-graphics.org, provides recipes to create various plots using R.

Dykes, B. (2019), *Effective data storytelling: How to drive change with data, narrative and visuals*, John Wiley & Sons. This book discusses a growing field of data storytelling putting an emphasis on building a compelling narrative from data.

Wilke, C. O. (2019), *Fundamentals of data visualization: A primer on making informative and compelling figures*, O'Reilly Media. As the of the book says, this books is "a guide to making visualizations that accurately reflect the data, tell a story, and look professional" (Wilke 2019). The online version can be freely assessed at https://clauswilke.com/dataviz/

5.4 Summary

We have discussed how to describe quantitative data using summary measures and graphs. We covered measures of central tendency and measures of dispersions using SPSS and various functions in R. Two graphs commonly mostly appropriate to describe quantitative data covered in this chapter are histogram and boxplots. They are excellent tools to describe data distribution and are helpful in detecting potential outliers – values that are distinct from the majority of cases.

5.5 Review Questions

1. Here is the daily order received by a book store in the past 10 days: 1, 2, 3, 5, 12, 14. Draw a boxplot to summarize the data and identify outliers.
2. Draw a box plot of this set of values: 1, 2, 3, 3, 3. Comment on the shape of the boxplot.

5.6 Exercises

1. Use the R base function hist() to plot a histogram of these values: 1, 2, 2, 2, 3, 3, 4, 5, 5, 3, 5, 6, 7.
2. Using the same data in question 1, use geom_histogram.

6

Normal Distribution

Many real-life phenomenon (e.g. exam scores) can be described by a distribution called a normal distribution or also referred to as a Gaussian distribution. This chapter discusses a normal distribution and its properties such as kurtosis and skewness. The chapter also discusses how to work out areas under the distribution and its corresponding values, and vice versa. In the last section of the chapter, the distinction between an empirical and theoretical distribution is explained.

Learning Objectives:

- Understand the characteristics of a normal distribution.
- Know how to obtain a standard normal distribution from a normal distribution.
- Know how to use SPSS to create a histogram.
- Know how to use SPSS macros to find areas under a normal curve.
- Know how to standardize a variable.

6.1 The Bell-Shaped Curve

Let us use SPSS again to recreate a histogram for weekend spending as we had done in the previous chapter: *Graphs* → Legacy Dialogs → Histogram. Note that in an SPSS version 29, the path is *Graphs* → Histogram. This time, I ticked a small box 'Display normal curve', which is below the 'Variable' box. As a result of ticking the box, you will obtain a histogram with a normal curve being imposed on the histogram (see Figure 6.1).

As you can see in Figure 6.1, there is a smooth bell-shaped curve superimposed in the histogram. The curve is known as a normal distribution curve, also known as a Gaussian distribution named after Carl Friedrich Gauss, the famous 18th-century German physicist and mathematician (1777–1855).

The normal distribution curve depends on two parameters μ and σ^2, which are the mean and variance of the distribution. The y-axis reflects the density where the relationship between the density and x value is given by Equation 6.1. The area under the normal distribution is a unit of 1 or 100% (see Figure 6.2).

$$y = \frac{1}{\sigma\sqrt{2\pi}} e^{-\frac{(x-\mu)^2}{2\sigma^2}} \tag{6.1}$$

DOI: 10.4324/9781003407225-8

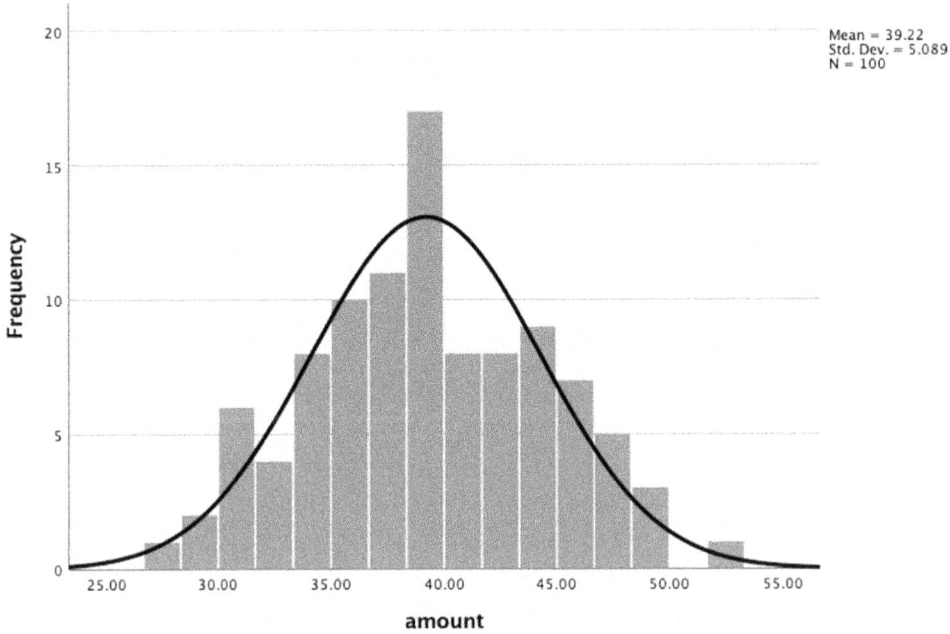

FIGURE 6.1
A histogram of weekend spending.

CARL FRIEDRICH GAUSS

Gauss was a child prodigy. Once, when he was just 10 years old, he amused his teacher by calculating the sum of numbers from 1 to 100 in just a few second. Can you do that? (The answer is 5050.)

Long time before Gauss was born, Abraham de Moivre (1667–1754) actually has proven the existence of the normal curve in 1733 (Stigler 1986; Stahl 2006; Snedecor & Cochran 1989). Pierre Simon de Laplace (1749–1827), a French mathematician, has also been credited as the inventor of the normal distribution. However, it was Gauss mostly credited for finding the mathematical formula for the normal distribution.

To describe a variable that is normally distributed, researchers typically use a shorthand notation $X \sim N(\mu, \sigma^2)$, which can be read as: X is normally distributed with mean μ and variance σ^2. For an illustration, if satisfaction score follows a normal distribution and the mean and standard deviation of the scores is 2 and 0.5, respectively, you can express it as $satisfaction \sim N$ (2, 0.25).

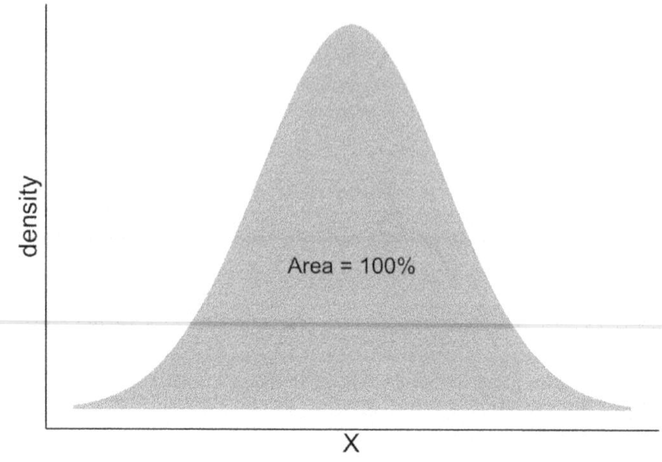

FIGURE 6.2
A normal distribution.

6.2 Standard Normal Distribution

A normal distribution having mean of 0 and standard deviation of 1 described as $X \sim N(0, 1)$ is called a standard normal distribution or z-distribution.

As you can see in Figure 6.3, the area under the curve is 1 or 100%. The curve is symmetrical. The mean and the median are the same and cut the curve into two halves. The small area under the curve to the left of –1.96 (left tail) is 2.5%, and similarly the area to the right of 1.96 (right tail) is 2.5% of the total area.

If a variable follows or is assumed to follow a normal distribution, its properties are really helpful. For example, suppose that you have records of satisfaction scores of 1000 customers and satisfaction is measured on a continuous scale from 0 to 100. Let us assume that the scores follow a normal distribution and the point on the curve from which the area to the right tail equals 5% is 7.5. This means that 5% of the 1000 customers (i.e. 50 customers), have satisfaction scores greater than 7.5.

6.2.1 R Code

The beautiful standard normal curve in Figure 6.3 is created using this R code:

```
rm(list=ls())
library(ggplot2)

lowerx <- -4
upperx <- 4
upper95 <- round(qnorm(.975, mean=0, sd=1),2)
dat<-data.frame(z = c(lowerx, to=upperx))
ggplot(data=dat, aes(x=z))+
  stat_function(fun = dnorm, xlim=c(lowerx,-upper95),
```

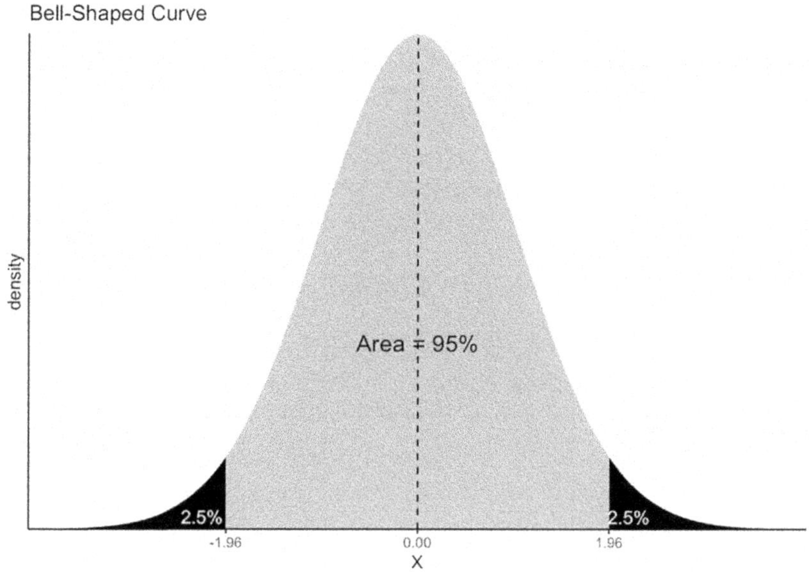

FIGURE 6.3
A standard normal distribution.

```
                   geom="area", fill="black")+
    stat_function(fun = dnorm, xlim=c(-upper95,upper95),
                   geom="area", fill="gray") +
    stat_function(fun = dnorm, xlim=c(upper95,upperx),
                   geom="area", fill="black")+
    labs(x = "X", y = "density") +
    scale_y_continuous(expand = c(0, 0),
                     breaks = NULL) +
    scale_x_continuous(expand = c(0, 0),
                     breaks = c(-upper95,0, upper95)) +
    annotate("text", x = 0, y = 0.15,
             label = " Area = 95% ",
             color="black", size=5)+
    annotate("text", x = -2.18, y = 0.01,
             label = "2.5% ",
             color="white", size=4) +
    annotate("text", x =    2.19, y = 0.01,
             label = "2.5% ",
             color="white", size=4) +
    geom_vline(xintercept = 0,
             linetype="dashed",
             color = "black", size=0.5) +
    theme(axis.text.x = element_text(size = 15)) +
    theme(axis.title = element_text(size = 20))  +
    ggtitle("Bell-Shaped Curve") +
    theme_classic()
```

6.3 Finding Area Under a Normal Curve

6.3.1 SPSS Action: NORMDIST Macro

To find an area under a normal curve, in the old days people use a standard normal distribution table, or use Excel. I have written an SPSS macro called `NORMDIST` to perform the task.[1] After you managed to install the macro on SPSS, you can find it on

SPSS menu by clicking: Analyze → NORMDIST by Ahmad Daryanto.

For an illustration, suppose that we want to find an area to the left of –1.96 under a standard normal distribution. You must enter: x = –1.96, mean = 0, and standard deviation = 1 (see Figure 6.4). The area is equal to 0.025 (see the `NORMDIST` macro in Figure 6.5), which is illustrated in Figure 6.6.

6.3.2 R Action: pnorm()

A function`pnorm` from R base can be used to find area to the left of 1.96.

```
pnorm(1.96, mean = 0, sd = 1)

 [1] 0.9750021
```

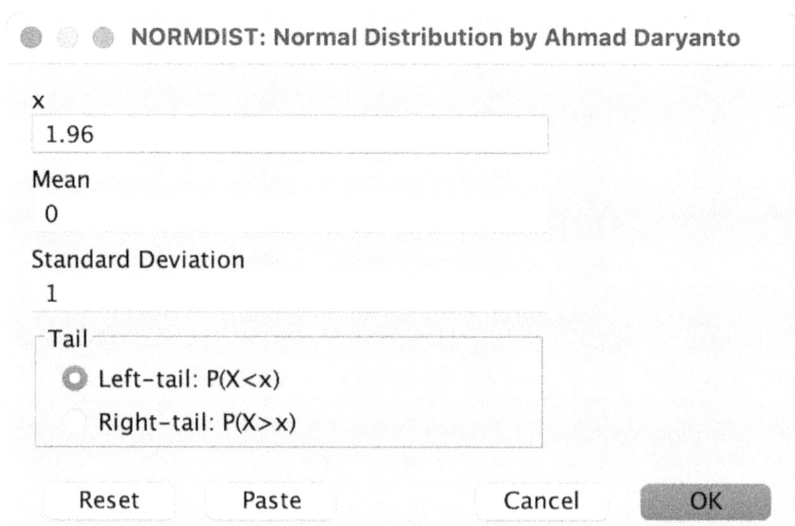

FIGURE 6.4
Screenshot of the NORMDIST macro.

[1] The macro and all other macros of other distributions discussed in the next chapter can be downloaded at the book's online support.

```
Matrix

Run MATRIX procedure:

Left-tail probability (%)
    .97500

X =
   1.95996

------ END MATRIX -----
```

FIGURE 6.5
Output of the NORMDIST macro.

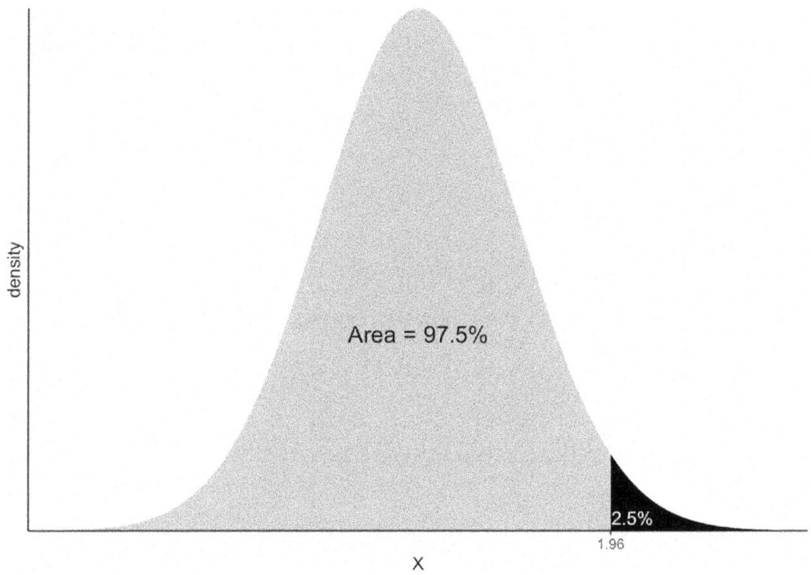

FIGURE 6.6
The area in black is associated with P(X < 1.96).

In the function argument, mean is set to zero and standard deviation (sd) is set to 1, which corresponds to a standard normal curve. The code can also be written simply as `pnorm(1.96)` because the default values are mean = 0 and sd = 1.

6.4 Finding *x* Values for Certain Areas Under a Normal Curve

6.4.1 SPSS Action: QNORMDIST Macro

You can find a certain value that is associated with a certain area under the normal distribution curve. This is the reverse of the problem discussed in the previous section. If

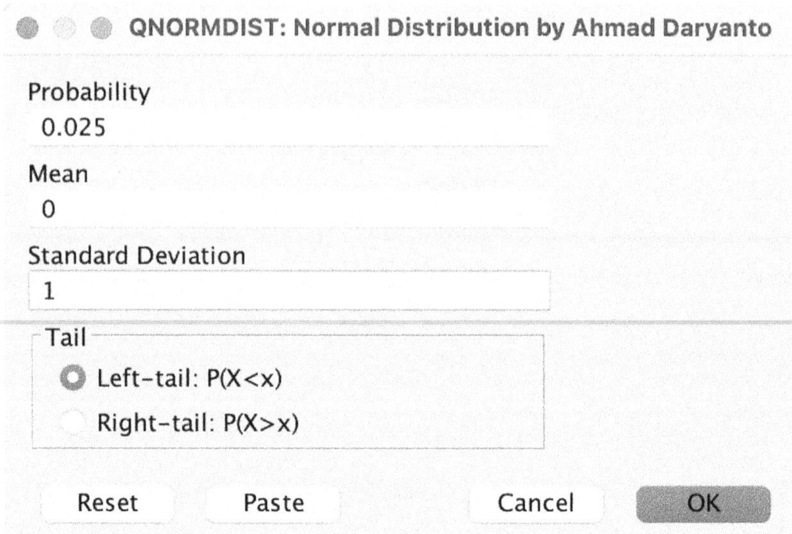

FIGURE 6.7
QNORMDIST macro.

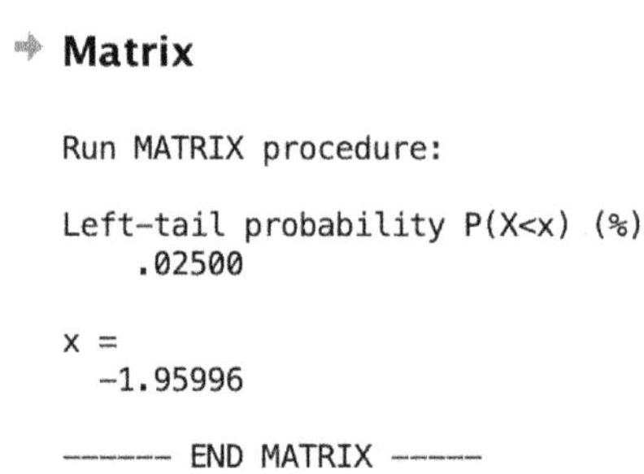

FIGURE 6.8
Output of QNORMDIST macro.

the area to the left of a certain value is 0.025, can you find that value? The answer is –1.96 as we have seen earlier.

I have written another SPSS macro `QNORMDIST` that can help you find a value under a normal curve if the probability is known. After you managed to install the macro on SPSS, you can find it by clicking: Analyze → QNORMDIST by Ahmad Daryanto.

6.4.2 R Action: qnorm()

A function `qnorm()` from R base can be used to find a value at which 25% of the area under the standard normal distribution lies to the left:

```
qnorm(0.025, mean = 0, sd = 1, lower.tail=TRUE)
```

```
## [1] –1.959964
```

In the function argument, mean is set to zero and standard deviation (sd) is set to 1, which corresponds to a standard normal curve. The lower.tail is set to TRUE. The code can also be written simply as `qnorm(0.025)`, without typing mean, sd, and lower.tail because the default values are mean = 0, sd = 1, and lower.tail = TRUE.

6.5 Z-Transformation

We can transform a normal distribution to a standard normal distribution. If we apply formula Equation 6.2) to normally distributed satisfaction scores, $satisfaction \sim N$ (μ, σ), then Z will be distributed according to standard normal distribution, $Z \sim N\ (0, 1)$. The resulting new variable is usually called a $z - score$.

$$Z = \frac{X - \mu}{\sigma} \tag{6.2}$$

There is an advantage if a variable is transformed into a z score. Using a z score, we will know how many deviations away an observation is from the mean of the data. For example, you will be able to say that Jack's exam score is 2 standard deviations above the mean scores of his cohort.

Illustration 1

Suppose that Andy is a manager of a car showroom in the UK who managed to sell 60 cars in a month. The sales mean score calculated from all managers in the country is 50 cars with a standard deviation of 5. Mark is the car manager of the same company in Germany. Mark managed to sell 80 cars in that month. The sales mean score in Germany is 70 cars with a standard deviation of 10. Assuming sales in both countries are normally distributed, which managers perform better relative to their peers in the same country?

$$Andy's\, z - score = \frac{60 - 50}{5}$$

$$Mark's\, z - score = \frac{80 - 70}{10}$$

The performance of the UK manager is 2 standard deviations above the mean, while the performance of the German manager is 1 standard deviation above the mean. Although Mark sold more car than Andy did, Andy actually performed better in the eyes of their peers.

Illustration 2

A variable is normally distributed with μ = 102 and σ = 10, answer the following questions.

a. What is the probability that a randomly selected variable X is less than 95?
b. What is the probability that a randomly selected variable X is between 80 and 110?

You can use the NORMDIST macro to answer these questions, which require you to calculate a certain area under a normal curve. There are two routes to answer the questions: calculating areas under a normal or those under the standard normal curve.

Answer (a):

In a shorthand notation, we want to find $P(X < 95)$.

In the NORMDIST macro, you can enter: x = 95, mean = 102, and standard deviation = 10, which gives 0.242.

If you want to work with a standard normal distribution using NORMDIST macro, work out the z-score (see the following calculation). The z-score is −0.70. Next, on the macro, enter x = −0.70, mean = 0, and standard deviation = 1. The answer is 0.242.

$$P(X < 95) = P\left(\frac{X-\mu}{\sigma} < \frac{95-102}{10}\right)$$
$$= P\left(Z < \frac{-7}{10}\right)$$
$$= P(Z < -0.70)$$

Answer (b):

In a shorthand notation, we want to find $P(80 < X < 110)$.

Using NORMDIST, we find $P(X < 80) = 0.023$, $P(X < 110) = 0.841$. Therefore, $P(80 < X < 110) = P(X < 110) - P(X < 80) = 0.818$.

NOTE

You probably heard a management approach called **Sig-Sigma**. Many management practitioners are dreaming of getting a 'Sig-Sigma' black belt (just like when you want to get a black belt in karate). The term Sig-Sigma is derived from the normal distribution curve, that is, six deviation (6σ) below or above the mean. It serves as a gold standard to achieve an optimal quality of business processes or engineering outputs. If a car manufacturer performance achieves Sig-Sigma, it is expected that the firm produces faulty cars only 3.4 times in a million times.

6.5.1 SPSS Action: Creating Z-Scores in SPSS

Data: sales.sav

- Click Analyze → Descriptive Statistics → Statistics.
- Insert *Sales* and *Adv* into the 'Descriptives' box.
- Tick 'Save standardized values as variables'.
- Click OK or Paste if you want to work with an SPSS syntax.

SPSS syntax:

```
DESCRIPTIVES VARIABLES=Sales Adv
  /SAVE
  /STATISTICS=MEAN STDDEV MIN MAX.
```

Now, inspect your data. Two new columns are added: *Zsales* and *ZADV*. The first one contains the z-score for *sales* and the second contains the z-score for *ADV*.

I have developed a special macro that can be used to standardize variables called the `CENTERING` macro.[2] Install the macro, after which you can run it by clicking Transform → CENTERING.

Using data *Sales.sav*, the variable *Sales* and *Adv* were standardized using the `CENTERING` macro. You must tick the `standardize` box, then click OK (I do not recommend to click `Paste` unless you want to see the source code of the macro).

Inspect your SPSS window. Look for a new data with name as **Untitled [MERGED_DATA]**. Open the data, new variables are created as zx1 and zx2.

6.5.2 SPSS Action: Mean-Centring

As explained in Section 6.5.1, mean-centring can be undertaken by using the CENTERING macro. Alternatively, we can use the SPSS built-in procedure 'Aggregate' and 'Transform'. For an illustration, suppose what we want to mean-centre the variable *Adv*. That is, we want to subtract the average of *Adv* from every value of *Adv* in the data.

Steps:

- Click Data → Aggregate.
- Under 'Aggregate Variables'. Insert *Adv* into the 'Summaries of Variable(s)' box.
- Once we have inserted the variable, in the 'Summaries of Variable(s)' box, 'Adv_mean = Mean(Adv)' is shown. This means that a new variable, *Adv_mean*, will be created whose values equal the mean of *Adv*.
- Click `OK` or `Paste` if you want to work with an SPSS syntax.
- Inspect the SPSS data. A new column 'Adv_mean' appears now in the data.
- Next, Transform → Compute variable.
- In the 'Target Variable' box, type in 'Adv_c'.

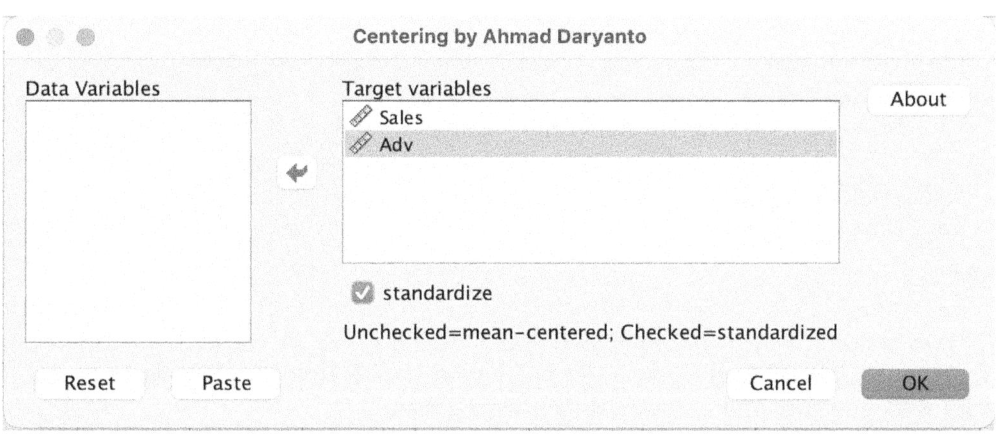

FIGURE 6.9
Standardize using the CENTERING macro before the columns of the original data.

[2] It can be downloaded at the book's online support.

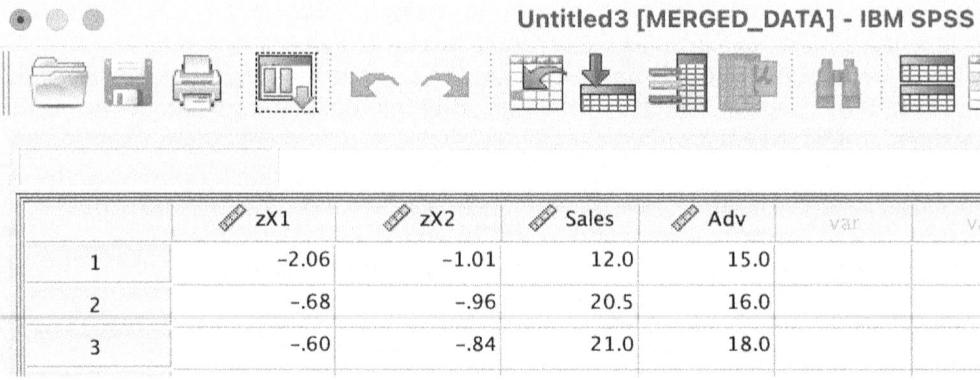

	zX1	zX2	Sales	Adv	var	va
1	-2.06	-1.01	12.0	15.0		
2	-.68	-.96	20.5	16.0		
3	-.60	-.84	21.0	18.0		

FIGURE 6.10
The first three rows of the new data. The variables zx1 and zx2 are z-scores for Sales and Adv, respectively.

- In the 'Numeric Expression' box, type in this expression: Adv-Adv_mean. Click OK or `Paste` if you want to work with an SPSS syntax.
- Inspect the data. The new variable *Adv_c* appears in the dataset containing the mean-centred values.

6.5.3 R Action

Let us use R to standardize the 60 cars that Andy had managed to sell. The mean score is 50 with a standard deviation of 5.

```
# Target value to standardize
x <- 60

# Mean and standard deviation of the distribution
mean_value <- 50
sd_value <- 5

# Calculate the Z-score (standardized value)
z_score <- (x - mean_value) / sd_value

print(z_score)
```

[1] 2

This expression may be impractical if you want to repeatedly calculate z-scores of different values. Alternatively, you could write your own R function. The basic syntax for a user-defined function in R takes the following format:

```
function_name <- function(parameters){
  function body
}
```

My z-score function looks like this:

```
# My z-score function
zscore <- function(target, themean, thesd){
    (target - themean) / thesd
}
print(zscore(60, 50, 5))
```

[1] 2

Let me explain the code. The name of my function is *zscore*. Executing the code will create an R object called *zscore* that will be available in the R environment. The name of the function is quite informative as it will create a z-score. The *zscore* function has three parameters, which generally refers to value that varies from task to task. They are variables. In R terminology, parameters can be called as the arguments of the function. The *zscore* function has three arguments: *target, themean, thesd.* I chose these names so that you can see how flexible it is to declare an argument. In the body of the function, the mathematical expression `(target - themean) / thesd` is placed inside the curly braces. Every time the expression is executed, the result is passed to the R object *zscore.*

6.6 Skewness and Kurtosis

Skewness is a measure of (a)symmetry. For example, a normal distribution is perfectly symmetrical. The skewness value of a normal distribution is zero. For a distribution that is not normal, the skewness value can be either positive of negative. For a left-tailed distribution – the flatness of the distribution is on the left, the skewness value is negative. For a right-tailed distribution – the flatness of the distribution is on the right, the skewness value is positive. Figure 6.11 illustrates the difference between right-tailed and left-tailed distributions.

Kurtosis is a measure of how peaked or flat a distribution is. For a normal distribution, kurtosis value is equal to 3. If the kurtosis value is less than 3, the distribution is called platykurtic, whilst if the kurtosis value is greater than 3, it is called leptokurtic. Figure 6.12 shows the comparison of the leptokurtic, platykurtic, and a standard normal distribution. I created the three distributions using R. The leptokurtic distribution has a standard deviation of 0.7, and the platykurtic distribution has a standard deviation of 2. Thus, values in the leptokurtic is less varied than those of the standard normal distribution, whilst values in the platykurtic distribution is more dispersed than those of the normal distribution.

6.6.1 R Code

I used the following R code to produce Figure 6.12. You can play around with the code by changing the value of *sd* in the line that starts with args.

```
# Comparing a normal distribution with
# a leptokurtic and platykurtic distributions
```

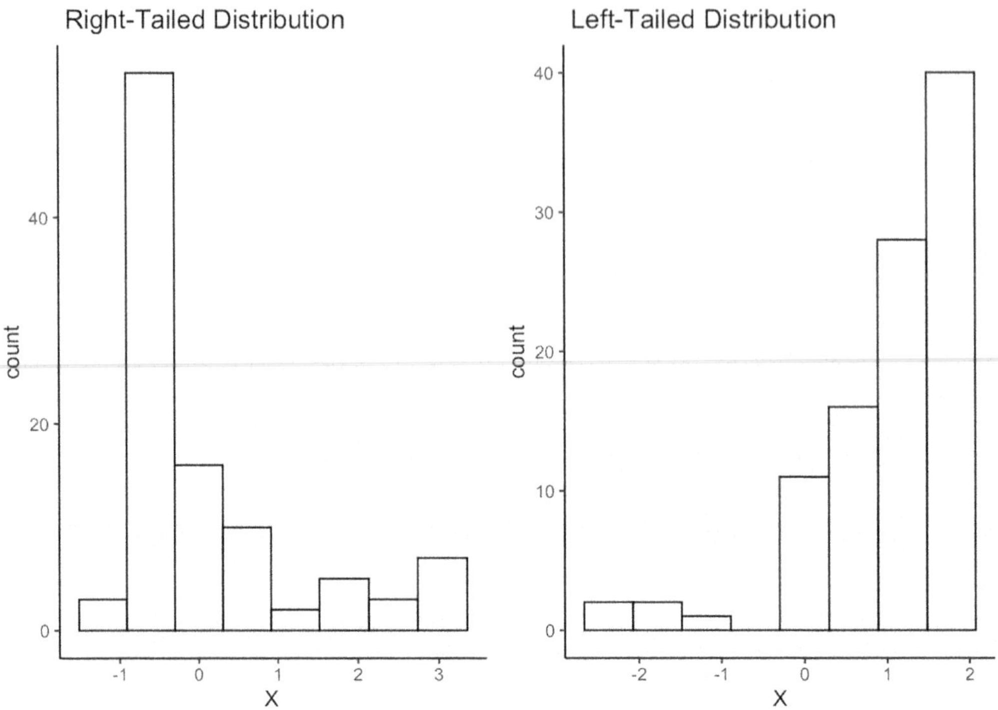

FIGURE 6.11
Right-tailed and left-tailed distributions.

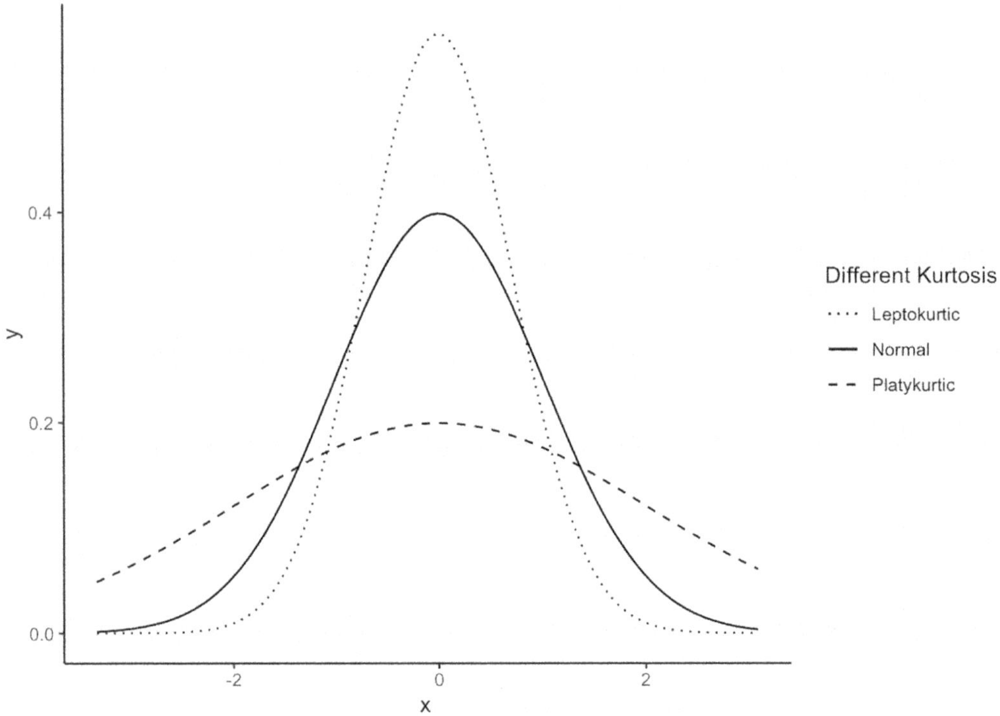

FIGURE 6.12
A normal distribution and leptokurtic and platykurtic distributions.

```
set.seed(2)
library(ggplot2)
set.seed(1492)
ggplot(data.frame(x = rnorm(1000)), aes(x)) + geom_
  function(aes(linetype=
  "Normal"),
    fun = dnorm, colour = "black",
    args = list(mean = 0, sd = 1)) +
  geom_function(aes( linetype="Platykurtic"),
    fun = dnorm, colour = "black",
    args = list(mean = 0, sd = 2)) +
  geom_function(aes(linetype="Leptokurtic"),
    fun = dnorm, colour = "black",
    args = list(mean = 0, sd = 0.7)) +
  scale_linetype_manual(name ="Different Kurtosis",
    values = c("Normal" = "solid",
            "Platykurtic" = "dashed",
            "Leptokurtic" = "dotted")) +
  theme_classic()
```

6.6.2 SPSS Action

Data: spending.sav

The goal of using SPSS is to check the skewness value of the variable *amount* in the *spending.sav* data.

- Click Analyze → Descriptive Statistics → Statistics.
- Insert amount to the `Variable(s) box`.
- Click `Options`.
- Under `Distribution`, tick `Kurtosis` and `Skewness`.
- Click `OK` or `Paste` if you want to work with an SPSS syntax.

SPSS syntax:

```
/STATISTICS=MEAN STDDEV MIN MAX KURTOSIS SKEWNESS.
```

6.6.3 R Action

Now, let us R to check for the skewness value and kurtosis value of the *amount* variable. For this purpose, we are using the R function moments (Komsta 2022).

```
Install the package.

install.packages("moments")
library(ahdar) library(moments)

dat <- spending
```

```
# skewness
skewness(dat$amount)

## [1] 0.04837932
# kurtosis
kurtosis(dat$amount)

## [1] 2.472581
# Inspect the distribution
hist(dat$amount)
```

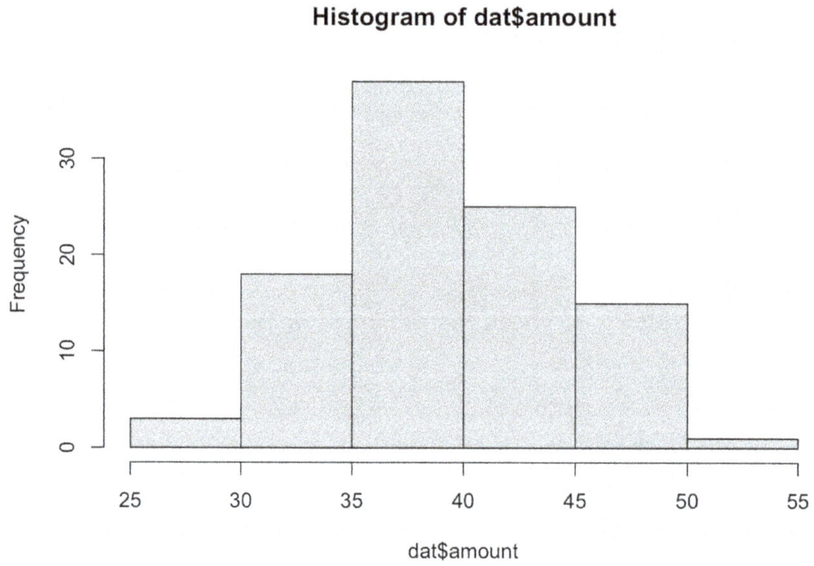

FIGURE 6.13
A histogram of amount produced by the hist() function.

NOTE

1. A normal distribution is symmetrical with skewness = 0 and kurtosis = 3.
2. A standard normal distribution has a mean of 0 and standard deviation of 1.
3. The area under the normal curve within –1.96 standard deviation below the mean and 1.96 standard deviation above the mean, namely, within the interval –1.96 σ, 1.96 σ is 95% of the total area. If the curve is standard normal where total area is 1, then the total area withing that interval is just 0.95 (see the blue area in Figure 6.3). If memory always fails you, just remember ±2 as a good estimate for ±1.96.

4. If data is normally distributed or assumed to be, we can find an answer of these kinds of questions:
    - What is the proportion of customers who spent £100 in a shopping trip? You can write the question succinctly as $P(Spending > 100) = ?$
    - What is the proportion of customers who spent less than £61 in a shopping?
    - What is the proportion of customers who spent from £60 to £80? You can write the question succinctly written as $P(60 < Spending < 80) = ?$

6.7 Checking Whether a Distribution Is Normal

We may want to inspect whether our data exhibits a normal distribution. This is because many statistical assumptions require a normality assumption, although in a large data, this assumption is not strictly required. One visual tool that can be used for this purpose is a quantile-quantile plot or Q-Q plot, for short (Gnanadesikan & Wilk 1968). In a Q-Q plot, the quantiles of our data distribution on the y-axis are plotted against those of another distribution on the x-axis. If the quantiles of the distribution on the x-axis is a theoretical normal distribution, it is called a normal Q-Q plot. In a normal Q-Q plot, if the plot looks linear, then the distribution of our data can be assumed to be normal.

6.7.1 SPSS Action

Data: spending.sav

Here, we use SPSS to produce a Q-Q plot. The variable we use from the spending.sav data is *amount*.

- Click Analyze → Descriptive Statistics → Q-Q Plots.
- Insert amount to the `Variable(s)` box.
- Under `Test Distribution`, `Normal` is given as a default.
- Click `OK` or `Paste` if you want to work with an SPSS syntax.

SPSS syntax:

```
PPLOT
  /VARIABLES=amount
  /NOLOG
  /NOSTANDARDIZE
  /TYPE=Q-Q
  /FRACTION=BLOM
  /TIES=MEAN
  /DIST=NORMAL.
```

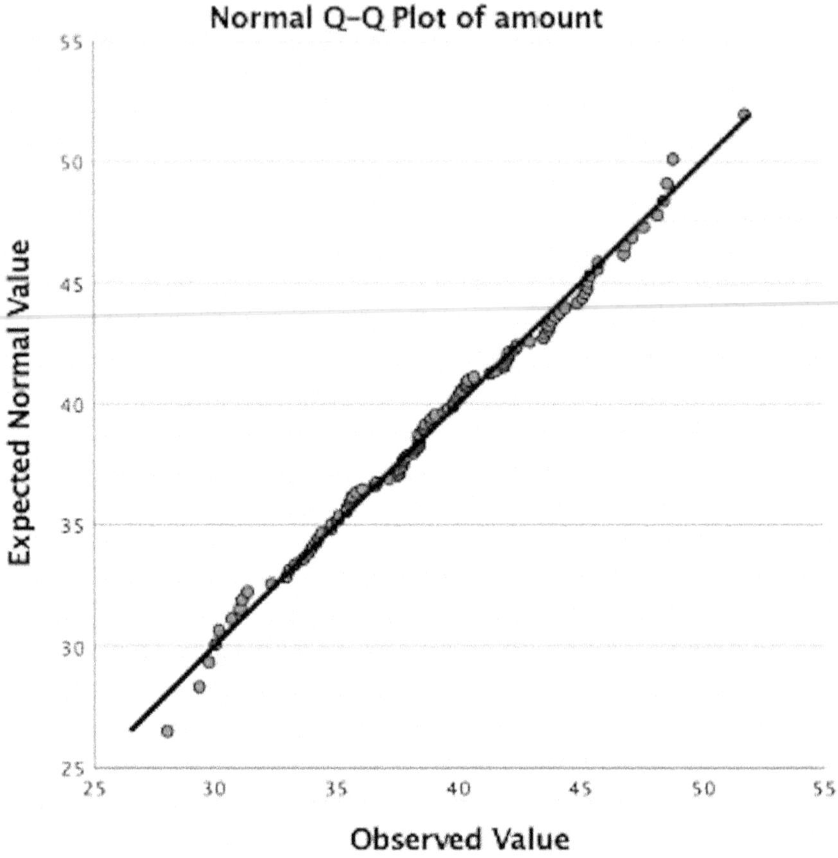

FIGURE 6.14
A Q-Q plot from SPSS. The R code to produce the qqplot is presented here.

Now, inspect the output. The Q-Q plot produced in the output can be seen in Figure 6.15. As can be seen in the figure, majority of the points – except few points at the end – lie on a straight line linear, so the data can be assumed to be fairly normal.

6.7.2 R Action

We can use the R base functions `qqnorm` to create a Q-Q plot, and by using `qqnorm`, a reference line, which is a straight line, can be added to the plot.

```
library(ahdar)

dat <- spending

qqnorm(dat$amount, pch = 1, frame = FALSE)
```

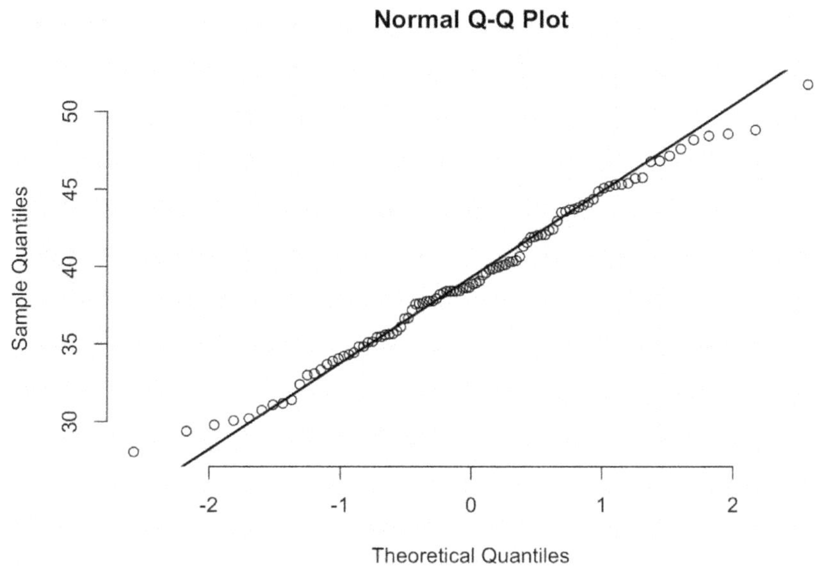

FIGURE 6.15
A Q-Q plot from R.

```
# add a reference line
qqline(dat$amount, col = "black", lwd = 2)
```

Histogram vs. Q-Q plot. Why can't we just use a histogram to assess whether our data distribution is normal? Yes, we can use a histogram, but it is not a perfect tool. As we have learned in the previous section, the shape of histogram depends on the number of bins we selected and the sample size; therefore, our assessment is not really accurate. Although the interpretation of a Q-Q plot also involves subjectivity, it is a better choice than histogram because skewness might not be easily spotted by eyes in histogram. For a demonstration, we can use the `sn package` (Azzalini & Azzalini 2015) to generate a skewed distribution, and plot a histogram, and a Q-Q plot. The code is given here. As can be seen in Figure 6.16, the distribution of the generated data looks normal in the histogram, but the Q-Q plot shows that the distribution is apparently skewed as there are strong deviations from a linear line at the tails of the distribution.

```
# set a random seed for replicability
set.seed(10)

# load library sn.
# install if it is not on your machine
```

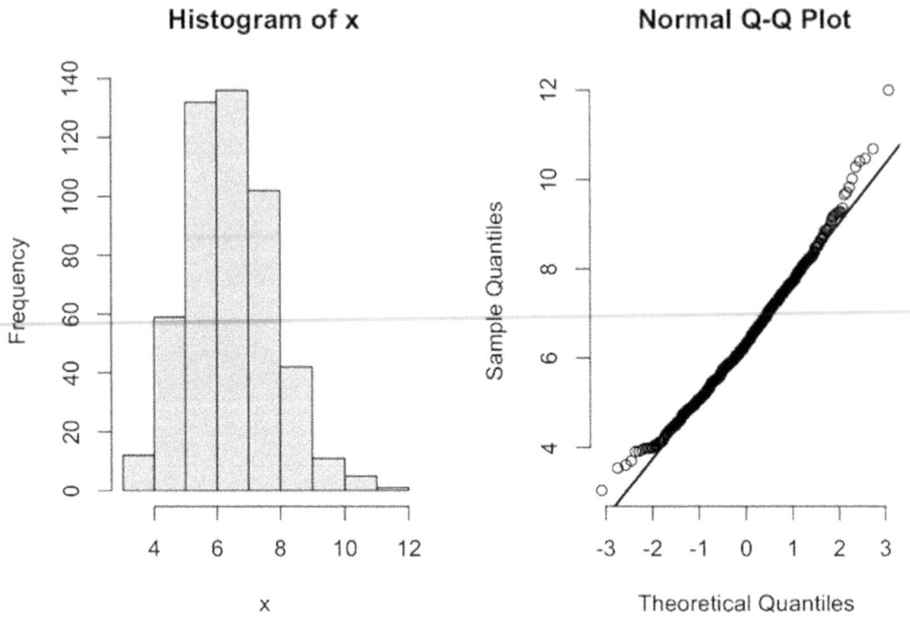

FIGURE 6.16
A histogram and its associated Q-Q plot. The distribution looks normal in the histogram, but the Q-Q plot detects skewness in the distribution.

```
library(sn)

# generate data
# the values in the bracket are the parameters values
# 500 is a sample size
# experimenting with the last value

x<- rsn(500, 5, 2, 2)

# prepare two plots in one window
par(mfrow = c(1, 2))

# plot a histogram and a q-q plot
hist(x)
qqnorm(x,     pch = 1, frame = FALSE)
qqline(x, col = "black", lwd = 2)
```

6.8 Empirical and Theoretical Distribution

When we construct a frequency distribution from our data, the distribution is empirical. If we create a distribution using a mathematical formula, such as the normal distribution formula described in Equation 6.1, the distribution is theoretical. For a theoretical normal distribution, the curve looks very smooth. A Q-Q plot compares the empirical distribution with the theoretical normal distribution. In reality, we never have such a perfect normal curve with our empirical data. In research, sometimes the interest lies in finding how close an empirical distribution is to a theoretical distributions, hence the use of a Q-Q plot as a visual inspection. In other words, can we fit a theoretical distribution to an empirical distribution? The activity is called curve-fitting.

6.9 Further Reading

Altman, D. G. & Bland, J. M. (1995), 'Statistics notes: The normal distribution', *BMJ* **310**(6975), 298.

Ghasemi, A. & Zahediasl, S. (2012), 'Normality tests for statistical analysis: A guide for non-statisticians', *International Journal of Endocrinology and Metabolism* **10**(2), 486.

6.10 Summary

This chapter discussed a normal distribution and its properties. This chapter also covers how to work out areas under a normal curve associated with a certain value and, conversely – given an area under a normal curve – find the value associated with the area; how to calculate a z-score; and how to assess visually whether a distribution is normal by using a Q-Q plot. The chapter briefly explains how to create a user-defined function, which is very useful if the same tasks are to be repeated with different input values.

6.11 Review Questions

1. To draw a normal distribution, you need to know two values. What are they?
2. What is a standard normal distribution?
3. What do I mean by an empirical and theoretical distribution in this chapter?

6.12 Exercises

1. A variable is normally distributed with $\mu = 50$ and $\sigma = 5$.
   - What is the probability that a randomly selected variable X is greater than 60?
   - What is the probability that a randomly selected variable X is between 20 and 40?

2. If satisfaction scores follow a standard normal distribution, and the probability to the right of a score is 0.03, what is the value of the score?
3. If scores on perceived quality are normally distributed with mean = 50, and standard deviation = 10, what is the probability of finding a value greater than 80%?
4. Create your own function to calculate the sum of two z-scores. It must be able to compute the sum of the z-scores for Andy and Mark (see illustration 1).
5. Use SPSS to calculate the skewness and kurtosis values of variable amount in spending.sav.

7

Distributions Derived from Normal Distribution

Some well-known distributions such as the chi-square, *F*, and *t* distributions, are derived from a normal distribution. Therefore, the normal distribution can be seen as the parent of these distributions. Knowing these distributions are useful in understanding the statistical tests discussed in the subsequent chapters. For instance, chi-square distribution is used in testing sample proportions, and the extent to which marketing variables are related. F-test and t-test are used in examining the effect of marketing variables via an experimentation using the analysis of variance (ANOVA) and a regression analysis. Proportion is enhanced if one understands the chi-square distribution. In this chapter, the properties of these three non-normal distributions are explained without focusing any formulas in details. The focus is on how those distributions are derived from a normal distribution, being familiar with the shapes of the distribution, and being able to read the area under the distributions curve and p-value associated with each of the non-normal distributions. The learning in this chapter is facilitated by the use macros that I have written. These macros are easy to install and use. In the last section, obtaining a chi-square distribution with a certain degree of freedom from a normal distribution is demonstrated.

Learning Objectives:

- Know some distributions derived from normal distribution *t*, *F*, and chi-square distribution.
- Know how to use SPSS macro and R to calculate areas under a non-normal distribution curve.

7.1 Chi-Square Distribution

Chi-square distribution commonly represented by this Greek's symbol 'χ^2', which appears later when we discussed proportion test and Crosstabs, is a continuous distribution. The shape of the distribution is determined by one parameter called its degrees of freedom (*df*). A chi-square distribution with *n* degrees of freedom can be constructed from *n* standard normal random variables. That is, by taking the sum of the squared of the *n* standard random variables, the resulting variable is distributed according a chi-square distribution with *n* degrees of freedom. Using a mathematical expression, if $V = X_1^{\ 2} + X_2^{\ 2} + \ldots + X_n^{\ 2}$, then *V* follows a chi-square distribution with *n* degrees of freedom. We can write *V* by using this notation: $V \sim \chi_n^2$ (read: *V* follows a chi-square distribution with *n* degrees of freedom). Figure 7.1 displays chi-square distributions at various degrees of freedom (*df* = 1, 5, 10 and 30).

DOI: 10.4324/9781003407225-9

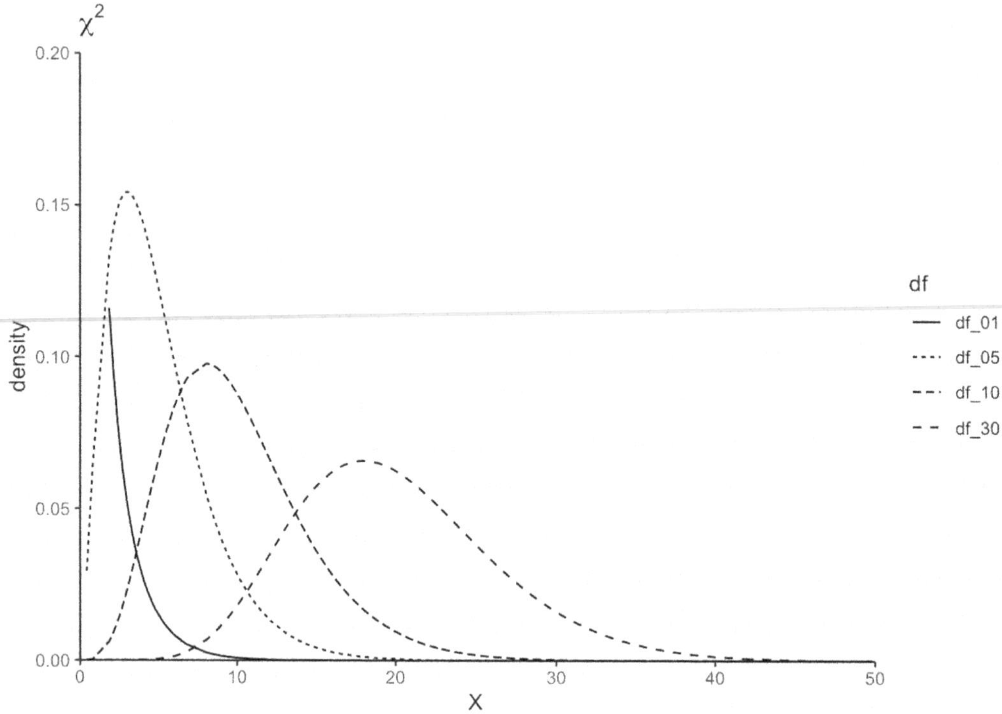

FIGURE 7.1
Chi-square distributions at df = 1, df = 5, df =10, and df = 30.

INSTALLING DISTRIBUTION MACROS

In this chapter, we use certain macros to work out the distribution of variables. I have written these macros, e.g. `QDIST`; therefore, they are not available under the standard SPSS menu. These macro needs to be installed. After a successful installation, the macro can be found the SPSS menu by clicking Analyze → the name of the macro. For example, `QDIST`, can be found by clicking **Analyze → QFDIST by Ahmad Daryanto**

7.1.1 Finding an Area Under the Chi-Square Distribution Curve

If X follows a chi-square distribution with $df = 5$, what is the probability of finding a value of X that is less than 10? We can use the CHIDIST macro, and the answer is about 92.5% (see Figure 7.2).

7.1.2 Finding a Value Associated with an Area Under a Chi-Square Distribution Curve

If X follows a chi-square distribution with $df = 5$, and the probability of finding a value greater than `something` is 5%, what is the value of the `something`? We can use the QCHIDIST macro, and the answer is 10.0705 (see Figure 7.4).

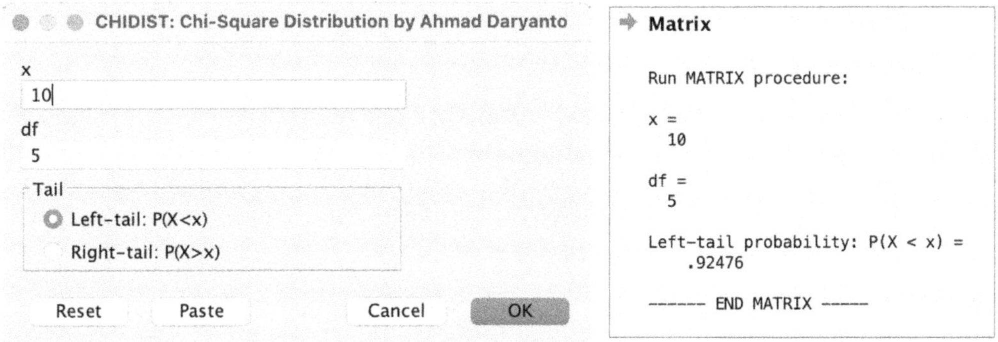

FIGURE 7.2
CHIDIST macro.

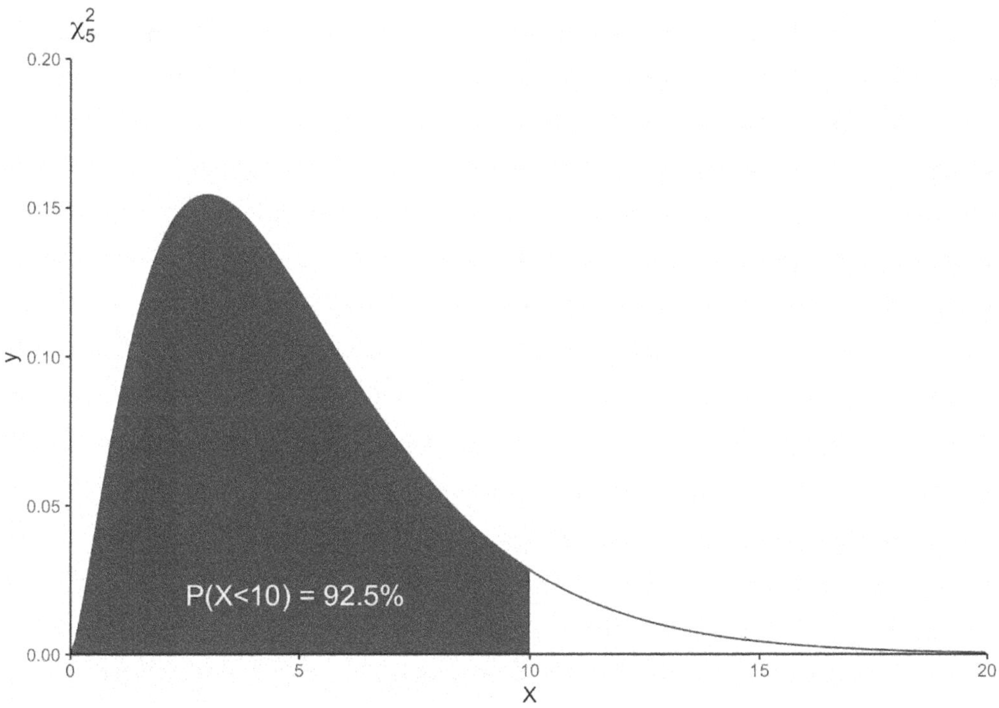

FIGURE 7.3
Visualization of the area under the curve to the left of X = 10.

We have seen the visualization of the area under the curve of a distribution (Figure 7.3 and Figure 7.5); in the next section, I will not present those types of visualizations.

7.2 *T* Distribution

Student's *T* distribution or *T* distribution, for short appears later when we learn regression techniques to test the significance of the regression parameters (see Chapters 12 and 13).

STUDENT

At the time when a British statistician, William Sealy Gosset Jr (1876–1837) worked on his paper to introduce his new discovery of *T* distribution, he was working in a beer company that did not allow its employees to publish a paper that revealed the name of the company. To avoid breaking the rule, he chose a pseudonym 'Student'.

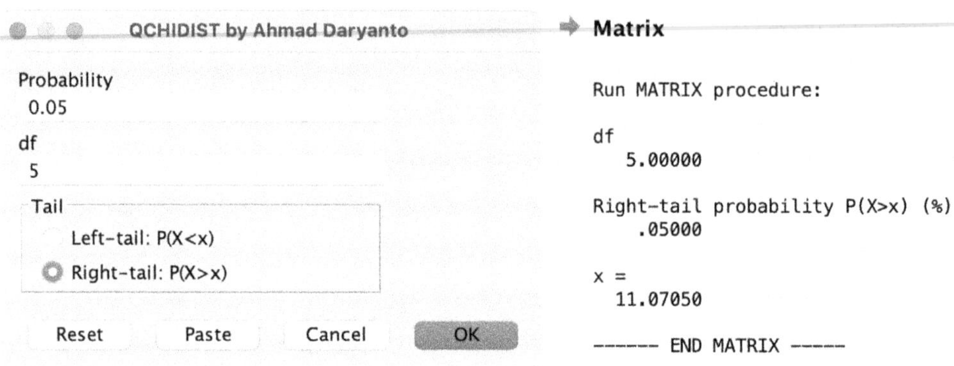

FIGURE 7.4
QCHIDIST macro.

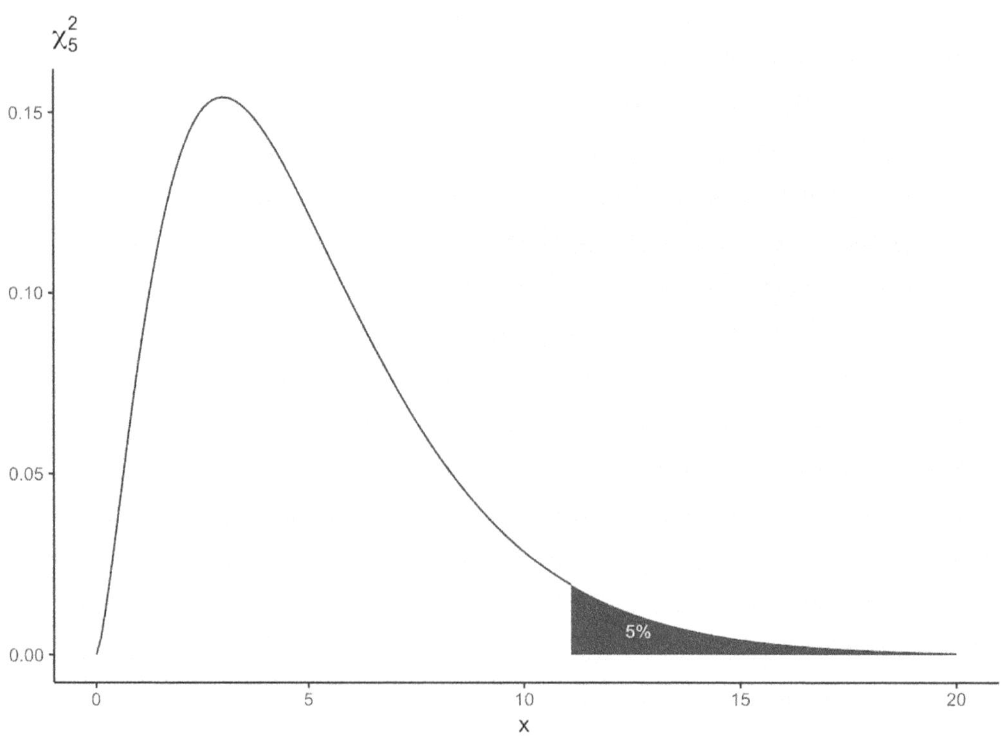

FIGURE 7.5
The area in red is 5% associated with X = 11.0705.

The T distribution, theoretically, is constructed from a standard normal and a chi-square distribution. If $Z \sim N(01), U \sim X_n^{\ 2}$ are independent random variables, then the distribution of $t = \dfrac{Z}{\dfrac{U}{\sqrt{n}}}$ is called t distribution with n degrees of freedom. Another form, which is more familiar for practical users of statistics takes the following equation:

$$t = \frac{\bar{X} - \mu}{\dfrac{S}{\sqrt{n}}} \tag{7.1}$$

where t in Equation 7.1 follows a t distribution with $n-1$ degrees of freedom. This formula appears in the context of taking a random sample from a normal population, where $\bar{X}$ and S are the mean and standard deviation of the random sample, and n is the sample size. The form resembles the standard normal Z in Equation 6.2 rewritten here: $Z = \dfrac{X - \mu}{\sigma}$ (if we replace X with $\bar{X}$ and σ with $\dfrac{S}{\sqrt{n}}$, then we get Equation 7.1). We will present again Equation 7.1 in the chapter where we discussed sampling distribution of sample means.

The shape of the T distribution depends on its degree of freedom n. Figure 7.6 shows three t curves. As we can see in the figure, T distribution is symmetrical around 0

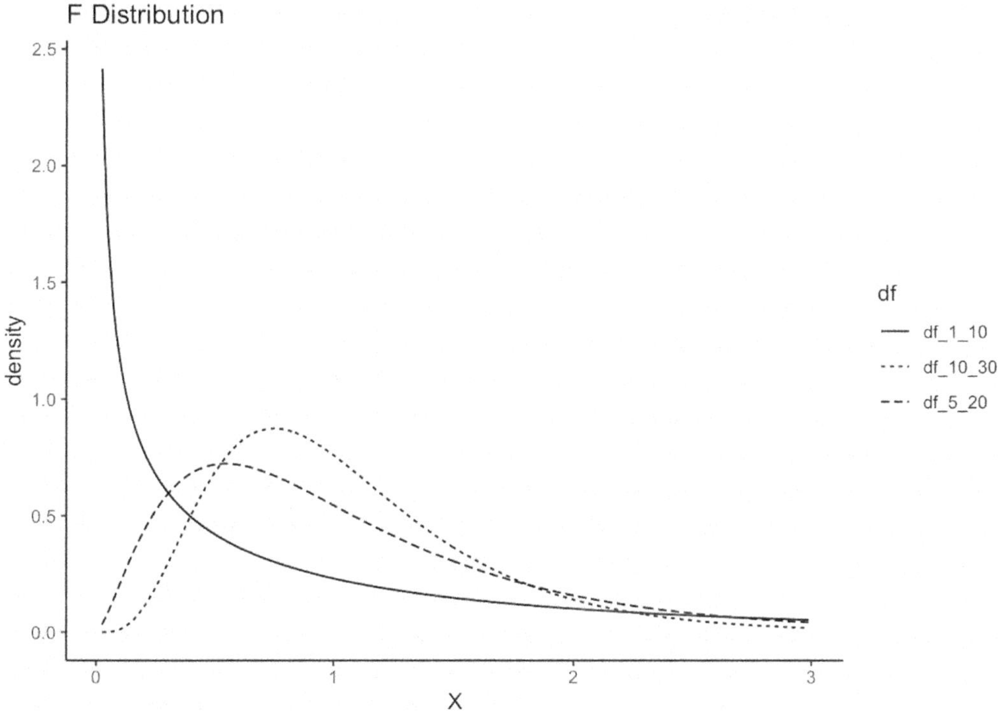

FIGURE 7.6
T distributions at various degrees of freedom. At a very large degrees of freedom, the distribution is approximately.

and has fat tails compared to that of standard normal distribution. *T* distribution will approach normal when its degree of freedom gets very large. At degrees of freedom equals 30, *T* distribution looks fairly normal.

> **NOTE: DEGREES OF FREEDOM**
>
> Degrees of freedom is related to sample size. If a sample size gets larger, degrees of freedom also get larger. The meaning of the degrees of freedom can be explained as follows: Suppose that I want you to mention 5 numbers that you like. However, the mean of the 5 numbers must be 10. While you can arbitrarily choose the first 4 numbers, the last number must be fixed to ensure that the mean score is 10. In this example, your degree of freedom is 4 – you are losing one degree of freedom because the mean score is certain. If you were to mention 15 numbers with the mean score is kept at a certain value, then your degrees of freedom is 14. It is obvious that in these two illustrations, your degree of freedom is equal to $N - 1$, where N is the sample size. Hence, when sample size gets larger, the degrees of freedom also get larger.

7.2.1 Finding an Area Under the *T* Distribution Curve

We can use `TDIST` macro to find the probability associated with a certain value. For example, if a variable follows a *t* distribution with $df = 2$, we can run the macro to find the probability of finding a value less than a certain value. Suppose that we want to find the probability of finding a value less than 1. In the macro, we must enter 1 in the x box, insert 2 in the `Degrees of Freedom` box, and select `P(X<x)` (see Figure 7.7).

7.2.2 Finding a Value Associated with an Area Under a *T* Distribution Curve

We can also calculate the areas under the *T* distribution curve if the probability and the degrees of freedom are given. Suppose we want to calculate at what value of *X* that $P(X < x) = 0.78868$. The answer is $X = 1.00003$ (see Figure 7.8).

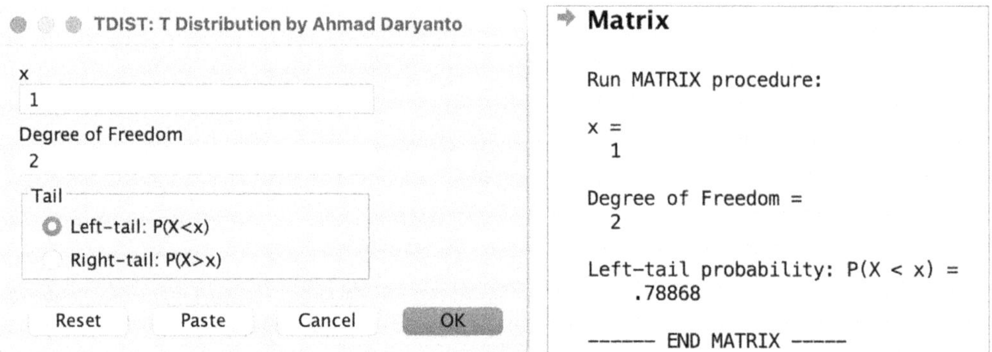

FIGURE 7.7
TDIST macro.

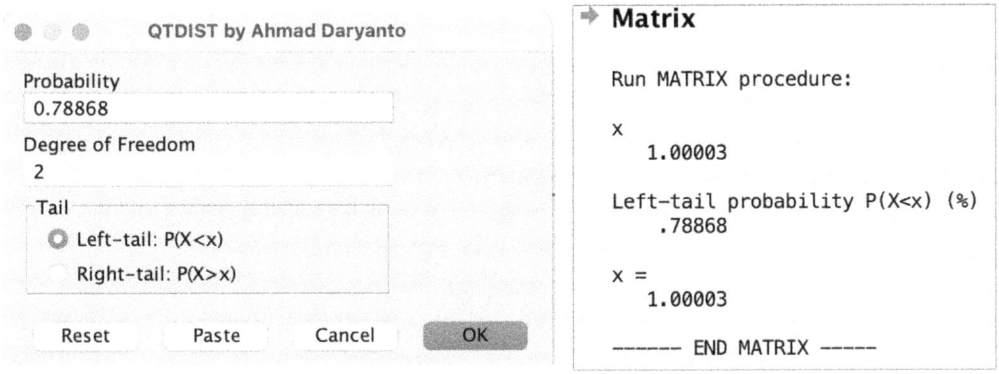

FIGURE 7.8
QTDIST macro.

7.3 *F* Distribution

F distribution appears later when we learn crosstabs and ANOVA. The shape of the distribution is determined by two degrees of freedom. The *F* distribution is denoted by $F(df1, df2)$ where $df1$ and $df2$ are the first and the second degrees of freedom. *F* distribution always have positive values and skewed to the right. Theoretically, *F* distribution is constructed from two chi-square distributions. If U is a chi-square distribution with m degrees of freedom ($U \sim \chi_m^2$) and V is another chi-square distribution with n degrees of freedom ($V \sim \chi_n^2$), then $X = \frac{U/m}{V/n}$ will be distributed according to *F* distribution with m and n degrees of freedom, denoted by $F(m,n)$. Figure 7.9 shows $F(1,10)$, $F(5,20)$, and $F(10,30)$ distributions.

7.3.1 Finding an Area Under the *F* Distribution Curve

We can use `FDIST` macro to find the probability associated with a certain value. For example, if a variable follows an *F* distribution with $df\ 1 = 1$ and $df\ 2 = 200$, we can run the macro to find the probability of finding a value, say, less than 1.96. We must enter 1.96 in the `x` box, insert 1 in the `df1` box, insert 200 in the `df2` box, and select $P(X < x)$. The screen image of the macro and its outputs are displayed in Figure 7.10.

7.3.2 Finding a Value Associated with an Area Under an *F* Distribution Curve

We can use `QFDIST` macro to find a value of x associated with a certain area under the *F* distribution curve. This is the reverse of the problem discussed in the previous section. If a variable follows an *F* distribution (with $df\ 1 = 5$, $df\ 2 = 20$), and the area to the right of a certain value is 0.055, can we find that value? The answer is 2.71089 (see Figure 7.11).

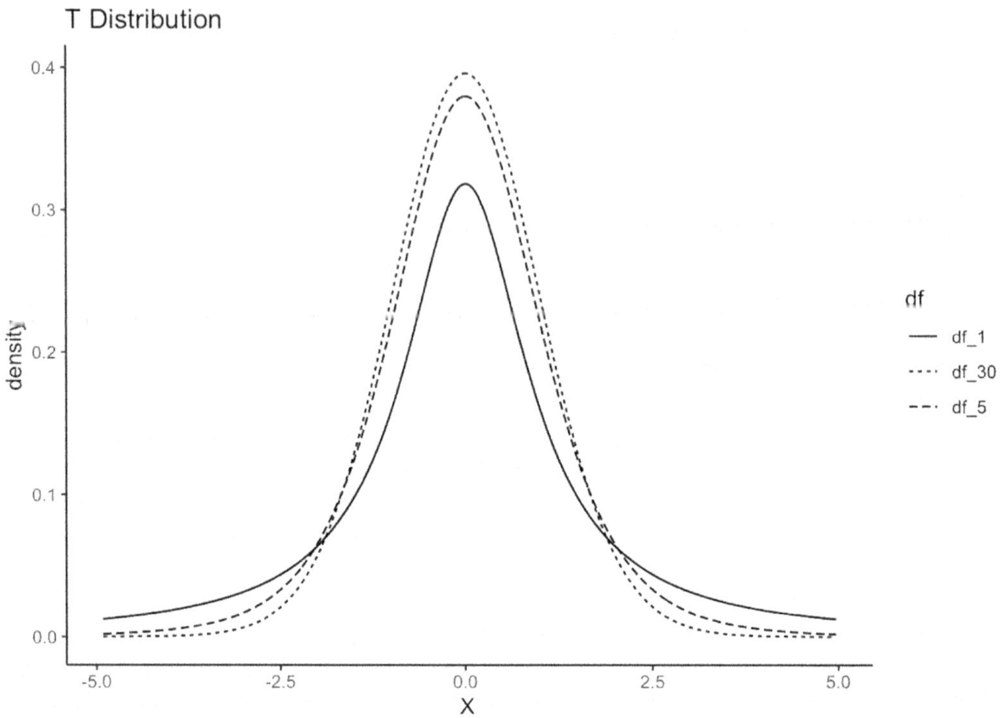

FIGURE 7.9
F distributions.

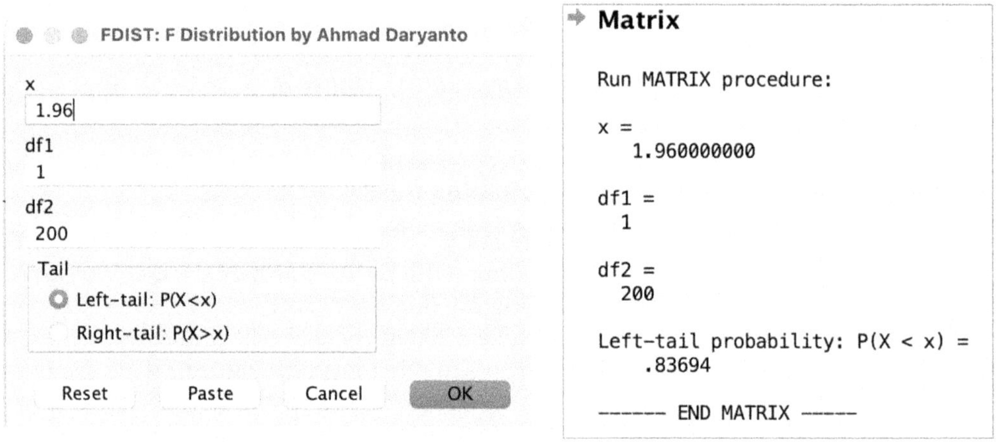

FIGURE 7.10
FDIST macro and its outputs.

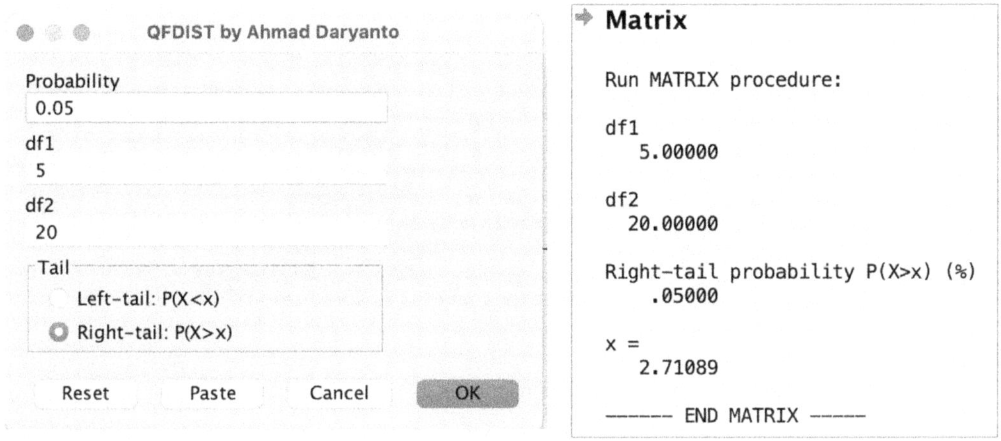

FIGURE 7.11
QFDIST macro.

7.4 Seeing Is Believing

We have learned that if $V = X_1^2 + X_2^2 + \ldots + X_n^2$, where X s are independent standard normal random variable, then V follows a chi-square distribution with n degrees of freedom (i.e. $V \sim X_n{}^2$). We could use *simulation* to prove this.

- Generate n standard normal random variables, e.g. $n = 5: x_1, x_2, x_3, x_4, x_5$
- Take the squared: $x_1^2, x_2^2, x_3^2, x_4^2 + x_5^2$
- Take the sum $V = x_1^2 + x_2^2 + x_3^2 + x_4^2 + x_5^2$
- Produce the histogram of V by clicking Graphs → Legacy Dialogs → Histogram.

I provide the SPSS syntax and the R code in the block codes here. To run the SPSS syntax, on the SPSS menu, click File → New → Syntax. Paste the code. Next, click Run → All.

7.4.1 SPSS Code to Simulate a Chi-Square Distribution

Here I present the SPSS code to simulate a chi-square distribution.

Before running the syntax, in the SPSS data view, prepare empty rows in the SPSS Data View to which data will be placed. It is easy to prepare 500 values in Excel, say from 1 to 500, and paste these values onto a column in the SPSS Data View. These values will be replaced with new values after we run the code, and new columns will be added depending on how many variables are generated.

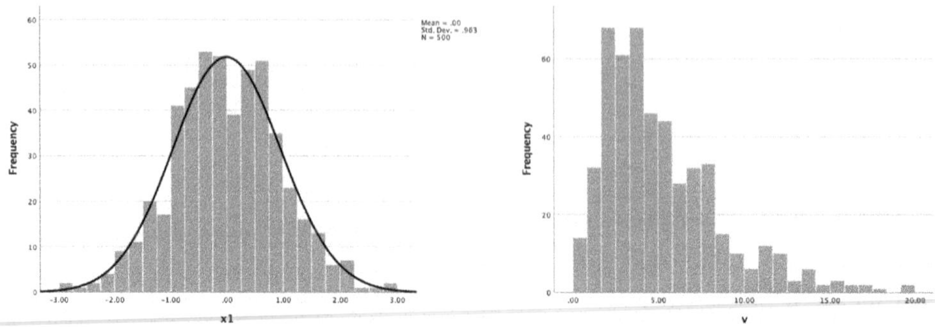

FIGURE 7.12
A normal distribution and a chi-square distribution from SPSS.

```
/* SPSS Syntax
/* Demonstrating Chi-Square Distribution with df=5.

set seed 12345

/* set seed allows us to replicate the results.

/* Generate five standard normal random variables.

COMPUTE x1 = rv.normal(0,1).
COMPUTE x2 = rv.normal(0,1).
COMPUTE x3 = rv.normal(0,1).
COMPUTE x4 = rv.normal(0,1).
COMPUTE x5 = rv.normal(0,1).

/*Squared each of xs.

Compute x1sq = x1**2.
Compute x2sq = x2**2.
Compute x3sq = x3**2.
Compute x4sq = x4**2.
Compute x5sq = x5**2.

/* Sum of squared.
Compute v = x1sq + x2sq + x3sq + x4sq + x5sq.

EXECUTE.
/* plot histogram of x1

GRAPH /HISTOGRAM(NORMAL) = x1.
/* plot histogram of v
GRAPH /HISTOGRAM = v.

EXECUTE.
```

7.4.2 R Code to Simulate a Chi-Square Distribution

```
set.seed(12345)

# Set a sample size
n <- 500

# Generate five standard normal random variables.

x1      <- rnorm(n,  0,1)
x2      <- rnorm(n,  0,1)
x3      <- rnorm(n,  0,1)
x4      <- rnorm(n,  0,1)
x5      <- rnorm(n,  0,1)

# Squared

x1sq <- x1**2
x2sq <- x2**2
```

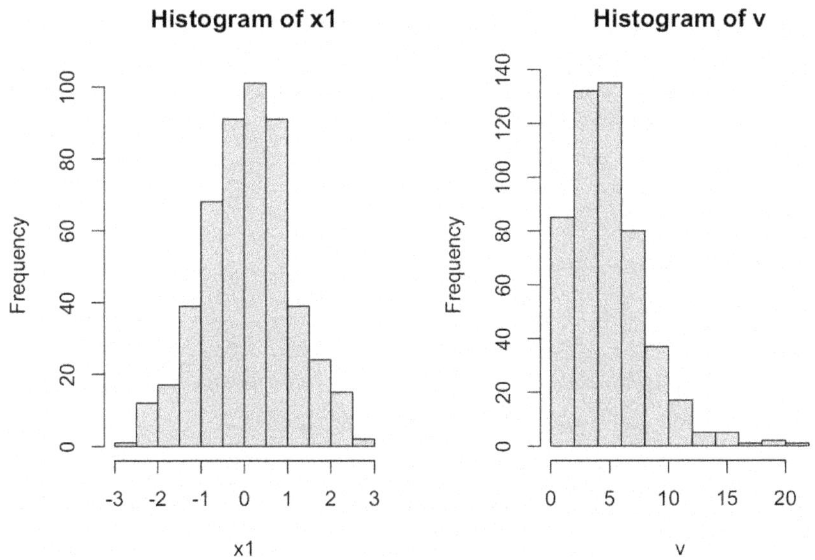

FIGURE 7.13
A normal distribution and a chi-square distribution plotted with R.

```
x3sq <- x3**2
x4sq <- x4**2
x5sq <- x5**2
```

```
# Sum of squared.

v <- x1sq + x2sq + x3sq + x4sq + x5sq

# Prepare a window for multiple plots
# c(1,2) means two images in one row

par(mfrow = c(1, 2))

# plot histogram of x1
  hist(x1)

# plot histogram of v
  hist(v)
```

7.5 Summary

In this chapter, we have discussed three distributions that are originated from normal distributions: T, F, and chi-square (χ^2) distributions. I have also demonstrated on how to work out the area under each distribution using my macros. Of course, there are many resources out there in the internet[1] to perform the same task; however, I found it quite handy to have the macros installed on the SPSS without necessarily visiting external resources. In the last section, I have demonstrated how to construct a chi-square distribution with *n* degrees of freedom by taking the sum of squares of *n* standard normal distributions.

7.6 Review Questions

1. To draw an *F* distribution, you need to know two values. What are they?
2. A variable follow chi-square distribution with df = 1.
   - What is the probability that a randomly selected variable *X* is greater than 5?
   - What is the probability that a randomly selected variable *X* is between 2 and 5?

7.7 Exercise

Modify the R code or SPSS code in Section 7.4. Show how F distribution can be produced from two chi-square distributions.

1 e.g. https://www.statskingdom.com/distribution-calculator.html.

8

Sampling Distribution

In this chapter, one of the important concepts in statistics is explained, that is, the central limit theorem. In the first part of the chapter, to facilitate the explanation of the concept, the story of the Lady Tasting Tea is used to illustrate the distribution of sample proportion when sample size gets larger. The chapter provides the R section code that can be used to investigate the sampling distribution of the proportion by changing the parameters of the experiment: probability of success and the number of cups. The importance of the sampling distribution is emphasized. In The second part of the chapter, the sampling distribution of sample means and the standard error of the mean are explained.

Learning Objectives:

- Understand what a sampling distribution is.
- Understand the importance of the central limit theorem and its implication to practice.
- Know the normal approximation to the binomial distribution.
- Understand how to calculate the standard error of the mean.

8.1 The Lady Tasting Tea

The story of 'The Lady Tasting Tea' captivated me from the first time I heard about it. The year was 2004. I was attending a three-day PhD workshop on structural equation modelling at the University of Groningen. Groningen is the largest city in the northern part of the Netherlands. It took me nearly a five-hour train journey from Maastricht, which is located in the southern part of the country. On the first day of the workshop, for the reason that I could not recall, the course instructor who is a sociologist and well-known statistician, Professor Anne Boomsma, with glittering eyes told me about the story of 'The Lady Tasting Tea'. It was taken from the title of the first chapter of a book written by Salsburg (2001). The phrase is also part of the book's title. It is a history book on statistics and important names with their discoveries in the 20th century. The book is a science popular book aimed at general readers. Without waiting the workshop to end, I immediately ordered the book online.

Here is an excerpt from the first chapter of the book:

> It was a summer afternoon in Cambridge, England, in the late 1920s. A group of university dons, their wives, and some guests were sitting around an outdoor table for

DOI: 10.4324/9781003407225-10

> afternoon tea. One of the women was insisting that tea tasted different depending upon whether the tea was poured into the milk or whether the milk was poured into the tea. The scientific minds among the men scoffed at this as sheer nonsense. What could be the difference? . . . A thin, short man, with thick glasses and a Vandyke beard beginning to turn gray, pounced on the problem. 'Let us test the proposition,' he said excitedly.
>
> (Salsburg 2001)

Later, the book revealed that the Vandyke-bearded man was Ronald Aylmer Fisher, the statistical giant of the 20th century.

8.2 Sampling Distribution

The reason I am telling you about 'The Lady Tasting Tea' is I will use the simplified version of the story to understand of what we mean by sampling distribution of a statistics.

Let us begin – note that this is the original story but modified to make it simple without losing the essence of what I am trying to explain here. Imagine that we presented the lady with 5 cups. In each cup, we ask her whether this is the cup into which the tea was poured into the milk or whether the milk was poured into the tea. Next, we record the number of correct answers she obtained. Before we move on, let me provide the definition of sampling distribution, which can be read as follows:

IMPORTANT: DEFINITION OF A SAMPLING DISTRIBUTION

Sampling distribution is the distribution of a statistic over a very large collection of samples (e.g. thousands, millions), each of which is randomly selected from a single population.

In this definition, a statistic is a value calculated from sample, which varies from sample to sample. Fisher named such variable as a variate (Fisher 1970), but today a random variable is the convention. For example, the average marks of group of students, the number of correct guesses of 5 trials in the Lady Tasting Tea experiment are statistics. What about population? In everyday conversation, people refer population to real entities or objects such as consumers, students, cities, firms, etc. To fit with the exact definition of population, population is actually a large pool of values, which can be infinitely large. If we are analysing the average mark of students in a sample of students, the population is actually the large pool of the marks not the students. The notion of population as a collection of values becomes obvious in the Lady Tasting Tea experiment where population is a large collection of either wrong or correct guesses made by the lady.

Now, let us consider the sampling distribution of the number of correct *guesses* or *answers* – I used these words interchangeably in this chapter. What constitutes a *sample*? If we presented the lady with 5 cups, then the values obtained from the 5 cup trials constitutes as a **sample**. One sample will consist of 5 values of which can be coded as either 0 for wrong guess or 1 for correct guess.

If we believe that the lady has no magical ability and just makes a random guess, then her chance of making a correct answer in a cup is half (see Figure 8.1) for an illustration with 5 cups). If the lady can endure the test forever, we could present her with another 5 cups, and another 5 cups, and another 5 cups, and so on.

Now, let us image that we could repeat the experiment again and again by presenting her with 1000 sets of 5 cups (i.e. 1000 samples) (see Figure 8.2). In each sample, we calculate the number of correct guesses. Therefore, when the whole experiments are finished, we would obtain 1000 values of correct guesses.

At this point, the definition of the sampling distribution can be expressed as:

> *The sampling distribution of the number of correct guess under a random guess is the distribution of the correct guess that would be obtained if the lady is making a random guess over a large number of experiments.*

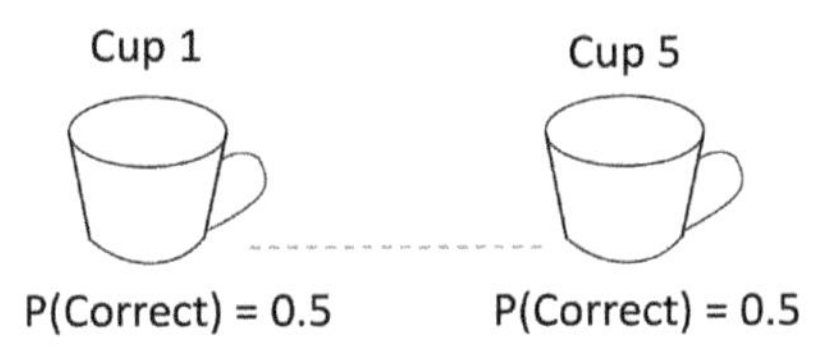

FIGURE 8.1
A hypothetical scenario of the Lady Tasting Tea experiment.

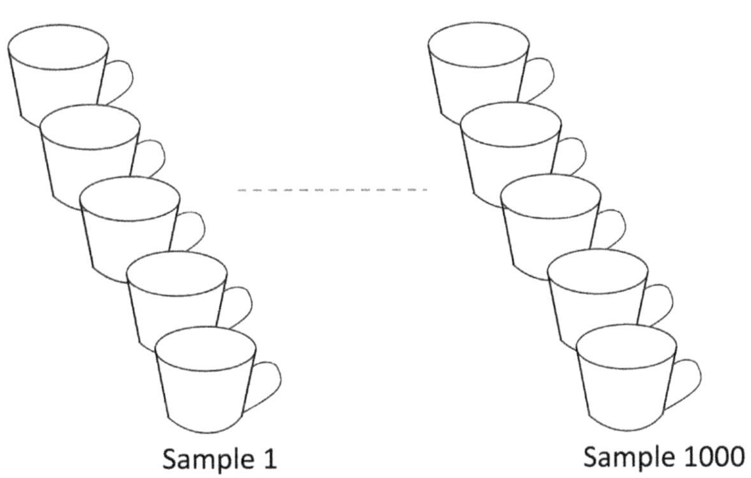

FIGURE 8.2
1000 experiments of which contains 5 cups.

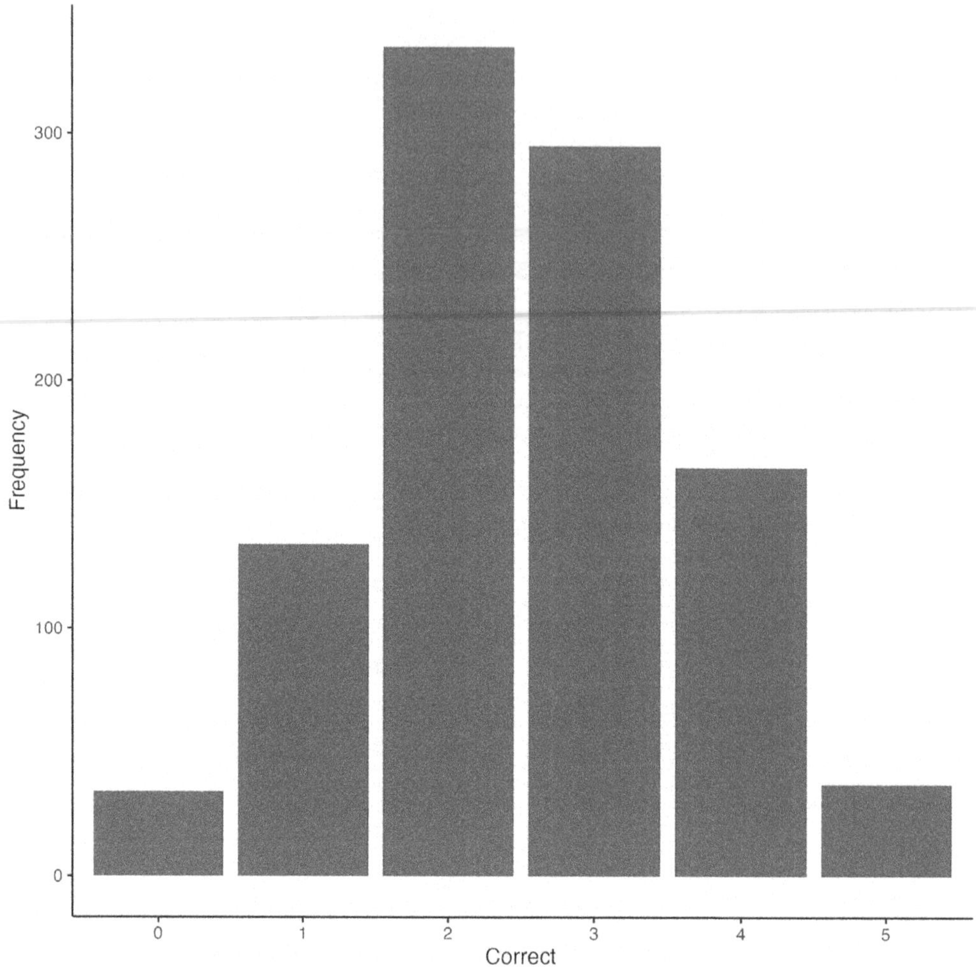

FIGURE 8.3
Frequency distribution of the number of correct guesses, n = 1000, p = 0.5.

8.3 Central Limit Theorem

Let us continue our story. From the 1000 samples, suppose that we obtain the distribution of the correct answer as displayed in Figure 8.3, which looks fairly normal.

Instead of presenting the lady with 5 cups, we could have asked her to guess 5 or 30 cups. Furthermore, let us assume that she just made a random guess. Thus, her chance of making a correct guess is a half, $p = 0.5$. We would obtain frequency distributions for each condition as displayed in Figure 8.4.

As you can see from Figure 8.4, when the number of cups is set to 5, the distribution of the correct guesses looks symmetrical and the counter of its peak seemingly follow a bell-shaped pattern. When the number of cups is set to 30, the bell-shaped pattern becomes more noticeable.

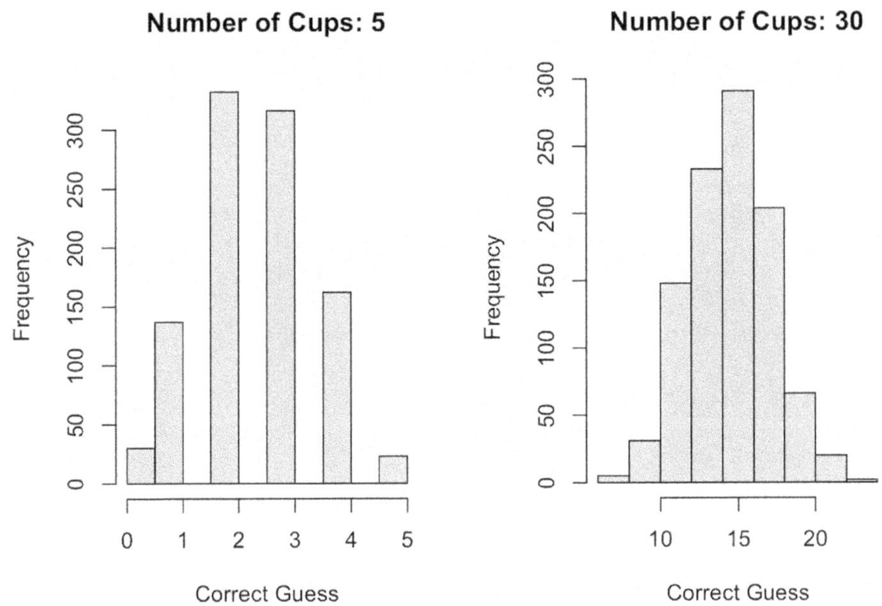

FIGURE 8.4
Frequency distribution of the number of correct guesses, p = 0.5.

The phenomenon whereby if the number of cups is nearly equal to 30 has been discovered many years ago and has been summarized in one of the most elegant theorems in statistics called the **central limit theorem (CLT)**.

IMPORTANT: CENTRAL LIMIT THEOREM

If a sample size is equal or greater than 30, the sampling distribution of a value will be normal regardless of the distribution of the value in a population.

There are minor variations in the wordings of the central limit theorem in other textbook, but they essentially convey the same information: sampling distribution approaches a normal distribution when a sample size gets larger. Sample size equals 30 is considered as the minimum sample size that produces a sampling distribution that is normal.

8.3.1 R Action

This R code can be used to simulate the Lady Tasting Tea experiment.

```
set.seed(120823)
rm(list=ls())
# set parameters
# nsamples # number of experiment
# ncups # number of cups
# pcorrect # probability of a correct guess

tastingtea <- function(nsamples, ncups, pcorrect){

   title _ text <- paste("Number of Cups:", ncups)

   chance <- c(1-pcorrect, pcorrect)

# prepare an R object to store
# the number of correct guesses
# in each experiment/sample.

ncorrect = rep(NA, nsamples)

for (i in 1:nsamples) {
    cups <- sample(0:1, ncups,
           replace = TRUE, prob = chance)
   ncorrect[i] <- sum(cups)
}

tastingtea <- hist(ncorrect, main=title _ text,
                   xlab="Correct Guess")

}

# Arrange spaces for plots
par(mfrow = c(1, 2))

print(tastingtea(1000, 5, 0.5)) # nsamples=1000, ncups=5.
print(tastingtea(1000, 30, 0.5)) # nsamples=1000, ncups=30.
```

8.4 Distributions of the Sample Means

In the previous section, we have learned about the sampling distribution of the sample proportions. Importantly, we learned about the concept of the `central limit theorem` restated as follows: if the sample size gets larger (>30), the distribution of the sample proportion will approach a normal distribution.

In this section, we look at the sampling distribution of the sample means – the distribution of means of various samples. Sample mean is just the average score of something. For example, you may want to know the average spending during a weekend of consumers in your defined population. You asked everyone in a town during a weekend (Saturday and Sunday) with this question: 'How much do you spend in a weekend (£)?' In each weekend, say, you managed to ask 30 customers, and calculate the average spending of the 30 customers. Now, let us imagine that you would do this for in another 499 weekends (more than 9 years!). My question is, what would be the distribution of the average spending of the 500 averages?

The answer of the question is that the `central limit theorem` will hold provided that the sample is around 30 or more. That is, the distribution of the average spending will be normal. Even if the distribution of the average spending in the population is not normal, the sampling distribution of the average spending will be normal.

This can be easily demonstrated in R. The benefit of using R to illustrate the concept is that you can try out generating different types of non-normal distribution, change the number of samples you want to draw, and change the number of cases in each sample. To generate a non-normal distribution for my fake population data, I use the mnonr() function from the *mnonr* R package (Qu et al. 2020). The *mnonr* function permits user to set different values for skewness and kurtosis of a distribution.

First, I create the fake population data of weekend spending. The population size that I choose is 10000. The code is shown here, and the resulting histogram can be seen in Figure 8.5.

```
rm(list = ls(all=TRUE)) # make a fresh start.
library(mnonr)

set.seed(16) # to make this illustration reproducible.

# create a normally distributed population.

pop_size = 10000 # population size

  dat <- mnonr(n=10000,p=1,ms=7,mk=15,
        Sigma=matrix(c(1),1,1),initial=NULL)
  # ms = a value for skewness.
  # for a normal distribution, ms = 0.
# mk = value for kurtosis.
# for a standard normal distribution, mk = 0.

hist(dat)
```

Now, I take a sample of 30 cases randomly from the population data and continue this process 500 times. Next, I calculate the mean of each sample. That is, in total, I will have 500 means. Next, I construct a histogram of the 500 means. The distribution of the sample means will look *normal*. The code is shown here, and the resulting histogram can be seen in Figure 8.6.

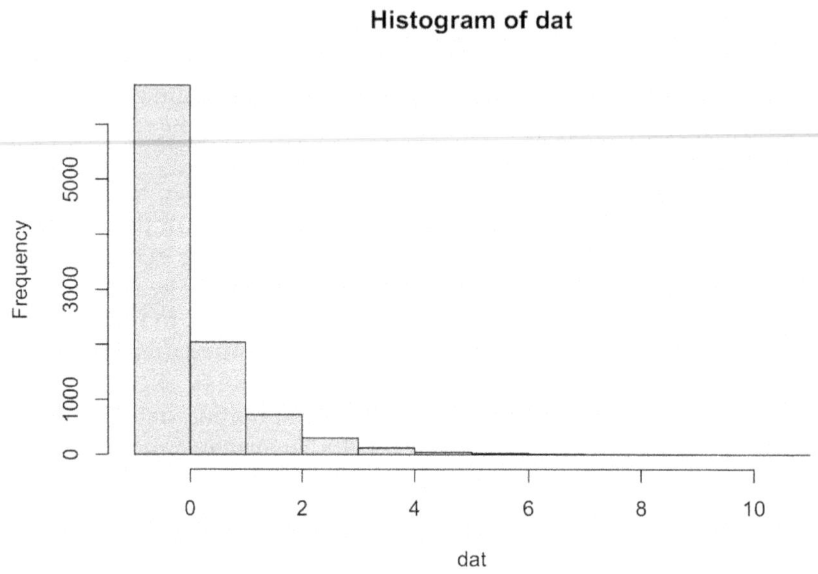

FIGURE 8.5
Histogram of variables generated with mnonr R function.

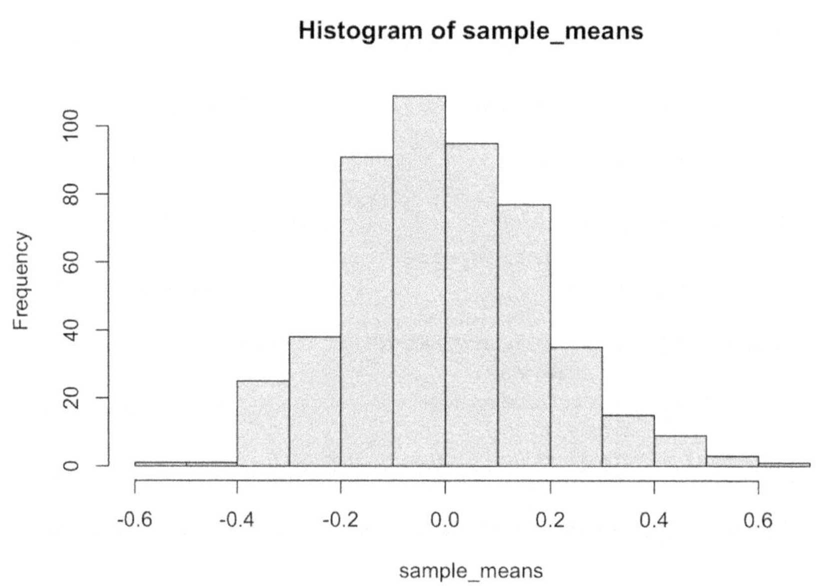

FIGURE 8.6
Histogram of the sample means distribution.

```
# Resampling from a population

nsamples <- 500 # set the number of samples sample _
size <- 30 # set the number cases in a sample

# prepare an R object to store the sample means
sample _ means = rep(NA, nsamples)

for(i in 1:nsamples){
  mysample <- sample(dat, sample _ size, replace = TRUE)

  sample _ means[i] = mean(mysample)
}

hist(sample _ means)
```

8.4.1 Standard Error of the Mean

As you learned from Chapter 6, a normal distribution is centred around its mean (μ) and its spread can be described by its standard deviation (σ). Likewise, the sampling mean distribution is also normal, so it can also be characterized by its mean and standard deviation. The mean of the sampling mean distribution is equal to population mean. As we do not know the population, it can be estimated with sample mean. The standard deviation of the sampling mean distribution given is called the standard error of the mean. I use the abbreviation *SE (mean)* in this book. *SE(mean)* is given by this formula:

$$SE(mean) = \frac{\sigma}{\sqrt{(n)}} \tag{8.1}$$

where σ is the standard deviation of the population distribution and n is a sample size. In practice, you will never know the value for σ, which can be replaced with the sample standard deviation. In the next section, I illustrate the use of our knowledge about the standard error of the mean.

8.4.2 Illustration

Suppose that satisfaction score of a population of consumers is 5.3 with a standard deviation is equal to 2.3. If you take a random sample of 50 consumers, what is the probability that the sample average is less than 5.5?

Answers: To answer this question, the central limit theorem must be applied, which we repeat here: *when sample size is large, then the distribution of the sample mean* $(\bar{X})$ is normal. The normal distribution has mean equals the population mean (μ), and its standard deviation equals the standard error of the mean $SE\ (mean) = \frac{\sigma}{\sqrt{n}}$, succinctly written as

$\bar{X} \sim N(\mu, SE)$, where σ is the population standard deviation, and n is the sample size. Next step is to calculate areas under the normal distribution curve.

First, let us calculate the standard error of the mean.

$$SE = \frac{\sigma}{\sqrt{n}} = \frac{2.3}{\sqrt{50}} = 0.325$$

This question can be written as: what is $P(\bar{X} < 5.5)$?

Now, you can transform $\bar{X}$ to a Z-score and do the same for 5.5 to maintain the inequality expression.

$$P(\bar{X} < 5.5) = P\left(\frac{\bar{X} - \mu}{SE} < \frac{5.5 - 5.3}{0.325}\right)$$
$$= P\left(Z < \frac{0.2}{0.325}\right)$$
$$= P(Z < 0.615)$$

Using `NORMDIST` macro (see Figure 7), we find P(Z < 0.615 =0.731). That is, the chance of getting a sample mean of less than 5.5 is about 73%.

You can directly use `NORMDIST` macro to find the answer without necessarily transforming $\bar{X}$ to z-score as we have done earlier. You must enter $x = 5.5$ into the 'x' box, 5.3 into the 'mean' box, the standard error of the mean 0.325 into the 'standard deviation' box, and tick left-tail probability P(X < x).

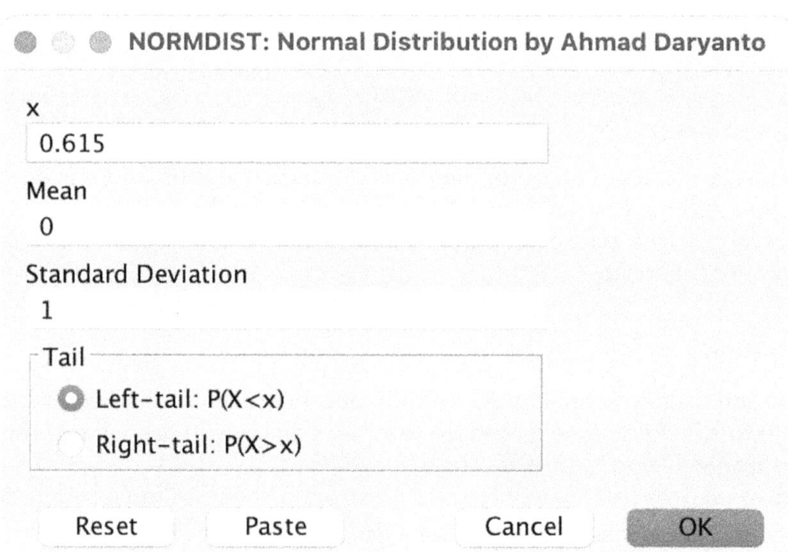

FIGURE 8.7
Finding P(Z < 0.61488).

Matrix

```
Run MATRIX procedure:

X =
   .6150000000

Left-tail probability: P(X < x) =
   .73072

------ END MATRIX -----
```

FIGURE 8.8
$P(Z < 0.61488)$ with NORMDIST macro.

8.5 Summary

In this chapter, I started with the 'Lady Tasting Tea', a story that captivated me since I was a graduate student. Using the story as a vehicle, I explained the concept of the central limit theorem, which is a famous theorem in statistics. This is one of the reasons why we should not collect a small sample because we want to ensure that the sample proportions to be normal. I also discussed the sampling distribution of the sample means and explained the concept of the standard error of the mean.

8.6 Further Reading

Richardson, J. T. (2021), 'A closer look at the lady tasting tea', *Significance* **18**(5), 34–37. This is an interesting article attempting to provide the precise account of the story of the lady tasting tea.

Salsburg, D. (2001), *The lady tasting tea: How statistics revolutionized science in the twentieth century*, Macmillan. This is the book that inspires me to share the stories of the lady tasting tea in this chapter. This book is beautifully written, which tells the stories about statistics, its advancement, and people that involves in its development.

8.7 Review Questions

1. What is a sampling distribution?
2. What is the central limit theorem and why it is important know it?
3. What does the central limit theorem say about populations that are not normally distributed?
4. Explain what the standard error of the mean?

8.8 Exercise

1. Suppose that satisfaction score of a population of consumers is 4.5 with a standard deviation is equal to 1.4. If you take a random sample of 200 consumers, what is the probability that the sample average is larger than 4.5?
2. Use the R code that I used to illustrate the sampling distribution of the sample means, change *sample_size* to 2, 5, 10, and 20. Comment on the distributions of the sample means.
3. Play around with the R code that I used to simulate the lady tasting tea experiment. In the line: `print(tastingtea(1000, 5, 0.5))`, 1000 refers to the number of experiment, 5 is the number of cups used in an experiment, and 0.5 is the probability of making a correct guess when a cup is presented. Change the probability value to 0.3 and 0.7. Inspect the shape of the distribution. State your conclusion.

Part III

Hypothesis Testing and Basic *Statistical Tests*

9

Hypothesis Testing and Significance

Assessing whether our data supports what we believe about a population requires a statistical procedure called hypothesis testing. This chapter covers the concept of hypothesis testing and how to decide whether the results of the test validate our hypothesis. The notion of hypothesis testing is explained, followed by the explanation of the difference between the null and the alternative hypothesis. Deciding whether to reject H0 depends on the p-value associated with a statistical test. The concept of p-value is explained with an intuitive explanation and its limitations are discussed. Next, the link between research objectives and research hypotheses, and how to build a survey item to gather data to test the hypothesis are explained. Last section of the chapter explains the difference between Type-1 error and Type-2 error that might happen in testing a hypothesis. Lastly, the concept of a statistical power is explained in brief.

Learning Objectives:

- Understand the concept of hypothesis testing.
- Know how to formulate null and alternative hypothesis.
- Understand the concept of p-value and its relation to a hypothesis testing.
- Be aware of the limitations of the p-value approach in hypothesis testing.

9.1 Making an Inference

Hypothesis testing is about testing a statement or proposition about a population. For example, your friend could make this claim: 'Postgraduate students in our university are satisfied with their accommodation provided by the university.' This is a statement that need to be supported by data. As it will not be practical to ask every student in the university, you may rely on opinions from several students to investigate whether the claim can be supported by data. The number of students you would ask constitutes your research sample.

The goal in hypothesis testing is not to say something about the student sample but to say something about all postgraduate students in the university. That is, using information obtained from a sample, you want to form judgements or conclusions about population of students. That is, you want to make an inference from a sample about a certain population of your interest. Using sample data, you will embark on data analysis to produce results that will or will not support your claim about the population. Figure 9.1 illustrates the research process where you start from obtaining a random

DOI: 10.4324/9781003407225-12

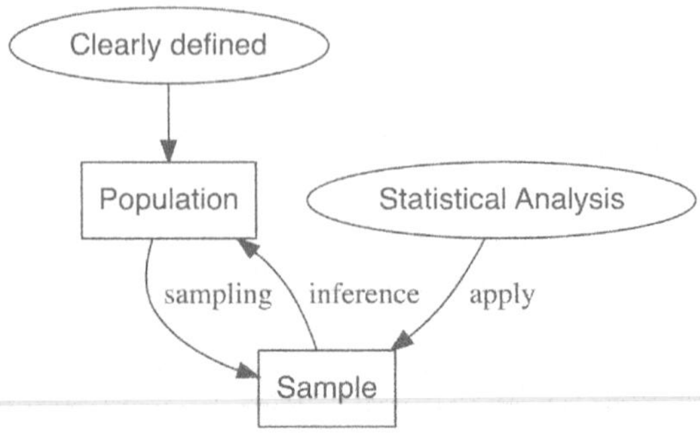

FIGURE 9.1
From a random sample to making an inference about a population.

sample, conduct data analysis, and use the statistical results to make an inference about population.

Information that we obtained from a sample is referred to as a *statistic* whose value is varied from sample to sample. For example, sample mean or sample average is a statistic – nearly everyone understands what an average is. As a sample is drawn from a population, therefore, the quality of sample data used in hypothesis testing depends on the quality of the sampling procedure (i.e. how you select a student to be in your sample). To ensure that a sample is a good representation of population, the sampling method that most researchers use is a random sampling. In a random sampling, everyone in the population has an equal chance of being selected as a member of the sample. The advantage of the random sampling is that it is easy and cheap to administer.

9.2 Null and Alternative Hypothesis

In hypothesis testing, two types of hypotheses are used: null and alternative hypothesis.

Null hypothesis is statement about status quo represented by a symbol H_0. The following statements with keywords written in bold are examples of null hypothesis:

- There is **no difference** between male vs. female students' satisfaction toward their university.
- There is **no relationship** between perceived quality of housing accommodation and satisfaction toward university.
- There is **no effect** of providing a lengthy feedback of students' course evaluation.
- There is **no association** between satisfaction and performance.

The opposite of the null hypothesis is known as the **alternative hypothesis**, represented by a symbol H_1 or H_A. The alternative hypothesis is actually a statement that we really want to know. Unfortunately, we never really test it. What we do here in the hypothesis testing is whether we can reject or not reject the null hypothesis. If we reject the null hypothesis, we are in favour of the alternative hypothesis – this does not mean we are directly testing it.

9.3 Intuitive Explanation

I knew a particular student known as Bob. Bob took an exam a week ago. There were two possibilities regarding how Bob prepared for the exam. I stated the possibilities of Bob's situation in terms of null and alternative hypothesis:

H_0: Bob had not studied at all before the exam.

H_A: Bob had studied before the exam.

Bob told you he just got his result that he passed the exam. He confessed that he had not studied at all before the exam despite having an excellent result. Would you believe Bob that he had not studied at all before the exam?

You came to an admin office and gathered data about student performance from an experimental study that the school conducted last year. The admin refused to let you see all the results. Instead, he randomly picked 100 names from his database and disclosed the exam results without mentioning further details about the students except that *these students had not been told about the exam before participating*. You assumed that these students' profiles were identical to those of Bob (e.g. they took the exam at the same year where Bob is now), males, like spaghetti.

You found out that 30 out of 100 students passed the exam. As these students had not been not informed about the exam, they had not chance to do some preparation. Let me write *H0* as 'Students had not studied at all before the exam' (just like the *H0* for Bob). I can write this information succinctly as **P(pass|H0 is true) = 0.3**, which reads 'The probability of passing the exam given that H_0 is true is equal to 0.3.' In light of this information, would you believe in Bob? You might be tempted to say that passing the exam without studying is very likely (only 30 out 100 students passed it). Because the chance of passing the exam without preparation is quite large (30%), and the fact that Bob passed the exam, you might believe that Bob was honest – Bob might have not studied before the exam. The exam seems to be quite easy as someone with lack of preps can still pass the exam.

Supposed that the information you obtained from last year is this: **P(pass|H0 is true) = 0.02**. Would you believe in Bob? The new information indicates that the chance of passing the exam if one had not studied is only 2%, which is very small – the exam was hard. In light with this information, you would incline to say that Bob was dishonest – he might have studied before the exam and concealed this fact.

Now, let us learn an important term in hypothesis testing. The probability of passing the exam given H_0 is true is called the probability value. It has more than one name – significance value (abbreviated as sig.value) and p-value. We use the p-value to make a decision as to whether H_0 is rejected or retain. The p-value from the first scenario is 30%, which is quite large and from the second one is 2%, which is quite small that warrant us to reject H_0. The question is, *how small the p-value must be that would protect us from making a wrong decision?*

9.4 P-Value and How Do You Get It?

To decide whether to reject or retain H_0, we need to compare p-value to the what so-called significance level, abbreviated as alpha (α). α is our tolerance level. Researchers' consensus is to use $\alpha = 0.05$, which means we can only afford to make a wrong decision 1 out of 20. Legend told that it was actually the famous statistician Ronald Aylmer Fisher who suggested to use α as equal to 0.05 (see Salsburg 2001).

Any statistical tests we undertake with SPSS, the SPSS will output p-value associated with the test. Your task is to simply read the p-value, compare it with $\alpha = 0.05$, and make a decision:

- **If p-value > 5%, retain H0.**
- **If p-value < 5%, reject H0.**

9.5 Test Statistic

I have explained the decision criteria in hypothesis testing using p-value. Software like SPSS does not only report p-value but also output a test statistic, hereafter abbreviated as $T-statistic$. In fact, SPSS uses this $T-statistic$ to calculate the p-value. Like p-value, we can also use $T-statistic$ to make an inference. What we need to do is to compare the $T-statistic$ to what a so-called a `t critical value` (t_{crit}). We reject the null hypothesis in favour of the alternative hypothesis if the $T-statistic$ is more extreme that would be expected if $H0$ were true (i.e. more extreme than t_{crit}). That is, in the Bob's situation we reject $H0$ if

$$P\left(T \geq t_{tcrit} \middle| H0\right) \leq \alpha.$$

The value of t_{crit} is determined by the choice of α. It is a value based on a theoretical distribution where the distribution is informed by the sampling distribution of the $T-statistic$. If the sampling distribution of the $T-statistic$ is normal, the calculation of the critical value uses a normal distribution. For a normal distribution and $\alpha = 0.05$, the critical value for a `one-sided test` is 1.96. If the probability that the $T-statistic$ is greater than 1.96 is equal to 0.0001 ($PT > 1.96 = 0.0001$), we would reject H_0 because it is less than α. At this stage, you probably sense that $P(T > 1.96 = 0.0001)$ is a p-value. You are correct.

Thus, you have two ways to make an inference, use either a $T-statistic$ or a p-value. Either way, your conclusion would be the same.

IMPORTANT

Steps in testing hypothesis using $T - statistic$:

1. Formulate the null hypothesis H_0 and alternative hypothesis H_1.
2. Using the sample data and assuming H_0 is true, calculate *statistic*.
3. Choose the significance level α, say 0.05, and from a known theoretical distribution, determine the critical value *tcrit*.
4. Compare the $T - statistic$ with the critical value t_{crit}.
5. Reject H_0 is $T - statistic > t_{crit}$; otherwise, do not reject H_0.

9.6 Limitations of P-Value

What I have discussed is the answer of the question 'What is the probability that Bob passed an exam given H_0 is true?' expressed as $P(pass|H_0\ is\ true)$. But what you want to know probably is not the answer to that question. But, perhaps, given that Bob passed the exam, you might want to find out the possibility that he had not studied before the exam which can be expressed as a shorthand notation like this:

$P\ (H_0|Pass)$. If you have this kind of question, you have just engaged in a Bayesian thinking. How would we go about answering your Bayesian question? To answer this question requires an adventure in the world of `Bayesian statistics`, which is beyond the scope this book.

The online book https://www.bayesrulesbook.com provides a good start and in my opinion, one of the best resources in learning Bayesian statistics.

P-value approach is the dominant approach in a hypothesis testing, but it is not the only one approach. At this point, you have gotten to know another approach called Bayesian thinking briefly describe earlier. The main criticisms of the p-value approach are as follows. First, it is often interpreted as the evidence of a meaningful result, where in fact, the results might not be practical (e.g. the effect size is very small). Second, the use of p-value would lead to a dichotomous decision: significant vs. not significant due to a certain threshold (e.g. 5% significant level). It is very problematic when the p-value is close to the threshold. Imagine if you obtained $p = 0.055$ by which you would conclude that the result is not significant while your friends found the p-value in their studies to be $p = 0.045$ deemed as significant. Third, p-value associated with a study depends on a sample size. Large sample tends to lead to a significant result ($p < 0.05$) although the result is not practically relevant. Fourth, many findings that are not significant – as a result of using the cut-off value of 5% significance level – never get published in scientific journals. This leads to a publication bias where significant findings are over-represented, which means the whole story of the effect being studied will never fully be understood.

Despite these limitations, the p-value approach is still ubiquitous in marketing research in testing hypotheses. However, it is not the only tool, and furthermore, we should be responsible in using the approach. Nowadays, confidence interval and effect size are seen as the alternative of reporting p-value. These two statistics are seen as more meaningful and informative in testing a hypothesis. For instance, the null hypothesis would be rejected if a 95% confidence interval does not include the value that is being tested or specified in the null hypothesis.

9.7 Presenting Hypotheses in Academic Papers

You can pick any academic papers that use empirical data and contain statistical analysis, and the chance is high that you will find research hypotheses. These hypotheses are alternative hypotheses. Researchers do not write null hypotheses. In most articles, researchers want to convince readers that they have data or evidence to support alternative hypotheses. If researchers embark on a research project, they want to demonstrate that what they believe is supported by data – this is the quest for the alternative hypothesis. If they fail, that does not mean that the null hypothesis is true. It actually means that they do not have sufficient evidence to reject the null hypothesis.

9.8 Formulating a Research Problem and Hypotheses

Research problem can be a real issue that needs to be solved because it can affect individuals, firms, or society possibly with cost (social or financial) implications. For example, a new advert promoting a new brand does not translate to sales, which sparks research of investigating how consumers process the advert: Does the funny advert actually denigrates the brand? Will consumers approve the ad?

Research problem may not be seen as a 'problem' from a layperson's point of view. Many researchers conduct research not because they see a real problem faced by firms that needs an immediate solution, but they feel something needs to be better understood. Their lack of understanding on a certain phenomenon is seen as a 'problem' from their point of view. For example, in one of my research, my co-authors and I are curious as to whether individuals' attachment to the place where they live has an impact on their pro-environmental behaviours (Daryanto & Song 2021). As we do not know much about the subject, we see this as a 'problem'.

Research problem is usually formulated into a problem statement or research objective, which in turn produces one or multiple research question. The approach I adopt in this book is that one research question translates to one research hypothesis. This way, I hope students will not be confused with how a research question is generated from problem statement. Figure 9.2 shows the connection between a research problem, problem statement or research objective, research questions, and hypotheses. As the figure suggests, a research problem is expressed as a problem statement, which produces multiple research questions where one research question correspond to one hypothesis.

For an illustration of how to apply diagram depicted in Figure 9.2, let us work on the following research problem: We have to put nutritional information on our food product packages as it is required by law and demanded by consumers. The problem statement can be formulated as follows: To what extent does putting nutritional information on

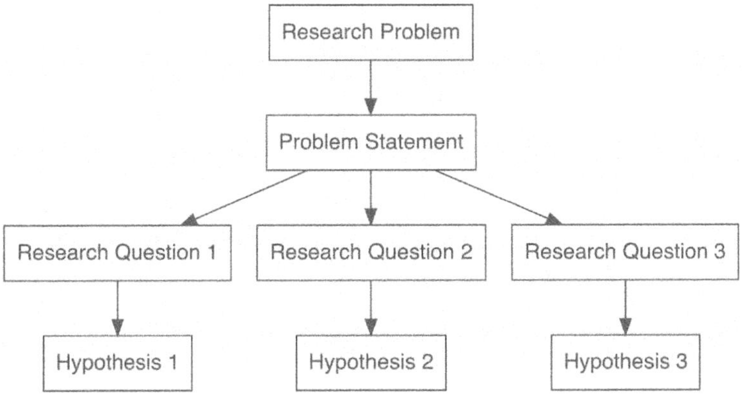

FIGURE 9.2
From a research problem to hypotheses.

food packages (e.g. wrappers) influence consumers' purchase intention? The research objective can be written as 'To examine the effect of nutritional information on food packages (e.g. wrappers) on consumers' purchase intention'. This research objective can produce multiple research questions. Our first research question could be: Does putting nutritional information influence intention to buy? And the second research questions can be presented as 'Is there a difference in intention to buy between adult and teenage consumers?' Finally, we can formulate our research hypothesis. Our research hypothesis can be one-sided (H1: putting nutritional information has an impact on intention to buy [two-sided hypothesis]) or two-sided (H1: putting nutritional information increases customers' intention to buy [one-sided hypothesis]). If we are no knowledge about the direction, two-sided hypothesis can be formulated, such as H2: There is a difference between adult and teenage consumers in their intention to buy (two-sided hypothesis); otherwise, a one-sided hypothesis can be formulated (H2: teenage consumers are more willing to buy than adult consumers).

9.8.1 R Code

R code to create Figure 9.2:

```
#| fig-cap: From Research Problem to RQs

# Basic plot

DiagrammeR::grViz("digraph{

  graph [rankdir = TD]

node [shape = box, fontname = Helvetica]
  rp [label = 'Research Problem']
  ps [label = 'Problem Statement']
  rq1 [label = 'Research Question 1']
```

```
    rq2 [label = 'Research Question 2']
    rq3 [label = 'Research Question 3']
    hypo1 [label = 'Hypothesis 1']
    hypo2 [label = 'Hypothesis 2'] hypo3
    [label = 'Hypothesis 3']

  edge []
      rp -> ps
      ps -> {rq1 rq2 rq3}
      rq1 -> hypo1
      rq2 -> hypo2
      rq3 -> hypo3

    {rank=sink;hypo1;hypo2;hypo3}

  }")
```

9.9 Non-Directional and Directional Hypothesis

When you hypothesize that there is a difference between males and females in their intentions to buy a product, your hypothesis is non-directional – it just tells the difference, not the nature of the difference. Similarly, if you hypothesize that providing a discount has an impact on consumer loyalty, the hypothesis is also non-directional – it just tells there is an effect but did say whether it will reduce or increase loyalty. In a non-directional hypothesis, the direction of the effect or relationship you are investigated is not specified. When you build this kind of hypothesis, you think that there will be a difference or there will be an effect, you are just not sure the nature of the difference or the nature of the effect. Another term for a non-directional hypothesis is a two-sided hypothesis. Statistical test used to test the two-sided hypothesis is commonly called a two-sided test or two-tailed test.

Non-directional hypothesis is uninteresting and may not be useful as it did not give you a specific detail of what you really want to know. What is more useful is to test the direction of the difference or the effect. For example, it would be more useful if you can state female is more willing to buy a product, or providing a discount generates more spending. From a managerial point of view, a directional hypothesis is more useful than the non-directional hypothesis. If discount boost sales, managers should not stop using this promotional tactic to enhance consumer loyalty. Another term for a directional-hypothesis is a one-sided hypothesis. The statistical test used to test the one-sided hypothesis is commonly called a one-sided test or one-tailed test.

9.10 From Hypothesis to Questionnaire

At this point, I hope you are aware that your research question or hypothesis must contain words depicting constructs or variables by which your hypotheses can be empirically tested. These variables will be transformed into questions, which in turn dictates how questions in a questionnaire should be presented (i.e. questionnaire items).

Let us look at the following example.

Research question: Are customers loyal toward a store?

H_0: Customers are not loyal toward a store.

H_A: Customers are loyal toward a store.

The key phrase in the alternative hypothesis is **customers are loyal**, which is an adjective from of customer loyalty. Customer loyalty is a construct. How would you *define* and *measure* customer loyalty?

When we define a construct, we should not use the name of the construct itself in our definition; otherwise, we would just state the same thing. This is a tautology. If a construct customer loyalty describes how loyal customer is, this definition will not take us further as loyal can be interpreted differently, not only by consumers who are filling in your questionnaire but also by researchers who read your research report. Customer loyalty can be defined differently. It can be referred to as the extent to which customers are committed to visit the same store again in the future (i.e. behavioural loyalty [Oliver 1999]) or the extent to which customers like the store more than other convenience stores (i.e. attitudinal loyalty [Yi & Jeon 2003]). If we use this operational definition, in terms of developing a questionnaire item, we can use this statement 'I like the store more than other convenience stores' measured with either a 5-point (1= strongly disagree, 5 = strongly agree) of 7-point (1= strongly disagree, 7 = strongly agree) Likert scale.

9.11 Managerial vs. Statistical Formulation

In the previous section, we have hypothesized: customers are loyal toward a store. Managers would understand this expression. Therefore, I call this the managerial formulation of the hypothesis. Nevertheless, statistical software needs to produce information (i.e. statistics such as an average score) to be processed by a statistical procedure to test the hypothesis. We also knew from the previous section that we will gather information by asking consumers to respond to this statement by using a 5-point Likert scale: 'I like the store more than other convenience stores.' The average score of this statement would give us an indication whether the consumers like or dislike the store by comparing the score with the midpoint of the scale. The midpoint of the scale is 3 = neither dislike nor like (neutral). Therefore, if the average score of the response answers is above the midpoint, this indicates that on average consumers like the store. Likewise, if the average score is below the midpoint, this indicates that on average the consumers do not like the store. Of course, you can use other values above the midpoint (say, loyal = 5) if you want the evidence to be much stronger. With this logic, we can reformulate the hypothesis, which I called as the statistical formulation of a hypothesis H_A:

$$H_0: \text{Loyal} = 3$$

$$H_A: \text{Loyal} > 3$$

TABLE 9.1

Managerial vs. Statistical Formulation

Managerial Formulation	Statistical Formulation
Customers are loyal	Loyal > 3

where Loyal is the name of the variable we use to store the respondents' responses in our spreadsheet. I summarize these two types of formulating an alternative hypothesis in Table 9.1.

Note that in discussing the managerial and statistical formulation of a hypothesis, there is only one construct involved and the useful statistics is the average score. What if you want to test the relationship between two constructs (e.g., satisfaction has a positive impact on loyalty)? The issue will be covered in Chapters 12 and 13.

9.12 Type-1 Error, Type-2 Error, and Power

In testing a hypothesis, you may make either of these two mistakes: Type-1 error or Type-2 error. Type-1 error occurs when you reject a null hypothesis when in fact it is true in the reality. For example, if someone is indeed guilty but released by your verdict as a jury in court, you commit a Type-1 error. Type-2 error occurs when you do not reject a null hypothesis when in fact it is false in the reality. Similarly, if someone is innocent but convicted, you commit a Type-2 error. In statistics, these two types of errors are expressed as a chance or probability of committing them. Type-1 error is the significance value of α that you set when testing a hypothesis. When $\alpha = 0.05$, this means you allow yourself to make a mistake 1 out of 20 if the null hypothesis is true. Type-2 error is denoted by β. The expression $p = 1 - \beta$ is called **the statistical test power, or the power of the test**, or **power**, for short, defined as the probability of rejecting null hypothesis when it is false (i.e. probability of making a correct rejection). The bigger the power of a test, the more chance that you make a correct decision. Understanding the concept of **power** is helpful in deciding the minimum number of participants or sample size you need for testing your hypothesis (you want a small sample in order to reduce your research cost while would still be able to reject H_0). Discussion of power, however, is beyond the scope of this book. If you want to know more about this concept and how to utilize it in research, you can start with Kraemer & Blasey (2015).

9.13 Summary

We have discussed the concept of hypothesis testing, null vs. alternative hypothesis, how to translate manager formulation to statistical formulation of a hypothesis, the concept of test statistics, and an overview on Bayesian perspective in hypothesis testing.

In deriving a hypothesis, we started with recognizing a problem – a real-life problem or a scientific enquiry, formulating a problem statement, and creating a research question followed by a research hypothesis. The approach I used is that a problem statement can lead to multiple research questions, whilst one research question corresponds to one hypothesis.

9.14 Further Reading

Kraemer, H. C. & Blasey, C. (2015), *How many subjects?: Statistical power analysis in research*, Sage Publications.

Murphy, K. R., Myors, B. & Wolach, A. (2014), *Statistical power analysis: A simple and general model for traditional and modern hypothesis tests*, Routledge.

9.15 Review Questions

1. Formulate H_0 or H_A – whichever is missing in the formulation – for the following research questions and specify whether the alternative hypothesis is directional or non-directional.
   - RQ1: Are customers satisfied with promotional offers? H_0: Customers are not satisfied with promotional offers? H_A: . . .
   - RQ2: Is there an effect of gender on store loyalty? H_0: . . .

     H_A: Male consumers are more loyal to a store than female consumers.
   - RQ3: Is there an effect of gender on store loyalty? H_0: . . .

     H_A: There are differences between male and female consumers in their loyalty toward a store.
   - RQ4: Does gender affect shopping time?

     H_A: There is no association between gender and shopping time at SPAR. H_A: . . .
   - RQ5: What affects store loyalty?

     H_0: Store image has no influence on loyalty.

     H_A: . . .
2. Using a scale, 1 = Sad and 7 = Happy, you measured how consumers feel after receiving a faulty product. Present the managerial and statistical formulation of your hypothesis.

10

Testing Proportions

Examining a sample proportion is very common in marketing research. For example, knowing the percentages of consumer who bought brand A versus brand B is useful for marketing managers to shape their marketing strategies. Two types of sample proportion tests, namely, single proportion and the difference between two proportions tests are covered in the chapter. The former is a statistical procedure used to assess whether the proportion of a particular attribute or outcome in a sample is significantly different from a hypothesized population proportion. The step-by-step procedure in SPSS and R were also provided. The latter is used to assess whether the proportion in two difference samples differ from a hypothesized population difference. To test the difference in two samples, D2prop SPSS macro developed by the author is demonstrated. Finally, the relevant R functions to undertake the tests were also covered.

Learning Objectives:

- Know how to conduct a sample proportion test in SPSS and R.
- Know how to conduct a statistical test of the difference in two proportions using D2prop macro in SPSS and R.

10.1 Testing a Single Proportion

10.1.1 Hypothesis Formulation

Let us revisit the lady testing tea experiment explained in Chapter 8. Supposed that the lady can make 24 correct guesses out of 30 attempts. Thirty attempts seem to be realistic. On the basis of the result of this one experiment, can we say something about the lady's ability to detect which cups where milk was poured into the cups prior to the tea and which cups where the tea was poured into the tea prior to the milk.

Let us formulate the null hypothesis as follows:

H_0: The lady has no ability.

H_A: The lady has an ability.

With the null hypothesis, we are merely saying that the lady makes a random guess, and she is no better than flipping a coin. With the alternative hypothesis, we want to confirm that the lady indeed has an ability. However, we have never been 100% sure but we need evidence to support this hypothesis.

DOI: 10.4324/9781003407225-13

Our null and alternative hypotheses are easy to understand for any living human beings but are not that helpful for a statistical software to understand. So we need to transform the formulation of hypothesis to one that are meaningful for statistical software to calculate.

If the lady does not have an ability, she would just make a random guess just like tossing a coin. When she does this, her chance of making a correct guess is just a half (p = 0.5). If she does have an ability, her chance of making a correct guess would be greater than a half ($p > 0.5$). We can formulate the null and alternative hypotheses as follows:

$H_0: p = 0.5$
$H_A: p > 0.5$ (one-sided hypothesis)

If the null hypothesis is true, how likely was she to be correct 24 out of 30 times? Can we calculate the probability of making 24 correct guesses from 30 trials, which we call p-value? The answer of these queries is yes. SPSS will produce the p-value we want to find. Let us move on to the next section.

10.1.2 SPSS Action: Chi-Square test

Data: magicLady.sav

The first 10 observations of in the data Ads.sav are displayed in Figure 10.1. Guess is a binary variable, which is equal to 1 if the lady made a correct guess, or 0 otherwise.

	Guess
1	1.00
2	1.00
3	.00
4	1.00
5	1.00
6	1.00
7	.00
8	1.00
9	1.00
10	1.00

FIGURE 10.1
First 10 observations. Guess is a binary variable, 1 = Correct, 0 = Wrong. Follow the following steps to conduct the test.

- Analyze → Nonparametric Tests → Legacy Dialogs → Chi-Square.
- After the SPSS windows appear on your screen, move the variable Guess into the `Test Variable List` box.
- Next, click `OK` or `Paste` if you want to work with an SPSS syntax. SPSS syntax:

```
NPAR TESTS
  /CHISQUARE=Guess
  /EXPECTED=EQUAL
  /MISSING ANALYSIS.
```

SPSS produces two outputs (see Figure 10.2), namely, the descriptive table for **Guess** and test statistics table. The Guess table has three columns. The first column displays the frequency of 'Wrong' and 'Correct', which is equal to 4 and 26, respectively. The second column displays the expected values for Wrong and Correct, each is equal to 15. The expected value is the value you would have expected to get if the null hypothesis was true. Under the null hypothesis, the chance of making either a wrong or correct guess in a trail is $p = 0.5$. If you have 30 trials, you would expect to get $0.5 * 30 = 15$ wrong results. Likewise, you would also expect to get the same amount for correct results due to the equal chance. The third column displays the `Residual = Observed - Expected`.

Guess

	Observed N	Expected N	Residual
Wrong	6	15.0	-9.0
Correct	24	15.0	9.0
Total	30		

Residual – Observed - Expected

Test Statistics

	Guess
Chi-Square	10.800[a]
df	1
Asymp. Sig.	.001

a. 0 cells (0.0%) have expected frequencies less than 5. The minimum expected cell frequency is 15.0.

= ((-9)2 /15+ 92/15)

df = degrees of freedom
= number of categories - 1

P-value

FIGURE 10.2
Results of the chi-square test.

NOTE

Residual = Observed – Expected

The second table provides the chi-square value (denoted by χ^2) and p-value associated with the test.

The chi-square value (χ^2) is given by Equation 10.1:

$$\chi^2 = \sum\nolimits_{i-1}^{n} \frac{(O_i - E_i)^2}{E_i} \tag{10.1}$$

where O = observed value, E = expected value, n = number of categories (equal to 2 in our example: wrong and correct cell).

In this example:

$$\chi^2 = \frac{-9^2}{15} + \frac{9^2}{15} = 10.8 \tag{10.2}$$

The p-value reported by the output is very small $p < 0.001$ (see Figure 10.2) meaning that we have sufficient evidence to reject the null hypothesis. The lady might have an ability to detect which cups the milk was first poured before the tea, and which cups the tea was first poured before the milk ($p < 0.001$).

10.1.3 R Action: Chi-Square Test

```
library(ahdar)

# Read data from ahdar library

dat <- magiclady
```

Use the `chisq.test(x, p)` R function included in the R base, where x: a collection of values.

p: a collection of probabilities associated with each values in x. Record the information needed:

```
nsuccess <- sum(dat)
ncups <- nrow(dat)
nfails <- ncups - nsuccess
dat <- c(nsuccess, nfails)
```

Run the test:

```
res <- chisq.test(dat, p = c(0.5, 0.5))
res
```

```
Chi-squared test for given probabilities data:     dat
X-squared = 10.8, df = 1, p-value = 0.001015
```

```
# View the expected values
res$expected
```

[1] 15 15

In the next section, I demonstrate another test that we can use to test proportion, namely, the binomial test.

10.1.4 SPSS Action: Binomial Test

Data: MagicLady.sav

In the previous section, I have explained how to use a chi-square test to assess a single proportion. The test is based on a chi-square distribution. SPSS produced the p-value associated with the test. This p-value is related to the distribution of χ^2, which is distributed according a chi-square distribution.

Another test called *binomial test* is available on SPSS to conduct the proportion test. It uses a normal distribution approximation to calculate a p-value of the test.

i NOTE

If a sample is large, the chi-square distribution will approximate a normal distribution.

From Chapter 8 we know that if a sample size is large (>30), the sampling distribution of the proportion (p) is assumed to be normal. We also know that sampling distribution of the mean is will also be normal. For 0,1 variable, the sample mean is just the proportion. For example, 8 corrects out of 10 trials gives $p = 0.8$, whereas the mean (the sum of 0s and 1s) is also 0.8.

We follow these steps to undertake the test:

- Analyze → Nonparametric Tests → Legacy Dialogs → Binomial.
- Click `OK` or `Paste` if we want to work with a SPSS syntax.
- We can click `Option` and tick `Descriptives`, which instructs SPSS to print out the mean and standard deviation of the sample proportion.

By default, the test value *p* is set by SPSS to 0.5 – we leave it as it is. SPSS syntax:

```
NPAR TESTS
  /BINOMIAL (0.50)=Guess
  /STATISTICS DESCRIPTIVES
  /MISSING ANALYSIS.
```

The main output is displayed in Figure 10.3.

As we can see from the result, we got the same p-value, which is less than 0.001; therefore, we have the same conclusion as that of the chi-square test.

10.1.5 R Action: Binomial Test

```
library(ahdar)

# Read data from ahdar library
dat <- magiclady
```

Calculate the number of success and number of trials from the data.

```
nsuccess <- sum
(dat) ncups <- nrow(dat)
```

Use a function `prop.test(nsuccess, ncups, p)` where

nsuccess = number of success
ncups = number of trials
p = probability

Binomial Test

		Category	N	Observed Prop.	Test Prop.	Exact Sig. (2-tailed)
Guess	Group 1	Correct	24	.80	.50	.001
	Group 2	Wrong	6	.20		
	Total		30	1.00		

FIGURE 10.3
Results of the binomial test.

```
res <- prop.test(nsuccess, ncups, 0.5)
res
```

```
1-sample proportions test with continuity correction
data:  nsuccess out of ncups, null probability 0.5
X-squared = 9.6333, df = 1, p-value = 0.001911
alternative hypothesis: true p is not equal to 0.5
95 percent confidence interval:
  0.6086926 0.9159524
sample estimates:
  p
0.8
```

IMPORTANT

Assumptions of the binomial test.

1. The minimum expected value in a cell is at least 5.
2. The minimum sample size is 30 (see Chapter 8) for the test to provide a reliable result.

10.2 Testing the Difference Between Two Proportions

10.2.1 Hypothesis Formulation

Imagine that you are developing two types of video ads (say, ad A and ad B) to promote green behaviours. Because of your budget constraint, only one ad will be in the actual production. You decide to run an experiment by randomly assign customers to watch either ad A or ad B for few minutes. After they finished watching the video clips, you asked them to engage in a task unrelated to the ads. Next, you asked the consumers whether they could recall the name of your new brand. You obtained the following results (see Table 10.1).

The proportion of participants who can recall brand in ad A and ad B is 60% (60 out of 100) and 73.9% (85 out of 115), respectively. The difference between the two proportions is 13.9%. Is the difference significant?

TABLE 10.1

Ads Experiment

Ad	Yes	No	N
A	60	40	100
B	85	30	115

Let $p1$ and $p2$ be the proportion difference of two independent populations. The proportion difference, $p1 - p2$ can be estimated from sample proportion difference. The hypothesis for the proportion difference test can be formulated as follows:

$H_0 : p1 - p2 = 0$

$H_A : p1 - p2 \neq 0$ (two-sided test).

You can also conduct a one-sided test, $H_A : p1 - p2 < 0$ or $H_A : p1 - p2 > 0$.

10.2.2 SPSS Action: D2prop Macro

Data: Ads.sav

SPSS does not have a specific procedure to test the difference between two proportions. For this, we can use the `D2prop` macro that I developed (Daryanto 2022). You can download the macro from this website https://www.tqmp.org/RegularArticles/vol18-2/p181/ or the book's online support.

`D2prop` macro requires a special format for its input. For the ad experiment, you can see the input data written in the SPSS data view as displayed in Figure 10.4. The rows in the in the input data represent groups or samples. The columns represent the variables that you are testing, e.g. proportion of 'Yes'.

You can install it via the SPSS pull-down menu by clicking: Extensions → Utilities → Install Custom Dialog. After you managed to install the macro, it will appear in the SPSS pull-down menu.

Follow these steps:

- Analyze → D2prop by Ahmad Daryanto.
- Insert variable *Yes* into the `Success` box. *Yes* is a variable that contains the frequency of success. In this box, you can enter multiple variables at once and the macro will calculate the proportion of success for each of them.
- Insert variable *Total* into the `Total` box.
- In the `Confidence Level` (%) box, set a confidence level you want to, say 95 for the 95% confidence level. This confidence level will be printed out at the end of the macro's outputs.
- Click `OK`. Do not click `Paste` – if you do so, you will see a long list of codes in a syntax file.

	Condition	Yes	No	Total
1	Ad A	60	40	100
2	AD B	85	30	115

FIGURE 10.4
Input data of the ads experiment.

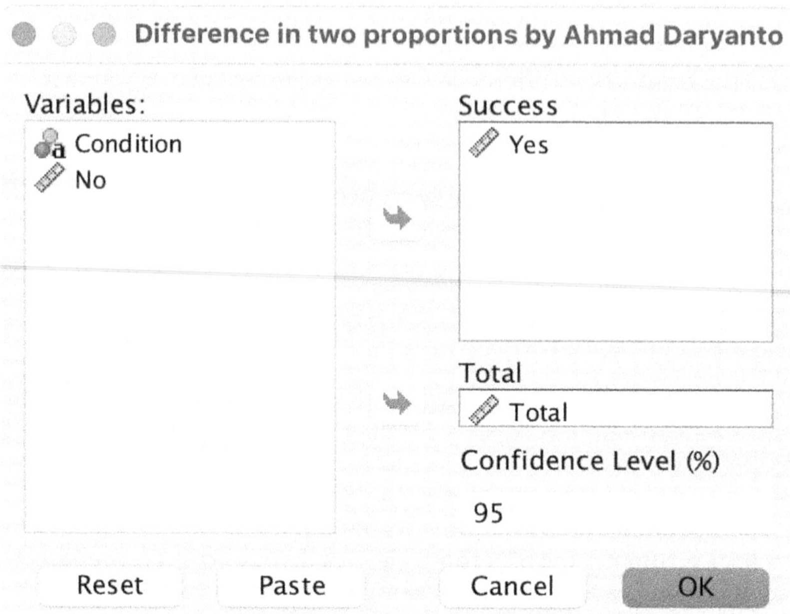

FIGURE 10.5
Screenshot of the D2prop macro.

On your screen, you should see the macro window as displayed in Figure 10.5.

The outputs of the `D2prop` macro for testing whether 13.9% is significant or not, is displayed in Figure 10.6.

`D2prop` tests the absolute difference between two proportions denoted by $\rho 1 - \rho 2$. This means the difference, its standard error (se) and its confidence interval are always positive. In an everyday conversation, you probably never say the difference between your exam mark and your friend is negative if your exam mark is lower than that of your friend. You probably would say 'The difference is 10 points, hers is higher than mine.' This is the reason that `D2prop` reports the difference of proportions in an absolute term.

However, when $p1$ is smaller than $p2$, you have to multiply the results with –1 if you want to be consistent in reporting the results. For example, if $p1 < p2$ and `D2prop` displays $|p1 - p2| = 0.12$ with a 95% confidence interval is (0.11, 0.13), you can write down your results as: $p1 - p2 = -12$ with a 95% confidence interval is (–0.13, –0.11).

For our hypothetical problem, the 13.9% proportion difference is significant (two-sided p-value = 0.03 < 5%) with a 95% confidence interval is (0.013, 0.261).

10.2.3 R Action: Testing the Difference in Two Proportions

```
library(ahdar)

# Read data from ahdar library

dat <- ads
```

```
 Written by Ahmad Daryanto - https://sites.google.com/view/ahmaddaryanto/

 March, 2022

=====================================

Data
   Yes Total
    60   100
    85   115

==========

Success variable:
 Yes


          Yes Total
Group 1    60   100
Group 2    85   115

Proportion of success
Group 1    .60000
Group 2    .73913

=====================================

Difference in proportions of success (absolute value of p1-p2)

 z and sig.values
          z    1-sided    2-sided
    2.17149     .01495     .02989

 Difference
   |p1-p2|        se
    .13913    .06385

Confidence interval (AC = Agresti-Caffo)
            LB         UB
Wald      .01397     .26429
Yates     .02332     .27363
AC        .01270     .26131

Confidence level (%)
  95
```

FIGURE 10.6
Outputs of the D2prop macro.

Use library(DescTools). Install this library by typing:

install.packages("DescTools") in your RStudio console.

library(DescTools)
Call a function BinomDiffCI(x1,n1,x2,n2, method="ac"), where
x1 = number of successes for the first group.
n1 = number of observations in the first group.
x2 = number of successes in the second group.
n2 = number of observations in the second group. conf.level = confidence level. The default is 0.95.

```
## Call the function
dprop<- BinomDiffCI(85,115,60,100,conf.level= 0.95,method="ac")
res<-round(dprop,3) # the result is rounded to 3 decimal places.
```

Output is produced by typing:

```
res
est lwr.ci upr.ci [1,] 0.139     0.013  0.261
```

NOTE

You can read here more information about what the function can do at the following website: https://rdrr.io/cran/DescTools/man/BinomDiffCI.html or by typing `?BinomDiffCI` in your console.

10.3 Crosstabs Analysis

Crosstabs stands for cross-tabulation. A crosstabs table, also referred to a contingency table, consists of rows representing one qualitative variable (nominal or ordinal) and columns representing another qualitative variable. The cells of the table typically contain counts or percentages. Crosstabs analysis can be used to examine the association between two qualitative (nominal or ordinal) variables. The null hypothesis and the alternative hypothesis can be formulated as follows:

H_0: There is no association between variable A and variable B.

H_A: There is an association between variable A and variable B.

Another formulation:

H_0: No association exists between variable A and variable B.

H_A: An association between variable A and variable B.

We can also formulate it this way:

H_0: Variable A is not associated with variable B.

H_A: Variable A is associated with variable B.

Choosing one of the formulations is just a matter of taste. They are essentially the same. If fact, we can also replace the word 'association' with 'relationship'.

What does it entail if two variables have an association? Variable A will have an association with variable B, if a certain value of A is more likely to occur with a certain value of B. Suppose that we want to know if gender (male vs. female) is associated with type of product that consumers buy (hedonic vs. utilitarian). If a hedonic product is preferred by male consumers, and a utilitarian product is also preferred by male consumers, the proportion of males who preferred each type of product would be higher than that of females. The same pattern would be observed in the utilitarian product category. This

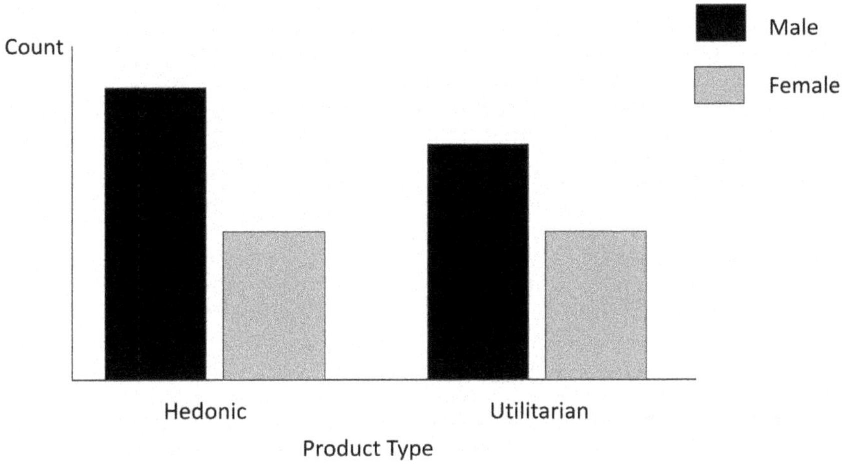

FIGURE 10.7
There is no association between gender and type of product. The are more males than females in the utilitarian and the hedonic categories.

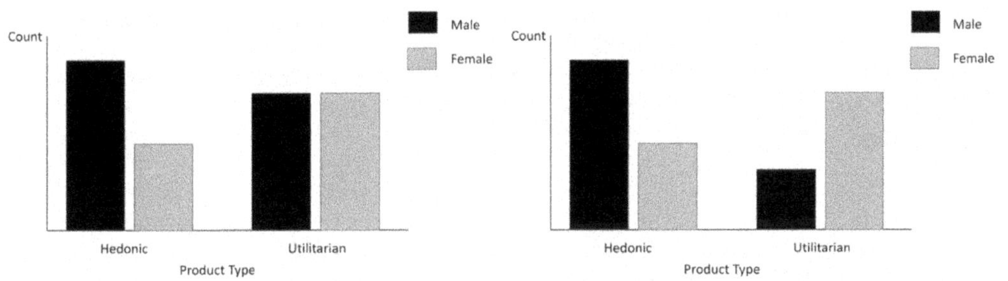

(a) Association in the utilitarian category. (b) Association in the hedonic category.

FIGURE 10.8
Association of product type and gender.

situation can be visualized in Figure 10.7. The pattern of the relationship reflects the situation of no association between gender and product type. That is, either types of product cannot be associated with male or female customers.

Now, let us look at Figure 10.8a and Figure 10.8b. The two figures describe an association between gender and types of products. In Figure 10.8a, in the hedonic product category, proportion of males is higher than that of females. In other words, males are associated with the hedonic product.

However, in the utilitarian product category, the proportion of males and females are relatively the same. In Figure 10.8b, the pattern of the association in one category is reversed in the other category. In this case, hedonic product is associated with male customers, whereas the utilitarian product is associated with female customers. Using sample data, these patterns of association can just occur by chance. For this reason, we need a statistical test, namely, crosstabs analysis, to ascertain how likely the association would occur in a population.

A crosstab analysis is carried out using the chi-square test of independence. Assuming that the null hypothesis is true, we look at the differences between the observed or actual values and the expected values. The expected values are the value we would have observed had the null hypothesis was true. The difference between the observed and the expected values make up a chi-square statistic that will be distributed according to a chi-square distribution. The chi-square statistic is calculated by using Equation 10.1 seen earlier.

10.3.1 SPSS Action

Data: store satisfaction. sav
Steps

- Analyze → Descriptive Statistics → Crosstabs.
- Insert variable *Gender* into Column(s) box.
- Insert variable *Prod* into a Row(s) box.

NOTE

The choice of which variable is entered into which box follows this rule of thumb: if A influences B, enter A into the Column(s) box and enter B into the Row(s) box.

- Next, click `Statistics` and tick `Chi-square` and `Phi` and `Cramer's Phi`.
- And tick percentages `Row`.
- Click `OK` or `Paste` if you want to work with a SPSS syntax pasted here:

```
CROSSTABS CROSSTABS
    /TABLES=prod BY gender
    /FORMAT=AVALUE TABLES
    /STATISTICS=CHISQ PHI
    /CELLS=COUNT EXPECTED ROW
    /COUNT ROUND CELL
    /BARCHART.
```

Outputs

The first output (see Figure 10.9) shows the crosstabs table showing the actual values, expected values, and gender proportion in each product types. This crosstabs table has a 2 (product type: hedonic vs. utilitarian) × 2 (gender: male vs. female) dimension.

As we can see from the table, within the hedonic product category, 56.5% of the customers are males. In contrast, within the utilitarian, 83.8% are females. This pattern of relationship is displayed in Figure 10.11. The association is significant because the p-value of the test is smaller than 0.05 (see Figure 10.12). The small footnote in the table shows that no cells have an expected count is less than 5. This satisfies one of the assumptions in crosstabs.

prod * gender Crosstabulation

			gender		
			male	female	Total
prod	hedonic	Count	13	10	23
		Expected Count	7.3	15.7	23.0
		% within prod	56.5%	43.5%	100.0%
	utilitarian	Count	6	31	37
		Expected Count	11.7	25.3	37.0
		% within prod	16.2%	83.8%	100.0%
Total		Count	19	41	60
		Expected Count	19.0	41.0	60.0
		% within prod	31.7%	68.3%	100.0%

FIGURE 10.9
A crosstabs of gender and product type from SPSS.

Symmetric Measures

		Value	Approximate Significance
Nominal by Nominal	Phi	.421	.001
	Cramer's V	.421	.001
N of Valid Cases		60	

FIGURE 10.10
Effect sizes of the crosstabulation of gender and product type.

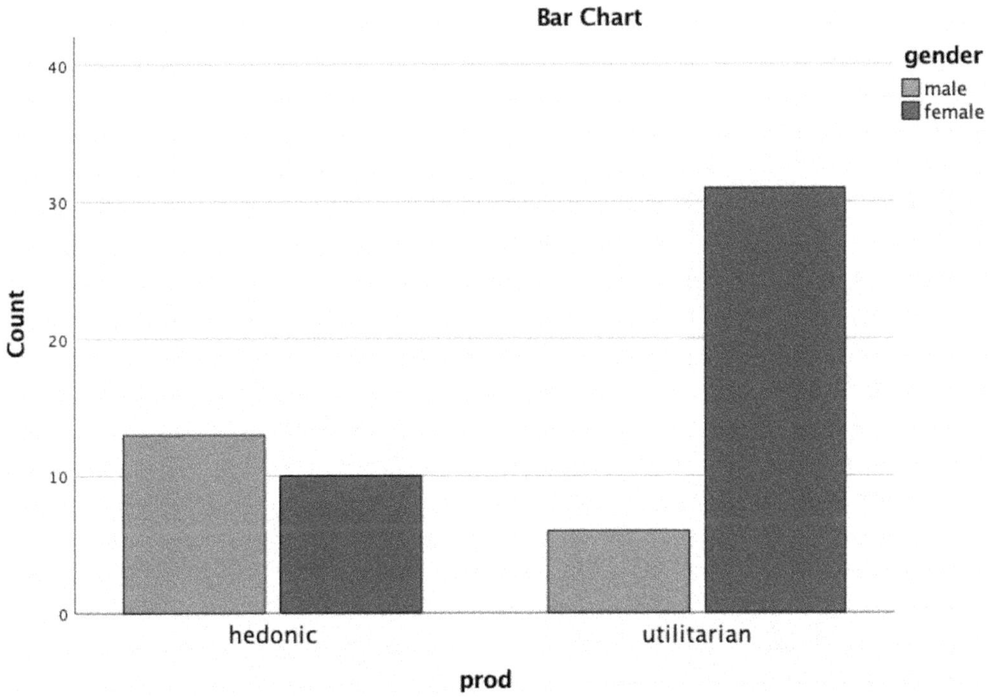

FIGURE 10.11
A clustered bar chart of gender and product type produced by SPSS.

Chi-Square Tests

	Value	df	Asymptotic Significance (2-sided)	Exact Sig. (2-sided)	Exact Sig. (1-sided)
Pearson Chi-Square	10.648[a]	1	.001		
Continuity Correction[b]	8.867	1	.003		
Likelihood Ratio	10.628	1	.001		
Fisher's Exact Test				.002	.001
Linear-by-Linear Association	10.471	1	.001		
N of Valid Cases	60				

a. 0 cells (0.0%) have expected count less than 5. The minimum expected count is 7.28.

b. Computed only for a 2x2 table

FIGURE 10.12
Statistical outputs of the crosstabs analysis showing the p-value.

ASSUMPTIONS

Crosstabs should satisfy the following assumptions: (1) no cells should have an expected count less than 0, and (2) no more than 20% of the cells have expected counts less than 5.

The strength of the association is identified by the phi (ϕ) value = 0.421 (see Figure 10.10), which is considered as a medium effect size according to Cohen's guidelines (1988):

- 0.1 as small
- 0.3 as medium
- 0.5 as large

If the dimension of the crosstabs table is larger than 2×2, the recommendation is to rely on the Cramer's V as a measure of effect size.

i How to Calculate the Effect Sizes

$$\text{Phi}\phi = \sqrt{\frac{x2}{n}}$$

$$Cramer'sv = \sqrt{\frac{X^2}{n(L-1)}},$$

where

n= number of observations, L = the smaller of the number of categories of the two variables. In the example, $X^2 = 10.648, n = 60, L = 2$. Therefore,

$$Phi(\phi) = \sqrt{\frac{10.648}{60}} = 0.421.$$

$$Cramer's V = \sqrt{\frac{10.648}{60(2-1)}} = 0.421$$

Crosstabs

prod	*gender* male	female	***Total***
hedonic	13 56.5 %	10 43.5 %	23 100 %
utilitarian	6 16.2 %	31 83.8 %	37 100 %
Total	19 31.7 %	41 68.3 %	60 100 %

χ^2=8.867 · df=1 · ϕ=0.421 · Fisher's p=0.002

FIGURE 10.13
Crosstabs of type of product vs. gender using R.

10.3.2 R Action

The function that we can use in R is the `xtab()` function from the sjPlot library (Lüdecke 2023).

```
install.packages("sjPlot")
library(sjPlot)
library(ahdar)
library(tidyverse)
# Read data from ahdar libary
dat <- storesat

 tab_xtab(var.row = dat$prod,
    var.col = dat$gender,
    title = "Crosstabs", show.row.prc = TRUE)
```

If you look at the output, the χ^2 value is 8.867. This value can be found in the SPSS output (see Figure 10.12) next to 'continuity correction'. This is the chi-square adjusted for continuity correction (also known as the Yates' correction [Yates 1934]). The Yates' correction adjusts the formula Equation 10.1 by subtracting 0.5 from the difference between each observed value and its expected value. This was suggested because the chi-square distribution that is continuous is used to calculate the p-value from distribution of values in the crosstabs table that are discrete.[1]

1 See https://en.wikipedia.org/wiki/Yates%27s_correction_for_continuity.

R code to draw a clustered bar chart (see Figure 10.14):

```
library(ahdar)
library(tidyverse)

# Read data from ahdar library

dat <- storesat

# Proportion chart
# bars sum to 100% within Recycle

table_dat <- dat %>%
# Specify as factors
mutate(prod = as_factor(prod)) %>%
mutate(gender = as_factor(gender)) %>%

# Compute frequency within each combination
group_by(prod, gender) %>%
summarize(count = n()) %>%

# Compute proportions within prod
# n is the default variable created by count()

group_by(prod) %>%
mutate(percent = round(count/sum(count)*100,2))
table_dat %>%
ggplot(aes(x = prod, y = count, fill = gender)) +
 geom_bar(position = 'dodge', stat = 'identity') +
 scale_fill_grey() +
 labs(y = "Count",
      x = "Type of Product",
      fill = "Gender") +
geom_text(aes(label = paste(percent,"%")),
 colour = "black", size = 5,
 vjust = 0.1, position = position_dodge(0.9)) +

theme_classic()

table_dat
```

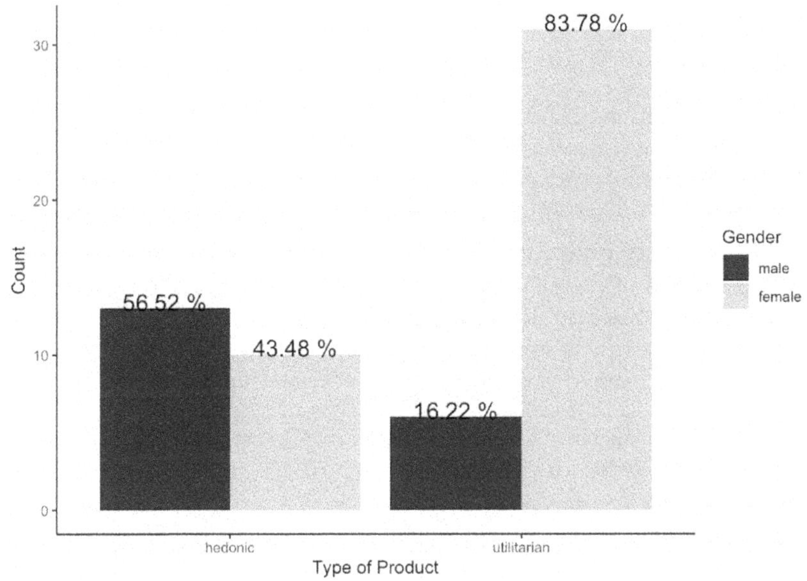

FIGURE 10.14
A clustered bar chart produced with R.

10.4 Summary

In this chapter, we have discussed how to test a single proportion and two samples proportion differences. In the single proportion, we have used the chi-square test and the binomial test in SPSS and R. In testing differences between two proportions, we have used the `D2prop` SPSS macro and the R function `BinomDiffCI()`.

10.5 Further Reading

Daryanto, A. (2022), 'Testing difference in two proportions using D2prop macro in SPSS', *The Quantitative Methods for Psychology* **18**(2), 181–185.

10.6 Review Questions

1. What statistical tests can you use to test one sample proportion?
2. What are the statistical assumptions in the binomial test?
3. In the previous exercise with `D2prop` macro, if I inserted `No` instead of `Yes` as a test variable, the results would be identical. Why is that so?
4. Explain the meaning of association in a crosstabs analysis.

10.7 Exercises

1. A market research had conducted a survey asking potential consumers on their opinions about a new product recently launched by a technological company. Out of 40 consumers surveyed, 60% of consumers indicated that they are willing to buy the product. Assess whether the result is significant (use data **Prop_ex1.sav**).
2. A sample of loyalty program (LP) members were sent an email from a retailer to remind them that they can redeem their LP points by the end of next week. They can redeem their points either to get reward A or reward B. After the data is gathered, the result is given in the following table. Is the proportion of LP members who redeemed reward A is the same as that of reward B?

Number of LP members	Reward A	Reward B
Redeemed	120	90
Not redeemed	50	40

3. Use D2prop macro to test the difference in 'No' proportions of data displayed in Figure 10.4. Compare the results with those of the 'Yes' proportions. Why are the results the same?

11

Correlation

Correlation is a word that can be heard in an everyday conversation. It is frequently used when one wants to make a reference to how things are related. Correlation is a statistical term. It requires data to fully appreciate its meaning. In this chapter, correlation as a summary measure of the relationship between two quantitative variables is discussed. The concept of spurious correlation and partial correlation are also covered. Spurious correlation occurs when a common cause affects two correlated variables. The use of the partial correlation and semipartial correlation to remove the effect of the common cause is demonstrated. As measurement errors can affect the correlation coefficient, the correction for attenuation for correlation coefficient is also covered in this chapter. Finally, the use of SPSS and R in calculating correlation, partial correlation, and semipartial correlation and creating a scatter plot are explained.

Learning Objectives:

- Understand the concept of covariance and correlation.
- Know how to interpret a scatter plot.
- Know how to assess the strength of correlation.
- Understand the concept of spurious correlation, and partial correlation.
- Understand the influence of outliers on correlation.
- Know how to correct correlation for attenuation.
- Know how to use SPSS and R to conduct correlation analysis

11.1 What Is Correlation?

Correlation is a statistical concept to describe a relationship between two variables. It measures a linear relationship, which means that a change in one variable relates proportionally to a change in another variable. As correlation informs whether two variables are linearly related. However, it does not give more information beyond the linear relations. It cannot say much about as to whether one variable causes the other as subsumed in the famous saying: *correlation does not imply causation.* That is, correlation does not infer causality. For instance, If *Age* and *Performance* are correlated, this does not mean that a change in *Age* causes a change in *Performance.* What we can only say is that changes in *Age* is related to changes in *Performance* in a linear fashion – as *Age* increases, performance improves or decreases. Inspecting how variables are correlated is the first step before conducting regression analysis, which will be discussed in Chapters 12 and 13.

DOI: 10.4324/9781003407225-14

11.2 Scatter Plot

A scatter plot is a useful graphical device to inspect correlation. A scatter plot is a type of plot that uses a coordinate system to display values for two variables. If two variables are linearly related, the positions of the values in the scatter plot would resemble a straight line.

Figure 11.1 shows a scatter plot of advertising expenditure and sales.

In inspecting a scatter plot, there are four points that we need to pay attention to:

1. **Form** of the relationship suggested by a scatter plot. Do points in the scatter plot suggest a linear or nonlinear relationship? If a variable relates to another variable in a non-linear fashion, a change in one variable is not proportionally related to a change in another variable. For example, if an increase in sales is doubled by a one unit increase in advertising, advertising and sales have a non-linear relationship. Two types of the nonlinear relationships widely discussed in marketing are the U-shaped and the inverted U-shaped relationships (see Haans et al. 2016). Figure 11.2 sketches the U-shaped and the inverted U-shaped relationship.

An example of the nature of the inverted U-shaped relationship that nearly everyone can relate to himself/herself is the relationship between the amount of workload and work performance as displayed in Figure 11.3. The figure illustrates that an increase in workload leads to an increase in work performance but only up to a certain point, beyond

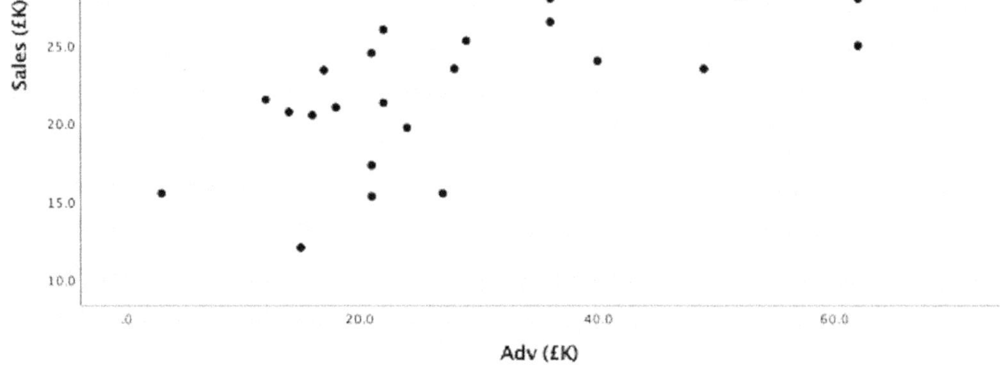

FIGURE 11.1
A Scatter plot of advertising expenditure and sales.

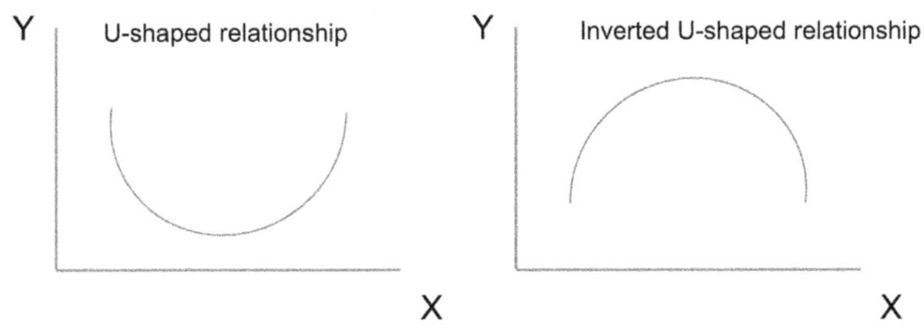

FIGURE 11.2
Forms of U-shaped and inverted U-shaped relationship.

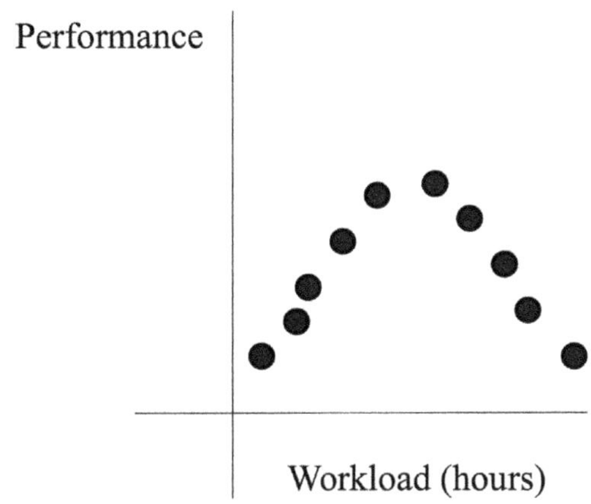

FIGURE 11.3
A scatter plot showing an inverted U-shaped relationship between workload and performance.

which performance suffers. Although workload and work performance is related, however, their inverted U-shaped relationship cannot be captured by a correlation.

The same construct can have both a U-shaped and an inverted U-shaped relationship but with different constructs. For example, Mu & Zhang (2021) found that the reputation of a brand (brand reputation) has an inverted U-shaped relationship with browsing duration. Here, browsing duration is defined as the time it took for consumers – looking for a specific brand – to browse an e-commerce platform. Interestingly, brand reputation has a U-shaped relationship with consumers' post-purchase negative feelings.

2. **Direction** of the relationship. Does the direction of the points in the scatter plot suggest a negative or a positive relationship, or neither?

Figure 11.1 illustrates a positive correlation between advertising expenditure and amount of sales. As an advertising expenditure goes up, the amount of sales also goes up. Figure 11.4 illustrates a negative correlation between brand liking and brand switching. Brand liking is defined as the extent to which a consumer likes a brand, and brand switching is defined as the extent to which a consumer will switch to another brand.

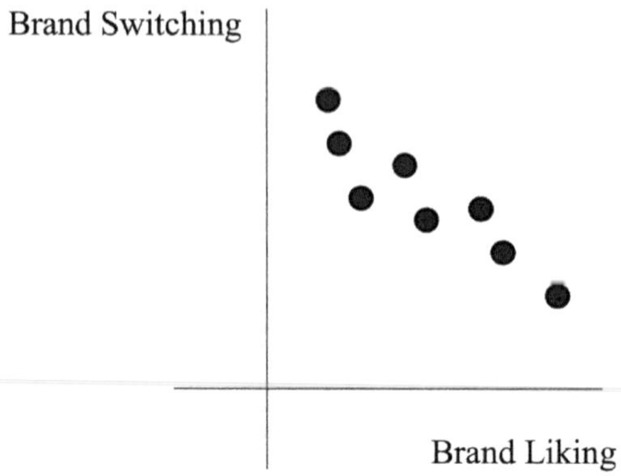

FIGURE 11.4
A scatter plot showing a negative correlation.

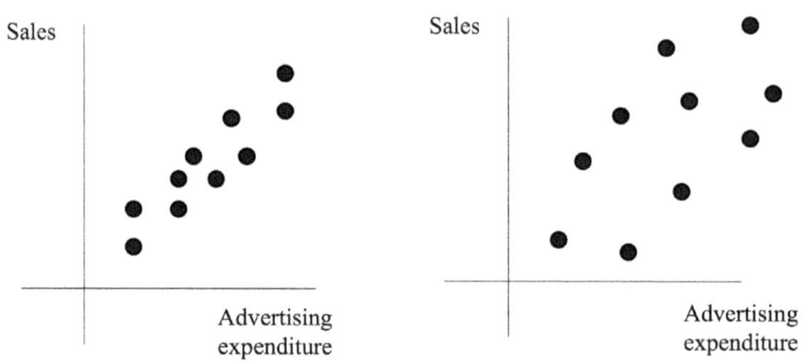

FIGURE 11.5
Correlation between advertising expenditure and sales. The left image shows a stronger correlation than the right image.

The negative correlation suggests that the more a consumer likes a particular brand, the less likely he/she will switch to another brand.

3. **Strength** of the relationship. How scattered are the points?

Figure 11.5 shows two scatter plots of the relationship between advertising expenditure and amount of sales. The two graphs show us that the relationship described by the graph on the left-hand side is stronger than that of the graph on the right-hand side because the points on the former is less scattered than those of the latter.

4. Presence of unusual points or **outliers**. Are there any points that are far from groups of points?

Figure 11.6 shows one point that is far from the clouds of points on the graph. The point can be considered as an outlier, whose inclusion can weaken the correlation and might change the direction of the relationship from positive to negative, or vice versa. In the

FIGURE 11.6
A scatter plot can show the presence of a potential outlier.

next section, I discuss how the presence of an outlier can distort the strength and the direction of the correlation.

11.3 Pearson's Correlation Coefficient

If two quantitative variables have a linear relationship, the strength of the relationship can be described by the Pearson's product moment correlation, or a Pearson's correlation for short, invented by Karl Pearson. Hereafter, for brevity, I use the term correlation instead of the Pearson's correlation.

The symbol for the correlation between two variables in a population is ρ, and the symbol for sample correlation is r where ρ or r takes a value between −1 and 1. The sign of the correlation coefficient tells the direction of the relationship where a minus sign refers to a negative relationship and a positive sign informs a positive relationship.

How to Calculate r

A formula to calculate correlation coefficient r of a sample is given by:

$$r = \frac{S_{xy}}{\sigma_x \sigma_y} \tag{11.1}$$

where r is a correlation coefficient, $S_{x,y}$ is a sample covariance between X and Y, and σ_x and σ_y are standard deviation for x and y, respectively. The formula suggests that the sample correlation is the *standardized* form of the sample covariance. The sample covariance between x and y is given by Equation 11.2:

$$S_{xy} = \frac{\Sigma_{i=1}^{N}(x_i - \overline{x})(y - \overline{y})}{N - 1} \tag{11.2}$$

Table 11.1 shows two datasets: ($x1$, $y1$) and ($x2$, $y2$) pairs. The two datasets are identical except that the $x2$–$y2$ pair contains an unusual pair ($x2 = 20$, $y2 = 3$), which appears in the last row of the table. The pair is a suspected outlier. While $x2 = 20$ is unusual given the range of $x2$, $y2 = 3$ alone cannot be an outlier as this value is within the range of $y2$. It is

TABLE 11.1

(x1, y1) and (x2, y2) Pairs Are Identical Except for the Values in the Last Row

X1	y1	x2	y2
1	2	1	2
2	4	2	4
3	5	3	5
4	4	4	4
2	4	2	4
3	6	3	6
2	5	2	5
5	9	5	9
5	8	5	8
4	7	4	7
NA	NA	20	3

Note: [a] NA = Not Available; [b] r(x1, y1) = 0.865; r(x2, y2) = −0.127

the combination of (*x*2, *y*2) that constitutes a *multivariate outlier.* That is, it is the combination of *x*2 and *y*2 that makes the point an outlier. If only one variable that makes a point an outlier, it is called a univariate outlier. The *x*1–*y*1 pair yields $r = 0.865$, the x2–y2 pair produces $r = -0.127$. The presence of (20,3) values really distorted the magnitude and the sign of the correlation.

11.4 Anscombe Quartet

Data: anscombe.sav

Anscombe created a four datasets known as Anscombe quartet. What is unique about Anscombe dataset is that the four pairs *xy* (x_1, y_2; x_2, y_2; x_3, y_3; x_4, y_4) have different scatter plots (see Figure 11.7) yet each produces the same correlation coefficients. Thus, merely calculating a correlation coefficient without inspecting a scatter plot does not give sufficient information about how the variables are related.

11.5 Strength of Correlation

Cohen (1988) provides a guideline to assess the strength of correlation between two variables.

- r = 0.1 small
- r = 0.3 moderate
- r = 0.5 strong

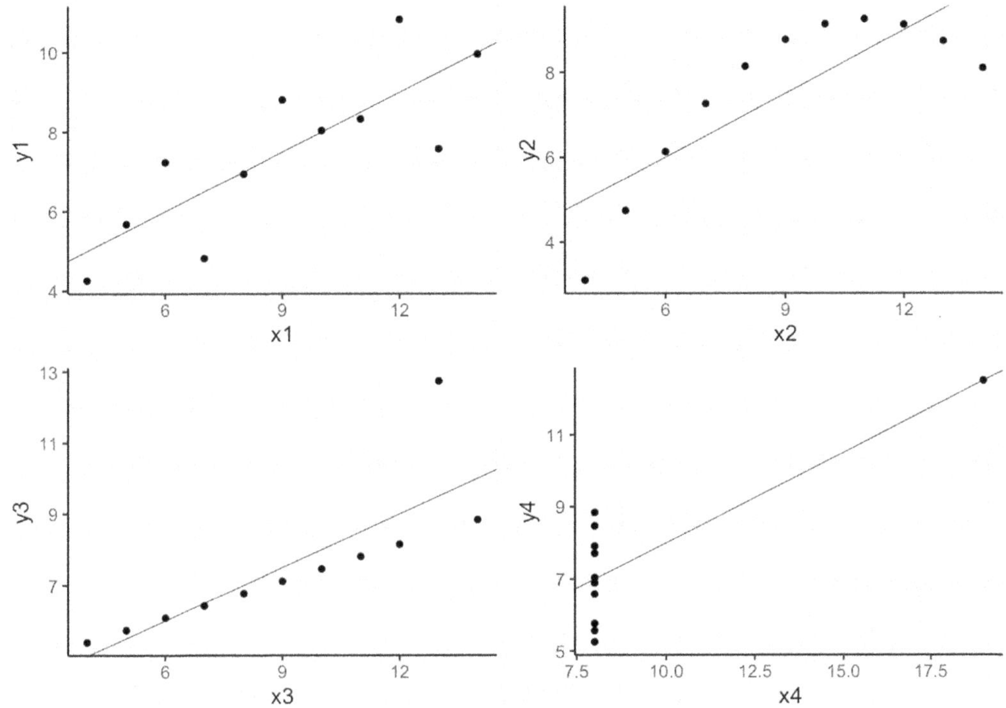

FIGURE 11.7
Scatter plots of the Anscombe quartet. The straight lines are the same regression line.

To memorize this guideline, I refer to the guidelines as the *135 rule* where the numbers refer to the last digit.

IMPORTANT

Before you assess the correlation between two quantitative variables, these three conditions must be checked:

- Type of variables. Pearson's correlation only applies to quantitative variables (interval, ratio).
- Linearity. Correlation measures the strength of the linear association only.
- Outliers. The presence of unusual observations or outliers can distort correlation coefficient. Therefore, outliers must be removed before conducting correlation analysis.

11.6 SPSS Action

Data: sales.sav

Does advertising expenditure (*Adv*) and sales (*Sales*) correlate? We have presented earlier the scatter plot of these two variables in Figure 11.1.

Steps:

- Analyze → Correlate → Bivariate.
- Insert *Adv* and *Sales* into `variables box`.
- Click `OK` or click `Paste` if you want to run the syntax.

The syntax:

```
CORRELATIONS
  /VARIABLES=Sales Adv/PRINT=TWOTAIL NOSIG FULL
  /MISSING=PAIRWISE.
```

As can be seen from the SPSS output displayed in Figure 11.10, the correlation between *Adv* and *Sales* is 0.668. The correlation coefficient is significant at p = 0.01 (see note at the bottom of the output).

11.7 R Action

Let us use R to reproduce our results computed using SPSS. Read data sales.sav:

```
library(haven)
dat <- read_spss("/Users/ahmaddaryanto/Documents/Data1/sales.sav")

# alternatively, load data from library(ahdar)
```

Draw a scatter plot:

Sample Size

Correlation Coefficient r

Correlations

		Sales	Adv
Sales	Pearson Correlation	1	.668**
	Sig. (2-tailed)		.000
	N	36	31
Adv	Pearson Correlation	.668**	1
	Sig. (2-tailed)	.000	
	N	31	31

**. Correlation is significant at the 0.01 level (2-tailed).

FIGURE 11.8
SPSS correlation table of variables Sales and Adv.

```
library(ggplot2)
p1 <- ggplot(data=dat, aes(x=Adv, y=Sales))+ geom_point() +
   labs(x= "Monthly Advertising Expenditure (£K)", y = "Sales") +
   theme_classic()
p1
```

Calculate correlation coefficient:

```
cor(dat$Adv, dat$Sales)
```

[1] 0.6677633

Test the correlation coefficient:

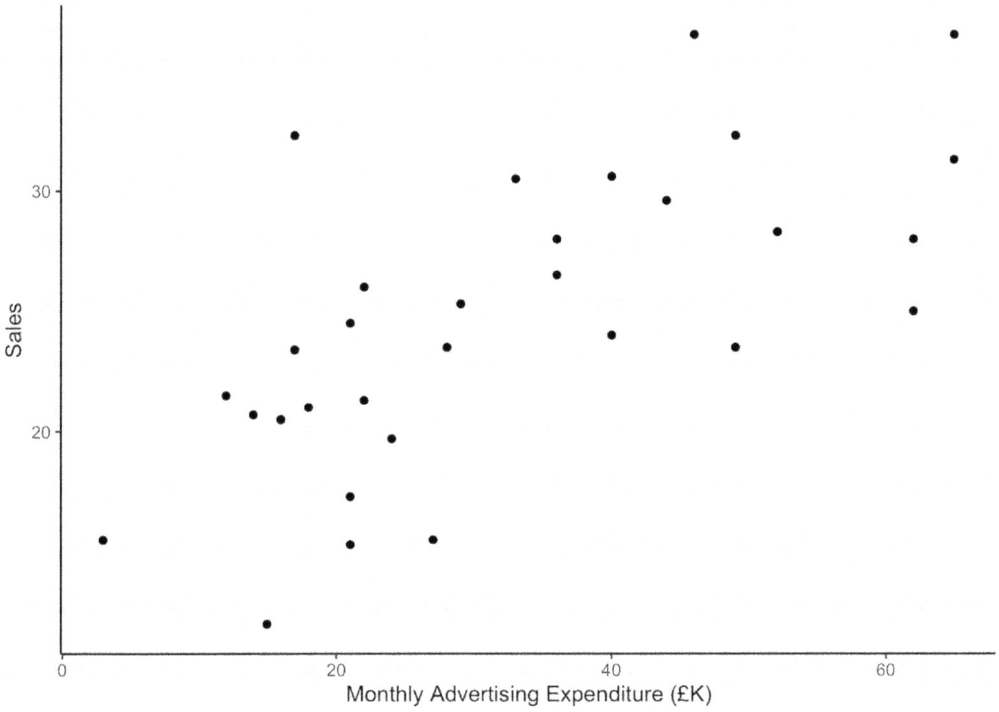

FIGURE 11.9
A scatter plot of Sales and Adv produced by R.

```
res <- cor.test(dat$Adv, dat$Sales, method = "pearson") res
##
##     Pearson's product-moment correlation
##
## data:       dat$Adv and dat$Sales
## t = 4.8309, df = 29, p-value = 4.058e-05
## alternative hypothesis: true correlation is not equal to 0
## 95 percent confidence interval:
##     0.4105704 0.8265330
```

sample estimates:
cor
0.6677633

As described in Chapter 3, we can also use the ggscatter() function from the ggpubr() package to the produce a scatter plot for this data.

```
library("ggpubr")
p2 <- ggscatter(dat, x = "Adv", y = "Sales", add = "reg.line",
      conf.int = FALSE, cor.coef = TRUE, cor.method = "pearson",
      xlab = "Monthly Advertising Expenditure (£K)", ylab =
      "Sales")
p2
```

As we can see in the graph, it produces correlation coefficient (cor.coef = TRUE), the p-value associated with it, and a straight line. This straight line is a regression line, which is a topic discussed in Chapter 12.

11.8 Spurious Correlation

There may be situations where correlation appears to exist even though there is no obvious relationship between the variables. For example, for growing children, their

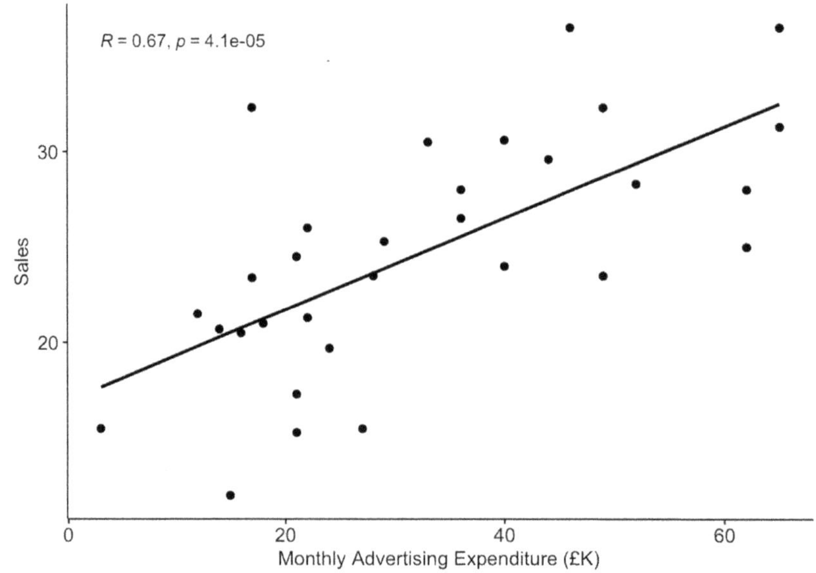

FIGURE 11.10
A scatter plot of Sales and Adv produced by ggscatter() function.

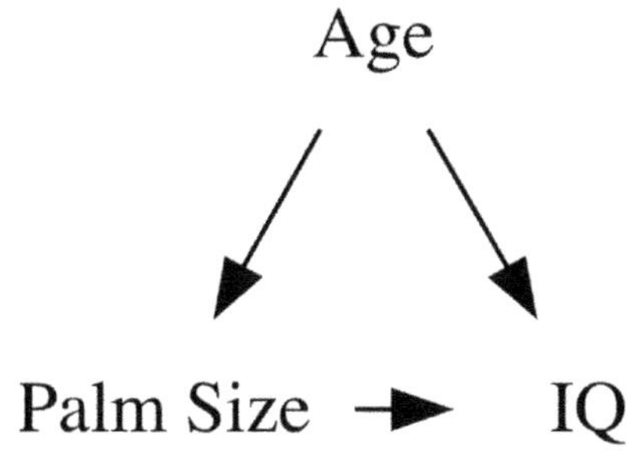

FIGURE 11.11
A diagrammatic representation of the spurious correlation between IQ and palm size that can be detected in children's data.

intelligence measured with their IQ scores and palm size might be correlated even though we cannot say intelligence causes palm size or vice versa. The reason of why the IQ scores and the palm sizes of children below 5 years is correlated because both variables are affected by a common cause, that is, age. This correlation occurs because age is related to the mental development of the children through education. In other words, because age is both related to IQ scores and palm size, this makes IQ scores and palm sizes to be correlated. If we look at the correlation between the IQ scores and the palm sizes of the children of the same age, the correlation between the IQ scores and the palm sizes would disappear. By looking at the correlation at a specific age group, we are controlling for age. That is, by accounting for age, IQ scores and palm sizes would not by correlated for children in that specific age group.

11.9 Partial Correlation

If a correlation is suspected to be spurious, the true nature of the correlation can be revealed by calculating a partial correlation. Suppose that Z is a third variable that exerts its influence on both X and Y. The idea in partial correlation between X and Y is that the influence of Z on both X and Y are removed in the calculation of the correlation. The partial calculation between X and Y is calculated using this formula:

$$r_{YX|Z} = \frac{r_{YX} - r_{YZ} r_{XZ}}{\sqrt{\left(1 - r_{YZ}^2\right)\left(1 - r_{XZ}^2\right)}} \tag{11.3}$$

The "$YX \mid Z$" reads Z is removed from both X and Y. For an illustration, suppose that a correlation coefficient among X, Y, and Z is as described in Figure 11.12. The correlation in the figure refers to the *zero-order correlation* coefficients. The partial correlation between X and Y, that is, the correlation after *controlling* for Z, is 0.09. This value which is a lot lower than their zero-order correlation, suspecting the magnitude of the zero-order correlation is spurious (can you check this calculation?).

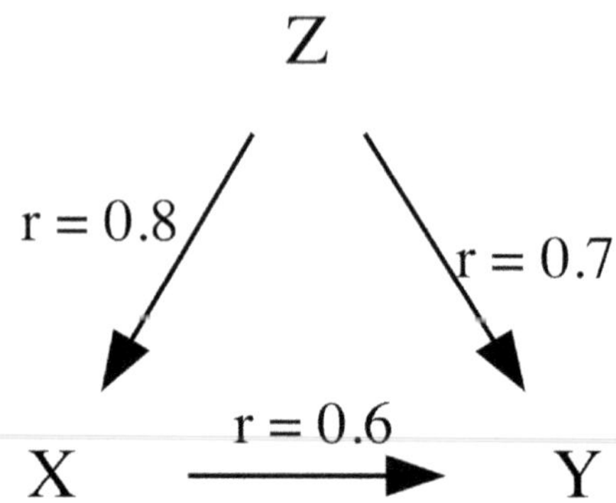

FIGURE 11.12
An illustration of the zero-order correlations among X, Y, and Z. Z is a third variable that influences both X and Y.

11.9.1 R Code

Figure 11.12 looks simple and can be drawn in a PowerPoint, but actually I created it using the following R code.

```
library(DiagrammeR)
grViz("
  digraph{
  graph []

  node [shape = plaintext]
    X [label = 'X']
    Y [label = 'Y']
    Z [label = 'Z']

  edge []

    X -> Y [label = 'r = 0.6', fontsize = 12]
    Z -> X [xlabel = 'r = 0.8', fontsize = 12]
    Z -> Y [label = 'r = 0.7',
            labeldistance = 5,
            fontsize = 12]
{rank = same; X; Y}
}")
```

11.9.2 SPSS Action

Data: spurious.sav
Here, we use SPSS to calculate correlation coefficient. Steps:

- Analyze →Correlate → Partial.
- Insert *x* and *y* into `Variable(s)` box.
- Insert *z* into `Controlling For` box.
- Click `Options` and tick `Zero-order correlations`.
- Click `OK` and inspect the output window.

If we click `Paste`, SPSS yields the following syntax:

```
PARTIAL CORR
  /VARIABLES=x y BY z
  /SIGNIFICANCE=TWOTAIL
  /STATISTICS=CORR
  /MISSING=LISTWISE.
```

The SPSS outputs of the partial correlation procedure are displayed in Figure 11.13. Because the options `zero-order correlations` is ticked, SPSS produces two blocks of outputs. The upper block displayed the zero-order correlations, and the lower block displayed the correlation between x and y accounting for z. The results show $r_{xy} = 0.630$ and the partial correlation $r_{xy.z} = 0.090$.

11.9.3 R Action

To calculate the partial correlation of two quantitative variables, we can use the `pcor.test()` function from `ppcor` package (Kim 2015). To use `pcor.test()` function for calculating Pearson's bivariate partial correlation between x and y controlling for z, it has the form `pcor.test(x, y, z, method = "Pearson")`. The output produces the correlations, the p-values, and the t-value, respectively.

```
library(ppcor)
```

Correlations

Control Variables			x	y	z
-none-[a]	x	Correlation	1.000	.630	.824
		Significance (2-tailed)	.	<.001	<.001
		df	0	298	298
	y	Correlation	.630	1.000	.722
		Significance (2-tailed)	<.001	.	<.001
		df	298	0	298
	z	Correlation	.824	.722	1.000
		Significance (2-tailed)	<.001	<.001	.
		df	298	298	0
z	x	Correlation	1.000	.090	
		Significance (2-tailed)	.	.121	
		df	0	297	
	y	Correlation	.090	1.000	
		Significance (2-tailed)	.121	.	
		df	297	0	

a. Cells contain zero-order (Pearson) correlations.

FIGURE 11.13
Two blocks of correlation tables produced by SPSS showing zero-order correlations (upper block) and partial correlation between x and y controlling for z (lower block).

```
## Loading required package: MASS
##
## Attaching package: 'MASS'
## The following object is masked from 'package:dplyr':
##
##     select
```

```
library(ahdar)
dat <- spurious
pcor.test(dat$x,dat$y,dat$z,method= c("pearson"))
```

```
##       estimate    p.value   statistic   n   gp   Method
##    1 0.08975519  0.1214686  1.553081   300   1   pearson
```

If we want to remove the influence of two variables (e.g. Z and T) from X and Y and correlate the remaining part of X with the remaining part of Y denoted by a symbol ($r_{YX|Z,T}$), we can use a syntax:

```
pcor.test(dat$x,dat$y, dat[,c("z","t")],method=xsc("pearson"))
```

```
  estimate    p.value    statistic   n    gp   Method
1 0.0896065   0.1227208  1.547875   300   2    pearson
```

11.10 Semipartial Correlation

In the partial correlation, we remove the influence of Z on both X and Y. If we remove the influence of Z only on X, and correlate the remaining part of X with Y, we obtain a semipartial correlation. We can use a symbol $r_{Y(X|Z)}$ to denote the semipartial correlation. The '$X|Z$' reads Z is removed from X. Likewise, we could remove the influence of X on Z, and correlate the remaining part of Z with Y. This semipartial correlation can be denoted by the symbol $r_{Y(Z|X)}$. You can see how I interchange the position of X and Z from the previous symbol to denote the new semipartial correlation. In the literature, semipartial correlation also refers to as part correlation. The formula for the semipartial correlation related to the symbol$r_{Y(X|Z)}$ is given here:

$$r_{Y(X|Z)} = \frac{r_{YX} - r_{YZ}r_{XZ}}{\sqrt{\left(1 - r_{XZ}^2\right)}} \tag{11.4}$$

11.10.1 SPSS Action

The correlation procedure in SPSS does not provide the calculation for semipartial correlation. However, it can be obtained from the multiple regression procedure. I will discuss multiple regression in details in Chapter 13. For our purposes, I provide the following syntax of the multiple regression procedure to calculate the zero-order, partial, and semipartial correlation.

Coefficients[a]

Model		Unstandardized Coefficients B	Unstandardized Coefficients Std. Error	Standardized Coefficients Beta	t	Sig.	Correlations Zero-order	Correlations Partial	Correlations Part
1	(Constant)	-3.775E-17	.044		.000	1.000			
	x	.104	.067	.110	1.553	.121	.630	.090	.062
	z	.620	.069	.632	8.966	<.001	.722	.462	.358

a. Dependent Variable: y

FIGURE 11.14
Regression outputs showing semipartial correlations that are displayed in the last column.

Data: spurious.sav

```
REGRESSION
  /MISSING LISTWISE
  /STATISTICS COEFF OUTS R ANOVA ZPP
  /CRITERIA=PIN(.05) POUT(.10)
  /NOORIGIN
  /DEPENDENT y
  /METHOD=ENTER x z.
```

The SPSS output is displayed in Figure 11.14. The block of correlation outputs the zero-order, partial, and semipartial (part) correlation. For instance, the semipartial correlation between *X* and *Y* with *Z* is removed from *X* is 0.062. The semipartial correlation of *Z* and *Y* with *X* is removed from *Z* is 0.358.

11.10.2 R Action

Here, we can use `spcor()` function from the ppcor package to calculate semipartial correlation.

```
library(ppcor)
library(ahdar)

dat <- spurious

spcor.test(dat$y,dat$x,dat$z,method=c("pearson"))
```

	estimate	p.value	statistic	n	gp	Method
1	0.06205636	0.2848033	1.071525	300	1	pearson

If we want to remove the influence of two variables (e.g. *Z* and *T*) from *X* and correlate the remaining part with *Y* denoted by ($r_{Y(X|Z,T)}$), we can use this syntax:

```
spcor.test(dat$y,dat$x,dat[,c("z","t")],method=c("pearson"))
```

	estimate	p.value	statistic	n	gp	Method
1	0.06170616	0.2883498	1.06366	300	2	pearson

11.11 Correction for Attenuation

Error in measuring a construct can occur. For example, respondents may not state his or her true opinion due to various reasons. This measurement error can also affect correlation coefficient. The good news is that correlation coefficient can be corrected for attenuation, thus resulting in a true correlation coefficient. The formula for correlation coefficient corrected for attenuation is given by:

$$r_c = \frac{r}{\sqrt{r_{xx} r_{yy}}} \tag{11.5}$$

where r is correlation coefficient, r_{xx} and r_{yy} are reliability coefficient (Cronbach's alpha) for x and y, respectively.

IMPORTANT

Correlation coefficient corrected for attenuation can be greater than 1 if the correlation coefficient is high and the reliability coefficients for variables involved are low. For an illustration, suppose $r = 0.90$, $r_{xx} = r_{yy} = 0.4$. Therefore, $r_c = 2.25$.

11.12 Correlation and Covariance Matrix

If there are more than two variables involved, correlation among variables can be represented by a correlation matrix, and for the same variables, the covariance among variables is represented by a covariance matrix. In the covariance matrix, its main diagonal is occupied by variance terms, and the off-diagonal is made up of the covariance terms. Table 11.2 show a correlation matrix among X, Y, and Z. Table 11.3 shows a covariance

TABLE 11.2

A Lower-Diagonal Correlation Matrix

X	Y	Z
1		
0.68	1	
0.12	0.26	1

TABLE 11.3

A Lower-Diagonal Covariance Matrix

X	Y	Z
1.03		
0.79	1.32	
0.21	0.51	2.84

matrix of the same data. In the correlation matrix, values in the main diagonal are 1 because the correlation between a variable and itself is one. However, values in the main diagonal of a covariance matrix are not necessarily 1. As correlation between *X* and *Y* is just the same as the correlation between *Y* and *X*, we can present either a lower-diagonal matrix (i.e. showing values below the main diagonal) as in Table 11.2 or an upper-diagonal matrix (i.e. showing values above the main diagonal).

The following R code produces correlation and covariance matrices among the variables in Table 11.2 and Table 11.3.

```
library(tidyverse)
library(ahdar)

dat <- empathy

dat2 <- dat |>
   dplyr::select(MI1, MI2, MI3)

cor.out <- round(cor(dat2),2) # correlation
cov.out <-round(cov(dat2),2) # covariance
cor.out
```

	MI1	MI2	MI3
MI1	1.00	0.68	0.12
MI2	0.68	1.00	0.26
MI3	0.12	0.26	1.00

cov.out

	MI1	MI2	MI3
MI1	1.03	0.79	0.21
MI2	0.79	1.32	0.51
MI3	0.21	0.51	2.84

Knowing a covariance matrix is important when it comes to learning a confirmatory factor analysis (CFA) (see the CFA section of Chapter 22). This is because CFA is based on the covariance matrix and the matrix can be used as an input data that is processed by a specialized statistical program for CFA such as AMOS, Lisrel, Mplus, EQS, and lavaan. From a methodological perspective, CFA estimates parameters of a model to produce a covariance matrix that is as close as possible to the sample covariance matrix.

11.13 Summary

In this chapter I have discussed Pearson's correlation as a technique to summarize the relationship between two quantitative variables, which is regarded as the first step prior to regression analysis. Being unaware of the presence of a third variable that influences both variables can result in correlation to be spurious. I have demonstrated how to calculate partial correlation to account for the third variable.

11.14 Further Reading

Haans, R. F., Pieters, C. & He, Z. L. (2016), 'Thinking about U: Theorizing and testing U-and inverted U-shaped relationships in strategy research', *Strategic Management Journal* **37**(7), 1177–1195.

Lind, J. T. & Mehlum, H. (2010), 'With or without U? The appropriate test for a U-shaped relationship', *Oxford Bulletin of Economics and Statistics* **72**(1), 109–118.

11.15 Review Questions

1. Explain what is meant by spurious correlation? And how would you check its potential presence?
2. What are the three conditions that you must check in analysing correlation?
3. Mention the criteria for assessing the strength of correlation between two quantitative variables.
4. Explain how the presence of outliers can distort correlation.

11.16 Exercises

1. Given the zero-order correlation in Figure 11.12, calculate semipartial correlation between X and Y when Z is removed from X only.
2. Repeat number 1, but this time Z is removed from Y only.

Part IV

Regression Analysis

12

Simple Linear Regression

This chapter discusses a simple linear regression model, which captures the relationship between an independent variable and a dependent variable. The method of ordinary least squares (OLS) and its assumptions are explained. Through the use of SPSS outputs, key concepts and key regression outputs are highlighted. The use of a simple linear regression model to assess group means was explained. The use of R in conducting a simple linear regression is also provided covering three popular R functions: `lm()`, `anova()`, and `summary()`, and two R packages `stargazer()` and `jtools()`. Finally, a slight modification of the specification of the simple linear regression model is explained, covering the log-linear and log-log models.

Learning Objectives:

- Understand the concept of simple linear regression.
- Be able to distinguish between independent and dependent variables.
- Know how to interpret the meaning of the regression coefficient.
- Be able explain the key assumptions of simple linear regression, which includes linearity, homoskedasticity, no auto-correlation, no endogeneity, and normality.
- Be able to use simple linear regression to assess mean differences.
- Be able to interpret the regression coefficient of the log-linear and log-log simple linear model.

12.1 Which Line Is Best?

You have seen earlier in Section 11 that in a scatter plot, you can see whether the scatter points illustrate a certain pattern. If you and your friends were stranded in an island and only have a paper and pencil to draw a straight line, each of you might have to come up with different lines as displayed in Figure 12.1.

So, which line will you choose? I intuitively will choose the middle line. Choosing something in the middle feels right to me as it carries the impression of choosing the average, which compromises any alternatives, which reminds me of a compromise effect – see the following box. Compared to the other two lines or any straight lines that you can draw, the middle line is the closest to all points in the scatter plot.

DOI: 10.4324/9781003407225-16

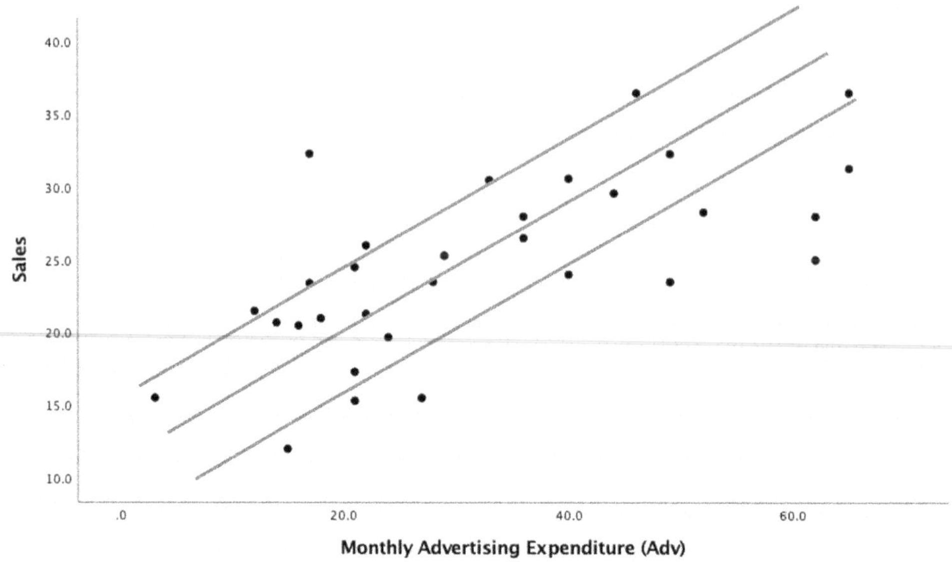

FIGURE 12.1
Which line is best?

INFO

A bit of a consumer behaviour theory here: a compromise effect is well-documented in a consumer research (Simonson 1989), showing that consumers will choose an option among other alternatives when it is perceived as a middle option, which can be construed as a compromise.

Finding the best line by manually drawing every possible line on a graph is an error-prone endeavour. Everyone will draw a different line and yet declare their lines are the best! To overcome this subjectivity, regression methods – one of which is ordinary least square (OLS) – can be used to avoid the subjectivity. This technique was implemented by a statistical software such as SPSS and R, which can help us finding the best line, also referred to as the best regression line.

Figure 12.2 shows a regression line that is plotted according to an equation $Sales$ = 18+0.208 Adv. This equation is obtained by running a regression procedure from SPSS. The regression equation can be referred to as the regression model representing the relationship between sales and advertising expenditure. The equation tells you that if the advertising expenditure is increased by 1K, the sales go up by £0.24K. This equation can also be used to make a prediction. If Adv = £3K, sales are expected to be equal to $Sales$ = 0.240 * £3K + 16.933 = £17.653.

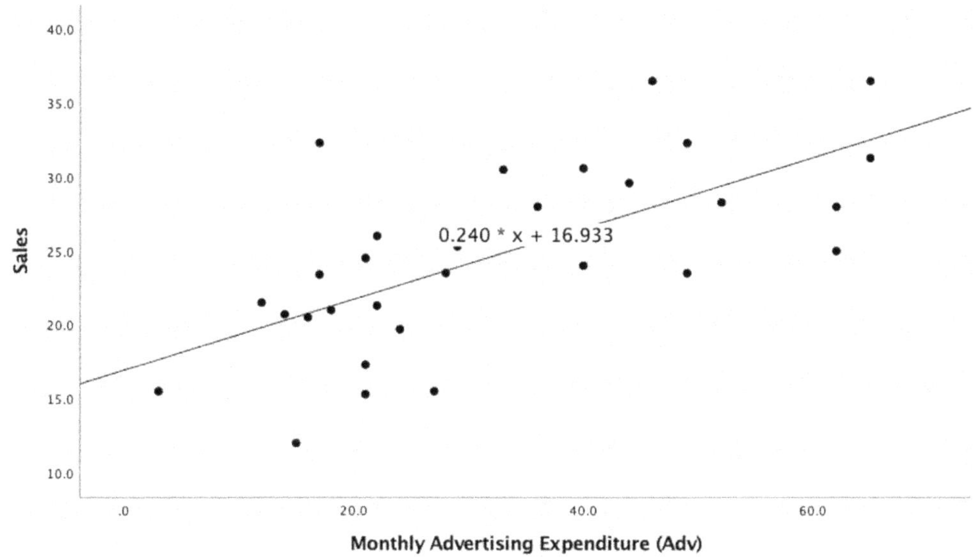

FIGURE 12.2
Predicted regression line with an equation.

IMPORTANT

In a regression of sales on advertising budget, all points on the sample regression line are expected values of *Sales* for any given values of *Adv*. They are predicted values. For this reason, a regression line can also be called a predicted regression line. If the observed value for *Sales* corresponding to *Adv* = 3 is £5.5K. The difference between the observed and predicted value is called a residual. The residual at *Adv* = £3K is £15.5 – £17.653= £–2.153.

12.2 Finding the Best Line

Finding the best straight line to summarize a relationship between two variables is about building a linear regression model used to estimate a population model. The population model takes the following form:

$$Y = \beta_0 + \beta_1 X + \varepsilon \tag{12.1}$$

This model tells us how changes in *X* affect changes in *Y* in a population. β_0 and β_1 are regression parameters whose values are fixed and unknown to us. *Y* is called a dependent variable, outcome variable, or response variable, most often abbreviated as *DV*. *X* is always referred to as an independent variable, most often abbreviated as an *IV*. Other names for *IV* are predictor variable and explanatory variable. ε denotes an error term representing any variables unrelated to *Y*.

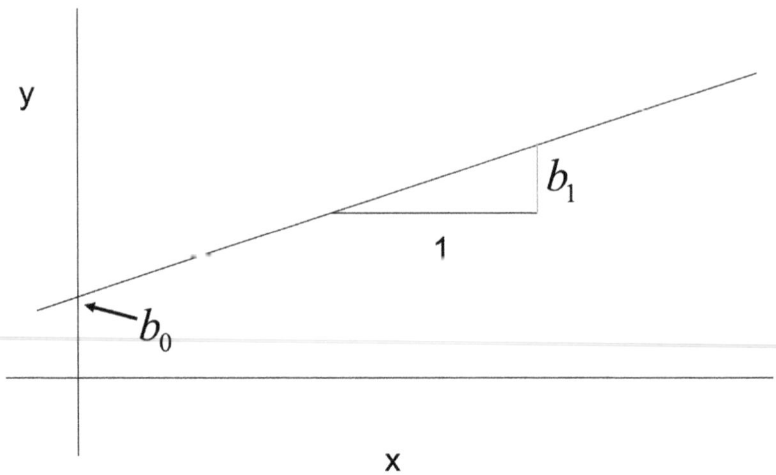

FIGURE 12.3
The intercept and slope of a regression line.

X and Y symbols are always reserved to represent an independent and a dependent variable, respectively. This is not a rule but a convention that has been adopted for hundreds of years to avoid confusion. Thus, they are not interchangeable. Putting them in the context of what affects what, then the influence goes from an independent variable to a dependent variable ($X \rightarrow Y$). Y can also affect X, known as a reverse relationship.

Using a random sample, the population model is estimated by a sample regression line, which is the best line illustrated:

$$Y = b_0 + b_1 X \tag{12.2}$$

where b_0 and b_1 are regression coefficients or estimates that are varied from sample to sample.

You may recall from your high school algebra that $y = mx+sc$ is an equation for a straight line, where m is the slope of the line and c is a point at which the line intersects the y-axis, which is called as the intercept. Equation 12.2 is essentially $y = mx+c$, where $m = b_1$ and $c = b_0$ (see Figure 12.3). From the figure, you see that the slope represents the expected change in y per one-unit change in x.

12.2.1 How to Find b_0 and b_1

A method called ordinary least squares (OLS) can be used to find b_0 and b_1. To appreciate the technique, look at Figure 12.4, which displays three observed values and a predicted regression line.

The objective of the OLS technique is to find a regression line from which the distance from the observed values is minimal. The vertical distance from an observed value point to the line reflects a regression error or a residual. A residual has a positive value when a point is above the line and has negative value when the point is below the line. The sum of all residuals is zero: $\sum_{i=1}^{3} e_i = e_1 + e_2 + e_3 = 0$ because the negative and positive residuals will be cancelled out each other. Because of this, nothing we can do to

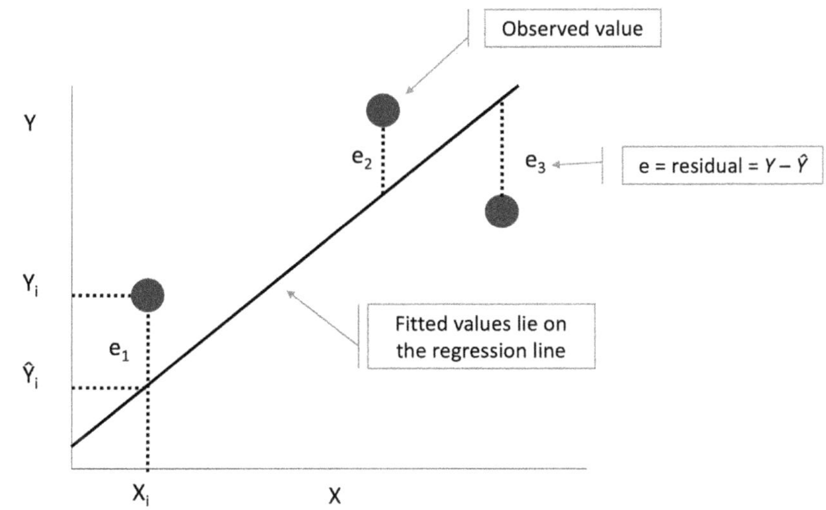

FIGURE 12.4
Observed values and distances to a predicted regression line.

minimise the sum of residuals that is always zero. Hence, a modification is made by taking the sum of squared residuals whose result would be nonzero. In this book, the sum of squared residuals is abbreviated as **SSE**, which stands for sum of squares errors. Now, the new objective is not to minimise the sum of all residuals but the sum of all squared residuals: $SSE = \sum_{i=1}^{3} e_1^2 + e_2^2 + e_3^2$.

In Section 5.1.3 we discussed how to calculate the variance of a variable. For a dependent variable *Y*, its population variance is estimated by this form:

$$Var(Y) = \frac{\sum_{i=1}^{n}(Y_i - \bar{Y})^2}{n-1}$$

In the context of regression, the form $\sum_{i=1}^{n}(Y_i - \bar{Y})^2$ is called the sum of squares regression, abbreviated as **SSR**.

In a simple linear regression model, b_0 and b_1 have an exact form that can be computed manually, expressed as the following:

$$b_1 = \frac{\sum_{i=1}^{n}(X_i - \bar{X})(Y_i - \bar{Y})}{\sum_{i=1}^{n}(X_i - \bar{X})} \quad (12.3)$$

$$b_0 = \bar{Y} - b_1\bar{X} \quad (12.4)$$

Where $\bar{X}$ is the mean score of the independent variable *X*, $\bar{Y}$ is the mean score of the dependent variable *Y*. However, SPSS implements a general computational procedure, not the given form, to calculate the regression coefficients. In Section 12.3.1, I provide a step-by-step calculation to illustrate how to work out the formula to calculate b_0 and b_1.

12.3 The Best Regression Line Contains Expected Values

I mentioned previously that, in the *Adv* ~ *sales* relationship, *all points on the sample regression line are predicted or expected values of Sales* for any given values of

Adv. At *Adv* = £3K, the expected *Sales* is equal to £19K. The phrase 'predicted Sales' can refer to *Sales* expected from a single firm if £3K is spent on advertising. The phrase 'expected Sales' refers to the average sales of a very large number of firms, if each spent 3K on advertising. The latter is the more precise statistical interpretation of values that lie on a regression line. That is, a sample regression line contains all values of the dependent variable that we would expect to get at any values of an independent variable. We can write this expression as

$$E(Y|X) = b_0 + b_1 X \tag{12.5}$$

where $E(Y|X)$ denote the expected value of Y at a given value of X. Expected value in (Equation 12.5) can also be interpreted as an average value. That is, you can also interpret the equation this way: at a given value of X, if your regression model is applied at different samples, it will produce different values of y, and $E(Y|X)$ is their average. In other words, $E(Y|X)$ is the mean of the distribution of y at a given value of X. The expression is referred to as *the conditional expectation of* Y at a given value of X. We can visualize this statement on a graph to understand this statement. Before presenting the graph, please read the following hypothetical scenario to put it into a context.

Imagine that there are 1000 advertising agencies allocating £3K each on advertising. After a while, each reported the amount sales generated from the spending. Despite each firm spent the same amount of budget on advertising, the amount sales from each firm will not be the same because they are targeted at different samples and there are factors other than advertising that also affect sales. Similarly, if all firms spend another budget, say, £5K, the amount of sales in each firm will also vary. The variation of sales at each spending can be captured by a probability distribution. In order the mechanics of regression to work, the probability distributions of sales at any value of advertising budget are assumed to be normally distributed. That is, at £3K, sales are assumed be normally distributed. Similarly, at £5K, sales are also assumed to be normal distributed. As we learned in the previous chapter, if sales follow a normal distribution, the centre of the distribution is the mean value of the sales. Figure 12.5 illustrates this interpretation. As you can see in the figure, the mean of sales at a particular advertising budget lies on the regression line.

From the figure, notice that the shapes of the two normal curves are the same. They have the same variance but different means.

IMPORTANT

The conditional distribution of Y at any value of X is assumed to be normal. All conditional distributions have the same spread. Recall from previous chapter that the spread of a normal distribution is quantified by its standard deviation denoted by σ, which is the square root of variance.

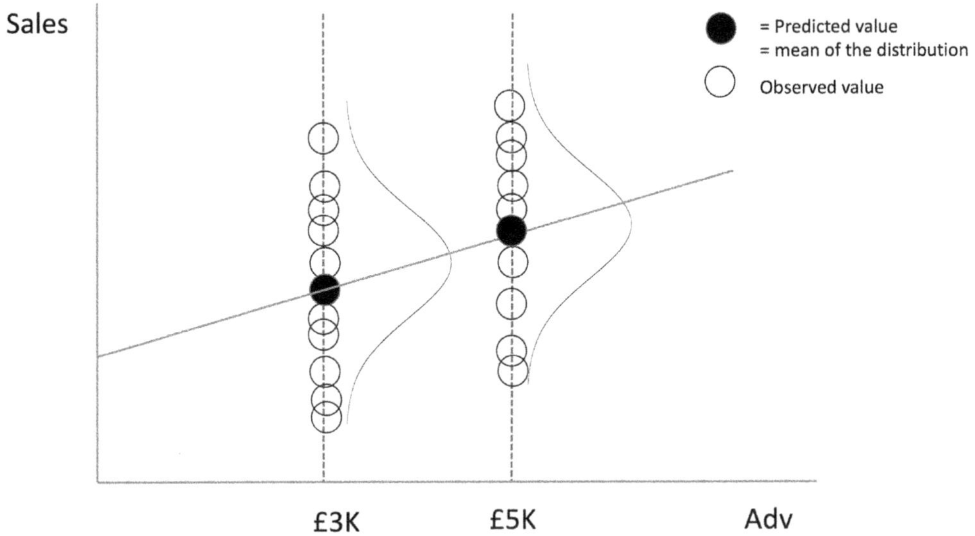

FIGURE 12.5
The conditional distribution of sales at Adv = £3K and £5K. The two normal distributions have the same variance.

12.3.1 Illustration

The following table shows you a step-by-step calculation to find the slope and intercept using the two formulas in Equation 12.3 and Equation 12.4. As I stressed before, you should not attempt to calculate the regression coefficient this way – let SPSS does the job for you.

X	Y	$X-\bar{X}$	$(X-\bar{X})^2$	$Y-\bar{Y}$	$(X-\bar{X})(Y-\bar{Y})$
5.83	5.2	0.056	0.003	1.166	0.065
5.33	6.2	0.542	0.293	0.006	0.003
7	7	0.872	0.761	0.518	0.452
5.17	6	0.803	0.645	0.078	0.063
7	7	0.872	0.761	0.518	0.542
$\bar{X}=6.07$	$\bar{Y}=6.28$			$\sum=2.463$	$\sum=1.036$

$$b_1=\frac{1.036}{2.463}=0.421$$

$$b_0=6.28-0.421*6.07=3.729$$

$$Y=3.729+0.421X$$

12.4 Assumptions in Simple Regression

Linear regression relies on several assumptions. Although the intercept b_0 and slope b_1 can be found algebraically, these assumptions are required in order to understand the statistical properties of the regression coefficients (e.g. sampling distribution of b_1), test their significance (e.g. are they greater than zero?), and construct the confidence intervals of the coefficients.

1. Linearity. This assumption requires that the relationship between an independent variable (IV) and dependent variable (DV) can be represented by a straight line represented by Equation 17.1. This means that any changes in the IV causes changes in the DV proportionally. For example, if $Sales$ = 1 +3 ADV, increasing ADV by one unit will increase sales by 3×1 units. An equation like $Y = \beta_0 + 3^{\beta_1 X} + \varepsilon$ is ruled out. This is an example of a nonlinear equation. For example, if $Sales$ = 1+3ADV, increasing ADV by one unit will not increase sales by 3×1 units. How about an equation like $Y = \beta_0 + \beta_1 X^2 + \varepsilon$? This quadratic equation, because of the X-squared, qualifies. In fact, you can replace the term X^2 with another variable, say, $Z = X^2$, to get the same form as Equation 17.1, i.e. $Y = \beta_0 + \beta_1 Z + \varepsilon$.
2. Homoskedasticity. This assumption requires that the regression error terms have constant variance. Non-constant variance is referred to as heteroskedasticity. Let us revisit Figure 12.5 presented earlier. From the figure, we see that at the two values of Adv, the two normal distributions have the same spread. This is an example of situation in which homoskedasticity assumption is satisfied. We discus homoskedasticity in more details in Section 14.
3. No endogeneity. Endogeneity refers to a modelling situation when the IV is correlated with the regression error term. The correlation occurs when an important variable that is not only correlated with the IV but also has an influence on the DV is omitted from the regression equation. We discuss endogeneity in more details in Section 17.
4. No perfect multicollinearity. Multicollinearity means a very high correlation among variables. This assumption only applies to multiple regression – model that incorporates more than independent variable, discussed in the next chapter. Perfect multicollinearity means that the variables are perfectly correlated to each other. For example, if you create another variable from ADV, such as ADV 2 = 3+ADV, then the regression model $Y = \beta_0 + \beta_1 ADV + \beta_2 ADV2 + \varepsilon$ is excluded. We discuss multicollinearity in more details in Section 14.2.
5. No autocorrelation. This assumption requires that the regression error term should not be correlated to each other. This situation can happen when we are dealing with time series data. For example, if you collected data on Saturday (t_1) and on another Saturday (t_2), the regression residual at t_1 can be correlated with that at t_2. Autocorrelation is not a concern if we are dealing with cross-sectional data. This type of data is collected at a single point in time. The term 'cross-sectional' comes from the fact that the data is collected across different observations at the same point in time.
6. Normality. The regression error terms are assumed to follow a normal distribution with a zero mean and a constant variance. The assumption is not very strict when sample size is very large. In a large sample, due to the central limit theorem, the distribution of the parameter estimates (i.e. the slope and intercept) will be approximately normal even if the error term is not normally distributed. Because of this, inspecting whether residual is not normal is not necessary to do when sample size is large.

We may be tempted to conduct a normality test for residuals and defended the practice by arguing normal residuals implied normal dependent variable. However, this is not always true: the dependent variable may not be normal even though the residuals are normal. For an illustration, the distribution of satisfaction displayed in Figure 12.6 does not follow a normal distribution but a bivariate normal distribution characterised by two humps. You can reconstruct the histogram using a dataset *satisfaction.sav*, which I also use in Section 12.8. If you inspect the residuals of the simple linear regression model regressing satisfaction on gender coded as either 0 or 1, the distribution of the residual will look normal (see Figure 12.7).

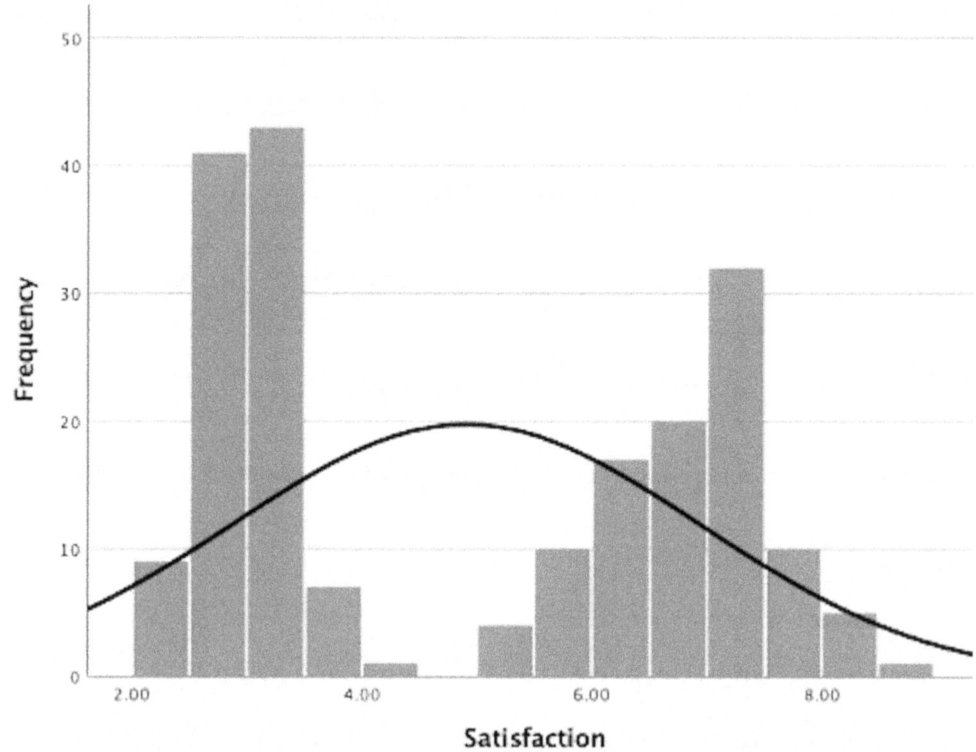

FIGURE 12.6
Satisfaction is bivariate normal. A normal curve is superimposed on the graph.

WARNING

Normality of residuals is not the same thing as normality of Y. For instance, normal residuals can be obtained from Y that is bivariate normal.

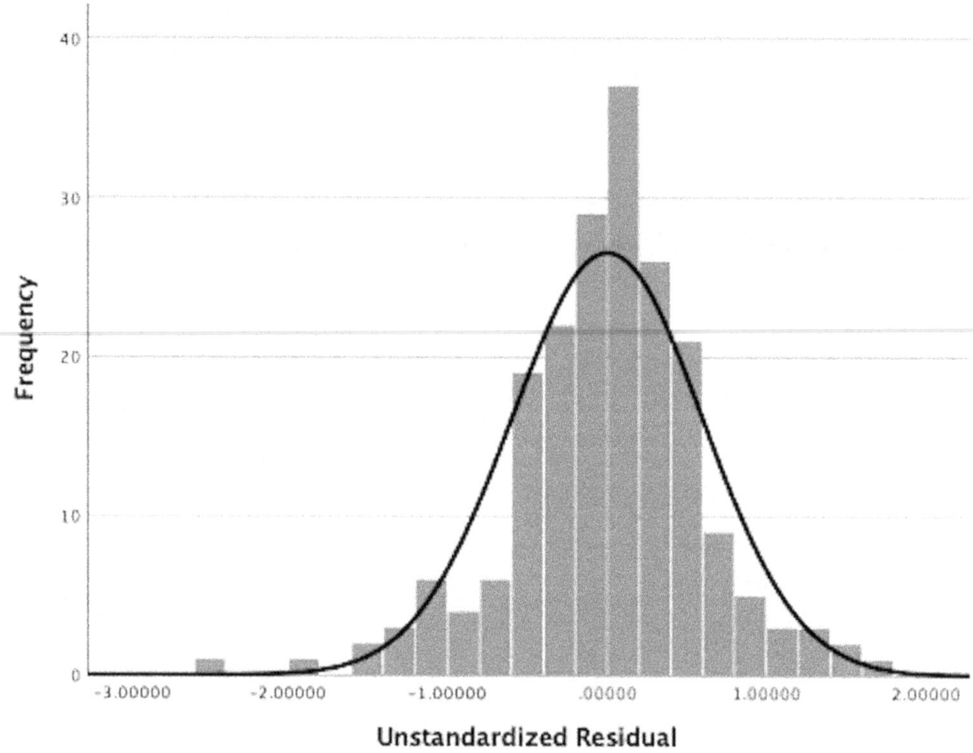

FIGURE 12.7
Histogram of residuals from regressing satisfaction on gender coded as either 0 or 1.

12.5 Testing the Significance of the Independent Variable

Let us write down again the formula of a simple linear regression model: $Y = \beta_0 + \beta_1 X + error$. The formula applies to a population. When the model is estimated by a random sample, we wrote down the formula as $Y = b_0 + b_1 x$. Using a different sample, we will get different values for b_0 and b_1. That is, these coefficients will vary from sample to sample. Thus, if we take 1000 random samples and conduct regression for each sample, we will obtain 1000 values for b_0 and b_1. As we will only be interested in β_1 estimate because this coefficient tells us whether X affects Y in the population, the question is then how would we know whether b_1, on average, will be different from, less than, or greater than zero? In other words, how would we know that the regression coefficient estimate (β_1) is significant or not? The mechanics of statistics prevent us from actually taking 1000 random samples in order to assess the significance of β_1. Using data only from a random sample, we would be able to assess the significance of the regression coefficients. We will not delve into more details on the mechanics of the test but will use a statistical software such as SPSS to assess the significance of the regression coefficient. I will demonstrate this in the next section.

In a simple regression model, our interest is to test the significance of the slope b_1. Depending our research objective, we can conduct either a two-sided test formulated as:

$$H_0 : \beta_1 = 0$$

$$H_A : \beta_1 \neq 0$$

or a one-sided test, which takes the following form:

$$H_0 : \beta_1 = 0$$

$$H_A : \beta_1 > 0$$

or the following form:

$$H_0 : \beta_1 = 0$$

$$H_A : \beta_1 < 0$$

12.6 SPSS Action and Interpretation

Data: sales.sav

This data contains two variables (monthly sales and monthly advertising expenditure) for 36 months of a particular product. Using SPSS, follow the following steps to conduct a simple regression analysis.

Steps:

- Analyze → Regression → Linear.
- Insert *Sales* into the `dependent box`.
- Insert *Adv* into the `independent box`.
- Next, click `Statistics`, and tick `Confidence Intervals` box.
- Click `OK` and inspect the outputs.

If in the last step you clicked `Paste`, an SPSS syntax is created:

```
get file '/Users/ahmaddaryanto/OneDrive - Lancaster University/
dataspss/sales.sav'
  REGRESSION
  /MISSING LISTWISE
  /STATISTICS COEFF OUTS CI(95) R ANOVA
  /CRITERIA=PIN(.05) POUT(.10)
  /NOORIGIN
  /DEPENDENT Sales
  /METHOD=ENTER Adv.
```

We will obtain four chunks of outputs. The first output is trivial as it just provides information on variable being entered. We focus on the remaining three chunks: `Model Summary`, `ANOVA`, and `Coefficients`.

12.6.1 Model Summary

The key statistics to look at the model summary output is R^2 (read: R-squared), also called as the coefficient of determination. It measures the proportion of variance in Y that can be explained by X. In a simple linear regression model, the square root of R^2 is just a correlation coefficient (you can check this by running correlation). The R^2 reported in Figure 12.8 is equal to 44.6%, which means that 44.6% of the variation in sales can be explained by the variation in advertising expenditure.

We can illustrate the variation in sales as a unit circle (see Figure 12.9). The area of the unit circle is equal to 100%. The R^2 reflects the area in the unit circle occupied by *Adv* is about 46.6%. The remaining 53.4% is the unknown area in the unit circle reflecting the proportion of variance attributed to unknown factors.

44.6% of variation in Sales is accounted for by Adv

Model Summary

Model	R	R Square	Adjusted R Square	Std. Error of the Estimate
1	.668[a]	.446	.427	4.6733

a. Predictors: (Constant), Adv

FIGURE 12.8
Model summary.

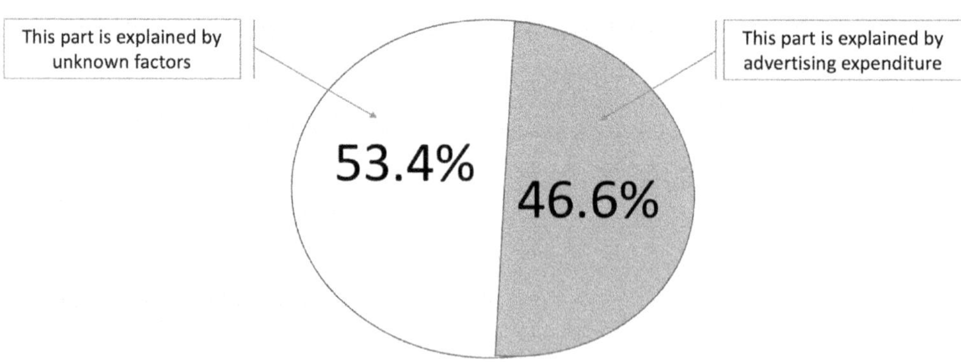

FIGURE 12.9
Variation in the dependent variable as a unit circle.

The output also shows the Adjusted R^2, which is R^2 value adjusted for the number of independent variables used in the regression model. Adjusted R^2 is used to prevent the inflation in R^2 simply due to more variables are being entered into the regression model – it is not relevant in the simple regression that has only one independent variable. R^2 should not be treated as a target that we want it to keep increasing in our research. What is more important is knowing whether X can explain Y.

12.6.2 ANOVA Table

SPSS produces an ANOVA table (see Figure 12.10).

ANOVA stands for analysis of variance. The first row of the table shows sums of squares regression (**SSR**). The second row shows sum of squared residuals (SSE). The last row shows the sum of squares total (**SST**). The definition of each term is explained in the following callout.

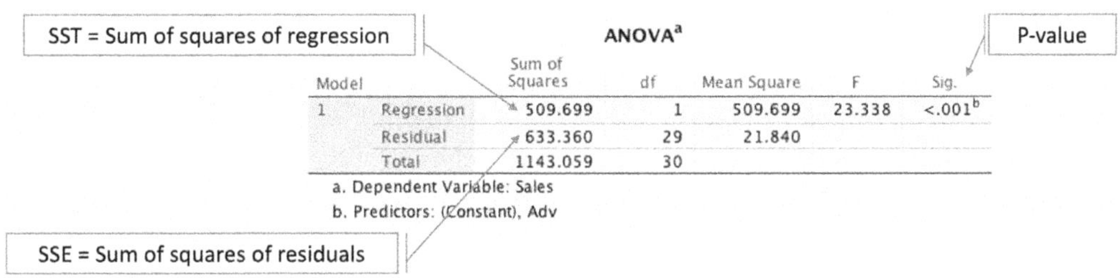

ANOVA[a]

Model		Sum of Squares	df	Mean Square	F	Sig.
1	Regression	509.699	1	509.699	23.338	<.001[b]
	Residual	633.360	29	21.840		
	Total	1143.059	30			

a. Dependent Variable: Sales
b. Predictors: (Constant), Adv

FIGURE 12.10
ANOVA table.

NOTE

SST = SSR + SSE

The expression can be expressed in terms of squared distance or variability.

- $SST = \sum(Y - \bar{Y})^2$ = sum of squared distances from the observed values to their mean Y.
- $SSR = \sum(\hat{Y} - \bar{Y})^2$ = sum of squared distances from predicted values to their mean.[1]
- $SSE = \sum(Y - \hat{Y})^2$ = sum of squared residuals.

[1] The mean of the predicted values is the same as the mean of the observed values.

From the first column of the ANOVA table, we have

- SSR = 509.699, and
- SSE = 633.360, so
- SST = 1143.059.

Knowing SST and SSR also allows us to calculate R^2. That is, $R^2 = SSR/SST =$ 509.699/1143.059 = 0.446$.

The third column of the table tell us the `degrees of freedom (df)`. The degrees of freedom are the number of information you are free to choose to estimate population values. The last column is the `mean square` calculated as **sum of squares/df**. The degrees of freedom associated with regression is equal to 1; therefore, the mean square for regression is **SSR/1**. The degrees of freedom for the residual is $N-2$ where N is the sample size, 2 is the number of parameters that needs to be estimated in the equation $Y = b_0 + b_1x$, which are the intercept (b_0) and slope (b_1).

The square root of mean square is the standard deviation of the residuals, which is the standard deviation of *Y*. SPSS called it `standard error of the estimate` printed in the `model summary` output – see the last column of Figure 12.8. You can check that $\sqrt{(21.840)} = 4.673$. The standard error of the estimate is a `conditional` standard deviation. If you look at Figure 12.11, this is the standard deviation associated with a normal curve at a certain point in *X*.

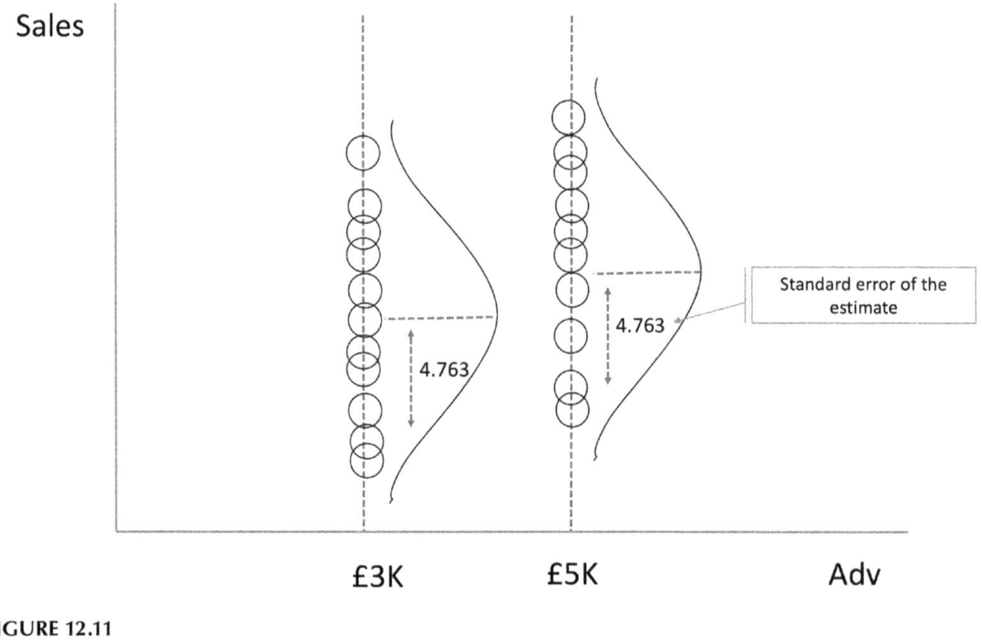

FIGURE 12.11
Standard error of the estimate.

The third column is the value calculated by dividing the mean square due to regression (MSR) by the mean square due to residual (MSE) $= \frac{MSR}{MSE} = \frac{509.699}{21.840} = 23.338$. This value follows an F distribution with $df1 = 1$, and $df2 = n - 2 = 29$. The last column shows the p-value associated with the following test:

$$H_0 : \beta_1 = 0$$
$$H_A : \beta_1 \neq 0$$

This test uses the F distribution. The test is significant as p-value is less than 0.000. Therefore, *Adv* is significant or the model is meaningful.

NOTE

The information in the ANOVA table actually is not necessary for a simple linear regression model as the information we need is already contained in the `coefficients` table discussed in next section.

You can check the p-value using the `FDIST` macro and tick the right-tail probability. This means you want to find $P(F > 23.388)$, which is less than zero. Figure 12.12 shows the screen image of the input and output of the macro.

In testing a hypothesis, you want to see a large F values, leading to a rejection of null hypothesis. If the null hypothesis is not rejected – b_1 is not significant, then the best regression line is a horizontal line at the mean of *Y*. In this case, your best guest for *Sales* at a certain value of *Adv* is the sales average value (see Figure 12.13).

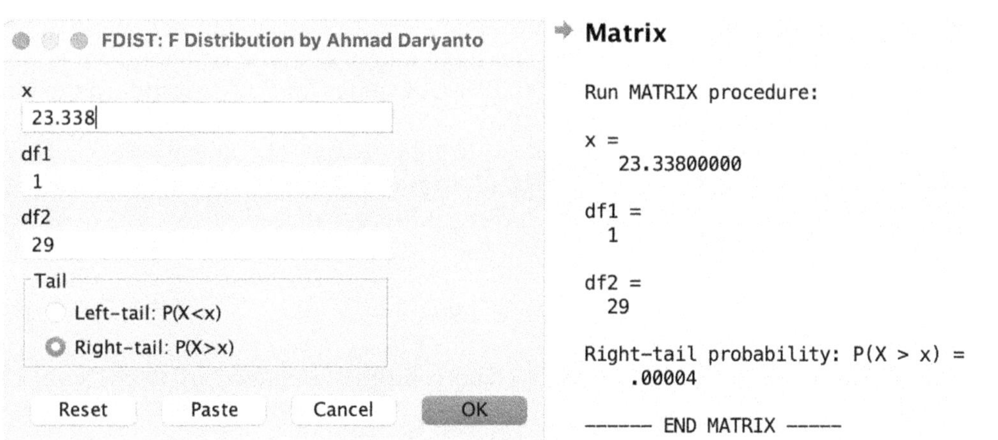

FIGURE 12.12
Calculating p-value using FDIST macro.

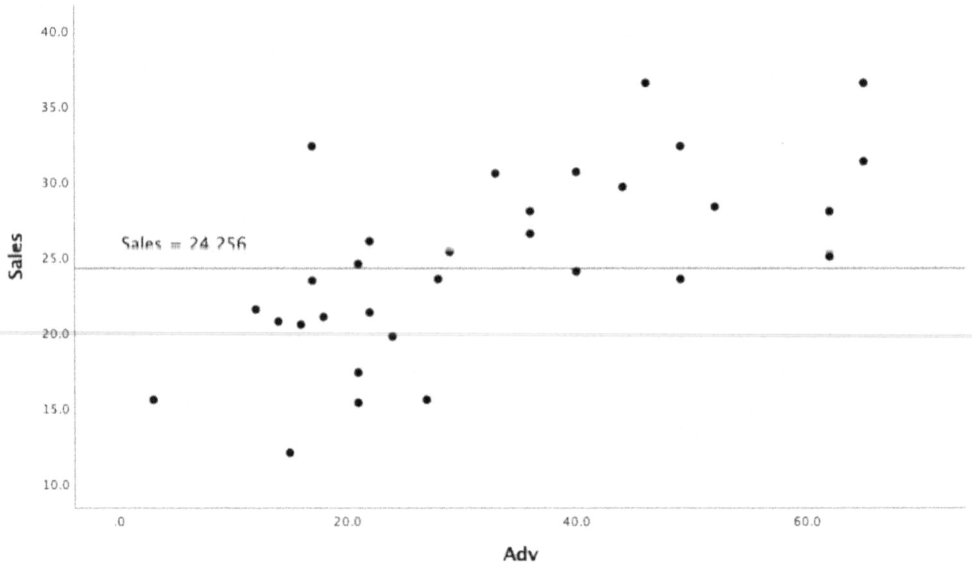

FIGURE 12.13
If Adv is not significant, the best regression line is the horizontal line at the mean value of sales.

12.6.3 Coefficients Table

The coefficients table (see Figure 12.14) produced by SPSS allows us to assess the significance of the regression coefficients and construct their confidence interval.

The first row of the coefficients table is for b_0 displayed as (Constant) in SPSS, and the second row is for the b_1. From the `Standardized Coefficients` part, we see $b_0 = 16.933$ and $b_1 = 0.240$. Knowing the constant and the slope, we can write down the equation for the best line as $Sales = 16.933 + 0.24Adv$.

The table also reports the standard error of the b_1, (the standard error for the constant is not very useful), $se = 0.05$, which informs us about the variability of sample slope. If you collect a large number of sample (say, 1000 samples), and conduct a simple linear regression for each then you will get 1000 different values for b_1. The standard deviation of the 1000 slopes is estimated as $se = 0.05$.

The 95% confidence interval for the slope is [0.138, 0.341]. This means we can be 95% confident that β_1 will fall between 0.0138 and 0.341. If you are curious where these numbers came from, you can compute the lower and upper bound of the 95% confidence interval manually using this formula

$$b_1 \pm 1.96se \tag{12.6}$$

where −1.96 and 1.96 are the 2.5th and 97.5th percentiles of the standard normal distribution, respectively.

The lower bound: 0.24 – 1.96 * 0.05 = 0.142

The upper bound: 0.24 + 1.96 * 0.05 = 0.338

Coefficients[a]

Model		Unstandardized Coefficients B	Std. Error	Standardized Coefficients Beta	t	Sig.	95.0% Confidence Interval for B Lower Bound	Upper Bound
1	(Constant)	16.933	1.815		9.331	<.001	13.222	20.645
	Adv	.240	.050	.668	4.831	<.001	.138	.341

a. Dependent Variable: Sales

FIGURE 12.14
Regression coefficients table.

The confidence interval computed manually is a bit different than the one reported by SPSS due to rounding errors. For instance, the standard error for the slope shown by in the SPSS output is not precisely 0.05 but has long decimal values (double-click the output, put your cursor in the cell, and double-click it again).

The next step is to assess the significance of the slope. The hypothesis test is

$$H_0 : \beta_1 = 0$$

$$H_A : \beta_1 \neq 0$$

The p-value (or Sig.value) associated with the test is given in the last column, $p = 0.000$. As this is less than 5%, *Adv* is significant.

IMPORTANT

SPSS version 27 and below reported a p-value associated with a two-sided test. Therefore, if you use the older version of SPSS to conduct a one-sided test (e.g. H1: $\beta_1 > 0$), you need to divide the p-value by half. For example, the p-values reported in the Sig. column of the coefficient table displayed in Figure 12.14 are associated with a two-sided test.

The p-value is calculated from the t statistics, $t = \dfrac{b}{se}$ = 4.831. You can use TNORM macro to find the p-value associated with the t-value by inserting 4.831 into the x box and inserting df = 29 to the degree of freedom box. You must choose right-tail probability $P(X > x)$. Figure 12.15 shows the screen image of the input and output. Next, you must multiply the p-value printed by the output by two (2*0.00002 = 0.00004) to obtain the two-sided p-value – this is the two-sided p-value reported in the SPSS output. You can check this by double-clicking the coefficient table, put your cursor in the p-value cell, and double-click it again. You will see that p = 0.000041 (see Figure 12.16).

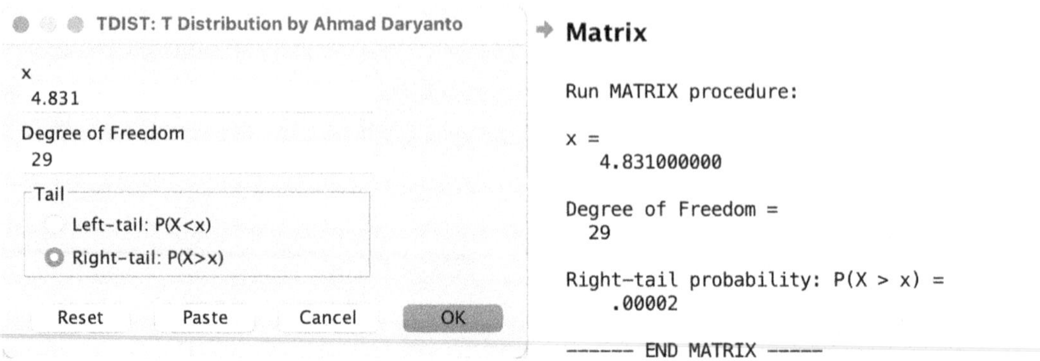

FIGURE 12.15
Using TDIST macro to calculate the p-value for Adv.

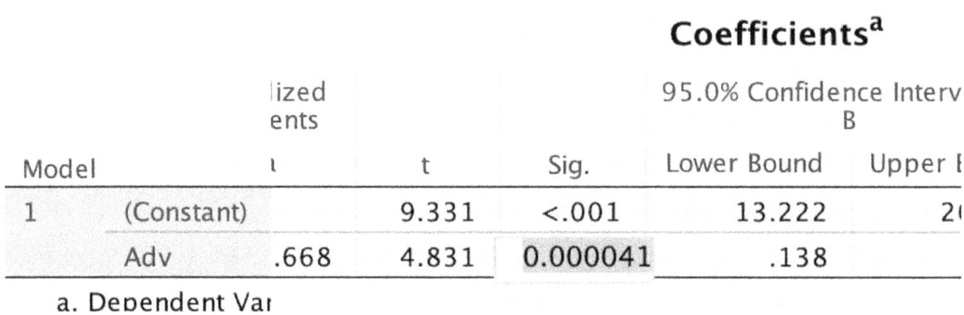

Coefficients[a]

Model		ized ents	t	Sig.	95.0% Confidence Interv B Lower Bound	Upper I
		ι				
1	(Constant)		9.331	<.001	13.222	2(
	Adv	.668	4.831	0.000041	.138	

a. Dependent Var

FIGURE 12.16
Zooming in the p-value.

Note that the hypothesis formulation is similar to the formulation presented earlier in the ANOVA section. This is the reason that the ANOVA table for simple linear regression does not really add more information in terms of testing whether the model is meaningful as the same information can be obtained from the coefficients table. You can also check that the *F* value from the ANOVA table ($F = 23.338$) is the same as $t^2 = 4.8312 =$ 23.339.

12.6.4 The Standardized Coefficients

SPSS also report the standardized coefficients. The standardized form of the estimated regression model is *Sales* = 0.668*Adv*. How did we get the slope = 0.668? The slope can be obtained by regressing the standardized form of *Sales* on the standardized form of *Adv* (remember, the standardized forms are also called z-scores, see Section 6.5.1). Do the following steps:

- Transform *Sales* and *Adv* to their z-scores (see Section 6.5.1), say the newly created variables are *Z Sales* and *Z Adv*.
- Conduct a regression of *Z Sales* on *Z Adv*.
- Inspect the slope of *Adv*, which should be equal to 0.668.

12.7 R Action

Let us use R to reproduce our results computed using SPSS. Read sales.sav.

```
library(haven)
dat <- read_spss("/Users/ahmaddaryanto/Documents/Data1/sales.sav")
# alternatively, library(ahdar) will load the data.
```

Conduct regression, save the results on lm_sales.

```
lm_sales <- lm(Sales ~ Adv, data = dat)
Extract ANOVA Table.
anova(lm_sales)
## Analysis of Variance Table ##
```

Response: Sales

```
##      Df Sum Sq Mean Sq F value  Pr(>F)
```

Adv 1 509.70 509.70 23.338 4.058e-05 ***
Residuals 29 633.36 21.84

Signif. codes: 0 '***' 0.001 '**' 0.01 '*' 0.05 '.' 0.1 ' ' 1

Output summary.

Produce

```
summary(lm _ sales)
```

```
##
## Call:
## lm(formula = Sales ~ Adv, data = dat)
##
## Residuals:
##     Min      1Q  Median      3Q     Max
## -8.5263 -2.7483 -0.1402   2.4901 11.2947
##
## Coefficients:
##              Estimate Std. Error t value   Pr(>|t|)
## (Intercept) 16.93331    1.81481     9.331  3.10e-10  ***
## Adv          0.23953    0.04958     4.831  4.06e-05  ***
## ---
```

```
## Signif. codes:  0 '***' 0.001 '**' 0.01 '*' 0.05 '.' 0.1 ' ' 1 ##
## Residual standard error: 4.673 on 29 degrees of freedom
## Multiple R-squared:   0.4459, Adjusted R-squared: 0.4268
## F-statistic: 23.34 on 1 and 29 DF,  p-value: 4.058e-05
```

The regression outputs produced by `summary()` function from R base did not produce standardized coefficients. The `lm.beta` package (Behrendt 2023) can be used to produce the standardized coefficients.

```
install.packages("lm.beta")
```

Use `lm.beta()` function to run regression, and with `summary()` function, set

```
library(lm.beta)
lm_sales_std <- lm standardized = TRUE.beta(lm_sales)
summary(lm_sales_std,standardized=TRUE)
```

```
##
## Call:
## lm(formula = Sales ~ Adv, data = dat)
##
## Residuals:
##     Min      1Q  Median      3Q     Max
## -8.5263 -2.7483 -0.1402 2.4901 11.2947
##
## Coefficients:
##              Estimate Standardized Std. Error t value Pr(>|t|)
##  (Intercept) 16.93331           NA    1.81481   9.331  3.10e-10 ***
##  Adv          0.23953      0.66776    0.04958   4.831  4.06e-05 ***
##  ---
##  Signif. codes:  0 '***' 0.001 '**' 0.01 '*' 0.05 '.' 0.1 ' ' 1
##
##  Residual standard error: 4.673 on 29 degrees of freedom
##  Multiple R-squared:  0.4459, Adjusted R-squared:   0.4268
##  F-statistic: 23.34 on 1 and 29 DF,   p-value: 4.058e-05
```

12.7.1 stargazer()

`Stargazer()` package (Hlavac 2015) can be used to produce regression results, which meet publication standards. Several options are available to format the outputs. For instance, in the following code, `single.row=TRUE` produces outputs in a row format, and `ci=TRUE` yields the 95% confidence intervals for the regression estimates. You can find all the options by looking at the package's help file (type in '?stargazer' in your R console).

```
library(stargazer)
stargazer(lm_sales, type = "text", single.row=TRUE, ci=TRUE)
```

```
##
## ===============================================
##                   Dependent variable:
##               ---------------------------
##                         Sales
## -----------------------------------------------
## Adv               0.240*** (0.142, 0.337)
## Constant         16.933*** (13.376, 20.490)
## -----------------------------------------------
## Observations                  31
## R2                          0.446
## Adjusted R2                 0.427
## Residual Std. Error    4.673 (df = 29)
## F Statistic         23.338*** (df = 1; 29)
## ===============================================
## Note:               *p<0.1; **p<0.05; ***p<0.01
```

12.7.2 jtools()

Another package worth exploring is `jtools()` (Long & Long 2017). In jtools, `summ()` function is used to product regression outputs, which is a replacement for the R base's `summary()` function. The package provides several options to format the regression outputs. You can run the `confint=TRUE`, which will produce the 95% confidence intervals for the regression estimates.

```
library(jtools)
summ(lm_sales, confint=TRUE)
```

12.8 Testing Means

12.8.1 Comparing Differences in Two Means

You can conduct a simple linear regression to compare mean differences of two samples. Suppose that you want to test whether mean satisfaction score of loyal is greater than that of non-loyal customers. You can build a simple regression model as presented in Equation 12.7:

$$Satisfaction = \beta_0 + \beta_1 Loyal + error \tag{12.7}$$

where Loyal is a categorical (0,1) variable, with $Loyal = 1$ if a customer is a loyal customer and = 0 if otherwise. It is important to code a categorical variable as 0,1 when you are dealing with two groups. Essentially, you are estimating two regression models (se Equation 12.8 and Equation 12.9) obtained by substituting the value of *Loyal*.

$$Satisfaction = \beta_0 + error, Loyal = 0 \tag{12.8}$$

$$Satisfaction = \beta_0 + \beta_1 + error, Loyal = 1 \tag{12.9}$$

Descriptive Statistics

Loyal		N	Minimum	Maximum	Mean	Std. Deviation
.00	Satisfaction	100	2.10	3.84	2.9790	.33430
	Valid N (listwise)	100				
1.00	Satisfaction	100	4.35	8.61	6.8293	.78425
	Valid N (listwise)	100				

FIGURE 12.17
Descriptive statistics of loyal and non-loyal customers.

Coefficients[a]

Model		Unstandardized Coefficients		Standardized Coefficients			95.0% Confidence Interval for B	
		B	Std. Error	Beta	t	Sig.	Lower Bound	Upper Bound
1	(Constant)	2.979	.060		49.418	<.001	2.860	3.098
	Loyal	3.850	.085	.955	45.163	<.001	3.682	4.018

a. Dependent Variable: Satisfaction

FIGURE 12.18
Coefficient table of regressing satisfaction on loyal.

From Equations 12.9, we can see that β_1 captures the difference between the satisfaction score of loyal and non-loyal customer. $\beta_1 > 0$ if the satisfaction score of loyal customer is greater than that of the non-loyal customers. Therefore, the hypothesis test is

$$H_0 : \beta_1 = 0$$

$$H_A : \beta_1 > 0$$

I use *satisfaction.sav* data to estimate the regression model. The descriptive statistics of the two groups are given in Figure 12.17. The sample size for the non-loyal group is 100, mean satisfaction = 2.9790, and standard deviation = 0.3343. The sample size for the loyal group is 100, mean satisfaction = 6.8293 and standard deviation = 78425. The mean difference is 6.8293–2.9790 = 3.8503. Is this significantly greater than zero?

The SPSS coefficient table is displayed in Figure 12.18.

The predicted regression model is

$$Satisfaction = 2.979 + 3.850 Loyal \tag{12.10}$$

The slope is greater than zero and significant ($\beta_1 = 3.850$, $p < 0.001$), and the 95% confidence interval does not include zero. We can conclude that the mean satisfaction score of the loyal customer is indeed significantly greater than that of the non-loyal customers, with the mean difference is equal to 0.3850.

12.8.2 Testing Population Mean

Can we use regression to test a population mean? For instance, is mean satisfaction score greater than 0? The answer is yes. Essentially, you are estimating a population mean using a model as presented in 12.11:

$$Satisfaction = \propto + error \tag{12.11}$$

where μ is the population mean. This model is the same as:

$$Satisfaction = \beta_0 + error \tag{12.12}$$

where the model has no slope and only the intercept $\beta_0 = \mu$.

Your hypothesis is

$$H_0 : \beta_0 = 0$$
$$H_A : \beta_0 > 0$$

SPSS Action

Here, I show how to use SPSS to test a single mean. Our objective is to test whether the mean of satisfaction variable is greater than 0. Before running a regression, the first step is to create a variable in the SPSS data containing only 1s.

Steps:

Data: satisfaction.sav

- Click Transform → Compute variable.
  - Type in *One* in the Target variable box. Next, put 1 in the Numeric Expression box.
  - Click OK or 'Paste' to generate a syntax as seen here:

```
COMPUTE One=1.
EXECUTE.
```

Now, inspect your data, which has a new column containing 1s. We can now run a regression using the One variable as an independent variable and satisfaction as the dependent variable.

- Click Analyze → Regression → Linear.
  - Insert *Sat* into the Dependent Variable box,
  - Insert *One* into the Independent(s) box.
- Click Options, then untick include constant in equation box.
- Click OK or Paste if you want to use an SPSS syntax.

```
REGRESSION
  /MISSING LISTWISE
  /STATISTICS COEFF OUTS R ANOVA
  /CRITERIA=PIN(.05) POUT(.10)
  /ORIGIN
  /DEPENDENT Sat
  /METHOD=ENTER One.
```

Coefficients[a,b]

Model		Unstandardized Coefficients B	Std. Error	Standardized Coefficients Beta	t	Sig.
1	One	4.904	.143	.925	34.309	<.001

a. Dependent Variable: Satisfaction

b. Linear Regression through the Origin

FIGURE 12.19
Testing population mean is greater than zero.

As you can see from the output, $\beta_0 = 4.904$. If you check the descriptive statistics, this value is just the sample mean, which is our best estimate for the population mean. The p-value associated with the test is significant ($p < 0.001$). Thus, we can conclude that the population mean is greater than zero at 5% significant level.

What if you want to test H_0:

$$H_0 : \beta_0 = 4$$
$$H_A : \beta_0 > 4$$

I choose the test value of 4 because it is the median value of a 7-point Likert scale used to measure satisfaction. Therefore, if the test rejects the null hypothesis, we have evidence that consumers in the population are significantly more satisfied.

Here, the trick is you have to subtract 4 for every value of satisfaction. For example, if Sat is the satisfaction variable, we can create a new variable, say, NSat, by subtracting 4 from Sat, e.g. NSat = Sat – 4. Next, we estimate:

$$NSatisfaction = \beta_0 + error \tag{12.13}$$

and test

$$H_0 : \beta_0' = 0$$
$$H_A : \beta_0' > 0$$

and follow the same procedure in SPSS (see exercise).

12.9 Modifying an SLR Model

12.9.1 Log-Linear Model

If we take the natural logarithm of the dependent variable, then we have a so-called log-linear model. For example, $Log(Sales) = 2.845 + 0.10 * Adv$ is a log linear model describing a relationship between log(*Sales*) and advertising expenditure (*Adv*). Suppose that the unit measurement for *Adv* is £1K. The regression coefficient for *Adv* in this particular example means that *sales increases by 0.10 × 100% (=10%) for every £1K spent on advertising.* A log-linear model is widely used for metrics data (ratio variables).

IMPORTANT

A regression coefficient in a log-linear regression model represents the estimated percent change in a dependent variable for a unit change in an independent variable.

12.9.2 Log-Log Model

Taking the natural logarithm at the both sides of the model give us the log-log model. For example, $Log(sales) = 2.282 + 0.269 * \log(Adv)$ is a log-log model describing a relationship between log(*Sales*) and log(*Adv*). Suppose that the unit measurement for *Adv* is £1K. The regression coefficient for *Adv* in this particular example means that *1% increase in Adv increases sales by 0.269%.* A log-log model is also known as a **constant elasticity model**.

IMPORTANT

A regression coefficient in a log-log model represents the estimated Elasticity: percent change in a dependent variable for a 1% unit change in an independent variable.

12.10 Summary

In this chapter, we have learned a simple regression model where there is only one independent variable in the model. Understanding a simple regression model is important as it provides a statistical foundation to understand a multiple regression model, which we discuss in the next chapter. In a multiple regression model, there are more than one independent variable in the model and the five assumptions in a simple regression model also apply to a multiple regression model. We have also discussed how to use a simple regression model to compare means across different samples. In the final two subsections, we discussed the specification of log-linear and log-log models modified from a simple linear regression model.

12.11 Further Reading

Gelman, A., Hill, J. & Vehtari, A. (2020), *Regression and other stories*, Cambridge University Press. R is used extensively in this book to explain regression and covers various topics, including Bayesian and causal inference.

12.12 Review Questions

1. Simple linear regression line will always pass through the means of X and Y. True or false?
2. When $b_0 = 0$, the simple regression line will pass through the origin. True or false?
3. Explain the meaning of E(Y|X).
4. Explain the difference between distribution of sales and conditional distribution of sales.
5. What is the standard error of the estimate?
6. What is the interpretation of the normal distribution curves in Figure 12.5?
7. Write down an equation for log-log and log-log linear regression model.
8. Explain the meaning of the coefficient in the log-log model.

12.13 Exercises

1. Using X and Y data in Section 12.3.1, use SPSS to find b_0 and b_1.
2. Interpret the meaning of the regression estimate associated with the independent variable in the result obtained in question 1.
3. Using satisfaction.sav, test whether sat score is greater than 4.

13

Multiple Regression

This chapter on multiple linear regression, or multiple regression, for short, extends simple linear regression discussed in the previous chapter by including more than one independent variable in a model. This chapter begins with the meaning of coefficients in a multiple regression model, and explains assumptions required in multiple regression. As there are more than one variable in multiple regression model, the chapter discussed the role of independent variables as control variables. Hierarchical regression analysis is introduced as a technique to account for the influence of control variables. The chapter also shows how to use multiple regression model to test series of hypothesis about relationship among variables depicted in a path model. In the final section, the use of SPSS and R to run multiple regression are demonstrated.

Learning Objectives:

- Understand that a multiple regression model is an extension of a simple linear regression model.
- Understand the role of control variables.
- Understand the meaning of regression coefficients in a multiple regression model.
- Know how to conduct a hierarchical regression.
- Know how to build a path model from series of hypotheses.
- Know steps in building a multiple regression model

13.1 Multiple Regression Model

Multiple regression model is a generalization of a simple linear regression model by having multiple independent variables to explain a dependent variable. The independent variables can accommodate different types of variables. These independent variables can be a mix of qualitative (i.e. nominal, ordinal) and quantitative variables (i.e. interval, ratio). However, the nominal or ordinal independent variables cannot be inserted into a model as such but must be transformed into multiple dichotomous variables so as to accommodate multiple categories in the measurement scale. Although a dependent variable can represent a nominal or an ordinal data, in this chapter, we consider the dependent variable as either an interval or ratio type that are treated as continuous variables. In general, multiple regression model can take many independent variables.

DOI: 10.4324/9781003407225-17

For simplicity, we consider the model with only three predictors represented with the following form

$$Y = \beta_0 + \beta_1 X_1 + \beta_2 X_2 + \beta_3 X_3 + \varepsilon \tag{13.1}$$

where all the βs denote regression parameters and ε denotes an error term. The error term represents any variables that are assumed to be unrelated to Y.

13.2 The Roles of Variables

In a multiple regression model, variables can serve various roles: as a dependent variable, independent variables or predictors, mediators and moderators, and control variables. The mediators and moderators are discussed in a different chapter, separately. Mediation is discussed in Chapter 15, and moderation is discussed in Chapter 16. In this section, I discuss the role of control variables.

Control variables, also known as covariates, are independent variables that influence a dependent variable but is not of a theoretical interest to the researchers in terms of theory testing. Its existence in a model is to capture extraneous influences that are not desirable because its inclusion can distort research findings pertaining to the researcher's theorized relationships. In Chapter 11, we have seen the case of a spurious correlation between children's palm sizes and their intelligence. To gauge the real correlation between palm size and intelligence, children's age must be controlled for. If we use a regression model to examine the effect of palm size on intelligence, then intelligence is treated as the dependent variable and palm size as the independent variable, where age should be included in the model as a control variable.

From a statistical perspective, the inclusion of a control variable in a multiple regression model helps eliminate the variation in the dependent variable associated with it. This, in turn, allows us to attribute the remaining variation in the dependent variable that is due to the independent variables that are the primary focus of the research.

As another example, suppose that a researcher aims to the examine the impact of consumers' waiting time on store satisfaction. However, if there are existing differences on the level of satisfaction between the older consumers and the younger consumers, the effect of waiting time on store satisfaction will be biased if age is ignored. Therefore, age could be a suitable control variable because pre-existing differences exist between the older and younger customers on their store satisfaction. With multiple regression, the variance in store satisfaction attributed to age can be controlled for, allowing us to isolate and examine the remaining variance in satisfaction that can be attributed to waiting time.

Consistent with this logic, the presence of a control variable means more than just being not the research focus, it influences how the roles of other independent variables are interpreted. You might have heard the phrase *ceteris paribus*. *Ceteris paribus* is a Latin phrase which means 'all other things being equal' or 'when everything else kept constant'.

Let us consider the following model:

$$StoreSatisfaction = \beta_0 + \beta_1 SubjectiveWaitingTime + \beta_2 Age + \varepsilon \tag{13.2}$$

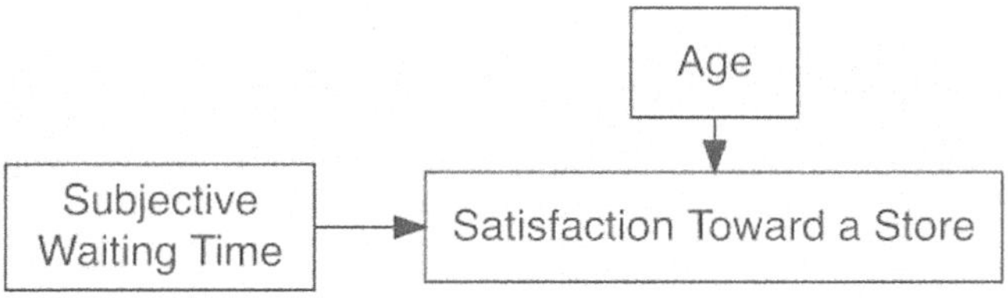

FIGURE 13.1
Waiting time affects satisfaction toward a store. Age is a control variable.

The model without an error term can be visualized in a diagram as displayed in Figure 13.1.

Age in Equation 13.2 serves as a control variable. The presence of *Age* enables us to say something like this: when *Age* is kept constant, the waiting time is positively related to store satisfaction. The phrase *when Age is kept constant* sounds ambiguous at first. What does that really mean? One way of keeping *Age* constant can be achieved by analysing data of groups of individuals of the same age, then we would be able to run a regression of store satisfaction on waiting time on a particular age group. As *Age* in a particular age group not varied, it would have no influence on the variation of store satisfaction. Controlling for *Age*, we would expect perceived negative waiting time to be negatively related to store satisfaction. That is, the longer they had waited in the queue, the more they were dissatisfied toward a store.

TO INCLUDE OR NOT TO INCLUDE

One of the methodological challenges that researchers often face when dealing with control variables is whether it is really necessary to include them. The recommendation is that the inclusion of control variables into a multiple regression model should be justified by a theory or thoughtful consideration. In fact, when in doubt, it is advisable to leave the control variables out (Becker et al. 2016; Spector & Brannick 2011; Carlson & Wu 2012). It is also advisable to run analyses with and without the control variables and compare the results (Becker et al. 2016). If the results are essentially the same, we can report the analysis without the control variables and include a statement indicating that their inclusion did not affect the initial results.

13.3 The Meaning of the Regression Coefficients

Like a regression coefficient in a simple regression model, the effect of independent variables on the dependent variable on a multiple regression model is captured by its regression coefficients. As there are more than one variable in the model, a regression coefficient associated with an independent variable in a multiple regression model is an estimate of the effect of the independent variable on the dependent variable when *ceteris paribus* holding other variables in the model constant.

PARTIAL REGRESSION COEFFICIENTS

Each regression coefficient in a multiple regression model is a partial regression coefficient. Why is it called a partial regression coefficient? This is because the coefficient is an estimate of the impact of its associated independent variable while removing the influence on the dependent variable of the other independent variables.

For an illustration, let us consider the hypothetical multiple regression model depicted in Equation 13.3 with its known coefficient estimates.

$$SatStore = 5.076 - 0.86WT - 0.01Age \quad (13.3)$$

where SatStore is satisfaction toward a store measured with a 7-point rating scale ranging from 1= very dissatisfied to 7 = very satisfied, which is a respond to a question: 'Please indicate how satisfied were you with this store'; SatEmp is a satisfaction toward service employees measured with a 7-point rating scale ranging from 1= very dissatisfied to 7 = very satisfied, which is a respond to a question: 'Please indicate how satisfied were you with the service employee of this store'; *WT* is a subjective waiting time measured in minutes, which is a respond to a statement 'How long do you time you had waited in the queue?'; and Age is the age of customers measured in years.

The coefficient estimate associated with *WT* or the partial regression coefficient is –0.86, which means that the effect of one point increase in the subjective waiting time will decrease the satisfaction score by 0.86 point, while holding *Age* constant. Similarly, if *Age* is increased by 1 point, the score on SatStore would go down by 0.01 point, while holding other *WT* in the model constant.

The partial regression coefficient for *WT* is –0.86. This coefficient can be found by removing the influence of *Age* on *WT* and use the remaining portion as the predictor of satisfaction.

13.3.1 SPSS Action

Data: store.sav

The following SPSS syntax shows how to obtain the partial regression coefficient associated with *WT* by conducting two regressions. In the first regression, *WT* is regressed on *Age*. The residual of the regression is saved and stored as RES_1. The residual RES_1 is the remaining part of *WT* that is not shared with *Age*. In the second regression, *SatStor e* is regressed on RES_1. In the regression output, the coefficient associated with RES_1 is the partial regression coefficient associated with *WT*.

```
REGRESSION
  /MISSING LISTWISE
  /STATISTICS COEFF OUTS R ANOVA
```

```
   /CRITERIA=PIN(.05) POUT(.10)
   /NOORIGIN
   /DEPENDENT wt
   /METHOD=ENTER age
   /SAVE RESID.
Execute.

REGRESSION
   /MISSING LISTWISE
   /STATISTICS COEFF OUTS R ANOVA
   /CRITERIA=PIN(.05) POUT(.10)
   /NOORIGIN
   /DEPENDENT satstore
   /METHOD=ENTER RES_1.
```

The regression output of the last step is displayed in

Coefficients[a]

Model		Unstandardized Coefficients B	Unstandardized Coefficients Std. Error	Standardized Coefficients Beta	t	Sig.
1	(Constant)	2.867	.055		51.986	<.001
	Unstandardized Residual	-.860	.053	-.906	-16.280	<.001

a. Dependent Variable: satstore

FIGURE 13.2
Output of the second regression. The partial regression coefficient associated with WT is –0.86.

13.3.2 R Action

The equivalent R code is given here:

```
library(ahdar)
dat <- store

# regress wt on age.
fit <- lm(wt ~ age, data = dat)

# extract the residuals and store to resid.
resid <- fit$residuals
```

```
# regress satstore on resid
fit2 <- lm(satstore ~ resid, data = dat)
summary(fit2)

Call:
lm(formula = satstore ~ resid, data = dat)
```

```
Residuals:
     Min        1Q    Median        3Q       Max
-1.02624  -0.18775  -0.03186   0.12705  1.15733

Coefficients:
            Estimate Std.  Error t  value    Pr(>|t|)
(Intercept)       2.86667  0.05514   51.99  <2e-16 ***
resid            -0.85967  0.05281  -16.28  <2e-16 ***
-
Signif. codes:  0 '***'  0.001 '**'  0.01 '*'  0.05 '.'  0.1 ' ' 1

Residual standard error: 0.4271 on 58 degrees of freedom
Multiple R-squared: 0.8204,      Adjusted R-squared: 0.8174
F-statistic:  265 on 1 and 58 DF, p-value: < 2.2e-16
```

13.4 Assumptions in Multiple Regression

The assumption in a simple regression model also applies to a multiple regression model. That is the expected form should be described by Equation 13.1, homoskedasticity, no autocorrelation, and no endogeneity. In addition to these, there is one more assumption in multiple regression that a simple regression model does not have, which is no *multicollinearity.*

Multicollinearity means high correlations among independent variables. The assumption in multiple regression is that the independent variables should not be highly correlated. I discuss multicollinearity issue in more details in Chapter 14.

13.5 Hierarchical Regression

When a regression model contains control variables, the common strategy that marketing researchers adopt to analyse the impact of an independent variable on a dependent variable is to perform a hierarchical regression analysis. A hierarchical regression analysis is a multiple regression analysis conducted in a step-by-step fashion. In a hierarchical regression analysis, the control variables are first entered into a model. That is, a dependent variable is first regressed on the control variables. This constitutes the first model. In the second step, the focal independent variables are entered. That is, a dependent variable is regressed on the control variables *and* the focal independent variables. This constitutes a second model. Because the control variables are also included in the second model, the first model is **nested** in the second model. In the second model, our objective is to find out whether the second model explains the dependent variable better than the first model. In other words, we want to examine whether the focal independent variables explain the dependent variable above and beyond the control variables that are already contained in the first model. Subsequently, the influence of the control variables on the dependent variable is analysed using the outputs of the first model. Next, the influence of the focal independent variables on the dependent variable are analysed using the outputs of the second model.

Conducting a hierarchical regression of model Equation 13.2, you have to run two regressions. In the first regression, *Store Satisfaction* is regression on *Age*. As there is only one independent variable, this is a simple linear regression model. In the second regression, *Store Satisfaction* is regressed on *Age* and *Subjective Waiting Time.*

13.5.1 SPSS Action

Data: store.sav

This section, I demonstrate how conduct a hierarchical regression analysis of model described by Equation 13.2 – examining the influence of *WT* and *SatEmp* on *SatStore* while controlling for *Age.*

Steps:

- Analyze →Regression → Linear.
- Insert *satstor e* into the dependent box.
- Insert *age* into the independent box.
- Click Next.
- In the second block, insert wt.
- Click Statistics, then tick R squared change.
- Click OK, and inspect the output windows.

Syntax

Clicking Paste instead of OK yielded the following script, which I provided in *hierachical.sps.*

```
REGRESSION
  /MISSING LISTWISE
  /STATISTICS COEFF OUTS R ANOVA CHANGE
  /CRITERIA=PIN(.05) POUT(.10)
  /NOORIGIN
  /DEPENDENT satstore
  /METHOD=ENTER age
  /METHOD=ENTER wt.
```

Model summary:

Model Summary

					Change Statistics				
Model	R	R Square	Adjusted R Square	Std. Error of the Estimate	R Square Change	F Change	df1	df2	Sig. F Change
1	.058[a]	.003	-.014	1.00633	.003	.194	1	58	.661
2	.908[b]	.824	.818	.42685	.820	265.382	1	57	<.001

a. Predictors: (Constant), age

b. Predictors: (Constant), age, wt

FIGURE 13.3
Model summary of a hierarchical regression.

Coefficients[a]

Model		Unstandardized Coefficients B	Std. Error	Standardized Coefficients Beta	t	Sig.
1	(Constant)	2.457	.938		2.620	.011
	age	.012	.027	.058	.440	.661
2	(Constant)	5.076	.429		11.830	<.001
	age	-.010	.012	-.049	-.875	.385
	wt	-.860	.053	-.912	-16.291	<.001

a. Dependent Variable: satstore

FIGURE 13.4
Model coefficients of a hierarchical regression.

From the outputs displayed in Figure 13.3, $R^2_{Model1} = 0.003$, $R^2_{Model2} = 0.824$, and R-square change $R^2_{Model1} - R^2_{Model2} = \Delta R^2 = 0.820$. This ΔR^2 is associated with $\Delta F(1,57) = 265.382$, corresponding to a very small p-value ($p<0.0001$), which means that adding *wt* in the second model provides a significant improvement over the first model. Looking at results displayed in Figure 13.4, variable *age* was not significant in explaining store satisfaction ($p=0.385$), whereas *wt* has a negative influence on store satisfaction ($b = -0.860$).

13.5.2 R Action

Performing a hierarchical regression is made easier with `stargazer()` R package. It produces regression outputs that are easily modified for publications. Testing the significance of R-square change can be performed by using the anova() function.

```
library(ahdar)
library(stargazer)

dat <- store

lm1 <- lm(satstore ~ age, data = dat)
lm2 <- lm(satstore ~ age + wt, data = dat)
```

```
stargazer(lm1, lm2, type = "text", single.row=TRUE)
##
## ===================================================================
##                              Dependent variable:
##
##                                   satstore
##                            (1)              (2)
##
## age                   0.012 (0.027)    -0.010 (0.012)
## wt                                     -0.860*** (0.053)
```

```
## Observations                  60                         60
## R2                           0.003                      0.824
## Adjusted R2                 -0.014                      0.818
## Residual Std. Error         1.006 (df = 58)        0.427 (df = 57)
## F Statistic                 0.194 (df = 1; 58) 133.230***(df = 2; 57)
## ================================================================
## Note:                                    *p<0.1; **p<0.05; ***p<0.01
```

Now, let us test whether the second model is better than the first, using the R function `anova()`:

```
anova(lm1, lm2)
```

```
## Analysis of Variance Table ##
## Model 1: satstore ~ age
## Model 2: satstore ~ age + wt
##     Res.Df RSS Df Sum of Sq     F      Pr(>F) ## 1   58 58.737
## 2   57 10.385    1      48.352 265.38 < 2.2e-16 *** ## ---
## Signif. codes:   0 '***' 0.001 '**' 0.01 '*' 0.05 '.' 0.1 ' ' 1
```

The results obtained are identical to those produced by SPSS.

13.6 Path Model

Multiple regression analysis can be used to test series of hypotheses represented by a path model. A research framework displayed in Figure 13.5 is an example of a path model that depicts relationship among subjective waiting time (*WT*), satisfaction toward service employees (*SatEmp*), and satisfaction toward a store (*SatStore*).

In a path model, relationships among constructs are described via multiple paths or arrows. Each path represents one hypothesis. That is, each path represents a researcher's idea about how a construct at the beginning of an arrow relates – as either positively or negatively, to another construct that is placed at the end of the arrow. The path model in Figure 13.5 contains three hypotheses where *Age* is treated as a control variable that needs not a hypothesis to predict its influence on the dependent variable.

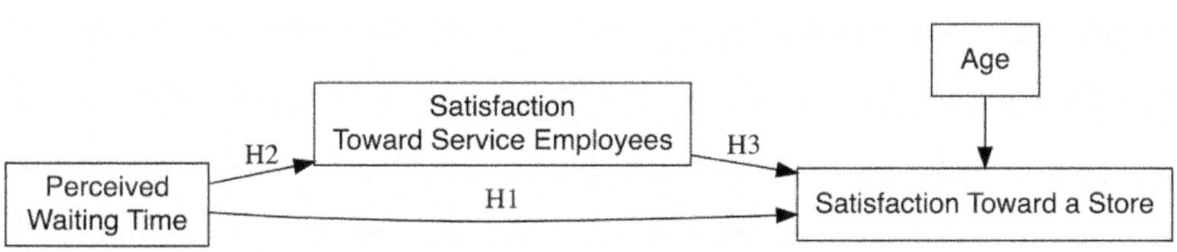

FIGURE 13.5
An example of a path model.

H1: Waiting time is negatively related to Satisfaction toward a store.

H2: Waiting time is negatively related to satisfaction toward service employees.

H3. Satisfaction toward service employees is positively related to satisfaction toward a store.

The hypotheses in the path model are tested using two regression models:

$$SatEmp = \beta_0 + \beta_1 * WT + error \tag{13.4}$$

$$SatStore = \beta_0 + \beta_1 * WT + \beta_2 * SatEmp + \beta_3 * Age + error \tag{13.5}$$

Figure 13.6 shows how the regression results are presented in the same path model. The number adjacent to the paths are regression coefficients – these can be reported as either the standardized or the unstandardized forms. In the figure, I reported the standardized coefficients.

Satisfaction Toward Service Employees has a unique position in the model – it is affected by *Subjective Waiting Time* as well as affects *Satisfaction Toward a Store.* Its role in the model explains one-way *Subjective Waiting Time* influence *Satisfaction Toward a Store. Subjective Waiting Time* can influence *Satisfaction Toward a Store* indirectly via *Satisfaction Toward Service Employees.* Such a role is known in literature as a mediating variable and the corresponding statistical analysis refers to as a mediation analysis. I discuss this topic in more details in Chapter 15.

IMPORTANT

The development of path analysis is widely credited to Sewall Wright (Wright 1934) who was also known for his work on population genetics. Sewall Wright used path analysis as a method to study the causal-effect relations among variables. According to Pearl & MacKenzie (2018, p. 307), 'Burks may actually have invented path diagrams independently of Sewall Wright.' Nowadays, regression-based path analysis is not considered as the best approach in causal modelling. To treat the relation between perceived waiting on store satisfaction as a causal relationship, an experiment might be the best approach. In this case, we would need to show that the causal effect of the manipulation of perceived waiting on store satisfaction. For instance, if we can establish that there are differences in the satisfaction score between group of individuals that were asked to wait for a short time and those that were asked to wait for a longer time, and no other factors influence satisfaction score, then a causal effect of subjective waiting time can be concluded with confidence.

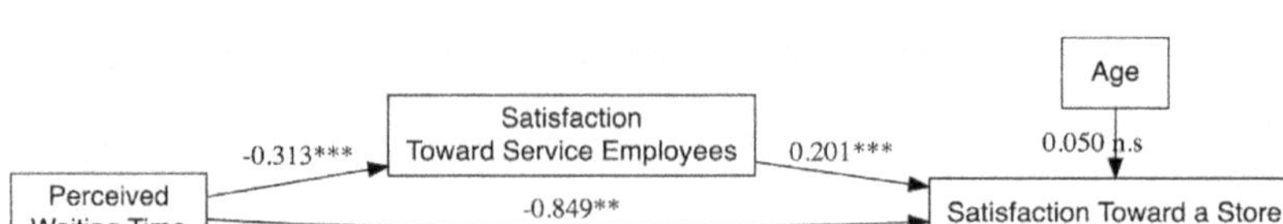

FIGURE 13.6
Path model with coefficient estimates obtained from two regressions.

13.6.1 R Code

R code to draw Figure 13.6:

```
DiagrammeR::grViz("digraph{

   graph [rankdir = LR]

node [fontname = Helvetica, shape = rectangle]

      wt [label = 'Perceived\nWaiting Time ']
      se [label = 'Satisfaction\nToward Service Employees']
      age [label = 'Age']
      ss [label = 'Satisfaction Toward a Store']

    edge[]
      wt -> se [label='-0.313***']
wt -> ss [label='-0.849**']
      se -> ss [label='0.201***']
      age -> ss [label='0.050 n.s']

{rank=same;ss;age}

    }")
```

13.7 Steps in Building a Model

We can summarize the steps in testing hypotheses using a multiple regression model as follows:

1. Define your research objectives and identify key constructs. In this step, you need to identity what the independent variables (IV) and the dependent variable (DV) are. Consider potential variables that can be treated as control variables.
2. Formulate your hypothesis. When you intend to use a multiple regression model, you are more likely to have multiple hypotheses. In formulating a hypothesis, you must specify the direction (i.e. negative or positive) of the relationship between each independent variable and the dependent variable. In other words, you must hypothesize the expected signs of the regression coefficient associated with each independent variable. Step 1 and Step 2 are often carried out in parallel.
3. Collect data. Collect data on the independent variables and dependent variable. If you use a survey, ensure that there are no missing values on the data. Treatment of missing values are a challenging topic, which unfortunately is beyond the scope of this book.
4. Prepare your data. This steps, you must clean your data, which include dealing with missing values, checking the actual values in the dataset, and inspecting potential outliers, e.g. using a scatter plot.

5. Specify your regression model, which includes inspecting the pattern and sign of the correlation between each of the independent variable and the dependent variable.
6. Check model assumptions. Your regression model should satisfy the regression assumption (e.g. no multicollinearity, homoskedasticity). The next chapter is devoted to checking these regression assumptions.
7. Conduct hypothesis tests to determine whether the regression coefficient associated with the independent variables are significant. You can read the p-value reported by a SPSS or R. If the p-value is less than 0.05, then regression coefficient is significant. This step includes checking the sign of the regression coefficient (does it conform to the hypothesized sign?).
8. Communicate your findings. Write down your results and communicate them in a concise and clear way. It usually takes only one or two paragraph to report your findings.
9. Draw conclusions. Tell your readers what the findings mean to them. For those who are primarily interested in theory, tell them how your results contribute to a deeper theoretical understanding of how the independent variables relate to the dependent variable. If the relationship between a construct and other construct has been known before, would you be able to say that the replication is need to increase the generalizability of the theory? If your readers are practitioners, tell them what they can do in practice in light of your findings. Can you offer actionable insights that can serve as a basis of informed practices?

13.8 Summary

We have discussed multiple regression model. A key decision in building a multiple regression model is in selecting sets of independent variables, which can pose a significant challenge as one may be tempted to include more independent variables that are not necessary or might miss out important variables in the model. Including more independent variables in the model will increase R^2 despite the variables are not explaining much of the variation in the dependent variable. One must not have a goal of maximizing R^2 in regression analysis. The best advice for selecting independent variables is to include independent variables that can be justified by a theory or learning from what others have done through reading relevant literature.

13.9 Further Reading

The following are articles that I think should be on the radar of those who are interested in control variables:

Becker, T. E., Atinc, G., Breaugh, J. A., Carlson, K. D., Edwards, J. R. & Spector, P. E. (2016), 'Statistical control in correlational studies: 10 essential recommendations for organizational researchers', *Journal of Organizational Behavior* **37**(2), 157–167.

Bernerth, J. B. & Aguinis, H. (2016), 'A critical review and best-practice recommendations for control variable usage', *Personnel Psychology* **69**(1), 229–283. This articles reviews the use of control variables in applied research and offers a decision tree for when to include control variables.

Breaugh, J. A. (2006), 'Rethinking the control of nuisance variables in theory testing', *Journal of Business and Psychology* **20**, 429–443. This article is helpful in under- standing the use of correlation, especially the semipartial correlation, in the context of control variables in a multiple regression analysis.

Carlson, K. D. & Wu, J. (2012), 'The illusion of statistical control: Control variable practice in management research', *Organizational Research Methods* **15**(3), 413–435. This article provides guidelines about the inclusion of control variables in empirical studies.

Spector, P. E. & Brannick, M. T. (2011), 'Methodological urban legends: The misuse of statistical control variables', *Organizational Research Methods* **14**(2), 287–305. This article has been cited more than 1200 citations and can be considered a classic paper on control variables.

13.10 Review Questions

1. What is meant by ceteris paribus condition? How is it related to multiple regression?
2. What do we care about multicollinearity issue?
3. When is it appropriate to conduct a hierarchical regression?

13.11 Exercises

1. Using *store.sav* data, uses SPSS to perform a hierarchical regression analysis of model in Equation 13.5 where Age is treated as a control variable.
2. Replicate the analysis using stargazer() package in R.

14

Regression Diagnostics

Regression diagnostics are set of activities or procedures to evaluate a regression model and determine whether it satisfies regression assumptions. This chapter focuses on two assumptions that can be violated when working with data collected at a fixed point in time (i.e. cross-sectional data), namely, constant residuals (homoskedasticity) and no multicollinearity. Violation of another assumption which requires a predictor to be uncorrelated with an error term is discussed separately in Section 17. The chapter explains how to use the HeteroskedasticityV3 macro to assess the homoskedasticity assumption and when to use the heteroskedasticity-adjusted standard errors. The use of SPSS and R in assessing the multicollinearity problems are explained.

Learning Objectives:

- Understand the concept of heteroskedasticity and multicollinearity.
- Know how to use the HeteroskedasticityV3 macro and interpret its outputs to detect heteroskedasticity.
- Know how to detect a multicollinearity problem and remedy it.

14.1 Homoskedasticity and Heteroskedasticity

Let us return to Figure 12.5. The normal distribution curves at $Adv = 3K$ and $Adv = 5K$ are identical. They have the same normal shapes because the variances of the two distributions are the same. This also implies that their residual variances are also the same. These constant residuals are called homoskedastic, also spelt as homoscedastic (using 'c' instead of 'k'). Homoskedastic residuals satisfies the regression's homoskedasticity assumption, which states that regression residuals should have the same spreads across any values of independent variables.

Compare these conditional distributions with those in Figure 14.1. Unlike the normal curves in Figure 12.5, the two normal curves in Figure 14.1 do not have the same variance. The distribution of satisfaction scores of loyal customers is more spread out than that of non-loyal customers. This also implies that the residuals of loyal customers are more spread out than that of the non-loyal customer. These residuals are called heteroskedastic residuals, whose existence violates the homoskedasticity assumption required in regression. When residuals are heteroskedastic, we can no longer rely on the standard regression outputs.

 DOI: 10.4324/9781003407225-18

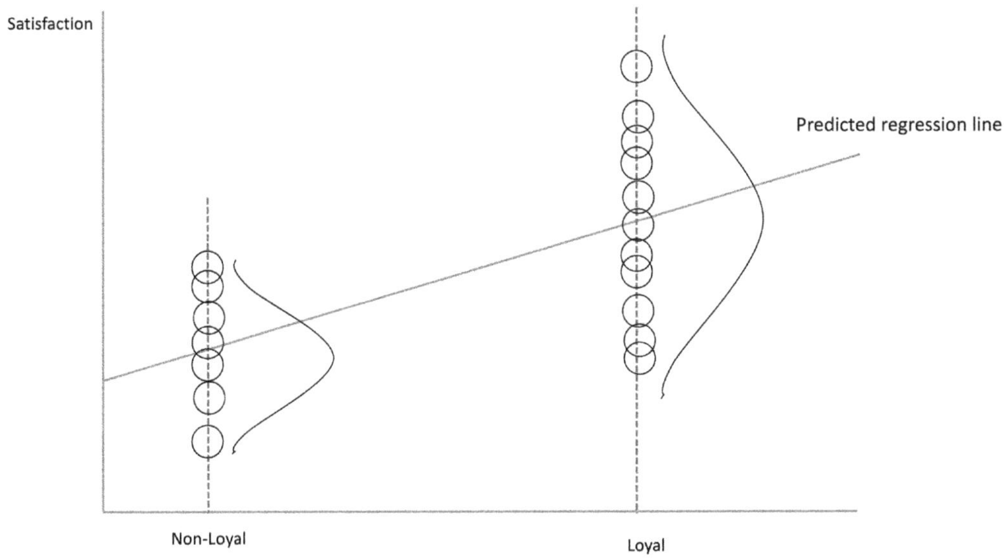

FIGURE 14.1
Heteroskedasticity exists. Satisfaction scores of loyal customers are more spread out than that of non-loyal customers.

14.1.1 Consequences of Heteroskedasticity

If regression residuals are heteroskedastic and we run a regression as usual in SPSS, the standard errors reported by SPSS are wrong. As a consequence, the t-value, p-value, and confidence intervals for b_0 and b_1 are wrong. If they are all wrong, our research conclusion is wrong. For example, non-significant relationship in a population can be significant in a sample when heteroskedasticity is present.

14.1.2 How to Detect Heteroskedasticity

Heteroskedasticity can be assessed in two ways, which can be done simultaneously using my `HeteroskedasticityV3` macro (Daryanto 2020*b*). The first method is by inspecting the plot of residuals against the independent variable or against the predicted values of the dependent variable. This is a rather subjective method but a good decision aid to start with. The second method is by conducting statistical tests, among which are the popular Breusch-Pagan and Koenker test. The null hypothesis of the tests is that error terms or residuals are homoskedastic. If p-value of the test is smaller than 0.05, we reject the null hypothesis and conclude that the error terms are likely to be heteroskedastic. Because we want to satisfy the homoskedasticity assumption, we want to have a large p-value. This means we do not want to reject the null hypothesis. If the null hypothesis is not rejected, we can conduct a regression analysis as usual without having to adjust the standard errors of the regression coefficients. The `HeteroskedasticityV3` macro (Daryanto 2020*b*) produces p-value associated with the tests and the plot of residual against the fitted values, which is called as **yfitted** in the outputs.

HOMOSKEDASTIC OR HETEROSKEDASTIC RESIDUALS?

In practice, it is more common to have heteroskedastic than homoskedastic residuals. Modern views regards homoskedastic residuals as an exception (Stock & Watson 2015).

14.1.3 Remedy

A simple remedy to address the heteroskedasticity problem is to adjust the standard errors of the regression coefficients using the heteroskedasticity-adjusted standard errors, or HC standard error, for short. Others prefer to use the term robust instead of adjusted, e.g. heteroskedasticity-robust standard errors. There are several types of these HC standard errors, namely, HC0 (or Eicker- Huber-White standard errors), HC1, HC2, HC3, and HC4. When we open the `HeteroskedasticityV3` macro, we can select one of these HC standard errors. HC4 is widely recommended, which is the latest version of the types (Daryanto 2020*b*). The recommendation is that we report our regression results with and without the adjusted standard errors.

14.1.4 SPSS Action: HeteroskedasticityV3 Macro

Data: satisfaction.sav

Download the HeteroskedasticityV3.spd macro from this website: https://www.tqmp.o rg/Vignettes/vol16–5/v008/index.html. To download the file, on the website, click Appendix. A folder containing the macro will be downloaded automatically. Please check your download folder in your computer. Alternatively, you can download the macro from the book's online support.

For an illustration, let estimate this model again.

$$Satisfaction = \beta_0 + \beta_1 Loyal + error \tag{14.1}$$

- Analyze → Regression → HeteroskedasticityV3 by Ahmad Daryanto.
- Insert *Sales* to the Outcome variable box.
- Insert Loyal to the Explanatory variable box.
- Leave the default HC4 as it is.
- Click OK and inspect the outputs. Do not click Paste because long list of syntax will be output to a new syntax file.

See Figure 14.2

The Macro's Outputs

The macro presents the regression results with and without the adjusted standard errors.

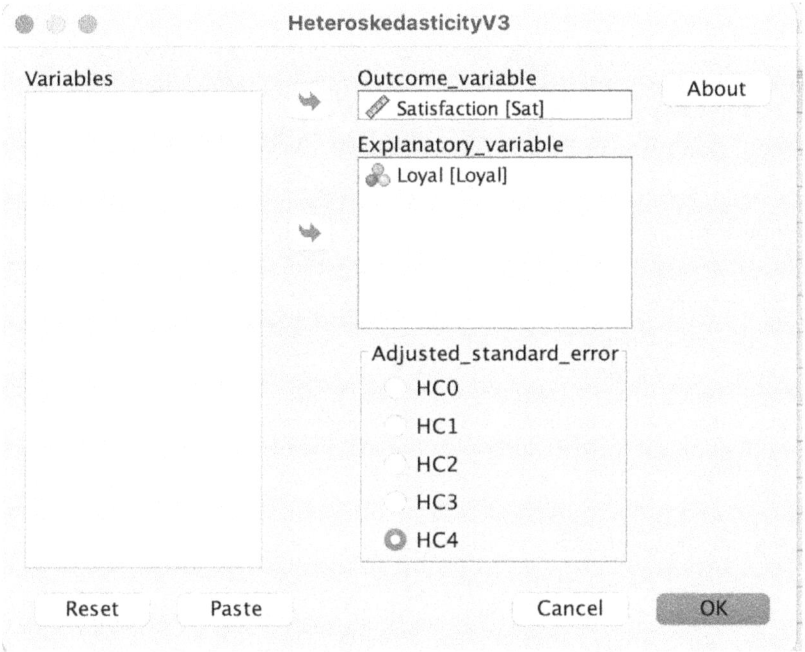

FIGURE 14.2
HeteroskedasticityV3 macro.

As we can see from the figure, the first part presents the standard regression outputs. The second part presents the regression results with adjusted standard errors. In both parts, the regression coefficients are the same. As expected, the standard errors are slightly different for the intercept, which is smaller in the adjusted standard error (se = 0.0603 vs. se(HC4) = 0.0334). In this particular example, Loyal is significant with and without adjusted standard errors. Despite minimal differences, we still need to decide which part of the outputs will be used, with or without adjusted standard errors? We have to look at the next outputs.

Statistical Tests

The macro conducts two tests called the Breusch-Pagan and Koenker test, and produces a test statistic called LM (Lagrange multiplier) and its associated p-value. In this example, the LM statistics of both tests are significant as both p-values are smaller than 0.05. Therefore, the null hypothesis of homoskedasticity is rejected. This means that heteroskedasticity is likely to be present in the data. Based on this result, we have to use the regression results with the adjusted standard errors.

The results of the Breusch-Pagan and Koenker test can be different. For example, the p-value of the Breusch-Pagan test can be significant while it is not for the Koenker test. The Breusch-Pagan test is more stringent than the Koenker test, which assumes that the residuals are normally distributed. When two results are different, the Koenker test is more preferable as it is robust against the departure from normality, especially if sample is large.

```
Run MATRIX procedure:

 written by Ahmad Daryanto

Original Regression model:

Dependent variable
 Sat

R-square
      .912

OLS outputs
                  b          se          t        sig      95%LB      95%UB
constant     2.9790       .0603    49.4180      .0000     2.8602     3.0979
Loyal        3.8503       .0853    45.1633      .0000     3.6822     4.0184

OLS outputs with heteroskedasticity-robust standard errors:
                  b          se          t        sig      95%LB      95%UB
constant     2.9790       .0334    89.1141      .0000     2.9131     3.0450
Loyal        3.8503       .0853    45.1633      .0000     3.6822     4.0184

* Note: standard error is HC4 variant
```

FIGURE 14.3
Outputs of the heteroskedasticity macro. It shows the regression results with and without the adjusted standard errors.

```
------- Breusch-Pagan and Koenker test statistics and sig-values --------
               LM         Sig
BP         47.9524       .0000
Koenker    26.0179       .0000

Null hypothesis: heteroskedasticity not present (homoskedasticity).

If sig-value less than 0.05, reject the null hypothesis.

Note: Breusch-Pagan test is a large sample test and assumes the residuals to be normally distributed.
```

FIGURE 14.4
Results of the Breusch-Pagan and Koenker tests.

Residual Plot

The plot of residuals against the fitted values is displayed in the last output of the macro. From the output, it is very obvious that the distribution of the residuals is not constant. The residuals of the loyal customer group are more spread out than that of the non-loyal customer group, which confirmed the results of the Breusch-Pagan and Koenker tests.

14.1.5 R Action

Data: Satisfaction.sav

The objective of this section is to show how to use R functions for testing for the potential presence of the heteroskedasticity in our data. If heteroskedasticity exists, our remedy is to correct for the standard errors of the coefficient estimates as an adjustment for the heteroskedasticity.

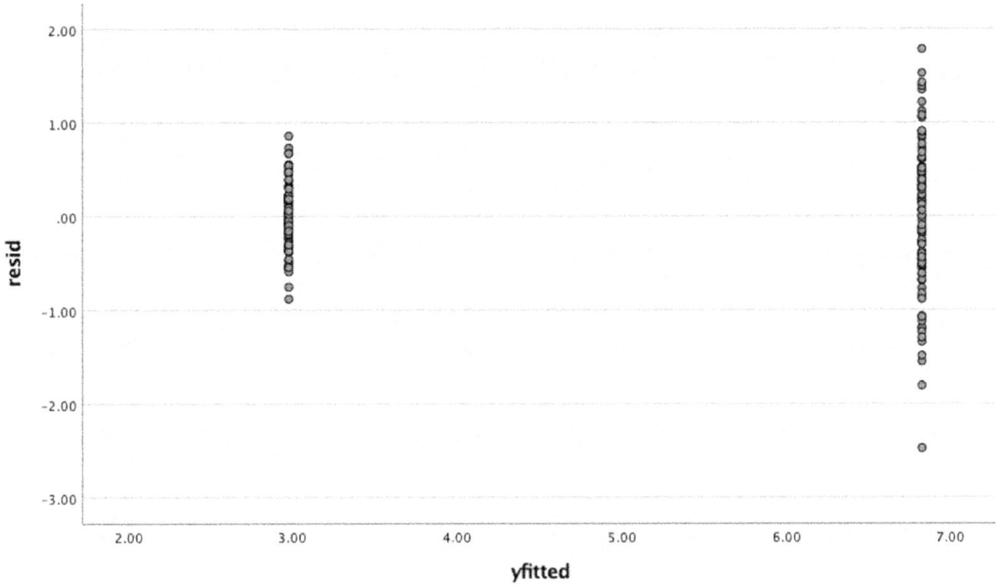

FIGURE 14.5
A scatter plot of the fitted values vs. residuals.

```
library(haven)
library(lmtest)
library(sandwich)
library(ahdar)

rm(list=ls()) # start from a clean slate.

# Reading data from ahdar package.
dat <- satisfaction

lm_model <- lm(Sat ~ Loyal, data = dat)
summary(lm_model)
```

```
Call:
lm(formula = Sat ~ Loyal, data = dat)

Residuals:
     Min         1Q    Median          3Q        Max
-2.47438 -0.32043   0.04031     0.33946    1.78460

Coefficients:
            Estimate Std. Error t value Pr(>|t|)
(Intercept)  2.97904    0.06028    49.42  <2e-16 ***
Loyal        3.85027    0.08525    45.16  <2e-16 ***
-
Signif. codes:    0 '***' 0.001 '**' 0.01 '*' 0.05 '.' 0.1 ' ' 1
```

```
Residual standard error: 0.6028 on 198 degrees of freedom
Multiple R-squared:  0.9115,    Adjusted R-squared:   0.9111
F-statistic:   2040 on 1 and 198 DF,   p-value: < 2.2e-16
```

We can product the plot of fitted values against the residuals to see whether the variance of the residuals are constants across Loyal – similar to that of Figure 14.5. We use plot() function. plot(lm_model) would produces several plots. We add an argument, which=c(1,1)) to select the fitted values vs. residuals plot.

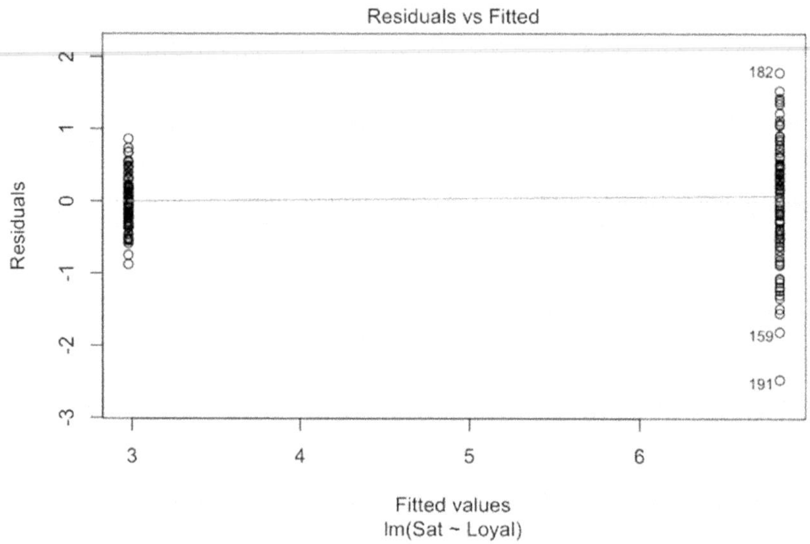

FIGURE 14.6
Fitted values against residuals.

```
plot(lm_model, which=c(1,1))
```

Next, let us conduct the Breusch-Pagan test:

```
# BP test
bp <- bptest(Sat ~ Loyal, varformula = NULL, studentize = FALSE
, data = dat)
bp
```

```
Breusch-Pagan test data:   Sat ~ Loyal
BP = 47.952, df = 1, p-value = 4.367e-12
To conduct a Koenker's test, set studentize = TRUE:
```

```
# Koenker test
kt <- bptest(Sat ~ Loyal, varformula = NULL, studentize = TRUE,
data = dat)
kt
```

```
studentized Breusch-Pagan test data:     Sat ~ Loyal
BP = 26.018, df = 1, p-value = 3.383e-07
```

The results of the BP and Koenker tests show that the null hypothesis of homoskedasticity were rejected. Next, we adjust the standard error using HC4. Calculate robust standard errors and compute their 95% confidence interval:

```
coeftest(lm_model,vcov = vcovHC(lm_model,type="HC4"))

t test of coefficients:

            Estimate Std. Error t value  Pr(>|t|)
(Intercept) 2.979039   0.033430  89.114 < 2.2e-16 ***
Loyal       3.850275   0.085252  45.163 < 2.2e-16 ***
-
Signif. codes:     0 '***' 0.001 '**' 0.01 '*' 0.05 '.' 0.1 ' ' 1
#compute 95%CI for robust se
covariance <- vcovHC(lm_model, type = "HC4")
t.critical <-qt(c(0.025,0.975),summary(lm_model)$df[2])
se <- sqrt(diag(covariance))
robust.ci <-coef(lm_model) + se %o% t.critical
```

```
robust.ci
```

	[,1]	[,2]
(Intercept)	2.913115	3.044962
Loyal	3.682156	4.018394

14.2 Multicollinearity

Multicollinearity refers to a high correlation among the independent variables of a regression model. A correlation coefficient greater than 0.9 is generally considered high; however, $r > 0.7$ can be an indicative of a multicollinearity problem. Multicollinearity causes the standard errors of the regression coefficients to be inflated, which makes the research conclusion to be misleading. For example, a regression coefficient can be insignificant when in fact it is in a population. For an illustration, if our regression results show us that satisfaction would not affect loyalty and we are not aware that the model suffers from a multicollinearity problem, we would ignore the true state of the relationship in the population that in fact satisfaction does affect loyalty. Furthermore, when multicollinearity exists, it is difficult to assess the relative importance of a variable while keeping another variable constant because it is difficult to assess the effect of one variable while isolating the effect of other variables as they are highly correlated. For example, if perceived product quality is highly correlated with perceived service quality, knowing the effect of perceived product quality alone on satisfaction would be difficult as the relationship is also contaminated by perceived service quality.

One of the frequently used diagnostic tools to assess multicollinearity is the variance inflation factor (*VIF*), which can be calculated for each predictor in a regression model. *VIF* measures how much the variance of the regression estimate associated with a predictor is inflated as compared to when the predictor is not correlated with other predictors in the model.

To understand the calculation of *VIF*, we have to know the concept of *Tolerance* because VIF is the inverse of *Tolerance* ($VIF = 1/Tolerance$). Tolerance is the percentage of variation in an independent variable that cannot be explained by other independent variables. If R^2 is the percentage of variation in an independent variable, then $Tolerance = 1 - R^2$. Thus, the *VIF* associated with the $kt\,h$ independent variable in a multiple regression model with several predictors can be written as:

$$VIF_k = \frac{1}{\left(1 - R_k^2\right)} = \frac{1}{Tolerance_k} \tag{14.2}$$

where R_k^2 is the R^2 produced by a regression of the $kt\,h$ variable in model on the remaining independent variables in the model. As mentioned, *VIF* indicates how much the variance of the regression estimate associated with a predictor is inflated due to its correlation with other predictors. The VIF value can be interpreted this way: if the *VIF* associated with a predictor is equal to 10 (i.e. Tolerance = 0.1), that means that the variance of the regression estimate associated with the predictor is 10 times higher than it would have been if the predictor had been uncorrelated with the other predictors in the model.

The largest *VIF* value exceeding 10 is often considered as a serious sign of a multicollinearity problem (Kutner et al. 2005). Others impose a more stringent value such as 5 (Studenmund 2014) or even 3 (Hair et al. 2009). The thresholds for the VIF values are rule of thumbs. They need to be interpreted 'in the context of other factors that influence the stability of the estimates of the *i*th regression coefficient' (O'brien 2007, p. 685).

For an illustration, consider data consisting 10 cases displayed in Figure 14.7. The data (collinearity.sav) is available to download from the book website.

	X	Z	Zadd	Y
1	.17	-.81	-.98	.37
2	.18	.57	-.40	.88
3	.82	-.92	1.33	2.42
4	.39	-.15	-.63	.97
5	-1.07	-1.12	-2.64	-1.20
6	-1.43	-.35	-3.57	.58
7	-.27	.73	-1.07	1.24
8	2.21	.29	3.51	3.18
9	.08	.52	1.33	2.29
10	-1.07	1.24	.75	.19

FIGURE 14.7
A hypothetical data of four variables, X, Z, Zadd, and Y (collinearity.sav). X and Z are uncorrelated. X and Zadd are correlated. Y is used as a dependent variable in regression.

X is uncorrelated with *Z* and highly correlated with *Zadd* with the correlation is greater than 0.8. In fact, *Zadd* is calculated as $Z + X + e$, where e is a standard normal random variable with mean 0 and variance 1. *Y* is the dependent variable.

Regressing *Y* on *X* and *Z* produces significant *X* and non-significant *Z* (see Figure 14.8). The VIF values of associated with both predictors that are uncorrelated to each other are 1 (their Tolerance are also 1; see the two right columns of the table). As Tolerance is equal to 1, the variation in *X* is fully unexplained by the variation by *Z*, which is another way of saying that they are uncorrelated.

Now, let us look at the results of regressing *Y* on *X* and *Zadd*. We are already suspicious that the result will suffer from a multicollinearity problem. The regression result is displayed in Figure 14.9 showing that both predictors are not significant (see Figure 14.9). Although the VIF value associated with each predictor is 2.833, which is below the recommended threshold, the model suffers from the multicollinearity problem – both predictors are highly correlated with $r > 0.8$. If we look at the standard error of the coefficient *X*, it is nearly twice as large as the standard error of the previous one. In this situation, the high correlation between the two predictors, as well as the non-significant *X* that is expected to be significant, are good indications of casting our doubt on the regression results.

14.2.1 SPSS Action

Data: store.sav

In this section, I am going to show how to produce the VIF values with SPSS, which we have seen previously. We consider again the influence of the subjective waiting time (*WT*) and satisfaction toward employees (*SatEmp*) and age (*Age*) on satisfaction toward *SatStore*. Respondents who waited long in the queue might give a lower rating

Coefficients[a]

Model		Unstandardized Coefficients		Standardized Coefficients			Collinearity Statistics	
		B	Std. Error	Beta	t	Sig.	Tolerance	VIF
1	(Constant)	1.092	.251		4.353	.003		
	X	.952	.248	.798	3.833	.006	1.000	1.000
	Z	.391	.334	.244	1.172	.280	1.000	1.000

a. Dependent Variable: Y

FIGURE 14.8
Regressing Y on X and Z, with X and Z being uncorrelated, resulting in the VIF values of 1 for both.

Coefficients[a]

Model		Unstandardized Coefficients		Standardized Coefficients			Collinearity Statistics	
		B	Std. Error	Beta	t	Sig.	Tolerance	VIF
1	(Constant)	1.153	.255		4.519	.003		
	X	.551	.417	.462	1.323	.227	.353	2.833
	Zadd	.257	.215	.418	1.196	.271	.353	2.833

a. Dependent Variable: Y

FIGURE 14.9
Regressing Y on X and Zadd, with X and Zadd being highly correlated, resulting in the VIF values of 2.833 for both. Both predictors are not significant.

on satisfaction toward employees (e.g. they could have done something to reduce the queue length, or speed up the process in the counter):

- Click Analyze → Regression → Linear.
- Insert *satstore* to the Dependent box.
- Insert *satemp, wt, age* to the Independent(s) box.
- Click Statistics and tick 'Collinearity diagnostics'.
- Click OK or click Paste if you want to work with a syntax file.
- Inspect the coefficient table in the output (see Figure 14.10).

```
REGRESSION
  /MISSING LISTWISE
  /STATISTICS COEFF OUTS R ANOVA COLLIN TOL
  /CRITERIA=PIN(.05) POUT(.10)
  /NOORIGIN
  /DEPENDENT satstore
  /METHOD=ENTER satemp wt age.
```

Tolerance = 1/ VIF

Coefficients[a]

Model		Unstandardized Coefficients B	Std. Error	Standardized Coefficients Beta	t	Sig.	Collinearity Statistics Tolerance	VIF
1	(Constant)	3.880	.497		7.814	<.001		
	satemp	.207	.054	.201	3.824	<.001	.902	1.109
	wt	-.800	.050	-.849	-16.051	<.001	.891	1.122
	age	-.010	.010	-.050	-.997	.323	.986	1.014

a. Dependent Variable: satstore

VIF values are below 10, thus multicollinearity is not an issue

FIGURE 14.10
Tolerance and VIF values.

SPSS printed two additional columns as a result of ticking 'Collinearity diagnostic', one of which is the VIF column that contains the VIF values associated with each independent variable. As we can see from Figure 14.10, the VIF values are very small; thus, multicollinearity is not be a concern.

14.2.2 R Action

Data: store.sav

Let us first run a multiple regression with the lm() function and output the results using stargazer() function.

```
library(haven)
library(stargazer)
library(ahdar)
rm(list=ls()) # start from a clean slate.
dat <- store
```

```
lm_model <- lm(satstore ~ satemp + wt + age, data = dat)
stargazer(lm_model, type = "text", single.row=TRUE)
```

```
===============================================
                         Dependent variable:
                              satstore
satemp                     0.207*** (0.054)
wt                         -0.800*** (0.050)
age                        -0.010 (0.010)
Constant                   3.880*** (0.497)
Observations                      60
R2                              0.860
Adjusted R2                     0.853
Residual Std. Error         0.383 (df = 56)
F Statistic              114.920*** (df = 3; 56)
===============================================
Note:  *p < 0.1; **p < 0.05; ***p < 0.01
```

To calculate VIF values, we have to rely on another package: car() library, that has a vif() function. Now, let us use the function to calculate the VIF values associated with each of the independent variable:

```
# Load the car library
library(car)
```

```
Loading required package: carData
```

```
# Calculate the VIF
round(vif(lm_model), 3) # round to 3 dp
```

```
satemp    wt     age
1.109  1.122   1.014
```

14.2.3 Remedy

There are three common ways to deal with multicollinearity. *First,* we can omit one or more highly correlated independent variables. For example, suppose that perceived product quality is explained by both brand image (BI) and product image (PI). However, if BI and PI are highly correlated, we drop one of them (either BI or PI) from the model.

Second, we can create a composite variable by averaging variables that are highly correlated. The new variable is the one that is used as an independent variable in a regression model. The drawback of averaging is that some information is lost and the meaning of the single variable is unclear. In this case, the interpretation of the meaning of the regression coefficient associated with the single variable is also unclear. Another way of creating a composite variable that is more meaningful than taking the average is by conducting a principal component analysis discussed in Chapter 21. Compared to averaging, PCA will retain most of the information from data when creating a new variable. In averaging, the original variables have equal contribution to the creation of the new variables, which is not the case in PCA. In PCA, the single variable is the weighted linear combination of the original variables. This means that the contributions of the original variables to the creation of the new variable are not the same: some original variables have more impact on the new variable than the other original variables.

Third, the model that suffers with multicollinearity can be used for prediction purposes only. For instance, we use the model to predict individuals' satisfaction score. However, the model that suffers from multicollinearity cannot be used for theory testing. For example, we cannot use the model to examine to what extent that subjective waiting time affect satisfaction because the regression coefficient associated with subjective waiting time will be biased.

14.3 Summary

In this chapter, we have discussed situations that lead to a biased in the estimates of the regression coefficients: heteroskedasticity – violating the constant variance or homoskedasticity assumption, and multicollinearity – high correlation among the predictor variables. The remedy for the heteroskedasticity situation suggested is to adjust the standard error of the regression coefficients. One of the remedies widely implemented by researchers in dealing with multicollinearity is to reduce the number of predictors into a few variables using principal component analysis, which is a topic of Chapter 21.

14.4 Further Reading

Daryanto, A. (2020), 'Tutorial on heteroskedasticity using heteroskedasticityV3 SPSS macro', *The Quantitative Methods for Psychology* **16**(5), 8–20. The section on homoskedasticity in this chapter is largely based on this article. The explanation in the article is more expanded than the section's.

Fox, J. (2019), *Regression diagnostics: An introduction*, Sage Publications. This is a definitive guide on regression diagnostics, which covers more material in depth, such as identifying outliers and influential observations. The presentation relies heavily on mathematical expressions and data, so reading this book would be challenging without a strong affinity for mathematical formulas.

14.5 Review Questions

1. What is an heteroskedasticity problem?
2. What is the null hypothesis in the Breusch-Pagan and Koenker tests?
3. Why must standard errors be adjusted if heteroskedasticity is detected?
4. Explain why multicollinearity problem can arise.
5. What are the criteria to detect a multicollinearity problem?

14.6 Exercise

Download **Teamstability.sav** from the book's website. Using DV = $tstability$ and IV = *team level debate*, run regression in SPSS and decide whether you would use results with or without adjusted standard errors.

Part V

Advanced Topics in Regression and ANOVA

15

Mediation

In this chapter, a mediation analysis is discussed with the aim of answering a research question of why a variable affects another variable. For example, a mediation analysis is required to test whether the relationship between sales employee's moral identity and moral empathy can be explained by the extent to which the sales employee can put himself/herself in the shoe of customers. The chapter begins with the diagrammatic representation of a mediation model, followed by the formulation of hypotheses involving mediation. Then, Baron and Kenny's approach is explained and its limitations are discussed. Next, some terminologies and how to report results of a mediation analysis are discussed. At the end of the chapter, testing mediation using a widely used PROCESS macro is illustrated. The concept of bootstrapping as a strategy to test the mediation effect is also explained.

Learning Objectives:

- Understand the concept of mediation.
- Know how to conduct mediation analysis using SPSS and R.
- Understand the concept of bootstrapping.
- Recognize the application of PROCESS macro.

15.1 What Is Mediation?

Imagine that you played chess online until midnight and woke up late for your exam. When your exam result was announced, your exam score was not good. What is the cause of your poor exam performance? Immediately the answer is lack of sleep, but why does lack of sleep affect your exam score? Engaging in this kind of 'why' thinking put your mindset in terms of developing what is called a mediation model whose basic skeleton is displayed in Figure 15.7.

WARNING

Mediation discussed in this chapter is a statistical term, which is not an everyday language. For a layperson, it might be interpreted as conflict resolution.

DOI: 10.4324/9781003407225-20

FIGURE 15.1
Basic mediation model.

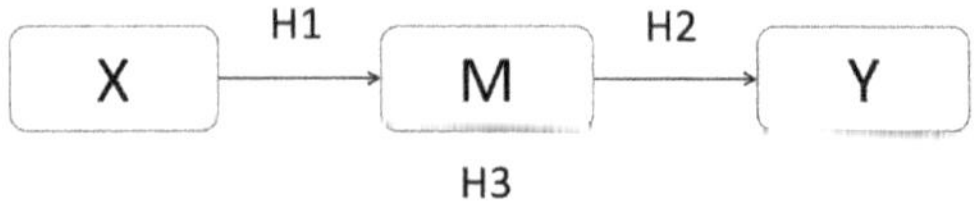

FIGURE 15.2
Mediation model with hypotheses.

Applying the model in the figure to our hypothetical example, X is lack of sleep, Y is exam score, and M can be the level of concentration that a student has during the exam – another candidate for M is the level of anxiety arisen due to lack of exam prep. However, both of these mechanisms can co-occur, in which case there are two Ms in the model. If you read the model from left to right, it sounds right: lack of sleep reduces concentration levels, which in turn leads to a poor exam performance. Alternatively, we can build a narrative that put a subject (e.g. individuals) into an action and tells the consequences of the action: if someone experiences a lack of sleep, his/her concentration level during an exam will be low, resulting in a lower exam score. The first one sounds more formal because it contains names of constructs involved and it is a typical version that you might find in academic papers. The second version is more informal and fits with how we talk to someone in a daily conversation.

The heart of the mediation is that we want to address how X affects Y or why X has an impact on Y. In other words, we want to uncover the underlying mechanism through which X influences Y. Researchers are sometimes so economical in expressing mediation that they could just state in their hypothesis: M mediates the effect of X on Y. In speaking about mediation, M is referred to as a mediator variable—Z symbol is also often used in the literature.

The famous example of the search for a mediator variable took place in the 18th century (Pearl & Mackenzie 2018). Many sailors expediting to arctic suffered from scurvy (the pirate disease). At that time, people discovered that citrus fruit prevented scurvy, but the reason was unknown until Albert Szent-Gyorgyi discovered the existence of vitamin C in fruits in 1930 – he won a Nobel Prize for his invention. Thanks to the Nobel Prize winner, nowadays, we understand that the correct path is: citrus fruits → vitamin C → scurvy. Vitamin C is the mediator of the effect of citrus fruits on scurvy. That is, vitamin C explains why citrus fruits prevents scurvy.

15.2 Hypotheses

To test a mediation hypothesis associated with the model in Figure 15.1, researchers typically present three hypotheses:

H1: X is positively related to M.
H2: M is positively related to Y.
H3: M mediates X on Y.

Nevertheless, nowadays, in the academic literature, one hypothesis in the form of H3 is often presented without H1 and H2. This is because the modern way of testing mediation does necessarily require testing H1 and H2 but facilitates testing H3 directly (see Zhao et al. 2010). Figure 15.2 modifies the previous figure by placing H1, H2, and H3 on the model.

15.3 Method of Analysis

Several methods exist to analyse a mediation model:

1. Regression using Baron and Kenny's approach
2. Regression with bootstrapping
3. Structural equation modelling (SEM)

In this book, I will explain Baron and Kenny's approach (Baron & Kenny 1986) as it is just the application of regression analysis that you have learned in Chapter 12 and Chapter 13. Next, I briefly explain the principle of the second method: regression with bootstrapping. I do not cover the SEM approach because it requires a book of its own right and is usually taught at a PhD level.

Nowadays, Baron and Kenny's approach, however, has lost its popularity among researchers largely due its limitations and because far better analysis, such as resampling with bootstrap and SEM approaches, are available. The reason I discuss it in this book is more for pedagogical and historical reasons because the logic is intuitively easy to grasp; therefore, it will be a good place to start with in learning mediation for those who are new to the topic.

i NOTE

Baron & Kenny (1986) is one of the most cited papers in social sciences. If you are curious how the authors developed their ideas on mediation, you can read Kenny (2008).

15.4 Baron and Kenny's (BK) Approach

To explain Baron and Kenny's approach, let us see Figure 15.3, which contains two models. In the models, a symbol adjacent to a path serves two purposes: denoting the path itself and representing a regression coefficient associated with that path.

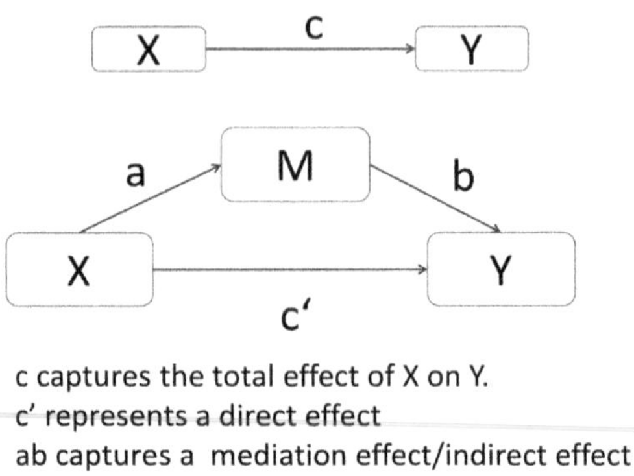

FIGURE 15.3
Simple mediation model with notations.

In the first model, path c connects X with Y. There is no *M* in this model. Path *c* captures the total effect of X on Y. The total effect can be decomposed into a direct and indirect effect: **total effect = direct + indirect effect**. The notion of the direct and indirect effects can be understood by looking at the second model.

In the second model, path *a* connects X with *M*, path *b* connects *M* with *Y*, and path c' (read: *c* prime) connects X with Y. The direct effect of X on Y is represented by path c′, and the indirect effect is obtained by the multiplication of $a \times b$.

Baron and Kenny's approach consists of three steps with the purpose of obtaining regression coefficients associated with path *a*, *b*, *c*, and c', These coefficients are obtained by running separate regressions.

Step 1: Test path *c* (i.e. $X \rightarrow Y$) by regressing *Y* on X. This is a simple linear regression as there is only one predictor unless there are control variables in the model (i.e. those that also directly affect Ys).

Step 1 is crucial in Baron and Kenny's approach. This step requires us to show that the effect or the relationship must exist. That is, the total effect should be significant, and its presence is regarded as a prerequisite in this approach. However, the modern approach on mediation does not require the step to be undertaken. For example, if there are two mediators (hence two indirect effects), the total effect can be zero if the two indirect effects have opposite signs; e.g. X has a negative effect on Y via M1 but has a positive effect on Y via M2.

Step 2: Test path $a(X \rightarrow M)$ using a simple linear regression. This is a simple linear regression as there is only one predictor unless there are control variables in the model.

Step 3: Test path *b* and c'. This is a multiple regression with two independent variables. If there are control variables, they should be included in the model.

I like to use a metaphor in describing these steps – sounds a bit silly, though, but I like it as it is easy to remember, and so far, none of my students have complained about it. Here is the story: if you want to explain how to get to London from Lancaster (look at a map), you must first determine whether there is a means of transportation from Lancaster to London. This is the essence of Step 1. If the answer is yes, then you have to determine further whether you can reach London via Manchester. As Manchester lies in the middle between Lancaster and London, the city is your *M* variable – the presence of M is tested in Step 2. If you are rich enough, you can also travel to London directly

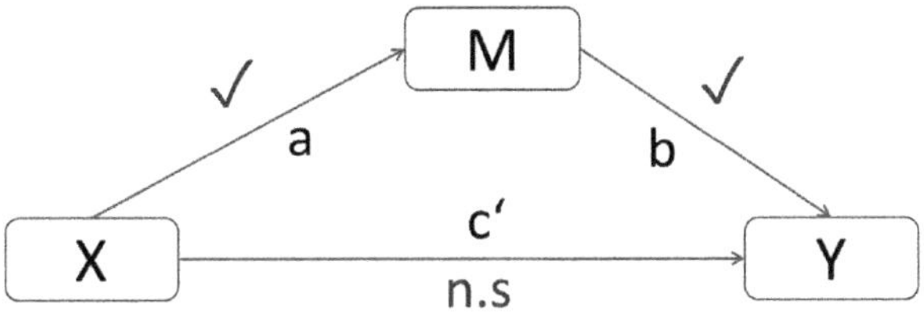

FIGURE 15.4
Full mediation: the direct effect is not significant. The check marks indicate significant paths.

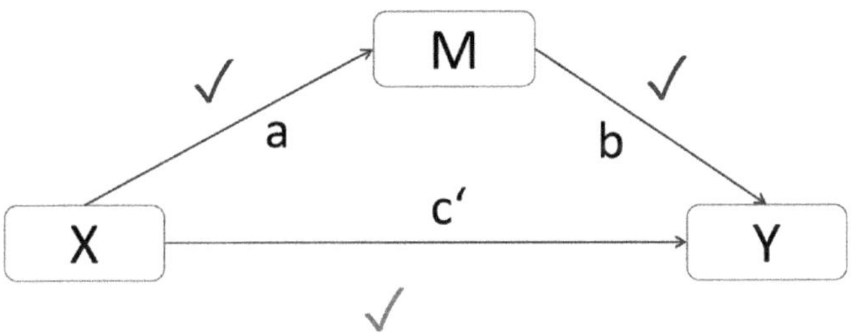

FIGURE 15.5
Partial mediation: all paths are significant. The check marks indicate significant paths.

by helicopter. Considering all these facts, this means that you can reach London both directly and indirectly from Lancaster. This possibility becomes apparent after conducting Step 3.

15.5 Terminology

Now, let us learn few terminologies in mediation that you can find anywhere in academic papers.

- Full mediation: this is a situation where *a* and *b* are significant, but c' is not significant. In this case, there is no direct effect where *M* fully explains the effect of *X* on *Y*.
- Partial mediation: in this situation, all paths are significant.

15.6 SPSS Action

Data: empathyV2.sav

In this illustration, we want to test the mediation model displayed in Figure 15.6. Our aim is to test whether customer-oriented perspective taking explains why store employee's

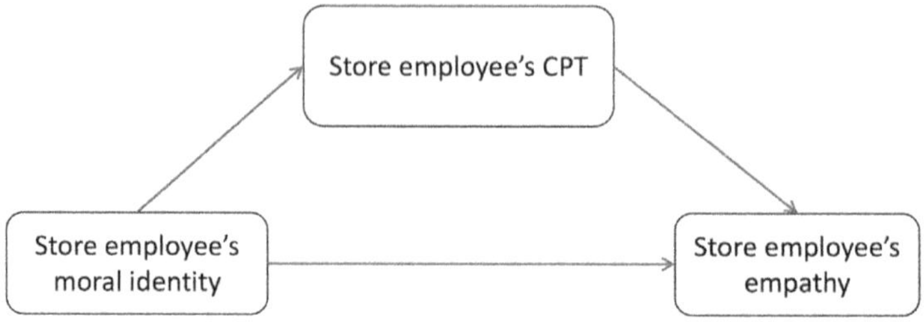

FIGURE 15.6
A mediation model explaining store employee's empathy; CPT = customer-oriented perspective taking.

TABLE 15.1
Cronbach's Alpha, Mean, Standard Deviation, and Correlation Among Constructs

Construct	Alpha	Mean (SD)	1	2	3
1. CPT	0.947	5.685 (1.079)	1		
2. CTEMP	0.922	5.586 (1.099)	0.734**	1	
3. MI	0.792	5.822 (1.012)	0.547**	0.504**	1

Note: ** $p < 0.01$. CPT = customer-oriented perspective taking; CTEMP = empathy toward customers; MI = moral identity; N = 206.

moral identity affects the store employee's empathy. In this context, customer-oriented perspective taking is defined as the extent to which a store employee is able and willing to take the perspective of customers he/she is serving. The construct empathy is defined as the extent to which a store employee empathizes with the customer, and moral identity reflects the importance of morality to the store employee's identity. These constructs were measured using existing scales that require respondents to indicate their opinions on a 7-point Likert scale ranging from 1 = strongly disagree to 7 = strongly agree.

Moral identity (MI) adapted from Aquino & Reed II (2002):

- It would make me feel good to be a person who has these characteristics.
- Being someone who has these characteristics is an important part of who I am.
- I would be ashamed to be a person who has these characteristics (R = reverse coded).
- Having these characteristics is not really important to me (R).
- I strongly desire to have these characteristics.

Customer-oriented perspective taking (CPT) adapted from Axtell et al. (2007):

- I imagine how things look from the customer's perspective.
- I think about how I would feel in their situation.
- I try to see things from their viewpoint.
- I try to imagine myself as a customer in a similar situation.

Empathy toward customers (CTEMP) adapted from Axtell et al. (2007):

- I feel concerned for customers if they are experiencing difficulties.
- I understand when customers get frustrated.
- I identify and empathize with the problems customers experience.

In applying Baron and Kenny's approach, we will work with mean values. Therefore, we will follow the following steps, which have learned in the previous chapters:

- Conduct a reliability analysis for each scale.
- Next, compute the average score for each scale.
- Using the average scores, conduct separate regressions to test for mediation.

The reliability and the correlations among these constructs can be seen in Table 15.1.
Applying BK's approach:
I strongly advise you to check the following calculations.

Step 1. Testing path *c*: moral identity empathy. Using a simple linear regression, we obtain the path coefficient *c* from the unstandardized regression coefficient 0.547, which is significant (p = 0.000).

Step 2. Testing path *a*: moral identity → customer-perspective taking. Again, using a simple linear regression, we obtain the path coefficient *a* from the unstandardized regression coefficient of 0.579, which is also significant (p = 0.000).

Step 3. Testing path *b* and *c*′. Finally, we conduct a multiple regression involving two predictors MI and CPT on $CTEMP$. The results show that the c′ path has an unstandardized regression coefficient of 0.154 (p = 0.011) and the b path has an unstandardized regression coefficient of 0.679.

Putting all results on a diagram:

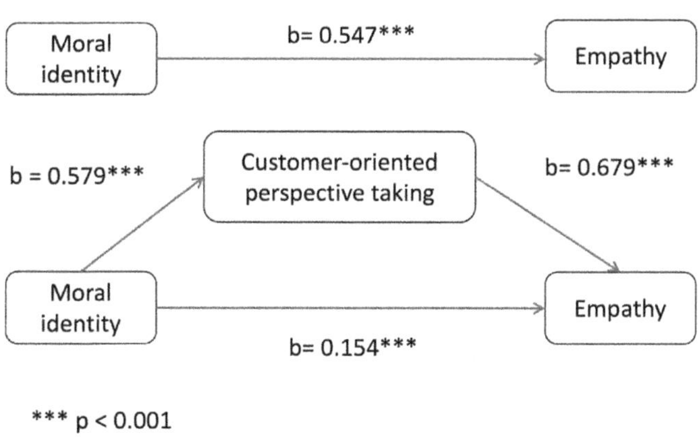

FIGURE 15.7
Presenting mediation results in diagrams.

As all path coefficients are significant, we have a partial mediation situation. That is, *M I* affects *CT E MP* indirectly via *CPT* but *M I* has also a direct impact on *CT E MP*.

15.6.1 SPSS Code

The SPSS code to run the Barron and Kenny's procedure explained earlier is given here:

```
# Reliability analysis: Cronbach's alpha.
RELIABILITY
   /VARIABLES=MI1 MI2 MI4R MI7R MI10
   /SCALE('ALL VARIABLES') ALL
   /MODEL=ALPHA.

RELIABILITY
   /VARIABLES=CPT1 CPT2 CPT3
   /SCALE('ALL VARIABLES') ALL
   /MODEL=ALPHA.

RELIABILITY
   /VARIABLES=CTEMP1 CTEMP2 CTEMP3
   /SCALE('ALL VARIABLES') ALL
   /MODEL=ALPHA.

*creating composite scores ie average.

COMPUTE MI_avg=mean(MI1,MI2, MI4R, MI7R, MI10).
COMPUTE CPT_avg=mean(CPT1,CPT2, CPT3).
COMPUTE CTEMP_avg=mean(CTEMP1,CTEMP2,CTEMP3).

EXECUTE.

*Step1. MI --> CTEMP

REGRESSION
   /MISSING LISTWISE
   /STATISTICS COEFF OUTS R ANOVA
   /CRITERIA=PIN(.05) POUT(.10)
   /NOORIGIN
   /DEPENDENT CTEMP_avg
   /METHOD=ENTER MI_avg.

*Step2. MI --> CPT

REGRESSION
   /MISSING LISTWISE
   /STATISTICS COEFF OUTS R ANOVA
   /CRITERIA=PIN(.05) POUT(.10)
   /NOORIGIN
   /DEPENDENT CPT_avg
   /METHOD=ENTER MI_avg.
```

```
*Step 3. MI + CPT --> CTEMP

REGRESSION
  /MISSING LISTWISE
  /STATISTICS COEFF OUTS R ANOVA
  /CRITERIA=PIN(.05) POUT(.10)
  /NOORIGIN
  /DEPENDENT CTEMP_avg
  /METHOD=ENTER MI_avg CPT_avg.
```

15.7 Testing $a \times b$

15.7.1 Sobel's Test

Mediation should be captured by the product $a \times b$. This is my metaphor to understand why we need the product to examine mediation: if your chance of going from Lancaster to Manchester is 0.3, and your chance of going from Manchester to London is 0.2, this means your chance of reaching London from Lancaster will be $0.3 \times 0.2 = 0.06$, which is quite small. This is the actual probability of going from Lancaster to London via Manchester.

The multiplication gives us the probability of what we really want to know. Using this logic, the mediation effect is the effect that what we really want to know. Knowing the separate effect of *a* and *b* does not yet give us the information about the mediation effect – the existence of both values seemingly gives us an idea about the presence of the mediation effect, but they are not the indirect effect we are looking for. Baron and Kenny's procedure only tests the significance of a and b separately. So far, we have no idea about what $a \times b$ is.

We can calculate the value of $a \times b$ easily as we have the ingredients for the calculation from the previous SPSS outputs. I have put the ingredients we need in Table 15.2 as well as other information that I will explain shortly. Using the information in the table, we can calculate $a \times b = 0.579 \times 0.679 = 0.393$.

Now, we know the value of the mediation effect. The next question is:

Is $a \times b$ significant?

TABLE 15.2

Calculating Sobel's T Statistics

Path	B	SE	T
a	0.579	0.062	
b	0.679	0.057	
ab	0.393	0.053	7.349

Note: T is the Sobel's T statistic; a and b are unstandardized regression coefficients, and SEs are their standard errors.

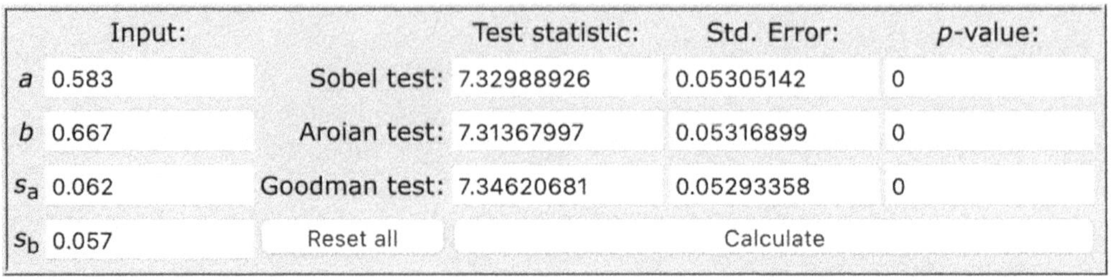

Input:		Test statistic:	Std. Error:	p-value:
a	0.583	Sobel test: 7.32988926	0.05305142	0
b	0.667	Aroian test: 7.31367997	0.05316899	0
s_a	0.062	Goodman test: 7.34620681	0.05293358	0
s_b	0.057	Reset all	Calculate	

FIGURE 15.8
Sobel's test calculator.

To test whether $a \times b$ is significant, $-ab$ is the shorthand version for the expression. Sobel (1982) introduced a formula that gives us the standard error for ab. If you remember from previous regression chapters, knowing a coefficient estimate and its standard error allows us to calculate the t value, which, in turn, can be converted to p-value. I have put the value for the standard error in Table 15.2. $S_{ab} = 0.053$ and the t value for ab is equal to $T_{ab} = 7.349$ (see t-value in the table). This large t-value is associated with a very small p-value – t is larger than 1.96, so ab is significant at 95% confidence level.

How did I get $S_{ab} = 0.053$? The answer is that I am using this online calculator http://quantpsy.org/sobel/sobel.htm. The applet produces standard error, t-value, and p-value associated with ab – see the first row of the screenshot of the applet presented in Figure 15.8.

15.7.2 Bootstrapping

Sobel's test requires a large sample. It assumes that a and b are normally distributed. However, even a and b are normal, ab is not necessarily normal. If ab is not normal, then we cannot use a normal distribution approach to calculate p-value. Another limitation is that when we have a small sample, Sobel's test will not be accurate because the distribution of a and b will be highly skewed. Largely to these reasons, researchers prefer to use another technique to test *ab*, which is called bootstrapping. This technique does not assume *a*, *b*, and ab to be normally distributed.

What Is Bootstrapping and How Do We Assess *ab*?

Bootstrapping is a resampling procedure. That is, we keep taking a sample repeatedly from our 'sample' – yes, the data from which the sample is drawn is regarded as a 'population'. A sample drawn from the 'population' is called a bootstrap sample. From each bootstrap sample, we calculate ab by running regressions as we had previously done. Say, we have 1000 values for ab gathered from the 1000 bootstrap samples. From these 1000 values, we can calculate the 95% confidence interval by arranging the values in an ascending order. What we need to look at is the value at 2.5th percentile and 97.5th percentile of the 1000 values. These are the lower and upper boundaries of the 95% confidence interval (referred to as the 95% bootstrap confidence interval), respectively. To simplify the task, if we have this data of 1000 $ab's$ in SPSS, we can use the SPSS frequency procedure to get the percentiles by clicking: Analyze → Descriptive Statistics → Frequencies. Click Statistics, and tick Percentiles. Next, enter 2.5 and 97.5. The 2.5th and

97.5th percentile are the lower and upper limit of the 95% confidence interval, respectively. Next, click OK and inspect the SPSS outputs.

A modern way of conducting mediation with bootstrapping is facilitated by the PROCESS macro (Hayes 2017), which covers various types of mediation models, and some of which combine mediation with moderation – we discuss moderation in Chapter 16.

15.8 R Action

The R code equivalent to the SPSS code presented previously to conduct Baron and Kenny's approach is presented. First, two variables are reverse coded (*MI4* and *MI7*) because they were worded negatively. The reversed coded variables actually already exist in the SPSS data, but here, I showed how to do it in R. Next, I created new different objects to store each new variables that contains the mean score of their associated original variables. Then, I combined them with the original data frame. After the data preparation has been taken care of, next, Baron and Kenny's approach was implemented step-by-step using the `lm()` function.

```
rm(list=ls())
library(tidyverse)
library(dplyr)
library(ahdar)
library(lm.beta)

# Read data from ahdar library

dat <- empathyv2

# Reverse code MI4 and MI7

dat <- dat %>%
  mutate(MI4R=8-MI4) %>%
  mutate(MI7R=8-MI7)

CPT <- dat %>%
  select(CPT1, CPT2, CPT3) %>%
  rowMeans()

CPT <- dat %>%
  select(CPT1, CPT2, CPT3) %>%
  rowMeans()

CTEMP <- dat %>%
  select(CTEMP1, CTEMP2, CTEMP3) %>%
  rowMeans()
```

```
MI <- dat %>%
    select(MI1, MI2, MI4R, MI7R, MI10) %>%
    rowMeans()

# Combine new variables with the original data frame
dat <- cbind(dat, MI, CTEMP, MI)

# Step 1: MI (Moral) - > CTEMP (Empathy)

  lm_step1 <- lm(CTEMP_avg ~ MI_avg, data = dat)

  # Calculate the standardized coefficients

  lm_step1_std <- lm.beta(lm_step1)
  summary(lm_step1_std,standardized=TRUE)
```

```
##
## Call:
## lm(formula = CTEMP_avg ~ MI_avg, data = dat)
##
## Residuals:
##    Min     1Q Median    3Q   Max
## -4.683 -0.459  0.098 0.749 1.974
##
## Coefficients:
##              Estimate Standardized Std. Error t value Pr(>|t|)
## (Intercept)    2.3984           NA     0.3884   6.18 3.5e-09 ***
## MI_avg         0.5474       0.5038     0.0657   8.33 1.2e-14 ***
## ---
## Signif. codes: 0 '***' 0.001 '**' 0.01 '*' 0.05 '.' 0.1 ' ' 1
##
## Residual standard error: 0.952 on 204 degrees of freedom
## Multiple R-squared: 0.254, Adjusted R-squared: 0.25
## F-statistic: 69.4 on 1 and 204 DF, p-value: 1.17e-14
```

```
# Step 2: MI - > CPT

  lm_step2 <- lm(CPT_avg ~ MI_avg, data = dat)

  # Calculate the standardized coefficients

  lm_step2_std <- lm.beta(lm_step2)
  summary(lm_step2_std,standardized=TRUE)
```

```
##
## Call:
```

```
## lm(formula = CPT_avg ~ MI_avg, data = dat)
##
## Residuals:
##    Min     1Q Median    3Q   Max
## -4.782 -0.362  0.102 0.638 2.260
##
## Coefficients:
##             Estimate Standardized Std. Error t value Pr(>|t|)
## (Intercept)   2.3083           NA     0.3671    6.29 1.9e-09 ***
## MI_avg        0.5790       0.5465     0.0621    9.32 < 2e-16 ***
## ---
## Signif. codes: 0 '***' 0.001 '**' 0.01 '*' 0.05 '.' 0.1 ' ' 1
##
## Residual standard error: 0.9 on 204 degrees of freedom
## Multiple R-squared: 0.299, Adjusted R-squared: 0.295
## F-statistic: 86.9 on 1 and 204 DF, p-value: <2e-16
```

```
# Step 3: MI + CPT - > CTEMP
  lm_step3 <- lm(CTEMP_avg ~ MI_avg + CPT_avg, data = dat)

  # Calculate the standardized coefficients

  lm_step3_std <- lm.beta(lm_step3)
  summary(lm_step3_std,standardized=TRUE)
```

```
##
## Call:
## lm(formula = CTEMP_avg ~ MI_avg + CPT_avg, data = dat)
##
## Residuals:
##    Min     1Q  Median     3Q    Max
## -3.920 -0.306   0.077  0.336  2.559
##
## Coefficients:
##             Estimate Standardized Std. Error t value Pr(>|t|)
## (Intercept)   0.8303           NA     0.3261    2.55   0.012 *
## MI_avg        0.1541       0.1418     0.0603    2.56   0.011 *
## CPT_avg       0.6793       0.6623     0.0569   11.93  <2e-16 ***
## ---
## Signif. codes: 0 '***' 0.001 '**' 0.01 '*' 0.05 '.' 0.1 ' ' 1
##
## Residual standard error: 0.732 on 203 degrees of freedom
## Multiple R-squared: 0.561, Adjusted R-squared: 0.557
## F-statistic: 130 on 2 and 203 DF, p-value: <2e-16
```

15.9 Mediation Test Using PROCESS Macro

Data: empathy2.sav

This dataset is just a copy of *empathyV2.sav* but I renamed the composite variable (e.g. *CTEMP_avg* to *CTEMP*) because PROCESS macro cannot accept variable name longer than 8 characters.

Go to this website to download the PROCESS macro (http://processmacro.org/download.html) and install it onto your SPSS.

Now, we are going to use the PROCESS macro to test a mediation model. By using this macro, we do not need to follow the three steps procedure suggested by Baron & Kenny (1986). The PROCESS macro includes a bootstrapping technique. As explained, bootstrapping is sampling technique where our data is treated as a population, and the macro keeps taking samples from our data with replacement according to a pre-specified number (the default of the program is 5000 samples). For each sample, the macro computes *a* and *b* and the product *ab*. Therefore, by having 5000 samples, there would be 5000 values of product *ab*. Using these 5000 values of the product *ab*, the macro calculates the confidence interval for the product *ab* – it is called a bootstrap confidence interval. If the interval does not include zero, the mediation effect is considered to be significant.

By default, the PROCESS macros set the level of bootstrap confidence at 95% level. We can change this value, but 95% is commonly used; therefore, leave the default as it is. For example, if the 95% bootstrap confidence interval for the size of the mediation effect is [0.04;0.25]. This means that we are 95% confident that the effect lies from 0.04 to 0.25. If the bootstrap confidence interval includes zero (e.g. [−0.3; 0.2]), the mediation effect is not significant.

15.9.1 Running the PROCESS Macro

- Click Analyze → Regression → Process.
- Insert CTemp into Y-variable box.
- Insert MI into X-variable box.
- Insert CPT into Mediators(M) box.
- Change model number to 4.

If you manage to follow these steps, on your SPSS screen, you should see the image displayed in Figure 15.9 on your screen.

- Click OK and inspect the output window. The outputs do not appear instantly as the macro takes a little while to complete its computation.

15.9.2 Outputs

Inspect the outputs. The most important output to look at is the last part of the outputs – see the following figure. It gives us the size of the mediation effect ($ab = 0.3886$), and the

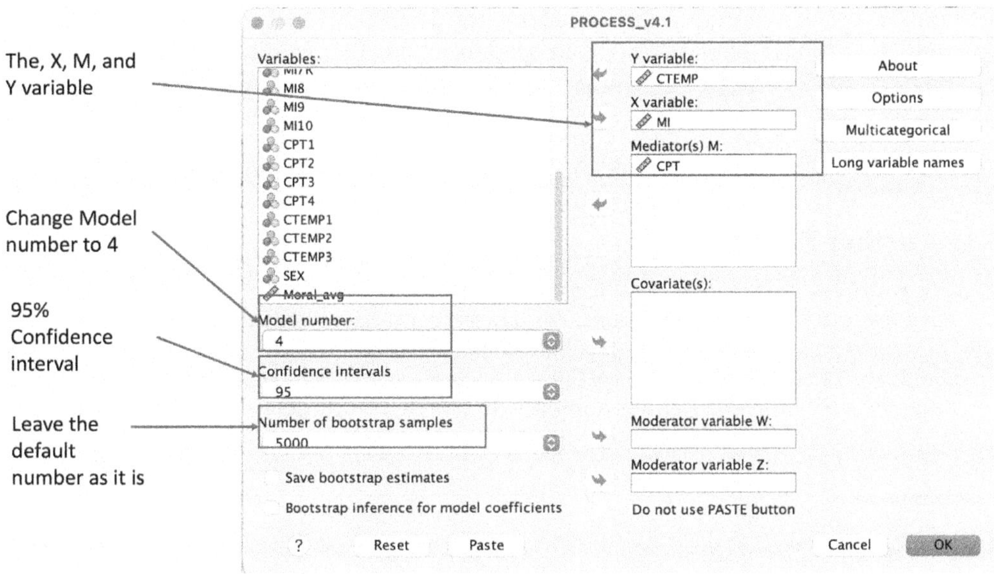

FIGURE 15.9
Process macro: model 4.

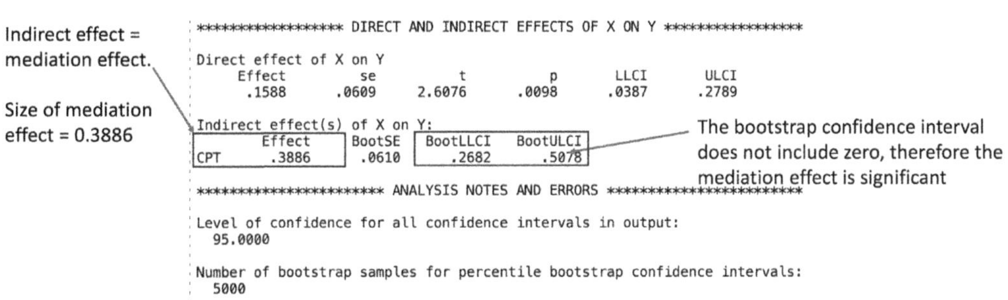

FIGURE 15.10
Outputs of the model 4 of the PROCESS macro showing mediation effect size.

lower and upper limit of the bootstrap confidence interval (0.2643; 0.5081). Because the 95% bootstrap confidence interval does not include zero, the mediation effect is significant.

15.10 Summary

In this chapter, we have discussed the concept of mediation, which can be used to find the underlying mechanism through which a variable affects another variable. I have explained how to analyse a simple mediation model using Baron and Kenny's approach and bootstrapping technique facilitated by the PROCESS macro. Baron and Kenny's approach is no longer recommended in academic journals, but it is quite useful in getting the basic understanding of the concept of mediation.

15.11 Further Readings

Hayes, A. F. (2017), *Introduction to mediation, moderation, and conditional process analysis: A regression-based approach*, Guilford Publications. This is a textbook discussing PROCESS macro in details.

Zhao, X., Lynch Jr, J. G. & Chen, Q. (2010), 'Reconsidering Baron and Kenny: Myths and truths about mediation analysis', *Journal of Consumer Research* 37(2), 197–206. This paper discusses the limitations of Baron and Kenny's approach and modern approach in addressing mediation.

15.12 Review Questions

1. A product can be imbued with a human characteristic – termed as product anthropomorphism. For example, we can add a 'human smile' sticker on a vacuum cleaner. Consumers may like this product simply due to the appearance of human elements on it. What do you think the best explanation for this causal mechanism: product anthropomorphism→ M→ liking? What is your best guess for *M*?
2. Explain Baron and Kenny's approach in testing mediation and its limitations.
3. What is bootstrapping? Explain how it can be used in mediation analysis.

15.13 Exercises

Download aad.sav from the book's online support. The SPSS data contains three variables: Aad (composite scores of attitude toward an ad), Aab (composite scores of attitude toward a brand), and PI (composite score of an intention to purchase a brand). Use PROCESS macro to find out whether Aab mediates the effect of Aad on PI.

16

Moderation

In this chapter, the concept of moderation is explained. Moderation refers to a situation in which the relationship between constructs, such as monetary incentives and sales performance, depends on the level of another construct. For example, the effect of a monetary incentives and performance of sales employee might depend on gender such that the relationship might be stronger for female than for male sales employees. The chapter begins with the diagrammatic representation of a simple moderation model, followed by a discussion on how to perform a moderation analysis as well as the graphical interpretation of the meaning of the moderation effect. Next, testing moderation using a widely used PROCESS macro is illustrated. At the end of the chapter, the concept of spurious moderation is explained.

Learning Objectives:

- Understand the concept of moderation.
- Know how to use hierarchical regression to test moderation effect.
- Understand moderation plots.
- Understand the concept of bootstrapping.
- Know how to use PROCESS macro to test moderation.

16.1 What Is Moderation?

When a linear relationship between two variables (*X* and *Y*) is affected by a value of another variable, say *Z*, we are dealing with a so-called moderation effect – interaction effect is another popular term, which seems to be a favourite by economists. I remember my experience presenting my moderation paper in a research seminar in other departments attended by some economists. One of them gave me a remark: 'Why do you call it a moderation effect, is it not just an interaction effect?'

Moderation can be best explained by using an example. Suppose that the effect of the amount of monetary incentive received by sale employees on performance differ across gender. That is, if male employees receiving money generate more sales than females receiving the same amount of money – if everything else constant – then we can say that gender moderates the relationship between the monetary incentive and performance. In this case, if you run a simple regression on performance of the amount of monetary incentive separately for female and male samples, you expect that the regression slope for male is larger than that of the female (see Figure 16.1). If the slope for male sample is the same as that of female sample, moderation effect does not occur. This situation is

DOI: 10.4324/9781003407225-21

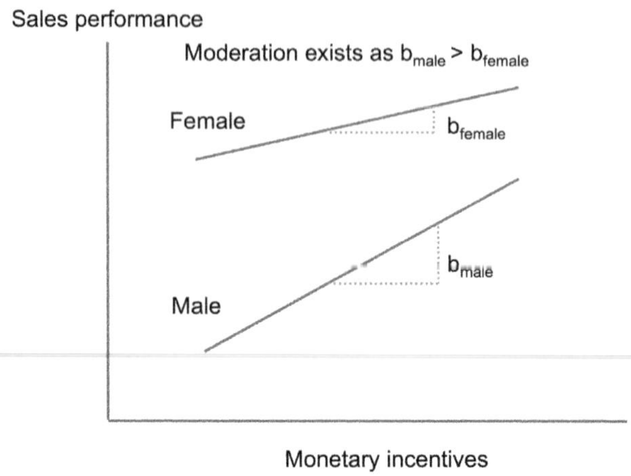

FIGURE 16.1
Moderation of gender on the relationship between monetary reward and performance.

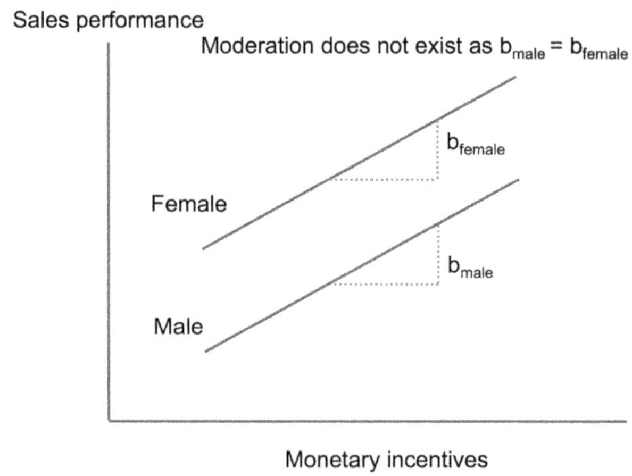

FIGURE 16.2
The lines are parallel suggesting no moderation.

depicted in Figure 16.2, where the two regression lines in the graph are in parallel, hence the same slope, implying that the effect of the monetary incentives on performance are the same across gender. A variable that moderates a relationship is referred to as a moderator variable, or moderator, for short. In this example, gender is the moderator variable of the relationship between monetary incentives and performance.

In this example, the moderator variable Z is a nominal variable (male vs. female). If Z is an interval or ratio variable, there may be a range of Z values where the effect of X on Y is detected as significant or non-significant.

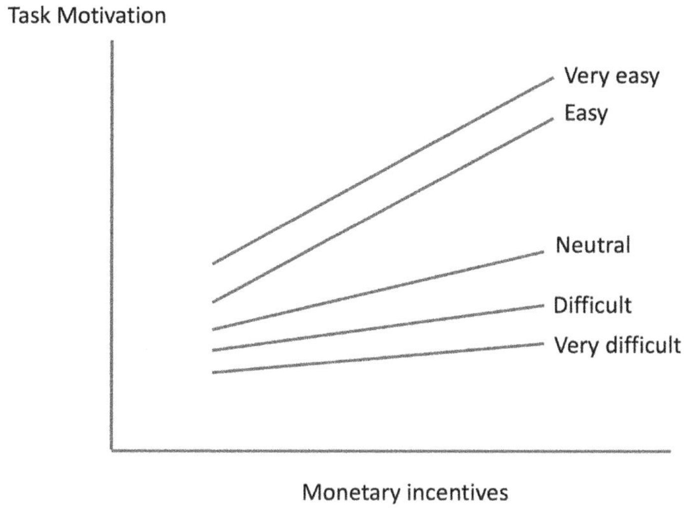

FIGURE 16.3
Relationship between monetary incentives and task motivation at various values of perceived task difficulty.

Let us consider another example. Suppose that sales employees were asked to rate the difficulty of negotiating with potential customers using a 5-point semantic differential scale ranging from 1 = very easy to 5 = very difficult. Let us call this construct as **perceived task difficulty**. They were also asked to rate their level of motivation to perform the task (1 = very unmotivated, 5 = very motivated). Let us call this construct as **task motivation**. Perceived task difficulty may influence the relationship between monetary incentives and motivation, hence a potential moderator variable: the relationship between incentives and motivation may vary at different values of perceived difficulty. Suppose that the relationship between monetary incentives and motivation at different values of perceived task difficulty is described by Figure 16.3.

The graph shows that the regression lines at `Easy` and `Very easy` are parallel suggesting the monetary incentives have the same effect on motivation for those who perceived the task as `easy` and `very easy`. Note that the slopes of both lines are quite steep, suggesting that the effect of incentives on motivation may be significant. Monetary incentives do matters for these employees who thinks the task are `easy` or `very easy`. The parallel lines suggest that the increase in monetary incentives produce the same effect on motivation. The regression lines for the other three values (`Neutral`, `Difficult`, and `Very difficult`) suggest that the effect of incentives is not as influential as that at `Easy` and `Very easy`. The differences in the regression slopes suggest that monetary incentives have a different impact on performance. In fact, the regression line at `Very difficult` is nearly flat, suggesting that monetary incentives have a very minor influence on motivation. In other words, if the task is perceived as very difficult or may be unrealistic to achieve, there is no obvious benefit of providing more incentives to boost employee's motivation. This is in line with the statement made by Locke (1968): 'people who do stop trying when confronted by a hard task are people who have decided the goal is impossible to reach and who no longer are trying' (p. 168).

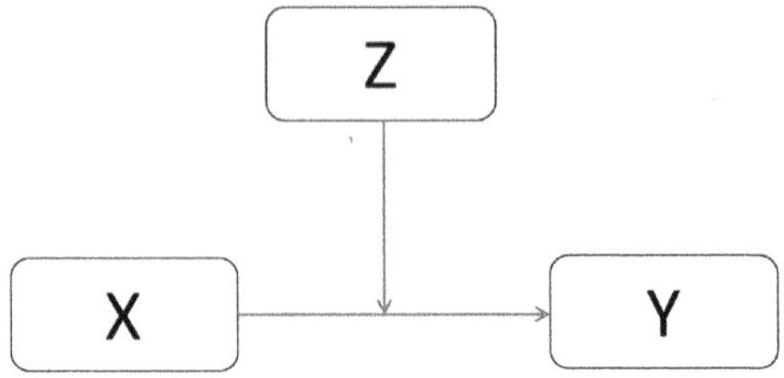

FIGURE 16.4
Diagram of a moderation model.

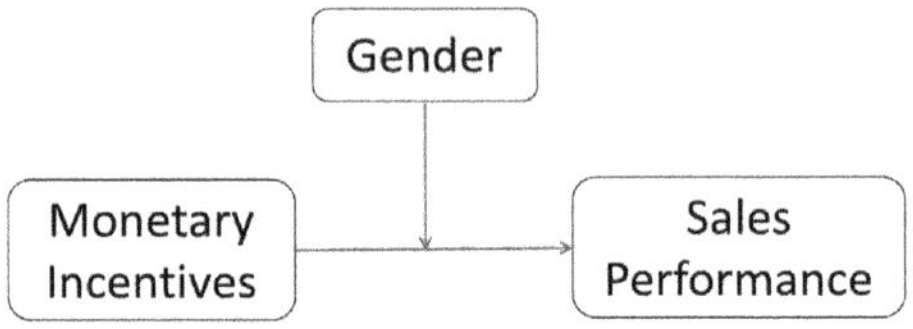

FIGURE 16.5
Gender moderates the relationship between monetary incentives and sales performance.

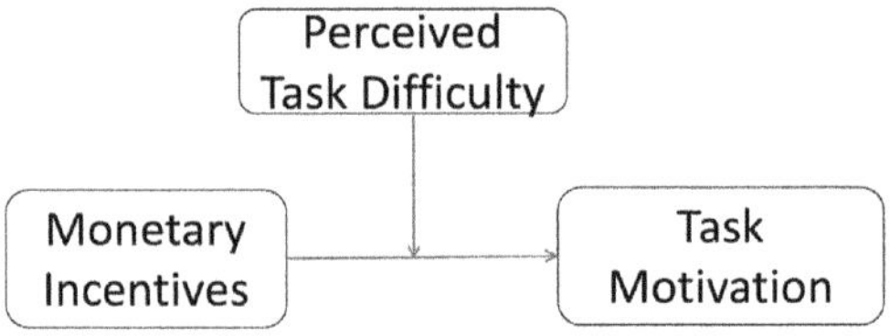

FIGURE 16.6
Perceived task difficulty as a moderator of the relationship between monetary incentives and task motivation.

16.2 Representing Moderation with a Diagram

Moderation can be presented in a diagram as displayed in Figure 16.4. As can be seen from the diagram, X is connected to Y by a directed arrow, showing that X influences Y. The moderator Z influences the relationship as indicated by an arrow that points to the line connecting X with Y. In our example earlier, with gender as a moderator variable, the relationship among the three variables can be described as a moderation model displayed in Figure 16.5. In the second example, with perceived task difficulty as a moderator, the moderation model is represented by a diagram displayed in Figure 16.6.

16.3 Capturing Moderation

A moderation model is just a regression model, in which moderation is captured by an interaction term $X Z$, which is the multiplication of X and Z. Such model is known as a

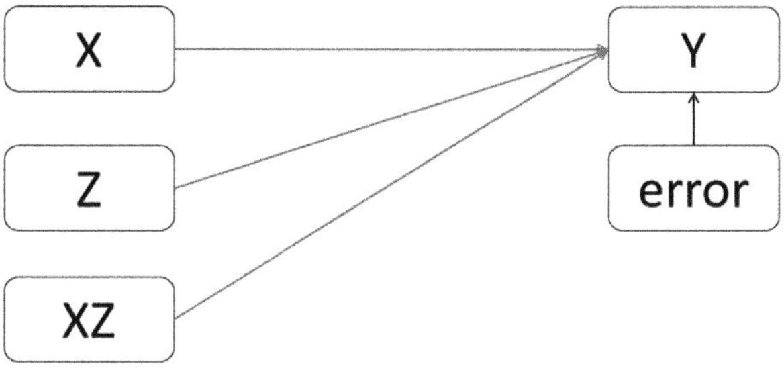

FIGURE 16.7
Translating a moderation equation into a diagram. X*Z is an interaction term.

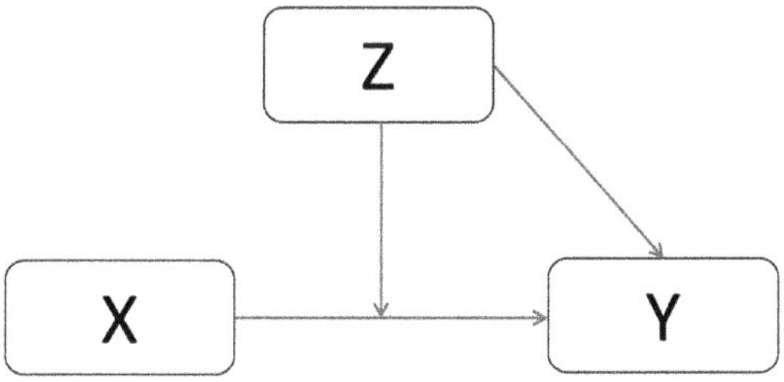

FIGURE 16.8
By construction, a moderator variable Z is also related to Y.

moderated regression model or by its longer version as a moderated multiple regression model. It takes the following form:

$$Y = \beta_0 + \beta_1 X + \beta_2 Z + \beta_3 XZ + \varepsilon \tag{16.1}$$

where ε is an error term.

The equation can also be represented by a diagram as displayed in Figure 16.7.

If we look at Equation 16.1, by construction, Z is related to Y. For this reason, it is often useful to describe a moderation model by also drawing an arrow from Z to Y, especially if you also want to present a hypothesis about the relationship between Z and Y. We extend Figure 16.4 to Figure 16.8 to incorporate the influence of Z on the dependent variable.

IMPORTANT

In a moderated regression model, both components of the interaction terms (X and Z) should exist as main terms in the model.

If a regression model takes this form:

$$Y = \beta_0 + \beta_1 X + \beta_3 XZ + \varepsilon \tag{16.2}$$

Equation 16.2 is not considered as a moderation model because Z does not appear in the model. The presence of the two main terms X and Z in the model occurs because, by definition, the moderated regression model arises when the coefficient associated with X is a function of a coefficient associated with Z. We will understand the meaning of this statement by rearranging Equation 16.1.

$$Y = \beta_0 + (\beta_1 + \beta_3 Z)X + \beta_2 Z + \varepsilon \tag{16.3}$$

As we can see from Equation 16.3, the coefficient associated with X is clearly a function of the coefficient associated with Z. We can simplify Equation 16.3 by rewriting as an additive model in the following form:

$$Y = a + bX + cZ + \varepsilon \tag{16.4}$$

where a, b, and c are regression parameters, and values of b depends on Z. I do not use the Greek symbols for denoting the regression parameters to avoid a confusion that might arise between the Greek symbols from the mentioned model and those of the moderation model. That is, b in Equation 16.4 and β_1 in Equation 16.1 are not the same.

Equation 16.4 is referred to as an additive model because the effect on Y of X and Z is assumed to be additive – Y is made of X and Z added together. In explaining moderation, we can also start from the additive model, then replace b with $\beta_1 + \beta_3 Z$, rearrange the equation, and rename the parameters to get Equation 16.1.

16.4 The Meaning of β_1

The alternative form of the moderated regression model as represented by Equation 16.3 informs us that the effect of X on Y at a particular value of Z is given by:

$$\beta_1 + \beta_3 Z \tag{16.5}$$

If Z takes only two values ($Z = 0$ for male, and $Z = 1$ for female), then β_1 gives the effect of X on Y for male. Similarly, if $Z = 1$, then the effect of X on Y for female is given by $\beta_1 + \beta_3$.

16.5 Mean Centring

If you read research papers that test moderation effects, many of the articles reported that X and Z are mean-centred prior to moderation analysis. Mean-centring means subtracting the mean of the variable for all observations in the data (see Section 6.5.2). It takes this form:

$$X_c = X - \bar{X} \quad (16.6)$$

$$Z_c = Z - \bar{Z} \quad (16.7)$$

X_c and Z_c are the mean-centred forms. By replacing X and Z with X_c and Z_c in Equation 16.3, the slope for X_c is given by:

$$\beta_1 + \beta_3 Z_c \quad (16.8)$$

Why did they do this? The answer is that mean-centring makes the interpretation more meaningful. First, look at again the form for the slope of X in Equation 16.5, β_1 gives us the effect of X on Y when $Z = 0$. However, $Z = 0$ will not make any sense if there are no cases with $Z = 0$. For example, perceived task difficulty (**Task**) was measured with 5-item scale, 1 = very easy to 5 = very difficult. There is no **Task** = 0. Second, look at again the form for the slope of X_c in Equation 16.8 if we set Z equals its mean value (i.e. $Z = Z$), then $Z_c = 0$; therefore, b_1 represents the effect of X at the mean of Z and mean of Z always exists.

IMPORTANT

There had been a misconception in the past about mean-centring that it will reduce the collinearity among variables in the moderated regression model and, thus, increase the power of detecting an interaction effect. The myth has been debunked (McClelland et al. 2017; Echambadi & Hess 2004). Mean-centring does reduce the collinearity, but it reduces the collinearity that is not useful for detecting a moderation effect. In other words, mean-centring does not change the results associated with the coefficient of the interaction (β_3) originally estimated without mean-centring.

16.6 Testing Moderation Hypothesis

How do we go about testing a moderation hypothesis while we also want to hypothesize the main effects of *X* and *Z*? For example, regardless of the perceived task difficulty, we want to know the effect of monetary incentives on performance – this is the main effect of *X*. Similarly, regardless of the monetary incentives, we want to know the effect of perceived task difficulty on performance – this is the main effect of *Z*.

A common strategy to test the main and the moderation effect hypotheses is to conduct a hierarchical regression analysis via two stages.

Stage 1. Testing main effects: Use the additive model (Equation 16.4), and examine the coefficients associated with X and Z.

Stage 2. Testing moderation effect: Enter the interaction term $X Z$, and examine the coefficient associated with the interaction term.

WARNING

A common mistake from a moderation beginner is to test the main effects (say, X) by assessing β_1 in Equation 16.1. As explained in the previous section, β_1 in Equation 16.1 is the effect of X at a particular value Z (i.e. conditional effect).

16.7 SPSS Action and Interpretation

Data: authenticity.sav

We consider whether authenticity (**aut_av**) and attractiveness (**att_av**) of an influencer affects consumers' attachment (**emot_av**) to the influencer. More importantly, we want to test a moderation model as displayed in Figure 16.9.

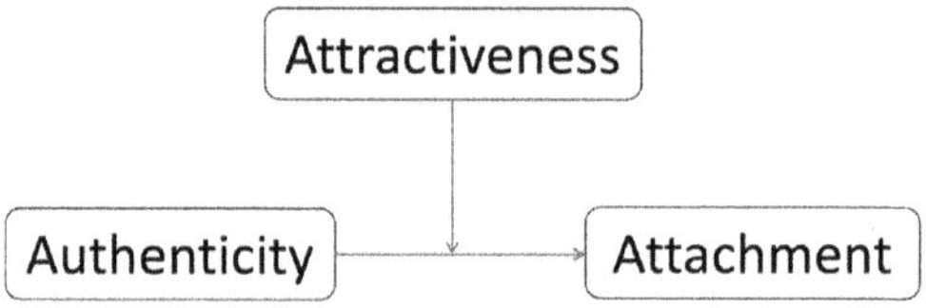

FIGURE 16.9
Attractiveness moderates the relationship between authenticity and emotional attachment.

Steps:

- Create an interaction term, say *att_aut*. Click **Compute** → **Transform**.
- Conduct a regression. Enter the main term: *att_av* and *aut_av*.
- Click Block and enter the interaction term *att_aut*.
- Next, click OK or Paste if you want to work with an SPSS syntax.

The SPSS syntax if you click paste is presented here:

```
* Testing moderation.
* Create an interaction term.

COMPUTE att_aut=att_av*aut_av.

* Hierarchical regression.
```

```
REGRESSION
  /MISSING LISTWISE
  /STATISTICS COEFF OUTS R ANOVA
  /CRITERIA=PIN(.05) POUT(.10)
  /NOORIGIN
  /DEPENDENT emo_av
  /METHOD=ENTER att_av aut_av
  /METHOD=ENTER att_aut.
```

The results of a hierarchical regression analysis are shown in Figure 16.10. The moderation effect is represented by the interaction term (*att_aut*).

Coefficients[a]

Model		Unstandardized Coefficients B	Std. Error	Standardized Coefficients Beta	t	Sig.
1	(Constant)	.129	.220		.587	.558
	aut_av	.131	.042	.158	3.089	.002
	att_av	.264	.036	.380	7.425	<.001
2	(Constant)	1.575	.453		3.479	<.001
	aut_av	-.184	.096	-.223	-1.917	.056
	att_av	-.128	.114	-.185	-1.132	.259
	att_aut	.081	.022	.801	3.635	<.001

a. Dependent Variable: emo_av

P-value Of The Main Effects

P-value Of The Interaction Effect

FIGURE 16.10
Results of a hierarchical regression.

The main effect of X and Z are given by the coefficients in the first block (Model 1). The moderation effect is given by the coefficient associated with the interaction term given in the second block (Model 2). In the results, the two main terms are significant, and the interaction term is also significant. These mean that authenticity and attractiveness have significant impacts on attachment. More importantly, the effect of authenticity on attachments depends on attractiveness. We discuss how to visualize the pattern of the moderation in the next section.

16.8 Graphical Interpretations of $\beta_1 + \beta_3 Z$

In this section, we will learn how to produce Figure 16.1, which shows us the pattern of the moderation. As a remainder, the line in the figure shows us the effect of X on Y at a particular value of Z where the slope represents the partial effect of X on Y given $\beta_1 + \beta_3 Z$.

16.8.1 When Z Is a Qualitative Variable

We consider how to plot the moderation when Z is nominal variable, such as gender (1 = male vs. 0 = female).

TABLE 16.1

Z Is a (0,1) Variable

Z	Intercept	Slope = $\beta_1 + \beta_3 Z$
0	β_0	β_1
1	$\beta_0 + \beta_2$	$\beta_1 + \beta_3$

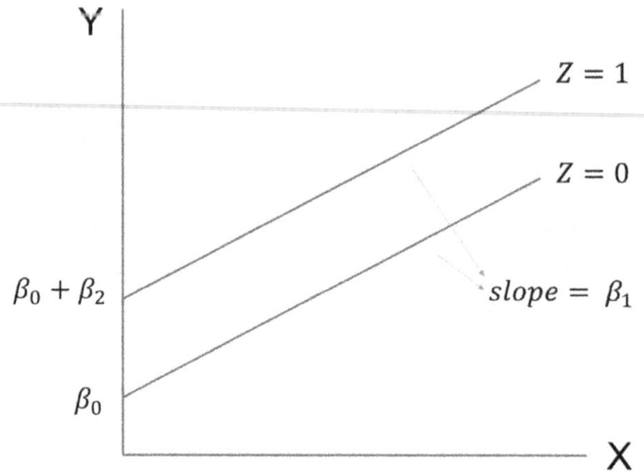

FIGURE 16.11
The relationship between X and Y do not differ across Z.

Let us tabulate, the value for intercept and slope at different values of *Z*, *Z* = 0, 1, if we use MMR model to estimate data.

We can easily see from the table that if there is no moderation (i.e. $\beta_3 = 0$), the slopes of the regression line at different values of *Z* are constant, which is equal to β_1. Thus, the regression lines for no interaction will be parallel because of the equal slopes – they can have different intercept, but only slopes that count (see Figure 16.11).

If moderation exists (i.e. β_3 is not zero), the pattern of relationship as shown in Figure 16.12 is one of the many possibilities in which the lines are not parallel. In this case, one of the slopes or both slopes of the lines are significant.

16.8.2 When Z Is Continuous

Now, we consider *Z* as a continuous variable. For a continuous moderator, typically researchers present the conditional effect of *X* on *Y* at three different values of *Z*: **mean, one standard deviation below the mean**, and **one standard deviation (SD) above the mean**. Researchers typically assign low and high level for construct value at one SD below and above the mean, respectively. For example, if *Z* is a perceived self-esteem, then score of one SD below the mean is assigned as low perceived self-esteem. There is a drawback on this practice. For example, if there are no respondents having a response at one SD below the mean, therefore, talking about low-self-esteem respondents makes no sense. Furthermore, value at one SD below the mean can be lower than zero.

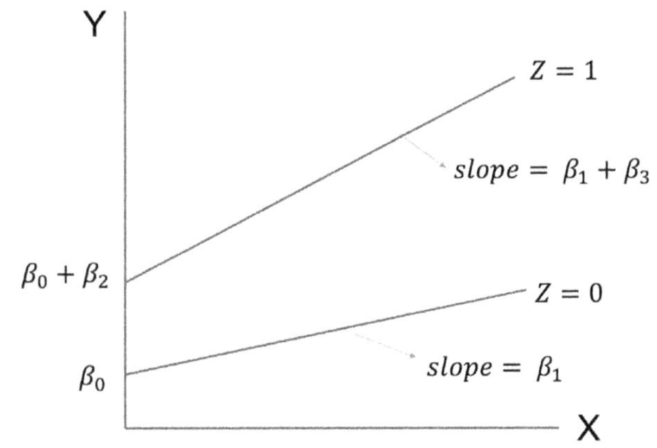

FIGURE 16.12
The relationship between X and Y differs across Z.

A recommended strategy to deal with a continuous moderator is to find and report values of *Z* where the effect of *X* change from significant to insignificant. The ranges of *Z* values where the effect of *X* on *Y* are significant is called the `Johnson-Neyman (JN) region of significance`. We can use a PROCESS macro (www.processmacro.org), also discussed in the previous chapter, to facilitate the calculations and plot the regions.

16.9 Moderation Test Using PROCESS

Data: authenticity.sav

Here, we are using PROCESS macro to test a moderation model displayed in Figure 16.9.

16.9.1 Running the PROCESS Macro

- Click **Analyze** → **Regression** → **Process.**
- Insert **emo_av** into `Y-variable` box.
- Insert **aut_av** `X-variable` box.
- Insert **att_av** into `Moderator variable(W)` box.
- Change model number to 1 (it is the default value). On your SPSS screen, you should see Figure 16.13.

- Tick `Generate code for visualizing interaction.`
- Under `Heteroscedasticity-consistent inference`, from the dropdown list, choose 'HC4 (Cribari-Neto).
- Click Option, and under `Conditioning Values`, tick `-1SD, Mean, +1SD`, and tick `Johnson-Neyman output.`

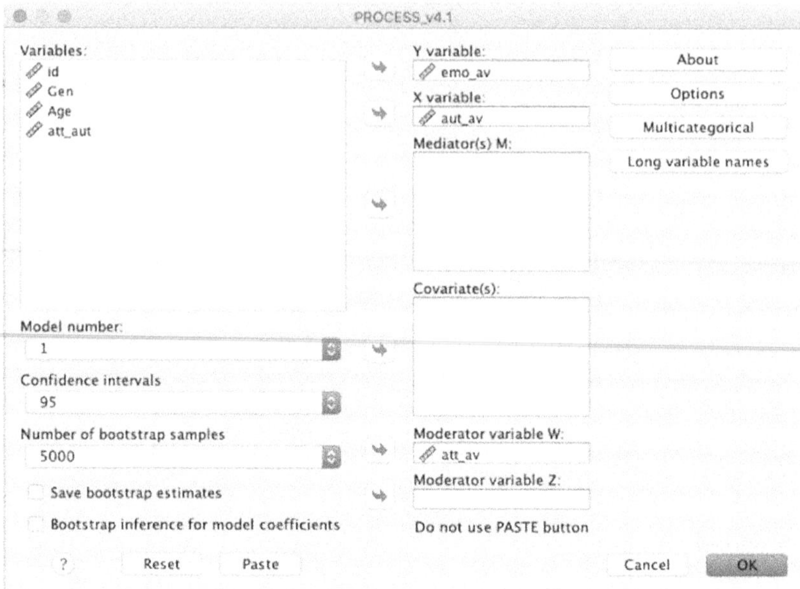

FIGURE 16.13
Model 1 of PROCESS macro.

On your SPSS screen, you should see Figure 16.14.

- Click Continue, and OK. The macro run for few seconds before you can see the outputs.

16.9.2 Outputs

PROCESS produces several outputs, which I split into several parts. I explained each part as follows. I skipped the beginning parts of the outputs which are trivial.

Regression

The first outputs display the regression results (see Figure 16.15). As you can see from the outputs, the interaction term is significant ($b = 0.0815, p < 0.05$). Next to the *X W* symbol, the macro produces the R^2 change, which is equal to 0.0294, which is significant. The R^2 change tells us that the inclusion of the interaction term to the main model without the interaction term can explain an additional variation in emotional attachment. This additional variation is nearly 3%.

Conditional Effect

Because we ticked `Conditioning Values`, and `-1SD, Mean, +1SD`, earlier, we obtained the outputs as displayed in Figure 16.16. The results show that at *att_av* = 2.686 (this value is -1SD below the mean of *att_av*), the effect of authenticity of on attachments is not significant ($p > 0.05$).

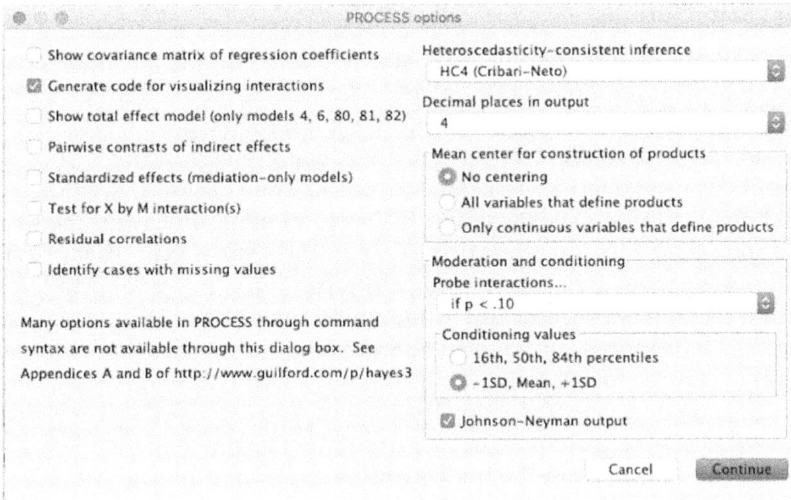

FIGURE 16.14
Clicking 'options' button in the PROCESS macro shows these options.

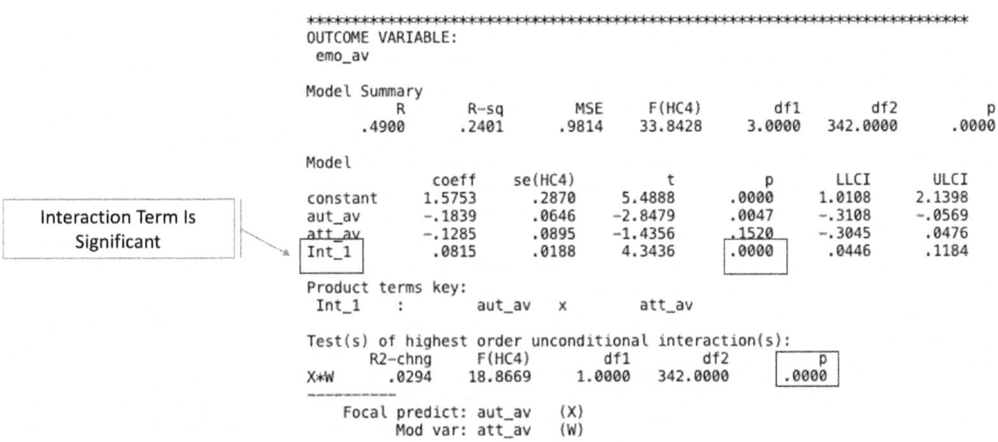


```
**************************************************************************
OUTCOME VARIABLE:
 emo_av

Model Summary
          R       R-sq        MSE     F(HC4)        df1        df2          p
      .4900      .2401      .9814    33.8428     3.0000   342.0000      .0000

Model
              coeff    se(HC4)          t          p       LLCI       ULCI
constant     1.5753      .2870     5.4888      .0000     1.0108     2.1398
aut_av       -.1839      .0646    -2.8479      .0047     -.3108     -.0569
att_av       -.1285      .0895    -1.4356      .1520     -.3045      .0476
Int_1         .0815      .0188     4.3436      .0000      .0446      .1184

Product terms key:
 Int_1    :        aut_av    x        att_av

Test(s) of highest order unconditional interaction(s):
       R2-chng     F(HC4)        df1        df2          p
X*W      .0294    18.8669     1.0000   342.0000      .0000
----------
    Focal predict: aut_av    (X)
          Mod var: att_av    (W)
```

FIGURE 16.15
Regression outputs.

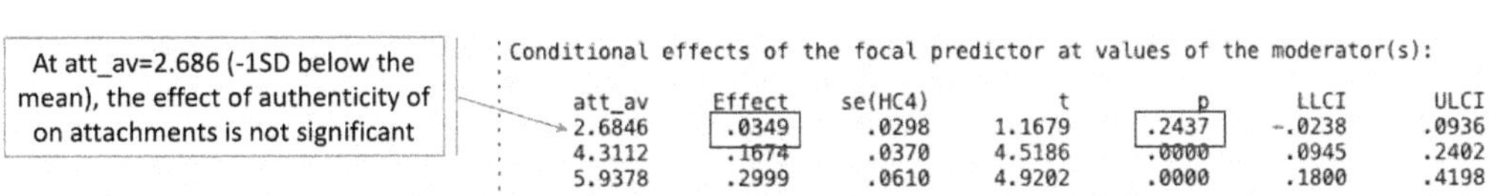


```
Conditional effects of the focal predictor at values of the moderator(s):

     att_av     Effect    se(HC4)          t          p       LLCI       ULCI
     2.6846      .0349      .0298     1.1679      .2437     -.0238      .0936
     4.3112      .1674      .0370     4.5186      .0000      .0945      .2402
     5.9378      .2999      .0610     4.9202      .0000      .1800      .4198
```

FIGURE 16.16
Outputs of the conditional effects of the PROCESS macro.

Johnson-Neyman Outputs

Because we ticked `Johnson-Neyman output`, we obtained outputs associated with the Johnson-Neyman (JN) region of significance. The JN region of significance tells us the values of the moderator at which the slope of the predictor goes from insignificant to significant and range of moderators where the slope are significant or not significant. The JN outputs are reported in two related parts. The first output informs us about values that defined the Johnson-Neyman (JN) region of significance. These values are $JN1 = 1.1331$ and $JN2 = 2.9571$ (see Figure 16.17). In the second output, it provides p-values associated with these two moderator values (for both, $p = 0.05$). Moderator values within $JN1$ and $JN2$ are not significant. Moderator values above $JN2$ are significant. This second output also produces confidence intervals associated with the moderator values. The JN region of significance is usually reported in a graph as displayed in Figure 16.19.

There is more than one way of plotting the JN plot. You can use Excel or R program (see Lin 2020). I used SPSS syntax to produce Figure 16.19. The name of the file is `JN-syntax.sps`, which you can obtain from the book's online support.

- Open the sps file on SPSS, and on the SPSS menu.
- Click **Run** → All.
- Inspect the output.

You can compare the resulting figure with Figure 16.20 produced by R (see Lin 2020).

The p-values of these thresholds are 0.05 (see next the output)

Moderator value(s) defining Johnson-Neyman significance region(s):

Value	% below	% above
1.1331	5.2023	94.7977
2.9571	19.9422	80.0578

FIGURE 16.17
Moderator values that define the Johnson-Neyman region of significance.

Moderator Values Defining the JN-Significance

Conditional effect of focal predictor at values of the moderator:

att_av	Effect	se(HC4)	t	p	LLCI	ULCI
1.0000	-.1024	.0485	-2.1101	.0356	-.1978	-.0069
1.1331	-.0915	.0465	-1.9669	.0500	-.1831	.0000
1.3158	-.0767	.0439	-1.7459	.0817	-.1630	.0097
1.6316	-.0509	.0396	-1.2848	.1997	-.1289	.0270
1.9474	-.0252	.0359	-.7030	.4825	-.0957	.0453
2.2632	.0005	.0327	.0160	.9873	-.0638	.0648
2.5789	.0262	.0304	.8637	.3884	-.0335	.0860
2.8947	.0520	.0291	1.7848	.0752	-.0053	.1093
2.9571	.0571	.0290	1.9669	.0500	.0000	.1141
3.2105	.0777	.0290	2.6768	.0078	.0206	.1348
3.5263	.1034	.0301	3.4337	.0007	.0442	.1627
3.8421	.1292	.0323	4.0008	.0001	.0657	.1927
4.1579	.1549	.0353	4.3857	.0000	.0854	.2243
4.4737	.1806	.0390	4.6289	.0000	.1039	.2574
4.7895	.2063	.0432	4.7744	.0000	.1213	.2913
5.1053	.2321	.0478	4.8566	.0000	.1381	.3261
5.4211	.2578	.0526	4.8991	.0000	.1543	.3613
5.7368	.2835	.0577	4.9170	.0000	.1701	.3969
6.0526	.3092	.0629	4.9200	.0000	.1856	.4329
6.3684	.3350	.0682	4.9139	.0000	.2009	.4691
6.6842	.3607	.0736	4.9025	.0000	.2160	.5054
7.0000	.3864	.0791	4.8881	.0000	.2309	.5419

FIGURE 16.18
Moderator values containing the Johnson-Neyman region of significance.

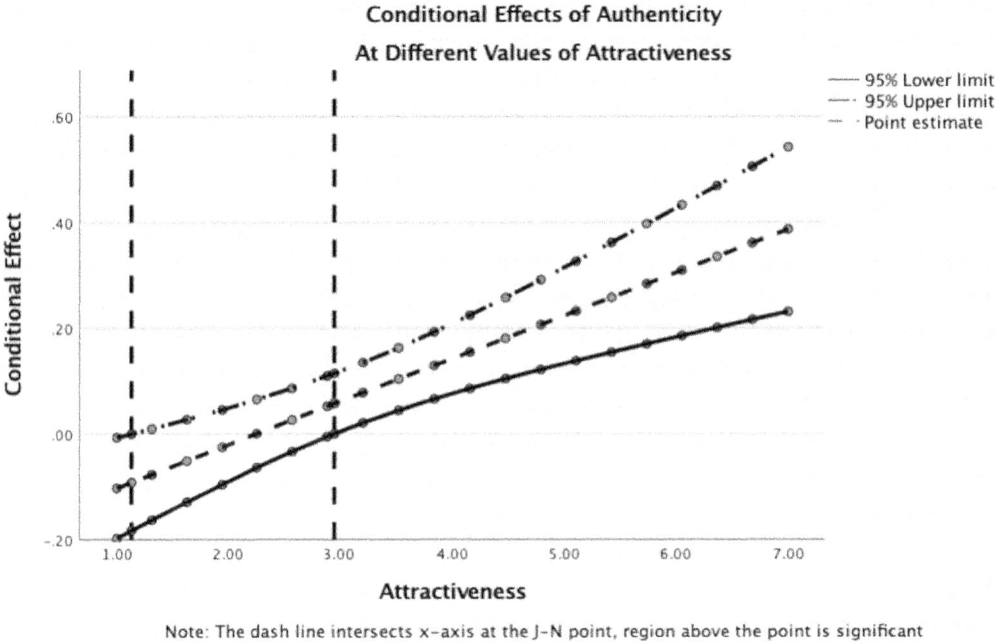

FIGURE 16.19
Johnson-Neyman plot. ns and p < 0.05 are manually added to the plot.

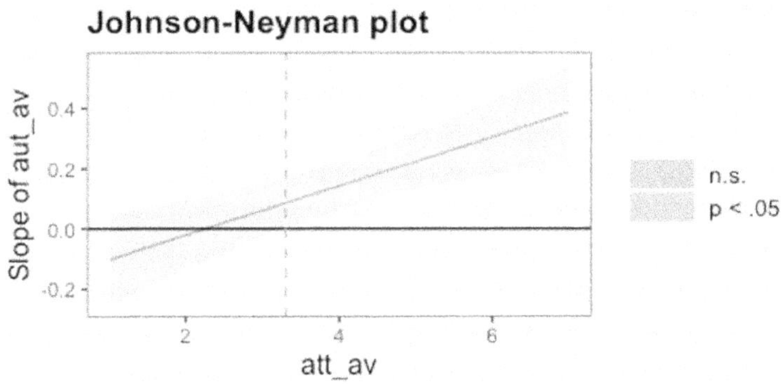

FIGURE 16.20
Johnson-Neyman plot produced by R.

16.10 Spurious Moderation

The word *spurious* means 'fake'. A spurious moderation means a fake moderation. A moderation effect is spurious when it is detected as a significant, but it is actually not. While spurious moderation can lead to misleading research conclusions, unfortunately, researchers rarely address this issue in empirical studies (Daryanto & Lukas 2022; Daryanto 2019). Daryanto & Lukas (2022) found that 'only 21 reported attempts to control for spurious moderation in marketing studies hypothesizing moderation published over the past 40 years' (p. 180). This is a very small number.

What causes a spurious moderation? Spurious moderation arises when a nonlinear effect (e.g. the relationship between X and Y resembles U-shaped) exists in a population and provided that the correlation between X and Z is nonzero, the nonlinear relationship can cause an interaction term $X\,Z$ to be significant in a sample. Technically speaking, when X and Z is correlated, the interaction terms $X\,Z$ will be correlated with the squared terms X^2 and Z^2 such that $X\,Z$ will capture variance due to the nonlinear terms and hence become significant in the regression model.

How to avoid spurious moderation? You can inspect the correlation coefficient and scatter plot of the relationship between either, Z, and Y. If the correlation is nonzero and patterns suggest nonlinear relationship, this may create the spuriousness issue. A simple solution to prevent spurious moderation effect is by inserting quadratic terms

X^2 and Z^2 into Equation 16.1. As a result, we obtain Equation 16.9. At this stage, we can compare the results of the resulting model with those of the initial model.

$$Y = \beta_0 + \beta_1 X^2 + \beta_2 Z^2 + \beta_3 X + \beta_4 Z + \beta_5 XZ + \varepsilon \tag{16.9}$$

where ε is an error term.

16.11 Summary

In this chapter, we have covered how to test a hypothesis involving moderation effect. Moderation effect is just an interaction effect captured by a cross-product term XZ in a multiple regression model called moderated regression model. A moderator Z can be a continuous or a categorical variable. When Z is a continuous variable, it is recommended to plot the JN region of significance to find out the points at which moderation is not significant. Moderation effect can be spurious when X and Z are correlated and the underlying relationship in population is non-linear. The easiest way of checking the potential spuriousness is by inserting quadratic terms X^2 and Z^2 into a moderated regression model.

16.12 Further Readings

Aguinis, H., Edwards, J. R. & Bradley, K. J. (2017), 'Improving our understanding of moderation and mediation in strategic management research', *Organizational Research Methods* **20**(4), 665–685.

Aguinis, H. & Gottfredson, R. K. (2010), 'Best-practice recommendations for estimating interaction effects using moderated multiple regression, *Journal of Organizational Behavior* **31**(6), 776–786.

Daryanto, A. (2019), 'Avoiding spurious moderation effects: An information-theoretic approach to moderation analysis', *Journal of Business Research* **103**, 110–118.

Daryanto, A. & Lukas, B. A. (2022), 'Controlling for spurious moderation in marketing: A review of statistical techniques', *Journal of Business Research* **144**, 180–192.

Hayes, A. F. (2017), *Introduction to mediation, moderation, and conditional process analysis: A regression-based approach*, Guilford publications.
Jaccard, J. & Turrisi, R. (2003), *Interaction effects in multiple regression*, Number 72, Sage.
Spiller, S. A., Fitzsimons, G. J., Lynch Jr, J. G. & McClelland, G. H. (2013), 'Spotlights, floodlights, and the magic number zero: Simple effects tests in moderated regression', *Journal of Marketing Research* **50**(2), 277–288.

16.13 Review Questions

1. Write down an equation for a moderation regression model.
2. What is the meaning of the regression coefficients in the model?
3. Why do some researchers mean-centre the predictors in the moderated regression model?
4. How would you test whether an interaction term between two variables is significant?

16.14 Exercises

Download robot.sav from the book's website, and use it to conduct a moderated regression analysis using PROCESS macro with consumer intention to join a loyalty program (`Intent`) as a dependent variable, environmental concern (`EC`) as an independent variable, and anticipated `Guilt` as a moderator.

1. Is the moderation effect significant? If yes, interpret the pattern of the moderation effect.
2. Plot JN region of significance and identify the points at which the moderation effect is not significant.

17

Endogeneity

One of the assumptions in regression is that the independent variable should be unrelated to the regression error term. However, if a variable affecting a dependent variable is also correlated with the independent variable but omitted from the regression model, the coefficient associated with the independent variable will be inaccurate. A regression model that breaks the assumption is said to suffer from an endogeneity problem. This chapter focuses on how to address the endogeneity problem and explains the use of two-stage least square (TSLS) that can be used to estimate the regression coefficients in the presence of endogeneity. The chapter discusses three key important tests used to assess endogeneity: Hausman's specification test, an overidentifying test, and a weak instrument test. The discussion is facilitated using an SPSS macro called `EndoS`, developed by the author.

Learning Objectives:

- Understand the concept of endogeneity.
- Have a basic understanding of how the TSLS estimator works.
- Be able to use EndoS macro to assess endogeneity.

17.1 What Is Endogeneity?

Lancaster, where I currently reside, is known as – at least by me – a city of barbershops. Despite it is a small town, there are more than ten barbershops around the city centre. Just to give you an idea, normally, it just took me from five to ten minutes to walk around the city centre. So, you can imagine that the competition among the barbershops in the Lancaster's city centre is quite intense. Although there are several alternatives for getting my hair cut, I prefer to stick to one barbershop because I found its background music is quite relaxing. This intrigues me. My modelling mindset leads me to contemplate whether background music really influences customers' intentions to visit a barbershop in the future. I would like to study individuals who visit the barbershop for the first time because they have not heard the types of music that are played there. For this, I can create a survey and ask new customers to indicate their likelihood of visiting the barbershop again in the future. I am prompting them with a question: will you visit the same barbershop in the future (1 = very unlikely, 5 = highly likely)? The response answers are stored in a variable called *REVISIT*. I will also measure their attitude toward the background music with a 5-point bipolar scale: how do you like the background music played in the barbershop (1 = extremely dislike it, 7 = like it very

 DOI: 10.4324/9781003407225-22

much)? The response answers are stored in a variable called *MUSIC*. Thus, I come up with the following simple linear regression model:

$$REVISIT = \beta_0 + \beta_1 MUSIC + \varepsilon \tag{17.1}$$

We know from Chapter 12, in the model, *REVISIT* is a dependent variable, *MUSIC* is a predictor, and ε is an error term. The error term ε can contain a variable, say, *O*, that may affect *REVISIT* – '*O*' stands for *omitted*. The variable *O* can be omitted from the model because either the data is missing, which can happen when all respondents in the survey refuse to answer particular questions, or I simply have limited knowledge about other variables that should be included in the model.

Of course, you can argue that *MUSIC* is not the only variable that can affect *REVISIT* and one factor that can be potentially included in the model is how customers like the barber (e.g. 'I like this barber', measured with a Likert scale ranging from 1 = strongly disagree to 7 = strongly agree) – stored in a variable *BARBER* (you bet, all customers will be more than happy to respond to this question). If this is the case, my revised model will look like this:

$$REVISIT = \beta_0 + \beta_1 MUSIC + \beta_2 BARBER + \varepsilon \tag{17.2}$$

If *BARBER* has no influence on *REVISIT* and is not correlated with *MUSIC*, and no other variables affect *REVISIT*, I can use Equation 17.1 to find the precise estimate of the influence of *MUSIC* on *REVISIT*. However, *BARBER* may have an impact on *REVISIT* and is also correlated with *MUSIC*. I expect there would be a correlation between the two, which might be quite small – you like the barber partly because he or she plays your favourite music. In this situation, the estimate for β_1 in Equation 17.1 will be biased. This means, the estimate will not reveal the true magnitude of the influence of *MUSIC* on *REVISIT* in a population because *BARBER* is omitted.

The modelling situation where a predictor is correlated with the error term is referred to as **endogeneity**. Because it is considered as a modelling 'problem', the term 'endogeneity problem' is also commonly used. The variable *MUSIC* in Equation 17.1 that is correlated with the error term is referred to as an **endogenous** variable. A variable that is not correlated with an error term is referred to as an **exogenous** variable.

IMPORTANT

Omitting an important variable from a model is not the only cause of an endogeneity problem. Endogeneity can also arise when (1) variables are measured with errors or (2) the causal effects run both from $X \rightarrow Y$ and from $Y \rightarrow X$, known in the regression literature as simultaneity.

17.2 Two-Stage Least Squares (TSLS)

One of the techniques to deal with endogeneity is the two-stage least squares (TSLS). Remember, we are dealing with Equation 17.1 where *BARBER* does not exist in our data – this is where TSLS can be applied. Our objective is to estimate β_1 in Equation 17.1 while taking into account for endogeneity. If we have the information about *BARBER*, we do not have to apply TSLS; we can simply include *MUSIC* and *BARBER* into our regression model.

However, there is a challenge in implementing TSLS as it requires us to find a variable known as an instrumental variable or instrument, for short. Let us call this variable as Z. To put Z for any use, it must satisfy the following assumptions:

- *Z* must be correlated with *MUSIC*. This is referred to as a relevance assumption.
- *Z* must be uncorrelated with an error term *O*. This is referred to as an exogeneity assumption.
- *Z* affects *REVISIT* only via *MUSIC*. This is referred to as an exclusion restriction assumption.

Figure 17.1 shows the relationship between the instrument *Z*, the endogenous variable, and the dependent variable *Y*.

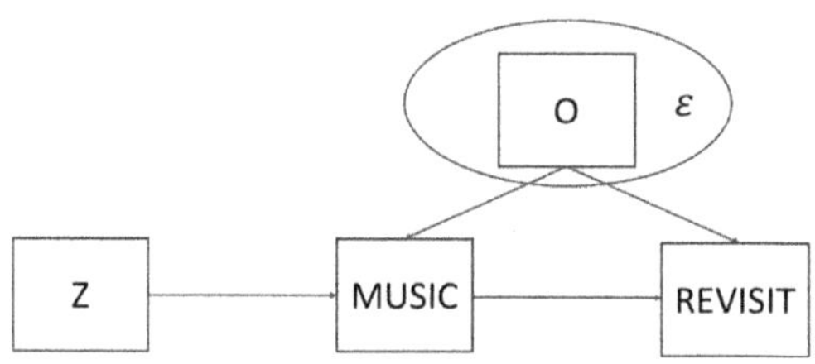

FIGURE 17.1
Z affects REVISIT indirectly via MUSIC.

In an endogeneity situation, the variation in *MUSIC* will consist of parts that are correlated and uncorrelated with the error term *O*. The role of *Z* is to capture the uncorrelated part and used it to replace *MUSIC* in Equation 17.1. As the TSLS acronym suggests, TSLS is conducted in two stages:

Stage 1. Use the OLS regression procedure in SPSS or R to conduct a simple regression because we only have one predictor. That is, *MUSIC* is regressed on *Z*. If we have other predictors, we can also enter them. Next, we save the predicted value of *MUSIC*. The predicted value of a variable has another symbol by putting a 'hat' above the variable. Here, the predicted value of our interest is $\widehat{MUSIC}$ (read: *MUSIC* hat), which is uncorrelated with the error term.

Stage 2. Conduct another regression wherein *REVISIT* is regressed on $\widehat{MUSIC}$. The resulting regression coefficient associated with $\widehat{MUSIC}$, denoted by β_{TSLS}, tells us the effect of *MUSIC* on *REVISIT*. This coefficient is more accurate than the coefficient obtained from the OLS regression procedure. Because the standard error for β_{TSLS} is obtained by using the ordinary least squares (OLS) estimator – one you usually use in SPSS regression – and we want to say something about the effect of *MUSIC* instead of $\widehat{MUSIC}$, the standard error obtained from these steps needs to be adjusted. This issue will not be a concern if you use a software that can calculate the correct standard error. One software that runs in the SPSS environment is one that I wrote: EndoS (Daryanto, 2020*a*).

17.3 Illustration

In this section, I demonstrate how to use EndoS to deal with an endogeneity problem. We stick to our example to find out the effect of a background music ($MUSIC$) on revisit intention to a barbershop ($REVISIT$).

We learned previously that estimating Equation 17.1 creates endogeneity as we don't include $BARBER$ in the model. If we have $BARBER$, then it can just be included in the model. Suppose that we do not have this variable in our data and still want to estimate the effect of background music on revisit intention. We will carry on by accounting for endogeneity. To overcome the endogeneity problem, we need to find a valid instrument Z. This is the hardest part. We can try. I am tempted to suggest my Z would be the number of music collections – this includes either CDs, vinyl records, and digital downloads – that a customer has, denoted by variable CDs. However, CDs must satisfy the relevance and the exogeneity assumptions explained previously. That is, to satisfy the relevance assumption, CDs should correlate with $MUSIC$. We can easily argue that if one has many music collections, one loves music and enjoys listening to a variety of genres or musicians which can be played in a barbershop. Therefore, we would expect CDs to be correlated with one's liking to the background music played in the barbershop.

To satisfy the exogeneity assumption, CDs should not be correlated with the error term. As we knew that $BARBER$ might be included in the error term, we can assume that CDs is not correlated with $BARBER$. Do you think the number of music CDs you have at home correlates with the extent to which you like the barber? You might like the barber because he put on your favourite music to play in the barbershop. But if your liking toward the barber is purely because of his skills, then we assume CDs and $BARBER$ to be uncorrelated. If this is the case, we satisfy the exogeneity assumption.

The relationship between the instrumental variable CDs, the endogenous variable $MUSIC$, and the dependent variable $REVISIT$ can be represented by a path diagram displayed in Figure 17.2

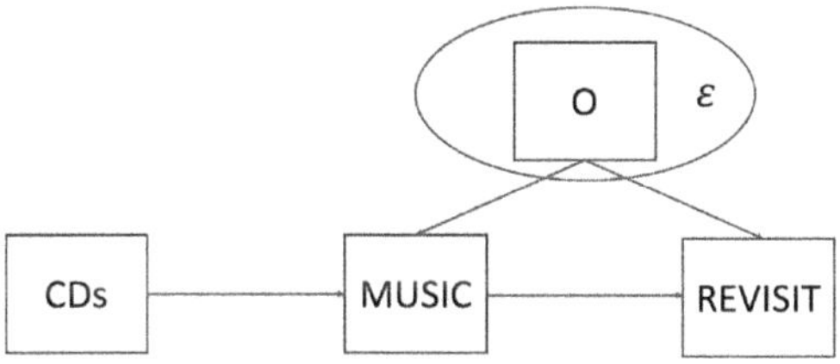

FIGURE 17.2
CDs affects REVISIT via MUSIC. CDs is an instrumental variable.

17.4 SPSS Action and Interpretation

Data: barbeshop.sav

I created a fictitious data barbershop.sav, which contains responses of 300 customers. The data contains four variables that are in the standardized forms (having mean of 0 and a standard deviation of 1): *MUSIC, CDs, REVISIT,* and *WAIT. WAIT* measures the amount of time an individual has to wait before being served by the barber. The model that we are examining is presented in Figure 17.3.

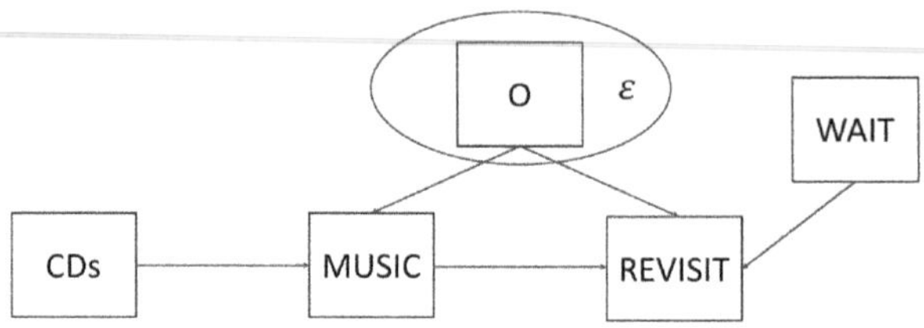

FIGURE 17.3
WAIT is a control variable affecting REVISIT.

Now, let us use the `EndoS` macro to examine the effect of background music on revisit intention while accounting for endogeneity. You need to install the software onto SPSS – you can download from the book's online support. After you have done this, find `EndoS` by clicking Analyze → Regression. You will see list of procedures including `EndoS` that you have successfully installed. The screen capture of the `EndoS` for this example can be seen in Figure 2.

As you can see from the figure, I have inserted *REVISIT* to the `dependent variable` box and *CDs* and *WAIT* into the `Independent variable` box. Notice in the `Instrument` box that I have inserted *CDs* and *WAIT*. It is important to note that *WAIT* appears both in the `Instrument` and in the `Independent variable` box. A variable that appears both in the `Independent variable` and `Instrument` box is considered as an instrument for itself. We call this an internal instrument. As you can also see, *CDs* appears in the `Instrument` box only. Entering *WAIT* and *CDs* in this fashion tells the macro that *CDs* is an instrument variable associated with *MUSIC*.

Now, click the 'Option' button, you can tick all boxes under the 'Diagnostic' tests (see Figure 17.5) to instruct `EndoS` to perform the three diagnostic tests that I will explain in the section.

As a result of ticking the options shown in Figure 17.5, `EndoS` produces a long list of outputs. I break down the outputs and discuss them into four sections. Note that in the first line of the outputs that you will see on your SPSS outputs, `EndoS` prints the number of missing cases that are discarded in the analysis. In the current dataset used for this illustration, there are no missing cases.

17.4.1 OLS Regression

`EndoS` produces OLS regression outputs obtained by applying the ordinary least squares (OLS) estimator (see Figure 17.6). As can be seen from the figure, the regression

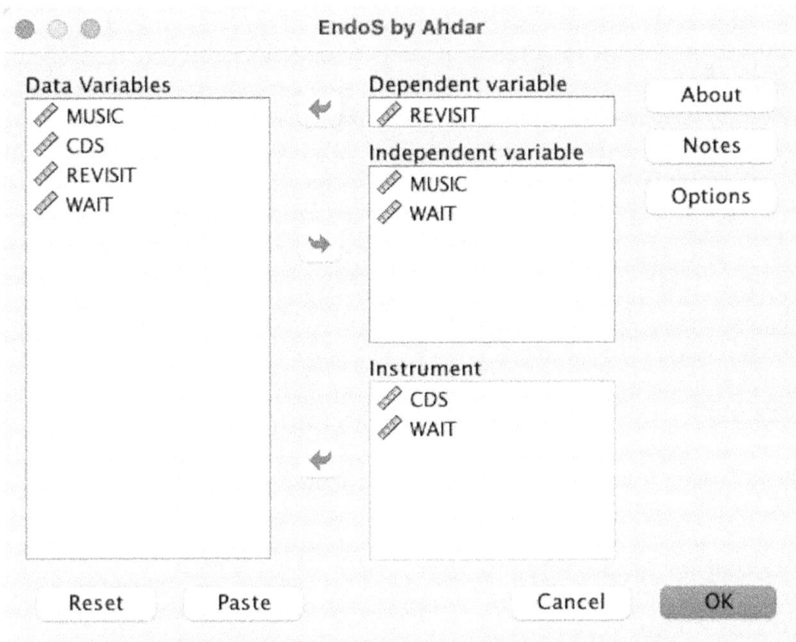

FIGURE 17.4
EndoS macro.

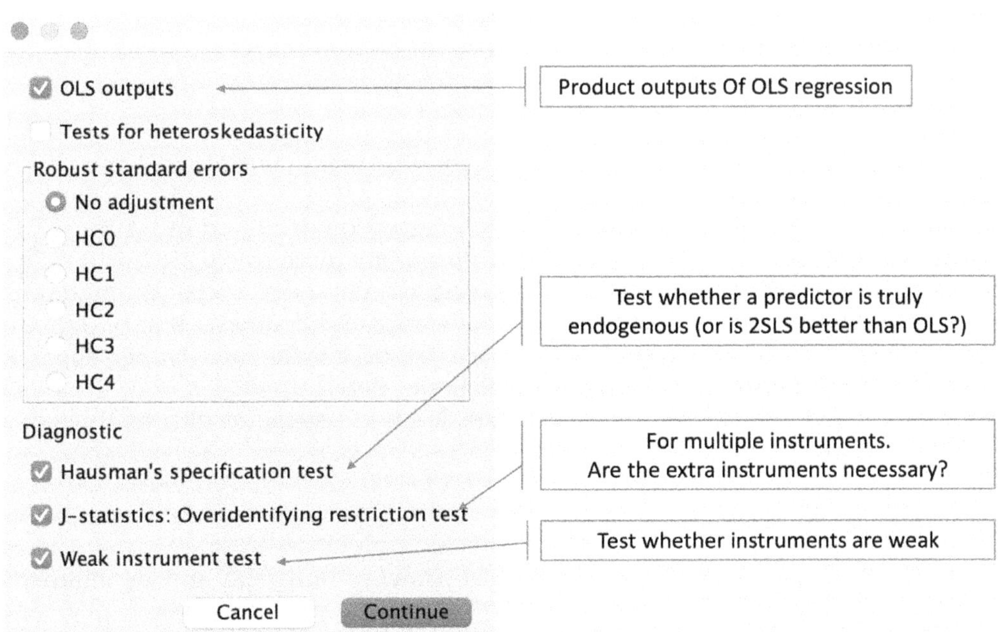

FIGURE 17.5
Options in EndoS.

```
Two-Stage Least Squares

written by Ahmad Daryanto

https://sites.google.com/site/ahmaddaryanto/

-----------------------------------------

OLS regression

Sample size (complete cases)f
  300

Dependent variable (DV)
   REVISIT

Independent variable (IVs)
   MUSIC       WAIT

Model summary
       R^2         Adj         SER
     .4227       .4168       .8295

Note: Adj = Adjusted R^2, SER = Std. error of regression.

OLS outputs
                    b          se           t         sig       95%LB       95%UB
constant         .000        .048        .000       1.000       -.094        .094
MUSIC            .583        .042      13.852        .000        .501        .666
WAIT             .169        .050       3.370        .001        .071        .267

* Note: standard errors are assumed to be homoskedastic--no adjustments.
```

FIGURE 17.6
OLS outputs produced by EndoS.

coefficient for *MUSIC* is 0.583, which is significant. This means that *MUSIC* has a positive influence on revisit intention.

However, if we look at the result of the TSLS regression displayed in Figure 17.7, the coefficient associated with *MUSIC* is not significant anymore ($p = 0.288 > 0.05$). Thus, after applying TSLS that accounts for endogeneity, we found that the background music has no influence on the revisit intention. Therefore, my hypothesis that background music will influence whether new customers to come back to the same barbershop is not supported by the data – after all, this is just fictitious data!

However, before we settle in this conclusion, let us assess the results the three diagnostic tests reported by `EndoS`.

17.4.2 Hausman's Specification Test

The Hausman's specification test assess the following null (H0) and its alternative hypotheses (H1):

H0: *MUSIC* is an exogenous variable (OLS is better).

H1: *MUSIC* is an endogenous variable (TSLS is better than OLS).

```
=========================================

Two-Stage Least Squares

Sample size (complete cases)
  300

Dependent Variable
   REVISIT

Endogeneous (instrumented) variable
   MUSIC

Instrument(s)
   WAIT       CDS

External instrument(s)
   CDS

Note: External instrument(s) is truly exogeneous, not part of the original model.

Model summary
       R^2        Adj        SER
     .1954      .1873      .9792


      df(m)    df(res)          F       Sig.
    2.0000   297.0000     9.7324      .0001

Note: Adj = Adjusted R^2, SER = Std. error of regression.

TSLS outputs
                     b          se          t        sig       95%LB       95%UB
constant          .000        .057       .000      1.000       -.111        .111
MUSIC             .128        .120      1.065       .288       -.108        .364
WAIT              .233        .061      3.816       .000        .113        .353

-----------------------------------------

* Note: standard errors are assumed to be homoskedastic--no adjustments.
```

FIGURE 17.7
TLS outputs produced by EndoS. Music is not significant.

To assess the significance of H1, we need to look at the significance of the 'resid' variable (i.e. resid1).

If we look at the results of the Hausman's test (Figure 17.8), $resid1$ is significant ($p < 0.001$). This test is associated with the p-value of the F statistic reported in the next line ($F = 24.113, p < 0.001$). Therefore, H0 is rejected and consequently we accept the alternative hypothesis that $MUSIC$ is indeed an endogenous variable – TSLS is better than OLS. Based on this result and the TSLS outputs, we are confident to conclude that background music has no influence on customers' revisit intentions.

17.4.3 Overidentifying Restriction Test

The next line of the outputs is those of the overidentifying test. The test is carried out if we used multiple instruments Z s. In our example, we have only one Z. The null (H0) and alternative hypotheses (H1) associated with the test are:

H0: All instruments are exogenous.

H1. One of the instruments is endogenous (i.e. correlated with the error term).

```
Hausman's specification test: Two-stage OLS regression using residuals as predictors.

Note: Results obtained via two stages.

Stage 1: Endogeneous variables are regressed on the IVs and external instruments.

Stage 2: DV is regressed on IVs and residuals obtained from stage 1.

The test assumes that the errors in stage 2 are homoskedastic.

Dependent variable
  REVISIT

Model summary
      R^2        Adj        SER
    .4695      .4623      .7964

    df(m)    df(res)          F      Sig.
   3.0000   296.0000    87.3303     .0000

Note: Adj = Adjusted R^2, SER = Std. error of regression.

=======
                b         se          t        sig      95%LB      95%UB
constant     .000       .046       .000      1.000     -.090       .090
MUSIC        .128       .098      1.310       .191     -.064       .320
WAIT         .233       .050      4.691       .000      .136       .331
resid1       .549       .107      5.114       .000      .339       .759

-----

Joint F test for the significance of the 'resid' variables
       df1        df2          F      Sig.
     1.000    296.000     24.113      .000

H0: Instrumented variables are exogeneous (OLS is efficient) (i.e., estimates of all resids are equal to zero).

H1: Instrumented variables are endogeneous.
```

FIGURE 17.8
Results of the Hausman's specification test produced by EndoS.

```
Overidentifying restrictions test (The J-statistic)
Value      .000
Sig.      1.000

H0: All instruments are exogenous.

The test assumes a large sample size, strong instruments, and homoskedastic errors.
```

FIGURE 17.9
Results of the overidentifying restrictions test produced by EndoS.

As we have only one instrument, therefore, this test is not applicable. For one instrument, the value of the *J* statistic is printed as 0 with p-value is equal to 1. For multiple instruments, if the test is not significant ($p - value < 0.05$), then all instruments are likely to be exogenous. Likewise, if the test is not significant, one of the instruments is related to the error term, in which case we should not use the variable as an instrument.

17.4.4 Weak Instrument Test

An instrument is considered as weak if it weakly correlates with the instrumental variable *Z*. To know whether *CDs* is a weak instrument, we look at the *F* statistic related to first-stage regression of the TSLS procedure. If the *F* statistic is less than 10, the instrument is considered as weak (Staiger & Stock 1997). In the output of Figure 17.10, the *F* statistic is larger than 10, so *CDs* is not a weak instrument.

```
Weak instrument tests

Cragg-Donald F-statistic
   61.2717

Stock-Yogo critical values for the weak instrument test based on TSLS size at 5% significance level:
        Size     Values
         .10      16.38
         .15       8.96
         .20       6.66
         .25       5.53

Stock-Yogo critical values for relative bias are not available for models with less than 3 instruments.

Note: For one endogeneous variable, Cragg-Donald F-statistic is the F-value of first stage regression.

For one endogeneous regressor, instruments are weak if the F-statistics is less than 10 (Staiger and Stock, 1997).

Note: Tables for the critical values (Stock & Yogo, 2002) are reproduced by permission—email communication (Stock, 16-11-2019).
```

FIGURE 17.10
Results of the weak instrument test produced by EndoS.

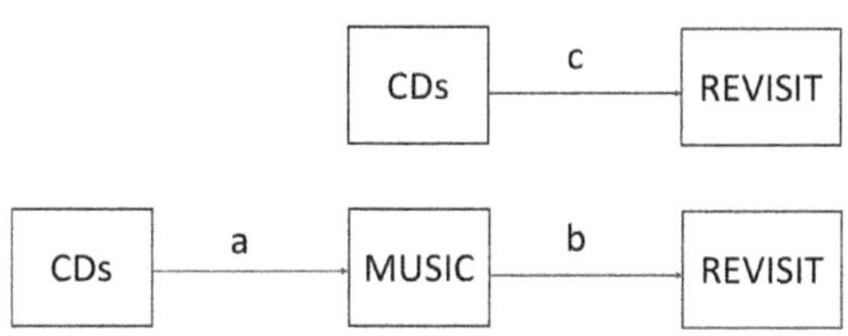

FIGURE 17.11
Model without (above) and with a mediator variable (below).

17.5 Instrument as a Part of a Mediation Model

The framework shown in Figure 17.1 is a mediation model (see Chapter 15). Let us see the two diagrams shown in Figure 17.11, which present two models: without and with a mediator *MUSIC*. For ease of presentation, a control variable WAIT is not shown in the models.

In the diagrams, *a* captures the effect of *CDs* on *MUSIC*, *b* captures the effect of *MUSIC* on *REVISIT* – this is our interest, and *c* captures the effect of *CDs* on *Revisit*, which represent a total effect in the language of mediation that we learned in Chapter 15.

As discussed in Chapter 15, total effect = direct effect + indirect effect. If you can recall, the direct effect was obtained by regressing the dependent variable on both the predictor and mediator: *REVISIT* on *CDs* and *MUSIC*. However, as you can see in Figure 17.11, there is no direct path from *CDs* to *REVISIT*, which means that the direct effect is assumed to be zero. Thus, total effect = indirect effect.

The indirect effect can be calculated by multiplying *a* with *b*. Therefore, total effect = $a \times b$.

The total effect *c* can be obtained by regressing *REVISIT* on *CDs* and *WAIT*. We found $c = 0.054$.

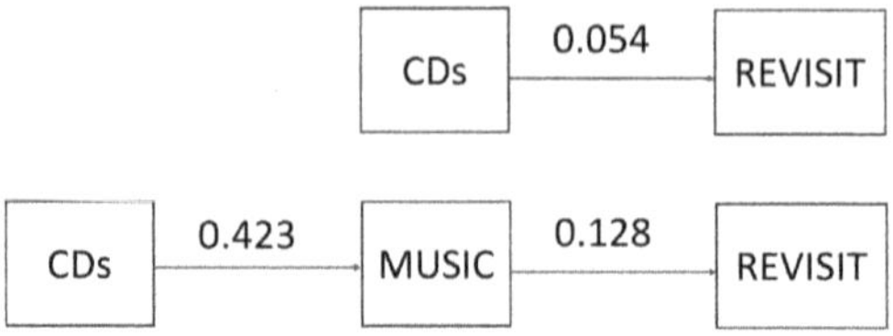

FIGURE 17.12
Running a series of regressions produce a coefficient estimate of the effect of MUSIC on REVISIT.

Now, regressing $MUSIC$ on CDs and $WAIT$, we obtain $a = 0.423$. Using these results, $b = \dfrac{0.054}{0.423} = 0.128$.

We know earlier from the TSLS outputs of the EndoS that this value is equal to β_{TSLS}. We can put these results together in a diagram as depicted in Figure 17.12.

The key takeaway from this exercise is that the estimate of the effect of $MUSIC$ on $REVISIT$ can be obtained by running a series of regression that follows a mediation model in which $MUSIC$ is treated as a mediator.

17.6 Summary

In this chapter I have discussed the concept of endogeneity and the principle of the two-stage least square (TSLS) estimation technique that can be used to estimate the effect of an independent variable on a dependent variable when endogeneity is present. The endogeneity analysis is facilitated by `EndoS` macro that I developed. Three key outputs of the macro are explained, which include the results of the Hausman's specification test, the overidentifying restriction test, and the weak instrument test. These tests are essential in an endogeneity analysis. I have also shown how to obtain the estimate of the coefficient of an independent variable that is similar to that of the TSLS by undertaking a mediation analysis.

17.7 Further Readings

Antonakis, J., Bendahan, S., Jacquart, P. & Lalive, R. (2014), 'Causality and endogeneity: Problems and solutions', *The Oxford Handbook of Leadership and Organizations* **1**, 93–117.

Busenbark, J. R., Yoon, H., Gamache, D. L. & Withers, M. C. (2022), 'Omitted variable bias: Examining management research with the impact threshold of a confounding variable (ITCV)', *Journal of Management* **48**(1), 17–48.

Daryanto, A. (2020), 'EndoS: An SPSS macro to assess endogeneity', *The Quantitative Methods for Psychology* **16**(1), 56–70.

Sande, J. B. & Ghosh, M. (2018), 'Endogeneity in survey research', *International Journal of Research in Marketing* **35**(2), 185–204.

17.8 Review Questions

1. Explain what an endogeneity problem is.
2. Explain assumptions that must be satisfied if a variable is chosen as an instrument.
3. What is the idea behind the weak instrument test?

17.9 Exercise

Using the barbershop.sav data, conduct a two-stage least square regression with EndoS by leaving out variable *WAIT* as a control variable.

18

Analysis of Variance

Many research endeavours in marketing require measurements of variables that are categorical (e.g. differences in purchase behaviours of loyal vs. non-loyal customers). Regression analysis involving a categorical variable with two categories can be used in such context. The analysis entails comparing group means using a dummy variable. When the comparisons involve more than two groups, more than one dummy variable is required in which one group serves as a baseline to which other groups' means are compared. This chapter focuses on how to assess mean differences using an analysis of variance (ANOVA), which can be used to compare means of more than two groups simultaneously.

Learning Objectives:

- Understand the concept of ANOVA.
- Know assumptions in ANOVA.
- Understand the meaning of between-groups and within-groups sum of squares.
- Understand the notion of effect size.
- Be able to analyse data using one-way ANOVA procedure in SPSS and R.

18.1 Comparing Means

When we use ANOVA, our aim is to compare means of several groups in a population. For example, we might be interested in comparing mean satisfaction scores of young, medium, and old-aged consumers. The null hypothesis in ANOVA is that the group means in the population are equal, and the alternative hypothesis that one of the means differ. The null and alternative hypotheses in a one-way ANOVA are formulated as follows:

$$H_0 : \mu_1 = \mu_2 = \mu_3$$
$$H_A\text{: one of the } \mu\text{'s differ}$$

μ_i is the population mean of group i. In this case we have three groups.

As there are three group means, if the null hypothesis is rejected, these situations are possible: μ_1 is different from $\mu_2 = \mu_3, \mu_2$ is different from $\mu_1 = \mu_3$, or the three means are completely different from each other, $\mu_1 \neq \mu_2 \neq \mu_3$. Detecting why the null hypothesis is rejected is tantamount to finding which of the possible situations

DOI: 10.4324/9781003407225-23

is possible. The endeavor is facilitated by conducting a post hoc test explained in Section 18.5.

Testing the null hypothesis in ANOVA is based on an *F* statistic calculated as:

$$F = \frac{Between\ -groups\ variance}{Within\ -groups\ variance}$$

As you can see from the expression, even though we are interested in comparing means, the analysis involves the calculations of variance. This is probably the reason the test is called the analysis of variance instead of the analysis of means. The calculation of between-groups variance is based on the variance of the sample means, whereas the calculation of within-groups variance is based on the variance of scores within each group. In the next section, I demonstrate how to calculate the *F* statistic using outputs from SPSS and in the following section, I show how to manually calculate sum of squares, which represents variability in the scores. Dividing sum of scores with its associated degrees of freedom produces variance.

NOTE

With different samples, you would obtain different values of *F*. Given the collection of *F* values, we can construct a sampling distribution. That is, if the null hypothesis is true, the *F* statistic will be distributed according to an *F* distribution (see Section 7.3).

18.1.1 SPSS Action

Data: repurchase.sav

I have created a fictitious data with a small sample size for an illustration on how to perform ANOVA Figure 18.1. The scenario could be as follows: The marketing manager was interested in determining whether there are differences across three groups of consumers classified into young, middle-aged, and elderly in their intentions to repurchase a product that is currently unavailable in his store shelf. The manager asked consumers who visited his store to fill in a questionnaire that contains an item measuring their repurchase intention: 'I want to repurchase product A if it is available again in this store.' Consumers indicated their answers on a 7-point Likert scale ranging from 1 = strongly agree to 7 = strongly agree. In the data, repurchase intention was stored as 'repurchase' variable, and age group was stored as `age` variable coded as 1 = young (n = 3), 2 = middle-age (n = 2), and 3 = elderly (n = 2) – the number in the brackets indicates the number of consumers who filled in the survey. In the data, the repurchase intention is stored in `repurchase` column, and age category is stored in `age column`. The `male` column recorded the gender of consumers (1 = male, 0 = female). We will use the `male` variable in Section 18.7.

	age	repurchase	male
1	1.00	1.00	.00
2	1.00	3.00	1.00
3	1.00	1.00	.00
4	2.00	4.00	1.00
5	2.00	6.00	.00
6	2.00	5.00	.00
7	3.00	6.00	.00
8	3.00	7.00	.00
9	3.00	4.00	1.00

FIGURE 18.1
Repurchase data.

Steps

- Analyze → Compare Means → One-Way ANOVA.
- Insert `repurchase` into `Dependent List box.`
- Insert `age` into `Factor` box.
- Uncheck 'Estimate effect size for an overall test'. We will need to check this box again when discussing effect size. For the time being, we leave it unchecked.
- Click `Options.`
- Under `Statistics, check Descriptive.`
- Check `Means plot.`
- Click OK.

If you click `Paste`, SPSS yields the following syntax:

```
ONEWAY repurchase BY age
   /STATISTICS DESCRIPTIVES
   /PLOT MEANS
   /MISSING ANALYSIS
   /CRITERIA=CILEVEL(0.95)
```

You will obtain three chunks of outputs: descriptive table, means plot, and ANOVA table.

Descriptive statistics and means plot

The descriptive statistics table shown in Figure 18.2 display means of the three groups and their standard deviations. As you can see from the table, the mean of the second group is relatively equal to that of the third group. The two groups' means are larger than that of the first group. These mean scores are plotted in a line graph displayed in Figure 18.3. The standard deviations of the three groups are also relatively equal.

The plot of the means is displayed in Figure 18.3. The plot is trivial as we have seen the means in the descriptive statistics after all. It would better to create a box plot, in this case three box plots, which give us more information about our data (see Figure 18.4)

The box plot in group 1 looks unusual – the lower whisker is missing and as if the median is also missing. But this is not surprising as the minimum and the median of repurchase intention in group 1 is the same (can you check that?).

Descriptives

repurchase

	N	Mean	Std. Deviation	Std. Error	95% Confidence Interval for Mean Lower Bound	Upper Bound	Minimum	Maximum
1.00	3	1.6667	1.15470	.66667	-1.2018	4.5351	1.00	3.00
2.00	3	5.0000	1.00000	.57735	2.5159	7.4841	4.00	6.00
3.00	3	5.6667	1.52753	.88192	1.8721	9.4612	4.00	7.00
Total	9	4.1111	2.14735	.71578	2.4605	5.7617	1.00	7.00

FIGURE 18.2
Descriptive statistics produced by SPSS one-way ANOVA.

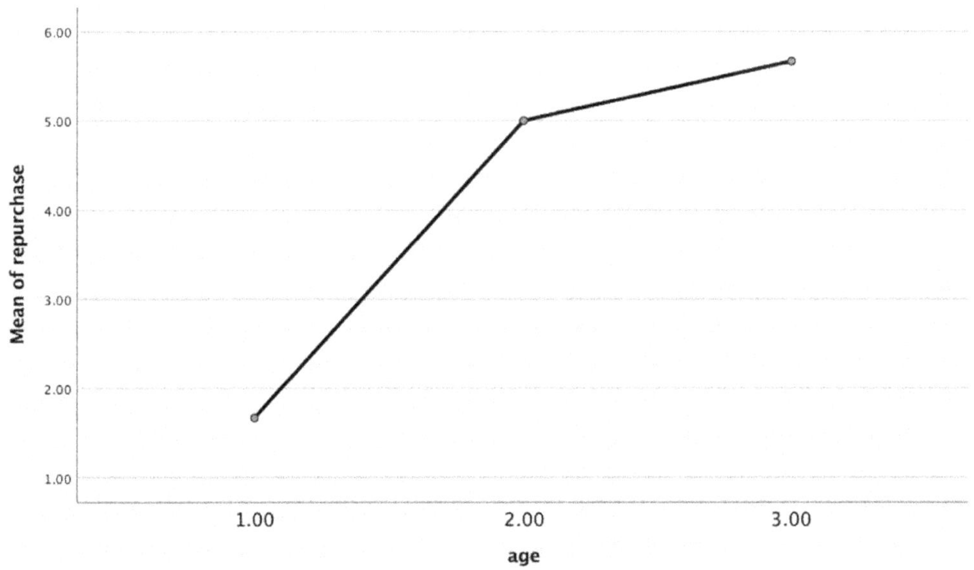

FIGURE 18.3
Means plot produced by the SPSS one-way ANOVA procedure.

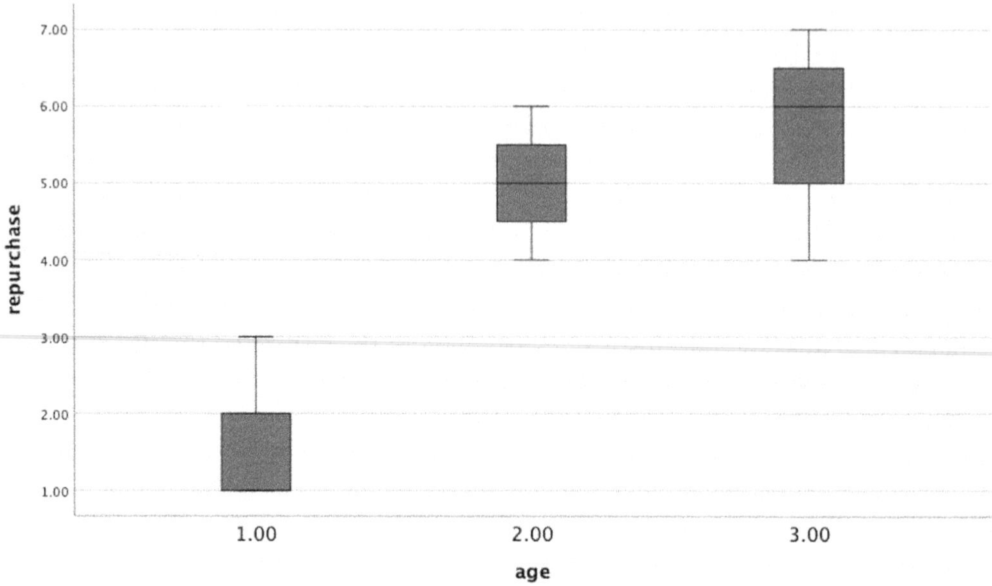

FIGURE 18.4
Box plots of each age category.

ANOVA

repurchase

	Sum of Squares	df	Mean Square	F	Sig.
Between Groups	27.556	2	13.778	8.857	.016
Within Groups	9.333	6	1.556		
Total	36.889	8			

FIGURE 18.5
One-Way ANOVA table.

ANOVA Table

The ANOVA table is shown in Figure 18.5.

- The sum of squares column displays the between-groups sum of squares, the within-groups sum of squares, and the total sum of squares. The total sum of squares is equal to between-groups sum of squares plus within-groups sum of squares.

$$SS_{Between} = 27.556$$
$$SS_{Within} = 9.333$$
$$SS_{Total} = 27.556 + 9.333$$
$$= 36.889$$

- The df column displays:
  - The degrees of freedom for the grouping variable (i.e. age) computed as the number of groups in the age variable minus 1 (i.e. $K - 1$), in this case $df_1 = 3 - 1 = 2$;
  - The degrees of freedom for the residuals calculated as the total number of observations minus the number of groups in the age variable (i.e. $N - K$), in this case $df_2 = 9 - 3 = 6$;
  - The degrees of freedom total (df_{Total}), which is the sum of df_1 and df_2, that is 2 + 6 = 8, alternatively it can be calculated by total number of observations minus one ($N - 1$), that is 9–1 = 8.
- The mean square column is the mean of the sum of squares, calculated by dividing the sum of squares by the degrees of freedom associated with each row.

$$\begin{aligned} MS_{Between} &= \frac{SS_{Between}}{df_1} \\ &= \frac{27.556}{2} \\ &= 13.778 \end{aligned}$$

$$\begin{aligned} MS_{Within} &= \frac{SS_{Within}}{df_2} \\ &= \frac{9.333}{6} \\ &= 1.556 \end{aligned}$$

- The F value column is the F statistic. The larger the F value, the more likely we are going to reject the null hypothesis.
- Last column is the p-value of the F statistic. The F statistic is calculated as:

$$\begin{aligned} F &= \frac{MS_{Between}}{MS_{Within}} \\ &= \frac{13.778}{1.556} \\ &= 8.857 \end{aligned}$$

To decide whether or not we reject the null hypothesis, we read the p-value of the F statistic. This F statistic is distributed according an F distribution with $df_1 = 2$, $df_2 = 6$. The $F = 8.857$ is associated with a $p - value = 0.016$, which is smaller than a 5% significance level. As the p-value is less than 5% significance level, we can reject the null hypothesis and conclude that three group means do not the same. Alternatively, you can compare the F statistic with F critical. You can use the `QFDIST` macro (see Chapter 7) by `Probability = 0.05`, `df1 = 2`, and `df2 = 6; under` Tail, `choose` Right-tail. The `screen image` of theQFDIST and the output are displayed in Figure 18.6. As you can see from the output, the F critical is given by $x = 5.143$. As the F statistic (8.857) is larger than the F critical (5.143), we reject the null hypothesis.

18.1.2 R Action

We can use the `aov()` function from R base to calculate the *F* statistic and p-value and produce the outputs using the `summary()` function. The expression in the `aov()` takes in this format: `aov(y ~ group, data = data)` where *y* is the variable that we use for a comparison – in this case `repurchase` – and `group` is the categorical variable – in this case is the `age`. However, when we read the SPSS data, `age` is considered as a numerical variable. For this reason, we need to convert `age` as a factor.

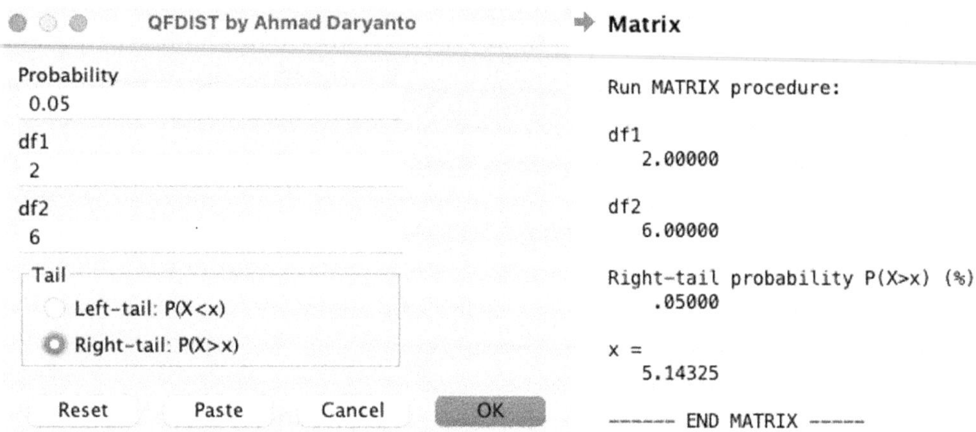

FIGURE 18.6
Finding F critical with QFDIST macro.

```
library(ahdar)
library(tidyverse)
library("ggpubr")
#| out.height: "40%"
#| out.width: "40%"
#| fig.align: "center"

# load data
dat <- repurchase

# convert "age" as a categorical variable.

dat <- dat |>
  mutate(age = as_factor(age))

# group the data by the factor "age"
dat <- dat |>
  group_by(age)

# calculate the number of observations,
# mean, standard deviation and for each group
```

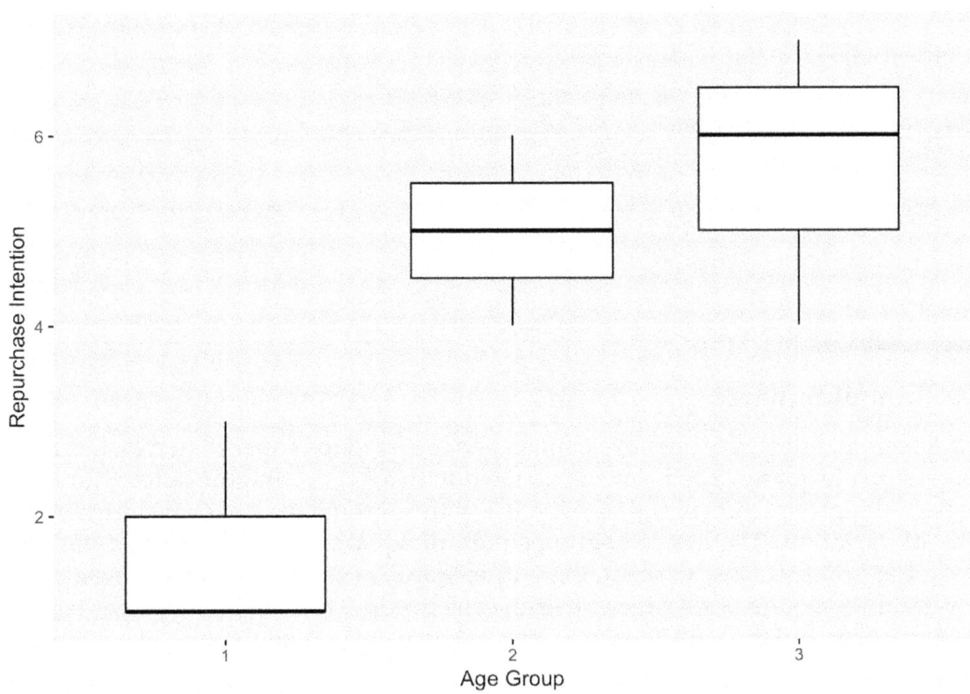

FIGURE 18.7
Box plots produced by the ggboxplot() R function.

```
desc_stats <- dat |>
  summarize(n = n(),
            mean = mean(repurchase),
            sd = sd(repurchase))

# print the descriptive statistics
desc_stats

## # A tibble: 3 x 4
##   age       n mean     sd
## <fct> <int> <dbl> <dbl>
## 1 1         3  1.67  1.15
## 2 2         3  5     1
## 3 3         3  5.67  1.53
Produce box plots
p <- ggboxplot(dat, x = "age", y = "repurchase",
          xlab="Age Group",
          ylab="Repurchase Intention") +
          theme_grey()

p
# perform ANOVA
fit <- aov(repurchase ~ age, data = dat)
# print summary
```

```
summary(fit)

##             Df Sum Sq Mean Sq F value Pr(>F)
## age          2  27.556  13.778   8.857 0.0162 *
## Residuals 6     9.333   1.556
## ---
## Signif. codes:  0 '***' 0.001 '**' 0.01 '*' 0.05 '.' 0.1 ' ' 1
```

18.2 Sum of Squares

In this section, I illustrate how to calculate between-groups sum of squares and within-groups sum of squares. The former is denoted with $SS_{Between}$, and the latter with SS_{Within}. The between-groups sum of squares and the within-groups sum of scores are both **measures of variation**. The between-groups sum of squares is an estimate of variability among the group means, whereas the within-groups sum of squares is an estimate of the variability among observations within each group. The sum of the between-groups sum of squares and the within-groups sum of squares is called the sum of squares total, denoted by SS_{Total}.

$$SS_{Total} = SS_{Between} + SS_{Within} \tag{18.1}$$

Dividing the between-groups sum of squares by its associated degrees of freedom (K-1) results in the between-groups variance, which quantifies the variance among scores that is due to group differences. Dividing the within-groups sum of squares by its associated degrees of freedom (N-K) results in the within-groups variance, which represents the variance that is due to differences among scores within groups.

The between-groups sum of squares is calculated as the sum of the squared differences between each group mean and the grand mean, which is the mean across all groups. In our example, it represents total variability in the scores that is explained by variable `age`. The within-groups sum of squares is calculated as the sum of the squared differences between each observation and the group mean, calculated for each group, and added all together. In our example, it represents the total variability that cannot be explained by variable age.

Manual calculations can be tedious if there are many observations. For the sake of illustration, I created **repurchase.sav** data with only a handful of observations, so we can work out the formulas by hand calculations. The between-groups and the within-groups are terminologies from SPSS. If you noticed, in R outputs, between-groups is replaced with the variable name `age _ cat`, and within-groups is replaced with `residuals` – as it is the same as residuals sum of squares representing variability due to errors. These two terminologies from R resemble the way the regression outputs were represented (see Figure 12.10 or Figure 12.6).

Before calculating between-groups sum of squares, let us find out where we can find the grand mean. It is printed in the descriptive statistics table displayed in

Figure 18.2. The grand mean is given in the cell with row `Total` of the mean column, $(Y) = 4.11$.

$$SS_{Between} = 3(1.67-4.11)^2 + 3(5.00-4.11)^2 + 3(5.67-4.11)^2$$
$$= 27.556$$

$$SS_{Within} = (1-1.67)^2 + (3-1.67)^2 + (1-1.67)^2 +$$
$$(4-5.00)^2 + (6-5.00)^2 + (5-5.00^2) +$$
$$(6-5.67)^2 + (7-5.67)^2 + (4-5.67)^2 +$$
$$= 9.33$$

$$SS_{Total} = (1-4.11)^2 + (3-4.11)^2 + (1-4.11)^2 +$$
$$\ldots + (6-4.11)^2 + (7-4.11)^2 + (4-4.11)^2$$
$$= 36.889$$

We can verify that $SS_{Total} = SS_{Between} + SS_{Within}$.

18.3 Effect Size

In the previous step, I unchecked 'Estimate effect size for an overall test'. If I leave the default as it is and run the one-way ANOVA test, several effect size measures will be printed (see Figure 18.8).

The most reported measure is the eta-squared (η^2). In this example, eta- squared represents the proportion of the total variance in `repurchase` that is accounted for by `age`. In other words, it measures the strength of the relationship between the age and repurchase intention. This interpretation is similar to how we interpret R^2 in regression. The eta-squared (η^2) is obtained by dividing between-groups sum of squares by total sum of squares:

$$\eta^2 = \frac{SS_{between}}{SS_{total}}$$
$$= \frac{27.556}{36.889}$$
$$= 0.747$$

Cohen (1988) provides a guideline on how to interpret eta-squared (η^2). The guideline can be considered as a rule of thumb rather than a strict rule to follow because the interpretation of an effect size can be quite subjective, which might depend on a research context – if consumers intend to file complaints about a delayed delivery service (short vs. long delay), a manager can view this as a large effect, although the effect size associated with intention to complain is statistically small – even a small delay triggers a complaint that is no difference than a long delay.

ANOVA Effect Sizes[a,b]

		Point Estimate	95% Confidence Interval Lower	Upper
repurchase	Eta-squared	.747	.049	.849
	Epsilon-squared	.663	-.269	.798
	Omega-squared Fixed-effect	.636	-.232	.779
	Omega-squared Random-effect	.466	-.104	.638

a. Eta-squared and Epsilon-squared are estimated based on the fixed-effect model.

b. Negative but less biased estimates are retained, not rounded to zero.

FIGURE 18.8
Table of effect sizes produced by one-way ANOVA.

- $\eta^2 = 0.01$, small effect
- $\eta^2 = 0.06$, medium effect
- $\eta^2 = 0.14$, large effect

The results in Figure 18.8 shows that the eta-squared is really large (0.747), meaning that age differences in repurchase intentions are very substantial.

18.4 ANOVA Assumptions

There are certain assumptions in a one-way ANOVA before we can rely on our results.

- Observations within each group should be independent. This means that the responses of one consumer in a group should not influence the responses of another consumer in that group.
- Normality: The population distribution within each group should follow a normal distribution. If population distribution is not normal, if a sample size is larger than 30, by the central limit theorem, the distribution of the sample means approaches a normal distribution. This means that, even if the observations within each group are not normally distributed, the means of the groups will be approximately normally distributed if the sample sizes are larger than 30. If the sample means are normally distributed, the *F* statistic will have an *F* sampling distribution.
- Equal variances: The variances of the observations within each group should be equal. This means that the spread of the responses should be similar across groups. This assumption may not be held in practice. In the next section, I will

discuss tests to adjust the violation of this assumption when we want to investigate why groups mean differ. However, when group sample sizes are not equal and one group has a standard deviation that is more than twice the smallest group standard deviation, the ANOVA results will be misleading (Agresti 2018)

Equal variance assumption is also known as the homogeneity of variance assumption. In the regression context, this is just the homoskedasticity assumption we learned in Chapter 12.

18.5 Finding Out Which Groups Differ

The result of the ANOVA test conducted showed that there were significant differences across the three groups of consumers. The descriptive statistics indicate that the mean of the first group is lower than that of the second and third group, and the mean of the second group looked the same as the mean of the third group. To ensure whether these findings are significant and not just occurring by chance, we need to conduct a post hoc test. There are many post hoc tests available – 18 tests in the one-way ANOVA procedure in SPSS. The choice of which test that we can use is guided by the results of the homogeneity of variance test or Levene's test. The null hypothesis in the homogeneity of variance test is that the variance of scores across groups are the same. In the case of three groups, $H_0 : \sigma_1^2 = \sigma_2^2 = \sigma_3^2$ against H_A: at least one group has a different variance. If the null hypothesis is rejected – hence, variances among three groups are not equal – the test commonly used is Games-Howell, whereas if the null hypothesis is not rejected, the recommended test to use is Tukey's test or Scheffe's test.

I presented the SPSS steps for conducting a homogeneity of variance test and a post hoc test in the following section. The steps are identical with the one presented earlier except that here I inserted new **Click** and **Ticks** written in bold.

18.5.1 SPSS Action Data: repurchase.sav Steps

- Analyze → Compare Means → One-Way ANOVA.

In SPSS version 29: Analyze → Compare Means and Proportions → One-Way ANOVA

- Insert `repurchase` into `Dependent List` box.
- Insert `age` into `Factor` box.
- Unchecked 'Estimate effect size for an overall test'. We will need to check this box again when discussing effect size. For the time being, we leave it unchecked.
- Click `Options`.
- Under `Statistics`, check '`Descriptive`'.
- Tick `Homogeneity of variance test`.
- Check `Means plot`.

- Click `Post Hoc`.
- `Under Equal Variances Assumed`, tick `Tukey`.
- Under `Equal Variances Unassumed`, tick `Games-Howell`.
- Click `OK`, or `Paste` if you prefer to work on the syntax.

```
ONEWAY repurchase BY age
  /STATISTICS DESCRIPTIVES HOMOGENEITY
  /PLOT MEANS
  /MISSING ANALYSIS
  /CRITERIA=CILEVEL(0.95)
  /POSTHOC=TUKEY GH ALPHA(0.05).
```

Figure 18.9 shows the results of the homogeneity of variance test that are based on different measures: mean, median, median with adjusted degrees of freedom, and trimmed mean. Of these options, Levene's test based on mean is commonly reported. However, if the distribution of scores in each group is skewed, the Levene's test based on median is the most appropriate choice (Carroll & Schneider 1985).

From the figure, the Levene's test based on mean yields a p-value that is larger than 5% significance level, so we retain the null hypothesis. In fact, when we inspected the descriptive table, the standard deviations of three groups are relatively equal. Based on this result, we read the `Tukey HSD` part of the `Multiple Comparisons` table displayed in Figure 18.10 – we can ignore the Games-Howell's results. The `Tukey HSD` part of the table shows the results of the Tukey's post hoc test.

The first block of the Tukey's HSD part, mean of group 1 is compared to those of the remaining groups. From the first row, the mean difference between group 1 and group 2 is significant ($p < 0.0001$). From the second row, the mean difference between group 1 and group 3 is significant ($p < 0.001$). From the second block, the mean of group 2 is compared to that of the remaining group. From the fourth row, the mean difference of group 2 and group 3 is not significant ($p = 0.165$). Mean comparisons of the third block is just the reverse of the previous comparisons. These comparisons are summarized in the homogeneous subsets table displayed in Figure 18.11.

Tests of Homogeneity of Variances

		Levene Statistic	df1	df2	Sig.
repurchase	Based on Mean	.462	2	6	.651
	Based on Median	.125	2	6	.885
	Based on Median and with adjusted df	.125	2	4.923	.885
	Based on trimmed mean	.424	2	6	.672

FIGURE 18.9
Results of the homogeneity of variance test.

Multiple Comparisons

Dependent Variable: repurchase

	(I) age	(J) age	Mean Difference (I-J)	Std. Error	Sig.	95% Confidence Interval Lower Bound	95% Confidence Interval Upper Bound
Tukey HSD	1.00	2.00	-3.33333*	1.01835	.039	-6.4579	-.2088
		3.00	-4.00000*	1.01835	.018	-7.1246	-.8754
	2.00	1.00	3.33333*	1.01835	.039	.2088	6.4579
		3.00	-.66667	1.01835	.797	-3.7912	2.4579
	3.00	1.00	4.00000*	1.01835	.018	.8754	7.1246
		2.00	.66667	1.01835	.797	-2.4579	3.7912
Games-Howell	1.00	2.00	-3.33333*	.88192	.043	-6.5064	-.1603
		3.00	-4.00000	1.10554	.053	-8.0793	.0793
	2.00	1.00	3.33333*	.88192	.043	.1603	6.5064
		3.00	-.66667	1.05409	.813	-4.7171	3.3837
	3.00	1.00	4.00000	1.10554	.053	-.0793	8.0793
		2.00	.66667	1.05409	.813	-3.3837	4.7171

*. The mean difference is significant at the 0.05 level.

FIGURE 18.10
Results of the post hoc test. Read the Tukey's part as the Levene's test shows equality of variances can be assumed.

repurchase

	age	N	Subset for alpha = 0.05: 1	2
Tukey HSD[a]	1.00	3	1.6667	
	2.00	3		5.0000
	3.00	3		5.6667
	Sig.		1.000	.797

Means for groups in homogeneous subsets are displayed.
a. Uses Harmonic Mean Sample Size = 3.000.

There is no significant difference between the means of these two groups. Each mean is significantly different from the mean of group 1

FIGURE 18.11
Table of the homogeneous subsets.

18.5.2 R Action

We can use the `leveneTest()` function from car package.

```
install.packages("car")

Let us conduct the Levene's test:
library(tidyverse)
library(ahdar)
library(car) # to run leveneTest() function

# load data from ahdar library

dat <- repurchase

# convert "age" as a categorical variable.
```

```
dat <- dat |>
        mutate(age = as_factor(age))

# Run the Levene's test

leveneTest(repurchase ~ age, data = dat, center="mean")

Levene's Test for Homogeneity of Variance (center = "mean")
        Df F value Pr(>F)
group  2       0.4615       0.651
        6
```

As the Levene's test is not significant, we can run Tukey's post hoc test by using the `TukeyHSD()` function indexR function!TukeyHSD(). The function uses the object from that we stored when running the ANOVA test.

```
fit <- aov(repurchase ~ age, data = dat) # run anova

TukeyHSD(fit) # run Tukey's post hoc test

   Tukey multiple comparisons of means
     95% family-wise confidence level
Fit: aov(formula = repurchase ~ age, data = dat)

$age
           diff          lwr          upr       p adj

2-1   3.3333333   0.2087556  6.457911  0.0389374
3-1   4.0000000   0.8754223  7.124578  0.0181426
3-2   0.6666667  -2.4579111  3.791244  0.7967638
```

From the output we can see that the p-value is exactly one (obviously greater than the significance level of 0.05). We obtain a similar result that we have seen previously with SPSS that the variance across can be assumed to be equal.

18.6 GLM Procedure

SPSS provides other procedure for conducting a one-way ANOVA, that is the *General Linear Model (GLM) procedure,* which also refers to as an *UNIANOVA* procedure. Follow these steps:

- Analyze → General Linear Model →Univariate.
- Insert `repurchase` to the `Dependent Variable` box.

- Insert `age` to `Fixed Factor(s)` box.
- Click `Options`, tick `Descriptive statistics` and `Estimates of effect size`.
- Click `Continue`.
- Click `OK`.

If you click `Paste`, SPSS yields the following syntax:

```
UNIANOVA repurchase BY age
  /METHOD=SSTYPE(3)
  /INTERCEPT=INCLUDE
  /PRINT ETASQ DESCRIPTIVE
  /CRITERIA=ALPHA(.05)
  /DESIGN=age.
```

In the outputs, you will see the descriptive statistics and ANOVA tables. Here, I only present the ANOVA table, which you can see in Figure 18.12.

As you can see from Figure 18.12, the sum of squares associated with Age is the between-groups sum of squares, and the sum of squares associated with Error is the within-groups sum of squares. This way of reporting is similar to that of the R output.

GLM procedure can produce more outputs required for analysis that can be requested by clicking other features. For instance, by clicking `Option` and ticking `Homogeneity tests`, it will produce the Levene's test output. If you click `Post Hoc`, insert age to `Post Hoc test for` box, and under `Equal Variances Assumed`, tick `Tukey`, and it will produce the Tukey's post hoc test result.

18.7 Two-Way ANOVA

We have examined differences in repurchase intention among groups of consumers defined by their age: young, middle-aged, and elderly. Surely, there are other

Tests of Between-Subjects Effects

Dependent Variable: repurchase

Source	Type III Sum of Squares	df	Mean Square	F	Sig.	Partial Eta Squared
Corrected Model	27.556[a]	2	13.778	8.857	.016	.747
Intercept	152.111	1	152.111	97.786	<.001	.942
age	27.556	2	13.778	8.857	.016	.747
Error	9.333	6	1.556			
Total	189.000	9				
Corrected Total	36.889	8				

a. R Squared = .747 (Adjusted R Squared = .663)

Effect Size Estimate

Age Is Significant ($p < 0.05$)

FIGURE 18.12
GLM outputs.

differences among these consumers. For instance, our data *repurchase.sav* contains the variable `male` to denote the gender of consumers (male = 1, female = 0). It would be more interesting to include also gender in our analysis. As we are now considering two categorical variables, analysing mean differences on repurchase intentions requires us to use a two-way ANOVA. In SPSS, the two-way ANOVA is conducted using the GLM procedure.

18.7.1 SPSS Action

Steps:

- Analyze → General Linear Model → Univariate.
- Insert `repurchase` to the `Dependent Variable` box.
- Insert `age` and `male` to `Fixed Factor(s)` box.
- Click `Plots`, and insert `age` into `Horizontal Axis` box and `male` into `Separate Lines` box. Click `Add`.
- Click `Options` and tick `Descriptive Statistics` and `Estimates of effect size`. Click `Continue`.
- Click `OK`.

If you click `Paste`, SPSS yields the following syntax:

```
UNIANOVA repurchase BY age male
   /METHOD=SSTYPE(3)
   /INTERCEPT=INCLUDE
   /PLOT=PROFILE(age*male) TYPE=LINE ERRORBAR=NO MEANREFERENCE=NO
    YAXIS=AUTO
   /PRINT ETASQ DESCRIPTIVE
   /CRITERIA=ALPHA(.05)
   /DESIGN=age male age*male.
```

Descriptive statistics

The descriptive table produced by the GLM procedure is displayed in Figure 18.13. I actually rerun the GLM procedure by changing the order of the entry: insert `male` and `age` to the `Fixed Factor(s)` box in order to show how different arrangement of table is produced by GLM – of course, the tables are identical.

The descriptive statistics in one of the tables in Figure 18.13 would be convenient to our eyes if we manually reconstruct it into a 2 × 2 table as displayed in Table 18.1.

Descriptive Statistics

Dependent Variable: repurchase

age	male	Mean	Std. Deviation	N
1.00	.00	1.0000	.00000	2
	1.00	3.0000	.	1
	Total	1.6667	1.15470	3
2.00	.00	5.5000	.70711	2
	1.00	4.0000	.	1
	Total	5.0000	1.00000	3
3.00	.00	6.5000	.70711	2
	1.00	4.0000	.	1
	Total	5.6667	1.52753	3
Total	.00	4.3333	2.65832	6
	1.00	3.6667	.57735	3
	Total	4.1111	2.14735	9

(a) Age is entered first.

Descriptive Statistics

Dependent Variable: repurchase

male	age	Mean	Std. Deviation	N
.00	1.00	1.0000	.00000	2
	2.00	5.5000	.70711	2
	3.00	6.5000	.70711	2
	Total	4.3333	2.65832	6
1.00	1.00	3.0000	.	1
	2.00	4.0000	.	1
	3.00	4.0000	.	1
	Total	3.6667	.57735	3
Total	1.00	1.6667	1.15470	3
	2.00	5.0000	1.00000	3
	3.00	5.6667	1.52753	3
	Total	4.1111	2.14735	9

(b) Male is entered first.

FIGURE 18.13
Descriptive statistics of age by male.

TABLE 18.1
Means

Group	Male	Female	Mean
Group 1	3.0000	1.0000	1.6667
Group 2	4.0000	5.5000	5.0000
Group 3	4.0000	6.5000	5.6667
Mean	4.3333	3.6667	4.1111

Figure 18.14 displays the plot of the mean of repurchase intention for each combination of age and male. The plot provides us an indication of the presence of an interaction effect. Interaction effect refers to a situation where the effect of one variable depends on the value of another variable. The presence of an interaction effect can be indicated by non-parallel lines. If the lines look parallel, it might that there is no interaction effect. Whether the interaction effect is statistically significant, we have to inspect the ANOVA table presented in Figure 18.15.

18.7.2 R Action

```
library(tidyverse)
library(ahdar)
library(car) # to run leveneTest() function

# load the data
```

```
dat <- repurchase

# convert "age" as a categorical variable.
dat <- dat |>
  mutate(age = as_factor(age))

# perform a two-way ANOVA
# age:male is the same as age*male
# age:male is an interaction term

fit <- aov(repurchase ~ age + male + age:male, data = dat)

# print summary
summary(fit)
```

```
##             Df  Sum Sq  Mean Sq  F value    Pr(>F)
## age          2  27.556   13.778   41.333  0.00655**
## male         1   0.889    0.889    2.667   0.20098
## age:male     2   7.444    3.722   11.167   0.04075*
## Residuals    3   1.000    0.333
## ---
## Signif. codes:    0 '***' 0.001 '**' 0.01 '*' 0.05 '.' 0.1 ' ' 1
```

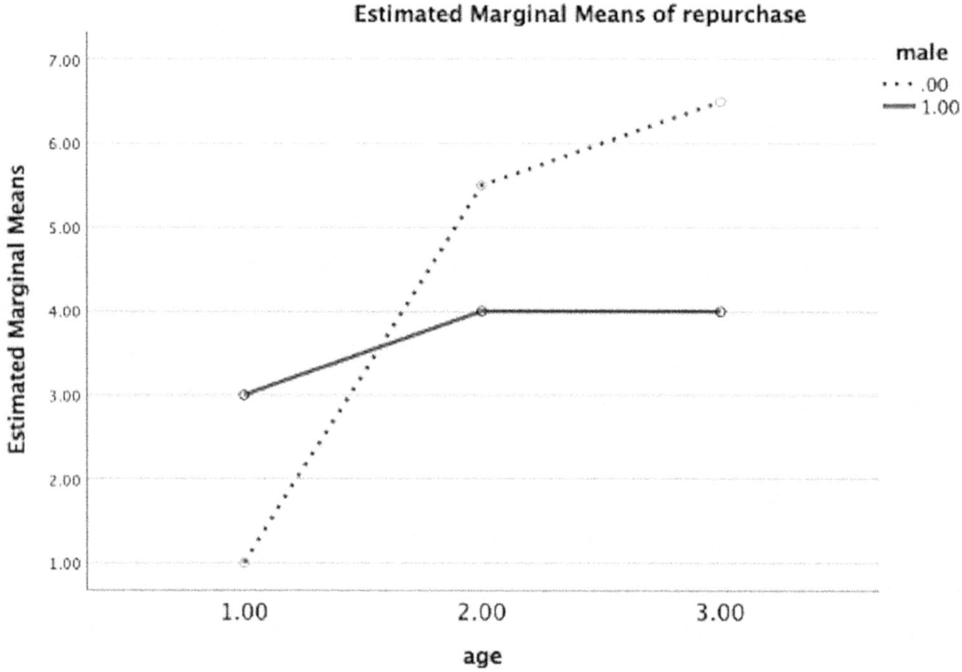

FIGURE 18.14
Means plot. Original plots from SPSS produced solid lines with colour.

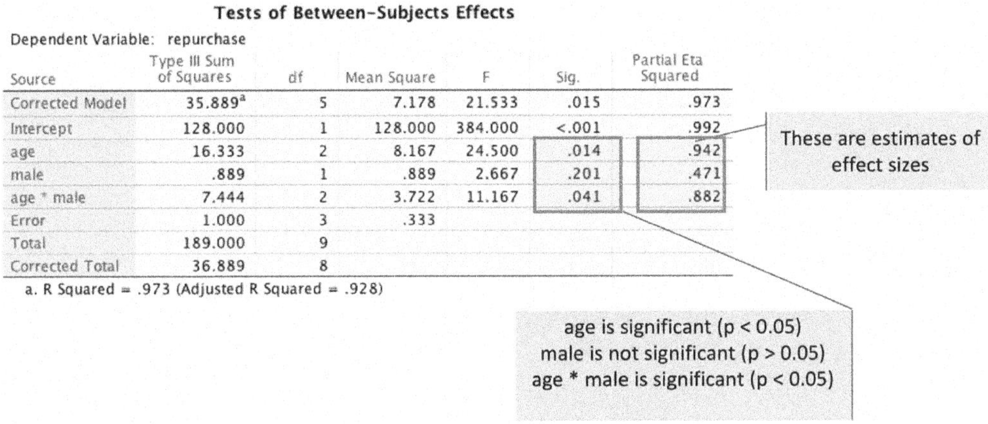

Tests of Between-Subjects Effects

Dependent Variable: repurchase

Source	Type III Sum of Squares	df	Mean Square	F	Sig.	Partial Eta Squared
Corrected Model	35.889[a]	5	7.178	21.533	.015	.973
Intercept	128.000	1	128.000	384.000	<.001	.992
age	16.333	2	8.167	24.500	.014	.942
male	.889	1	.889	2.667	.201	.471
age * male	7.444	2	3.722	11.167	.041	.882
Error	1.000	3	.333			
Total	189.000	9				
Corrected Total	36.889	8				

a. R Squared = .973 (Adjusted R Squared = .928)

FIGURE 18.15
GLM results.

18.8 Summary

We have discussed analysis of variance (ANOVA) that can be used to compare means of several samples, usually for more than two groups. ANOVA is an extension of the two independent samples T-test, which can also be used to replace the two-independent samples T-test. Nonetheless, T-tests were not covered in the book because it can be easily done by using a regression analysis.

18.9 Further Reading

Rutherford, A. (2011), *ANOVA and ANCOVA: A GLM approach*, John Wiley & Sons. Note: This book discusses ANOVA, and ANOVA with control variables (ANCOVA) as a general linear model.

18.10 Review Questions

1. How would you formulate the null and alternative hypothesis in a one-way ANOVA test?
2. Explain the assumptions of a one-way ANOVA test.
3. What do between-groups and within-groups sum of squares represent?

4. Explain how the *F* statistic is calculated in a one-way ANOVA test.
5. Explain the difference between a one-way ANOVA and a two-way ANOVA.
6. If the result of a one-way ANOVA is significant, how would you proceed?

18.11 Exercises

Using *repurchase.sav*, use the GLM procedure to conduct a one-way ANOVA with a post hoc test.

19

Experiment

The concept of experiment or experimentation is discussed in this chapter. Experiment enables marketing researchers to test the effect of a marketing intervention on consumers' attitudes and behaviours. The chapter begins by explaining the conceptual meaning of an experiment as the manipulation of a marketing variable. Key concepts and procedures in experiment are then explained, including randomization of participants, the distinction between treatment and control groups, manipulation of the experimental variable, average treatment effect, selection bias, and the analysis of experimental data with the SPSS GLM procedure and R.

Learning Objectives:

- Understand what an experiment is.
- Understand the concept of confounding effect.
- Be able to recognize threats to internal and external validity.
- Familiar with the term of a main effect and an interaction effect.

19.1 Concept

A long time ago, whenever I heard about the word 'experiment', the first thing that came to my mind was someone with a white lab coat working with mice in a research lab. To be clear, I am referring to small rodent, not the small device you use to navigate your laptop. While my imagination about an experiment was not entirely wrong, many years later I learned that social scientists also conduct experiments, not with rodents, but with people– to understand why they behave the way they do, why they show certain emotions, and what drives their actions.

As a human being, we are gifted with a curious mind. We want to understand why things occurred, and whether some causes trigger some actions. For instance, teachers want to know why students' grades are poor, managers are interested in finding out whether price discounts increase consumer purchase intention, advertisers want to know which types of ads affect viewers' attention, and some of you want may to know whether taking quantitative research method class will put you in a better job position in the future. These kinds of goals involve examining cause-effect, or causal relationship. In the causal relationship, one event (the cause) directly influences the other (the effect). That is, the cause precedes the effect – temporal precedence – and the cause changes the status of the next event (e.g. price discount changes the intention level of

DOI: 10.4324/9781003407225-24

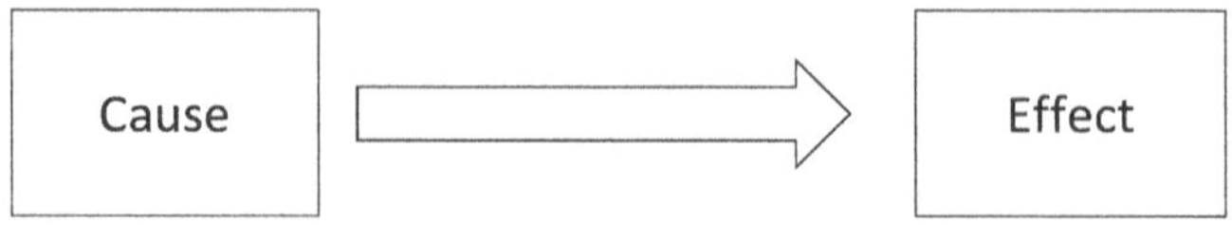

FIGURE 19.1
Experiment is to test the cause-effect relationship.

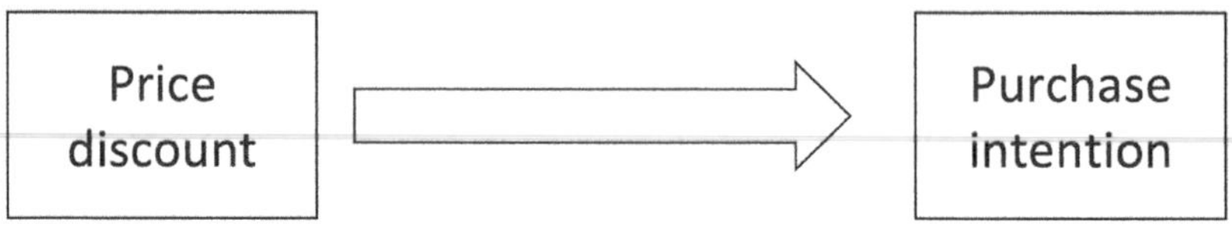

FIGURE 19.2
Price discount affects purchase intention.

consumers). Experiment is considered to be the most appropriate research method to answer these kinds of relationships.

The key feature of an experiment is that it involves manipulating a variable of interest – a variable that researchers are focusing on to study. The effect of the manipulation of the variable can be observed by examining the outcomes of the experiment. What do we mean by 'manipulating a variable of interest'? An illustration will help us in understanding the phrase. For example, a researcher wants to know whether price discounts affect consumers' purchase intentions. In this example, the variable of interest is the price discount, and consumers' purchase intentions are the outcomes of the experiment (see Figure 19.2). To manipulate price discount, the simplest way is by introducing two types of price discount: no discount and 5% discount.

IMPORTANT

Conducting an experiment entails manipulating a variable of interest.

To make it more real, imagine that a researcher selects a group of consumers in random from a population. Next, some of the consumers from the sample receive a 5% price discount, and others receive no discount. The random assignment of the consumers into these two groups can be easily done by flipping a coin: those who get heads are assigned the discount condition, and tails to the no discount condition.

By having two experimental conditions (5% discount vs. no discount), in the language of experiment, the researcher is manipulating a price discount variable. Here, price discount is a nominal variable having two levels, which can be coded as either 1 for 5% price discount or 0 for no discount. The 5% price discount condition constitutes a **treatment** condition whereas no discount acts as a **control** condition. Note that, instead of 'condition', the word 'group' is also commonly used by researchers. The design of this hypothetical experiment having two conditions (treatment vs. control) with random

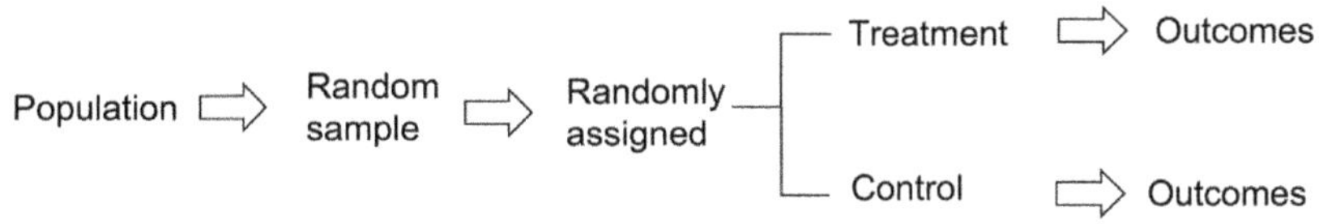

FIGURE 19.3
Randomized two-group design.

RANDOM ASSIGNMENT

Random assignment is allocating participants to different experimental conditions in a purely random manner (e.g. by flipping a coin).

assignment can be described as a **randomized two-group design**. This whole research process can be described by a flow chart presented in Figure 19.3.

19.2 Creating Experimental Conditions

There are various ways of creating different experimental conditions, and the choice is guided by our research objectives. We discussed the approaches in this section.

19.2.1 Experimental Group vs. Control Group

As explained, we can create two experimental conditions: treatment group vs. control group. The treatment group is the condition in which a group of participants receives a treatment, and the control group consists of a group of participants to whom no experimental treatment is administered. We have seen earlier that the group that received no discount condition is a control group and the group receiving a 5% price discount is the treatment group. In medicine, to test the effect of flu vaccine, individuals who receive a placebo is a called a control group, and those who received a vaccine is referred to as a treatment group.

19.2.2 Several Experimental Levels

Another way of manipulating an experimental variable is by creating several treatment levels (e.g. low vs. medium vs. high treatment). In the price discount example, a researcher can introduce 1% discount (low condition), 10% discount (medium condition), and 40% discount (high condition). In another illustration, if a marketing manager is interested in the effect of store displays on weekly unit sales of a product, the manager can create different experimental conditions by arranging different number of displays in a store (see Figure 19.4).

19.2.3 Two Manipulated Variables

Experiment can involve manipulating more than one variable. For example, two variables can be manipulated such that each has two levels. This will create four experimental conditions. For an illustration, suppose that we are interested in the effect of training delivery time and types of training on sales employee engagement. Two variables being manipulated are types of training delivery time and types of training. Types of training delivery time has two levels: morning vs. evening. Types of training also have two levels: technical vs. non-technical. The objective of this experiment is to determine the most appropriate time for delivering a specific type of training. The design of the experiment can be described as a 2 × 2 experiment.

The description can be made more specific by displaying the experimental condition, such as a 2 (delivery time: morning vs. evening) × 2 (technical vs. non-technical) randomized design. The term 'randomized' can be replaced by other popular term called 'between-subject design', which indicates that participants are randomly assigned to the four experimental conditions (see Figure 19.5).

FIGURE 19.4
Three experimental conditions operationalized differently and weekly sales are measured in each condition.

Experiment	Technical training	Non-technical training
Morning	Randomly-allocated Participants	Randomly-allocated Participants
Evening	Randomly-allocated Participants	Randomly-allocated Participants

FIGURE 19.5
2 × 2 randomized experimental design.

19.3 What a Random Assignment Does

To assess the effect of 5% price discount vs. no discount, ideally, we would use the same participants. However, we would avoid assigning the same individuals to different experimental conditions because if they had been exposed to one of the treatment conditions that would affect how they react to another treatment. As an illustration, if you were given a 5% price discount, you would certainly be more unhappy if later you were told that you didn't receive a discount. Another drawback of being exposed to different conditions simultaneously is that participants might learn the real objective of the experiment, which will distort the results of the experiment. For instance, they could be motivated to provide answers that they believed are expected by the researcher, which is known as social desirability bias.

As we avoid assigning the same participants to both treatment and control conditions, however, we could imagine their potential responses had they been assigned to a different condition. For example, for participants being assigned to the treatment group, we could imagine what their scores would have been if they had been assigned to the control group instead. Similarly, for participants being assigned to the control group, we could imagine what their scores would have been if they had been assigned to the treatment group.

Table 19.1 presents responses of 5 participants assigned to a treatment condition (5% discount) (column `Observed`). The table also records the answers that the participants might have provided had they been placed in a control condition (column `Potential`). The third column in the table provides the effect of price discount for each individual calculated as the difference between observed and potential (`Treatment = Observed - Potential`). For Alex, the effect of price discount is equal to $5-2=3$, whereas for Bella, it is $6-5=1$.

The sixth row of the table provides the average score for each column. The average score of the `Observed` column is 5, and the average score of the `Potential` column is 3.2. The difference between the two average score is $5-3.2=1.8$. This value is referred to as the **average treatment effect (ATE)**. It has the same value as the average of the values in the column O-P. This shows that the average individual treatment effect is the same as the difference in the group means: observed means – potential means.

TABLE 19.1

Purchase Intention: Observed vs. Potential

	Price Discount	No Price Discount	Treatment Effect
Participant	**Observed (O)**	**Potential (P)**	**O-P**
Alex	5.0	3.0	2.0
Bella	6.0	5.0	1.0
Jen	5.0	3.0	2.0
Dylan	4.0	2.0	2.0
Millam	5.0	3.0	2.0
Mean	**5.0**	**3.2**	**1.8**
ATE	**1.8**		

Note: ATE = average treatment effect.

The 5 participants in the treatment group are not going to be assigned to the control group to avoid bias. Therefore, we will not be able to observe values in the column `Potential`. As a consequence, we would like to assign different participants to the control group that are identical to those in the treatment group. We could achieve this by randomly assigned participants of the same population to either the treatment or the control group.

If we do not randomly assign participants to different experimental conditions (e.g. assigning them because of our liking), we might get unbalanced individual characteristics.

For instance, non-random assignment might place participants in one experimental condition where they might have a tighter budget spending compared to those in the other condition. This non-random assignment can affect the experimental results. For another illustration, imagine that one of your products is facing a tough competition due to the newly launched competitor product, and you decide to introduce a 5% price discount to stay competitive. You test your idea by conducting an experiment by approaching consumers that enter your store in random. For some consumers, you ask them whether they would be willing to purchase your product today if they were given a 5% price discount – they are assigned to a treatment group. For others, you simply ask whether they would be willing to buy the product today – they are assigned to a control group. If you happen to select consumers in the treatment group who generally have a tighter budget spending than those in the control group, they would be more likely to be attracted to the 5% price discount. In this case, the **ATE** score will reflect differences in consumers' budget spending rather than showing the effect of price discount, resulting a biased result.

What you want to determine is whether consumers with equal budgets for that day would find a 5% discount attractive. There are other factors that might affect how they react to the 5% price discount. For example, some are more price-conscious than others. For example, consumers that are highly price-conscious will be more likely to search for more information when exposed to a discount that those who are lowly price-conscious (Alford & Biswas 2002).

This difference in price consciousness will influence how consumers react to the price discount. Because of these differences in the consumer characteristics exist, you want these factors to be kept constant prior to concluding the existence of the causal effect of price discount on purchase intention. One way of keeping price consciousness constant is by finding individuals are equally price-conscious. In reality, this approach is very unrealistic.

CETERIS PARIBUS

Keeping everything else constant is known as a ceteris paribus assumption.

Existing differences among individuals that affect the results of an experiment beyond the treatment effect is known as a **selection bias** problem. In general, differences between treatment and control are equal to treatment effect plus selection bias. If selection bias does not exist, the difference between the treatment and control reflects a treatment effect.

IMPORTANT

Treatment effect – control = Treatment effect + selection bias

The random assignment will not eliminate existing individual differences (e.g. gender, race, education, price consciousness, sale proneness, etc.). But it ensures that these existing differences will be more or less equal among participants in the treatment vs. control group in a large sample. That is, random assignment removes selection bias that may arise due to existing differences among participants if a sample size is large.

19.4 Key Factors in Designing an Experiment

Based on the illustration presented, let us summarize that there are four key factors that need to be considered in designing an experiment.

1. Unit of analysis or test unit. In the price discount illustration, our test unit is consumer.
2. What independent variables or treatments are to be manipulated. In the pricing illustration, the independent variable is the pricing discount manipulated into two types: 5% discount (treatment) vs. no discount (control).
3. What outcome variables (just another name for dependent variables) are to be measured.

Choosing how to measure the outcome variables is closely related to the formulation of a research problem. For example, if the research problem is about knowing the behaviour of individuals, then the outcome variables should contain measures about behaviours.

There are three broad types of outcome measures:

- Self-reported attitudinal measures such as liking (I like brand A), awareness (are you aware of brand A?)
- Self-reported behaviours
  - Intention, e.g. will you buy brand A?
- Real behaviours
  - Frequency of buying (how many products did you buy last week?)
  - Present vs. absent (e.g. bought brand A vs. not bought)

Types of outcome measures employed in an experiment determines the choice of statistical test appropriate to analyse the data. In this book, we will consider outcome measures measured using interval or ratio scales, which allow us to compare the mean of a construct, and use it for mean comparisons, e.g. comparing the mean of different experiment conditions. Having the construct mean scores also allow us to use regression to analyse the experimental data.

4. Consider factors that might affect results beyond the treatment effect. That is, consider the potential confounding factors that need to be controlled. For example, in studying the effect of price discount on purchase intention, sale proneness can be considered as a confounding factor that must be measured and controlled.

19.5 Analysing Experimental Data

There are two ways of analysing the experimental data: comparing means using statistical techniques called ANOVA (analysis of variance), which we have discussed in Chapter 18, and regression. The first method is widely used in the psychology, marketing, health, and related fields. The second method is very popular in the economic discipline. In this section, I will focus on the regression procedures.

19.5.1 Comparing Two Groups

To analyse data of two groups such as treatment against control, we can use a regression analysis with a binary independent variable, as explained in Section 8.1 of Chapter 12, and adding control variables or covariates – the covariate is assumed to have an influence on the dependent variable. For example, if there are two covariates, the model takes the following form:

$$Y = \beta_0 + \beta_1 X + \beta_2 A_1 + \beta_3 A_2 + \varepsilon \tag{19.1}$$

where X is randomly assigned and equal to 1 if an individual is assigned to a treatment group or 0 otherwise, and A_1 and A_2 are the covariates. In the language of experiment, an independent variable is referred to as a *factor.*

19.5.2 Comparing Two Groups Involving an Interaction

The causal effect of treatment X might depend on the value of a covariate. This modelling situation can be captured by creating an interaction term X A. For example, the following model contains a binary variable X (1 = treatment, 0 = control or other condition) and covariate A, and the interaction term X A (shortened as X A) to capture the effect of treatment that might depend on the value of A.

$$Y = \beta_0 + \beta_1 X + \beta_2 A + \beta_3 AX + \varepsilon \tag{19.2}$$

The covariate *A* can also be a categorical variable (e.g. gender). Therefore, the interaction term will capture the effect of treatment that differ at the different levels of the covariate. For example, our study might find that the effect of treatment is stronger for male than female.

19.6 SPSS Action

Data: nature.sav

In this exercise, we are interested in examining the effect on pro-environmental behaviours (PEB) of communicating nature as in terms of either mother-nature or father-nature. The study can be conducted using an experiment. Participants are asked to read an article about nature. In one article, nature is framed as a mother-nature and, in another article, as a father-nature. Participants are randomly assigned to read one of these two types of articles. As there are some studies showing that males and females are not equally engaged in PEB (Coelho et al. 2017; Vicente-Molina et al. 2018), gender is treated as a covariate or control variable. In addition to gender differences on PEB, males and females might react differently toward how nature was framed. That is, the effect of framing on nature might depend on gender. We can describe this modelling situation as a 2 (*Gender*: male vs female) × 2 (*Framing*: mother-nature vs. father-nature) design, with Framing being randomized.

$$PEB = \beta_0 + \beta_1 Framing + \beta_2 Gender + \beta_3 Framing \times Gender + \varepsilon \tag{19.3}$$

For this illustration, I have created a fictitious data mother nature experiment.sav, which contains five variables: Framing, Gender, PEB, Age, and inter.

Framing: 1 = mother-nature, 0 = father-nature

Gender: 1 = Female, 0 = Male

PEB: This is an average score of several items measuring pro-environmental behaviour. Each item is measured using a 7-point Likert scale (1 = strongly disagree, 7 = strongly agree)

To analyse data from this experiment, we use the GLM (general linear model). Steps:

- Click: Analyze → General Linear Model → Univariate.
- Insert *PEB* into the `Dependent` box.
- Insert *Framing* and *Gender* into the `Fixed Factor(s)` box.
- Click `Options`.
- Tick `Descriptive statistics` and `Estimates of effect size`.
- Click `Plots`.
- Insert *Framing* into the `Horizontal Axis` box.
- Insert *Gender* into the `Separate Lines` box.

- Click `Add`.
- Under `Chart Type`, tick `Bar Chart`.
- Under `Error Bar`, tick `Include Error Bars`.
- Choose 95% Confidence Interval.
- Click `OK`, or `Paste` if you prefer to work with syntax (see the following).

```
UNIANOVA PEB BY Framing Gender
   /METHOD=SSTYPE(3)
   /INTERCEPT=INCLUDE
   /PLOT=PROFILE(Framing*Gender) TYPE=BAR
     ERRORBAR=CI MEANREFERENCE=NO
   /PRINT ETASQ DESCRIPTIVE
   /CRITERIA=ALPHA(.05)
   /DESIGN=Framing Gender Framing*Gender.
```

19.6.1 Descriptive Statistics

The first output printed by the GLM procedure is a table displaying the allocation of participants across the experimental conditions (see Figure 19.6). As you can see from the figure, there are 70 participants assigned to the father-nature condition, and 70 participants to the mother-nature condition.

In the next output, the descriptive statistics table is presented. The table shows the mean score of PEB, the standard deviation, and the number of participants in each cell (see Figure 19.7). For instance, there are 35 males in the father-nature condition with PEB's mean score of 4.039 and SD of 0.208.

19.6.2 Results

The key output is the table presented in Figure 19.8, which allows us to assess the significant of the experimental manipulation (*Framing*), the main effect of *Gender*, and the interaction effect between *Framing* and *Gender*. As you can see from the figure, *Framing* is significant ($p < 0.05$), *Gender* is significant ($p < 0.001$), and the interaction effect of *Framing* × *Gender* is also significant ($p < 0.001$).

The descriptive statistics data can guide us to justify the results. For example, males' PEB mean score is higher (M = 4.32) than that of females (M = 4.07), which qualifies

Between-Subjects Factors

		Value Label	N
Framing	.00	Father-nature	70
	1.00	Mother-nature	70
Gender	.00	Male	70
	1.00	Female	70

Allocation of participants. There are 70 participants in each condition

FIGURE 19.6
Allocation of participants in the type of framing × gender experiment.

Descriptive Statistics

Dependent Variable: PEB

Framing	Gender	Mean	Std. Deviation	N
Father-nature	Male	4.0394	.20811	35
	Female	4.2837	.19095	35
	Total	4.1616	.23334	70
Mother-nature	Male	4.6148	.21005	35
	Female	3.8586	.19162	35
	Total	4.2367	.42993	70
Total	Male	4.3271	.35644	70
	Female	4.0712	.28617	70
	Total	4.1991	.34671	140

35 males assigning to the Father-nature condition. Mean score of PEB = 4.039, SD = 0.208

FIGURE 19.7
Descriptive statistics: mean, standard deviation, and sample size.

Framing is significant, p < 0.05

Gender is significant, p < 0.001

Framing x Gender is significant, p < 0.001

Tests of Between-Subjects Effects

Dependent Variable: PEB

Source	Type III Sum of Squares	df	Mean Square	F	Sig.	Partial Eta Squared
Corrected Model	11.248[a]	3	3.749	93.378	<.001	.673
Intercept	2468.581	1	2468.581	61480.737	<.001	.998
Framing	.198	1	.198	4.922	.028	.035
Gender	2.292	1	2.292	57.082	<.001	.296
Framing * Gender	8.758	1	8.758	218.131	<.001	.616
Error	5.461	136	.040			
Total	2485.290	140				
Corrected Total	16.709	139				

a. R Squared = .673 (Adjusted R Squared = .666)

FIGURE 19.8
GLM results.

why *Gender* is significant. Similarly, if you change the order of the entry – in the syntax enter *Gender* prior to *Framing* – you would find the mean score of the two types of framing regardless of gender of the participants. The mean score of PEB in the mother-nature condition (M = 4.23) is slightly higher than that of the father-nature condition (M = 4.20). The main interest in the 2 × 2 experiment is to find out whether the interaction term is significant. In the output, the interaction effect is significant. The nature of the interaction can be seen by inspecting Figure 19.9. As you can see from the figure, females are more likely to exhibit PEB if nature is communicated as father, whereas males are more likely to exhibit PEB if nature is communicated as mother.

19.6.3 Effect Size

The last column of the main table displayed in Figure 19.8 shows the effect size associated with each independent variable of the GLM model. Effect size is about addressing a question: how big is the effect? The effect size reported by the table is the partial eta-squared symbolized as partial η^2. In this context, it is defined as the proportion of variation in PEB that is explained by a factor after partialling out the variation due to

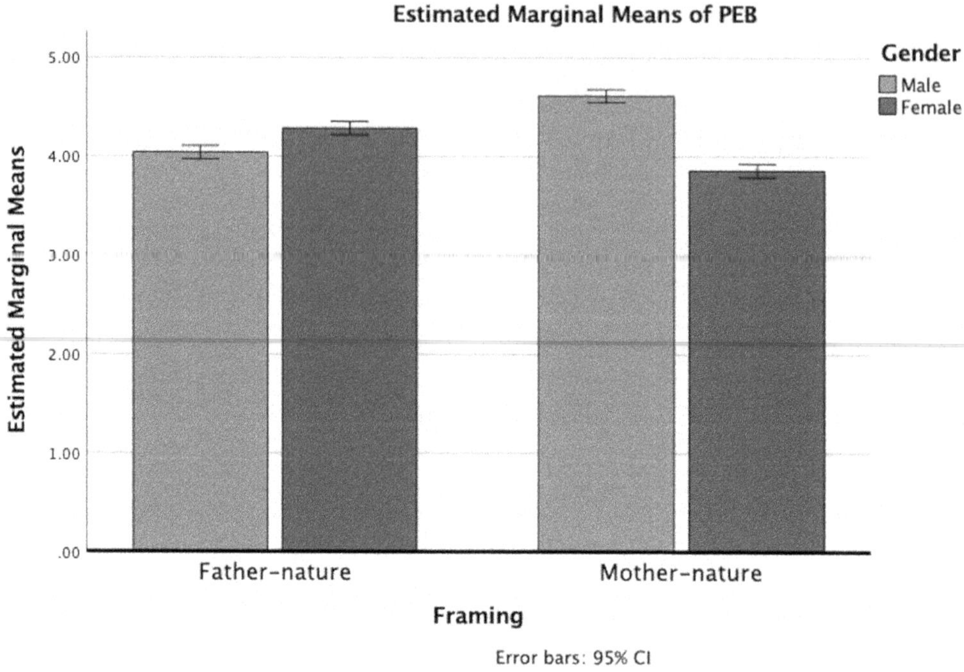

FIGURE 19.9
Interaction between framing and gender.

the other factors. For example, the partial eta-squared associated with Framing is 0.035. This means that 3.5% of variation in PEB can be explained by *Framing* holding out other factors constant. How do we assess this effect? The rule thumb is that a small effect is indicated by partial $\eta^2 = 0.01$, a medium effect is indicated by partial $\eta^2 = 0.06$, and a large effect is considered if partial $\eta^2 = 0.14$ (Cohen 2013). Thus, the effect of framing in the fake data is small.

NOTE

partial $\eta^2 = \frac{SS_{factor}}{SS_{factor} + SS_{error}}$, where SS stands for sum of squares. In the example,

partial η^2 associated with Framing is $\frac{0.198}{0.198+5.461} = 0.035$

19.7 R Action

Here, we use the `aov()` function, which we have used in Chapter 18, to analyse the data. To calculate partial eta-squared, I used the *lsr* package (Navarro 2015).

```
install.package("lsr")
```

The R code to conduct the experimental data is as follows:

```
rm(list=ls())
library(tidyverse)
library(haven)
library(ahdar)
library(lsr)

# get 'nature' data from the ahdar package.
# stored to data.

dat <- nature

# convert "Framing" and "Gender"
# as categorical variables (Factors).

dat <- dat |>
  mutate(Framing = as_factor(Framing)) |>
  mutate(Gender = as_factor(Gender))

fit <- aov(PEB ~ Framing + Gender + Framing:Gender, data = dat)

# print summary
summary(fit)
```

```
                Df   Sum Sq  Mean Sq  F value  Pr(>F)
Framing         1    0.198   0.198    4.922    0.0282    *
Gender          1    2.292   2.292    57.082   5.52e-12  ***
Framing:Gender  1    8.758   8.758    218.131  < 2e-16   ***
Residuals       136  5.461   0.040
---
Signif. codes: 0 '***' 0.001 '**' 0.01 '*' 0.05 '.' 0.1 ' ' 1
```

```
# calculate effect size
# partial eta-squared

etaSquared(fit)
```

```
                  eta.sq  eta.sq.part
Framing         0.0118269 0.03492428
Gender          0.1371723 0.29563661
Framing:Gender  0.5241835 0.61596127
```

```
# partial eta-square is given in the last column of the output.
```

19.8 Learning from Published Research

Nowadays, many researchers made their data publicly available as a way to increase research transparency. Open Science Forum (https://osf.io) facilitates such initiatives. This is a great way of studying how researchers conduct their research, especially if they use experiments. You can visit the website and browse around to find studies that might be of your interests.

19.9 Further Reading

Kail, R. V. (2019), *Scientific writing for psychology*, Sage. This is not a statistic book. It teaches how to prepare a scientific article with the emphasis on writing experimental studies.

Reichardt, C. S. (2019), *Quasi-experimentation: A guide to design and analysis*, Guilford Publications. Quasi-experiment is a type of experiment in which participants are not randomly assigned to experimental conditions. This situation is more realistic to encounter in field research when we cannot assign participants to treatment conditions, for example, due to ethical reasons – assigning consumers to receive bad services. This is a comprehensive book that discusses this type of experiment.

19.10 Review Questions

1. Explain why randomization is crucial in experimentation.
2. What do experimenters need to be aware of potential confounding factors?
3. Explain how to compute ATE (average treatment effect).
4. Explain the internal and external validity of an experiment.
5. Explain how to test an interaction effect using an experiment.

19.11 Exercise

Age might influence PEB over and above *Framing* and *Gender* (i.e. old individuals exhibit more PEB than young participants), so it can be treated as a covariate (control variable). The inclusion of the role of the covariate is to remove variation in the PEB that is caused by existing differences that is more likely to be certain. Conduct a GLM procedure using data mother nature experiment.sav. This time, insert *Age* into `Covariate(s)` Box. Interpret the outputs.

Part VI

Advanced Statistical Methods

20

Cluster Analysis

Cluster analysis involves categorizing objects or entities, such as customers, organizations, markets, products, events, and so on, into groups or clusters based on similarities in their characteristics, attitudes, behaviours, or preferences. The classification resulting from a cluster analysis would enable marketers to gain a deeper understanding of their target audience and adjust their marketing strategies that resonate with those segments. For this purpose, this chapter focuses on a hierarchical clustering technique with Ward's method where the measurement items are quantitative variables. In the last part of the chapter, a clustering technique called a latent class analysis (LCA) is introduced where the measurement items are qualitative variables. Using a hypothetical data with predefined clusters, the use of SPSS and R for clustering are demonstrated putting an emphasis on the interpretations of their outputs. For LCA, the use of the R package poLCA is demonstrated.

Learning Objectives:

- Understand the principles of a hierarchical clustering technique.
- Know how to perform a cluster analysis using a hierarchical clustering with SPSS and R, which includes:
  - Knowing how to read a proximity matrix table.
  - Knowing how to read a dendrogram.
  - Knowing how to interpret a cluster solution.
- Understand the principle of validation for checking the quality of cluster solutions.

20.1 Why Cluster Analysis

We tend to classify objects of our interests or entities (e.g. consumers, products, markets, organizations, events, etc.) into groups. These objects may belong to a natural group carried out from birth (e.g. family role: parents vs. children). An object can also emerge from the tendency to classify objects based on their shared characteristics or attributes. Such man-made orderings will create set of homogeneous groups where members of one group share the same characteristics with other members for a specific period. This classification may be dynamics where an object can switch from one group to another and vice versa (e.g. consumer status: loyal vs. non-loyal). These classifications are motivated by our tendency to seek better understanding, which allows us to compare the objects in terms of their similarities and dissimilarities. For marketers, knowing groups of consumers, products, events, and organizations will aid them to formulate their

DOI: 10.4324/9781003407225-26

marketing decisions (e.g. tailoring promotions to specific groups of consumers or business organizations). For example, McAlister et al. (2022), using a cluster analysis, classify marketing organizations into three types: growth champions, service providers, and marcom leader; Harvey (1990) discovered that fund-raising donors can be categorized into five categories: managers, low involvement, sceptics, guardians, and crusaders.

Classification can be created using one dimension or variable. For example, we can easily classify students based on their exam performance. For example, those receiving below 40% are considered as a fail and those above it as a pass. Similarly, marketers can group consumers based on how long it takes for them to adopt a new product (e.g. early adopters vs. laggards). When classifications involve more than one variable, segmenting customers into homogeneous groups can be very challenging. For example, if consumers' attitude toward a brand and their income are used to segment consumers, marketers are confronted with a problem of whether to use the two single scales, or combine the two measurements into a single scale, or use both scales by plotting objects as points in a scatter plot. For the two dimensions, a scatter plot can reveal a pattern such as favourable ratings can be associated with high income, and conversely, unfavourable rating is associated with low income. When there are several dimensions involved, clustering becomes very difficult to understand, let alone visualize it. For example, visualizing objects in a three-dimensional space is hard, but how about in a four-dimensional space? This is just impossible. Thanks to cluster analysis, classifications based on several variables are no longer impossible. According to Green et al. (1967), who provided one of the earliest definition of a cluster analysis, 'cluster analysis is a generic label applied to a set of techniques in order to identify "similar" entities from characteristics (categorical or measured) possessed by the entities'. Cluster analysis has become a popular statistical tool across several disciplines, especially in marketing. Although cluster analysis is deemed as scientific, the interpretations of its results involve subjective judgements.

With the emergence of the field of artificial intelligence and machine learning, cluster analysis becomes more associated with these fields as it is considered as one of the machine learning techniques called **unsupervised learning**. The idea of a machine learning is that a computer can be trained, using data, to *think* like human in making a classification (unsupervised learning) or prediction (supervised learning). In unsupervised learning algorithms, computers seek pattern from data – this is what cluster analysis and factor analysis do. In supervised learning algorithms, computers were given an input and output data to seek a model to connect the two. For example, regression is a supervised learning technique.

20.2 Distances

Cluster analysis is based on the principle of similarity. That is, two objects that are `similar` are merged, and other objects were combined in successive orders based on their similarity with the previous objects or clusters. At the end, objects in one cluster have small differences (i.e. small within-cluster variance), but large differences with those in other clusters (i.e. large between-cluster variance).

When I judge two individuals, I can tell how similar or dissimilar they are. But computer does not have this perceptual ability. To enable computer to compare objects based on similarity, *similarity is translated into distances*. If distances among objects are known, the computer, using a *specific algorithm*, will group objects that are close to each other into a cluster. The specific algorithm we are focusing in this chapter is a hierarchical clustering with Ward's method, which is widely used in practice and academic research.

IMPORTANT

Cluster analysis is essentially 'a numerical procedure for computing distances among points and grouping points according to their **closeness** in the *n*-dimensional space' (Green et al. 1967, p. 389).

There are many distance measures offered by SPSS and R, such as Euclidean distance, squared Euclidean distance, Pearson's correlation, Block, Minkowski, etc. To illustrate the concept of distance, I focus on the Euclidean distance. This measure is easy to understand and its calculation is quite simple. The Euclidean distance is suitable for many types of data and can be used along with different types of clustering algorithms, such as K-means and hierarchical clustering with Ward's method (see Section 20.3). Euclidean distance is defined as the square root of the sum of the squares of the differences between the coordinates of two points. I hope you still remember your high school algebra: the Euclidean distance is the length of the longest side of a right-angled triangle (i.e. the length of the hypotenuse), which can be found by applying a Pythagorean theorem: $c^2 = a^2 + b^2$ where c is the hypotenuse, a and b are each side of the right-angled triangle (see Figure 20.1).

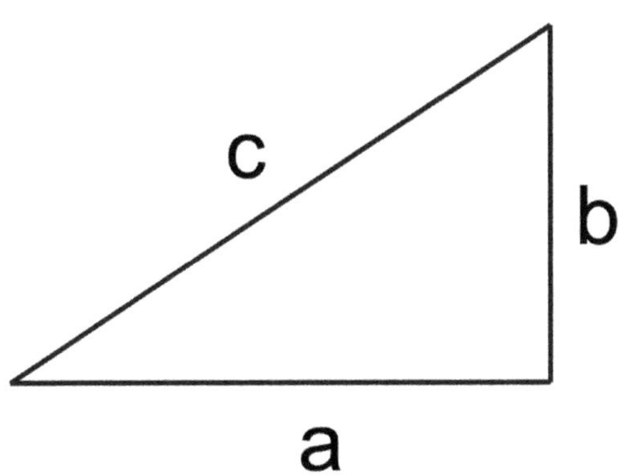

FIGURE 20.1
c is the hypothenuse. Its length is the Euclidean distance.

If an object has a coordinate (x_1, y_1), and another object has a coordinate (x_2, y_2) in a scatter plot. The Euclidean distance is given by Equation 20.1:

$$d = \sqrt{(x_2 - x_1)^2 + (y_2 - y_1)^2} \tag{20.1}$$

If two objects are measured with three variables x, y, and z, therefore, an object's coordinate is (x_1, y_1, z_1), and another object's coordinate is (x_2, y_2, z_2), the Euclidean distance is given by Equation 20.2 – imagine there are two balls in a room, one in the floor, and one is in your hand, and you measured how far the ball on the floor to the ball in your hand.

$$d = \sqrt{(x_2 - x_1)^2 + (y_2 - y_1)^2 + (z_2 - z_1)^2} \tag{20.2}$$

To illustrate on how to compute a Euclidean distance, I present data containing only two objects measured with two variables, x and y (see Figure 20.2; the data file on the book website is xyobjects.sav if you are not so keen to manually type those numbers in SPSS). The x and y variables constitute coordinates of the objects, which allow us to plot them in a scatter plot.

Applying Equation 20.1, the Euclidean distance between the two points is (see Figure 20.3):

$$\begin{aligned} d &= \sqrt{(3-1)^2 + (2-1)^2} \\ &= \sqrt{5} \\ &= 2.236 \end{aligned} \tag{20.3}$$

You do not have to compute distances between objects manually. SPSS or R will do the job for you internally as a part of their clustering procedures. In R you can request it to display the distances among objects. In SPSS clustering menus, there is an option to display the distances – see next section. However, you could also request it via `Correlation` menu by clicking:

- *Analyze* → Correlation → Distance.
- Insert variables into `Variables` box.

	x	y
1	1.00	1.00
2	3.00	2.00

FIGURE 20.2
Two objects measured with two variables: x and y.

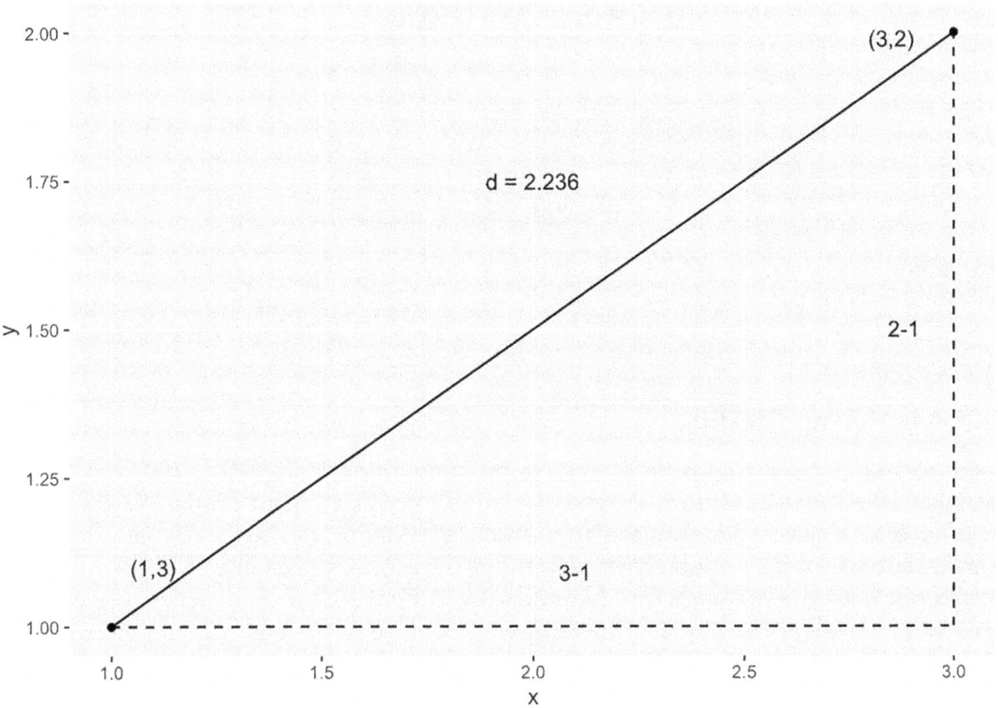

FIGURE 20.3
A proximity matrix shows the Euclidean distance of two objects.

- Under `Compute Distances`. Choose `Between cases` (the default).
- Under `Measure`, tick `Dissimilarity` (the default).
- Click `Measures`, and choose `Euclidean distance` (the default) *Clustering Method* 329.
- Click `OK`, or `Paste` if you prefer to work with syntax (see the following). Inspect the output window.

```
PROXIMITIES x y
  /VIEW=CASE
  /MEASURE=EUCLIDE
  /STANDARDIZE=NONE
```

Figure 20.4 shows distance between two objects given by the `Correlation` menu.

Proximity Matrix

	Euclidean Distance	
	1	2
1	.000	2.236
2	2.236	.000

This is a dissimilarity matrix

FIGURE 20.4
Euclidean distance of two objects.

20.3 Clustering Method

There are many clustering methods. Two popular methods are K-means and Ward's methods (also called Ward's minimum variance). In this chapter I focus on the Ward's method (Ward 1963), which is widely used in marketing (Punj & Stewart 1983; Saunders 1980) and fits naturally with our objective of findings the number of clusters from our data that we did not know beforehand. The two methods differ in their approaches. K-means is a centroid-based algorithm, where it attempts to minimize the sum of squared distances between each object (or data points) and its nearest centroid (e.g. a cluster mean). K-means requires us to specify, at the outset of the analysis, the number of *K* clusters we want to obtain from our data. Ward's method is a hierarchical clustering algorithm where the algorithm starts by treating each object as its own cluster, and in a successive fashion merges other closest objects or clusters until all objects are included in a single cluster – when this is reached, the algorithm stops. The objective of the Ward's method is to minimize the variance within clusters and maximize the variance between clusters at each step of the merging process. In other words, it merges an object or cluster that results in the least increase in the preceding object of cluster. The algorithm produces a tree-like structure referred to as a dendrogram, which shows the progression of merging clusters at each step of the clustering process. I discuss how to read the dendrogram in the SPSS Action section.

20.4 Evaluating Cluster Solutions

The interpretation of the cluster solutions can be very subjective. For instance, you might arrive at 2, 3, or 4-cluster solutions. One thing for sure that you do not want to choose 1-cluster solution in which case there is no point of conducting a cluster analysis at all. You also do not want to choose too many clusters, say 10 clusters as this is impractical. It is too costly for a firm to target 10-customer segments with various marketing plans. The recommendation for marketing applications is to choose 4–5 clusters (Thomas 1980).

To decide as to whether the cluster solutions is the final solution deemed as useful, you need to *validate* the result. That is the validity and accuracy of the solutions needs to be checked. One method recommended in the marketing literature is to check the quality of the cluster solution via a split-sample validation in which a sample is randomly split into a calibration and a validation sample of equal sizes (Punj & Stewart 1983; Saunders 1980). First, the analysis is conducted using a calibration sample. The centroids (or the means) of the cluster are saved. Objects in the validation sample are assigned to one of the identified clusters on the basis of the smallest Euclidean distance to a cluster centroid (Punj & Stewart 1983, p. 146). The cluster solutions of the two samples were then compared, and the agreement regarding cluster assignments were assessed.

In the language of machine learning, calibration and validation data are called *a training set* and *a test set*, respectively.

Rousseeuw (1987) proposed a 'silhouette method' for evaluating the quality of clustering solutions. Silhouette is a graphical method that can be used as a decision aid to interpret and validate the cluster solutions: 'Each cluster is represented by a so-called silhouette, which is based on the comparison of its tightness and separation. This silhouette shows which objects lie well within their cluster, and which ones are merely somewhere in between clusters' (Rousseeuw 1987, p. 53). A good clustering solution will have a high average silhouette score. Unfortunately, the current SPSS does not cover the method. In R, it requires `cluster` package to compute silhouette score of each case, and `factoextra` package to visualize the silhouette. I provide the demonstration in the R Action section.

20.5 Profiling Clusters

After we have decided the number of clusters we want to obtain, we want to describe the profiles of the clusters by comparing the clusters on several variables. This is called cluster profiling. For instance, we can use one-way ANOVA to compare clusters on the mean of variable(s) of our interests. You might think that you can compare cluster on the variables you used for clustering. In fact, many empirical papers implemented this practice (Brusco et al. 2017). However, comparing clusters with variables used in the clustering process as the dependent variables adds little value in understanding differences between clusters. The one-way ANOVA results are more likely to be significant as these cluster variables contribute to splitting data into multiple groups. The recommendation from literature is to use external variables that were not used as cluster variables in the clustering process (Brusco et al. 2017).

Split-sample validation and silhouette scores are examples of internal validation. Their aims are to evaluate the quality of cluster solutions (e.g. which objects belong to which clusters) without using external information. Profiling with external variables can be considered as external validation. It evaluates the quality of cluster solutions by using variables that are not used to create clusters.

20.6 Procedure

The whole procedure of conducting a cluster analysis can be summarized by a flowchart presented in Figure 20.5. At the first step, we determine the variables that are going to be used as input variables. If there are many candidate variables, factor analysis can be used to reduce these variables into smaller dimensions. For example, principal component scores (PCA) scores can be used as the input variables. In the second step, we choose measure of a proximity (e.g. a Euclidean or a squared Euclidean distance). Next, we select a clustering method. As aforementioned in the previous section, we use Ward's method, which is widely used in practice and recommended in the literature (Brusco et al. 2017; Punj & Stewart 1983). After this step, by using a software, we determine the number of clusters we want to retain (i.e. by reading a dendrogram). This is our initial cluster solution. The next step is validation with the aim of validating the stability of the cluster solutions. Lastly, after the validation process, cluster profiles can be built by using external variables that were not part of the clustering process.

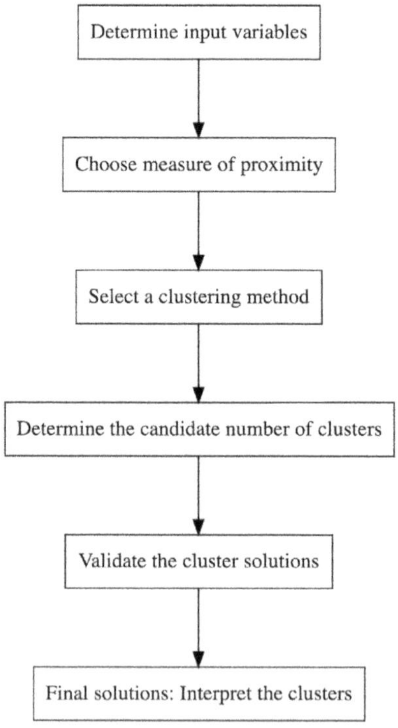

FIGURE 20.5
A procedure in conducting a cluster analysis.

20.7 SPSS Action and Interpretation

Data: youtube.sav

This is a hypothetical data about 10 YouTube influencers (see Figure 20.6). The data contains ten rows where each row corresponds to each influencer and three variables: *Likes*, which is the average likes (in thousands) that an influencer received on a new post on YouTube, and *Subscribers*, which is the number of subscribers (in millions).

The first column of the data is a grouping variable where I manually assigned the 10 influencers into three clusters based on the number of likes and number of subscribers they have. Having the information about cluster membership would allow me to compare the cluster assignment given by the SPSS results. The three clusters are as follows: influencers number 1 to 3 who received less than 1K or 2K likes and a number of subscribers of either 2M or 3M, were assigned to the first cluster. Influencers number 4 to 7, who received 11K–12K likes and had number of subscribers of either 4M or 5M, were assigned to the second cluster. Finally, influencers number 8–10, who received more than 20K–23K likes and had a number of subscribers of either 6M or 7M, were assigned to the third cluster. Figure 20.7 presents a scatter plot of *Subscribers* against *Likes*. It clearly indicates three clusters.

Steps

- Analyze →Classify → Hierarchical Cluster.
- Insert *Likes* and *Subscribers* into the `Variable(s)` box.
- Under `Cluster`, `Cases` is ticked by default.
- Under `Display`, `Statistics` and `Plots` are ticked.

	Group	Likes	Subscribers
1	1.00	1.00	3.00
2	1.00	2.00	2.00
3	1.00	1.00	3.00
4	2.00	12.00	4.00
5	2.00	11.00	5.00
6	2.00	12.00	4.00
7	2.00	9.00	5.00
8	3.00	21.00	6.00
9	3.00	22.00	7.00
10	3.00	23.00	7.00

FIGURE 20.6
youtube.sav (fictitious data).

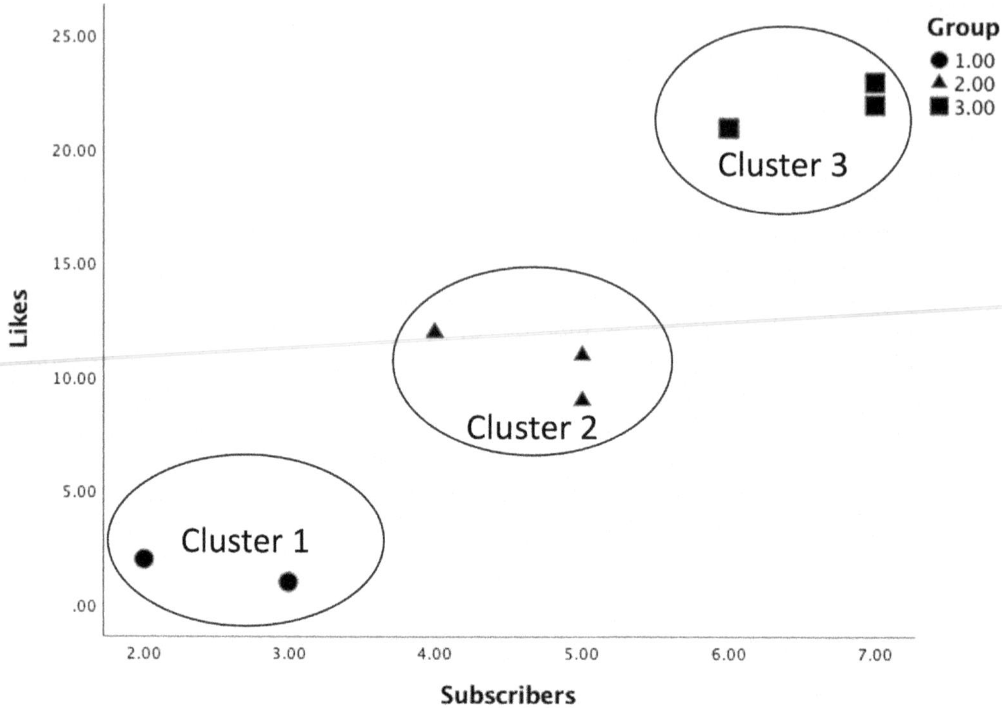

FIGURE 20.7
Three predefined clusters from youtube.sav.

- Click `Statistics`. `Agglomeration schedule` was ticked by default.
- You can tick `Proximity matrix` to display distances among cases. The matrix can get very large if there are many cases, therefore, I leave it unchecked.
- Click `Plots` and tick `Dendrogram`.
- Under `Orientation`, `Vertical` was ticked by default.
- Click `Method`, and next to the `Cluster Method` choose `Ward's method`.
- Under `Measure`, `Interval` was clicked by default. This option is to choose for a metric input variable. Next to the `Interval` option, change the default of `Squared Euclidean Distance` to `Euclidean Distance`. The squared Euclidean distance is simply the square of the Euclidean distance. You can use the default as it is actually compatible with the objective of minimizing variance in the Ward's method – calculating variance involved sum of squares and this is proportional to the squared Euclidean distance between cluster centres (Murtagh & Legendre 2011, p. 5). In the exercise, you are asked to use the squared Euclidean distance.
- Under `Transform Values`, choose `z-scores`. This step is not necessary if there is only one variable in the data. However, there are two variables (*Likes* and *Subscribers*) as input variables that are measured differently, so we choose this option.
- Click `Continue`.
- Click `OK` and inspect the output window.

If in the last step you clicked `Paste`, an SPSS syntax is created:

```
DATASET DECLARE D0.5678863817867955.
PROXIMITIES Likes Subscribers
  /MATRIX OUT(D0.5678863817867955)
  /VIEW=CASE
  /MEASURE=EUCLID
  /PRINT NONE
  /STANDARDIZE=VARIABLE Z.
CLUSTER
  /MATRIX IN(D0.5678863817867955)
  /METHOD WARD
  /PRINT SCHEDULE
  /PLOT DENDROGRAM VICICLE.
Dataset Close D0.5678863817867955.
```

Two key outputs are worth discussing. The first output is a chart showing the agglomeration schedule presented in Figure 20.8.

The agglomeration schedule shows the order in which cases were combined into clusters, followed by clusters into clusters. It starts from order zero where each case was treated as its own cluster. The procedure stops when all cases were combined into one big cluster. The decision which cases or clusters were merged was guided by the distance between the merged cluster measured using distance metric, in this case a squared Euclidean distance. In the agglomeration table, the distance is described by `Coefficients` column. The agglomeration schedule can be very long if there are many cases involved. Since we have only 10 cases, all ordering sequence can be fully displayed in the figure.

In Stage 1, case 4 and case 6 were merged into a cluster because the distance between the two cases shown in the `Coefficients` column is the smallest distance between any two cases. The next step involving this cluster is stage 7 (see value of the last column of the table). In stage 7, case 5 was merged into this cluster that were already contained case 4, case 5, case 6, and case 7 (case 7 was combined with case 5 in stage 5. Similarly, in stage 2, case 1 and case 3 were also combined into a cluster. Next step involving this cluster is stage 5.

The second output is a dendrogram – a tree-like structure, displayed in Figure 20.9, which shows the progression of merging clusters at each step of the clustering process, similar to the agglomeration schedule.

As the dendrogram in the figure displayed horizontally, we read it from left to right. As we can see from the dendrogram, cases 4, 5, 6, and 7 were merged into one cluster; case 1, case 2, and case 3 were merged into another cluster; case 8, case 9, and case 10 were merged into another cluster. To be consistent with the classification displayed in Figure 20.7, I refer to these clusters as cluster 2 (cases 4, 5, 6, and 7), cluster 1 (cases 1, 2, and 3), and cluster 3 (cases 8, 9, and 10). Clusters 1 and 2 were merged at a distance near 10, and three clusters were merged into one cluster at a distance 25. This is where subjectivity comes in. If there are many distances at which clusters were combined, you can stop at any distances arriving at a certain number of clusters. You could end up having a big argument with your teammates as to whether having four or five clusters, the solution of which might depend on your research goals and other statistical considerations discussed earlier in Section 20.4.

Agglomeration Schedule

Stage	Cluster Combined		Coefficients	Stage Cluster First Appears		Next Stage
	Cluster 1	Cluster 2		Cluster 1	Cluster 2	
1	4	6	.000	0	0	7
2	1	3	.000	0	0	6
3	9	10	.059	0	0	5
4	5	7	.176	0	0	7
5	8	9	.565	0	3	9
6	1	2	.962	2	0	8
7	4	5	1.542	1	4	8
8	1	4	3.772	6	7	9
9	1	8	7.715	8	5	0

FIGURE 20.8
Agglomeration schedule.

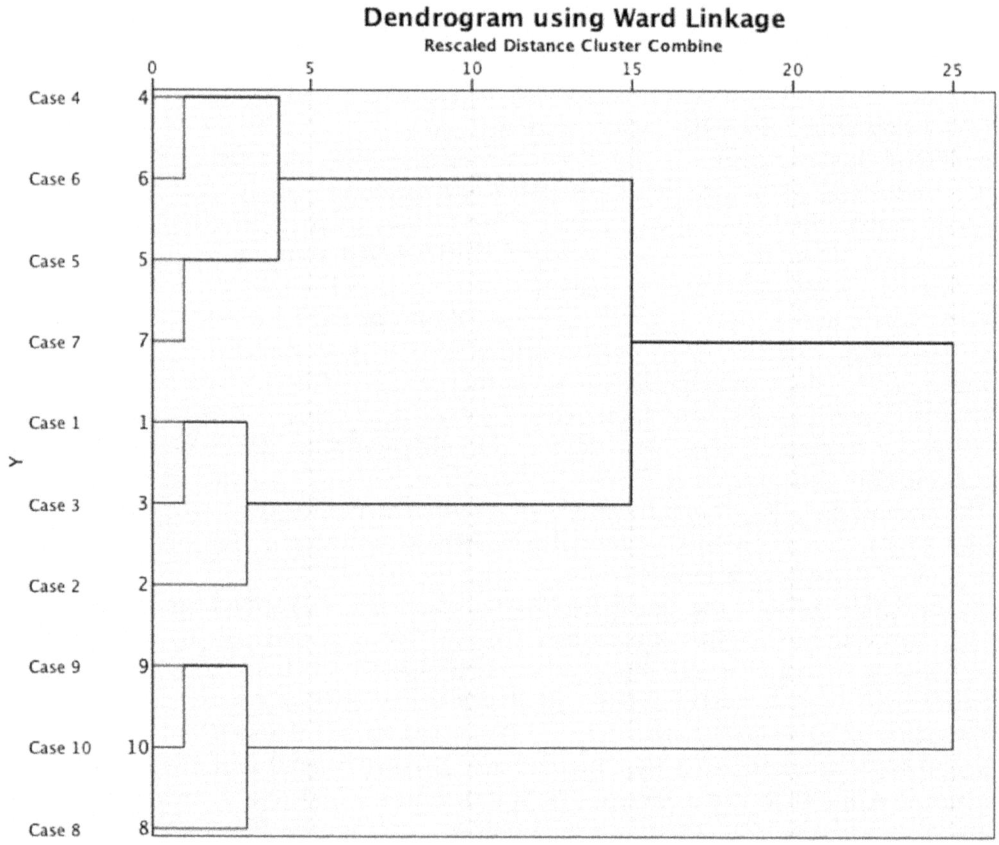

FIGURE 20.9
Dendrogram.

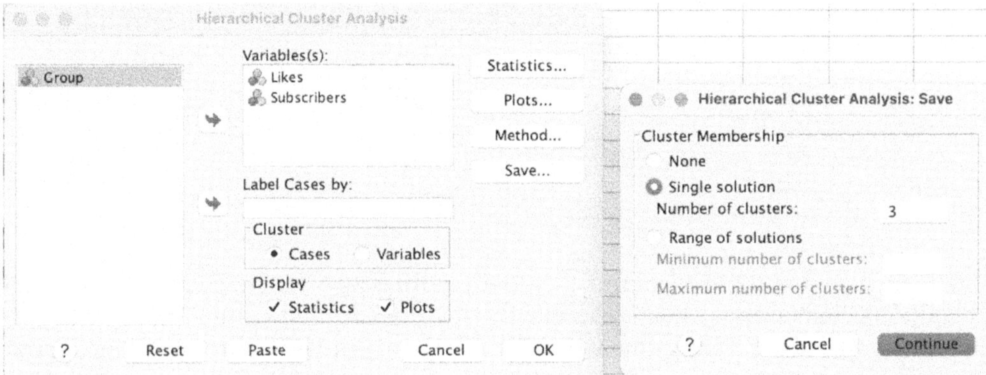

FIGURE 20.10
Saving a cluster membership.

	Group	Likes	Subscribers	CLU3_1
1	1.00	1.00	3.00	1
2	1.00	2.00	2.00	1
3	1.00	1.00	3.00	1
4	2.00	12.00	4.00	2
5	2.00	11.00	5.00	2
6	2.00	12.00	4.00	2
7	2.00	9.00	5.00	2
8	3.00	21.00	6.00	3
9	3.00	22.00	7.00	3
10	3.00	23.00	7.00	3

FIGURE 20.11
CLU3_1 is a new variable created by SPSS denoting cluster assignment.

To save cluster membership, redo the analysis. This time, you can click `Save`, then `under Membership`, tick `Singe solution`, and insert 3 in the `Number of cluster` box.

The SPSS syntax of the procedure is displayed here. It is identical with the previous syntax except that the `/SAVE CLUSTER(3)` command is added as we instructed SPSS to save cluster membership.

```
DATASET DECLARE D0.680961199734334.
PROXIMITIES Likes Subscribers
  /MATRIX OUT(D0.680961199734334)
  /VIEW=CASE
  /MEASURE=EUCLID
  /PRINT NONE
  /STANDARDIZE=VARIABLE Z.
```

```
CLUSTER
   /MATRIX IN(D0.680961199734334)
   /METHOD WARD
   /PRINT SCHEDULE
   /PLOT DENDROGRAM VICICLE
   /SAVE CLUSTER(3).
Dataset Close D0.680961199734334.
```

In the SPSS data view, a new column is added. In this case, `CLU3 _ 1` is the new variable that contains cluster assignment. Comparing my manual assignment denoted by variable `Group` and the SPSS assignment in `CLU3 _ 1`, there is a 100% agreement between the two variables as if they are exact copies of each other.

20.8 R Action

The following R code replicate our results obtained with SPSS: a hierarchical clustering using Ward's method. First, I used `dist()` function from R base to create a distance matrix among cases. Next, `hclust()` from R base was used to perform Ward's method. I plot the dendrogram using command `plot(fit)` where `fit` is the R object I used to store the results of Ward's method. In the next step, I used `cutree()` function from R base by specifying the desired number of clusters (in this case $k = 2$) and assigned cases to clusters. I added a new column containing cluster assignment to the original data. Finally, I used the `silhouette()` function to evaluate the clustering solutions obtained. A step-by-step procedure is presented here:

Load libraries and read data:

```
rm(list=ls())
library(tidyverse)
library(ahdar)
library(cluster)
library(factoextra) # to use fviz_silhouette()

# Read data from ahdar package
dat <- youtube
```

Calculate a proximity matrix:

```
distance_matrix <- dist(dat, method = "euclidean")

# round the results to 3 decimal places

round(distance_matrix,3)
```

```
##        1      2      3      4      5      6      7      8      9
## 2  1.414
## 3  0.000  1.414
## 4 11.091 10.247 11.091
## 5 10.247  9.539 10.247  1.414
## 6 11.091 10.247 11.091  0.000  1.414
```

```
##         1      2      3      4      5      6      7      8      9
## 7   8.307  7.681  8.307  3.162  2.000  3.162
## 8  20.322 19.519 20.322  9.274 10.100  9.274 12.083
## 9  21.471 20.712 21.471 10.488 11.225 10.488 13.191 1.414
## 10 22.450 21.679 22.450 11.446 12.207 11.446 14.177 2.236  1.000
```

Perform a hierarchical clustering with Ward's method:

```
fit <- hclust(distance_matrix, method = "ward.D")

fit
```

```
##
## Call:
## hclust(d = distance_matrix, method = "ward.D")
##
## Cluster method   : ward.D
## Distance         : euclidean
## Number of objects: 10
```

Plot the dendrogram:

```
plot(fit)
```

From a dendrogram of Figure 20.12, we can cut the tree into 3 clusters.

Assign objects to clusters using a `cutree()` function. To use the `cutree()` function, specify the number of cluster k. In this case $k = 3$, which refers to three clusters.

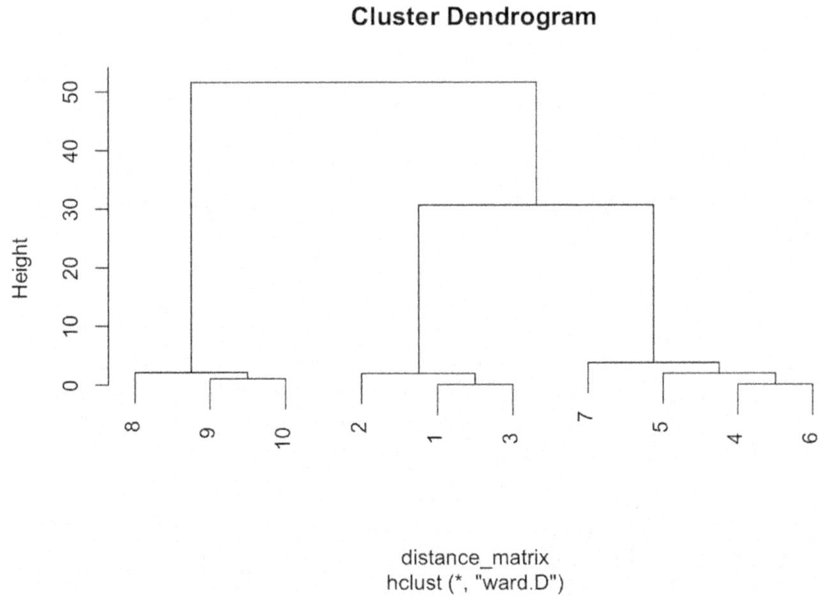

FIGURE 20.12
Dendrogram in R.

```
cut_dendrogram <- cutree(fit, k = 3)
cut_dendrogram
```

```
##     [1] 1 1 1 2 2 2 2 3 3 3
```

Now, we want to validate the three-cluster solutions. I use a silhouette method.

```
evaluate _ cluster <- silhouette(cut _ dendrogram, distance _ matrix)

  evaluate _ cluster
```

```
        cluster    neighbor  sil_width
  [1,]        1           2  0.9305646
  [2,]        1           2  0.8500083
  [3,]        1           2  0.9305646
  [4,]        2           3  0.8533516
  [5,]        2           1  0.8392308
  [6,]        2           3  0.8533516
  [7,]        2           1  0.6573466
  [8,]        3           2  0.8207562
  [9,]        3           2  0.8936284
 [10,]        3           2  0.8686529

attr(,"Ordered")
[1] FALSE
attr(,"call")
silhouette.default(x = cut_dendrogram, dist = distance_matrix)
attr(,"class")
[1] "silhouette"
```

The results show the silhouette width of each object. The silhouette width is a value that can be used to assess the fit of an object to a cluster. All the silhouette widths are above 0.8 indicating an excellent fit.

We can calculate the average silhouette width per cluster by using the *fviz_silhouette()* function from the *factoextra* package.

```
fviz_silhouette(evaluate_cluster)
```

As can be seen from the Figure 20.13, the average value of the silhouette width is above 0.8, showing an excellent fit. Satisfying with the solutions, let us add a new column named *cluster* to the data to record the cluster assignment.

```
dat <- dat %>%
  mutate(cluster=cut_dendrogram)

# let us view the data
dat
```

```
  cluster size ave.sil.width
1       1    3          0.90
2       2    4          0.80
3       3    3          0.86
```

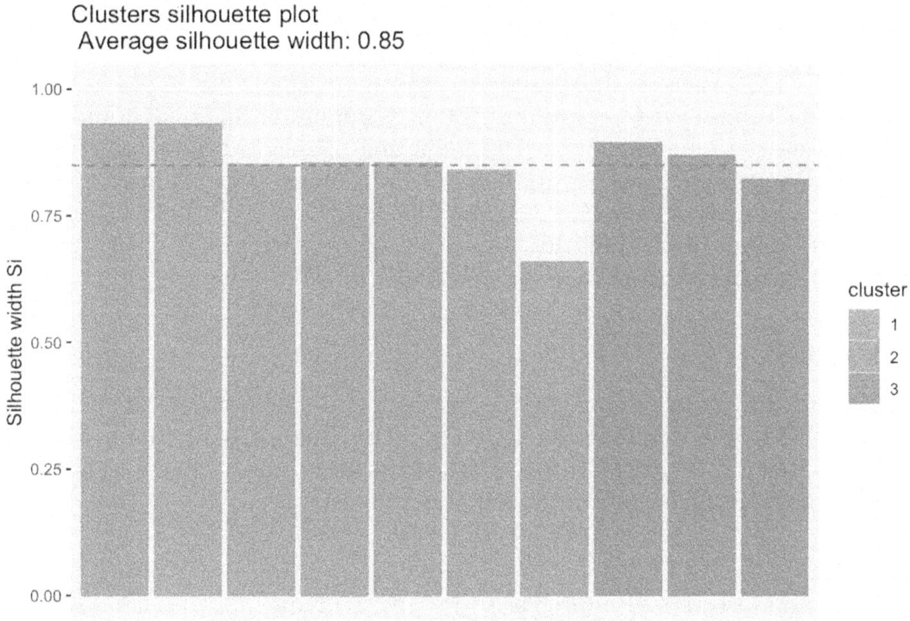

FIGURE 20.13
Output of the fviz_silhouette() function.

```
## # A tibble: 10 x 4
##   Group Likes Subscribers cluster
##   <dbl> <dbl>       <dbl>   <int>
## 1     1     1           3       1
## 2     1     2           2       1
## 3     1     1           3       1
## 4     2    12           4       2
## 5     2    11           5       2
## 6     2    12           4       2
## 7     2     9           5       2
## 8     3    21           6       3
## 9     3    22           7       3
## 10    3    23           7       3
```

Despite cluster analysis has been invented quite sometime ago, this field is still growing. This can be demonstrated by the number of R packages available for conducting cluster analysis covering vast array of basic and advanced techniques (see the full list at https://CRAN.R-project.org/view= Cluster.

20.9 Latent Class Analysis

Another popular statistical tool used for clustering in marketing research is a latent class analysis (LCA). Unlike the hierarchical clustering that uses similarity measures such as distance to classify objects, LCA is a probabilistic clustering technique. It calculates the probability of individuals being assigned to a cluster given their responses to several measurement items. LCA assumes that unobserved groups exist and the responses to the items differ across the unobserved subgroups. The LCA applies an iterative numerical procedure to estimate class memberships. The traditional LCA used categorical variables as the measurement items (e.g. yes/no questions). LCA can be conducted in specialized commercial programs, such as LatentGold (Vermunt & Magidson 2013) and MPlus (Muthén & Muthén 2019). To date, SPSS does not have a procedure to run LCA. LCA can be run in R using the R package `poLCA` (Linzer & Lewis 2011), which is relatively easy to use.

20.9.1 R Action

To demonstrate how to use `poLCA`, I have created a fictitious dataset `resort.sav`, which is also available in the dataset package `ahdar`. This dataset is fictitious. The possible scenario is as follows. Visiting a resort, 500 tourists were approached and asked to participate in a survey, which contain the following four items:

- Y1: Do you like the place? (1 = Yes, 2 = No)
- Y2: Are you satisfied with the place? (1 = Yes, 2 = No)
- Y3: Will you visit the place again in the future? (1 = Yes, 2 = No)
- Y4: Will you recommend the place to your friends? (1 = Yes, 2 = No)

The R code is presented here.

```
library(poLCA)
library(haven)
library(tidyverse)
library(ahdar)

# Read data

dat <- resort

attach(dat)

# Define model formula.

   f <- cbind(Y1,Y2, Y3, Y4)~1

   # Estimate LCA model with two classes (default).
   # One class is not permitted.
   # maxiter speficied 6000 iterations to find the solutions.
```

```
resort_lc2 <- poLCA(f, dat, nclass=2, maxiter = 6000)

## Conditional item response (column) probabilities,
##  by outcome variable, for each class (row)
##
## $Y1
##            Pr(1)  Pr(2)
## class 1:  0.4839 0.5161
## class 2:  0.6737 0.3263
##
## $Y2
##            Pr(1)  Pr(2)
## class 1:  0.4648 0.5352
## class 2:  0.5783 0.4217
##
## $Y3
##            Pr(1)  Pr(2)
## class 1:  0.3908 0.6092
## class 2:  1.0000 0.0000
##
## $Y4
##            Pr(1)  Pr(2)
## class 1:  0.4721 0.5279
## class 2:  0.6971 0.3029
##
## Estimated class population shares
##  0.7781 0.2219
##
## Predicted class memberships (by modal posterior prob.)
##  0.826 0.174
##
## =========================================================
## Fit for 2 latent classes:
## =========================================================
## number of observations: 500
## number of estimated parameters: 9
## residual degrees of freedom: 6
## maximum log-likelihood: -1379.571
##
## AIC(2): 2777.142
## BIC(2): 2815.074
## G^2(2): 5.404041 (Likelihood ratio/deviance statistic)
## X^2(2): 5.349472 (Chi-square goodness of fit)
##
```

I have created the data such that respondents in a particular cluster have a higher probability of responding to 'Yes' to every item. For example, as we can see from the outputs associated with Y1, respondents assigned to Cluster 2 have the probability of answering 'Yes' of about 67%.

Based on this output, Cluster 2 can be assigned as a 'loyal' cluster, and those in Cluster 1 can be assigned as a 'non-loyal' cluster. This is because respondents assigned to Cluster 2 indicate that they like the place, are satisfied with the place, are more likely to visit the place again in the future, and are more likely to recommend the place.

From the outputs, the *Estimated class population shares* and *Predicted class memberships* provide the estimate size of the clusters in terms of proportion of membership calculated in two different ways. The *Estimated class population shares* calculates the proportions based on share observations in each class. From the output, 78% of respondents are assigned to the first cluster. The *Predicted class memberships* calculates the proportion using posterior probabilities – the probability of a respondent being assigned to a class given his or her scores on the items used to create the classes. From the output, 83% of respondents are assigned to the first cluster. As a rule of thumb, if the two values are similar, that indicates a good model fit.

`resort_lc2` is an R object that contains several attributes, one of which is the predicted class membership. We can print the predicted class membership with the following code:

```
# Predicted class membership of the first six rows.
head(resort_lc2$predclass)
```

[1] 1 1 1 2 1 1

20.9.2 How Many Clusters?

We have estimated two-cluster solution. We are pondering whether three-cluster solution might be a better model. Let us rerun the model again by setting `nclass = 3`. I have to increase the maximum iteration to 2000 (`maxiter = 2000`) to find the solutions because below this value, the solution does not converge.

```
# Estimating 3-cluster solutions.
resort_lc3 <- poLCA(f, dat, nclass=3, maxiter = 20000)
```

```
## Conditional item response (column) probabilities,
##  by outcome variable, for each class (row)
##
## $Y1
##             Pr(1)  Pr(2)
## class 1:  0.6817  0.3183
## class 2:  0.0050  0.9950
## class 3:  0.4870  0.5130
##
## $Y2
##             Pr(1)  Pr(2)
## class 1:  0.5724  0.4276
## class 2:  0.0000  1.0000
## class 3:  0.4829  0.5171
##
## $Y3
##             Pr(1)  Pr(2)
```

```
## class 1:  0.8053  0.1947
## class 2:  0.3838  0.6162
## class 3:  0.4059  0.5941
##
## $Y4
##            Pr(1)   Pr(2)
## class 1:  0.7345  0.2655
## class 2:  1.0000  0.0000
## class 3:  0.3935  0.6065
##
## Estimated class population shares
##  0.303 0.0415 0.6554
##
## Predicted class memberships (by modal posterior prob.)
##  0.232 0.768
##
## =========================================================
## Fit for 3 latent classes:
## =========================================================
## number of observations: 500
## number of estimated parameters: 14
## residual degrees of freedom: 1
## maximum log-likelihood: -1378.11
##
## AIC(3): 2784.221
## BIC(3): 2843.225
## G^2(3): 2.482268 (Likelihood ratio/deviance statistic)
## X^2(3): 2.462864 (Chi-square goodness of fit)
##
```

From the results, the three-cluster solution does not provide a good model fit. The `Estimated class population shares` and `Predicted class memberships` is very different, indicating a poor fit. When comparing between alternative solutions, we can rely on the AIC (Akaike Information Criterion) and the BIC (Bayesian Information Criterion) values. The rule is that the model with a lower AIC/BIC value should be selected as the best model compared to other alternatives. In this example, the AIC value of the two-cluster solution is 2777.142 and the AIC value of the three-cluster solution is 2784.222. We obtained similar conclusion with BIC values. Based on this result, the two-cluster solution is better than the three-cluster solution. Hence, the two-cluster solution should be selected as the best and final model to use.

20.9.3 Creating Fake Data

Fake data where the solutions are known beforehand is good for learning purposes. `poLCA` package has the capability of generating data by specifying the number and size of clusters as well as the probability of responding to measurement items. The `poLCA.simdata()` function serves this purpose. Data for LCA in this chapter were created by using this function. The following R code demonstrate how to create data by specifying two clusters are known probability of responding to four measurement items (Y1, Y2, Y3, and Y4) if individuals belong to a cluster.

```
set.seed(1243)

probs <- list(

    # Conditional response probability to Y1
    matrix(c(0.6, 0.4,
             0.4, 0.6),
             ncol = 2,
             byrow = TRUE),
    # Conditional response probability to Y2
    matrix(c(0.6, 0.4,
             0.4, 0.6),
             ncol = 2,
             byrow = TRUE),
    # Conditional response probability to Y3
    matrix(c(0.6, 0.4,
             0.4, 0.6),
             ncol = 2,
             byrow = TRUE),
    # Conditional response probability to Y4
    matrix(c(0.4, 0.3, 0.3,
             0.2, 0.6, 0.2),
             ncol = 3,
             byrow = TRUE))

simdat <- poLCA.simdata(N=500,probs,P=c(0.5,0.5))

# Save the raw data to mydata.

mydata <- simdat$dat

# Estimate LCA solutions with two clusters.
# This part is not a part of data creation process.

f <- cbind(Y1,Y2,Y3,Y4)~1
lc2 <- poLCA(f,mydata,nclass=2, maxiter=5000)
```

```
## Conditional item response (column) probabilities,
##  by outcome variable, for each class (row)
##
## $Y1
##             Pr(1)   Pr(2)
## class 1:   0.7344  0.2656
## class 2:   0.4916  0.5084
##
## $Y2
##             Pr(1)   Pr(2)
## class 1:   1.0000  0.0000
## class 2:   0.4058  0.5942
```

```
##
## $Y3
##           Pr(1)  Pr(2)
## class 1:  0.6982 0.3018
## class 2:  0.4976 0.5024
##
## $Y4
##           Pr(1)  Pr(2)  Pr(3)
## class 1:  0.4264 0.2636 0.3101
## class 2:  0.2885 0.5157 0.1958
##
## Estimated class population shares
##  0.1417 0.8583
##
## Predicted class memberships (by modal posterior prob.)
##  0.092 0.908
##
## =========================================================
## Fit for 2 latent classes:
## =========================================================
## number of observations: 500
## number of estimated parameters: 11
## residual degrees of freedom: 12
## maximum log-likelihood: -1556.154
##
## AIC(2): 3134.308
## BIC(2): 3180.669
## G^2(2): 18.63481 (Likelihood ratio/deviance statistic)
## X^2(2): 17.79277 (Chi-square goodness of fit)
##
```

Here are the explanations of the code.

- The code generates four items: Y1, Y2, Y3, and Y4. Items Y1, Y2, and Y3 have two categories (e.g. Yes/No), and Y4 has three categories (e.g. Yes/No/Maybe)
- The code generates two latent clusters.
- The probability of answering to each category of an item, given an individual belongs to a cluster, is given by probs object.
- The line after # `Conditional response probability to Y1` provides the probability of responding to each category of Y1, given an individual belongs to a cluster. The numbers after the first matrix corresponds to these probabilities. In the first matrix associated with 'Y1', the probability of responding to the first category of Y1 (say, 'Yes'), given in the first cluster, is 0.6, whereas the probability of responding to the second category of Y1 (say, 'No'), given in the second cluster, is 0.4. The sum of the probability must be 1. Likewise, for individuals in the second cluster, the probability of responding to the 'Yes' is 0.4, and the probability of responding to the 'No' is 0.6. The response probabilities for Y2, Y3, and Y4 are given in the subsequent matrices and should be interpreted in this way.

- `poLCA.simdata(N=500, probs, P=c(0.5,0.5))` tells the program to generate 500 individuals whose patterns of response to each measurement item are given in `probs`. The last term `P=c(0.5,0.5)` specifies the expected size of the clusters, i.e. the proportion of individuals in each cluster.

20.10 Summary

In this chapter we learned about cluster analysis, which is a statistical method to classify objects or entities into groups. It is one of the most frequently used techniques in marketing research (Kumar et al. 2017). There are many methods for clustering algorithms. We focus on Ward's method, which is more suitable for quantitative variables and widely used in marketing. We also touched on the validation step for checking the quality of cluster solutions. Finally, in the last part of the chapter, we learned how to conduct a latent class analysis (LCA) using R package poLCA, where the measurement items are qualitative (nominal/ordinal) variables.

20.11 Further Reading

Harvey, J. W. (1990), 'Benefit segmentation for fund raisers', *Journal of the Academy of Marketing Science* **18**(1), 77–86. Note: An example of the applications of cluster analysis in marketing.

Punj, G. & Stewart, D. W. (1983), 'Cluster analysis in marketing research: Review and suggestions for application', *Journal of Marketing Research* **20**(2), 134–148. Note: This is a highly cited article in marketing on cluster analysis. It can be considered a seminal paper on the topic in marketing due to its comprehensive reviews on the marketing applications prior to year the article was published, and suggests guidelines to conduct a cluster analysis, which includes how to validate cluster solutions.

Romesburg, C. (2004), *Cluster analysis for researchers*, Lulu.com. Note: This book is very ideal for beginners who want to know the bolts and nuts of hierarchical clustering.

Wedel, M. & Kamakura, W. A. (2000), *Market segmentation: Conceptual and methodological foundations*, Springer Science & Business Media. Note: A classic book on a wider topic of market segmentation, including latent class analysis.

20.12 Review Questions

1. Explain why the concept of distance is important in a cluster analysis.
2. Explain how to read a dendrogram.
3. Why is validation step in a cluster analysis necessary?
4. Explain why a cluster analysis is considered as a supervised learning technique.

20.13 Exercises

1. Open instagram.sav. This is the abridged version of data downloaded from kaggle.com.[1]

It contains two attributes of 200 Instagram influencers:

score = score of the influencers calculated on basis of mentions, importance, and popularity
posts = number of posts they have made followers = number of followers

Perform a cluster analysis using a squared Euclidean distance and Ward's cluster method.

2. Split instagram.sav into two equal-sized sub-samples; perform a cluster analysis in each sub-sample. Would you able to obtain the same number of clusters in both samples?
3. Use hotel.sav or hotel data in the R package ahdar; conduct a latent class analysis with poLCA in R. How many clusters will you retain?

[1] https://www.kaggle.com/datasets/surajjha101/top-instagram-influencers-data-cleaned

21

Principal Component Analysis

This chapter discusses a statistical technique called principal component analysis (PCA). PCA is a data reduction technique with the primary goal of reducing the dimensionality of data to just a few variables called principal components. The new variables or principal components can then be used to describe the data for subsequent analysis. For example, PCA is typically conducted prior to a regression analysis because having a small number of variables can avoid a multicollinearity problem (see Chapter 14). Retaining only a few variables without losing much of information from data is the main goal of PCA. This chapter provides the basic principle of PCA and shows how to conduct a PCA analysis using SPSS and various functions in R. The R section demonstrates how to reproduce SPSS results with the widely used R functions, which include prcomp(), pca(), and principal() functions.

Learning Objectives:

- Understand the basic principles of principal component analysis (PCA).
- Know how to use SPSS and R to conduct PCA.
- Know how to interpret the PCA outputs.
- Understand the principle of PCA from a geometric perspective.

21.1 Why PCA?

To explain the principle of PCA, let us start with a simple illustration. Suppose that we have collected data from customers on 10 variables associated with their purchase of a brand. We have recorded their answers on SPSS and assigned names to each variable as V_1, V_2, V_3, V_4, up to V_{10}. For example, V_1 records the average number of purchases made in a month, and V_6 records the number of brands that were available when they made a purchase. Later, we realize that having 10 variables makes it too difficult to describe the data. So, we run a PCA procedure on SPSS. As a result, we managed to reduce the 10 variables into two just two new variables such that $V_1 \ldots V4$ are completely related to a new variable, and $V5 \ldots V10$ to another new variable (this is an ideal situation that never happens in practice). Despite having just two variables, thanks to the PCA procedure, the resulting two new variables still retain most of the information from our data. In the PCA terminology, they are referred to as principal components.

DOI: 10.4324/9781003407225-27

NOTE

PCA has a long and rich history. Pearson (1901) and Hotelling (1933) were considered the early pioneers of PCA (Jolliffe 2022, 2002). Although PCA was invented prior to what we consider the artificial intelligence and machine learning era, nowadays in a modern data analysis, PCA is classified as one of the most important machine learning techniques due to the proliferation of big data – those with too many variables and cases. It falls under the broader umbrella of unsupervised learning – a computer algorithm is tasked with seeking a pattern in data without being provided with any predefined labels or categories. In the supervised learning, there is no such thing as a dependent and independent variables, which is also the case in PCA.

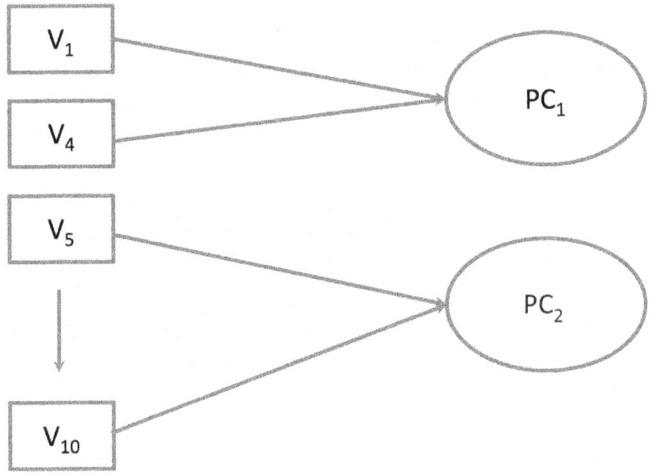

FIGURE 21.1
Ten variables are reduced to two principal components: PC_1 and PC_2.

Figure 21.1 provides a simple graphical representation of how the 10 original variables relate to the two principal components. In the figure, the 10 items are reduced to two principal components, each labelled as PC_1 and PC_2. For simplicity, V_1 up to V_4 exactly relate to PC_1 and none of them relate to PC_2. Likewise, V_5 up to V_{10} exactly relate to PC_2 and none of them relate to PC_1. Reading the wording of the original variables that belong to PC_1 and PC_2, for instance, PC_1 can be renamed as a consumer budget, and PC_2 can be renamed as a market structure.

IMPORTANT

The PCA procedure discussed in this chapter is for either interval or ratio variables. That is, the internal computational PCA procedure here applies for quantitative variables only, not qualitative variables (i.e. nominal or ordinal).

The goal of PCA is to derive principal components that account for variance in the data where the relationship between the principal components and the original variables are assumed to be linear. Nevertheless, PCA for qualitative variables based on a different principle does exist and called as a categorical principal components analysis (CATPCA), which is beyond the scope of our discussion.

21.2 How PCA Works

The PCA procedure works this way: it finds new variables that explain variations in the data. That is, it extracts the maximum variance by finding the first principal component. Next, it will find the second principal component that extracts the remaining variation that is not accounted for by the first principal component, and the second principal component must be uncorrelated with the first principal component. Next, it will find the third principal component that accounts for the remaining variance unexplained by the second principal components, and the third principal component must be uncorrelated with the second principal component. The PCA procedure works in that way and will stop if adding a new principal component will not explain much additional variance left in the data. So if the procedure results in three principal components (PC_1, PC_2, PC_3), the variance of PC_1 will be greater than that of PC_2, and variance of PC_2 will be greater than that of PC_3, and these PCs are uncorrelated to each other.

Mathematically speaking, a principal component is a weighted linear combination of the original variables. In general, if we have 10 variables that are reduced to 2 principal components, each principal component is a weighted linear combination of the 10 variables. For simplicity, following our previous illustration, our principal components PC_1 andPC_2 are formed from different sets of variables. That is, $V_1 \ldots V_4$ are reduced to PC_1, and $V_5 \ldots V_{10}$ are reduced to PC_2). Such relationships can be represented by the following equations:

$$\begin{aligned} PC_1 &= b_1V_1 + b_2V_3 + b_3V_3 + b_4V_5 \\ PC_2 &= b_6V_6 + b_7V_7 + b_8V_8 + b_9V_9 + b_{10}V_{10} \end{aligned} \tag{21.1}$$

where b_1, $b_2 \ldots b_{10}$ are called loadings or weights or path coefficients – the latter if the relationship between the original variables and principal components are described as a path model (see Figure 21.2).

Equation 21.1 might remind you of the equation that you have seen in a multiple regression model discussed in Chapter 13. Indeed, it resembles a multiple regression

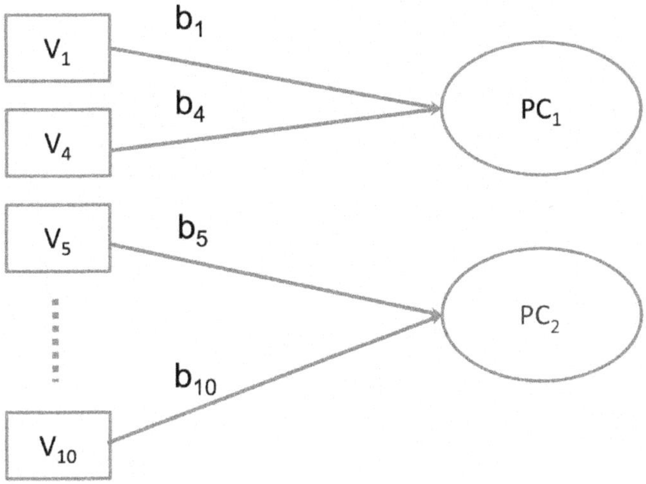

FIGURE 21.2
PCA as a path model. b's are path coefficients.

equation. However, they are not quite the same. In PCA, there is a constraint that is imposed by the PCA procedure regarding how the coefficients in the equations must be chosen. Normally, the sum of the squared loadings must be equal to a certain value, which is typically set to 1:

$$b_1^2 + b_2^2 + b_3^2 + b_4^2 = b_6^2 + b_7^2 + b_8^2 + b_9^2 + b_{10}^2 = 1 \qquad (21.2)$$

NOTE

Setting up values for the sum of squared loadings is referred to as *normalization*.

PCA procedure in SPSS or R can use a correlation matrix among the observed variables as input data. As we can recall in Chapter 11; a correlation matrix is derived from a covariance matrix: dividing each value of the covariance matrix by the product of the standard deviations of the corresponding variables. The PCA procedure, therefore, will find the path coefficients ($b_1, b_2 \ldots b_{10}$) to maximize the correlation between the PC and the original variables. Therefore, the observed variables that are represented by their principal component should be highly correlated with each other. In our example, V_1 up to V_4 are highly correlated with each other as they can be represented by the principal component PC_1. Likewise, V_5 up to V_{10} are also highly correlated with each other as they can be represented by the principal component PC_2.

IMPORTANT

Principal components are made of original variables that are combined in a linear fashion. Principal components are mutually uncorrelated.

21.3 Illustration

For an illustration, suppose that we have five observed variables. The correlations among these variables are represented by a correlation matrix as displayed in Figure 21.3.

From the correlation matrix in the figure, we can see that V_1 and V_2 are correlated (r = 0.5), whereas the remaining variables are correlated to each other: the correlation between V_3 and V_4 is 0.6, the correlation between V_3 and V_5 is 0.6, and the correlation between V_4 and V_5 is 0.7. Without using SPSS or R to run PCA, based on this correlation matrix alone, we can actually decide to reduce our data into two principal components. That is, V_1 and V_2 will be reduced to one principal component because these the two original variables are highly correlated to each other and each of them has low correlation with the three remaining variables. Similarly, V_3, V_4, and V_5 will be collapsed into another principal component because the three original variables are correlated to each other and each of them has low correlation with either V_1 or V_2.

In multiple regression discussed in Chapter 13, the squared correlation (R^2) is a measure of the amount of variance in the dependent variable that is explained by the independent variables in a regression model. The PCA procedure in statistical software such as SPSS also calculates this kind of statistic. That is, the procedure calculates the proportion of variance in the data that can be explained by each principal component, in short, which is referred to as the proportion of variance explained. Running PCA (whose procedure is explained in the next section) using the correlation matrix will indeed produce two principal components: V_1 and V_2 load to one principal component, and V_3, V_4, and V_5 load to another principal components. The two principal components account for about 75% variance in the data that is summarized by the correlation matrix.

	V_1	V_2	V_3	V_4	V_5
V_1	1				
V_2	.5	1			
V_3	0.1	0.1	1		
V_4	0.1	0.1	.6	1	
V_5	0.1	0.1	.6	.7	1

FIGURE 21.3
Correlation matrix of five variables.

21.4 SPSS Action

Data: fakedatapca.sav

In this section, I use fake data, which I created for the sake of demonstration. The correlation coefficients among variables in the fake data are identical to those displayed in Figure 21.3.

There are two ways of using SPSS to conduct PCA: (1) using `FACTOR` command and its subcommands on a syntax file with a correlation matrix as an input for PCA and (2) using a point-and-click procedure from the SPSS menu.

21.4.1 Option 1: Correlation Matrix as an Input

In this option, we use the correlation matrix of variables subject to PCA as an input data. Therefore, raw data is not required. SPSS will perform PCA based on the given correlation matrix. The following section shows we can create a correlation matrix in a format that can be processed by SPSS.

Preparing a correlation matrix

First open fakedatapca.sav. This dataset has five variables: V1, V2, V3, V4, and V5. The correlation matrix of these variables can be created by using `corrmat.spd` macro that I developed, which can be installed on SPSS. The macro produces a correlation matrix that can be copied and pasted into a syntax file. After the macro is installed on SPSS, we can follow the following steps:

- Analyze → Descriptive Statistics → Corrmat.
- Insert V1 up to V5 into the `Target List`, and click `OK` and inspect the outputs.
- Copy the correlation matrix from the output and paste it to your PCA syntax file.
- Transform the correlation matrix into a lower diagonal matrix by deleting values above its main diagonal.

Running PCA

Type the following code in an SPSS syntax file. It contains the correlation matrix of the five variables created in the previous section.

```
/*Comment: This syntax uses the correlation matrix as an input.
/* In the subcommand 'EXTRACTION PC',
/* PC indicates that PCA is requested.
MATRIX DATA
```

```
  VARIABLES=ROWTYPE_ V1 V2 V3 V4 V5.
BEGIN DATA.
N 500 500  500 500  500
COR 1.000
COR .520   1.000
COR .109    .107    1.000
COR .110    .109     .609   1.000
COR .113    .111     .623    .722  1.000
END DATA.
FACTOR
  /MATRIX=IN(COR=*)
  /ANALYSIS V1 V2 V3 V4 V5
  /KMO ROTATION
  /INITIAL EXTRACTION
  /EXTRACTION PC
  /PLOT EIGEN
  /ROTATION VARIMAX.
```

I provide the annotations of the following syntax:

In the syntax file, the text after /* is not processed by SPSS. Texts following / are SPSS subcommands, which tell SPSS to run tasks that are being specified in code.

The first line of the syntax begins with MATRIX DATA, followed by DATA which requires us to define variables in the order in a correlation matrix. The BEGIN DATA and END DATA commands contain the information about the sample size and the correlation matrix. The sample size is duplicated five times in the syntax to conform with the number of variables or columns in the correlation matrix. The next line starts with the FACTOR command that tell SPSS to run factor analysis. In the SPSS environment, factor analysis is a general term for a data reduction technique called exploratory factor analysis (EFA), which is conceptually different than PCA. Lines after FACTOR contain commands to run specific procedures in factor analysis.

- /MATRIX=IN(COR=*). This command tells SPSS that the data specified within the BEGIN DATA and END DATA commands is a correlation matrix.
- /ANALYSIS V1 V2 V3 V4 V5. The /ANALYSIS subcommand and the five variables next to it indicate variables that are going to be analysed with PCA. We have included the variables in the dataset; however, if we want to use the first four variables, *V*5 can be omitted from the list.
- /INITIAL EXTRACTION KMO ROTATION. This line contains four sub commands. INITIAL will print the initial communalities and the sub command EXTRACTION will print the final estimates of the communalities (see Section 21.4.8. KMO will perform the Kaiser-Meyer-Olkin (KMO)

test after performing a rotation specified in the ROTATION command (see Section 21.4.3). The KMO test measures the adequacy of the sample size for PCA. That is, if there is enough correlation in the data to justify using PCA for dimension reduction.

- /EXTRACTION PC. The /EXTRACTION subcommand specifies what type of factor analysis or estimation methods we want to use. For PCA, the keyword is PC. Other methods are available such as ML (maximum likelihood) and PF (principal axis factoring).
- /PLOT EIGEN. The /PLOT subcommand tells SPSS to produce a plot. The EIGEN specifies that a scree plot is requested (see Section 21.4.4, which is the common plot reported in PCA studies.
- /ROTATION VARIMAX. The /ROTATION subcommand specifies types of com- ponent rotation, which is helpful for ease of interpretation of the PCA solutions. In general, rotation will produce loadings that are large for a particular principal component and small for other loadings achieving a so-called *simple structure*. The varimax method rotates the PCA solutions by retaining uncorrelated principal components (see Section 21.4.7.

The syntax produces four outputs: table of communality, table of total variance explained, scree plot, component matrix, and rotated component matrix. These outputs will also be produced by running another option to run PCA using a syntax explained in the following.

21.4.2 Option 2: Requesting a PCA Procedure from SPSS Menu

In this option, a raw data format is required. Here, we use fakedatapca.sav. PCA is requested from the SPSS menu by clicking:

- Analyze → Dimension Reduction → Factor.
- Click `Extraction` and `under Method`, select `Principal Components`. Under `Analyze, correlation matrix` is ticked by default, which we leave it as it is. Under `Extract, eigenvalues greater than 1` is set as a default. Under `Display`, tick `Unrotated factor solution`, and `Scree plot`.

Click Continue.

- Click `Rotation`. For this illustration, I choose `VARIMAX`. Then, click `Continue`.
- Click Scores. Under Save `Variables`, choose `Regression`, which is the default option.
- Click `Option` (this is optional but I always click it). Under `Coefficient Display Formats`, tick `Supress small coefficients`, and next to Absolute value below, type in 0.4.
- Click `OK` or `Paste`.

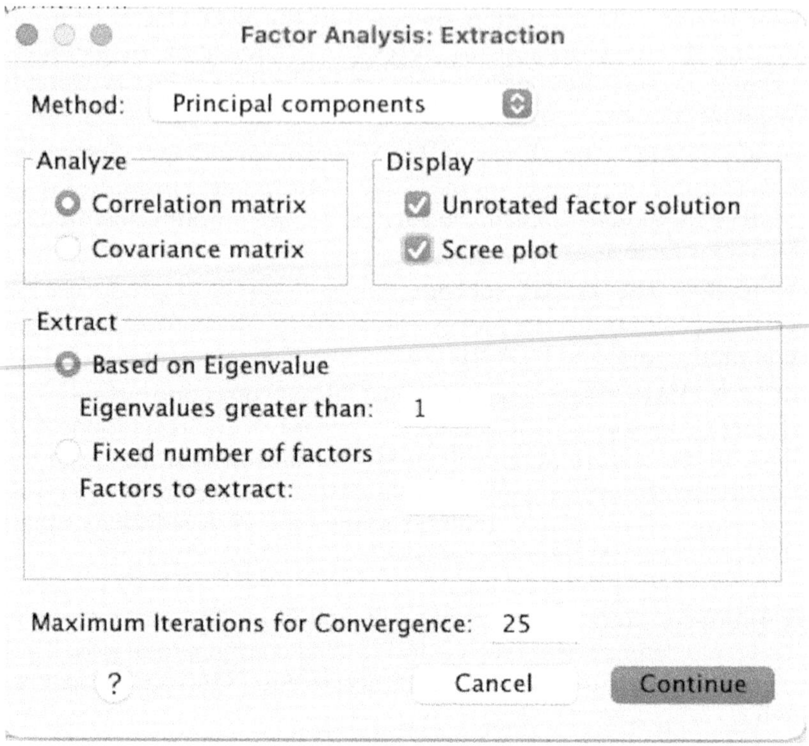

FIGURE 21.4
PCA interface in SPSS.

Clicking `Paste` in the last step produces the following syntax:

```
FACTOR
   /VARIABLES V1 V2 V3 V4 V5
   /MISSING LISTWISE
   /ANALYSIS V1 V2 V3 V4 V5
   /PRINT INITIAL EXTRACTION KMO ROTATION
   /FORMAT BLANK(.4)
   /PLOT EIGEN
   /CRITERIA MINEIGEN(1) ITERATE(25)
   /EXTRACTION PC
   /CRITERIA ITERATE(25)
   /ROTATION VARIMAX
   /SAVE REG(ALL)
   /METHOD=CORRELATION.
```

Lines after FACTOR command contain subcommands to run specific procedures in factor analysis. Some lines have been used in Option 1. The new lines in Option 2:

- /FORMAT BLANK(.4). This subcommand specifies the outputs to display only loading greater than 0.4. Values below 0.4 will be shown as empty.

- /SAVE REG(ALL). This subcommand prints principal component scores into the original data file. As a result, SPSS produces two new columns in the fakedatapca.sav, each contains scores of the two extracted principal components.

We will discuss key outputs produced by the syntax in the next section.

21.4.3 KMO and Bartlett's Test

PCA assumes that variables in data should be correlated. Related to this is the question: **Is it appropriate to use PCA?** Correlated data is required in PCA because if the variables are not correlated, they cannot be represented with a principal component. This assumption must be met prior to reading other outputs reported by SPSS. Two statistical test outputs that are typically reported by researchers are the (1) the p-value of the Bartlett's test of sphericity and (2) KMO criterion. Both are reported in one table (see Figure 21.5).

Bartlett's sphericity test. This statistical test informs us whether this there is enough correlation in the data to justify using PCA for dimension reduction. The Bartlett's sphericity test reports a p-value associated with the following null and alternative hypotheses:

H0: The variables are not correlated (PCA is inappropriate).

HA: The variables are correlated (PCA is appropriate).

The Bartlett's sphericity test's output for our data is displayed in Figure 21.5.

In the output, the p-value is less than 5%; therefore, we can reject H0, meaning that reducing the dimension of our data with PCA is justified.

KMO criterion. The first line of the output displayed in Figure 21.5 shows the Kaiser-Meyer-Olkin measure of sampling adequacy (typically shortened as KMO criterion), which is equal to 0.680. The KMO criterion is a statistical index to assess whether the data is suitable or PCA. The KMO index takes a value from 0 to 1. The threshold value for KMO is 0.6 under which PCA is not recommended to do. In the output, the KMO index is slightly above 0.6, which means that PCA is acceptable.

21.4.4 Scree Plot

Scree plot provides an answer to the question: how many principal components should be retained? A scree plot, which was introduced by Cattell (1966), displays `eigenvalues`

KMO and Bartlett's Test

Kaiser-Meyer-Olkin Measure of Sampling Adequacy.		.680
Bartlett's Test of Sphericity	Approx. Chi-Square	821.519
	df	10
	Sig.	<.001

FIGURE 21.5
KMO and Bartlett's sphericity of fakedatapca.sav.

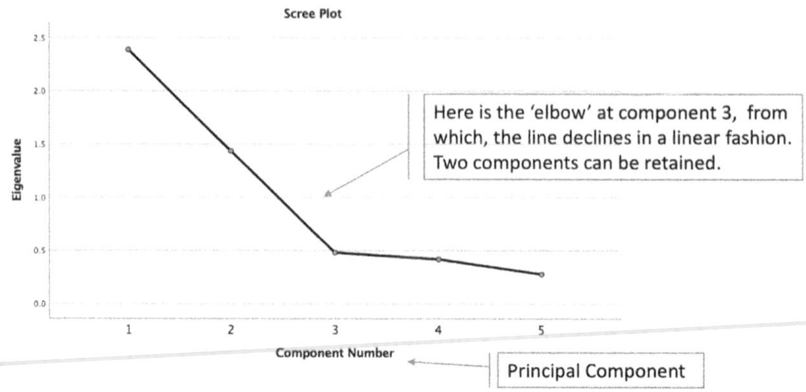

FIGURE 21.6
A scree plot.

of each principal component on the y-axis and the corresponding principal components on the x-axis. Figure 21.6 shows the scree plot produced by PCA of our data.

IMPORTANT

An eigenvalue associated with a principal component is the variance of the principal component.

NOTE

You have read the word `eigen` multiple times already. It is everywhere in this chapter. The origin of the word `eigen` is from the German language that means 'own' or 'characteristic'. Instead of 'eigenvalue', other researchers may prefer to use the word 'characteristic root', or 'root' for short. You might be curious about to who we should thank for adding this term to our vocabulary. Most sources that I read refer to the German mathematician David Hilbert who introduced the term in the early 20th century.

What we want to find in the scree plot is an 'elbow' beyond which the line in the plot goes from steep to flat. After the elbow is found, retain the principal component numbers that are below the elbow. The rationale is that after the elbow, the eigenvalues are relatively stable, which means that the remaining principal components may not capture as much meaningful variation in the data.

Reading a scree plot is quite subjective. Another criterion frequently used in practice is Kaiser's rule that suggests retaining only principal components with eigenvalues greater than 1. If, for example, all our variables ($V_1 \ldots V_5$) cannot be reduced, then each variable is a principal component. In this case, each variable or principal component has an eigenvalue, which is equal to 1. Therefore, a principal component should account for variance greater than 1. In other words, a principal component should explain more variance than a single original variable. However, Kaiser's eigenvalue greater than 1 is also not ideal as it can overestimate the number of principal components to retain. Furthermore, a principal component with an eigenvalue greater than 1 can still capture noise or random fluctuations in the data rather than meaningful variance (Zwick & Velicer 1986; Preacher & MacCallum 2003).

21.4.5 Horn's Parallel Analysis

The eigenvalue-greater-than-one rule and scree plot have received criticism in the literature as criteria to decide the number of components to retain as both criteria can lead to sub-optimal solutions (e.g. retaining more or fewer components than are necessary) (Zwick & Velicer 1986; Preacher & MacCallum 2003). Instead, researchers recommend conducting Horn's parallel analysis. This procedure involves comparing eigenvalues from actual data with those from random data. Principal components will be retained if the eigenvalue from the actual data is greater than the corresponding eigenvalue from the random data. The comparison is easier to do by looking at the point at which the scree plot of the original data crosses with that of the random data.

`Horn's` parallel analysis is not available on the standard SPSS menu but can be run after installing `Horn.spd`. The macro is an SPD version of the `rawpar.sps` that I converted. The SPS file was developed by O'Connor (2000).[1]

Steps:

- Open a data file fakedatapca.sav.
- Download `Horn.spd` from the book website and install on the SPSS.
- Click Analyze → Dimension Reduction → Horn's Parallel Analysis
- Insert V1, V2, . . . , V5 into the `Items` box.
- Click `OK` and inspect the outputs.

The macro outputs the specification used to generate random data that are specified by a user under the menu: *Ncases* is the number of cases in one dataset, which is equal to 500. *Nvars* is the number of variables, which is equal to 5. *Ndatsets* is the number of datasets generated by the program, which is set by default at 100, and *Percent* is the percentile of the distribution of the eigenvalues of the random data, which is set at 95 as the default. Using this specification, the macro generated 100 datasets and in each dataset performs a PCA (i.e. computes eigenvalues). At the end of the program, the macro computes the means of the eigenvalues, and values at the 95th percentile of the eigenvalue distributions. A list of eigenvalues of the actual and random data can be seen in the annotated outputs displayed in Figure 21.8.

[1] See https://oconnor-psych.ok.ubc.ca/nfactors/nfactors.html.

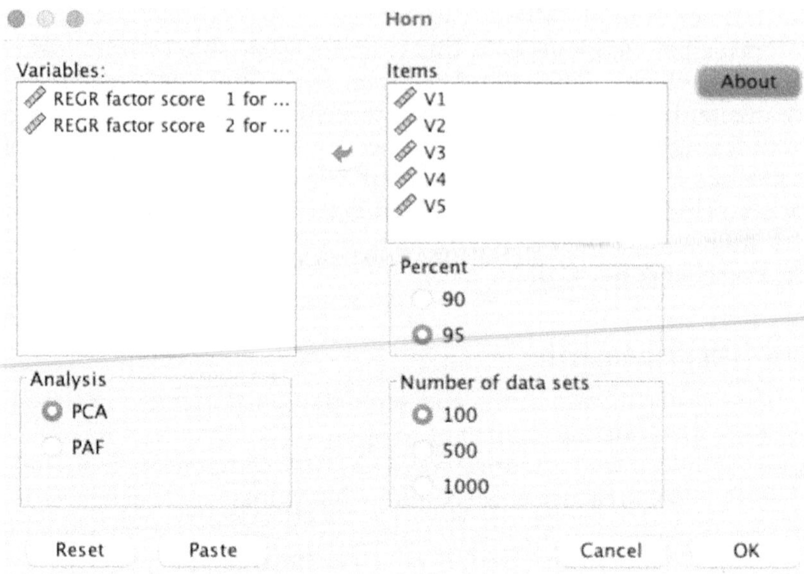

FIGURE 21.7
An interface of the Horn macro.

```
Run MATRIX procedure:

PARALLEL ANALYSIS:

Principal Components & Raw Data Permutation

Specifications for this Run:
Ncases      500
Nvars         5
Ndatsets    100
Percent      95

Raw Data Eigenvalues, & Mean & Percentile Random Data Eigenvalues
       Root     Raw Data      Means     Prcntyle
   1.000000     2.387726   1.127347     1.175045
   2.000000     1.436075   1.055421     1.098277
   3.000000      .480491    .999108     1.030214
   4.000000      .418388    .944855      .977615
   5.000000      .277320    .873269      .918588

------ END MATRIX -----
```

Specifications for random data generation. 100 data sets were generated each having 500 cases and 5 variables. 95th percentile of eigen values distributions is set.

95th percentile of eigen values of random data distribution

Mean eigen values of random data

Eigen values of actual data

FIGURE 21.8
Horn's outputs: eigenvalues of the actual and random data.

The annotated scree plot that also contains 'scree plots' of the means of the eigenvalues and the 95th percentile eigenvalues of random data (both are straight lines) can be seen in Figure 21.9.

The macro also produces a new SPSS file called *screedata.sav* containing a list of eigenvalues of an actual data, and those of the random data (see Figure 21.10).

screedata.sav can be used to create a scree plot manually by using the SPSS `Graphs` menu. In fact, the Horn's parallel analysis macro reads this data to create the scree plot shown in Figure 21.9. I have recreated a scree plot that shows the scree plot of the actual data and the 95th percentile by following this step:

- On the SPSS menu, click Graphs → Line.
- Choose `Multiple`.
- Tick `Summaries of separate variables`.
- Insert rawdata and percntyl into the 'Lines represent' box.
- Insert root into the `Category Axis` box.
- Click OK. See the output that will show Figure 21.12. Note that the lines will have different colours. I have modified the colours and line type by double-clicking the graph.

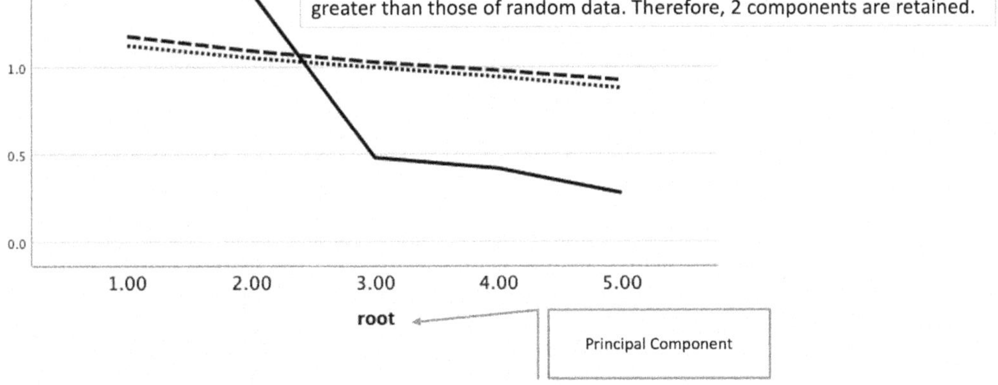

FIGURE 21.9
A scree plot of actual data, random data, the mean eigenvalues, and 95th percentiles eigenvalues.

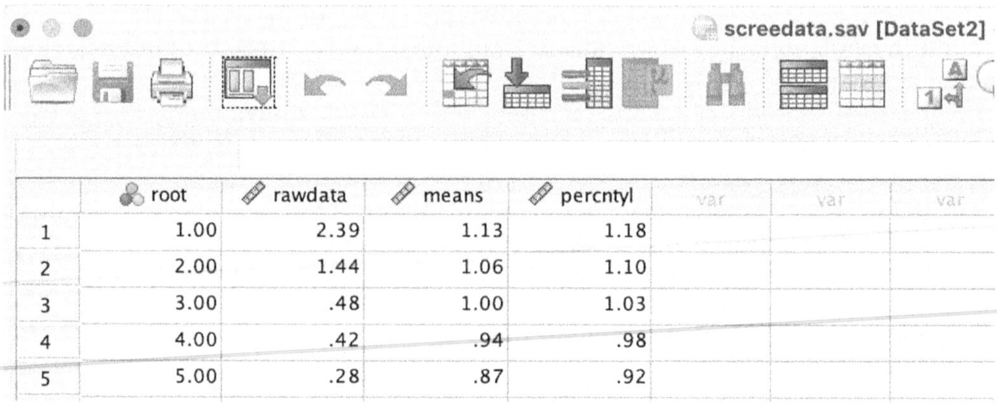

screedata.sav [DataSet2]

	root	rawdata	means	percntyl	var	var	var
1	1.00	2.39	1.13	1.18			
2	2.00	1.44	1.06	1.10			
3	3.00	.48	1.00	1.03			
4	4.00	.42	.94	.98			
5	5.00	.28	.87	.92			

FIGURE 21.10
screedata.sav generated by the Horn macro.

FIGURE 21.11
Creating a scree plot on SPSS's graph menu using screedata.sav data.

21.4.6 Unrotated Component Matrix

Figure 21.13 shows the component matrix showing the values of the correlation between the principal components (called `principal component loadings or loadings`, for short) and the original variables.

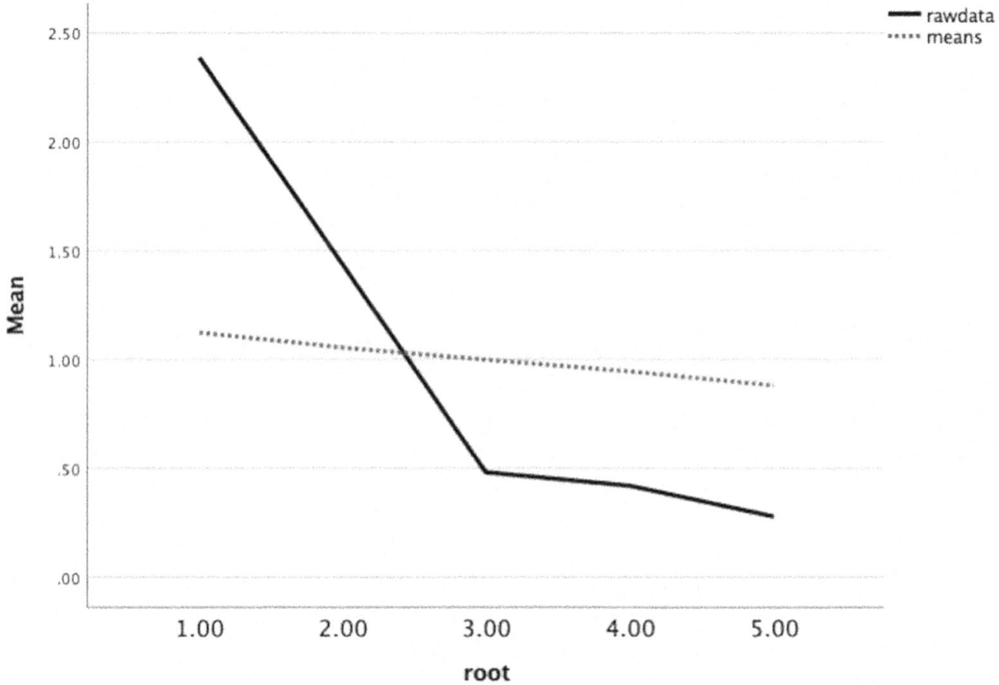

FIGURE 21.12
A scree plot of the actual data and the plot of 95th percentile eigenvalues.

Component Matrix[a]

	Component 1	Component 2
V1	.324	.809
V2	.323	.810
V3	.821	-.193
V4	.864	-.211
V5	.871	-.210

Extraction Method: Principal Component Analysis.

a. 2 components extracted.

These values are the correlations between variables and their principal components. They are called 'loadings'.

The correlation between V1 and PC1 is 0.324

The correlation between V1 and PC2 is 0.809

$0.324^2 + 0.809^2 = 0.76$ = **communality of v1**

Communality is the proportion of variance in a variable explained by principal components.
76% of variance in V1 is explained by PC1 and PC2.

FIGURE 21.13
Unrotated component matrix showing principal component loadings. The loading is the correlation between a variable and a principal component.

Rotated Component Matrix[a]

	Component 1	Component 2
V1	.064	.869
V2	.062	.869
V3	.841	.065
V4	.887	.061
V5	.893	.064

Extraction Method: Principal Component Analysis.
Rotation Method: Varimax with Kaiser Normalization.

a. Rotation converged in 3 iterations.

Rotated Component Matrix[a]

	Component 1	Component 2
V1		.869
V2		.869
V3	.841	
V4	.887	
V5	.893	

Extraction Method: Principal Component Analysis.
Rotation Method: Varimax with Kaiser Normalization.

a. Rotation converged in 3 iterations.

Loadings below 0.4 are not shown.

FIGURE 21.14
The original rotated component matrix (left) and the modified rotated component matrix (right).

For example, the correlation between V_1 and the first principal component is 0.324, whereas the correlation between V_1 and the second principal component 2 is 0.809.

21.4.7 Rotated Component Matrix

Figure 21.14 shows the rotated component matrix. A rotated component matrix shows the values of the correlation between the principal components (called loadings) and the original variables after the PCA solutions have been rotated. Rotated solutions mean that principal components initially produced by the PCA procedure are rotated geometrically for ease of interpretation.

Rotation with varimax in PCA preserves the uncorrelated principal components. Although, PCA reduces a set of possibly correlated variables into a smaller set of uncorrelated variables called principal components, rotation is still helpful for ease of interpretations of the factor solutions. Rotation is typically used in exploratory factor analysis (EFA) – explained in the next chapter. Rotation might not be necessary if the PCA solutions already suggest that a simple structure exists where we could see clearly how variables load into the principal components.

Back to our example, in the rotated solutions, the correlation between V_1 and the first principal component is 0.064, whereas the correlation between V_1 and the second principal component is 0.869. Thus, in the rotated solutions, V_1 appears to be strongly correlated to the first principal component and weakly correlated to the second principal component. The pattern of the relationship between the variables and the two principal components gets clearer when we look at other correlations: PC1 is highly correlated with V_3, V_4, and V_5, and its correlation with V_1 and V_2 is so small that their correlations can be ignored. Similarly, PC2 is highly correlated with V_1 and V_2, and its correlations with V_3, V_4, andV_5 are so small that their correlations can be ignored. The correlation between the two principal components and the original variables while ignoring small correlations can be visually described in the right-hand table of Figure 21.14 and visually displayed in the PCA model in Figure 21.15.

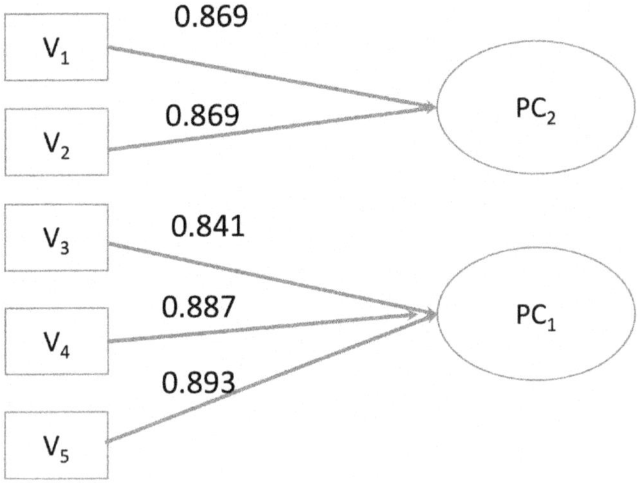

FIGURE 21.15
PCA model ignoring small loadings and cross-loadings (loadings to other components).

Communalities

	Initial	Extraction
V1	1.000	.760
V2	1.000	.760
V3	1.000	.711
V4	1.000	.791
V5	1.000	.802

Extraction Method: Principal Component Analysis.

Each variable's Initial estimate of communality is 1. This value is taken from the main diagonal of the correlation matrix.

Communality associated with V1 = 76%. This means 76% of variance in V1 is explained by the principal components.

FIGURE 21.16
Communality table.

21.4.8 Communality

Communality is the proportion of variance in a variable (e.g. in *V*1) accounted for by the principal components. Communality associated with a variable is calculated as the sum of squared loadings for that item. It can be manually calculated from the loading printed in the unrotated or rotated component matrix. For example, we can calculate the communality associated with *V*1 from the rotated component matrix as follows:

- Inspect the rotated component matrix.
- Read the correlation between V1 and PC1, which is 0.064.
- Read the correlation between V1 and PC2, which is 0.869.
- Take the sum of the squared loadings: $0.0642^2 + 0.8692^2 = 0.76$.

- Thus, the proportion of variance in *V1* explained by PC1 and PC2 is 76%. Table 21.16 display the initial and the final communality estimates.

21.4.9 Total Variance Explained

Figure 21.17 shows the 'Total Variance Explained' table. It is a part of a big table not entirely shown here. What is displayed in the figure is the part that shows the solutions after the principal components are rotated. It displays the eigenvalues of each principal component, its proportion of the total, and the cumulative of the percentage variance. As can be seen in the table, the eigenvalue associated with PC1 is 2.300, which is 46% of the total variance. Note that the total variance is equal to 5, which is always the same as the total number of variables being used for PCA if a correlation matrix is used an input data for PCA – the default in the SPSS (see Figure 21.4).

= 2.3/total eigenvalues
= (2.3/5)*100% = 46%

Total Variance Explained

	Rotation Sums of Squared Loadings		
Component	Total	% of Variance	Cumulative %
1	2.300	46.005	46.005
2	1.524	30.471	76.476

Extraction Method: Principal Component Analysis.

Proportion of variance accounted for by two PCs after rotation (76.48%)

FIGURE 21.17
Table of 'Total Variance Explained'.

WARNING

In the PCA perspective, the amount of information in the data is the sum of the variances of the individual variables, which is the total variance. PCA can be based on either a covariance matrix or a correlation matrix. If we choose the option of using a correlation matrix as an input to PCA (see Figure 21.4), the individual variables are standardized meaning that each of the original variable has a 0 mean and variance equals to 1. Therefore, the amount of information in the data is just the same as the number of the original variables, each with variance that is equal to 1. If we have 5 standardized variables, the amount of variance in the data is just 5. If we choose the option of using a covariance matrix ((see Figure 21.4), the total variance is the sum of the variances of the individual variables in their original forms. However, running PCA with the covariance matrix will not give the same results as those produced by PCA with a correlation matrix. The recommended procedure is to conduct a correlation based PCA – leaving the SPSS default 'correlation' as it is.

21.4.10 Principal Component Scores

The Option 2 syntax includes subcommand /SAVE REG(ALL) instructing SPSS to produce principal component scores. This command cannot be used in the Option 1 syntax as SPSS requires raw data to perform the operation. Executing the command will create two new columns on the data file. These columns are the scores of the first and the second principal components, respectively. Figure 21.18 shows the principal component scores of the PCA with unrotated and rotated solutions. The former are produced by PCA without rotation, and the latter are produced by rerunning PCA with varimax rotation.

The principal component scores, or component scores, for short, provide information about the contribution of each observation to the principal components. They can be interpreted as the score of an individual on the principal components. The principal component scores are in the standardized forms with mean 0 and variance 1 (please check).

The availability of these scores allows us to check the correlation between the variables *V*1 . . . *V*5 and *PC*1, *PC*2, or loadings that we have seen in Figure 21.14. The advantage of having the component scores is that they can be used in a regression analysis. For example, if we treat the PC1 and PC2 as two independent variables explaining a dependent variable, the scores are the values of the independent variables. In some applications, obtaining the principal components are the primary research objective. In many empirical works, the principal component scores are used prior to undertaking further analysis. For example, one of the earliest PCA papers in marketing conducted PCA as a precursor of a regression analysis (Farley 1964).

Standardized PC Scores from rotated solutions

	V1	V2	V3	V4	V5	FAC1_1	FAC2_1
1	-.18	-.04	-1.27	-1.32	-1.45	-1.51667	-.00314
2	-1.70	-.94	-.25	-.97	-1.36	-.88908	-1.30146
3	-.87	-.80	-1.60	.14	-1.00	-.84638	-.81054
4	.27	-.30	1.52	-.40	-.56	.16842	-.02742
5	-.23	1.14	-.80	-.37	-.33	-.59454	.52693

FIGURE 21.18
The last two columns are the principal component scores.

These correlations are the loadings of V1 on PC1 and PC2

Correlations

		V1	REGR factor score 1 for analysis 1	REGR factor score 2 for analysis 1
V1	Pearson Correlation	1	.064	.869**
	Sig. (2-tailed)		.154	<.001
	N	500	500	500
REGR factor score 1 for analysis 1	Pearson Correlation	.064	1	.000
	Sig. (2-tailed)	.154		1.000
	N	500	500	500
REGR factor score 2 for analysis 1	Pearson Correlation	.869**	.000	1
	Sig. (2-tailed)	<.001	1.000	
	N	500	500	500

**. Correlation is significant at the 0.01 level (2-tailed).

FIGURE 21.19
Correlation between V1 and factor scores associated with PC1 and PC2, which are the loadings of V1 on PC1 and PC2.

21.5 R Action

There are three widely used functions in R to run PCA: `prcomp()`, `pca()`, and `principal()`.[2] The first function is from the stats package included in the R base and can therefore be called directly without loading any other packages. Other package from R base is princomp(). I do not include princomp() here because it is slightly less flexible in handling types of input data compared to prcomp(), and in general prcomp() is more popular than princomp(). The second function, `principal()`, is from the `psych` library. The third function, `pca()`, is from the `FactoMiner` package. I show how to replicate results reported by SPSS using prcomp(), pca(), and principal() because they are user-friendly, and with little modification, we can reproduce outputs identical to SPSS's results.

NOTE

This section contains mathematical calculations which – to fully appreciate them – requires the knowledge of vectors, matrices, and their operations typically covered in a special course called matrix algebra. A variable in a SPSS data is a vector (*V1* in our data is a vector). A matrix is a collection of vectors (our data

[2] others are dudi.pca() from the package ade4 and the acp() from the package amap

is a matrix). To understand the mechanics of PCA, knowing matrix algebra is an obvious advantage, which is beyond the scope of this book. My goal in this section is more on the use of various R functions to replicate the SPSS results discussed in the preceding section rather than discussing the mechanics of PCA, and try to show you where those SPSS values come from without getting into the details of the calculations.

21.5.1 Prcomp() Function

prcomp() is very popular for running PCA because its computation is quite fast and is part of the R base. prcomp() uses a PCA algorithm called a singular value decomposition (svd) – essentially, it is an engine that drives prcom().

```
rm(list=ls()) # start from a clean slate.
library(ahdar) # load data package

# load fakedatapca.
# save to a new object.
# short name is better than a long name.

dat <- fakedatapca

apply prcomp():

# based on correlation matrix
res <- prcomp(dat, center=TRUE, scale=TRUE)

summary(res)
```

```
## Importance of components:
##                           PC1    PC2    PC3     PC4     PC5
## Standard deviation     1.5452 1.1984 0.6932 0.64683 0.52661
## Proportion of Variance 0.4775 0.2872 0.0961 0.08368 0.05546
## Cumulative Proportion  0.4775 0.7648 0.8609 0.94454 1.00000
```

prcomp() produced results stored in R objects, which include:

sdev: The standard deviations of the principal components.

rotation: The matrix of loadings (eigenvectors) representing the directions and contributions of the original variables to the principal components.

x: The matrix of principal components (component scores).

center and *scale*: Information about centring and scaling applied to the data. Calculate eigenvalues:

```
eigen_va7l <- res$sdev^2 # variance of the pcs
print(round(eigen_val,3))
```

```
## [1] 2.388 1.436 0.480 0.418 0.277
```

Calculate proportion of variance explained by principal components:

```
var_explained = round((eigen_val / sum(eigen_val)) * 100,2)
print(var_explained)
```

```
## [1] 47.75 28.72  9.61   8.37   5.55
```

To reproduce the SPSS's loadings:

- Get the eigenvector. Store the results in *eigen_vec*.
- Get the standard deviation of the principal component. Store the results in *sd_pc*.
- SPSS loadings are obtained by multiplying *eigen_vec* with *sd_pc*.

```
ncomp <-2 # number of components
eigen_vec <- res$rotation[,1:ncomp] # eigen vector
sd_pc <- diag(res$sdev,ncomp,ncomp)
loadings <- eigen_vec %*%  sd_pc
print(loadings) # SPSS loadings
```

```
##              [,1]         [,2]
##   V1   0.3244469    0.8089314
##   V2   0.3226646    0.8097865
##   V3   0.8206675   -0.1934289
##   V4   0.8641721   -0.2110154
##   V5   0.8706658   -0.2097823
```

NOTE

You can pause for a while before we proceed. As promised, I am back to the topic of normalization.

Let us calculate this expression:

```
round(t(loadings[,1]) %*% loadings[,1],6)
```

```
##          [,1]
## [1,] 2.387726
```

The expression means that we take the sum of the squares of the elements of loadings. The result is 2.387726. As we knew before, this value is just the variance (or eigenvalue) of the first principal component. SPSS reports the loading associated with the first principal component with this eigenvalue. Now, the mystery is revealed that the normalization constraint that seemed to be imposed by SPSS is that the sum of the squared loadings associated with the first principal component is equal to the variance of the principal component.

```
# Eigenvalue or variance of the first principal component

eigen_val[1]
## [1] 2.387726
```

Now, let us reproduce the SPSS's principal component scores. Follow these steps:

- Standardize all variables in the data; i.e. each variable has a mean of zero and variance of 1.
- Calculate principal component scores by multiplying the standardized variables with their associated loadings. Store the results in *pc*.
- Standardize *pc*. Store the values in *zpc*.

```
# Standardize all variables.
zdat <- scale(dat, center=TRUE, scale=TRUE)

# Multiply the standardized variables with loadings
pc <- zdat %*% loadings # pc scores.

# Standardize pc scores.
zpc <- scale(pc, center=TRUE, scale=TRUE)

print(head(zpc))
```

```
##              [,1]           [,2]
## [1,] -1.4462280     0.45687676
## [2,] -1.2418385    -0.97061839
## [3,] -1.0522996    -0.51575300
## [4,]  0.1521744    -0.07719234
## [5,] -0.4067802     0.68239450
## [6,]  0.4914366    -2.18704185
```

The values for *zpc* are similar to those of the principal component scores from the SPSS's unrotated PCA solutions (see Figure 21.18).

Let us create a scatter plot using the ggplot() function. We need to use `var _ explained` created in the previous step, which contains the eigenvalues. This object is stored in another object, called `dat _ eigen` in the following syntax.

```
#create scree plot
library(ggplot2)

dat_eigen <- data.frame(pc=c(1:length(eigen_val)), var_explained)
```

Now, we are ready to use ggplot(). I use geom_line() to draw the graph, and geom_point() to draw points at the positions of the eigenvalues. I display the eigenvalues on the graph by using geom_text(). I also display the eigenvalues on the graph by using labels in the mapping, and use paste0() to include the '%' sign next to the eigenvalue.

```
p <- ggplot(data = dat_eigen,
         mapping = aes(x = pc,
                       y = var_explained,
                       label = paste0(var_explained, '%')))+
         geom_line() +
         geom_point() +
         geom_text(nudge_y = 1.4, nudge_x = 0.3) +
         labs(x = "Principal Component",
              y = "% Variance Explained",
              title = "Scatter Plot") +
         ylim(0, 50)+
         theme_classic()
p
```

21.5.2 PCA() Function

pca() function belongs to the FactoMiner package (Lê et al. 2008). The package provides various results that are stored in R objects. The objects can be selected and integrate well with the ggplot() for visualization. We are going to use another package `factorextra` to produce a scree plot, which can be easily customized according to our need. Furthermore, thanks to their developers, the package has its own official website with many useful resources, which is hosted at http://factominer.free.fr/index.html. Let us install the package.

WARNING

The component scores as produced by the PCA() function from FactoMiner index-principal component analysis!R package!FactoMiner package will not be the same as those of SPSS.

Let us read fakedatapca and save it to R object `dat`. Note that, if you worked on an SPSS data using fakedatapca.sav, it should contain five variables only. If you happen to save the principal component scores onto your data from previous SPSS session, please delete them.

```
# Load the necessary library

library(ahdar)
library(FactoMineR)
```

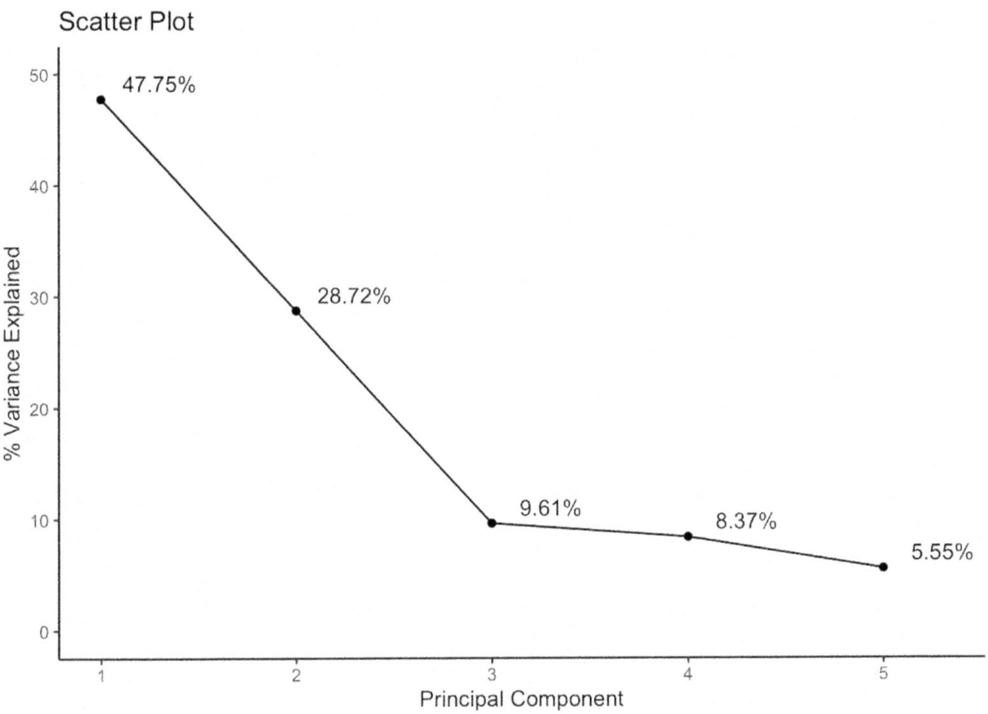

FIGURE 21.20
Scree plot created by the ggplot().

```
Read data and store to a new object dat:
```

```
dat <- fakedatapca
```

```
Call the pca() function to run PCA.
res <- PCA(dat, graph = FALSE)
print(res)

## **Results for the Principal Component Analysis (PCA)**
## The analysis was performed on 500 individuals, described by 5
   variables
## *The results are available in the following objects: ##

##       name                  description
##    1  "$eig"                "eigenvalues"
##    2  "$var"                "results for the variables"
```

```
##    3  "$var$coord"          "coord. for the variables"
##    4  "$var$cor"            "correlations variables
                              - dimensions"
##    5  "$var$cos2"           "cos2 for the variables"
##    6  "$var$contrib"        "contributions of the variables"
##    7  "$ind"                "results for the individuals"
##    8  "$ind$coord"          "coord. for the individuals"
##    9  "$ind$cos2"           "cos2 for the individuals"
##   10  "$ind$contrib"        "contributions of the individuals"
##   11  "$call"               "summary statistics"
##   12  "$call$centre"        "mean of the variables"
##   13  "$call$ecart.type"    "standard error of the variables"
##   14  "$call$row.w"         "weights for the individuals"
##   15  "$call$col.w"         "weights for the variables"
```

From these outputs, there are 15 objects produced by PCA. We are not going to use all of them. Let us start with showing the variance of the principal components:

```
eigen <- res$eig
print(eigen)
```

```
## eigenvalue percentage of variance cumulative percentage of variance
## comp 1    2.3877258      47.754516                           47.75452
## comp 2    1.4360750      28.721500                           76.47602
## comp 3    0.4804915       9.609829                           86.08585
## comp 4    0.4183877       8.367753                           94.45360
## comp 5    0.2773201       5.546402                          100.00000
```

We obtain similar results to those produced by SPSS. The first two principal components have eigenvalues greater than one and explain 76.5% of variation in the data. Let us create a scree plot.

Install the `factoextra` package:

```
install.packages("factoextra")
```

Use the fviz_screeplot() function to display a scree plot:

```
library(factoextra)

p <- fviz_screeplot(res, addlabels = TRUE,
                    geom ="line", ncp = 5) +
                    theme_classic()
p
```

```
# Setting addlabels = TRUE, shows eigenvalues.
# geom ="line" requests a line graph.
# ncp is the number of component to display.
# The output is a ggplot()'s style graph.
```

As we would be retaining the first two principal components, we want to show the loadings: the correlation between the variables and the principal components.

```
ncomp <- 2 # number of components
loadings <- res$var$cor[,1:ncomp]
print(loadings)
```

```
##            Dim.1        Dim.2
##    V1   0.3244469    0.8089314
##    V2   0.3226646    0.8097865
##    V3   0.8206675   -0.1934289
##    V4   0.8641721   -0.2110154
##    V5   0.8706658   -0.2097823
```

To reproduce the SPSS's principal component scores, first we have to standardize all variables in the original data matrix:

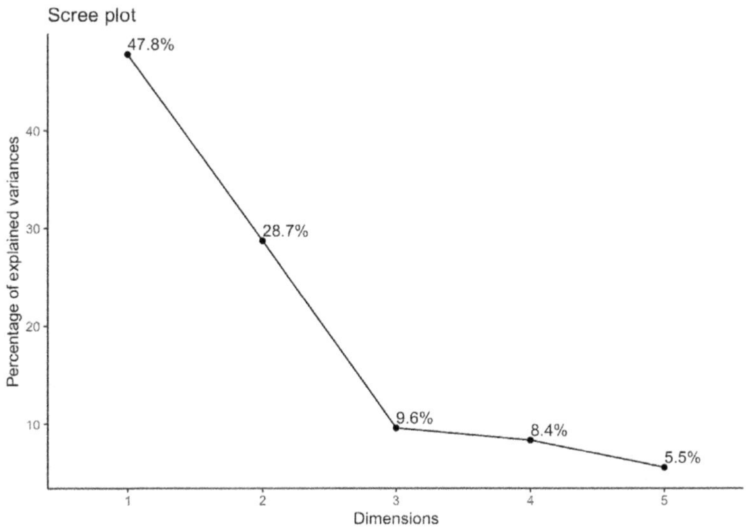

FIGURE 21.21
Scree plot created by the fviz_screeplot().

```
# standardize all variables in the data
zdat <- scale(dat, center=TRUE, scale=TRUE)
```

next, calculate the factor scores by multiplying *zdat* with the loadings:

```
pc <- zdat %*% loadings # principal component scores.
```

The next step is to standardize the principal scores obtained using the scale() function by setting center=TRUE and scale=TRUE.

```
zpc <- scale(pc, center=TRUE, scale=TRUE)

## Print top rows of the variable
print(head(zpc))
```

```
##             Dim.1        Dim.2
## [1,]   -1.4462280   0.45687676
## [2,]   -1.2418385  -0.97061839
## [3,]   -1.0522996  -0.51575300
## [4,]    0.1521744  -0.07719234
## [5,]   -0.4067802   0.68239450
## [6,]    0.4914366  -2.18704185
```

As FactoMiner also produces principal components scores, but they are not the same as *zpc* or SPSS's principal component scores:

```
fsc <- res$ind$coord[, 1:ncomp]
print(head(fsc))
```

```
##          Dim.1        Dim.2
## 1   -2.2369884   0.54805274
## 2   -1.9208440  -1.16431851
## 3   -1.6276700  -0.61867854
## 4    0.2353795  -0.09259713
## 5   -0.6291972   0.81857562
## 6    0.7601416  -2.62349585
```

These values are calculated from the multiplication of unstandardized loadings and the standardized variables. We can calculate this 'manually' by getting the loadings with prcomp() and multiply it with the standardized data (all column variables are standardized):

```
res_pr <- prcomp(dat, center=TRUE, scale=TRUE)

# Standardize data.
datz <- scale(dat, center=TRUE, scale=TRUE) #
# Calculate pc scores
```

```
eigen_vec2 <- res_pr$rotation[,1:2]
pc2 <- datz %*% eigen_vec2
head(pc2)
```

```
##              PC1          PC2
##  [1,] -2.2347503   0.54750442
##  [2,] -1.9189222  -1.16315361
##  [3,] -1.6260415  -0.61805955
##  [4,]  0.2351440  -0.09250448

## [5,] -0.6285677  0.81775663
## [6,]  0.7593810 -2.62087104
```

21.5.3 principal() Function

This time, we will use the principal() from the psych package (Revelle et al. 2018) using the same data as before.

```
rm(list=ls())
library(psych)
library(ahdar)
dat <- fakedatapca

Now we call the principal() function
res <- principal(dat, nfactors=5, rotate="none")

# print rest
print(res)
```

```
## Principal Components Analysis
## Call: principal(r = dat, nfactors = 5, rotate = "none")
## Standardized loadings (pattern matrix) based upon correlation matrix
##       PC1   PC2    PC3    PC4    PC5  h2       u2  com
##  V1 0.32  0.81  -0.49   0.00   0.00   1  -2.2e-16  2.0
##  V2 0.32  0.81   0.49   0.00   0.00   1   1.9e-15  2.0
##  V3 0.82 -0.19   0.00   0.54   0.03   1  -2.2e-16  1.9
##  V4 0.86 -0.21   0.00  -0.28   0.36   1   0.0e+00  1.7
##  V5 0.87 -0.21   0.00  -0.23  -0.38   1   1.1e-16  1.7
##
##                          PC1   PC2   PC3   PC4   PC5
##  SS loadings            2.39  1.44  0.48  0.42  0.28
##  Proportion Var         0.48  0.29  0.10  0.08  0.06
##  Cumulative Var         0.48  0.76  0.86  0.94  1.00
##  Proportion Explained   0.48  0.29  0.10  0.08  0.06
##  Cumulative Proportion  0.48  0.76  0.86  0.94  1.00
##
```

```
## Mean item complexity = 1.9
## Test of the hypothesis that 5 components are sufficient. ##
## The root mean square of the residuals (RMSR) is 0
## with the empirical chi square 0 with prob < NA
##
## Fit based upon off diagonal values = 1
```

Given the results, we would retain two principal components. These two principal components account for 76% of variance in the data. We will call again the principal() function by setting nfactors equal to 2.

```
ncomp <- 2 # number of components to retain
new_res <- principal(dat, nfactors= ncomp)
print(new_res)
```

```
## Principal Components Analysis
## Call: principal(r = dat, nfactors = ncomp)
## Standardized loadings (pattern matrix) based upon correlation matrix
##      RC1    RC2   h2   u2  com
## V1  0.31   0.82 0.76 0.24  1.3
## V2  0.31   0.82 0.76 0.24  1.3
## V3  0.82  -0.18 0.71 0.29  1.1
## V4  0.87  -0.19 0.79 0.21  1.1
## V5  0.87  -0.19 0.80 0.20  1.1
##
##                        RC1  RC2
## SS loadings           2.39 1.44
## Proportion Var        0.48 0.29
## Cumulative Var        0.48 0.76
## Proportion Explained  0.62 0.38
## Cumulative Proportion 0.62 1.00
##
## Mean item complexity =  1.2
## Test of the hypothesis that 2 components are sufficient.
##
## The root mean square of the residuals (RMSR) is   0.1
## with the empirical chi square 100.55 with prob < 1.2e-23
##
## Fit based upon off diagonal values = 0.94
```

We can print the loadings

```
loadings <- res$loadings
print(loadings)
```

```
##       Loadings:
##
##        PC1          PC2      PC3      PC4      PC5
##   V1   0.324        0.809   -0.490
##   V2   0.323        0.810    0.490
##   V3   0.821       -0.193             0.537
##   V4   0.864       -0.211            -0.281    0.360
##   V5   0.871       -0.210            -0.226   -0.383
##
##                       PC1      PC2      PC3      PC4      PC5
##   SS loadings        2.388    1.436    0.480    0.418    0.277
##   Proportion Var     0.478    0.287    0.096    0.084    0.055
##   Cumulative Var     0.478    0.765    0.861    0.945    1.000
```

Let us save the principal component scores into a new object.

```
zpc <-new_res$scores
```

Now let us print the top rows of the object.

```
head(zpc)
##                  RC1           RC2
##      [1,]   -1.4550655    0.42789739
##      [2,]   -1.2222028   -0.99523030
##      [3,]   -1.0417875   -0.53666965
##      [4,]    0.1536860   -0.07413728
##      [5,]   -0.4203298    0.67413297
##      [6,]    0.5350245   -2.17678911
```

As you can see, the values for *zpc* are similar to those of the *pc* scores from the SPSS's unrotated PCA solutions (see Figure 21.18).

21.6 Geometric Perspective

Having shown how to conduct PCA with either SPSS or R. It would be a good time to see PCA from a geometric perspective as PCA has a strong geometrical interpretation. I present this geometric perspective after the discussing the PCA results with the hope that you can relate the results to how the points are presented graphically. For simplicity, we consider data with only two variables (pca_mini_data.sav is available on the book's website). The dataset contains six cases (see Figure 21.22).

With small data that has only two dimensions, we could show the data points in a scatter plot as displayed in Figure 21.23.

	V1	V2
1	1.00	2.00
2	1.50	4.00
3	2.00	5.00
4	1.50	5.00
5	1.25	1.00

FIGURE 21.22
The mini data.

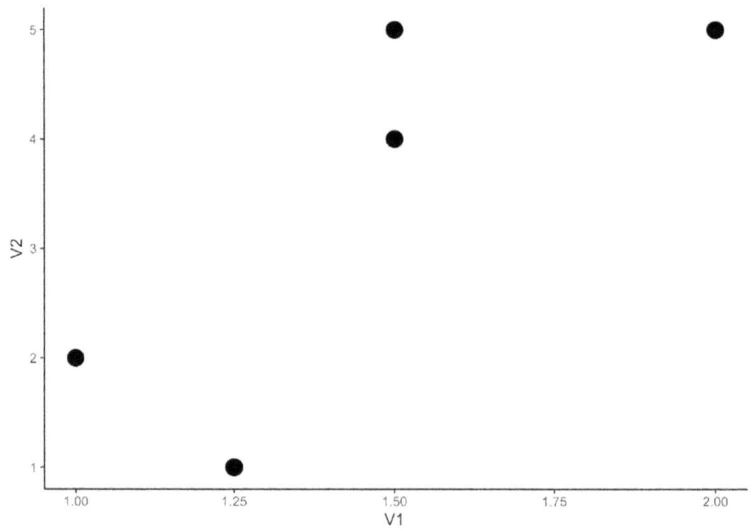

FIGURE 21.23
A scatter plot of the mini data.

What we want to do now is to find a straight line – a principal component – to represent the data. In other words, we want to reduce the dimension of our data from two dimensions to one dimension only. In doing so, we would lose some information in the original data. With the correlation matrix as an input, the amount of information in the original data is the variance of the original data, which is just the number of original variables. If we would not lose too much information, we would be fine to describe our data with one dimension only.

To represent the original data points that have coordinates from *V*1 and *V*2 means that the original data points are projected *perpendicular* to the principal component line. Figure 21.24 shows the projection of the original data points onto a line PC (or a principal component PC). The projected data points on the PC line are displayed as small solid rectangles. This graph resembles the graph we have seen in the regression chapter (see Figure 12.4), but they are not the same. In Figure 21.24 points are projected along the

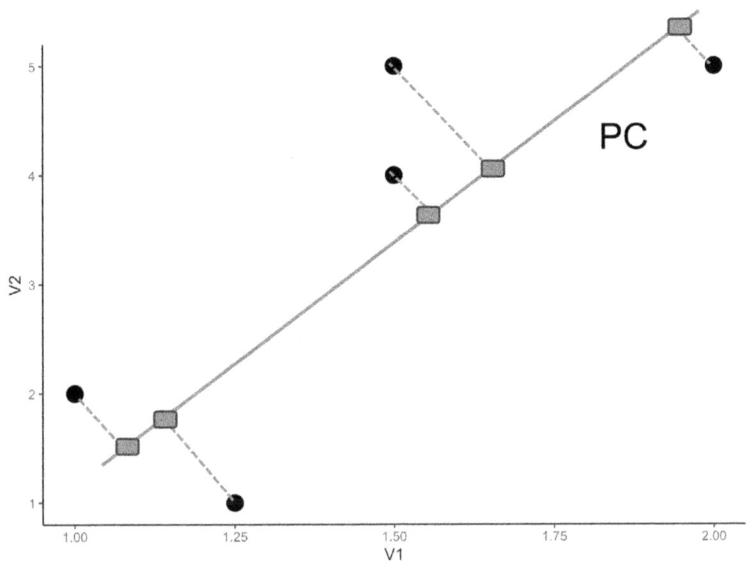

FIGURE 21.24
Projecting original data points onto a principal component. The original points are perpendicular to the line. The small solid rectangles on the line are the projected data points.

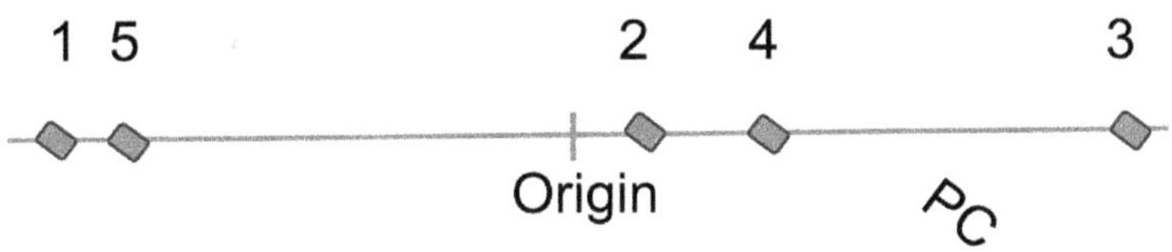

FIGURE 21.25
Projecting original data points onto a principal component.

dashed lines, which form 90-degree angles with the principal component line, whereas in Figure 12.4, points are projected vertically onto the regression line.

Ignoring the horizontal line *V*1 and the vertical line *V*2 as they are no use anymore, we would need one line only to locate the original points. This line is the PC line. The spread of the original data points with respect to the principal component (PC line) is displayed in Figure 21.25.

Conducting PCA with SPSS, the eigenvalue of the first principal component is greater than 1 (1.779), and the eigenvalue of the second principal component is less than 1 (0.221). The first principal component accounts for nearly 90% of variance in the original data (see Figure 21.26). Therefore, we are losing only 10% of information in the original data if we reduce the dimension of our data to one variable only, which is the principal component PC. Note that a scree plot is not of a much use here as we know from the beginning that our goal is to reduce the dimension of our data into one variable only – this variable is the principal component.

How would we describe the spread of the five data points on the PC line? The answer is given by the variance of the principal component, which is its eigenvalue (1.779).

The correlation between each of two variables with the principal component is 0.943, which is very high. This means that the proportion of variance explained in each of the variables (communality) is nearly 90% (see Figure 21.26). As can be seen in Figure 21.26, values in the first row of the 'Initial Eigenvalues' block and those of the 'Extraction Sums

Total Variance Explained

Component	Initial Eigenvalues Total	% of Variance	Cumulative %	Extraction Sums of Squared Loadings Total	% of Variance	Cumulative %
1	1.779	88.969	88.969	1.779	88.969	88.969
2	.221	11.031	100.000			

Extraction Method: Principal Component Analysis.

FIGURE 21.26
Mini data: the 'Total Variance Explained' table, also showing initial eigenvalues.

Component Matrix[a]

	Component 1
V1	.943
V2	.943

Extraction Method: Principal Component Analysis.

a. 1 components extracted.

Communalities

	Initial	Extraction
V1	1.000	.890
V2	1.000	.890

Extraction Method: Principal Component Analysis.

FIGURE 21.27
Mini data: the loadings and communality of the PCA solutions.

of Squared Loadings' are the same. This is because there is only one principal component extracted from data. That is, the dimension of the data is reduced to a line. Solutions that are reduced to a line cannot be rotated as rotation requires at least two axes or dimensions as it involves changing the orientation of the components in the multidimensional space. For this reason, a rotated component matrix is not applied, and thus, only a component (unrotated) matrix is produced in the output (see left hand image of Figure 21.27.

The position of the data points on the PC line are the component scores shown in the last two columns of the data in Figure 21.28: $FAC1_1$ is the principal components score produced by SPSS having mean of and variance of 1. *ManPC* is the principal component scores that I calculated manually by multiplying the loadings and standardized original variables: $0.943 \times ZV1 + 0.943 \times ZV2$. For example, the principal component scores of the first case: $0.943 \times -1.2136 + 0.943 \times -0.7707 = -1.8711$. If *ManPC* is standardized, we obtain *FAC1_1*. Using the principal component scores, we can see the positions of the data points on the PC line by displaying their row number in original data (see Figure 21.28). For example, case 5 is plotted at the position of –0.986 on the line.

The R code for the mini data PCA using prcomp() is given here:

```
rm(list=ls())
library(ahdar)

dat <- pca_mini_data
```

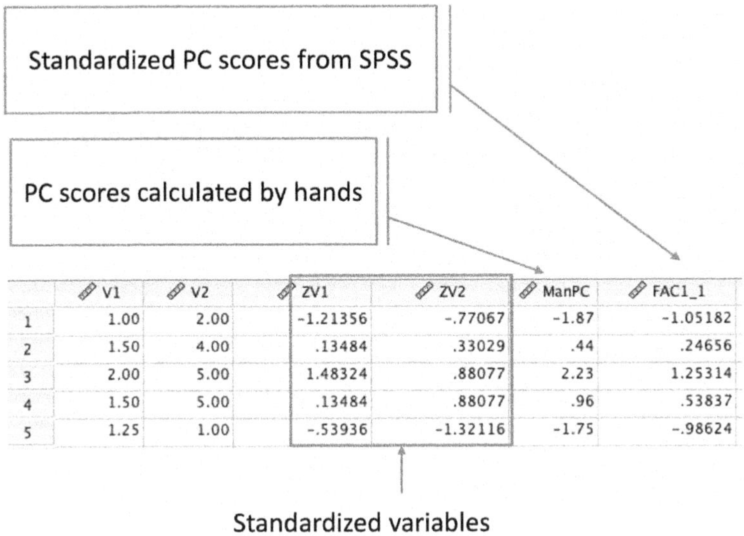

	V1	V2	ZV1	ZV2	ManPC	FAC1_1
1	1.00	2.00	-1.21356	-.77067	-1.87	-1.05182
2	1.50	4.00	.13484	.33029	.44	.24656
3	2.00	5.00	1.48324	.88077	2.23	1.25314
4	1.50	5.00	.13484	.88077	.96	.53837
5	1.25	1.00	-.53936	-1.32116	-1.75	-.98624

FIGURE 21.28
Mini data: principal component scores.

FIGURE 21.29
Principal component scores are the positions of points on the PC line. The number above the data points are their associated row number in the original data.

```
# Based on correlation matrix
res <- prcomp(dat, center=TRUE, scale=TRUE)
summary(res)
```

```
##  Importance of components:
##                              PC1     PC2
##  Standard deviation       1.3339  0.4697
##  Proportion of Variance   0.8897  0.1103
##  Cumulative Proportion    0.8897  1.0000
```

```
eigen_val <- res$sdev^2 # variance of the pcs
print(round(eigen_val,3))
```

```
## [1] 1.779 0.221
```

```
#calculate total variance explained by each principal component
var_explained = (eigen_val / sum(eigen_val)) * 100
print(var_explained)
```

```
## [1] 88.96915 11.03085
```

```
ncomp <-1 # number of components to retain
eigen_vec <- res$rotation[,1:ncomp] # eigen vector
sd_pc <- diag(res$sdev,ncomp,ncomp)
loadings <- eigen_vec %*%  sd_pc
print(loadings) # loadings
##           [,1]
## [1,] 0.9432346
## [2,] 0.9432346

# standardized data matrix.
zdat <- scale(dat, center=TRUE, scale=TRUE)
pc <- zdat %*% loadings # principal component scores.

# standardized pc scores.
zpc <- scale(pc, center=TRUE, scale=TRUE)

# Positions of points on the principal component print(zpc)
```

```
##               [,1]
##   [1,]    -1.0518244
##   [2,]     0.2465607
##   [3,]     1.2531403
##   [4,]     0.5383660
##   [5,]    -0.9862426
## attr(,"scaled:center")
## [1] 2.442491e-16
## attr(,"scaled:scale") ## [1] 1.779383
## attr(,"scaled:scale") ## [1] 1.779383
```

21.7 Summary

In this chapter, we have learned one of the popular techniques in data analysis, called principal component analysis (PCA), that can be used to reduce data into smaller dimensions while retaining as much information as possible. When writing a report for PCA, the minimum information that can be reported are: criteria used to retain the number of components, number of principal components that are retained possibly with their assigned names, scree plot with a parallel analysis plot, proportion of variance accounted for by principal components, and how principal components scores can be used for subsequent analysis. Many individuals, including experienced researchers, mistakenly use PCA to uncover latent constructs, especially those who use SPSS. One of the reasons is that in SPSS, PCA is placed under 'Factor Analysis'. To uncover latent constructs in the exploratory phase of research, one needs to conduct an exploratory factor analysis (EFA) instead of PCA, which is the subject of the next chapter.

21.8 Further Reading

Farley, J. U. (1964), 'Why does "brand loyalty" vary over products?', *Journal of Marketing Research* **1**(4), 9–14. This article is one the earliest paper that discussed the application of PCA in marketing. The author used PCA to find factors that explain brand purchases. Next, the factor scores of three principal components produced from PCA were used to explain brand switching using a multiple regression analysis.

Holbrook, M. B. (1993), 'Gratitudes and latitudes in MBA attitudes: Customer orientation and the business week poll', *Marketing Letters* **4**, 267–278. The author used PCA with a varimax rotation to summarize several measures of the quality of MBA education (e.g. average number of job offers to graduates, annual tuition) into two dimensions: cost and job-oriented quality. These two principal components account for more than 89% variation in their data. Further, they used the components' factor scores to create a perceptual map that describes the position of top business schools along these two dimensions.

Holbrook, M. B. & Batra, R. (1987), Assessing the role of emotions as mediators of consumer responses to advertising, *Journal of Consumer Research* **14**(3), 404–420. The authors performed PCA with varimax rotation to reduce 66 adverts' content scales, each measured with a semantic differential scale, e.g. humorous–serious, into six dimensions: emotional, threatening, mundane, sexy, cerebral, and personal.

21.9 Review Questions

1. Explain the goal of conducting PCA.
2. What are principal components and how are they related to their associated original variables?
3. Explain the use of a scree plot in deciding the number of principal components.
4. What is the benefit of conducting PCA before running a regression?
5. How would you use the results of PCA for another analysis such as regression?
6. I have 15 nominal variables each coded as either 0 or 1. I want to use PCA to reduce the data into a smaller number of variables that would be easier to deal with. What would you suggest?

21.10 Exercises

1. Using SPSS data: fakedatapca.sav, calculate communalities of $V2$ up to $V5$ by hand. Check your results with those of the communality table produced by Option 1's syntax.
2. Download place.sav from the book website, and conduct PCA on the variables in the data. How many dimensions would you retain?

22

Factor Analysis

This chapter discusses techniques to uncover and examine the underlying structure of data where responses from consumers are assumed to be influenced by unobserved common factors also called latent factors of latent constructs. The statistical technique for this purpose, which is the focus of this chapter, is the exploratory factor analysis (EFA) that is closely related to principal component analysis (PCA). While the primary goal of PCA is data reduction, EFA achieves more than that by identifying underlying common factors that give rise to consumers' responses. The SPSS syntax and R code on EFA with principal axis factoring and oblique rotation were discussed. Practical guidelines on EFA based on recent literature were also provided. Finally, the chapter ends with brief discussion on a confirmatory factor analysis (CFA), which is a statistical technique to examine an already known factorial structure.

Learning Objectives:

- Understand the basic principles of EFA.
- Understand the different between EFA and PCA.
- Understand the basic principles of CFA.
- Be able to use SPSS and R to conduct EFA.
- Know how to interpret the results of EFA.

22.1 Why EFA?

Exploratory factor analysis (EFA) is a technique to uncover the underlying factors that influence how individuals respond to set of items in the questionnaire. As a result, EFA automatically reduces the dimensions of data to a few meaningful variables called common factors or latent constructs. Similar to PCA, in EFA, common factors are derived from correlation matrix of observed variables. Variables that are mutually correlated can lead to a common factor because the common factor influences the variables in a meaningful way. For example, three variables that are meant to be measured satisfaction are correlated because the scores on the three variables reflect their satisfaction level. In other words, their satisfaction toward the store give rise to the scores on the three variables.

The assumption that a latent construct or a common factor influences observed variables does not exist in PCA. This is a stark difference between EFA and PCA, conceptually and statistically. In PCA, a principal component is just a linear weighted combination of several variables. That is, in PCA, the scores on the items are not caused by a latent construct; rather, the scores create the principal component, not the other way around. PCA is regarded as

 DOI: 10.4324/9781003407225-28

purely a data reduction method and says nothing about the presence of a latent construct. In EFA, a latent construct is assumed to exist (e.g. satisfaction toward a store). Even if you do not yet have items to measure satisfaction, consumers always experience a certain level of satisfaction. Items on a satisfaction scale serve as a means to tap into the satisfaction level. The scale is really akin to a thermometer that measures your body temperature.

Nevertheless, despite a philosophical difference between PCA and EFA, many researchers use PCA instead of EFA to uncover latent constructs. The culprit of the mistake is that both PCA and various techniques of EFA do not have a separate route in the SPSS menu – they are all considered factor analysis techniques. When an SPSS syntax is used, as you can see in the SPSS action later, the PCA and EFA syntax look identical. Another reason of the negligence (I hope this does not sound harsh) is that in many situations the PCA solutions and the EFA solutions are fairly identical, especially when there are large number of items involved and the items are highly correlated (Bandalos 2018). I will discuss the methodological difference between PCA and EFA in the next section where I explain how EFA works.

NOTE

The father of EFA is mostly credited to Charles Spearman, a British psychologist (Bartholomew 1995; Lovie & Lovie 1993). Spearman analysed correlation among observed variables that are meant to measure intelligence (Spearman 1904). According to Spearman, an item aimed at measuring intelligence captures both a general factor of ability and a factor specific to the item. The general factor, which he called the *g* factor, is common with other items that are also used to measure intelligence. The specific factor, which he called the *s* factor, is unique to the factor and reflects the influence of the specific feature of the item (e.g. wording). This theorizing of how unobserved general factor and specific factor influence an item serves as a theoretical foundation of factor analysis. If you read Spearman's 1904 seminal paper, you would not find the EFA terminologies discussed in this chapter that are common today, such as principal axis factoring, oblimin, communalities, scree plot, etc., as these techniques were brought to the EFA literature sometime later. According to Loehlin (2004),

Spearman's factor analysis of intelligence is more aligned with the philosophy of a confirmatory factor analysis (CFA) than an exploratory factor analysis (EFA).

22.2 How EFA Works

22.2.1 The EFA Model

To explain how EFA works, it is best by using an illustration that puts the method in a practical context. Let me tell the story of my student who wants to know what consumers think about a local grocery store that the consumers usually go for a grocery shopping. These consumers were asked to respond to five items in a questionnaire. Each item was measured by using a 7-point Likert scale ranging from 1 = strongly disagree to 7 = strongly agree. The five items are listed here:

- The grocery store's staff always solve my queries (V_1).
- The grocery store's staff are always polite to me (V_2).
- It is easy for me to move around the grocery store and to push my trolley or carry my basket (V_3).
- The layout at this grocery store makes it easy for me to find what I need (V_4).
- At the payment counters, there is enough space for me to move around and to pack purchases (V_5).

How did my student come up with these items? What he did was he approached a group of customers and asked what they think about the quality of the grocery store they used to go for their grocery shopping. Based on the customers' responses, the student ended up creating the five items.

Looking at the wording of the five items, they all seem to tap into how consumers perceive the service quality of the grocery store they usually go. The construct can be labelled as perceive store quality, which is a latent construct. However, reading the wording items in more detail, they might tap into different dimensions of store quality.

V_1 and V_2 are more identical than the rest as both are targeted toward the quality of the store staff, while the rest are geared toward the quality of store space. These are sub-latent constructs that can be revealed by EFA: perceived quality of staff and perceived quality of store space. EFA is needed here as no prior evidence exists to support the student's theory.

In an ideal (or extreme) situation, V_1 and V_2 loads into one common factor (say, F_1 = perceived quality of staff) and V_3, V_4, and V_5 load into another common factor (say, F_2 = perceive store space quality). The relationship between the two latent constructs F_1 and F_2 and items that are tied to them can be described in a two-factor EFA model as shown in Figure 22.1. As shown in the model, the double-headed arrow indicates that the two common factors are correlated. In an extreme situation, the common factors are not mutually uncorrelated, hence no double-headed arrow. The influence of a common factor to items are called factor loadings. In the figure, it is presented by the *b* symbol.

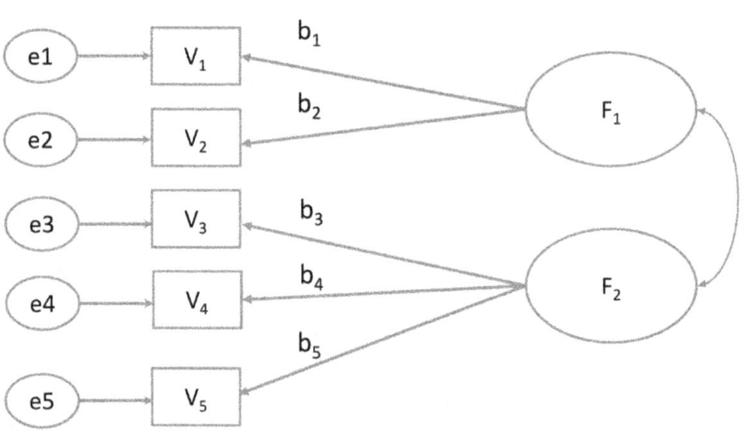

FIGURE 22.1
A two-factor EFA model. The b's are factor loadings. The double-headed arrow indicates that the two factors are correlated.

In reality, especially with a survey data, a common factor would exert an influence on other items that belong to another factor. That is, F_1 will have a little influence on V_3, V_4, V_5, and F_1 will have a little influence on V_1 and V_2.

Figure 22.1 is not quite the same as Figure 21.1, which we have seen previously in PCA. The differences between the two figures are noticeable:

- The direction of the arrow. In Figure 21.1, the directions of the arrows are from items to a factor, suggesting that the items make up the factor. In other words, the factor exists because of the items. In Figure 22.1, the directions of the arrows are from factors to items suggesting that changes in the factors would cause changes in the items. In EFA, the factors are assumed to exist and the items are the device to read them.
- Extra features. In Figure 22.1, five symbols 'e' ($e_1, \ldots, e_5$) are added to the model. Each of them is pointing to an item with a single-headed arrow. The 'e' symbol is used for brevity that stands for error. However, it actually captures two types of unobserved influence on the item that cannot be explained by common factors: a specific factor and measurement error. The specific factor is a systematic influence on the item that affects only the item (e.g. bias in the wording of the item). The measurement error captures the random influence on the item that can vary from person to person. For example, two different respondents can assign a different score on the item because the survey is administered at a different time of the day (e.g. morning vs. afternoon), which affects the mood of the respondents. An ambiguous wording can also contribute to measurement error. Although the symbol 'e' captures two types of influence on the item, for brevity, I called it an error term. The variance of the error term is known as the *unique variance* and the variance due to the common factors is called the *common variance*. PCA do not distinguish these two types of variances.

The factor model of Figure 22.1 can be described by the following sets of mathematical equations:

$$\begin{aligned} V_1 &= b_1F_1 + e_1 \\ V_2 &= b_2F_1 + e_2 \\ V_3 &= b_3F_2 + e_3 \\ V_4 &= b_4F_2 + e_4 \\ V_5 &= b_5F_2 + e_5 \end{aligned} \qquad (22.1)$$

Each of the equation is a type of regression equation. While in the regression equation, the independent variables are observed scores, the F in each of the equation is not an observed score. One of the goals of the EFA is to estimate the scores for the F, whose values are referred to as factor scores (akin to principal component scores in PCA).

Important

EFA assumes the relationships between the observed variables and the latent common factors to be linear as described by Equation 22.1.

22.2.2 How EFA Produces Common Factors

The heart of EFA lies in how it extracts common factors from a correlation matrix of observed variables. There are several techniques to extract common factors from the correlation matrix. SPSS provides six options for EFA: principal axis factoring, maximum likelihood, unweighted least squares, generalized least squares, alpha factoring, and image factoring – these options can be found under the factor analysis menu in SPSS. Note that you will also find PCA in the list, but, as explained in the previous chapter, PCA is not considered as an EFA technique. In this chapter, I focus on the principal axis factoring (PAF) as an extraction method because it is commonly used in research and from a methodological point of view is closely related to PCA.

Unlike PCA, PAF does not use the correlation matrix of observed variables where values in the main diagonal of the matrix are 1. Instead, PAF replaces the ones in the main diagonal of the correlation matrix with the estimates of communalities associated with each item. We have learned what communality is in the context of PCA: the proportion of variance in a variable accounted for by the principal components. In the context of EFA, communality is the proportion of shared variance explained by the common factors. In PCA, the initial estimates of the communalities of each variable is '1', which is taken from the main diagonal of the correlation matrix of the observed variables (please check the communality table of the PCA output). In PAF, the ones in the main diagonal of the correlation are replaced by squared multiple correlation (*SMC*s) as the initial estimates of communality. The squared multiple correlation associated with an item is just an R^2 from regressing the item on the remaining variables. For example, an *SMC* associated with V_1 is the R^2 of the regression model:

$$V_1 = b_1V_2 + b_2V_3 + b_3V_4 + b_4V_5 + error$$

where all the items are in the standardized forms – the same result would be obtained using items in their original forms, which means a constant must be added to the regression equation.

It makes sense to use *SMC* as an estimate of communality because it captures variance that is shared with other variables. Using *SMC* as an initial estimate of communality, PAF will use an iterative procedure to extract common factor, estimate factor loadings, and calculate new communalities given the factors loadings. The new communalities are then compared with those obtained in the previous cycle until the new communalities did not differ significantly with the previous one or the maximum number of iterations have been reached.

IMPORTANT

When communalities are very high (i.e. close to 1), the results of PCA and PAF are identical. In this situation, common factors almost account for all variations in the data – uniqueness in the items (e.g. measurement error) was less of a concern.

22.3 SPSS Action

Data: fa_qual.sav

In this section, I illustrate how to use SPSS to conduct EFA using data collected by my student. I have explained the research context in the previous section.

22.3.1 Option 1: Using SPSS Syntax with a Correlation Matrix as an Input

The first option to use EFA with SPSS is by using a syntax file in which the correlation matrix of the observed variable is provided as input for EFA. This option is similar to that I have presented in PCA section. I have explained how to obtain the correlation matrix in the PCA section; therefore, I will not repeat the procedure here again.

The EFA syntax is given here:

```
/* EFA syntax.
/* Correlation matrix as an input.
/* Method of extraction is PAF = Principal Axis Factoring.
/* Method of factor rotation is oblimin

MATRIX DATA
  VARIABLES=ROWTYPE_ V1 V2 V3 V4 V5.
BEGIN DATA.
N 243 243 243 243 243
COR    1.000
COR  .544  1.000
COR  .333   .414 1.000
COR  .186   .152  .560 1.000
COR  .193   .213  .529  .593 1.000
END  DATA.
FACTOR
  /MATRIX=IN(COR=*)
  /ANALYSIS V1 V2 V3 V4 V5
  /DIAGONAL 0.312 0.367 0.466 0.444 0.409
  /EXTRACTION PAF
  /PLOT EIGEN ROTATION
  /ROTATION OBLIMIN.
```

The syntax is identical to the PCA syntax in Section 4.1 of Chapter 21 on PCA with few modifications.

- The /DIAGONAL subcommand specifies values that need to be used to replace the ones in the main diagonal of the correlation matrix. These values are the *SMC* of each variable according to the order of the variable in the / VARIABLES subcommand. In essence, PAF algorithm will use the following correlation matrix at the start of its iterative procedure to extract common factors:

```
0.312
 .544  0.367
 .333   .414  0.466
 .186   .152   .560  0.444
 .193   .213   .529   .593  0.409
```

- The /EXTRACTION subcommand sets factor extraction method to PAF.
- /PLOT EIGEN ROTATION subcommands create two factor plots: solutions before rotation (EIGEN) and after rotation (ROTATION). The first plot shows the positions of variables in a coordinate system using the unrotated solutions. The second plot used the rotated solutions.
- The /ROTATION subcommand sets the rotation method to oblimin, which is an oblique rotation that allows factor solutions to be correlated.

The SPSS outputs of the syntax are explained in Section 22.3.3.

IMPORTANT

PCA and EFA (with PAF) are both aimed at extracting factors from a correlation matrix. In PCA, values in the main diagonal of the correlation matrix are '1'.
In PAF, all the ones in the input correlation matrix are replaced by the estimates of communalities. Commonly used estimates of communalities are the squared multiple correlations (*SMC*s). An *SMC* associated with an item is the R^2 from regressing the item on the remaining items.

NOTE

In the factor analysis terminology, a correlation matrix with ones in the diagonal is referred to as the unreduced correlation matrix, whereas a correlation matrix with SMCs in the main diagonal is called the reduced correlation matrix.

22.3.2 Option 2: Requesting EFA Procedure from SPSS Menu

In this option, EFA is requested from the SPSS menu. All the steps are similar to those we learned in PCA with few steps added.

- Analyze → Dimension Reduction → Factor.
- Insert *V*1, . . ., *V*5 into the `Variables` box.
- Click `Descriptives`. Under `Statistics`, tick `Univariate descriptive`. This will produce the descriptive statistics of the variables such as means and standard

deviations. This step is optional – I will skip the outputs in Section 22.3.3. My aim is to show that it is possible to inspect the means and standard deviations of items in the data without going to the main menu: Analyze → Descriptive Statistics → Descriptives.

- Tick `Initial Solution`. Under `Correlation Matrix`, tick `KMO and Bartlett's test of sphericity`. Click `Continue`.
- Click `Extraction`. Under `Method`, select `Principal Axis Factoring`. Under `Analyze, correlation matrix` is ticked by default, leave it as it is. Tick `scree plot`. Under `Extract, eigenvalues greater than 1` are set as the default.
- Click `Rotation`. Under `Method`, select `Direct Oblimin`. Under `Display`, tick `Rotated solution` and `Loading plot(s)`. Click `Continue`.
- Click Scores. Under `Save Variables`, choose Regression, which is the default option.
- Click `Option` (this is optional but I always click it). Under `Coefficient Display Formats`, tick `Supress small coefficients`, and next to `Absolute value below`, type in 0.4.
- Click `OK` or `Paste`.

Clicking `Paste` in the last step produces the following syntax:

```
FACTOR
  /VARIABLES V1 V2 V3 V4 V5
  /MISSING LISTWISE
  /ANALYSIS V1 V2 V3 V4 V5
  /PRINT UNIVARIATE INITIAL KMO EXTRACTION ROTATION
  /FORMAT BLANK(0.40)
  /PLOT EIGEN
  /CRITERIA MINEIGEN(1) ITERATE(25)
  /EXTRACTION PAF
  /CRITERIA ITERATE(25) DELTA(0)
  /ROTATION OBLIMIN
  /SAVE REG(ALL)
  /METHOD=CORRELATION.
```

22.3.3 Interpretations of the Outputs

KMO And Bartlett's Test

As in PCA discussed in Chapter 21. We start by looking at the KMO and Bartlett's test results to see if EFA is really needed. We address the question: is there enough correlation in the data? The Bartlett's test is significant (p-value < 0.05) suggesting that dimension reduction as a result of EFA is warranted. The KMO's value is equal nearly 0.7, which is above the threshold value of 0.6 suggesting that EFA is acceptable.

Communality

Communality table is the first table that SPSS produces in EFA. It contains communalities of items in the analysis. As we have learned in PCA, communality of an item

KMO and Bartlett's Test

Kaiser-Meyer-Olkin Measure of Sampling Adequacy.		.699
Bartlett's Test of Sphericity	Approx. Chi-Square	353.446
	df	10
	Sig.	<.001

FIGURE 22.2
KMO and Bartlett's sphericity outputs.

is the proportion of variance that is accounted for by principal components. In EFA, it is interpreted in the same way: proportion of variance in the item that is accounted for by the common factors. However, in PCA, the communality accounts for total variance as there is no separation between the common variance and the unique variance. In EFA, communality represents the amount of shared variance, which is the variance that is **shared** among other variables. In EFA, if communality of an item is high, this means that the common factors can strongly explain the variation in the item. In other words, the common factors have a strong influence on the item. For example, if communality is 1, the variation in the item is solely due to the common factors. In contrast, if the communality is low, the variation in the item is not largely due to the common factors. With a low communality, the common factors have a weak influence on the item. As an extreme example, if communality is zero, latent factors have totally no influence on the item, which means the variation in the item is fully caused by specific factors and measurement errors. Figure 22.3 shows the communality of each item used in the analysis.

How Many Factors to Retain

The scree plot of the output suggests that two factors can be retained as the elbow occurs at factor 3. A scree plot of the actual and the scree plot of the means and the 95th percentile eigenvalues also suggest that two factors can be retained. This is because at factor equals 2, the eigenvalues of the actual are greater than those of random data.

Now, let us look at the table of total variance explained. As we can see from Figure 22.6, two factors account for more than 74% of variation in the data. This value is calculated as the sum of the variance of the first two factors. Therefore, retaining two common factors can explain majority of the variation in the data. The table is not quite the same as the one we have seen in Chapter 21. In the PCA chapter, I used an orthogonal rotation varimax, which allows factors to be uncorrelated. In this case, the total variance accounted for by the factors is the same as the sum of the squared factor loadings. The table from EFA with oblimin produced a footnote, which states: *'When factors are correlated, sum of squared factor loadings cannot be added to obtain a total variance.'*

EFA Solutions: Factor Matrix, Pattern Matrix, and Structure Matrix

The EFA procedure in SPSS produces three types of outputs in regard to factor loadings when oblique rotation is applied: factor matrix, pattern matrix, and structure matrix. The factor matrix shows factor loadings before rotation is applied. The pattern matrix

Communalities

	Initial	Extraction
V1	.312	.397
V2	.367	.750
V3	.466	.580
V4	.444	.662
V5	.409	.538

Extraction Method: Principal Axis Factoring.

FIGURE 22.3
Communalities.

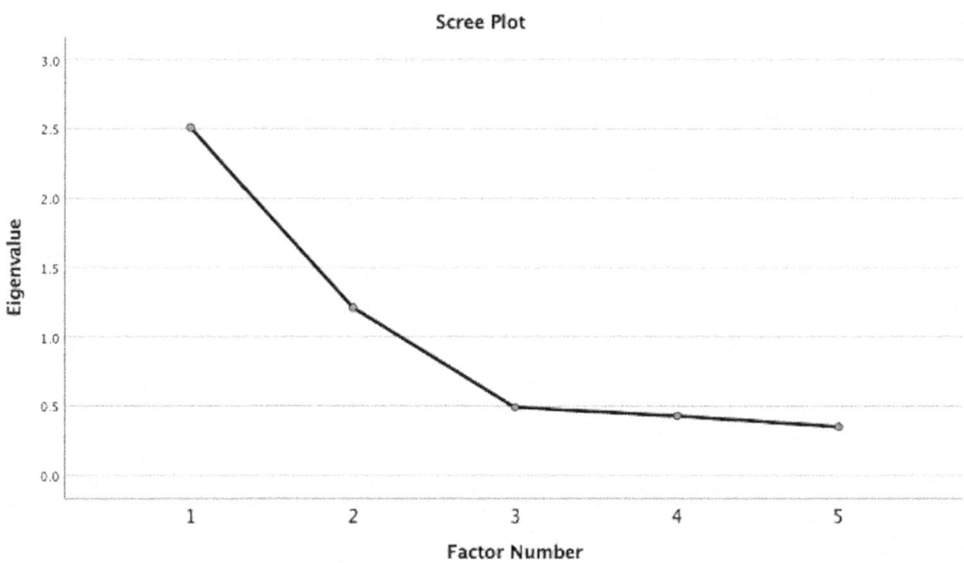

FIGURE 22.4
A scree plot.

and structure matrix are solutions that are specifically produced when oblique rotation is implemented.

Factor Matrix

Figure 22.7 shows two factor matrix tables that contains factor loadings of *unrotated solutions*. The table on the right of the figure does not show loadings below 0.4 as instructed

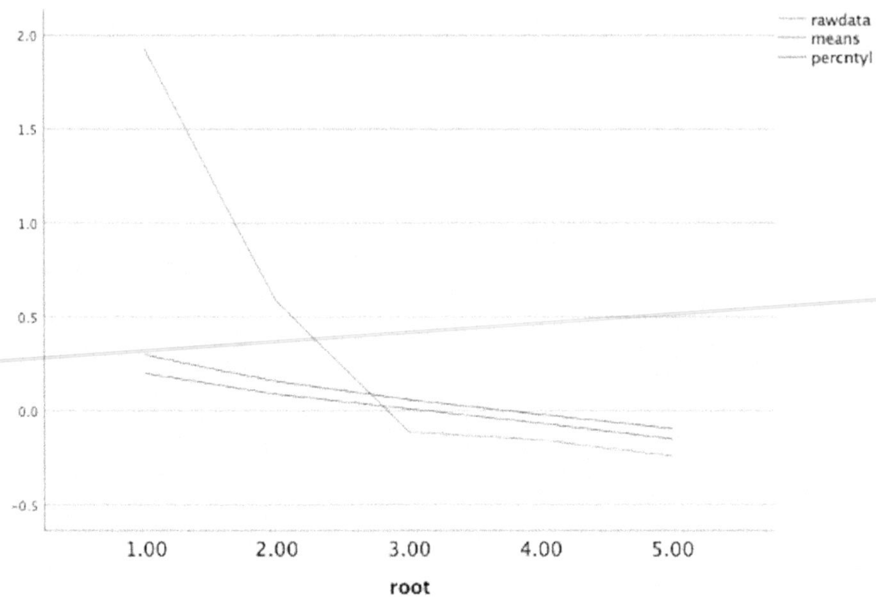

FIGURE 22.5
Scree plots from the Horn's parallel analysis.

Proportion of variance accounted for by two PCs before rotation

Sum of the percentage variance

Total Variance Explained

Factor	Initial Eigenvalues Total	% of Variance	Cumulative %	Extraction Sums of Squared Loadings Total	% of Variance	Cumulative %	Rotation Sums of Squared Loadings[a] Total
1	2.511	50.218	50.218	2.104	42.089	42.089	1.874
2	1.212	24.232	74.450	.823	16.454	58.543	1.521
3	.492	9.839	84.289				
4	.432	8.637	92.926				
5	.354	7.074	100.000				

Extraction Method: Principal Axis Factoring.

a. When factors are correlated, sums of squared loadings cannot be added to obtain a total variance.

FIGURE 22.6
The 'Total Variance Explained' table.

by the subcommand /FORMAT BLANK(0.40) that makes the table easier to read and interpret. The table on the left is the output of EFA without the subcommand

/FORMAT BLANK(0.40). The factor matrix table can also be obtained separately by running EFA without rotating the extracted factors using the subcommand /ROTATION.

NOROTATE. The unrotated factor loadings can be interpreted as the correlations between items and the common factors.

Factor Matrix[a]

	Factor 1	Factor 2
V1	.493	.393
V2	.609	.616
V3	.757	-.084
V4	.693	-.426
V5	.661	-.317

Extraction Method: Principal Axis Factoring.

a. Attempted to extract 2 factors. More than 25 iterations required. (Convergence=.004). Extraction was terminated.

Factor Matrix[a]

	Factor 1	Factor 2
V1	.493	
V2	.609	.616
V3	.757	
V4	.693	-.426
V5	.661	

Extraction Method: Principal Axis Factoring.

a. Attempted to extract 2 factors. More than 25 iterations required. (Convergence=.004). Extraction was terminated.

FIGURE 22.7
Factor matrix showing the loadings of unrotated factors. The right table hides loadings below 0.4 as specified in the /FORMAT subcommand.

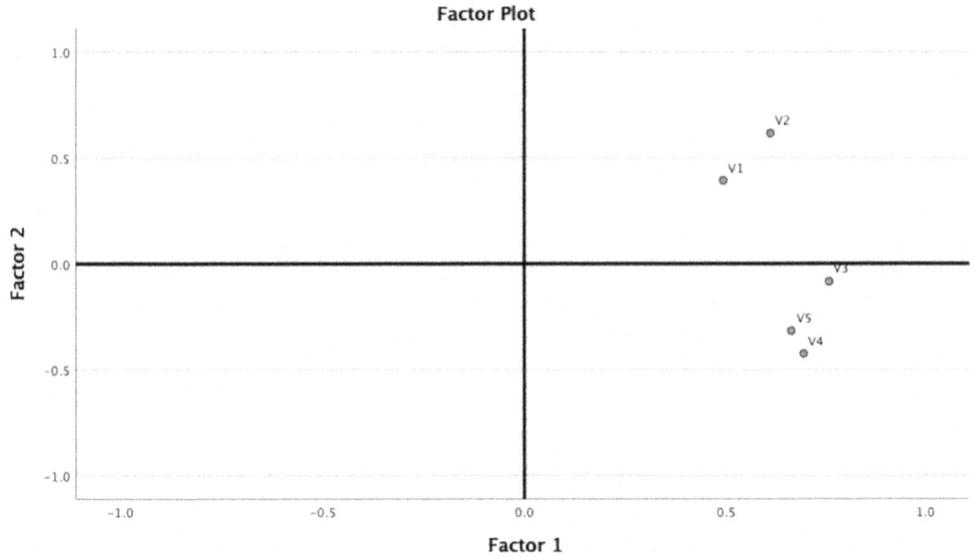

FIGURE 22.8
Factor plot of unrotated solutions.

If you looked at the factor loadings greater than 0.4, it seems that all items contribute to the first factor and cross-loadings occur for two items (*V*2 and *V*4), one of which has a negative sign (*V*4). If we choose to show loadings greater than 0.3, cross-loading can also easily be visible for *V*1. This result is not easy to interpret. It does not provide a clear indication of the presence of a simple structure.

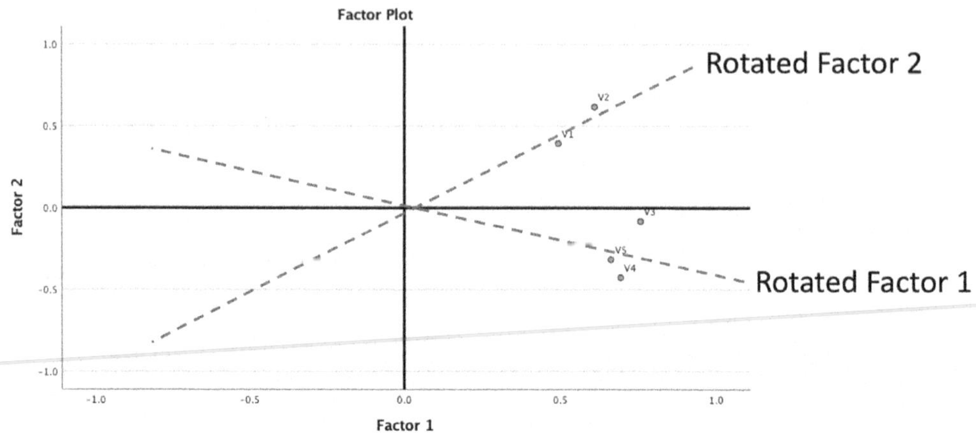

FIGURE 22.9
Factor plot of unrotated solutions with rotated factors are illustrated.

The factor loadings constitute the coordinate of items in a factor plot as shown in Figure 22.8. As you can see from Figure 22.8, Factor 1 is presented by the horizontal line, and Factor 2 is represented by the vertical line. It is clear from the figure that all variables are plotted at the positive side of Factor 1. With respect to Factor 2, two variables are in the positive side and three variables are in the negative side.

What we want to obtain is whether Factor 1 and Factor 2 can be reoriented by rotation such that *V*1 and *V*2 are closed to Factor 1 and the remaining variables are closed to Factor 2. The oblique rotation that we have chosen provided the answer. Figure 22.9 illustrates how Factor 1 and Factor 2 are rotated using direct oblimin such that *V*1 and *V*2 are aligned with Factor 2 and the remaining variables are aligned with Factor 1. The *ROTATION* argument in subcommand /FORMAT produces a factor plot of the rotated solutions in which Factor 1 and the rotated Factor 2 become the new axes. The coordinate of the item relative to the new axes are given by the factor loadings of the rotated factor loadings.

Communality of each item can be calculated by taking the sum of the unrotated squared factor loadings associated with the two common factors. For example, the calculation of the V_1's communality and V_2's communality can be shown here:

- Communality of $V_1 = 0.493^2 + 0.393^2 = 0.397$.
- Communality of $V_2 = 0.609^2 + 0.619^2 = 0.754$.

Pattern Matrix and Structure Matrix

Patten matrix and structure matrix are tables specifically printed when oblique rotation such as direct oblimin is used. You will not obtain these tables if you used an orthogonal varimax rotation.

The pattern matrix from our EFA analysis is shown in Figure 22.11. The left table is the pattern matrix that shows all factor loadings, whereas the right table hides loadings below 0.4. The left table is obtained by rerunning EFA without the subcommand/

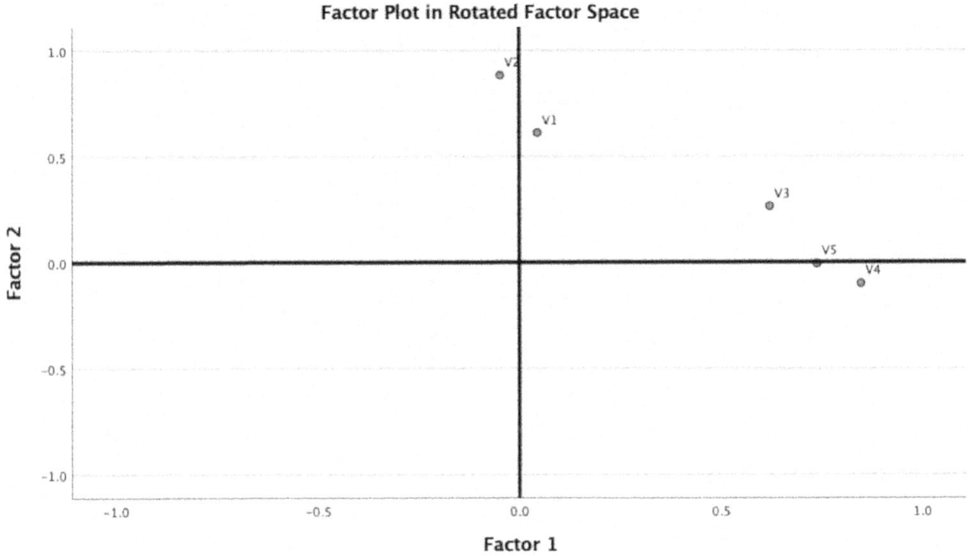

FIGURE 22.10
Factor plot of rotated solutions.

Pattern Matrix[a]

	Factor	
	1	2
V1	.045	.611
V2	-.047	.883
V3	.620	.265
V4	.847	-.100
V5	.736	-.007

Extraction Method: Principal Axis Factoring.
Rotation Method: Oblimin with Kaiser Normalization.

a. Rotation converged in 5 iterations.

Pattern Matrix[a]

	Factor	
	1	2
V1		.611
V2		.883
V3	.620	
V4	.847	
V5	.736	

Extraction Method: Principal Axis Factoring.
Rotation Method: Oblimin with Kaiser Normalization.

a. Rotation converged in 5 iterations.

FIGURE 22.11
Pattern matrix. The right table hides loadings below 0.4.

FORMAT BLANK(0.40). Pattern matrix shows factor loadings associated with each item. The meanings of the loadings are not the same with those of the factor matrix. The loadings in each row of the pattern matrix are obtained by regressing the item, in a standardized form, on the factors. As there are two factors extracted in our example, the coefficients capture the influence of a factor on an item when another factor is

Structure Matrix

	Factor	
	1	2
V1	.279	.629
V2	.290	.865
V3	.721	.502
V4	.808	.224
V5	.733	.275

Extraction Method: Principal Axis Factoring.
Rotation Method: Oblimin with Kaiser Normalization.

Structure Matrix

	Factor	
	1	2
V1		.629
V2		.865
V3	.721	.502
V4	.808	
V5	.733	

Extraction Method: Principal Axis Factoring.
Rotation Method: Oblimin with Kaiser Normalization.

FIGURE 22.12
Structure matrix. The right table hides loadings below 0.4.

held constant. Taking the square of the coefficient, it represents the amount of variance explained by a factor holding other factor constant.

The structure matrix from our EFA analysis is shown in Figure 22.12. The left table is the structure matrix that shows all loadings, whereas the right table hides loadings below 0.4. The left table is obtained by rerunning EFA without the subcommand / FORMAT BLANK(0.40). The loadings in the structure matrix can be interpreted as the correlation between the correlation between the items and the factors. The loadings in the structure matrix are calculated by multiplying the loadings in the structure matrix by factor correlations. Before showing you how to calculate the loadings of the structure matrix, let us first discuss factor correlations.

IMPORTANT

If the factors are uncorrelated the pattern matrix and the structure matrix is the same.

Factor correlations. The correlation between the two common factors is shown in Figure 22.13, which is equal to 0.383. This coefficient is printed automatically when the oblique rotation is chosen as the factor rotation method.

Knowing factor correlations, let us calculate the loadings of the structure matrix as I promised previously. The ingredients we need are the loadings of the factor matrix and factor correlations. The calculation involves matrix computation: the whole pattern matrix is multiplied by the whole pattern correlation matrix. In principle, the [*i*, *j*] coefficient in the structure matrix is obtained by multiplying the *i*th row of the pattern matrix by the *j* column of the factor correlation matrix.

Factor Correlation Matrix

Factor	1	2
1	1.000	.383
2	.383	1.000

Extraction Method: Principal Axis Factoring.
Rotation Method: Oblimin with Kaiser Normalization.

FIGURE 22.13
Correlation matrix showing the correlation between the two common factors extracted from EFA.

I provide the illustrations here:

- The loading of the first item associated with the first factor in the structure matrix is 0.279. This value is calculated as follows: $0.045 \times 1 + 0.611 \times 0.383 = 383.656$. In essence, what I am doing here is multiplying the elements of the first row of the pattern matrix [0.045, 0.611] with the elements of the first column of the factor correlation matrix [1, 0.383].
- Let us take up another example. The loading of the second item associated with the second factor in the structure matrix is 0.865. This value is calculated as follows: $-0.047 \times 0.383 + 0.883 \times 1 = 0.865$. In essence, what I am doing here is multiplying the elements of the second row of the pattern matrix with the elements of the second column of the factor correlation matrix.

i Note
Structure matrix = Pattern matrix × Factor correlations

Factor Scores

As previously done in the PCA chapter, SPSS produces factors scores by processing subcommand /SAVE REG(ALL) in the syntax. The factor scores of the two common factors will be printed in the data file. The factor scores have the same interpretation as the component scores in PCA. That is, it is the score of an individual on the underlying factors. If you have an ability to read the latent factors, those are the scores you would have obtained. Unlike the component scores in PCA that are in the standardized forms, the factors scores with oblique rotation have a mean of zero but the variance is not equal to 1. This is because, with oblique rotation, the factors are allowed to be correlated. The rotation makes the points less dispersed, hence reducing the variance. If we inspect the factor plot with the oblique rotation, the items look less spread out compared to those in the original factor plot. If you use varimax rotation that allows factors to be uncorrelated, the variance of the factor scores remains 1.

22.4 R Action

In this section, we will perform EFA using the fa() function from the *psych* package (Revelle et al. 2018). We used the same data that we have analysed previously with SPSS. Before you start your R session with EFA, install the following two R packages: (1) *psych* package (`install.packages(psych)`) which contains the `fa()` function; (2) *GPArotation*. This package is required for factor rotation.

The code to run EFA and produce main results is given here:

```
rm(list=ls())  # make a fresh start
library(psych) # load the psych package
library(ahdar) # load data package

rcor <- cor(fa_qual)
KMO(rcor)
cortest.bartlett(rcor, n = 243)
fa.parallel(fa_qual, fm="pa", fa="fa", n.obs=243,
    main="Scree Plots")
fa_res <- fa(fa_qual, fm="pa", nfactors = 2, rotate = "oblimin")
fa_res$communality
print(fa_res$loadings, cutoff = 0.4)
print(fa_res$Structure, cutoff = 0.4)
fa_res$Phi
fa.diagram(fa_res, digits=3)
fs_scores <- factor.scores(fa_qual, fa_res, method = "Thurstone")
head(fs_scores$scores)
```

Explanations of these commands are as follows.

The first four lines: remove all objects from previous R sessions if you do not start R from fresh, load *psych*, and load data package ahdar.

```
rm(list=ls()) # make a fresh start
library(psych) # load the psych package
library(ahdar) # load data package
```

- The next line calculates the correlation matrix of all variables listed in the `sfc` data using the `cor()` function, which an R base function. `sfc` only contains variables that we are going to use for EFA. If your data contains demographic variables or variables that are not relevant, you have to deselect them first. The correlation is stored in the object `rcor`.

```
rcor <- cor(sfc)
```

- The next line performs the Bartlett's test of sphericity of the object rcor. $n = 243$ specifies the sample size being used in the test.

```
cortest.bartlett(rcor, n = 243)

## $chisq
## [1] 616.3791 ##
## $p.value
## [1] 5.727445e-117 ##
## $df
## [1] 21
```

- The next line runs a parallel analysis and produce scree plots of the actual data and values at the 95th percentile of the eigenvalue distributions. fm="pa" used a principal axis factoring as the extraction method. `fa=fa` used the eigen values of the principal axis factoring.

```
fa.parallel(sfc, fm="pa", fa="fa", main = "Scree Plots")
```

- Next, we calculate the KMO value of the correlation matrix `rcor`.

```
KMO(rcor)

## Kaiser-Meyer-Olkin factor adequacy
## Call: KMO(r = rcor)
## Overall MSA =     0.83
## MSA for each item =
## SFC1  SFC2  SFC3  SFC4  EA1   EA2   EA3
## 0.80  0.87  0.90  0.81 0.85  0.77  0.79
```

- The next line will run EFA, which performs the extraction procedure on the `sfc` data. The 1s in the diagonal of the correlation matrix of the items are replaced with SMC, which is set at the default of the argument as SMC=TRUE.
- fm = "pa" sets the EFA method to principal axis factoring. fm stands for factoring method that allows users to specify the EFA method that they preferred. "pa" is not the default, so it must be explicitly written in the argument.
- nfactors = 2, this argument sets the number of factors to be extracted. Here, it is set to 2.

- rotate = "oblimin" sets the rotation method to oblimin, which is an oblique rotation that allows factors to be correlated. Oblimin is the default in the argument; it is not necessary to include in the syntax. However, making it explicit in the syntax is a good practice to enhance clarity because sometimes we do not remember what the default arguments are. There are many rotation methods available, which you can read in documentation of the function by typing `?fa` in your R console.

The code requires R package *GPArotation*, which is needed for factor rotation. You can install it by running on your console: `install.packages("GPArotation")`

```
fa_res <- fa(sfc, fm="pa", nfactors =  2, rotate =  "oblimin")
```

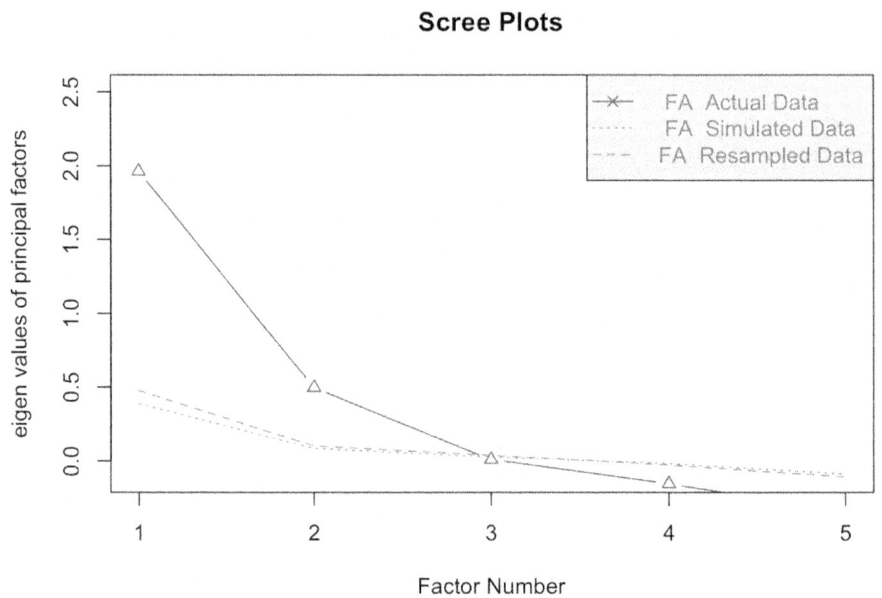

FIGURE 22.14
Scree plots produced by the fa.parallel() function.

```
Loading required namespace: GPArotation
```

- We print the communality of each item with:

```
round(fa_res$communality,3)
```

```
## SFC1  SFC2  SFC3  SFC4   EA1   EA2   EA3
## 0.766 0.578 0.456 0.739 0.180 0.361 0.523
```

- The next line prints all factor loadings of the pattern matrix that are greater than the cutoff = 0.4. It also prints the sum of squared loadings (SS loadings), proportion of variance accounted for by each factor, and the cumulative variance. These values are the psych's equivalents of the SPSS's total variance explained table.

```
print(fa_res$loadings, cutoff = 0.4)
```

```
##
## Loadings:
##      PA1    PA2
## SFC1  0.902
## SFC2  0.764
## SFC3  0.617
## SFC4  0.838
## EA1
## EA2                0.608
## EA3                0.719
##
##                   PA1     PA2
## SS loadings     2.510   1.002
## Proportion Var  0.359   0.143
## Cumulative Var  0.359   0.502
```

- The next line prints all factor loadings of the structure matrix that are greater than the cutoff = 0.4.

```
print(fa_res$Structure, cutoff =  0.4)
```

```
## Loadings:
##
##           PA1     PA2
## SFC1    0.874
## SFC2    0.760
## SFC3    0.669  0.413
## SFC4    0.859  0.462
## EA1
## EA2            0.601
## EA3            0.723
##
##                  PA1     PA2
## SS loadings     2.854   1.727
## Proportion Var  0.408   0.247
## Cumulative Var  0.408   0.654
```

- We print the factor correlation matrix with the following:

```
fa_res$Phi
```

```
##             PA1          PA2
## PA1  1.0000000   0.5021054
## PA2  0.5021054   1.0000000
```

FIGURE 22.15
EFA diagram produced by the fa.diagram() function.

- Next, let us produce a path diagram of the EFA model using information stored in the object `fa _ res`. The path diagram also shows the three-digit values of factor loadings of the pattern matrix and factor correlations.

```
fa.diagram(fa_res, digits=3)
```

- In the next line, calculate the factor scores and store the results in the R object `fs _ scores`. The factor scores in SPSS are listed under the Regression method, which is the default. In the *psych* package, it is called 'Thurstone'. The `fs _ scores`object contains several sub objects one which is the factor scores a space that we are looking for. We use `head()` function to show the top rows of the factor scores.

```
fs_scores <- factor.scores(sfc, fa_res, method = "Thurstone")
head(fs_scores$scores)
```

```
##              PA1          PA2
##   [1,]   1.1012857   1.50309696
##   [2,]   0.7246077   1.24959595
##   [3,]   0.9976341  -0.03875131
##   [4,]  -0.4627170  -0.84395516
##   [5,]   0.4025161   0.83136336
##   [6,]   1.2559573   1.07510706
```

IMPORTANT

Using our illustration data, the conclusion derived from the results of the EFA procedure using PAF and oblimin rotation from SPSS and *psych* package are the same (e.g. which items contribute to which factors). Nevertheless, the implementation of the principal axis factoring in SPSS vs. *psych* package have been known to produce different factor solutions if we use other types of rotation (i.e. promax) despite the analysis settings are set the same (see Grieder & Steiner 2022). Therefore, when reporting EFA results, it is important to disclose all the information regarding the details of the EFA implementation, which allows readers to develop a better understanding of the conclusions drawn from EFA.

22.5 Practical Guidelines

Conducting EFA can be confusing as each step of the EFA procedures, we are provided with multiple options (e.g. method of factor retention) by SPSS or by the `fa()` function from the *psych* package. I present here practical guidelines or rules of thumbs based on recent literature around five themes commonly encountered in a practical EFA analysis: sample size, number of items per factor, quality of data, factor retention, extraction method, and factor rotation.

22.5.1 Sample Size

Minimum sample size recommended is 300. Smaller sample is appropriate if communalities is high. In the dataset that I used in the previous section, the sample size is lower than 300, however only one variable (i.e. *V*2) has a high communality larger than 0.7. In this case, more observations could have been collected. As we never knew what communalities we would obtain prior to running EFA, a minimum sample size of 400 is strongly recommended so as to provide a more reliable results (Goretzko et al. 2021). Recommendation has been made in the literature regarding the number of observations required in relation to the number of items that is subject to EFA. The rule of thumb is to collect more than 10 observation per items. So, if you have 20 items, you should aim for at least $10 \times 20 = 200$ observations. Nevertheless, if you can achieve at least 400 observations, you will be safeguarding yourself for at least 40 items in your questionnaire. This amount is quite daunting, which might create another problem when respondents fill in your questionnaire without paying too much attention to it contributing to a common method bias (Podsakoff et al. 2003).

22.5.2 Quality of Data

The same procedures as in PCA were recommended regarding the quality of data. It refers to the issue of whether there is enough correlation in the data. Two tests were suggested: Bartlett's sphericity test and KMO criterion. In the Bartlett's sphericity test, the null hypotheses of no correlation should be rejected, and the KMO value should exceed 0.6.

22.5.3 Factor Retention

We have discussed several methods to retain principal components with PCA in Chapter 21 such as Kaiser's rule (i.e. eigen value >1), scree plot, and Horn's parallel analysis. Those techniques also apply in EFA. The recommended procedure is to use those approaches together. It is advisable to avoid sole reliance on Kaiser's rule, as it may lead to the extraction of more factors than necessary (Ruscio & Roche 2012).

22.5.4 Extraction Method

The extraction method discussed in this chapter is the principal axis factoring (PAF). Among other factor extraction methods available, PAF is the mostly used technique in research (Goretzko et al. 2021). Although PCA is listed in SPSS under `factor`, `PCA` should not be used as a technique to uncover latent constructs unless communalities are close to 1 because the results would be similar to those of PAF. Nonetheless, communalities closer to 1 is very rare in practice, so sticking to PAF is conceptually and methodologically sound.

Checking the distribution of items before deciding which extraction method to choose has been recommended in literature (Costello & Osborne 2005; Fabrigar et al. 1999). If the items were normally distributed, it is recommended to choose the maximum likelihood estimation method. However, in a survey data with Likert scale, where normality is often violated, the recommendation is to use PAF (Costello & Osborne 2005).

Despite PCA is not an EFA technique, it has been shown to be used in a combination with PAF (Yong et al. 2013; Lattin et al. 2003). First, PCA is used to reduce the dimensions of the data, next PAF is used by setting the number of factors based on the number

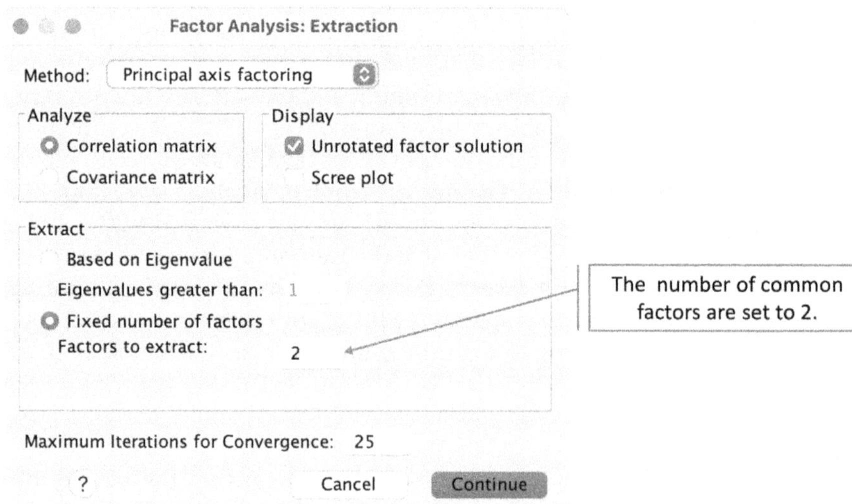

FIGURE 22.16
Specifying the numbers of factors to be extracted.

of factors extracted in the PCA step. The second step is done in SPSS by ticking `Fixed number of factors` and entering the number of factors to be extracted.

Using fa() function in R, the number of factors to be extracted is set up with the nfactors argument, which has been shown in Section 22.4 – rewritten here:

```
fa_res <- fa(your_data, nfactors = 2, rotate = "oblimin")
# Number of factors to be extracted is equal to 2.
```

22.5.5 Factor Rotation

Rotating factor solutions are sometimes necessary to improve the interpretation of the factor solutions. The aim of factor rotation is to achieve a simple structure in which the relationship between items and common factors are easier to see – which items load highly into common factors and which ones don't. There are two broad types of factors rotation: orthogonal and oblique. An orthogonal rotation produces common factors that are uncorrelated, whereas an oblique rotation allows factors to be correlated. The oblique rotation is recommended to use when the aim of EFA is to uncover the underlying latent constructs because in social and behavioural sciences, they are typically correlated (Goretzko et al. 2021). Furthermore, they are mostly assessed by self-reported measures using scales, which will allow items of distinct factors to be correlated (e.g. tendency to tick closely related options answers).

A study by Goretzko et al. (2021) reported that 74% of published articles in psychology used oblique rotation, and most of these studies use promax rotation, followed by oblimin rotation as a second preferred option. One practical reason of why oblique rotation is the most favourite options by researchers is that no information is lost if an oblique rotation is applied to uncorrelated factors – oblique rotation would produce uncorrelated factors, if they are uncorrelated (Hancock et al. 2010; Bandalos 2018; Costello & Osborne 2005). This logic reminds me of the rationale of applying heteroskedasticity-adjusted standard errors in regression – even heteroskedasticity is not present in the data, applying heteroskedasticity-adjusted standard errors will produce homoskedastic standard errors (see Chapter 12). The varimax rotation that I used in Chapter 21 is not recommended to use if a general factor is expected to emerge from data. A general factor is the factor that accounts for most variation in the data, that is, majority of items will load onto this general factor. The drawback of varimax rotation is that it reduces 'the tendency to obtain a general factor' (Bandalos 2018, p. 333). Despite the plethora of choices regarding factor rotation, the best practice is to try both rotations (e.g. varimax vs. direct oblimin) and inspect the solutions of both techniques, and chose the solutions that are easiest to interpret and theoretically defensible (Bandalos 2018).

22.6 A Glimpse of CFA

Having known how common factors relate to items either from a prior EFA study or from the psychometric scales developed by other researchers, the next logical step is to confirm the already known factor structure by conducting a confirmatory factor analysis (CFA). CFA is a complex subject. This section only discussed CFA briefly. You can consult a specialized book on CFA. I have listed one of my favourite books in the 'Further Reading' section.

When working with data, EFA and CFA should not be used on the same dataset; otherwise, there is no point of reconfirming a factorial structure using CFA on the same sample that had been used to discover the structure with EFA. The CFA solutions will provide the estimates for each parameter of the CFA model, which includes factor loadings, the variances of the latent factors, the covariances among the latent factors, and often times the covariances among the error terms (if the error items are allowed to be correlated). Having these ingredients, CFA software would be able to calculate covariance matrix of the items (Σ). A good model will produce Σ that is close to the covariance matrix calculated from a sample (S).

IMPORTANT

The goal in CFA is to determine how well a proposed CFA model aligns with observed data. CFA will compare the predicted covariance matrix of observed variables Σ with the sample covariance matrix S. A good fit occurs when Σ and S do not differ greatly. A perfect fit occurs when $\Sigma = S$. However, a perfect fit never happens in a real-life setting.

CFA can only be undertaken using as a specialized software, such as AMOS, LISREL, EQS, Mplus, or an R package *lavaan*. AMOS is now a part of SPSS, but it does not come automatically with SPSS; therefore, it must be installed separately. *lavaan* is increasingly popular nowadays, and has a very good documentation.

For an illustration, I analysed data that contains responses of consumers on five items of sustainable fashion consumption scale (SFC1–SFC5) and three items of awareness of consequences for the biosphere. The sustainable consumption scale is adapted from the consciousness for sustainable consumption's scale developed by Balderjahn et al. (2013). The items are as follows:

- I now buy clothing that is durable ($SFC1$).
- It is made from recycled materials ($SFC2$).
- I will buy clothing that is safe to the environment ($SFC3$).
- I will not buy new clothing items, if I already have previous dresses in usable state ($SFC4$).

The *lavaan* code to run CFA is presented here:

```
rm(list = ls(all=TRUE)) # make a fresh start
library(lavaan)
library(lavaanPlot)
```

```
library(semTools)
library(ahdar)

sfc_model <- '
    SFC =~ SFC1 + SFC2 + SFC3 + SFC4
'
fit <- cfa(sfc_model, data=sfc)
summary(fit, standardized=TRUE)
fitMeasures(fit,c("chisq","df","rmsea","srmr","cfi","tli"))

# plotting the CFA path model

labels = list(SFC = "SFC")
pl <- lavaanPlot(model = fit, labels = labels,
           graph_options = list(rankdir = "TB"),
           node_options = list(shape = "box",
           fontname = "Helvetica"),
           edge_options = list(color = "grey"),
           coefs = TRUE, stand = TRUE)
pl

# calculate composite reliability
reliability(fit)
```

The breakdown explanations of the code are as follows:

- We load the required libraries and data package ahdar to make sfc data available.

```
library(lavaan) # do the CFA
library(lavaanPlot) # plot CFA path diagram
library(semTools) # calculate composite reliability
library(ahdar)
```

- The CFA model is specified within the ' ' symbols. A latent factor is formulated in the form of a string where the left-hand side of the =~ symbol specifies the factor and the right-hand side specifies the items. The R object's name that I chose for the CFA model in the code is *sfc_model*. The CFA model that I specified has only one latent factor (*SFC*) measured with four items (*SFC*1, *SFC*2, *SFC*3, *SFC*4).

```
sfc_model <- '
    SFC =~ SFC1 + SFC2 + SFC3 + SFC4
'
```

- The data is then fitted to the model with `cfa()` function, and the summary of the model fit is provided using summary(`fit, standardized=TRUE`). The argument `standardized=TRUE` will print the standardized solutions. In the standardized solutions, the variances of the factors are fixed to 1, and the factor loadings are in the standardized form with mean of 0 and variance of 1.

```
fit <- cfa(sfc_model, data = sfc)
summary(fit, standardized=TRUE)
```

```
## lavaan 0.6.16 ended normally after 23 iterations ##
##   Estimator                                ML
##   Optimization method                            NLMINB
##   Number of model parameters                          8
##
##   Number of observations                            309
##
##   Model Test User Model:
##
##   Test statistic                                  2.373
##   Degrees of freedom                                  2
##   P-value (Chi-square)                            0.305
##
##   Parameter Estimates:
##
##   Standard errors                              Standard
##   Information                                  Expected
##   Information saturated (h1)                 Structured
     model
##
##   Latent Variables:

##              Estimate  Std.Err  z-value  P(>|z|)   Std.   Std.all
                                                        lv
##   SFC =~
##     SFC1        1.000                               1.225    0.870
##     SFC2        0.874    0.057   15.417    0.000   1.071    0.764
##     SFC3        0.814    0.064   12.673    0.000   0.997    0.662
##     SFC4        1.011    0.056   17.899    0.000   1.238    0.864
##
##   Variances:
##                Estimate  Std.Err  z-value  P(>|z|) Std.lv  Std.all
##     .SFC1       0.482    0.067    7.239    0.000   0.482    0.243
##     .SFC2       0.817    0.080   10.196    0.000   0.817    0.416
##     .SFC3       1.272    0.113   11.219    0.000   1.272    0.561
##     .SFC4       0.523    0.070    7.507    0.000   0.523    0.254
##      SFC        1.501    0.164    9.156    0.000   1.000    1.000
```

```
fitMeasures(fit,c("chisq","df","rmsea","srmr","cfi","tli"))
```

```
## chisq      df rmsea     srmr   cfi    tli
## 2.373   2.000 0.025    0.010 0.999 0.998
```

The last function produces six indices commonly reported in CFA studies: chi-square statistic (*chisq*) divided by model's degrees of freedom (*df*), root mean square error of approximation (*RMSE A*), standardized root mean square residual (*SRM R*), comparative fit index (*CF I*), and Tucker-Lewis Index (*TLI*).

TABLE 22.1

Model Fit Guidelines

Index	Meaning	Criteria	Decision
chisq/df	chi-square/degree of freedom	< 2	Excellent
CFI	Comparative Fit Index	0.90 – 0.95	Acceptable
		> 0.95	Excellent
TLI	Tucker-Lewis Index	0.90 – 0.95	Acceptable
		> 0.95	Excellent
RMSEA	Root Mean Square Error Approximation	0.05 – 0.08	Acceptable
		> 0.08	Excellent
SRMR	Standardized Root Mean Square Residual	0.05 – 0.08	Acceptable
		> 0.05	Excellent

Table 22.1 provides benchmarks for model fit indices. These indices are commonly reported in published research and have been shown to be reliable in evaluating the fit of the model with data (Hu & Bentler 1998). For each of the fit indices, the table shows the cut-off values above which the model is considered to have an acceptable or excellent fit to the data. This is how I report these indices in one of my papers (Daryanto et al. 2022):

"We performed a confirmatory factor analysis (CFA) to assess the appropriateness of the constructs used in our model framework, using the R package lavaan (Rosseel 2012). Our results showed that the CFA model had an adequate fit to the data (chi-square = 411.304, df = 254, RMSEA = 0.044, SRMR = 0.047, CFI = 0.965, TLI = 0.958."

Looking at the outputs, the fit indices of the CFA model are quite good, which means that the one factor CFA model fit well to the data. Standardized factor loadings are provided in the last column of the outputs under the heading *Std.All*. Three of the standardized loadings are above 0.7 (*SF*1, *SFC*2, *SFC*4), and one is above 0.6 (*SFC*3). Generally, loadings above 0.5 are considered acceptable, which means the latent factor can explain 25% of variation in the item. Because each item loads onto only one factor, the standardized loadings can be interpreted as the correlation between the item and the factor. Thus, the correlation between the items and the factor is all above 0.6, suggesting strong correlations.

- The lines after the comment # *plotting the CFA path diagram* are code to produce a path diagram of the CFA model specified in the previous line. One of the best R packages to produce a path diagram in *lavaan* environment is the *lavaanPlot* (Lishinski 2018). Install this package: install.packages("lavaanPlot")'. More information on how to modify the code can be read in the package's website: https://lavaanplot.alexlishinski.com/articles/intro_to_lavaanplot.

```
labels = list(SFC = "SFC")
pl <- lavaanPlot(model = fit, labels = labels,
                 graph_options = list(rankdir = "TB"),
                 node_options = list(shape = "box",
                 fontname = "Helvetica"),
                 edge_options = list(color = "grey"),
                 coefs = TRUE, stand = TRUE)
pl
```

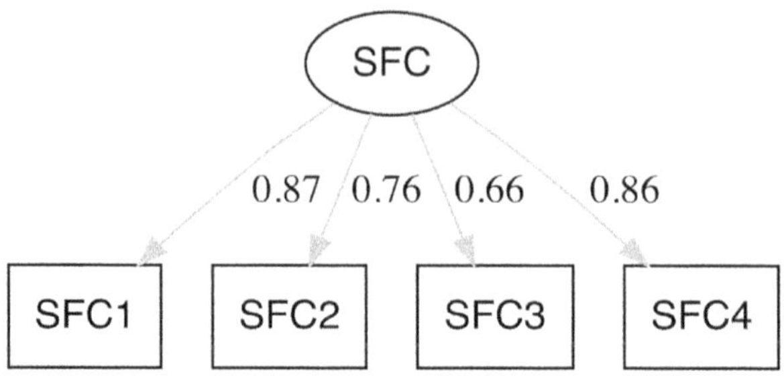

FIGURE 22.17
CFA model with item loadings (measurements errors are not shown).

- The `reliability()` function after the note # *calculate composite reliability* calculates composite reliability (*CR*). This function belongs to the *semTools* package (Jorgensen et al. 2016). The composite reliability is the CFA's version of the reliability coefficient. It is analogous to Cronbach's alpha that it reflects the extent to which items belong together in measuring a latent construct. If loadings of all items are equal, the composite reliability will be the same as the Cronbach's alpha.

```
# calculate composite reliability
reliability(fit)
```

```
##                 SFC
##      alpha  0.8667232
##      omega  0.8690913
##     omega2  0.8690913
##     omega3  0.8690953
##     avevar  0.6259281
```

The 'alpha' in the outputs gives the Cronbach's alpha of the four items, which is equal to 0.867. Of the remaining values, the recommended value to be reported for the composite reliability index is the omega value (0.869), which is not very different than the alpha.

22.7 Summary

We have covered an exploratory factory analysis (EFA) with principal axis factoring (PAF) as a method to extract underlying common factors, and applied an oblique rotation called direct oblimin as a method to rotate the factor solutions. We also discussed the SPSS syntax and R code to conduct an EFA study and the practical guidelines based on recent literature. In the chapter, Introduced a confirmatory factor analysis

(CFA) briefly when one wants to establish a known factorial structure and showed a *lavaan* code for a one-factor CFA model. I also discussed summary of fit indices to evaluate the fit of CFA model to data. Of course, the small section on CFA in this chapter is not sufficient for an actual empirical work. CFA is not just about connecting items with a latent factor. There are subtleties that must be understood (e.g. modifying the factorial structure to improve fit) when working with real data, which most often requires data cleaning.

22.8 Further Readings

Brown, T. A. (2015), *Confirmatory factor analysis for applied research*, Guilford Publications. This is a defining text on CFA. early chapters covered EFA.

Daryanto, A., Song, Z. & Soopramanien, D. (2022), 'The COVID-19 pandemic as an impetus for pro-environmental behaviours: The role of causal attribution', *Personality and Individual Differences* **187**, 111415. There are four different constructs discussed in the paper. I conducted a CFA to evaluate whether these constructs were indeed distinct. What I like about this paper is that it implemented a robust procedure to check the quality data, e.g. the calculation of the maximum number of steady responses provided by a respondent consecutively and attention quality check using the R package *careless* (Yentes & Wilhelm 2018).

22.9 Review Questions

1. Explain the goal of EFA.
2. Is EFA a supervised or an unsupervised learning? And why is that so?
3. Explain the philosophical and methodological difference between EFA and PCA.
4. Briefly explain how principal axis factoring (PAF) works.
5. Explain the meaning of the coefficients in the factor matrix, pattern matrix, and structure matrix when oblique rotation is used in EFA.

22.10 Exercises

1. The following is the output from Corrmat.spd macro. Using the information displayed in the figure, conduct EFA with PAF using SPSS. How many factors would you extract? How much variation in the data do the factors account for?

```
Run MATRIX procedure:

Calculating covariance and correlation matrix

written by Dr. Ahmad Daryanto, 2016

ahdar_2000@yahoo.com

=================================

 Number of variables
    7.00

 Number of cases
  362.00


          Mean        SD
V1       5.240     1.182
V2       5.105     1.321
V3       5.047     1.405
V4       5.044     1.441
V5       3.135     1.684
V6       3.069     1.844
V7       3.144     1.758

Correlation matrix
    1.000     .493     .499     .451    -.158    -.187    -.199
     .493    1.000     .593     .638    -.165    -.256    -.180
     .499     .593    1.000     .746    -.131    -.260    -.185
     .451     .638     .746    1.000    -.161    -.312    -.181
    -.158    -.165    -.131    -.161    1.000     .840     .886
    -.187    -.256    -.260    -.312     .840    1.000     .839
    -.199    -.180    -.185    -.181     .886     .839    1.000
```

FIGURE 22.18
Output from Corrmat.spd macro.

2. Are the underlying factors positively or negatively correlated?
3. sfc.sav data (download it from book website) contains three items that measure environmental awareness. Modify the CFA code that I used in the chapter by adding a new construct (say, EA) measured with these three items. Evaluate the model fit and comment on the standardized loadings.
4. In the code for plot, replace the line with coef with this one: *coefs = TRUE, stand = TRUE, covs=TRUE). covs=TRUE* will the draw a double-headed arrow between two latent factors. The plot will show the correlation between SFC and EA. Assess the correlation between the two latent constructs.

23

Binary Logistic Regression

In this chapter, a binary logistic regression model with a categorical dependent variable that takes only two discrete values (yes/no) is discussed. A binary logistic regression model is useful in modelling consumer decision making involving two choices (e.g. buying brand A or brand B). The chapter begins with a discussion of the characteristics of the binary logistic regression model. The model is used to examine whether number of years playing an acoustic guitar can explain consumers' ownership of an electric guitar. Next, the analysis is demonstrated using the SPSS binary logistic procedure and the `glm()` R function. The extensions of the binary logistic regression to multinomial logit and multinomial probit models are also discussed. In the last section, the property of the independence from the irrelevant alternatives is described.

Learning Objectives:

- Understand the principle of a logistic regression.
- Understand why a linear regression model with a continuous dependent variable cannot be used to model a choice.
- Understand the method used to estimate coefficients in a logistic regression.
- Know how to interpret key outputs of a logistic regression from SPSS binary logistic procedure and the `glm()` R function.

23.1 Building a Model

Imagine that we select a group of acoustic guitar owners in random from the population of acoustic guitar owners. Then, we asked them to indicate whether they owned an electric guitar and how many years they have been playing an acoustic guitar (in years).[1] Our question is: can the number of years playing an acoustic guitar explain whether someone owns an electric guitar? Anecdotal evidence suggests that many beginner players start with an acoustic or an electro-acoustic guitar because it is relatively quick and simple to use than the electric one. The main reasons are that the acoustic guitar does not need to be plugged into an amp, and there are many alternatives for some good budget-friendly brands on the market. Only after attaining a certain level of proficiency involving some years of experience that the aspiring musicians might switch to an electric guitar. The argument may not be entirely true as some beginners may jump directly to learning an electric guitar or after just a few months of playing.

[1] See this link for interesting facts from a survey in the US: https://www.pianodreamers.com/guitar-sales-statistics/

DOI: 10.4324/9781003407225-29

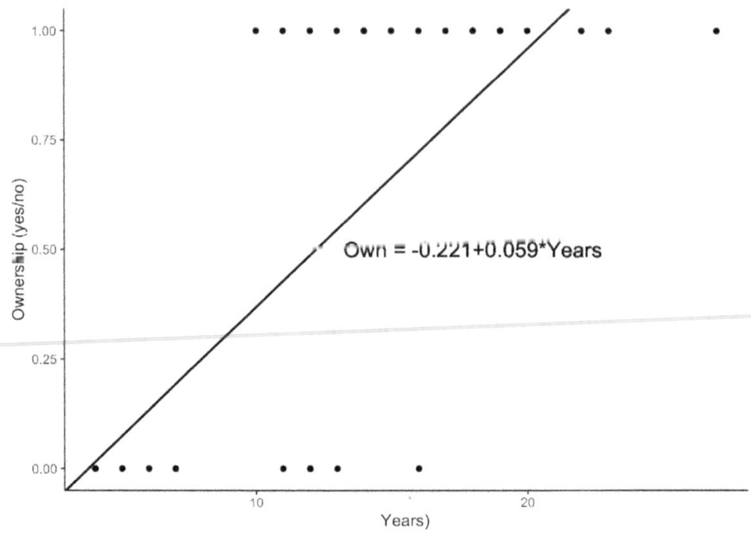

FIGURE 23.1
A scatter plot of Own against Years and a simple regression line.

To answer the question, we can develop the following regression model:

$$Own = \beta_0 + \beta_1 Years + \varepsilon \tag{23.1}$$

where *Own* denotes an electric guitar ownership with 1 = Owned, 0 = No, and *Years* = number of years playing an acoustic guitar, and ε denotes an error term. I have created fake data with 30 observations and plot *Own* against *Years*. I also used an ordinary least square (OLS) regression to estimate the coefficients of the model. The results show that the relationship between *Own* and *Years* can be described by this equation $Own = -0.221 + 0.059\ Years$. The scatter plot and a simple linear regression line is displayed in Figure 23.1:

Looking at the data, of the 30 responses, 60% consumers indicate that they owned an electric guitar. As *Own* is a 0, 1 dependent variable, the mean score of the variable is 0.6, which is exactly equal to the proportion. This proportion can also mean that *the probability of a random customer at a particular number of years of playing an acoustic guitar, to own an electric guitar is 0.6*. This result resembles tossing a coin that is biased with a 60% chance it will land on a head, that is, out of 30 coin tosses, we would expect 60% of them will land on a head.

However, if we use a simple linear regression model, our focus is in estimating what value of *Own* that we would expect from a customer with a certain value of *Years*. For example, for a customer with 23 years of playing an acoustic guitar, the value of $Own = -0.221 + 0.059 * 23 = 1.44$. If we treat 1.44, which is greater than 1, as the probability of owning a guitar, we run into a problem that probability can only take a value from 0 (impossible) to 1 (certain). Therefore, an OLS regression, covered in Chapter 13, is not appropriate for modelling the probability of owning an electric guitar.

NOTE

In general, if Y is a dependent variable that takes on two values where Y=1 is denoted as success, and Y=0 is denoted as a fail, and *X* is an independent variable:

$$E(Y|X) = 1 \times P(Y = 1|X) + 0 \times P(Y = 0|X) \tag{23.2}$$
$$P(Y = 1|X) \tag{23.3}$$

where $E(Y|X)$ is the conditional expectation of *Y* at a given value of *X*. In a layterm $E(Y|X)$ means, the value of Y that we would expect to obtain if a person is randomly selected with a certain value of *X*. To understand the right-hand side of the expression, we read the '+' sign as 'or'. That is, we would obtain either $Y = 1$ or $Y = 0$ at a certain value of *X*. The chance for Y=1 to occur is $P(Y = 1|X)$, and the chance for $Y = 1$ to occur is $P(Y = 0|X)$. The result is $E(Y|X) = P(Y = 1|X)$. That is, the conditional expected value of *Y* is the probability of getting a success.

To overcome the problem of modelling probability $P(Y > 0)$, the solution is by applying a logistic regression model. Because we are dealing with a categorical dependent variable that has two values coded as either 0 or 1, it is also known as a binary logistic regression model. It takes the following form:

$$P = P(Own = 1|\, Years) = \frac{e^{\beta_0 + \beta_1 Years}}{1 + e^{\beta_0 + \beta_1 Years}} \tag{23.4}$$

where *P* is the probability of owning an electric guitar at a certain value of *Years*. *Years* is the number of years playing an acoustic guitar, and *e* is a symbol for Euler's number, which is approximately equal to 2.718 (rounded to three decimal places). If we know the value of β_0 and β_1, we can calculate the probability of owning an electric guitar at a specific value of *Years*, say *Years* = 10. For example, if $\beta_0 = -6.192$ $\beta_1 = 0.509$, then $P = 0.249$. This means that there is nearly a 25% chance that someone owned an electric guitar having played an acoustic guitar for 10 years. The calculation is shown below:

```
p <- function(x){
    bx <- -6.192 + 0.509*x
    y <- exp(bx) / (1 + exp(bx))
    return(y),
}
round (p(10), 3)
```

```
## [1] 0.249
```

Plotting *P* against *Years* produces a curve that resembles an S-shaped curve as can be seen in Figure 23.2. The curve is known as a logistic curve because it is drawn from a standard cumulative logistic distribution or logistic function.

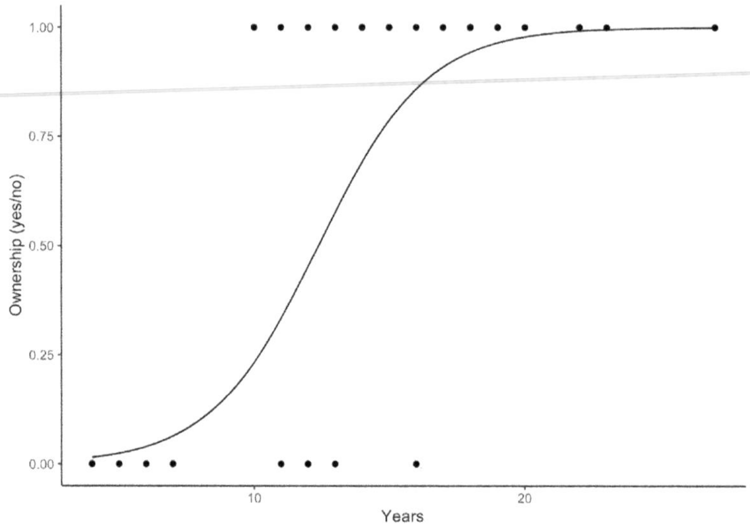

FIGURE 23.2
An S-shaped logistic curve showing the probability of owning an electric guitar given `Years`.

NOTE

A random variable is distributed according to a standard logistic distribution if its density function (y) has the following form:

$$y = \frac{e^x}{(1+e^x)^2}$$

The standard logistic distribution curve has a similar shape as the standard normal distribution curve but with heavier tails and shorter peak.

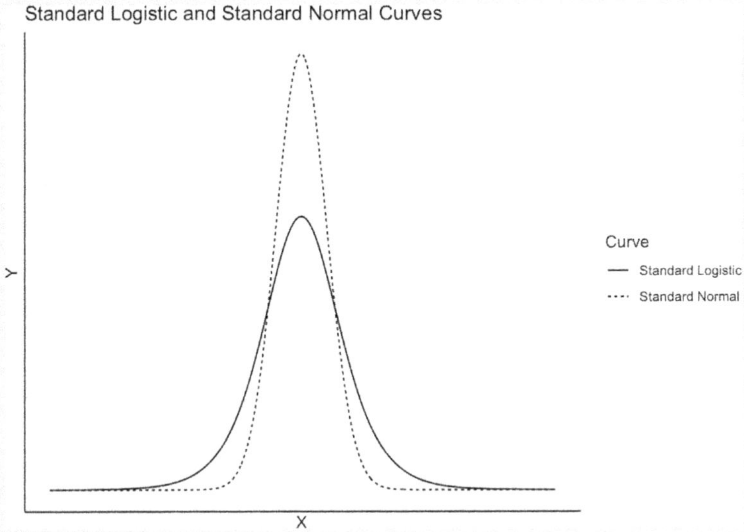

FIGURE 23.3
Standard logistic and standard normal distribution.

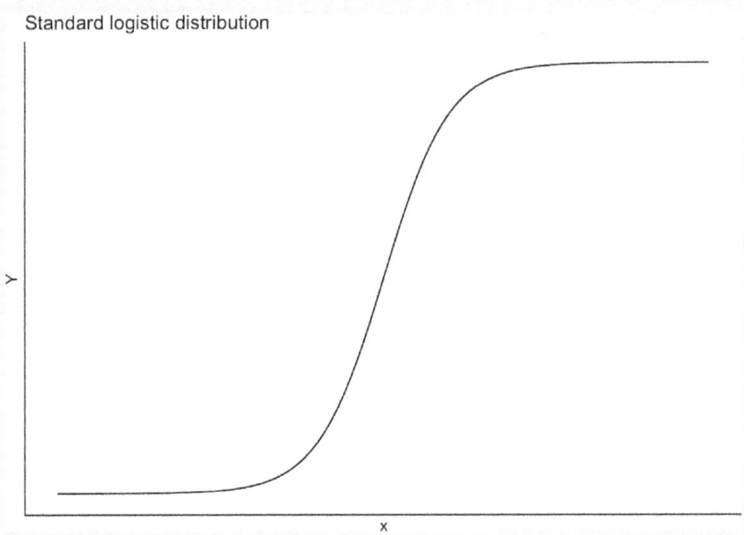

FIGURE 23.4
Standard logistic cumulative distribution.

And the cumulative standard logistic distribution is given by: $y = \dfrac{e^x}{1+e^x}$

The cumulative distribution function is synonymous with the logistic function because it has the same form. The logistic function was discovered by the Belgian mathematician Verhulst in 1838 in his attempt in modelling human population growth at that time in France, Belgium, Essex, and Russia (Cramer 2004). The standard cumulative distribution function or the logistic function described by the equation has an S-shaped curve.

23.2 Alternative Form

Estimating the two parameters in Equation 23.4 is computationally difficult, and the form of the equation looks complicated. An alternative formulation exists:

$$\text{In} = \frac{P}{1-P} = \beta_0 + \beta_1 Years \quad (23.5)$$

The left-hand side of the equation, $\frac{P}{1-P}$, is referred to as the odds ratio. As P is the probability of owning an electric guitar, $1-P$ is the probability of not owning, which is just the reverse. The expression $\frac{P}{1-P}$ is thus the ratio of the probability that a customer owns an electric guitar to the probability that an individual does not own an electric guitar.

I guess, the last sentence of the previous paragraph sounds very technical and is difficult to understand, let alone be used in an everyday conversation. To get the intuitive meaning of the odds ratio, we can trace how a probability is derived from odds. Imagine that out of 5 attempts in a sport competition, Mr X wins 3 of them. His odds of winning are 3:2 (3 wins and 2 losses). Turning the odds into a probability, his probability of wins is 3 out of 5 $\left(P = \frac{3}{5}\right)$, and his probability of losing is $1-P = \frac{2}{5}$. The odds ratio in favor of winning is therefore:

$$\frac{P}{1-P} = \frac{\frac{3}{5}}{\frac{2}{5}} = \frac{3}{2} = 1.5 \quad (23.6)$$

This means that the probability of winning is 1.5 higher than the probability of losing. '*ln*' in the expression $ln\frac{P}{1-P}$ stands for natural logarithm. *ln* is strongly connected to Euler's number. If $e^n = y$, then $ln(y) = n$. Compare this expression with this one: If $10^2 = 100$, then $\log(100) = 2$, where *log* stands for logarithm. I hope, you can see that $In(e) = \log(10) = 1$.

Now, let us look at the right-hand side of Equation 23.5: $\beta_0 + \beta_1$ *Years*, which is the same as the form in the right-hand side of Equation 23.1. The form $\beta_0 + \beta_1$ *Years* makes the left-hand side of both equations linear in the parameters β_0 and β_1. Estimating equations that are linear in parameters are much simpler compared to those in the original forms. To estimate β_0 and β_1, statistical software applied the estimation technique called the maximum likelihood estimation (MLE). Unlike, OLS, MLE uses an iterative computational procedure to find the coefficient estimates for the two parameters. The search procedure will stop if the values for the estimates converge wherein an additional search does not produce new values that are so different than the previous ones. $\text{Ln}\,\frac{P}{1-P}$ is often referred to as *logit* giving us the binary logit model:

$$\text{log}it(p) = \beta_0 + \beta_1 Years \tag{23.7}$$

23.2.1 R Code

R code to reproduce Figure 23.2 is given below:

```
rm(list=ls())
library(tidyverse)
library(haven)
library(ahdar)

p <- ggplot(data = guitar,
            mapping = aes(x = Years, y = Own)) +
     geom_point() +
     labs(x = "Years",
          y = "Ownership (yes/no)") + theme_classic()

# Estimate logit model
mylogit <- glm(formula = Own~Years, binomial(
               link = "logit"), data = guitar)

# Logistic curve

y_logit <- function(x){
    bx <- coef(mylogit)[2]*x + coef(mylogit)[1]
    y <- exp(bx) / (1 + exp(bx))

    # Alternative calculation
    # y <- plogis(bx, location = 0, scale = 1)
  return(y)
}
p + stat_function(fun = y_logit) + theme_classic()
```

23.3 SPSS Action

Data: guitar.sav
Steps:

- Analyze → Regression → Binary Logistic.
- Insert *Own* into the `dependent box`.

- Insert *Years* into the `independent box`.
- Change 'Method' to `Backward LR`.
- Click: `Save`, and under Predicted Values, tick `Probabilities` and `Group membership`.
- Click `Options`, and tick `Classification plots` and `Hosmer-Lemeshow goodness-of-fit`.
- Click `Continue` and click `OK`.
- Inspect the outputs.

If in the last step you clicked `Paste`, an SPSS syntax is created:

```
LOGISTIC REGRESSION VARIABLES Own
  /METHOD=BSTEP(LR) Years
  /SAVE=PRED PGROUP
  /CLASSPLOT
  /PRINT=GOODFIT
  /CRITERIA=PIN(0.05) POUT(0.10) ITERATE(20) CUT(0.5).
```

SPSS produces several outputs but we will discuss the most essential ones: `Variables in the Equation`, `Likelihood Ratio Test`, `Hosmer and Lemeshow Test`, and `Classification Table`.

23.3.1 Variables in the Equation

The outputs produce the coefficient estimates for β_0 and β_1, that is, $b_0 = -6.192$ and $b_1 = 0.509$ (see Figure 23.5). b_1 is significant ($\rho = 0.009$), which means *Years* is positively related to the probability of owning an electric guitar. The estimated logit model is given by:

$$logit(p) = -6.192 + 0.509Years \tag{23.8}$$

The meaning of b_1 is that it captures the effect on the logit of a one-unit increase in *Years*. In other words, for an additional one year of playing an acoustic guitar, the logit is expected to be increased by 0.509.

SPSS also produces odds ratios, which are often reported by researchers in their academic papers. In the SPSS outputs, the odds ratio is given by the entry of the last column, *Exp(B)*, where *B* is the entry of the first column. The odds ratio associated with the coefficient of *Years* is 1.664. As the heading of the column suggests, this value is obtained by this simple calculation $e^{0.509} = 1.644$, in reverse, $In(1.644) = 0.509$. How do we interpret this odds ratio?

Let us rewrite Equation 23.5 as follows:

$$Odds_{Years} = \frac{P}{1-P} = e^{\beta_0 + \beta_1 Years} \tag{23.9}$$

Variables in the Equation

		B	S.E.	Wald	df	Sig.	Exp(B)
Step 1[a]	Years	.509	.195	6.824	1	.009	1.664
	Constant	-6.192	2.532	5.982	1	.014	.002

a. Variable(s) entered on step 1: Years.

FIGURE 23.5
Logistic regression's coefficient estimates.

where $Odds_{Years}$ is an odds number at a particular value of *Years*. The odds ratio of an additional year will be:

$$Odds_{(Years+1)} = \frac{P}{1-P} = e^{\beta_0+\beta_1(Years+1)} \tag{23.10}$$

From the property of exponentiation, $e^{(a+b)} = e^a e^b$, we obtain:

$$Odds_{Years+1} = e^{\beta_0} e^{\beta_1 Years} e^{\beta_1} \tag{23.11}$$

$$= e^{\beta_0} + e^{\beta_1 Years} e^{\beta_1} \tag{23.12}$$

$$= Odds_{Years} e^{\beta_1} \tag{23.13}$$

That is, the odds of another year of playing is the odds of the current year multiplied by the odds ratio $e^{\beta}{}_1$. Based on our results, the odds of owning an electric guitar from an additional year of playing an acoustic guitar increase by 64.4%, as calculated here:

$$= (\frac{Odd \times se^{\beta_1} - Odds}{Odds}) \times 100\% \tag{23.14}$$

$$= (e^{\beta_1} - 1) \times 100\% \tag{23.15}$$

$$= (1.644 - 1) \times 100\% \tag{23.16}$$

$$= 64.4 \tag{23.17}$$

From this demonstration, we know that that in order to calculate the percentage increase in the odds of success ($Y = 1$), we can subtract one from the odds ratio associated with the predictor variable ($e^{\beta}{}_1$), and multiply it by 100%.

23.3.2 Likelihood Ratio Test

The likelihood ratio test compares an intercept-only model (no predictor) with our specified model (i.e. model with *Years*). The null hypothesis is that the model with the predictor is no better than the intercept-only model. Therefore, in this test, we want to *reject* the null hypothesis (i.e. obtaining a small p-value). The outputs relevant to likelihood ratio test can be produced by changing the `Method to Backward: LR`. If we are using the SPSS syntax, it can be requested by using /METHOD=BSTEP(LR). The outputs are displayed in Figure 23.6. As can be seen from the figure, the p-value of the test is very

Model if Term Removed

Variable		Model Log Likelihood	Change in -2 Log Likelihood	df	Sig. of the Change
Step 1	Years	-20.190	19.104	1	<.001

FIGURE 23.6
Results of the likelihood ratio test.

Hosmer and Lemeshow Test

Step	Chi-square	df	Sig.
1	4.043	7	.775

FIGURE 23.7
Results of the Hosmer and Lemeshow test.

small; therefore, we reject the null hypothesis and conclude that our model with predictor *Years* is better than the intercept-only model. We continue our discussion on the idea behind the calculation in the R Action section.

23.3.3 Hosmer and Lemeshow Test

The Hosmer and Lemeshow test is a goodness-of-fit test based on a chi-square statistic that provides an indication of how accurate is the prediction from the model. This test requires large number of cases (at least 50) (Hair et al. 2009; Hosmer et al. 2013). The null hypothesis is that the observed and the expected proportions are the same. In this test, we want to *retain* the null hypothesis, which means that our specified model is acceptable. The result in Figure 23.7 shows that the test is not significant ($p = 0.775$), which means that there are no significant differences between the observed proportions and those predicted by the model. Thus, the use of our model to predict ownership is statistically justified.

23.3.4 Classification Table

One way of measuring how accurate the prediction of our logit model is by assessing the classification table, which is a cross tabulation of the observed and the predicted values for the probabilities. If the model is good, we would see most of the cases in the main diagonal showing that the model can predict the probabilities well. The classification table of our example is given in Figure 23.8. As can be seen in the main diagonal of the table, there are 10 correctly predicted non-ownership and 15 correctly predicted ownership. The last column of the table shows the 'percentage correct'. The percentage correct obtained shown in the first row is 83.3%. This value is obtained from dividing the number of correct by total row: $10 | 12 = 0.833$. Similarly, the percentage correct in the second row: $15 | 18 = 0.833$. Finally, the overall percentage correct is given by the sum of cases in the main diagonal divided by the number of cases

Classification Table[a]

Observed			Predicted: Own .00	Predicted: Own 1.00	Percentage Correct
Step 1	Own	.00	10	2	83.3
		1.00	3	15	83.3
	Overall Percentage				83.3

a. The cut value is .500

2 non-owners were wrongly classified as owners.

Overall, 83.3 % cases were correctly classified: ((10+15)/30) x 100%.

FIGURE 23.8
Classification table.

in total: 15 | 30 = 0.833. This overall percentage tells us that 83.3% of the cases were correctly predicted by the model.

To see what is happening, we can instruct SPSS to produce the predicted probabilities and the predicted membership by clicking: `Save`, and under Predicted Values, tick `Probabilities` and `Group membership` (or with the syntax /SAVE=PRED PGROUP). As a result, two columns will be added to the data: PRE_1 containing predicted probabilities and PGR_1 containing predicted group membership (see Figure 23.9). You can also use Crosstabs from the SPSS descriptive statistics menu to create a cross tabulation of Own and PGR_1 to produce a classification table, but the percentage correct is not going to be printed.

Now, let us look at data in Figure 23.9. Let us focus on cases with `Own = 0`, that is those that do not own an electric guitar. Of the 12 cases, two cases were falsely classified as owners (`Own = 1` in case 5 and 12). The reason they were wrongly classified as `Own = 1` is because their predicted probabilities are greater than 0.5. For example, for case 5 with *Years* = 16, its predicted probability is given by:

```
Years <- 16
bx=-6.192+0.509* Years
p = exp(bx)/(1+exp(bx))
round(p,3) # 3 decimal places
```

```
[1] 0.876
```

The remaining cases with `Own = 0` have predicted probabilities lower than 0.5 and thus, are correctly assigned to non-ownership.

NOTE

We learned that if the probability of Own is greater than half, an individual is predicted to be in the ownership category; otherwise, it is assigned to the non-ownership category. Why is the threshold set to half? The answer is that it is quite intuitive to assign someone to predicted $Own = 1$ if the probability is better than a coin flip.

	Own	Years	PRE_1	PGR_1
1	.00	12.00	.47895	.00
2	.00	5.00	.02540	.00
3	.00	7.00	.06728	.00
4	.00	4.00	.01543	.00
5	.00	16.00	.87563	1.00
6	.00	11.00	.35589	.00
7	.00	12.00	.47895	.00
8	.00	12.00	.47895	.00
9	.00	4.00	.01543	.00
10	.00	6.00	.04156	.00
11	.00	7.00	.06728	.00
12	.00	13.00	.60462	1.00
13	1.00	14.00	.71783	1.00
14	1.00	16.00	.87563	1.00
15	1.00	11.00	.35589	.00
16	1.00	22.00	.99334	1.00
17	1.00	15.00	.80888	1.00
18	1.00	27.00	.99947	1.00
19	1.00	23.00	.99599	1.00
20	1.00	17.00	.92134	1.00
21	1.00	12.00	.47895	.00
22	1.00	18.00	.95119	1.00
23	1.00	20.00	.98180	1.00
24	1.00	19.00	.97008	1.00
25	1.00	19.00	.97008	1.00
26	1.00	18.00	.95119	1.00
27	1.00	18.00	.95119	1.00
28	1.00	14.00	.71783	1.00
29	1.00	13.00	.60462	1.00
30	1.00	10.00	.24932	.00

FIGURE 23.9
PRE_1 (predicted probability) and PGR_1 (predicted group membership) were added into the original data.

From a mathematical point of view, having the threshold equals half is the consequence of setting the expected value of this expression $\beta_0 + \beta_1$ *Years* to be greater than zero. Let us write the expected value as $U = b_0 + b_1$ *Years*, where b_0 and b_1 are the estimates of β_0 and β_1, respectively. If U is greater than zero, then an individual is assumed to derive some amount of utility U from owning an electric guitar; thus, the individual would be assigned to predicted $Own = 1$. If it is lower than zero, it is perceived that she/he did not get any benefits from owning an electric guitar; thus, the individual would be assigned to predicted $Own = 0$. The following simple calculation demonstrates this idea. If $U = 0$:

$$\begin{aligned} P &= \frac{e^{\beta_0 + \beta_1 X}}{1 + e^{\beta_0 + \beta_1 X}} \\ &= \frac{e^{U}}{1 + e^{U}} \\ &= \frac{e^{0}}{1 + e^{0}} \\ &= \frac{1}{1+1} \\ &= \frac{1}{2} \end{aligned} \tag{23.18}$$

23.4 R Action

In this section, we are going to reproduce the SPSS results using R.

23.4.1 Glm()

To run a binary logistic regression in r, we can use the `glm()` function, which is available in R base. glm stands for generalized linear model. As the name suggests the glm function can be used to run a wide variety of models. For our purpose, we focus on the binary logistic regression by setting the `family = "binomial"` or `binomial(link = "logit")`.

```
library(ahdar)
mylogit <- glm(formula = Own~Years,
               family = binomial(link = "logit"), data = guitar)
summary(mylogit)
##
## Call:
## glm(formula = Own ~ Years, family = binomial(link = "logit"),
```

```
##     data = guitar)
##
## Coefficients:
##                Estimate Std.   Error  z value   Pr(>|z|)
## (Intercept)     -6.1922       2.5318   -2.446   0.01445 *
## Years            0.5090       0.1948    2.612   0.00899 **
## ---
## Signif. codes:  0 '***' 0.001 '**' 0.01 '*' 0.05 '.' 0.1 ' ' 1
##
## (Dispersion parameter for binomial family taken to be 1)
##
##     Null deviance: 40.381 on 29 degrees of freedom
## Residual deviance: 21.277 on 28 degrees of freedom
## AIC: 25.277
##
## Number of Fisher Scoring iterations: 6
```

23.4.2 Likelihood Ratio Test

To calculate the likelihood test 'manually', we will utilize the outputs printed in the `summary(mylogit)`, particularly the `Null deviance` and the `Residual deviance`.

```
mylogit$null.deviance
```

```
[1] 40.3807
mylogit$deviance
```

```
[1] 21.2769
```

Deviance means lack of fit or, in our context, the deviance of predicted probabilities from observed probabilities. Null deviance is the deviance produced by the null model – model with an intercept only. The Residual deviance is the deviance produced after adding a predictor into the previous model. Deviance is reduced after adding a significant predictor. The amount of reduction can be tested by using a likelihood ratio test where the reduction is assumed to follow a chi-square distribution with certain degrees of freedom. The degree of freedom is calculated as the amount of parameters in the new model minus the number of parameter in the previous model – that is, the number of parameters in our specified model minus the number of parameter in the intercept-only model (null model). In our specified model, there are two parameters: β_0 and β_1. In the intercept-only model, there is only one parameter: β_0. Therefore, the degree of freedom equals 1.

```
# Compute the test statistic
# That is, the reduction in the deviance.

LR_test<-mylogit$null.deviance-mylogit$deviance
LR_test
```

```
[1] 19.1038
```

This value is the same as the value printed in the SPSS output of 'Model if Term Removed', in the column 'Change in -2 Log Likelihood'.

Now, let us compute the p-value of the test – that is, the p-value associated with the test statistic distributed according to a chi-square distribution with $df = 1$.

```
# Compute the p-value
df <- 1
LR_pvalue<-1-pchisq(LR_test,df)
LR_pvalue
```

```
[1] 1.237981e-05
```

23.4.3 Hosmer-Lemeshow Test

We can also conduct the Hosmer-Lemeshow Test in R by using the `hltest()` function from the glmtoolbox package (Vanegas et al. 2023).

```
library(glmtoolbox)
hltest(mylogit)
```

```
##   The Hosmer-Lemeshow goodness-of-fit test
##
##
##   Group     Size  Observed   Expected
##       1        3         0 0.05625312
##       2        3         0 0.17612298
##       3        3         2 0.96110739
##       4        4         1 1.91580576
##       5        4         3 2.64490558
##       6        3         2 2.56014745
##       7        4         4 3.77490270
##       8        3         3 2.92194676
##       9        3         3 2.98880826
##
##             Statistic = 4.04347
##   degrees   of freedom =  7
##             p-value    = 0.77476
```

23.4.4 Classification Table

```
library(tidyverse)
guitar <- guitar %>%
  mutate(predprob=round(fitted(mylogit),2))
guitar <- guitar %>%
  mutate(predgrp=ifelse(predprob >= 0.5, 1,0))
head(guitar)
```

```
# A tibble: 6 x 4
      Own   Years   predprob   predgrp
    <dbl>   <dbl>      <dbl>     <dbl>
1       0      12       0.48         0
2       0       5       0.03         0
3       0       7       0.07         0
4       0       4       0.02         0
5       0      16       0.88         1
6       0      11       0.36         0
```

```
# Create classification table
ctable<-table(guitar$Own,guitar$predgrp)
ctable
```

```
     0    1
0   10    2
1    3   15
```

```
# Accuracy
percent_correct <- sum(diag(ctable))/sum(ctable)*100
percent_correct
```

```
[1] 83.33333
```

23.5 Probit Model

An alternative to logit is the probit model. In the probit model, the probability of owning an electric guitar is calculated by using the cumulative standard normal distribution.

Recall that in Chapter 6 on normal distribution, we learned that we can calculate the probability of a random variable being less than or equal to a specific value by using `pnorm()` function. The syntax looks like this: `pnorm(z, 0, 1)`. For example, the probability of obtaining a value that is less or equal to 1.96 is `pnorm(1.96, mean = 0, sd = 1) = 0.975`. We will use the knowledge after running the probit regression. To run the probit regression using our data, we can use the glm function by setting `family = binomial(link = "probit")`.

```
library(ahdar)
myprobit <- glm(formula = Own~Years,
                family = binomial(link = "probit"),
```

```
##
## Call:
## glm(formula = Own ~ Years, family = binomial(link = "probit"),
##     data = guitar)
##
## Coefficients:
##               Estimate Std.  Error  z value  Pr(>|z|)
## (Intercept)     -3.6226     1.3247   -2.735   0.00625**
## Years            0.2975     0.1004    2.962   0.00306**
## ---

## Signif. codes: 0 '***' 0.001 '**' 0.01 '*' 0.05 '.' 0.1 ' ' 1
##
## (Dispersion parameter for binomial family taken to be 1) ##
##
##     Null deviance: 40.381 on 29 degrees of freedom
## Residual deviance: 21.003 on 28 degrees of freedom
## AIC: 25.003

##
```

```
# Printing the results of logit and probit library(stargazer)
## Number of Fisher Scoring iterations: 7
```

```
##
##  ===============================================
##                   Dependent variable:
##             ------------------------------------
##                          Own
##                   logistic        probit
##                     (1)            (2)
##  ---------------------------------------------------------------
                        ------------------------
```

```
##
## ===================================================
## Years              0.509*** (0.195) 0.298*** (0.100)
## Constant           -6.192** (2.532) -3.623*** (1.325)
## ---------------------------------------------------------
##
                      ------------------------
## Observations          30                 30
## Log Likelihood      -10.638            -10.501
## Akaike Inf.          25.277             25.003
   Crit.
## ===================================================
## Note:                      *p<0.1; **p<0.05; ***p<0.01
```

Based on the results of the probit regression shown:

$p = P(Own = 1 \mid years) = -3.623 + 0.298Years$

At *Years* = 10:

```
p <- -3.6226 + 0.2975*10
p
```

```
## [1] -0.6476
```

The probability of obtaining a value that is less than or equal to −0.6476 is given by `pnorm(-0.6476,0,1)`:

```
round(pnorm(p,0,1),3)
```

```
## [1] 0.259
```

That is, using probit, the probability that someone owned an electric guitar having played an acoustic guitar for 10 years is about 26%. Using logit calculated previously, the probability is equal to 25%, thus showing little difference between the two predicted values. Indeed, in practice, the difference between logit and probit is minimal. Despite their similarity, logit model is easy to be communicated because it has a closed form, as presented in Equation 23.4. The expression for the probability in the probit model does not have such kind of closed form.

The following code calculates the predicted probability of owning an electric guitar using logit and probit at four different values of *Years*: 0, 5, 10, and 20 years. As can be seen from the results, the predicted probabilities of the two models are similar.

```
library(ahdar)
Yrs <- c(0, 5, 10, 20)
mylogit <- glm(formula = Own~Years,
           family = binomial(link = "logit"),
           data = guitar)
myprobit <- glm(formula = Own~Years,
           family = binomial(link = "probit"),
           data = guitar)
p_logit <- predict(mylogit, list (Years = Yrs), type = "response")
p_probit <- predict(myprobit, list (Years = Yrs), type = "response")

res <- data.frame(Yrs, p_logit, p_probit)
           round (res, 3)
```

```
  Yrs  p_logit  p_probit
1   0    0.002     0.000
2   5    0.025     0.016
3  10    0.249     0.259
4  20    0.982     0.990
```

Figure 23.10 displays the estimated logit and probit curves, which coincide with each other, showing no substantial difference between the logit and probit models. This minimal difference occurs most of the time in practice.

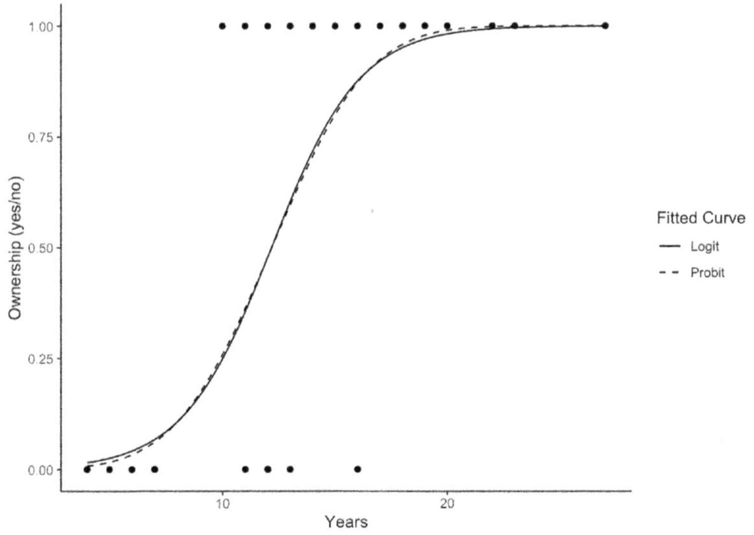

FIGURE 23.10
Fitting logit and probit curves.

23.5.1 R Code

R code to reproduce Figure 23.10 is given here:

```
rm(list=ls())
library(ggplot2)
library(tidyverse)
library(haven)
library(ahdar)

p <- ggplot(data = guitar,
            mapping = aes(x = Years, y = Own)) + geom_point() +
     labs(x = "Years",
          y = "Ownership (yes/no)")

x <- seq(from = 0, to = 30, by = 0.01)

# Estimate logit model
mylogit <- glm(formula = Own~Years,
               binomial(link = "logit"), data = guitar)

# Estimate probit model
myprobit <- glm(formula = Own~Years,
                binomial(link = "probit"), data = guitar)

# Logistic curve

y_logit <- function(x){
    bx <- coef(mylogit)[2]*x + coef(mylogit)[1]
    y <- plogis(bx, location = 0, scale = 1)
  return(y)
}

# Probit curve

y_probit <- function(x){
    bx <- coef(myprobit)[2]*x + coef(myprobit)[1]
    y <- pnorm(bx, mean = 0, sd = 1)
return(y)
}

# Plot
p <- p + stat_function(fun = y_logit,
   aes(linetype="Logit")) + stat_function(fun = y_probit,
   aes(linetype="Probit")) + scale_linetype_manual(name =
   "Fitted Curve",
   values = c("Logit"="solid","Probit"= "dashed")) +
   theme_classic()

p
```

23.6 Multiple Predictors

Having only one predictor is unrealistic in any modelling projects. We can extend our logit model by including another predictor to make it more realistic. Suppose that we include the extent to which an individual likes rock music measured by a Likert scale from 1 = strongly disagree to 7 = strongly agree, represented with a variable `Rock` as another predictor, our logit model would be:

$$In = \frac{P}{1-P} = \beta_0 + \beta_1 Years + \beta_2 Rock \tag{23.23}$$

How can we interpret the coefficient associated with `Years` (β_1) in the presence of `Rock`?

1. We can interpret the sign of `Years` in a similar way we interpret the sign of the coefficient in a regression model. For example, if *Years* has a positive sign, this means that *Years* is positively related to the probability of owning an electric guitar. In other words, the more experience an individual has with an acoustic guitar, the higher the chance that he or she owns an electric guitar.
2. What is the impact of one unit increase in *Years* on the probability of owning an electric guitar holding *Rock* constant? In the multiple regression context, we learned that the answer of this question is given by the regression coefficients, which is known as the marginal effect. In the logit model, the answer is not straightforward like this. The marginal effect is given by this formula: $b_1 p(1-p)$, where b_1 is the coefficient estimate associated with a predictor, and p is the predicted probability (Ramanathan 2002, p. 533; Studenmund 2014). That is, the marginal effect depends not only on the value of the regression coefficient but also on the value of the observation. Therefore, there would be a 'marginal effect' at each observation. To come up with a single number that can communicate a marginal effect, the commonly reported marginal effect is the average of the individual partial effect – this effect is the 'marginal effect' at an observation. Thus, we can calculate the partial effect for every observation, and take the average of the partial effects. Using R, this can be easily done by using the `logitmfx` (Fernihough et al. 2019). The following R code shows the calculation of the marginal effect via the calculation of the average of the partial effect and using the `logitmfx` function.

```
library(ahdar)

mylogit <- glm(formula = Own~Years,
family = "binomial", data = guitar2)

# Calculating partial effect at each observation.

yrs <- guitar2$Years

## calculating predicted probabilities at every observation.
```

```
pred <- predict(mylogit, newdata = data.frame("Years" = yrs),
type = "response")

## store the regression coefficient associated with Years.
b_years <- coef(mylogit)[2]
partial_effects <- b_years * pred * (1-pred)
# calculate the marginal effect
# – the average of the partial effects.
mean(partial_effects)
```

```
## [1] 0.05800399
```

```
# Calculating marginal effect using logitmfx function.
library(mfx)
logitmfx(mylogit, atmean=FALSE, data = guitar2)
```

```
## Call:
## logitmfx(formula = mylogit, data = guitar2, atmean = FALSE) ##
## Marginal Effects:
##          dF/dx Std.       Err.         z      P>|z|
## Years      0.058004   0.036672   1.5817   0.1137
```

3. Instead of calculating the average partial effect, we can compute the effect of change in *Years* at a specific `Years` on the predicted probabilities, holding *Rock* constant. For example, we can calculate the effect of an additional year of playing an acoustic guitar from 7 to 8 years.

```
predicted_prob <- predict(mylogit,
newdata = data.frame("Years" = c(7,8)), type = "response")
predicted_prob
```

```
         1            2
0.06728213   0.10714747
```

```
# Difference in the predicted probabilities.
diff(predicted_prob)
```

```
         2
0.03986534
```

The results show that having another year of experience in playing an acoustic guitar from 7 to 8 years increases the probability of owning an electric guitar by 3.9%, assuming the liking to a rock music is not changing during the years.

23.7 The Multinomial Logit Model

The multinomial logit model is the extension of the binary logit model. Similarly, the multinomial probit model is the extension of the binary probit model. In these models, the dependent variable has more than two categories (e.g. Brand A vs. Brand Brand B vs. Brand C). Multinomial logit model is widely used in marketing research to explain consumers' choices (e.g. Elshiewy et al. 2017; Guadagni & Little 1983) and firms' decisions (e.g. Wei et al. 2005; Wulff 2015). Back to our illustration, we can use a multinomial logit to explain the choice of three types of guitar: electric, acoustic, and electro-acoustic. This is a typical situation that aspiring musicians can have when they want to expand their guitar collection: which type of guitar to buy?

Let us only consider *Years* as the only predictor. The probability of buying a particular guitar given the number of years playing is:

$$P(Buy=j)=\frac{e^{\beta_{0,j}+\beta_{1,l}Yeras}}{\sum_{k=1}^{j}e^{\beta_{0,k}+\beta_{1,k}Yeras}} \tag{23.24}$$

for j = 1, . . ., J. Here, J = 3; j = 1 (acoustic), 2 = (electro-acoustic), 3 = (electric). For example, $P(Buy=1)$ is the probability of buying an acoustic guitar, and $\beta_{1,1}$ captures the impact of *Years* on the probability of buying an acoustic guitar – the influence of *Years* on the probability of buying is not the same across the three types of guitar. The expression in the nominator relates only to one type of guitar – the guitar j. The expression in the denominator considers all choices. If there are more than three types of guitars, say 4, we can replace J in the summation sign with 4. Because $P(Buy=1)+P(Buy=2)+P(Buy=3)$ must be equal to 1, one guitar must be selected as a base category. Without the base, we will have an issue in identifying the estimate of $\beta_{1,j}$ because there will be many solutions. This is called an identification problem, akin to solving $A+B=10$ where there are infinitely many values of the pair A and B that satisfy the equation.

Let us select acoustic guitar as the base. This means that we can set the parameters associated with it to be zero: $\beta_{0,1}=\beta_{1,1}=0$. Hence,

$$P(Buy=1)=\frac{1}{\sum_{k=2}^{j}e^{\beta_{0,k}+\beta_{1,k}Yeras}} \tag{23.25}$$

As you can see from the equation for the base, the expression in the denominator now depends on the remaining guitars: electro-acoustic (k = 2) and electric (k = 3).

Having the base category, each possible choice is compared to it. The logit (i.e. the log of the odds ratio) is given by:

$$In\frac{P(Buy=j)}{P(Buy=1)}=\beta_{0,j}+\beta_{1,j}Years \tag{23.26}$$

where $P(Buy=1)$ is the probability of buying an acoustic guitar – the base category.

For instance, if we are interested in comparing the choice of an electric guitar vs. acoustic guitar, the logit is given by:

$$In\frac{P(Buy=3)}{P(Buy=1)}=\beta_{0,3}+\beta_{1,3}Years \tag{23.27}$$

Similarly, for the choice of an electro-acoustic guitar, the logit is given by:

$$In\frac{P(Buy=2)}{P(Buy=1)}=\beta_{0,2}+\beta_{1,2}Years \tag{23.28}$$

23.7.1 Choosing the Base Category

In a multinomial logit model, from a mathematical point of view, choosing the base category is arbitrary. As there are multiple categories (e.g. acoustic, electro-acoustic, and electric guitar), we can choose any category that we want as the base. Nevertheless, from a research or practical point of view, which category to use as the base is a very relevant question because the base affects the interpretations of the solutions of the logit model. As we have seen, using acoustic as the base category, the model coefficients are interpreted with respect to the acoustic guitar. There is no a clear guideline in the literature about choosing the base category. However, in general, our research objectives dictate the choice of the base: choose a category that can answer our research questions. In our earlier example in the binary logit model, `Own = 0` is the base category because it gives us the probability of owning an electric guitar given `Years`. In general, when dealing with success and failure, failure condition can be selected as the base category. It helps us to examine factors that lead to success. Status quo can also be chosen as the base. As analogy, as you can recall, in a hypothesis testing, the null hypothesis represents a status quo (i.e. no effect; no difference), and the alternative hypothesis is formulated to capture the reverse (i.e. there is an effect; there is a difference). Status quo is a condition that we want to intervene. If we want to investigate the effect of price discount on buying, 'no purchase' can be selected as the base.

23.7.2 Independence from the Irrelevant Alternatives Property

We used *Years* earlier as the predictor. This variable is related to an individual's characteristic. Of all individuals who choose a particular guitar, the value of *Years* will vary. Now, let us add another predictor, price of a guitar, which is the characteristic of the guitar. We assume that price will have the same impact on the probability. Using acoustic as the base category, as done earlier, the logit associated with buying an electric guitar given *Years* is:

$$In\frac{P(Buy=3)}{P(Buy=1)}=\beta_{0,3}+\beta_{1,3}Years+\beta_2(Price_3-Price_1) \tag{23.29}$$

What is interesting about the right-hand side of the Equation 23.29 is that the logit depends on the individual characteristics and, more importantly, the price of the electric and acoustic guitar – the last term. While, an individual is contemplating of considering buying one of three types of guitar – acoustic, electro-acoustic, and electric – the odds ratio does not consider the price of the electro-acoustic. That is, the decision of buying either an acoustic or electric guitar does not depend on the price of the electro-acoustic that is also under consideration. This is known as the independence from the irrelevant alternatives (IIA) property. Is the property realistic? Well, maybe not – when we compare two alternatives, we might also consider the features of the other product under our consideration. There are ways of testing and relaxing the IIA property (e.g. nested logit model), which are beyond the scope of this chapter. The multinomial probit model does not need the IIA property but specifying the model is more complex than that of the multinomial logit model; hence, it is not very popular in practice.

The IIA property will be violated if features of the electro-acoustic guitar appear in the Equation 23.29. For instance, Equation 23.30 includes $\beta_3 Promo_2$ in the logit, where $Promo_2$ is a variable denoting whether the electric guitar is on promotion – if it is, an amp is given to the buyer as a bonus. This suggests that whether IIA property is valid or not, that depends on how a model is specified (McFadden et al. 1977, p. 41).

$$In\frac{P(Buy=3)}{P(Buy=1)} = \beta_{0,3} + \beta_{1,3} Years + \beta_2 (Price_3 - Price_1) + \beta_3 Promo_2$$

The classic example of the violation of the IIA property is the blue bus and red bus paradox. Imagine that the mode of transportation that you can choose is: a train and a bus painted in red (red bus). Suppose that your probabilities of choosing each transportation mode are 1/2 and 1/2. A new bus has just been introduced. This bus is painted in blue (blue bus). Because colour will not affect the length of your journey, you should not be indifferent between the two buses. Therefore, your probability of choosing either bus is 1/4. Now, the choice probabilities with respect to the train, the red bus, and the blue bus are 1/2, 1/4, and 1/4. These probabilities will be inconsistent with the IIA property. Why?

$$\text{Before the blue bus is introduced: } \frac{P(train)}{P(red\ bus)} = \frac{1/2}{1/2} = 1$$

$$\text{After the blue bus is introduced: } \frac{P(train)}{P(red\ bus)} = \frac{1/2}{1/4} = 2$$

To be inconsistent with the IIA property, after the introduction of the blue bus, $P\ (train)/P\ (red\ bus)$ should equal one, which is not the same as that of before the introduction.

23.7.3 The Origins of the IIA Property

The IIA property is also known in the literature as the Luce's axiom introduced by the prominent mathematical psychologist, R Duncan Luce (Luce 1959). According to Luce (1959): 'It is a natural probabilistic formulation on K. J. Arrow's famed principle of the independence of irrelevant alternatives, and as such it is a possible underpinning for rational, probabilistic theories of social behavior' (Luce 1977, p. 229). Kenneth J. Arrow, a Nobel Prize winner in economics, introduced the 'independence of the irrelevant alternatives' assumption, not property, in the context of voting. That is, the social preference of two political candidates, should not depend on the presence or absence of any other candidates. As you might have noticed, Luce used 'from' and Arrow used 'of' in the expression of the IIA. According to Luce (1959), the use of 'from' rather than 'of' is more appropriate to describe that the ratio of the probabilities (P_a / P_b) does not depend on any other alternatives. It is interesting to note that Luce (1959) derived the multinomial logit starting from the IIA property.

23.8 Summary

In this chapter, we learned how to build a binary logit regression model where the dependent variable is a categorial variable with only 0 or 1 values. The model can be used to explain the choice that individuals made when they were deciding between two alternatives. In this context, OLS regression should be avoided because a straight line from OLS cannot properly handle a (0,1) dependent variable. For instance, the OLS predicted values can fall outside the range of 0 and 1. Unlike an OLS regression model, the parameters in the logit model are estimated by using an iterative procedure. We discussed the interpretation of the coefficients in the logit model and relevant outputs. The difference between logit and probit model was also discussed. Finally, the form of the multinomial logit model, which is a direct extension of the binary logit model was presented. Finally, we discussed the independent of the irrelevant alternatives (IIA) property of the multinomial logit model.

23.9 Further Reading

Ben-Akiva, M. E. & Lerman, S. R. (1985), *Discrete choice analysis: Theory and application to travel demand*, Vol. 9, MIT Press. This is a classic graduate textbook on discrete choice modelling and widely cited in the literature.

Elshiewy, O., Guhl, D. & Boztuğ, Y. (2017), 'Multinomial logit models in marketing–from fundamentals to state-of-the-art', *Marketing: ZFP–Journal of Research and Management* **39**(3), 32–49. This article presents an overview of the application of the multinomial logit models in marketing.

Hosmer Jr, D. W., Lemeshow, S. & Sturdivant, R. X. (2013), *Applied logistic regression*, John Wiley & Sons. This is the standard textbook of logistic regression widely used in the courses across the fields of social sciences.

Train, K. E. (2009), *Discrete choice methods with simulation*, Cambridge University Press. This is the graduate level book on discrete choices suitable for those who have strong background in mathematics and statistics. The author provides the online version of the book for free at https://eml.berkeley.edu/books/choice2.html.

Wulff, J. N. (2015), 'Interpreting results from the multinomial logit model: Demonstrated by foreign market entry', *Organizational Research Methods* **18**(2), 300–325. This article presents a guideline of how to analyse and interpret the results of the multinomial logit model.

23.10 Review Questions

1. Explain the use of logistic function in the context of binary logit model.
2. Explain the difference between binary logit and binary probit model.
3. Discuss how to interpret the coefficient of a continuous predictor in a simple binary logit model (having only one predictor).
4. Explain the principle of the likelihood ratio test.
5. Discuss key SPSS and R outputs in the binary logit analysis.

23.11 Exercises

1. You want to build a logit model of how customers decide which two smartphones to choose: iPhones vs. Android phones. Assume that the most important variable is camera quality.
   (a) How would you measure camera quality, which you can use as a predictor in a logit model?
   (b) Build a logit model with camera quality as a predictor, and hypothesize its sign.
2. Imagine that a cellular operator company just developed a chatbot to serve its customers. Before the chatbot is put into use, a pilot study was conducted by asking a group of participants to interact with the new service chatbot. The following variables were recorded:

   Like: = 1 if a participant like the chatbot, 0 = otherwise. Age: age of participants in years.

   Duration: duration of a participant's session in minutes.

   For this exercise, use the SPSS data, `chatbot.sav` or if you use R, you can load the data from the `ahdar` R package. You are tasked with the following:

   (a) Build a binary logit model to examine whether Age and Duration affect `Like`.

(b) Assess the fit of your model.

(c) What is the impact of one unit increase in `Age` on the probability of `Like` holding `Duration` constant?

Bibliography

Agresti, A. (2018), *Statistical methods for the social sciences*, Pearson Education.

Aguinis, H., Edwards, J. R. & Bradley, K. J. (2017), 'Improving our understanding of moderation and mediation in strategic management research', *Organizational Research Methods* **20**(4), 665–685.

Aguinis, H. & Gottfredson, R. K. (2010), 'Best-practice recommendations for estimat- ing interaction effects using moderated multiple regression', *Journal of Oganiza- tional Behavior* **31**(6), 776–786.

Alford, B. L. & Biswas, A. (2002), 'The effects of discount level, price consciousness and sale proneness on consumers' price perception and behavioral intention', *Journal of Business Research* **55**(9), 775–783.

Altman, D. G. & Bland, J. M. (1995), 'Statistics notes: The normal distribution', *British Medical Journal* **310**(6975), 298.

Antonakis, J., Bendahan, S., Jacquart, P., Lalive, R. et al. (2014), 'Causality and endogeneity: Problems and solutions', *The Oxford Handbook of Leadership and Organizations* **1**, 93–117.

Aquino, K. & Reed II, A. (2002), 'The self-importance of moral identity', *Journal of Personality and Social Psychology* **83**(6), 1423.

Axtell, C. M., Parker, S. K., Holman, D. & Totterdell, P. (2007), 'Enhancing customer service: Perspective taking in a call centre', *European Journal of Work and Organizational Psychology* **16**(2), 141–168.

Azzalini, A. & Azzalini, M. A. (2015), 'Package 'sn'', *The skew-normal and skew-t distributions*, 1–3. https://cran.r-project.org/web/packages/sn/sn.pdf

Bache, S. M., Wickham, H., Henry, L. & Henry, M. L. (2022), 'Package 'magrittr'', *R. Package Version*.

Balderjahn, I., Buerke, A., Kirchgeorg, M., Peyer, M., Seegebarth, B. & Wiedmann, K.-P. (2013), 'Consciousness for sustainable consumption: Scale development and new insights in the economic dimension of consumers' sustainability', *AMS Review* **3**, 181–192.

Balducci, B. & Marinova, D. (2018), 'Unstructured data in marketing', *Journal of the Academy of Marketing Science* **46**(4), 557–590.

Bandalos, D. L. (2018), *Measurement theory and applications for the social sciences*, Guilford Publications.

Baron, R. M. & Kenny, D. A. (1986), 'The moderator–mediator variable distinction in social psychological research: Conceptual, strategic, and statistical considerations', *Journal of Personality and Social Psychology* **51**(6), 1173. https://cran.r-project.org/web/packages/lm.beta/index.html

Bartholomew, D. J. (1995), 'Spearman and the origin and development of factor analysis', *British Journal of Mathematical and Statistical Psychology* **48**(2), 211–220.

Bearden, W. O. & Netemeyer, R. G. (1999), *Handbook of marketing scales: Multi-item measures for marketing and consumer behavior research*, Sage Publications.

Becker, T. E., Atinc, G., Breaugh, J. A., Carlson, K. D., Edwards, J. R. & Spector, P. E. (2016), 'Statistical control in correlational studies: 10 essential recommendations for organizational researchers', *Journal of Organizational Behavior* **37**(2), 157–167.

Behrendt, S. (2023), 'Package 'lm. beta''. https://cran.r-project.org/web/packages/lm.beta/lm.beta.pdf

Ben-Akiva, M. E. & Lerman, S. R. (1985), *Discrete choice analysis: Theory and application to travel demand*, Vol. 9, MIT Press.

Bernerth, J. B. & Aguinis, H. (2016), 'A critical review and best-practice recommendations for control variable usage', *Personnel Psychology* **69**(1), 229–283.

Breaugh, J. A. (2006), 'Rethinking the control of nuisance variables in theory testing', *Journal of Business and Psychology* **20**, 429–443.

Brown, T. A. (2015), *Confirmatory factor analysis for applied research*, Guilford Publications.

Bruner, G. C., Hensel, P. J. & James, K. E. (2005), *Marketing scales handbook*, American Marketing Association, Chicago, IL.

Brusco, M. J., Singh, R., Cradit, J. D. & Steinley, D. (2017), 'Cluster analysis in empirical om research: Survey and recommendations', *International Journal of Operations & Production Management* **37**(3), 300–320.

Busenbark, J. R., Yoon, H., Gamache, D. L. & Withers, M. C. (2022), 'Omitted variable bias: Examining management research with the impact threshold of a confounding variable (ITCV)', *Journal of Management* **48**(1), 17–48.

Carlson, K. D. & Wu, J. (2012), 'The illusion of statistical control: Control variable practice in management research', *Organizational Research Methods* **15**(3), 413–435.

Carroll, R. J. & Schneider, H. (1985), 'A note on levene's tests for equality of variances', *Statistics & Probability Letters* **3**(4), 191–194.

Cattell, R. B. (1966), 'The scree test for the number of factors', *Multivariate Behavioral Research* **1**(2), 245–276.

Chang, W. (2018), *R graphics cookbook: Practical recipes for visualizing data*, O'Reilly Media.

Coelho, F., Pereira, M. C., Cruz, L., Simões, P. & Barata, E. (2017), 'Affect and the adoption of pro-environmental behaviour: A structural model', *Journal of Environmental Psychology* **54**, 127–138.

Cohen, J. (1988), *Statistical power analysis for the behavioral science*, Academic Press, NJ.

Cohen, J. (2013), *Statistical power analysis for the behavioral sciences*, Academic Press.

Costello, A. B. & Osborne, J. (2005), 'Best practices in exploratory factor analysis: Four recommendations for getting the most from your analysis', *Practical Assessment, Research, and Evaluation* **10**(1), 7.

Cramer, J. S. (2004), 'The early origins of the logit model', *Studies in History and Philosophy of Science Part C: Studies in History and Philosophy of Biological and Biomedical Sciences* **35**(4), 613–626.

Cronbach, L. J. (1951), 'Coefficient alpha and the internal structure of tests', *Psychometrika* **16**(3), 297–334.

Daryanto, A. (2019), 'Avoiding spurious moderation effects: An information-theoretic approach to moderation analysis', *Journal of Business Research* **103**, 110–118.

Daryanto, A. (2020*a*), 'EndoS: An spss macro to assess endogeneity', *The Quantitative Methods for Psychology* **16**(1), 56–70.

Daryanto, A. (2020*b*), 'Tutorial on heteroskedasticity using heteroskedasticityV3 spss macro', *The Quantitative Methods for Psychology* **16**(5), 8–20.

Daryanto, A. (2022), 'Testing difference in two proportions using D2prop macro in SPSS', *The Quantitative Methods for Psychology* **18**(2), 181–185.

Daryanto, A. & Lukas, B. A. (2022), 'Controlling for spurious moderation in marketing: A review of statistical techniques', *Journal of Business Research* **144**, 180–192.

Daryanto, A. & Song, Z. (2021), 'A meta-analysis of the relationship between place attachment and pro-environmental behaviour', *Journal of Business Research* **123**, 208–219.

Daryanto, A., Song, Z. & Soopramanien, D. (2022), 'The covid-19 pandemic as an impetus for pro-environmental behaviours: The role of causal attribution', *Personality and Individual Differences* **187**, 111415.

DeVellis, R. F. & Thorpe, C. T. (2021), *Scale development: Theory and applications*, Sage publications.

Dykes, B. (2019), *Effective data storytelling: How to drive change with data, narrative and visuals*, John Wiley & Sons.

Echambadi, R. & Hess, J. D. (2004), 'Mean-centering does nothing for moderated multiple regression', *Journal of Marketing Research*, 2–16.

Edmondson, D. R. (2005), 'Likert scales: A history', in Proceedings of the 12th conference on historical analysis and research in marketing (CHARM), 127–133.

Elshiewy, O., Guhl, D. & Boztuğ, Y. (2017), 'Multinomial logit models in marketing–from fundamentals to state-of-the-art', *Marketing: ZFP–Journal of Research and Management* **39**(3), 32–49.

Fabrigar, L. R., Wegener, D. T., MacCallum, R. C. & Strahan, E. J. (1999), 'Evaluating the use of exploratory factor analysis in psychological research', *Psychological Methods* **4**(3), 272.

Farley, J. U. (1964), 'Why does "brand loyalty" vary over products?', *Journal of Marketing Research* **1**(4), 9–14.

Fernihough, A., Henningsen, A. & Fernihough, M. A. (2019), 'Package 'mfx''. https://doi:10.32614/CRAN.package.mfx

Fisher, R. A. (1970). *Statistical methods for research workers*. Oliver & Boyd.

Fox, J. (2019), *Regression diagnostics: An introduction*, Sage Publications.

Gelman, A., Hill, J. & Vehtari, A. (2020), *Regression and other stories*, Cambridge University Press.

Ghasemi, A. & Zahediasl, S. (2012), 'Normality tests for statistical analysis: A guide for non-statisticians', *International Journal of Endocrinology and Metabolism* **10**(2), 486.

Gnanadesikan, R. & Wilk, M. B. (1968), 'Probability plotting methods for the analysis of data', *Biometrika* **55**(1), 1–17.

Goretzko, D., Pham, T. T. H. & Bühner, M. (2021), 'Exploratory factor analysis: Current use, methodological developments and recommendations for good practice', *Current Psychology* **40**, 3510–3521.

Green, P. E., Frank, R. E. & Robinson, P. J. (1967), 'Cluster analysis in test market selection', *Management Science* **13**(8), B–387.

Grieder, S. & Steiner, M. D. (2022), 'Algorithmic jingle jungle: A comparison of implementations of principal axis factoring and promax rotation in R and SPSS', *Behavior Research Methods* **54**(1), 54–74.

Guadagni, P. M. & Little, J. D. (1983), 'A logit model of brand choice calibrated on scanner data', *Marketing Science* **2**(3), 203–238.

Haans, R. F., Pieters, C. & He, Z.-L. (2016), 'Thinking about U: Theorizing and testing U-and inverted U-shaped relationships in strategy research', *Strategic Management Journal* **37**(7), 1177–1195.

Hair, J. F., Black, W. C., Babin, B. J., Anderson, R. E. & Tatham, R. (2009), *Multivariate data analysis: Global edition*, 7th Edition, Pearson Education.

Hancock, G. R., Mueller, R. O. & Stapleton, L. M. (2010), *The reviewer's guide to quantitative methods in the social sciences*, Routledge.

Harvey, J. W. (1990), 'Benefit segmentation for fund raisers', *Journal of the Academy of Marketing Science* **18**(1), 77–86.

Hayes, A. F. (2017), *Introduction to mediation, moderation, and conditional process analysis: A regression-based approach*, Guilford publications.

Heggestad, E. D., Scheaf, D. J., Banks, G. C., Monroe Hausfeld, M., Tonidandel, S. & Williams, E. B. (2019), 'Scale adaptation in organizational science research: A review and best-practice recommendations', *Journal of Management* **45**(6), 2596–2627.

Hlavac, M. (2015), *Stargazer: Beautiful latex, html and ascii tables from r statistical output*, Comprehensive R Archive Network (CRAN).

Holbrook, M. B. (1993), 'Gratitudes and latitudes in MBA attitudes: Customer orientation and the business week poll', *Marketing Letters* **4**, 267–278.

Holbrook, M. B. & Batra, R. (1987), 'Assessing the role of emotions as mediators of consumer responses to advertising', *Journal of Consumer Research* **14**(3), 404–420.

Hosmer Jr, D. W., Lemeshow, S. & Sturdivant, R. X. (2013), *Applied logistic regression*, John Wiley & Sons.

Hotelling, H. (1933), 'Analysis of a complex of statistical variables into principal components', *Journal of Educational Psychology* **24**(6), 417.

Hu, L.-T. & Bentler, P. M. (1998), 'Fit indices in covariance structure modeling: Sensitivity to underparameterized model misspecification', *Psychological Methods* **3**(4), 424.

Hyndman, R. J. & Fan, Y. (1996), 'Sample quantiles in statistical packages', *The American Statistician* **50**(4), 361–365.

Jaccard, J. & Jacoby, J. (2019), *Theory construction and model-building skills: A practical guide for social scientists*, Guilford publications.

Jaccard, J. & Turrisi, R. (2003), *Interaction effects in multiple regression*, Number 72, Sage.

Jarvis, C. B., MacKenzie, S. B. & Podsakoff, P. M. (2003), 'A critical review of construct indicators and measurement model misspecification in marketing and consumer research', *Journal of Consumer Research* **30**(2), 199–218.

Jolliffe, I. T. (2002), *Principal component analysis for special types of data*, Springer.

Jolliffe, I. T. (2022), 'A 50-year personal journey through time with principal component analysis', *Journal of Multivariate Analysis* **188**, 104820.

Jorgensen, T. D., Pornprasertmanit, S., Schoemann, A. M., Rosseel, Y. et al. (2016), *Package 'semtools'*. https://cran. r-project. org/web/packages/semTools/semTools. pdf

Kail, R. V. (2018), *Scientific writing for psychology: Lessons in clarity and style*, SAGE Publications.

Kenny, D. A. (2008), 'Reflections on mediation', *Organizational Research Methods* **11**(2), 353–358.

Kim, S. (2015), 'ppcor: An R package for a fast calculation to semi-partial correlation coefficients', *Communications for Statistical Applications and Methods* **22**(6), 665.

Komsta, L. (2022), *R package: Moments, technical report*. https://cran.r-project.org/web/packages/moments/index.html

Kraemer, H. C. & Blasey, C. (2015), *How many subjects?: Statistical power analysis in research*, Sage Publications.

Kumar, V., Sharma, A. & Gupta, S. (2017), 'Accessing the influence of strategic marketing research on generating impact: Moderating roles of models, journals, and estimation approaches', *Journal of the Academy of Marketing Science* **45**(2), 164–185.

Kutner, M. H., Nachtsheim, C. J., Neter, J., Li, W. et al. (2005), *Applied linear statistical models*, Vol. 5, McGraw-Hill Irwin Boston.

Lattin, J. M., Carroll, J. D. & Green, P. E. (2003), *Analyzing multivariate data*, Thomson Brooks/Cole Pacific Grove, CA.

Lazer, W. (1962), 'The role of models in marketing', *Journal of Marketing* **26**(2), 9–14.

Lê, S., Josse, J. & Husson, F. (2008), 'Factominer: An R package for multivariate analysis', *Journal of Statistical Software* **25**, 1–18.

Likert, R. (1932), 'A technique for the measurement of attitudes', *Archives of Psychology* **140**, 5–53.

Lin, H. (2020), 'Probing two-way moderation effects: A review of software to easily plot johnson-neyman figures', *Structural Equation Modeling: A Multidisciplinary Journal* **27**(3), 494–502.

Lind, J. T. & Mehlum, H. (2010), 'With or without U? the appropriate test for a u-shaped relationship', *Oxford Bulletin of Economics and Statistics* **72**(1), 109–118.

Linzer, D. A. & Lewis, J. B. (2011), 'poLCA: An R package for polytomous variable latent class analysis', *Journal of Statistical Software* **42**, 1–29.

Lishinski, A. (2018), 'lavaanplot: Path diagrams for lavaan models via diagrammer', *R package version 0.5 1*. https://github.com/alishinski/lavaanPlot

Locke, E. A. (1968), 'Toward a theory of task motivation and incentives', *Organizational Behavior and Human Performance* **3**(2), 157–189.

Loehlin, J. C. (2004), *Latent variable models: An introduction to factor, path, and structural equation analysis*, Psychology Press.

Long, J. A. & Long, M. J. A. (2017), *Package 'jtools'*. https://jtools.jacob-long.com

Lovie, A. D. & Lovie, P. (1993), 'Charles spearman, cyril burt, and the origins of factor analysis', *Journal of the History of the Behavioral Sciences* **29**(4), 308–321.

Luce, R. D. (1959), *Individual choice behavior*, Vol. 4, Wiley, New York.

Luce, R. D. (1977), 'The choice axiom after twenty years', *Journal of Mathematical Psychology* **15**(3), 215–233.

Lüdecke, M. D. (2023), *Package 'sjPlot'*. https://strengejacke.github.io/sjPlot/

McAlister, L., Germann, F., Chisam, N., Hayes, P., Lynch, A. & Stewart, B. (2022), 'A taxonomy of marketing organizations', *Journal of the Academy of Marketing Science* 1–19.

McClelland, G. H., Irwin, J. R., Disatnik, D. & Sivan, L. (2017), 'Multicollinearity is a red herring in the search for moderator variables: A guide to interpreting moderated multiple regression models and a critique of iacobucci, schneider, popovich, and bakamitsos (2016)', *Behavior Research Methods* **49**(1), 394–402.

McFadden, D., Tye, W. B. & Train, K. (1977), *An application of diagnostic tests for the independence from irrelevant alternatives property of the multinomial logit model*, Institute of Transportation Studies, University of California Berkeley.

Mikulić, J. & Ryan, C. (2018), 'Reflective versus formative confusion in sem based tourism research: A critical comment', *Tourism Management* **68**, 465–469.

Mu, J. & Zhang, J. Z. (2021), 'Seller marketing capability, brand reputation, and consumer journeys on e-commerce platforms', *Journal of the Academy of Marketing Science* **49**(5), 994–1020.
Murtagh, F. & Legendre, P. (2011), 'Ward's hierarchical clustering method: Clustering criterion and agglomerative algorithm', arXiv preprint arXiv:1111.6285.
Muthén, B. & Muthén, L. (2019), *Mplus: A general latent variable modeling program*, Muthén & Muthén.
Myors, B., Murphy, K. R. & Wolach, A. (2010), *Statistical power analysis: A simple and general model for traditional and modern hypothesis tests*, Routledge.
Navarro, D. (2015), *Learning statistics with R: A tutorial for psychology students and other beginners (Version 0.6), R package version 0.5.1*, University of New South Wales, Sydney, Australia. https://learningstatisticswithr.com
O'brien, R. M. (2007), 'A caution regarding rules of thumb for variance inflation factors', *Quality & Quantity* **41**, 673–690.
O'Connor, B. P. (2000), 'Spss and sas programs for determining the number of components using parallel analysis and velicer's map test', *Behavior Research Methods, Instruments, & Computers* **32**(3), 396–402.
Oliver, R. L. (1999), 'Whence consumer loyalty?', *Journal of Marketing* **63**(4_suppl1), 33–44.
Osgood, C. E. (1964), 'Semantic differential technique in the comparative study of cultures', *American Anthropologist* **66**(3), 171–200.
Pearl, J. & Mackenzie, D. (2018), *The book of why: The new science of cause and effect*, Basic books.
Pearson, K. (1901), 'LIII. On lines and planes of closest fit to systems of points in space', *The London, Edinburgh, and Dublin Philosophical Magazine and Journal of Science* **2**(11), 559–572.
Peter, J. P. (1981), 'Construct validity: A review of basic issues and marketing practices', *Journal of Marketing Research* **18**(2), 133–145.
Podsakoff, P. M., MacKenzie, S. B., Lee, J.-Y. & Podsakoff, N. P. (2003), 'Common method biases in behavioral research: A critical review of the literature and recommended remedies', *Journal of Applied Psychology* **88**(5), 879.
Podsakoff, P. M., MacKenzie, S. B. & Podsakoff, N. P. (2012), 'Sources of method bias in social science research and recommendations on how to control it', *Annual Review of Psychology* **63**, 539–569.
Podsakoff, P. M., MacKenzie, S. B. & Podsakoff, N. P. (2016), 'Recommendations for creating better concept definitions in the organizational, behavioral, and social sciences', *Organizational Research Methods* **19**(2), 159–203.
Preacher, K. J. & MacCallum, R. C. (2003), 'Repairing tom swift's electric factor analysis machine', *Understanding Statistics: Statistical Issues in Psychology, Education, and the Social Sciences* **2**(1), 13–43.
Punj, G. & Stewart, D. W. (1983), 'Cluster analysis in marketing research: Review and suggestions for application', *Journal of Marketing Research* **20**(2), 134–148.
Qu, W., Liu, H. & Zhang, Z. (2020), 'A method of generating multivariate non-normal random numbers with desired multivariate skewness and kurtosis', *Behavior Research Methods* **52**, 939–946.
Ramanathan, M. (2002), *Introductory econometrics with applications*, Harcourt College Pub, New York.
Reichardt, C. S. (2019), *Quasi-experimentation: A guide to design and analysis*, Guilford Publications.
Revelle, W. (2018), 'psych: Procedures for psychological, psychometric, and personality research'. https://personality-project.org/r/psych/
Richardson, J. T. (2021), 'A closer look at the lady tasting tea', *Significance* **18**(5), 34–37.
Romesburg, C. (2004), *Cluster analysis for researchers*, Lulu Press.
Rook, D. W. & Fisher, R. J. (1995), 'Normative influences on impulsive buying behavior', *Journal of Consumer Research* **22**(3), 305–313.
Rosseel, Y. (2012), 'Lavaan: An R package for structural equation modeling and more. version 0.5–12 (beta)', *Journal of Statistical Software* **48**(2), 1–36.
Rousseeuw, P. J. (1987), 'Silhouettes: A graphical aid to the interpretation and validation of cluster analysis', *Journal of Computational and Applied Mathematics* **20**, 53–65.

Ruscio, J. & Roche, B. (2012), 'Determining the number of factors to retain in an exploratory factor analysis using comparison data of known factorial structure', *Psychological Assessment* **24**(2), 282.

Rutherford, A. (2011), *ANOVA and ANCOVA: A GLM approach*, John Wiley & Sons.

Salsburg, D. (2001), *The lady tasting tea: How statistics revolutionized science in the twentieth century*, Macmillan.

Sande, J. B. & Ghosh, M. (2018), 'Endogeneity in survey research', *International Journal of Research in Marketing* **35**(2), 185–204.

Saunders, J. A. (1980), 'Cluster analysis for market segmentation', *European Journal of Marketing* **14**(7), 422–435.

Simonson, I. (1989), 'Choice based on reasons: The case of attraction and compromise effects', *Journal of Consumer Research* **16**(2), 158–174.

Snedecor, G. W. & Cochran, W. G. (1989), *Statistical methods*, 8th Edition, Vol. 54, Iowa State Universuty Press, Ames, Iowa, 71–82.

Sobel, M. E. (1982), 'Asymptotic intervals for indirect effects in structural equations models. S. Leinhart', *Sociological Methodology* 290–312.

Spearman, C. (1904), 'General intelligence, objectively determined and measured', *American Journal of Psychology* **15**, 201–292.

Spector, P. E. & Brannick, M. T. (2011), 'Methodological urban legends: The misuse of statistical control variables', *Organizational Research Methods* **14**(2), 287–305.

Spiller, S. A., Fitzsimons, G. J., Lynch Jr, J. G. & McClelland, G. H. (2013), 'Spotlights, floodlights, and the magic number zero: Simple effects tests in moderated regression', *Journal of Marketing Research* **50**(2), 277–288.

Stahl, S. (2006), 'The evolution of the normal distribution', *Mathematics Magazine* **79**(2), 96–113.

Staiger, D. O. & Stock, J. H. (1997), 'Instrumental variables regression with weak instruments', *Econometrica* **65**(3), 557–586.

Stigler, S. M. (1986), *The history of statistics: The measurement of uncertainty before 1900*, Harvard University Press.

Stock, J. H. & Watson, M. W. (2015), *Introduction to econometrics*, 3rd Edition, Pearson.

Studenmund, A. H. (2014), *Using econometrics a practical guide*, Pearson Education Limited.

Thomas, J. W. (1980), 'Market segmentation', *Quarterly Review of Marketing* **6**(1), 25–28.

Train, K. E. (2009), *Discrete choice methods with simulation*, Cambridge University Press.

Vanegas, L. H., Rondon, L. M. & Paula, G. A. (2023), 'Generalized estimating equations using the new R package glmtoolbox', *The R Journal* **15**(2), 105–133.

Vermunt, J. K. & Magidson, J. (2013), *Technical guide for Latent GOLD 5.0: Basic, advanced, and syntax*, Statistical Innovations Inc., Belmont, MA.

Vicente-Molina, M. A., Fernández-Sainz, A. & Izagirre-Olaizola, J. (2018), 'Does gender make a difference in pro-environmental behavior? the case of the basque country university students', *Journal of Cleaner Production* **176**, 89–98.

Ward Jr, J. H. (1963), 'Hierarchical grouping to optimize an objective function', *Journal of the American Statistical Association* **58**(301), 236–244.

Wedel, M. & Kamakura, W. A. (2000), *Market segmentation: Conceptual and methodological foundations*, Springer Science & Business Media.

Wei, Y., Liu, B. & Liu, X. (2005), 'Entry modes of foreign direct investment in china: A multinomial logit approach', *Journal of Business Research* **58**(11), 1495–1505.

Wickham, H. (2016), *ggplot2: Elegant Graphics for Data Analysis*, Springer.

Wickham, H., Çetinkaya-Rundel, M. & Grolemund, G. (2023), *R for data science*, O'Reilly Media, Inc.

Wilke, C. O. (2019), *Fundamentals of data visualization: A primer on making informative and compelling figures*, O'Reilly Media.

Wilkinson, L. (2012), *The grammar of graphics*, Springer.

Wright, S. (1934), 'The method of path coefficients', *The Annals of Mathematical Statistics* **5**(3), 161–215.

Wulff, J. N. (2015), 'Interpreting results from the multinomial logit model: Demonstrated by foreign market entry', *Organizational Research Methods* **18**(2), 300–325.

Yates, F. (1934), 'Contingency tables involving small numbers and the χ 2 test', *Supplement to the Journal of the Royal Statistical Society* **1**(2), 217–235.

Yentes, R. & Wilhelm, F. (2018), *Careless: Procedures for computing indices of careless responding [R package]*. https://github.com/ryentes/careless/

Yi, Y. & Jeon, H. (2003), 'Effects of loyalty programs on value perception, program loyalty, and brand loyalty', *Journal of the Academy of Marketing Science* **31**(3), 229–240.

Yong, A. G. & Pearce, S. (2013), 'A beginner's guide to factor analysis: Focusing on exploratory factor analysis', *Tutorials in Quantitative Methods for Psychology* **9**(2), 79–94.

Zarantonello, L. & Pauwels-Delassus, V. (2015), *The handbook of brand management scales*, Routledge.

Zhao, X., Lynch Jr, J. G. & Chen, Q. (2010), 'Reconsidering baron and kenny: Myths and truths about mediation analysis', *Journal of Consumer Research* **37**(2), 197–206.

Zwick, W. R. & Velicer, W. F. (1986), 'Comparison of five rules for determining the number of components to retain', *Psychological Bulletin* **99**(3), 432.

Index

For Product Safety Concerns and Information please contact our EU
representative GPSR@taylorandfrancis.com
Taylor & Francis Verlag GmbH, Kaufingerstraße 24, 80331 München, Germany

www.ingramcontent.com/pod-product-compliance
Ingram Content Group UK Ltd.
Pitfield, Milton Keynes, MK11 3LW, UK
UKHW050231200926
475702UK00020B/2976
* 9 7 8 1 0 3 2 5 2 5 6 4 8 *